WORLD WAR II: BOOKS IN ENGLISH, 1945-65

Hoover Bibliographical Series: XLV

WORLD WAR II: BOOKS IN ENGLISH, 1945-65

Compiled by

JANET ZIEGLER

HOOVER INSTITUTION PRESS
Stanford University • Stanford, California

The Hoover Institution on War, Revolution and Peace, founded at Stanford University in 1919 by the late President Herbert Hoover, is a center for advanced study and research on public and international affairs in the twentieth century. The views expressed in its publications are entirely those of the authors and do not necessarily reflect the views of the Hoover Institution.

Standard Book Number 8179-2451-5
Library of Congress Card Number 74-155297
Printed in the United States of America
©1971 by the Board of Trustees of the Leland Stanford Junior University
All rights reserved

To my Mother and Father

Margaret and Lew Ziegler

CONTENTS

	Page
Preface, by Robert Vosper	xi
Introduction: A Survey of Existing Bibliographical Coverage	xiii
I. General Works	3
A. Bibliographies and Guides	3
1. General	3
2. Specific Subjects	3
3. Guides to Collections and Archives	5
B. Chronologies	6
C. General Accounts (for general accounts of the war in and by specific countries, see IV)	7
D. Pictorial Histories	9
E. Atlas Histories	10
F. Historiography	10
G. Linguistic Studies	10
II. Prelude to the War: Origins and Outbreak (see also IV.B)	11
A. General	11
B. Europe	11
C. Far East	12
III. Military Aspects of the War	13
A. General Accounts	13
B. Memoirs and Biographies	15
1. American	15
2. British and Commonwealth	17
3. German	19
4. Japanese	20
5. Others	20
C. General Aspects	21
1. Strategy; High Command	21
2. Techniques and Technology; Logistics; Administration; Psychological Warfare (for the atomic bomb, see also III.D.3.c)	23
3. Medical Aspects	29
4. Espionage; Secret Services; Special Operations, Commando Operations (see also III.E)	33
5. Unit Histories	40
a. Australia	40
b. Canada	42
c. Great Britain	42
d. India	48
e. New Zealand	48
f. United States	49
g. Others	63
D. Campaigns and Operations (see also III.A and B)	64
1. Land Campaigns: European Theater	64
a. German-Polish (see also III.E.h and IV.D.1.a)	64
b. War in the West, 1939-40	64
Battle of Britain (see also III.D.3.b and IV.E.4.a)	65

	Page
c. Russo-Finnish War	66
d. Mediterranean	66
e. Africa and the Near East	67
f. The Balkans	70
g. German-Russian	71
h. European Theater, 1941-45	73
2. Land Campaigns: Far Eastern Theater	81
a. China	81
b. Philippines	81
c. Malaya; Singapore	82
d. Dutch East Indies	83
e. Burma	83
3. Aerial Operations	85
a. General	85
b. European Theater (see also III.D.1.b)	89
c. Pacific and Far Eastern Theater	95
The Atomic Bombing of Hiroshima and Nagasaki (see also III.C.2)	97
4. Naval Operations and Battles, Including Aircraft Carriers, Amphibious Operations, the Merchant Marine, and Submarines	97
a. General	97
b. Atlantic, Mediterranean, and the Arctic	102
c. The War in the Pacific	109
E. Underground and Resistance, Including the German Anti-Nazi Movement (see also III.C.4)	117
1. General	117
2. Europe (by country)	118
a. Albania	118
b. Belgium and the Netherlands	118
c. France	118
d. Germany and Austria	119
e. Greece	121
f. Hungary	121
g. Italy	121
h. Poland	121
i. Russia	121
j. Scandinavia and the Baltic States	122
k. Yugoslavia	123
3. Far East	123
IV. Political Aspects of the War	125
A. General Accounts	125
B. Memoirs and Biographies	126
C. The Axis Powers	129
1. General Diplomacy	129
2. Individual Countries	129
a. Germany	129
b. Italy	132
c. Japan	133
d. Others	133
3. War Aims	134
4. Propaganda	134
D. Axis-held Countries (see also III.E and VI.A)	134
1. Europe	134
a. Poland	134

	Page
b. Belgium and the Netherlands	136
c. Denmark	136
d. Norway	137
e. France	137
f. Yugoslavia	138
g. Greece	139
h. Baltic States	139
i. Channel Islands	139
2. Far East	140
E. United Nations Coalition	141
1. General Diplomacy	141
2. Big-Three Conferences	142
Territorial Questions	142
3. War Aims; United Nations Organization; Peace Treaties	143
4. Individual Countries	144
a. Great Britain	144
Commonwealth Nations	146
b. Russia	148
c. United States	149
General	149
Local	151
d. Others	153
5. Propaganda	153
V. Economic and Legal Aspects of the War	154
A. General	154
B. Axis Powers	154
C. Axis held Countries	155
D. United Nations Coalition	155
1. General	155
2. British Commonwealth	155
3. Russia	158
4. United States	158
E. Other Countries	162
VI. Social Impact of the War	163
A. Prisoner of War Camps; Concentration Camps, Relocation Camps; Atrocities, "The Final Solution"; Escape Accounts (see also VIII)	163
1. General	163
2. Europe	163
a. General	163
b. Atrocities, "The Final Solution"	163
c. Prisoner of War and Concentration Camps; Personal Accounts	166
d. Individual Camps	171
e. Escape Accounts	172
3. Far East	175
4. North America	179
B. Demographic Changes and Shifts; Displaced Persons; Children	180
C. Relief; Military Government; Civil Affairs; Red Cross, YMCA, USO, etc. (see also III.C.3)	182
D. Religious and Moral Aspects; Military Chaplains; Conscientious Objectors; Churches	185
E. The Arts and the War	187
F. Radio, Press, Censorship	188

	Page
G. Science, Education, Libraries	189
VII. Position of the Neutral Countries	191
VIII. War Crimes Trials (see also I.A and VI.A)	192
A. General	192
B. Germany	192
C. Japan	194
D. Eichmann Trial	194
Index	195

PREFACE

Since its inception in 1960, UCLA's Graduate School of Library Service has placed special focus on bibliography because of its fundamental importance to all types of library work. The impact of that conception is made real in this publication by Miss Ziegler, who is a product of the School.

The University of Chicago's great Professor Pierce Butler, who was among the first to give academic distinction to our profession, once stated that the young librarian's profit from his professional studies "will depend very largely upon his skill in reading the tabulations of formal bibliography as a shorthand of history." Obviously Miss Ziegler profited from her studies, and as one of her teachers I am honored to bear witness by this Preface. Just as obviously the profession at large and students in general will profit in turn from the imagination and diligence with which she has pushed this exacting project forward.

In my other guise as University Librarian, I am equally pleased by Miss Ziegler's creativity because, as the redoubtable Professor Fredson Bowers said here in 1966, bibliography—by which he of course particularly meant analytical bibliography—is "a significant and perhaps the basic ground of understanding between librarians and scholars." In an academic library of our sort, the establishment of that "ground of understanding" is essential to the health of the institution. As a member of our Library staff, Miss Ziegler has now filled us full of vitamins.

Under such circumstances, the UCLA Library would have been proud itself to publish the fruits of Miss Ziegler's efforts. Greater pride and service to all concerned will, however, stem from its issuance by the most appropriate of all publishers for this bibliography, the Hoover Institution on War, Revolution and Peace, which has supported Miss Ziegler's research with a grant.

Robert Vosper
University Librarian and
Professor in the Graduate School of Library Service
University of California, Los Angeles

INTRODUCTION

A SURVEY OF EXISTING BIBLIOGRAPHICAL COVERAGE OF THE WAR

To anyone interested in studying World War II in some depth, the bibliographical coverage of that conflict will be a source of much exasperation and some comfort. The searcher will be exasperated first by the fact that the enormous body of publications which has been amassed in the various countries throughout the world since 1945 lacks any sort of a comprehensive multilingual bibliography. Furthermore, the writings on the war that originated in the individual countries also are generally in need of national bibliographic coverage. With some minor exceptions (such as, for example, Poland and Yugoslavia) these publications have remained a largely unmapped labyrinth. This is particularly the case with English-language publications, and it is specifically the lack of bibliographic tools for the English-language publications on the war that this bibliography seeks to remedy.

To ease the task of the searcher, in the realm of bibliography of bibliographies, there are two notable surveys of bibliographies compiled in various countries for materials concerning the war. In his "Die Bibliographien zur Geschichte des zweiten Weltkrieges" (*Jahresbibliographie, Bibliothek für Zeitgeschichte*, 1961, pp. 511–565) Max Gunzenhaüser discusses the libraries, institutes, and archives specializing in World War II materials, and lists almost 500 bibliographies and other sources from countries throughout the world. Janet Ziegler's "Répertoire international des bibliographies publiées de 1945 à 1965 sur la seconde guerre mondiale (*Revue d'histoire de la deuxième guerre mondiale,* July 1966, pp. 69–80) includes 131 bibliographies which indicate the available national bibliographic coverage of the war for more than twenty-five countries, regions, and subject areas, as well as the coverage for general aspects of the war.* In addition, The Publichnaia Biblioteka in Moscow has issued a general bibliography of non-Soviet historical bibliographies under the title *Istorii zarubezhnykh stran (Europa, Amerika, Australiia)*, compiled by G. P. Pochepko and I. I. Frolova (Moscow, 1967), which contains numerous entries of bibliographies dealing with World War II.

In the realm of general bibliographies on the war, the International Commission for the Teaching of History has produced one of the only two existing multilingual tools: *The Two World Wars: A Selective Bibliography* (New York, 1964), which includes about 500 titles and sources on the Second World War in the major languages. It also describes archives and documentary collections and lists non-book materials, such as film and phonograph records. More extensive is Hans-Adolf Jacobsen's *Zur Konzeption einer Geschichte des zweiten Weltkrieges, 1939–1945* (Frankfurt am Main, 1964), which, in addition to an analytical discussion, includes a classified list of about 1,110 major works and sources on the war in the languages of the major participating countries.

Quarterly coverage of the publications on the war from all countries can be found in *Revue d'histoire de la deuxième guerre mondiale* (Paris, 1950–). Also a quarterly, the *Wojskowy przegląd historyczny* (Warsaw, 1956–) includes, in each issue since 1959, a section entitled "Materiały do bibliografii drugiej wojny światowej," which records books, articles, and book reviews published since 1957 in the various European languages. The Bibliothek für Zeitgeschichte-Weltkriegsbücherei in Stuttgart has recently published its *Alphabetischer Katalog* in 11 volumes, and *Systematischer Katalog* in 20 volumes (Boston, G. K. Hall, 1969), which display the substantial holdings of the library in various languages. The *Jahresbibliographie, Bibliothek für Zeitgeschichte-Weltkriegsbücherei* (before 1960 the *Bücherschau der Weltkriegsbücherei*) lists the annual acquisitions of the Library, supplementary to the published catalogs, and includes many short special bibliographies.

Among the useful general tools, also international in scope, are the *Foreign Affairs Bibliography, 1932–43; 1942–52;* and *1952–62* (New York, 1945; 1955; 1964): the *Library of Congress Catalog: Books: Subjects,* 1950–54; 1955–59; 1960–65, and annual cumulations of quarterly issues; the annual *International Bibliography of the Historical Sciences* (Paris, 1947–; the latest volume published in 1968, covers 1965); and the *Bibliographie zur Zeitgeschichte* issued quarterly in *Vierteljahreshefte zur Zeitgeschichte* published by the Institut für Zeitgeschichte in Munich. The Library of the Institut für Zeitgeschichte has also published its catalog in four sections: *Biographischer Katalog,* 1 volume; *Alphabetischer Katalog,* 5 volumes; *Länderkatalog,* 2 volumes; and *Sachkatalog,* 6 volumes (Boston, G. K. Hall, 1967).

---

*For bibliographies published since 1965, see the author's "Répertoire international des bibliographies publiées de 1945 à 1965: Supplement 1966–1969," *Revue d'histoire de la deuxième guerre mondiale* (to appear in 1970).

In general, the national bibliographic coverage of publications on the war in the individual countries is spotty and inadequate. In most countries some bibliographies on narrow aspects of the war have been published, but so far only a few attempts at general bibliography of a nation's writings on the conflict have materialized. In the survey that follows, only the major and latest general bibliographies are brought to attention. The reader may bear in mind that bibliographies on narrow aspects of the war which have been published before the appearance of a comprehensive bibliography are almost always included in it. Due to the compiler's language limitations, publications on the war in the Oriental languages have not been surveyed. However, the reader will find some useful United States compilations of Oriental publications listed in Part I of this bibliography.

German publications on the war are represented in three bibliographies which are not addressed exclusively to World War II and include materials in several languages: *Bibliographie zur Zeitgeschichte und zum zweiten Weltkrieg für die Jahre 1945–1950*, by Franz Herre and Hellmuth Auerbach (Munich, 1955; reprinted 1966); the quarterly *Bibliographie für Zeitgeschichte*, which continues Herre and Auerbach; and the previously discussed publications of the Bibliothek für Zeitgeschichte-Weltkriegsbücherei. In addition, Otto Diehn's *Bibliographie zur Geschichte des Kirchenkampfes, 1933–1945* (Göttingen, 1958) lists a great number of relevant titles. On the underground in Germany, Inter Nationes has published a short bibliography, *Resistance in Germany, 1933–1945: A Bibliography* (Bonn, 1964), and the *Bibliographie zur Geschichte des antifaschistischen Widerstandes* (East Berlin, 1959), compiled by Franz Karma and others and issued by the Deutsche Staatsbibliothek, lists East German materials.

So far as French publications on the war are concerned, bibliographic information is regularly provided by the *Revue d'histoire de la deuxième guerre mondiale*. Works on the resistance in France are discussed by Henri Michel in *Bibliographie critique de la résistance* (Paris, 1964). The products of the underground press in France are listed in the *Catalogue de périodiques clandestines, 1939–1945* of the Bibliothèque Nationale (Paris, 1954).

For Italy, the official *Saggio bibliographico sulla seconda guerra mondiale* (Rome 1955) with about 2,500 titles, and its second volume with 1,377 titles covering the years 1955–65 (Rome, 1966), list primarily Italian publications, but also include some French, German, and English works. Quarterly coverage of Italian publications on the war is provided by *Il movimento di liberazione in Italia* (Milan). Bibliographic information on the Italian resistance is available in *Resistenza: Panorama bibliographica* (Rome, 1957), compiled by Alfonso Bartolini and others, listing almost 3,000 principally Italian titles; and in Giampaolo Panza's *La resistenza in Piemonte; Guida bibliographica, 1943–1963* (Turin, 1965), containing 1,984 entries. The publications of the Italian resistance during the war years are listed in Laura Conti's *La resistenza in Italia, 25 luglio 1943–25 aprile 1945; Saggio bibliographico* (Milan, 1961), which includes almost 5,000 broadsides and other materials.

The principal publications about the Netherlands in the war are listed by Eduard Groeneveld in "Bibliographie Néerlandaise de la deuxième guerre mondiale" *(Revue d'histoire de la deuxième guerre mondiale,* April 1963, pp. 103–112). Three bibliographies cover the products of the underground press in the Netherlands: *De ondergrondse pers, 1940–1945* (The Hague, 1954) by L. E. Winkel, with 1,193 titles; *Catalogue van pamfletten, 1940–1945* (Amsterdam, 1952), which lists 301 titles from the collection of the Rijksinstituut voor Oorlogsdocumentatie; and *Het vrije boek in onvrije tijd: Bibliografie van illegale en clandestine belletrie* (Leiden, 1958), compiled by Dirk de Jong, which lists 1,019 entries and includes an index of pseudonyms.

For Belgium, Jacques Willequet's "La Belgique et la deuxième guerre mondiale: Orientation bibliographique" *(Bücherschau der Weltkriegsbücherei,* 1955, pp. 239–247) includes only 66 titles and is now very much out of date. "Belgische Literatur zum Westfeldzug 1940," by Klaus-Jürgen Müller in *Bücherschau der Weltkriegsbücherei,* 1959 (pp. 422–434), lists 92 titles. The products of the underground press in Belgium are listed in *Inventaire de la presse clandestine, 1940–1944, conservé en Belgique,* compiled by J. Dujardin and others, and issued by the Centre National d'Histoire des Deux Guerres Mondiales (Brussels, 1966) with 567 titles.

Scandinavian bibliographers have also provided little guidance for the student of World War II. For Denmark there is only the guide to underground publications, *Besaettelsestidens illegale blade og bøger* (Copenhagen, 1954) and its *Supplement og rettelser* (Copenhagen, 1960), both compiled by Leo Buschardt and others. For Norway there is Sigmund Skaard's *Bøker om Norges kamp: Bibliografiske samlinger* (Washington, 1945), containing about 1,000 titles. Sven Fritz, in "Schwedische Literatur über den zweiten Weltkrieg" *(Jahresbibliographie, Bibliothek für Zeitgeschichte,* 1963, pp. 573–603), lists and discusses 249 Swedish publications.

Works on Finland in the war are listed and discussed by Vilho Niitemaa in "Finland und der zweite Weltkrieg in der historischen Literatur" *(Bücherschau der Weltkriegsbücherei,* 1957, pp. 295–308), with 300 titles; and in Ernst Klink's "Zur Literatur über der finnisch-sowjetischen Winterkrieg, 1939–1940," in *Jahresbibliographie, Bibliothek für Zeitgeschichte* (1961, pp. 589–597), with 75 titles of books and articles.

By comparison, in Eastern Europe the bibliographic coverage of the war is much more comprehensive and current. For the Soviet Union, G. A. Kumanev's *Velikaia otechestvennaia voina Sovetskogo Soiuza 1941–1959 gg.* (Moscow, 1960) lists about 2,000 books, pamphlets, and articles. The Publichnaia Biblioteka, Moscow, has provided a more select list in its *Velikaia otechestvennaia voina Sovetskogo Soiuza, 1941–1945 gg.: Rekomendatel'nyi ukazatel' literatury* (Moscow, 1965), with about 600 annotated titles. In addition, the sixth volume of the *Istoriia velikoi otechestvennoi voiny Sovetskogo Soiuza, 1941–1945* (Moscow, 1965) includes almost fifty pages of bibliography of Soviet and non-Soviet works used in the writing of this six-volume history of the war. A classified list of almost 600 dissertations on the war written in the Soviet Union has been issued by the Institut Istorii of the Akademiia Nauk SSSR: *SSSR v period velikoi otechestvennoi voiny* (Moscow, 1961). Two additional tools may be of use: Michael Schatoff's *Bibliografiia osvoboditel'nogo dvizheniia narodov Rossii v gody vtoroi mirovoi voiny, 1941–1945* (New York, 1961), with more than 2,400 entries and a title page, table of contents, and introduction in English; and Alexander Dallin's *The German Occupation of the USSR in World War II: A Bibliography* (Washington, 1955).

Polish compilers have published several bibliographies on the war, the most comprehensive of which is *Bibliografia wojskowo II wojny swiatowej: Materialy za lata 1939–1958, czesc polska* (Warsaw, 1960), a classified list of about 6,500 titles of books and articles, produced by the Wojskowy Instytut Historyczny. Another tool by the Instytut is *Bibliografia walki wyzwolenczej narody polskiego przeciw hitlerowskiemu okupantowi, 1939–1945: Material z lat 1945–1960* (Warsaw, 1960), which includes almost 900 classified titles, with French translation of the title page, introduction, and each entry. Publications on the Nazi occupation of Poland are listed in *Bibliografia piśmiennictwa Polskiego za lata 1944–1953 o hitlerowskich zbrodniach wojennych* (Warsaw, 1955), compiled by J. Kosicki and W. Kozlowski, with 2,296 titles; and its supplement, *Materialy do bibliografii okupacji hitlerowskiej w Polsce, 1939–1945: Uzupelnicnia za lata 1944–1953* (Warsaw, 1957), compiled by W. Chojnacki and others, with 1,200 titles. More limited in scope are the two bibliographies by Marek Getter: *Wrzesièn 1939 w kziozce, prasii i filmii: Poradnik Bibliograficzny* (Warsaw, 1964), a classified list of 228 annotated titles; and *O walkach ludowego wojska polskiego, 1943–1945* (Warsaw, 1963), a classified list of 150 annotated titles, with author and subject indexes, maps, and illustrations. *Centralny katalog polskiej prasy konspiracyjney 1939–1945* (Warsaw, 1962), prepared by the Polska Akademia Nauk, Instytut Historii, provides a list of 1,146 titles of the Polish underground press, locates them in twenty-three libraries and archives in Poland, and includes summaries in Russian, French, and English.

For the Baltic countries, Erik Thomson has provided "Estland und Lettland während des zweiten Weltkrieges: Eine bibliographische Übersicht" in *Bücherschau der Weltkriegsbücherei* (1958, pp. 322–327), which includes 150 titles published between 1945 and 1958. About sixty works on the German occupation of Lithuania are covered by E. Lagauskieni in *Faktai kaltina: Literatūros apzvalgo* (Kaunas, 1961), published by Lietuwos TSR Valstybinė Respublikinė Biblioteka.

Publications dealing with the countries of Southeastern Europe in the war have basic bibliographic coverage in *Südost-Europa im zweiten Weltkrieg: Literaturbericht und Bibliographie* (Frankfurt am Main, 1962), compiled by Andreas Hillgruber, which includes 1,976 entries for Greece, Yugoslavia, Hungary, Rumania, Bulgaria, Albania, and Czechoslovakia.

Hungary's Fövarosi Szabó Ervin Könyvtár in Budapest has issued two bibliographies of Hungarian publications on the conflict: *A masodik vilaghabory története, 1939–1945: Vàalogatatt müvek bibliografiaja* (Budapest, 1955), compiled by Erzsebet Köves; and *Hazánk felzabodylása 1944–1945: Bibliografia es dokumentum gyütemeny* (Budapest, 1955). The latter includes about 5,300 classified entries of books, articles, leaflets, and broadsides. The Hungarian Jewish organization, Magyar Izraelitak Orsages Kipveselete, has published *A magyarorszagi fasimus zsidoüldözesenek bibliografiaja, 1945–1958* (Budapest, 1958), compiled by Arthur Geyer, listing about 1,000 annotated entries. Randolph L. Braham includes 752 titles in his *The Hungarian Jewish Catastrophe: A Selected and Annotated Bibliography* (New York and Jerusalem, 1962), published as number 4 in the Joint Documentary Projects, Bibliographical series, of the Yivo Institute for Jewish Research and the Yad Washem Martyrs' and Heroes' Memorial Authority.

For Czechoslovakia there are several tools of limited scope. Ruzena Machánková's *Zur Geschichte des slowakischen Nationalaufstandes 1944: Bibliographie* (Bratislava, 1961) lists about 100 annotated books and articles. Michal Fedor's *Súpis periodík v slovenskej účasti na Československom národnooslobodzovacom boja za druhej svetovy voiny, 1939–1945*, published for Matica Slovenska (Turciansky sv. Martin, 1959), includes 117 annotated titles. Michael Schwartz lists 225 titles in several languages in his "Bibliographie zur Geschichte des slowakischen Aufstandes 1944" (*Bücherschau der Weltkriegsbücherei,* 1961, pp. 458–473). For additional guidance, the searcher may turn to *25 ans d'historiographie tchécoslovaque, 1936–1960* (Prague, 1960), compiled by Jan Filip and others for the Akademie Ved, Historicky Ustav; it includes a discussion (pp. 344–363) of writings dealing with the period 1938–45.

A number of bibliographies provide access to Bulgarian literature on the war. A recent brief review of about 125 titles is available in J. Dolaptchieva's "Bibliographies sur la guerre et la résistance" (*Revue d'histoire de la deuxième guerre mondiale,* October 1968, pp. 83–93). *Partiiniiat i antifashistkiiat pechat v podgotovkata no Devetosetemvriiskoto narodno vustanie, 1941–1944: Bibliografski ukazatel* (Sofia, 1961), published by the Bulgarski Bibliografski Institute, and edited by V. Kovachev and I. Dancheva, includes 137 annotated titles. A listing of about 1,500 titles of books and articles is available in *Istoriia Bolgarii do 9 sentiabria 1944: Ukazatel' literatury, 1945–1958* (Moscow, 1962), pp. 383–444, compiled by N. V. Busse and others. Two additional compilations are: *Antifašistkata borba na bŭlgarskija narod, otrazena v chudožestvenata i memoarnata literatura: Bibliografija,* by Stephen Ivanov and P. Djugmedžieva (Sofia, 1964); and *Otechestvenata voina na Bulgariia, 1944–1945: Bibliografiia* (Sofia, 1966), by Tasho V. Tashev.

A bibliography of the works on Albania in the war is provided by the Imperial War Museum Library, London, in *Albania, 1939–1945: List of Selected References* (London, 1962). Rumanian publications on the war are listed by Vasile G. Ionescu in "L'historiographie Roumanie de la deuxième guerre mondiale" (*Revue d'histoire de la deuxième guerre mondiale,* April 1968, pp. 69–81), and by Ion Popescu-Puturi in "Recherches sur l'histoire de la résistance en Roumanie" (*Il movimento di liberazione in Italia,* no. 83, 1966, pp. 78–90).

Greek works on Greece's part in the war are discussed in *War and Postwar Greece: An Analysis Based on Greek Writings* (Washington, 1950), prepared by Floyd A. Spencer for the European Affairs Division of the Library of Congress. A few publications are listed in "Bibliographie sur l'occupation et la résistance en Grèce" (*Cahiers d'histoire de la guerre,* no. 3, 1950, pp. 132–135). To supplement these two outdated works, the searcher may turn to *Quinze ans de bibliographie historique en Grèce, 1950–1964* (Athens, 1966), published by the Comité National Hellénique de l'Association International d'Études de Sud-Est Européen. This bibliography is provided (pp. 255–256) with a "Table analytique des matières," in which the materials dealing with World War II are listed under "Histoire contemporaine."

Access to Yugoslav war literature is made possible by several good bibliographies, the most extensive of which is *Petnajst let bibliografiji o narodnoosvobodilnem boju slovencev, 1945–1959* (Ljubljana, 1962) by France Skerl-Bregar, which lists 6,461 books, articles, and other materials. Also useful are *Izbor dela o narodnooslobodilačkoj borbi: Bibliografiski priručnik* (Belgrade, 1962), compiled by L. Stankov and others and published by Savez Organzacija i Ustanova za Sirenje Knjige NR Srbije, with 1,060 titles; *Bibliografija na statii i knigi za N.O.B. vo Makejonija,* compiled by Netalija Dimik for the Institut za Nacionala Istorja in Skopje (1953), which lists 1,759 titles of books and articles; M. Todorovski's *Prilog kon bibliografijata za NOB vo Makejonija, 1952–1959* (Skopje, 1960), which supplements Dimik's work with 759 titles; and "Srbija u narodnooslobodilačkom ratu i narodnoj revoluciji: Bibliografija publikacija i clanaka u periodicnim izdanjima 1944 do 1960 godine," in *Istorijski glasnik* (1961, pp. 233–255), by Radmila Stefanovic. For the publications of the war years, Vojnoistorijski Institut in Belgrade has published an extraordinary bibliography, *Bibliografjia izdanja u narodnooslobodilačkom ratu, 1941–1945* (Belgrade, 1964), with more than 9,500 titles of books, pamphlets, newspapers, magazines, and bulletins. Two more general tools will also be found useful: *Dix années d'historiographie yougoslave, 1945–1955* (Belgrade, 1955) published by the Comité National Yougoslave des Sciences Historiques, which includes (pp. 575–660) a bibliographical article in English discussing works on military operations and the resistance; and *Historiographie yougoslave, 1955–1965* (Belgrade, 1965) published by the Fédération des Sociétés Historiques de Yougoslavie, which includes (pp. 419–448) a bibliographical discussion in French and a list of the works on the war published during the years 1955–65.

There are a few bibliographies available for Latin American publications on the war: *Fontes para a historia de F.E.B.: Ensaio* (Rio de Janeiro, 1958), compiled by Francisco Ruas Santos, listing 465 annotated Brazilian titles published during and after the war; "Brazilien Literatur über der zweiten Weltkrieg" (*Jahresbibliographie, Bibliothek für Zeitgeschichte,* 1960, pp. 427–437), by Werner Haupt, with 115 titles; *Guerra y postguerra: Bibliografía* (Buenos Aires, 1945), compiled by the Facultad de Ciencias Económias of the Universidad Nacional of Argentina, with 550 titles; *Bibliografía cubana de la II guerra mondial* (Havana, 1945), compiled by Fermin Peraza Sarausa, with about 500 titles; and finally, "Die lateinamerikanische Literatur über den zweiten Weltkrieg," by Werner Haupt, in *Wehrwissenschaftliche Rundschau* (February 1958, pp. 97–101), which includes a short bibliographical essay and a list of about 30 titles.

Several major bibliographies of special aspects of the war have been published and should prove useful. *Bibliografia dell'oppressione nazista fino al 1962* (Florence, 1964), by Andrea Devoto, provides a listing of 1,503 titles of books, articles, and pamphlets. Books and pamphlets published worldwide about Nazi concentration camps are listed in *Materialy do bibliografii hitlerowskich obozów koncentracyjnych: Literatura miedzynarodowa 1934–1962* (Warsaw, 1964), compiled by Wanda Kiedrzyńska for the Instytut Historii Polskiy Akademii Nauk, which includes 1,703 titles and has an English summary of the introduction. The Wiener Library in London has published *Persecution and Resistance Under the Nazis* (London, 1960), with more than 2,000 titles of books, pamphlets, and periodicals of Germans in exile, and pamphlets and periodicals of the Anti-Nazi Movement.

The Joint Documentary Project of the Yad Washem Remembrance Authority in Jerusalem and the Yivo Institute for Jewish Research in New York is publishing a bibliographic series in which the first and most useful bibliography is *Guide to Jewish History Under Nazi Impact* (New York, 1960), by Jacob Robinson and Philip Friedman, presenting more than 3,600 entries of bibliographical and archival sources and other research tools. The other volumes in the series are: *Bibliography of Books in Hebrew on the Jewish Catastrophe and Heroism in Europe* (Jerusalem, 1960), edited by Philip Friedman, 1,246 entries; *Bibliography of Yiddish Books on the Catastrophe and Heroism* (New York, 1962), by Philip Friedman and Joseph Gar, with more than 1,760 entries; *The Hungarian Jewish Catastrophe: A Selected and Annotated Bibliography* (New York, 1962), by Randolph L. Braham, with 752 classified titles; *The Jewish Holocaust and Heroism Through the Eyes of the Hebrew Press: A Bibliography* (Jerusalem, 1966), edited by Mendel Piekarz, in four volumes; and *Bibliography of Articles on the Catastrophe and Heroism in Yiddish Periodicals* (Vol. 1, New York, 1966) by Joseph Gar. The Centre de Documentation Juive Contemporaine in Paris has published a number of bibliographies of its holdings on the Jews in Europe during the war years: *Alfred Rosenberg dans l'action idéologique, politique et administrative du Reich hitlérien* (Paris, 1963) by Joseph Billig; *Les autorités allemandes en France occupée* (Paris, 1966) by Julien Steinberg; *La France; La Troisième Reich; Israël* (Paris, 1968); and *La France de l'affaire Dreyfus à nos jours* (Paris, 1964).

Publications concerning war crimes and trials are inadequately covered in two bibliographies which are out of date: Helen Conover's *The Nazi State, War Crimes and War Criminals* (Washington, 1945), compiled for the U.S. Library of Congress, with 1,084 titles; and Inge S. Neumann's *European War Crimes Trials: A Bibliography* (New York, 1952).

* * * * * *

The English-language literature on the war, as it was pointed out above, has sorely lacked bibliographic coverage. It has hitherto been necessary to make use of such general tools as the *Library of Congress Catalog: Books: Subjects,* the *Cumulative Book Index,* and the *British National Bibliography.* The *Harvard Guide to American History* (Cambridge, Mass., 1954) has provided a well-chosen but limited list of basic works, as has the American Historical Association's *Guide to Historical Literature* (New York, 1961). Books and articles on the war published during the war are listed by Henry O. Spier in *World War II in Our Magazines and Books, September 1939–September 1945* (New York, 1945). In his pamphlet, *Writings on World War II* (Washington, 1967), Louis Morton has provided an excellent but limited bibliographic discussion of major aspects and controversies of the war, together with the most important English-language works. Sponsored and published by the Service Center for Teachers of History, it is primarily intended for high school teachers and is thus limited in subject matter and in the number of titles it presents. Bibliographies on narrow aspects and specific subjects which do exist are listed in Section I.A of this bibliography.

The bibliography offered here attempts to provide comprehensive coverage of the books published in English during the years 1945 through 1965. The main sources which have been used in its compilation include: the *Library of Congress Catalog: Books: Subjects;* the *British National Bibliography;* the *Revue d'histoire de la deuxième guerre mondiale;* the *Foreign Affairs Bibliography; Foreign Affairs; International Affairs; Military Affairs; Bücherschau der Weltkriegsbücherei* and *Jahresbibliographie, Bibliothek für Zeitgeschichte;* the *International Bibliography of the Historical Sciences;* Herre and Auerbach's *Bibliographie zur Zeitgeschichte und zum zweiten Weltkrieg;* the *Bibliographie zur Zeitgeschichte;* and *Saggio bibliographico sulla seconda guerra mondiale.* A number of the bibliographies on special subjects listed in this bibliography, and a number of other general bibliographies, have also been scrutinized, as well as special lists of government publications on the war. The Library of Congress card catalog and its collections have been examined on two occasions, in 1963 and again in 1967, the latter trip having been partially supported by the UCLA University Library and the Hoover Institution on War, Revolution and Peace. The card catalog of the Hoover Institution on War, Revolution and Peace was consulted in 1963, on a trip supported by the Hoover Institution.

With the exception of a few entries in the section citing bibliographies and guides, the bibliography lists only works of fifty pages or more, including paperback editions. Government publications, except official histories and other primarily historical works, have been excluded. Also omitted are fiction, poetry, works of purely humorous or artistic content (cartoons, paintings), juvenile literature, statistical works (such as registers of the dead), and works on such postwar problems as claims and reconstruction.

The bibliographical information for each title has been kept at a minimum, in keeping, wherever possible, with that supplied by the Library of Congress in its catalogs. In cases involving multiple editions, chronological order is observed. The table of contents is made as detailed as possible, so as to serve as a limited subject index. Cross-references to related sections are given at the beginning of various subdivisions. To facilitate the locating of individual titles, an index is provided listing authors, joint authors, and government historical series. The user should refer not only to the table of contents, but invariably also to the index in trying to find a given work. This is especially true because many works defy easy classification (e.g., W. S. Churchill's *The Second World War,* which the compiler has classified under political memoirs and for which an argument can be made that it should be under general histories of the war).

* * * * * *

It is a great pleasure to be able, at long last, to thank the people who have helped make this publication possible. I am indebted to Professors Eugen Weber and Mortimer Chambers of the UCLA History Department whose interest and encouragement got the project past its embryonic stage. Mr. Robert Vosper and the UCLA Library and Mr. Karol Maichel and the Hoover Institution on War, Revolution and Peace have materially supported the project. My grandmother, Mrs. Myrtle Berg, spent hours of enthusiastic cutting, pasting, and filing. To my father, whose moral and financial support over the years is evident, and to my mother, who did most of the typing, filing, cutting, pasting, and arranging—with wonderful enthusiasm—my debt and gratitude are inexpressible.

BIBLIOGRAPHY

I. GENERAL WORKS

A. BIBLIOGRAPHIES AND GUIDES

1. General

1   International Commission for the Teaching of History.
THE TWO WORLD WARS: SELECTIVE BIBLIOGRAPHY. Oxford and New York, Pergamon Press, 1965. 246 p.

2   Morton, Louis.
WRITINGS ON WORLD WAR II. Washington, Service Center for Teachers of History, 1967. 54 p.

3   Spier, Henry O. (comp.).
WORLD WAR II IN OUR MAGAZINES AND BOOKS, SEPTEMBER 1939 TO SEPTEMBER 1945: A BIBLIOGRAPHY. New York, Stuyvesant Press, 1945. 96 p.

2. Specific Subjects

4   Barnhart, Edward N.
JAPANESE AMERICAN EVACUATION AND RESETTLEMENT: CATALOG OF MATERIAL IN THE GENERAL LIBRARY. Berkeley, General Library, University of California, 1958. 177 p.

5   Braham, Randolph L.
THE HUNGARIAN JEWISH CATASTROPHE: A SELECTED AND ANNOTATED BIBLIOGRAPHY. New York, Yivo Institute for Jewish Research, 1962. 86 p. (Yad Washem Martyrs' and Heroes' Memorial Authority, Jerusalem. Yivo Institute for Jewish Research, New York. Joint Documentary Projects. Bibliographical Series, No. 4)

6   Dallin, Alexander (comp.), with Conrad F. Latour.
THE GERMAN OCCUPATION OF THE USSR IN WORLD WAR II: A BIBLIOGRAPHY. Washington, External Research Staff, Office of Intelligence Research, Dept. of State, 1955. 76 p. (External Research Paper)

7   Dornbusch, Charles E.
HISTORIES OF AMERICAN ARMY UNITS, WORLD WAR I AND II AND KOREAN CONFLICT, WITH SOME EARLIER HISTORIES. Washington, Library and Service Club Branch, Special Services Division, Office of Adjutant General, Dept. of Army, 1956. 310 p.

8   Dornbusch, Charles E.
POST-WAR SOUVENIR BOOK AND UNIT HISTORIES OF THE NAVY, MARINE CORPS, AND CONSTRUCTION BATTALIONS. Washington, Office of Naval History, 1953. 14 l.

9   Ghent, Donald, Gladys Waltcher, and Edwin Beal (comps.).
MANPOWER, WAGES AND LABOR RELATIONS IN WORLD WAR II: AN ANNOTATED BIBLIOGRAPHY. Ithaca, New York State School of Industrial and Labor Relations, Cornell University, 1951. 93 p. (Cornell University. State School of Industrial and Labor Relations. Bulletin No. 19)

10   Hsueh Chun-tu.
THE CHINESE COMMUNIST MOVEMENT, 1937-1949: AN ANNOTATED BIBLIOGRAPHY OF SELECTED MATERIALS IN THE CHINESE COLLECTION OF THE HOOVER INSTUTITION ON WAR, REVOLUTION AND PEACE. Stanford, Hoover Institution on War, Revolution and Peace, 1962. 312 p. (Hoover Institution. Bibliographical Series)

11   Landis, Benson Y., and Inez M. Cavert (comps.).
CHURCH LITERATURE ON POST-WAR PLANNING: SELECTED REFERENCES. New York, Inter-Council Committee on Postwar Planning, 1945. 31 p.

12   London. Imperial War Museum. Library.
ALBANIA, 1939-1945: A LIST OF SELECTED REFERENCES. London, 1962. 3 p.

13   London. Imperial War Museum. Library.
BIBLIOGRAPHY OF ESPIONAGE AND TREASON IN WORLD WAR I AND II. London, 1955. 21 p.

14   London. Imperial War Museum. Library.
LIST OF BOOKS ON MILITARY OPERATIONS IN WESTERN EUROPE, 1939-1945. London, 1952. 8 p.

15   London. Imperial War Museum. Library.
MILITARY OPERATIONS IN GREECE AND CRETE. 1939-1945. London, 1955. 9 p.

16   London. Imperial War Museum. Library.
"OPERATION MARKET GARDEN": THE AIRBORNE LANDINGS AT ARNHEM, EINDHOVEN AND NIJMEGEN, SEPTEMBER, 1944: A LIST OF SELECTED REFERENCES. London, 1962. 13 p.

17   London. Imperial War Museum. Library.
SECOND WORLD WAR: MILITARY OPERATIONS IN ABYSSINIA. London, 1951. 5 p.

18   London. Imperial War Museum. Library.
SECOND WORLD WAR: MILITARY OPERATIONS IN MADAGASCAR. London, 1951. 2 p.

19   London. Imperial War Museum. Library.
SECOND WORLD WAR MILITARY OPERATIONS: THE NORTH AFRICAN CAMPAIGN. London, 1961. 43 p.

20   London. Imperial War Museum. Library.
SECOND WORLD WAR: PACIFIC THEATRE: MILITARY OPERATIONS. London, 1953. 11 p.

21   London. Imperial War Museum. Library.
THE SECOND WORLD WAR: THE BURMA CAMPAIGN; A LIST OF PERIODICAL ARTICLES. London, 1957. 11 p.

22   London. Imperial War Museum. Library.
THE SECOND WORLD WAR: THE BURMA CAMPAIGN; LIST OF SELECTED TITLES, BOOKS AND PAMPHLETS. London, 1960. 11 p.

23   London. Imperial War Museum. Library.
SECOND WORLD WAR: THE CAMPAIGN IN ITALY. London, 1951. 16 p.

24 London. Imperial War Museum. Library.
    SECOND WORLD WAR: THE INVASION OF NORMANDY, JUNE 1944; LIST OF SELECTED REFERENCES. London, 1959. 66 p.

25 London. Imperial War Museum. Library.
    THE WOMEN'S PART IN THE SECOND WORLD WAR: A SELECTION OF REFERENCES. London, 1956. 25 l.

26 London. Imperial War Museum. Library.
    YUGOSLAV PARTISANS: SELECTED LIST OF REFERENCES. London, 1963. 5 p.

27 Mote, Frederick W.
    JAPANESE-SPONSORED GOVERNMENTS IN CHINA, 1937-1945: AN ANNOTATED BIBLIOGRAPHY COMPILED FROM MATERIALS IN THE CHINESE COLLECTION OF THE HOOVER LIBRARY. Stanford, Hoover Institution on War, Revolution and Peace, 1954. 68 p. (Hoover Institution on War, Revolution and Peace. Bibliographical Series, No. 3)

28 Neumann, Inge S.
    EUROPEAN WAR CRIMES TRIALS: A BIBLIOGRAPHY. New York. Carnegie Endowment for International Peace, 1952. 113 p.

29 Perusse, Roland I.
    BIBLIOGRAPHY ON INTERNATIONAL PROPAGANDA: AN ANNOTATED LIST OF SELECT RECENT TITLES, TO INCLUDE PERTINENT ASPECTS OF INTERNATIONAL INFORMATION, INTERNATIONAL COMMUNICATION AND PSYCHOLOGICAL WARFARE. Washington, 195-. 31 l.

30 Robinson, Jacob, and Philip Friedman.
    GUIDE TO JEWISH HISTORY UNDER NAZI IMPACT. Forewords by Genzion Dinur and Salo W. Baron. New York, Yivo Institute for Jewish Research, 1960. 425 p. (Yad Washem Martyrs' and Heroes' Memorial Authority, Jerusalem. Yivo Institute for Jewish Research, New York. Joint Documentary Projects. Bibliographical Series)

31 Rothfeder, Herbert P. (comp.).
    CHECKLIST OF SELECTED GERMAN PAMPHLETS AND BOOKLETS OF THE WEIMAR AND NAZI PERIOD IN THE UNIVERSITY OF MICHIGAN LIBRARY. Ann Arbor, 1961. 214 l.

32 Scanlon, Helen L.
    WAR CRIMES: A SELECTED LIST OF BOOKS AND ARTICLES DEFINING WAR CRIMES UNDER INTERNATIONAL LAW AND DISCUSSING THEIR TRIAL AND PUNISHMENT, INCLUDING WORKS ON AN INTERNATIONAL CRIMINAL COURT. Washington, Carnegie Endowment for International Peace, Library, 1945. 16 p. (Select Bibliographies)

33 Schreiber, Thomas.
    HUNGARY AND THE SECOND WORLD WAR: AN ANNOTATED BIBLIOGRAPHY. Brussels, Imre Nagy Institute for Political Research, 1961. 18 p. (Les Carnets de l'Institut)

34 SELECT BIBLIOGRAPHY OF REVISIONIST BOOKS DEALING WITH THE TWO WORLD WARS AND THEIR AFTERMATH. Oxnard, Calif., Oxnard Press-Courier, n.d. 30 p.

35 Sharp, John C.
    IN JAPANESE HANDS: A LIST OF BOOKS DEALING WITH PRISONERS OF WAR. Birmingham, 1952. 24 p. Supplementary List, 1953, pp. 25-30; 1954, pp. 31-45.

36 Smith, Bruce L., and others.
    PROPAGANDA, COMMUNICATION, AND PUBLIC OPINION: A COMPREHENSIVE REFERENCE GUIDE. Princeton, N.J., Princeton University Press; London, Oxford University Press, 1946. 435 p.

37 Social Science Research Council. Committee on Civil-Military Relations Research.
    CIVIL-MILITARY RELATIONS: AN ANNOTATED BIBLIOGRAPHY, 1940-1952. New York, 1954. 140 p.

38 Special Libraries Association. Military Libraries Division.
    NAVAL OPERATIONS IN WORLD WAR II, 1939-1945: 100 TITLES FOR THE LARGE PUBLIC OF ACADEMIC LIBRARY. Compiled by Jack B. Goldman. n.p., U.S. Naval School, 1956. 7 p. (Military Bibliographies)

39 Stanford University. Hoover Institution on War, Revolution and Peace.
    LIST OF THE POLISH UNDERGROUND COLLECTION, 1939-45. Stanford, 1948. 18 p.

40 Taylor, Philip H., and Ralph J. D. Braibanti.
    ADMINISTRATION OF OCCUPIED AREA: A STUDY GUIDE. Syracuse, Syracuse University Press, 1948. 111 p.

41 Tompkins, Dorothy L. C. C.
    SABOTAGE AND ITS PREVENTION DURING WARTIME. Berkeley, Bureau of Public Administration, University of California, 1951. 53 l. (Defense Bibliographies)

42 United Nations. Dag Hammarskjöld Library.
    A BIBLIOGRAPHY OF THE CHARTER OF THE UNITED NATIONS. New York, United Nations, 1955. 128 p. (Bibliographical Series)

43 United Nations Information Office, New York.
    SELECTED READING LIST ON UNITED NATIONS RELIEF AND REHABILITATION ADMINISTRATION. New York, 1945. 10 p.

44 U.S. Adjutant-General's Office. Administrative Services Division.
    LIST OF UNOFFICIAL UNIT HISTORIES AND UNIT ASSOCIATIONS. Washington, 1947. 91 p.

45 U.S. Army. European Command. Historical Division.
    GUIDE TO FOREIGN MILITARY STUDIES, 1945-1954: CATALOG AND INDEX. Karlsruhe, 1954. 253 p.

46 U.S. Bureau of the Budget. Library.
    HISTORICAL REPORTS OF FEDERAL ADMINISTRATION IN WORLD WAR II: A CHECKLIST OF STUDIES LIMITED TO PUBLICATIONS AND MANUSCRIPTS DEALING WITH NON-MILITARY WARTIME ADMINISTRATION,

AVAILABLE IN THE BUREAU OF THE BUDGET LIBRARY. Washington, 1950. 17 p.

47   U. S. Dept. of the Army. Office of Military History.
GUIDE TO JAPANESE MONOGRAPHS AND JAPANESE STUDIES ON MANCHURIA, 1945-1960. Washington, 1962. 282 p.

48   U. S. Dept. of the Army. Office of Military History.
UNIT HISTORIES OF WORLD WAR II, UNITED STATES ARMY, AIR FORCE, MARINES, NAVY, REPRODUCED IN COLLABORATION WITH NEW YORK PUBLIC LIBRARY. Washington, 1950. 141 p.

Supplement, 1951:
Washington, Distributed by Library Section, Special Services Division, Dept. of Army, 1951. 50 p.

49   U. S. Library of Congress. European Affairs Division.
THE DISPLACED PERSONS ANALYTICAL BIBLIOGRAPHY. [By Helen F. Conover assisted by Hildegarde Lobel]. Report (supplemental) of a Special Subcommittee of the Committee on the Judiciary, House of Representatives, pursuant to H. Res. 238, a Resolution to Authorize the Committee on the Judiciary to Undertake a Study of Immigration and Nationality Problems. Washington, U. S. Government Printing Office, 1950. 82 p. (U.S. 81st Cong., 2d sess. [1950]. House. Report No. 1687)

50   U. S. Library of Congress. European Affairs Division.
WAR AND POSTWAR GREECE: AN ANALYSIS BASED ON GREEK WRITINGS. Prepared by Floyd A. Spencer, consultant. Washington, 1952. 175 p.

51   U. S. Library of Congress. General Reference and Bibliography Division.
DEMOBILIZATION: A SELECTED LIST OF REFERENCES. Compiled by Grace Hadley Fuller. Washington, 1945. 193 p.

52   U. S. Library of Congress. General Reference and Bibliography Division.
ITALY: ECONOMICS, POLITICS AND MILITARY AFFAIRS, 1940-1945. Compiled by Helen Conover, Washington, 1945. 85 p.

53   U. S. Library of Congress. General Reference and Bibliography Division.
MILITARY GOVERNMENT: A SELECTED LIST OF REFERENCES (SUPPLEMENTARY TO MIMEOGRAPHED LIST OF MARCH 1944). Compiled by Grace Hadley Fuller. Washington, 1946. 17 p.

54   U. S. Library of Congress. General Reference and Bibliography Division.
THE NAZI STATE, WAR CRIMES AND WAR CRIMINALS. Compiled by Helen F. Conover for the U. S. Chief of Counsel for the Prosecution of Axis Criminality. Washington, 1945. 132 p.

55   U. S. National Historical Publications Commission.
LIST OF WORLD WAR II HISTORICAL STUDIES MADE BY CIVILIAN AGENCIES OF THE FEDERAL GOVERNMENT. Washington, 1951. 53 p.

56   U. S. War Production Board.
SELECTED BIBLIOGRAPHY ON UNITED STATES PRIORITY CONTROLS INSTITUTED DURING WORLD WAR II. Washington, 1945. 8 p.

57   Wiener Library.
BOOKS ON PERSECUTION, TERROR AND RESISTANCE IN NAZI GERMANY. London, 1949. 45 p.

Other edition:
PERSECUTION AND RESISTANCE UNDER THE NAZIS. London, Vallentine, 1960. (Catalogue Series)

58   Wiener Library.
CATALOGUE OF NUREMBERG DOCUMENTS. London, 1961. 139 l.

3. Guides to Collections and Archives

59   American Historical Association. Committee for the Study of War Documents.
GUIDES TO GERMAN RECORDS MICROFILMED AT ALEXANDRIA, VA. Washington, National Archives, 1958-. Nos. 1-55 published.

60   Dull, Paul S., and Michael Takaaki Umemura.
THE TOKYO TRIALS: A FUNCTIONAL INDEX TO THE PROCEEDINGS OF THE INTERNATIONAL MILITARY TRIBUNAL FOR THE FAR EAST. Ann Arbor, University of Michigan Press, 1957. 94 p. (University of Michigan. Center for Japanese Studies. Occasional Papers)

61   Heinz, Grete, and Agnes F. Peterson (comps.).
NSDAP HAUPTARCHIV: GUIDE TO THE HOOVER INSTITUTION MICROFILM COLLECTION. Stanford, Calif., Hoover Institution on War, Revolution and Peace, 1964. 175 p. (Hoover Institution. Bibliographical Series)

62   United Nations. Communications and Records Division. Archives Section.
GUIDE TO RECORDS OF THE UNITED NATIONS WAR CRIMES COMMISSION, LONDON, 1943-1948. London, 1951. 14 p. (United Nations Archives Reference Guides)

63   United Nations. Dept. of Conference and General Services.
GUIDE TO RECORDS OF THE WAR CRIMES TRIALS HELD IN NÜRNBERG, GERMANY, 1945-1949. Prepared in Archives Section, Communications and Records Division. Lake Success, 1949. 3 p. (United Nations Archives Reference Guides)

64   U. S. Dept. of State. Historical Office.
A CATALOGUE OF FILES AND MICROFILMS OF THE GERMAN FOREIGN MINISTRY ARCHIVES, 1920-1945. Compiled and edited by George D. Kent. Stanford, Calif., Hoover Institution on War, Revolution and Peace, 1962-. 4 v. (Hoover Institution Publications)

65   U. S. Dept. of the Army. Office of Military History.
UNITED STATES ARMY IN WORLD WAR II: MASTER INDEX; READER'S GUIDE. Compiled by the Chief Historian. Washington, 1960. 145 p.

66   U. S. National Archives.
THE DETERMINATION OF REQUIREMENTS, 1939-1945: A GUIDE TO RECORDS IN THE NATIONAL ARCHIVES. Compiled by Elizabeth Bethel. Washington, 1951. 56 p.

67 U.S. National Archives.
FEDERAL RECORDS OF WORLD WAR II. Washington, U.S. Government Printing Office, 1950. 2 v.

68 U.S. National Archives.
HANDBOOK OF FEDERAL WORLD WAR II AGENCIES AND THEIR RECORDS, SAMPLE ENTRIES, WORLD WAR II RECORDS PROJECT. Washington, 1947. 238 p.

69 U.S. National Archives.
INVENTORY OF THE RECORDS OF THE RUBBER SURVEY COMMITTEE, AUGUST-SEPTEMBER 1942. Compiled by Philip P. Brewer. Washington, 1947. 21 p. (Inventories of World War II Records)

70 U.S. National Archives.
MATERIALS IN THE NATIONAL ARCHIVES RELATING TO THE HISTORICAL PROGRAMS OF CIVILIAN GOVERNMENT AGENCIES DURING WORLD WAR II. Washington, 1952. 117 p. (Reference Information Papers)

71 U.S. National Archives.
PRELIMINARY INVENTORY OF THE RECORDS OF THE FOREIGN ECONOMIC ADMINISTRATION. By H. Stephen Helton. Washington, 1951. 180 p. (Preliminary Inventories)

72 U.S. National Archives.
PRELIMINARY INVENTORY OF THE RECORDS OF THE OFFICE FOR AGRICULTURAL WAR RELATIONS, RECORD GROUP 16. Compiled by Harold T. Pinkett. Washington, 1952. 19 p. (Preliminary Inventories)

73 U.S. National Archives.
PRELIMINARY INVENTORY OF THE RECORDS OF THE OFFICE OF CENSORSHIP, RECORD GROUP 216. Compiled by Henry T. Ulasek. Washington, 1953. 16 p. (Preliminary Inventories)

74 U.S. National Archives.
PRELIMINARY INVENTORY OF THE RECORDS OF THE OFFICE OF WAR INFORMATION. By H. Stephen Helton. Washington, 1953. 149 p. (Preliminary Inventories)

75 U.S. National Archives.
PRELIMINARY INVENTORY OF THE RECORDS OF THE PETROLEUM ADMINISTRATION FOR WAR. By James R. Fuchs and Albert Whimpey. Washington, 1951. 152 p. (Preliminary Inventories)

76 U.S. National Archives.
PRELIMINARY INVENTORY OF THE RECORDS OF THE RETRAINING AND REEMPLOYMENT ADMINISTRATION. By Thayer M. Boardman. Washington, 1951. 17 p.

77 U.S. National Archives.
PRELIMINARY INVENTORY OF THE RECORDS OF THE SOLID FUELS ADMINISTRATION FOR WAR. By Edward F. Martin. Washington, 1951. 39 p. (Preliminary Inventories)

78 U.S. National Archives.
PRELIMINARY INVENTORY OF THE RECORDS OF THE WAR RELOCATION AUTHORITY, RECORD GROUP 210. Compiled by Estelle Rebec and Martin Rogin. Washington, 1955. 45 p. (Preliminary Inventories)

79 U.S. National Archives.
PRELIMINARY INVENTORY OF THE RECORDS OF THE WAR SHIPPING ADMINISTRATION (RECORD GROUP 248). By Allen M. Ross. Washington, 1951. 35 p. (Preliminary Inventories)

80 U.S. National Archives.
RECORDS OF THE OFFICE OF WAR MOBILIZATION AND RECONVERSION. By Homer L. Calkin. Washington, 1951. 156 p. (Preliminary Inventories)

81 U.S. National Archives.
RECORDS OF THE UNITED STATES WAR BALLOT COMMISSION. By Robert W. Krauskopf. Washington, 1951. 4 p. (Preliminary Inventories)

82 U.S. National Security Resources Board.
SELECTED LIST OF DOCUMENTS IN THE MOBILIZATION PLANNING FILE OF WAR PRODUCTION BOARD RECORDS PERTAINING TO PROBLEMS AND METHODS OF PRODUCTION CONTROL ADMINISTRATION DURING WORLD WAR II. Prepared by Office of Mobilization Procedures and Organization, National Security Resources Board. Washington, U.S. Government Printing Office, 1949. 373 p.

83 U.S. Strategic Bombing Survey.
EUROPEAN WAR: LIST OF REPORTS. Washington. U.S. Government Printing Office, 1946. 3 p.

84 U.S. Strategic Bombing Survey.
INDEX TO THE RECORDS OF THE UNITED STATES STRATEGIC BOMBING SURVEY. Washington, 1947. 317 p.

85 Weinberg, Gerhard L., and others.
GUIDE TO CAPTURED GERMAN DOCUMENTS: Maxwell Air Force Base, Ala., Human Resources Research Institute, Air University, 1952. 90 p. (Columbia University. Bureau of Applied Social Research. War Documentation Project Study)

Supplement:
Washington, General Services Administration, National Archives Records Service, 1959. 69 p.

B. CHRONOLOGIES

86 Daily Telegraph, London.
THE DAILY TELEGRAPH STORY OF THE WAR. Edited by David Merley. London, Hodder and Stoughton, 1942-46. 5 v.

87 Detroit News.
WAR...IN HEADLINES OF THE DETROIT NEWS, 1939-1945. Detroit, 1945. 104 p.

88 Fortune, Charles H.
THE WAR IN RETROSPECT: A DAY-TO-DAY RECORD OF WORLD WAR II. Dunedin, N.Z., Evening Star Co., 1944-45. 2 v.

89 Glover, Charles C.
   A WASHINGTON DIARY OF WORLD WAR II. Washington, 1963. 324 p.

90 Hopkins, John A. H.
   DIARY OF WORLD EVENTS, BEING A CHRONOLOGICAL RECORD OF THE SECOND WORLD WAR PHOTOGRAPHICALLY REPRODUCED FROM THE AMERICAN AND FOREIGN NEWSPAPER DISPATCHES AS REPORTED DAY-BY-DAY, INCLUDING MAPS, PICTURES, CARTOONS, ANECDOTES, OFFICIAL MESSAGES, REPORTS AND DECLARATIONS, AND CONGRESSIONAL ACTS. Baltimore, National Advertising Co., 1942-48. 54 v.

91 Husted, H. H.
   THUMB-NAIL HISTORY OF WORLD WAR II. Boston, Humphries, 1949. 442 p.

92 Kinnaird, Clark (ed.).
   IT HAPPENED IN 1945. New York, Essential Books, Duell, Sloan and Pearce, 1946. 464 p.

93 Neilson, Francis.
   THE TRAGEDY OF EUROPE: A DAY-TO-DAY COMMENTARY OF THE SECOND WORLD WAR. Appleton, Wis., Nelson, 1940-46. 5 v.

94 New York Herald Tribune.
   FRONT PAGE HISTORY OF THE SECOND WORLD WAR, INCLUDING HISTORICALLY-IMPORTANT PHOTOGRAPHS OF LEADING WAR PERSONALITIES AND INCIDENTS, A CHRONOLOGY OF EVENTS, AND ARTICLES OF SURRENDER. New York, 1946. 112 p.

95 Richard, Dorothy E.
   THE U.S. NAVY IN WORLD WAR II: A CHRONOLOGY. Washington, 1949. 2 v.

96 Royal Institute of International Affairs.
   CHRONOLOGY OF THE SECOND WORLD WAR. London, 1947. 374 p.

97 St. Joseph News-Press.
   THE HISTORY OF WORLD WAR II, AS TOLD IN THE HEADLINES, MAPS AND CARTOONS FROM THE ST. JOSEPH NEWS-PRESS AND ST. JOSEPH GAZETTE, ST. JOSEPH, MISSOURI. St. Joseph, 1945. 264 p.

98 San Francisco Examiner.
   HISTORY OF THE WAR IN FRONT PAGES: ACTUAL REPRODUCTIONS OF NEWSPAPER FRONT PAGES, SELECTED FROM THE SAN FRANCISCO EXAMINER, COVERING MAJOR EVENTS IN WORLD WAR II, PLUS COMPLETE TEXT OF UNITED NATIONS SAN FRANCISCO CHARTER AND STATUTE OF WORLD COURT. San Francisco, 1945. 61 p.

99 U.S. Air University.
   CHRONOLOGY OF WORLD WAR II. Compiled by Major F. E. Bates. Maxwell Field, Ala., Air War College, Air University, 1947. 106 p.

100 U.S. Naval History Division.
    UNITED STATES NAVAL CHRONOLOGY, WORLD WAR II. Washington, U.S. Government Printing Office, 1955. 214 p.

101 U.S. Office of Naval History.
    CHRONOLOGY OF THE NAVY'S WAR IN THE PACIFIC, WORLD WAR II. Washington, 1947. 116 p.

102 Williams, Mary H. (comp.).
    CHRONOLOGY, 1941-1945. Washington, Office of Chief of Military History, Dept. of Army, 1960. 660 p. (U.S. Army in World War II: Special Studies)

C. GENERAL ACCOUNTS (for general accounts of the war in and by specific countries, see IV)

103 Associated Press.
    REPORTING TO REMEMBER: UNFORGETTABLE STORIES AND PICTURES OF WORLD WAR II BY CORRESPONDENTS OF THE ASSOCIATED PRESS. New York, 1945. 71 p.

104 Broad, Lewis.
    THE WAR THAT CHURCHILL WAGED. London, Hutchinson, 1960. 472 p.

105 Brookhouser, Frank.
    THIS WAR YOUR WAR: AN ANTHOLOGY OF GREAT WRITINGS FROM WORLD WAR II. Garden City, N.Y., Doubleday, 1960. 498 p.

106 Commager, Henry S. (ed.).
    THE STORY OF THE SECOND WORLD WAR. Boston, Little Brown, 1945. 578 p.
    Other edition:
    THE POCKET HISTORY OF THE SECOND WORLD WAR. New York, Pocket Books, 1945. 574 p.

107 Compton's Pictured Encyclopedia.
    SUMMARY OF THE SECOND WORLD WAR AND ITS CONSEQUENCES; AN ALPHABETICAL REFERENCE BOOK: PERSONS, PLACES AND EVENTS, SCIENTIFIC AND MILITARY DEVELOPMENTS; AND POSTWAR PROBLEMS IN PRESERVING PEACE. Chicago, Compton, 1947. 134 p.

108 Deborin, Grigorii A.
    THE SECOND WORLD WAR: A POLITICO-MILITARY SURVEY. Edited by I. Zubkov; translated from Russian by Vic Schneierson. Moscow, Progress Publishers, 1962-. 559 p.

109 DeGruchy, Francis A. L.
    WAR DIARY: AN OVERALL WAR PICTURE, 1939-1945. Aldershot, Eng., Gale and Polden, 1949. 187 p.
    Other edition:
    Aldershot, Eng., Gale and Polden, 1950.

110 Dennis, Geoffrey P. (ed.).
THE WORLD AT WAR: A HISTORY DEALING WITH EVERY PHASE OF WORLD WAR II ON LAND, AT SEA, AND IN THE AIR, INCLUDING THE EVENTS WHICH LED UP TO THE OUTBREAK OF HOSTILITIES. London, Caxton Publishing Co., 1951. 4 v.

111 Encyclopedia Americana.
A CONCISE HISTORY OF WORLD WAR II. Vincent J. Esposito, advisory editor. New York, Praeger, 1964. 434 p.

Other edition:
London, Pall Mall, 1965.

112 Ensor, Robert C. K.
A MINIATURE HISTORY OF THE WAR DOWN TO THE LIBERATION OF PARIS. New York, Oxford University Press, 1945. 153 p.

113 Falls, Cyril.
THE SECOND WORLD WAR: A SHORT HISTORY. 3d ed., rev. London, Methuen, 1950. 312 p.

114 Fenston, Joseph.
VICTORY CAVALCADE. London, Heath Cranton, 1950. 304 p.

115 Flower, Desmond, and James Reeves (eds.).
THE TASTE OF COURAGE: THE WAR, 1939-1945. New York, Harper, 1960. 1120 p.

Other edition:
THE WAR, 1939-1945. London, Cassell, 1960. 1130 p.

116 Hall, Walter P.
IRON OUT OF CAVALRY: AN INTERPRETATIVE HISTORY OF THE SECOND WORLD WAR. New York, Appleton-Century, 1946. 389 p.

117 Hansen, Harold A., John G. Herndon, and William B. Rangsdove (eds.).
FIGHTING FOR FREEDOM: HISTORIC DOCUMENTS. Philadelphia, Winston, 1947. 502 p.

118 Hasluck, Eugene L.
THE SECOND WORLD WAR. London, Blackie, 1948. 358 p.

119 Hirsch, Phil (ed.).
GREAT UNTOLD STORIES OF WORLD WAR II. New York, Pyramid, 1963. 191 p.

120 Holt, Edgar.
THE WORLD AT WAR, 1939-45. London, Putnam, 1956. 272 p.

Other edition:
London, Hamilton, 1959. 187 p. (Panther Books)

121 Langsam, Walter C. (ed.).
HISTORIC DOCUMENTS OF WORLD WAR II. Princeton, N.J., Van Nostrand, 1958. 192 p. (Anvil Original)

122 Le Vien, Jack, and John Lord.
THE VALIANT YEARS: A DRAMATIC NARRATIVE OF THE SECOND WORLD WAR. London, Harrap, 1962. 216 p.

Other editions:
WINSTON CHURCHILL: THE VALIANT YEARS. New York, Bernard Geis Associates; distributed by Random House, 1962. 411 p.

London, Transworld, 1963. 286 p. (Corgi Books)

123 McInnes, Edgar.
THE WAR. London and New York, Oxford University Press, 1940-45. 6 v.

124 Miller, Francis T.
HISTORY OF WORLD WAR II. Philadelphia, Winston, 1945. 966 p.

Other editions:
THE COMPLETE HISTORY OF WORLD WAR II. Chicago, Progress Research Corp., 1948. 999 p.

WAR IN KOREA AND THE COMPLETE HISTORY OF WORLD WAR II. Philadelphia, Winston, 1952. 2d ed., 1954; 3d ed., 1955. 999 p.

125 The New Yorker.
THE NEW YORKER BOOK OF WAR PIECES. New York, Reynal and Hitchcock, 1947. 562 p.

126 Nicoll, Peter H.
BRITAIN'S BLUNDER: AN OBJECTIVE STUDY OF THE SECOND WORLD WAR, ITS CAUSE, CONDUCT AND CONSEQUENCES. London, 1949. 134 p.

127 O'Neill, Herbert C. (Strategicus, pseud.).
A SHORT HISTORY OF THE SECOND WORLD WAR AND ITS SOCIAL AND POLITICAL SIGNIFICANCE. London, Faber and Faber; New York, Praeger, 1950. 345 p.

128 O'Neill, Herbert C. (ed.).
ODHAMS HISTORY OF THE SECOND WORLD WAR. Contributors: E. C. Anstey and others. London, Odhams Press, 1951. 2 v.

129 Padmanabhan, C. E.
HITLER-STALIN AXIS WAR. Madras, Short, Bewes, 1962. 657 p.

130 Reader's Digest.
SECRETS AND STORIES OF THE WAR: A SELECTION OF ARTICLES AND BOOK CONDENSATIONS IN WHICH THE READER'S DIGEST RECORDED THE SECOND WORLD WAR. London, Reader's Digest Association, 1963. 2 v. 720 p.

131 Rothberg, Abraham (ed.).
EYEWITNESS HISTORY OF WORLD WAR II. New York, Bantam Books, 1962. 4 v.

132 Savage, Katharine.
A STATE OF WAR, EUROPE, 1939-1945. London, Blond, 1964. 72 p. (Today Is History)

133 Savage, Katharine.
THE STORY OF THE SECOND WORLD WAR. London, Oxford University Press, 1957. 230 p.

Other edition:
New York, Walck, 1958. 271 p.

134 Sellman, Roger R.
    THE SECOND WORLD WAR. London, Methuen, 1964. 111 p. (Methuen's Outlines)

135 Shugg, Roger W., and Harvey A. DeWeerd.
    WORLD WAR II: A CONCISE HISTORY. Washington, Infantry Journal, 1946. 538 p.

136 Snyder, Louis L.
    MASTERPIECES OF WAR REPORTING: THE GREAT MONUMENTS OF WORLD WAR II. New York, Messner, 1962. 555 p.

137 Snyder, Louis L.
    THE WAR: A CONCISE HISTORY, 1939-1945. Foreword by Eric Sevareid. New York, Messner, 1960. 579 p.

Other edition:
London, Hale, 1962. 594 p.

138 The Stars and Stripes.
    THE STARS AND STRIPES STORY OF WORLD WAR II. Edited by Robert Meyer. New York, McKay, 1960. 504 p.

139 Storrs, Ronald, and Philip Graves.
    A RECORD OF THE WAR. London, Hutchinson, 1940-47. 24 v.

140 U.S. War Department. General Staff. Military Intelligence Division.
    THE WORLD AT WAR 1939-1944: A BRIEF HISTORY OF WORLD WAR II. Washington, Infantry Journal, 1945. 410 p.

141 Van Sinderen, Adrian.
    THE STORY OF THE SIX YEARS OF GLOBAL WAR. New York, Price, 1946. 393 p.

142 Verni, Vicente.
    TWENTY WAR FRONTS: A LATIN VISION OF WORLD WAR II. Translated by Enrique A. Lorenzo and Robert B. Aice. Mexico City, 1945. 193 p.

143 Wiener Library.
    ON THE TRACK OF TYRANNY: ESSAYS PRESENTED TO LEONARD G. MONTEFIORE. London, Valentine, Mitchell, 1960. 232 p.

144 Wilmot, Chester.
    THE STRUGGLE FOR EUROPE. London, Collins; New York, Harper, 1952. 766 p.

Other editions:
London, Collins, 1959. 830 p. (Fontana Books)
London, Collins, 1965. 766 p.

145 Yust, Walter (ed.).
    TEN EVENTFUL YEARS: A RECORD OF EVENTS OF THE YEARS PRECEDING, INCLUDING AND FOLLOWING WORLD WAR II, 1937 THROUGH 1946. Chicago, Encyclopedia Britannica, 1947. 4 v.

D. PICTORIAL HISTORIES

146 Detzer, Karl W.
    THE MIGHTIEST ARMY. Pleasantville, N.Y., Reader's Digest Associates, 1945. 168 p.

147 Disabled American Veterans.
    LEST WE FORGET: A PICTORIAL HISTORY. Maplewood, N.J., Hammond, 1964. 80 p.

148 The Evening Bulletin, Philadelphia.
    WORLD WAR II IN HEADLINES AND PICTURES: THE IMPORTANT EVENTS OF WORLD WAR II VIVIDLY TOLD BY 56 FRONT PAGES OF THE EVENING BULLETIN AND MORE THAN 150 ACTION PHOTOGRAPHS. Philadelphia, 1946. 112 p.

149 Evening News, London.
    HITLER PASSED THIS WAY: 170 PICTURES FROM THE LONDON EVENING NEWS. London, Alabaster, Passmore, 1945. 1 v.

150   FROM BEACH-HEAD TO BERLIN: A STORY IN PICTURES OF A GREAT FEAT OF ARMS. DES GREVES DE NORMANDIE A BERLIN: L'HISTOIRE EN PHOTOGRAPHIES D'UN GRAND FAIT D'ARMES. London, H. O. Loescher, Ltd., 1945. 128 p.

151 Great Britain. British Information Services.
    BRITAIN AGAINST GERMANY: A RECORD IN PICTURES. New York, 1945. 127 p.

152 Groth, John.
    STUDIO: EUROPE. Introduction by Ernest Hemingway. New York, Vanguard Press, 1945. 282 p.

153 Hatlem, John C., and Kenneth E. Hunter, with Margaret E. Tackley (comps.).
    THE WAR AGAINST GERMANY AND ITALY: MEDITERRANEAN AND ADJACENT AREAS. Washington, Office of Chief of Military History, Dept. of the Army, 1951. 465 p. (U.S. Army in World War II: Pictorial Record)

154 Hodge, Clarence L., and Murray Befeler (eds.).
    PEARL HARBOR TO TOKYO. Honolulu, Tongg, 1945. 156 p.

155 Hutchinson, Walter (ed.).
    PICTORIAL HISTORY OF THE WAR: A COMPLETE AND AUTHENTIC RECORD IN TEXT AND PICTURES. London, Hutchinson, 1939-45. 26 v.

156 Life (Chicago).
    PICTURE HISTORY OF WORLD WAR II. New York, Time Inc., 1950. 368 p.

157 Martin, Ralph G., and Richard Harrity.
    WORLD WAR II: A PHOTOGRAPHIC RECORD OF THE WAR IN EUROPE FROM D-DAY TO V-E DAY. Greenwich, Conn., Gold Medal Books, 1962. unpaged. (Original Gold Medal Book)

158 Martin, Ralph G.
    WORLD WAR II: A PHOTOGRAPHIC RECORD OF THE WAR IN THE PACIFIC FROM PEARL HARBOR TO V-J DAY. Greenwich, Conn., Fawcett Publications, 1965. 224 p. (Gold Medal Books)

159 Meeking, Charles, and N. Bartlett (eds.).
    PICTORIAL HISTORY OF AUSTRALIA AT WAR, 1939-45. Canberra, Australian War Memorial, 1958. 5 v.

160 Morris, Herman C., and Harry B. Henderson (eds.).
    WORLD WAR II IN PICTURES. New York, Journal of Living Publishing Corp., 1945. 3 v.

161 Museum of Modern Art, New York.
    POWER IN THE PACIFIC. New York, U.S. Camera, 1945. 144 p.

162 Newnes, George, Ltd.
    OUR FINEST YEARS: A 25TH ANNIVERSARY PICTORIAL PRESENTATION OF THE SECOND WORLD WAR (1939-1945). Foreword by Field Marshal the Viscount Montgomery of Alamein. London, Newnes, 1964. 100 p.

163 PICTORIAL HISTORY OF THE SECOND WORLD WAR: A PHOTOGRAPHIC RECORD OF ALL THEATERS OF ACTION CHRONOLOGICALLY ARRANGED. New York, Wise, 1944-49. 10 v.

164 PICTORIAL HISTORY OF WORLD WAR II: THE GRAPHIC RECORD OF YOUR ARMED FORCES IN ACTION THROUGHOUT EVERY PHASE OF GLOBAL CONFLICT. Veterans of Foreign Wars Memorial Edition. New York, 1951. 2 v.

165 THE PICTURE HISTORY OF WORLD WAR II, 1939-45. New York, Grosset and Dunlap, 1960. 272 p.

    Original edition:
    COLLIER'S PHOTOGRAPHIC HISTORY OF WORLD WAR II. 1946. 272 p.

166 Topolski, Feliks.
    THREE CONTINENTS, 1944-45. London, Methuen, 1946. 224 p.

167 Whitcombe, Fred (ed.).
    THE PICTORIAL HISTORY OF CANADA'S ARMY OVERSEAS, 1939-1945. Narrative by Blair Gilmour. Montreal, Whitcombe, Gilmour, 1947. 280 p.

168 Ziegler, Richard.
    FACES BEHIND THE NEWS. London, Dobson, 1946. 126 p.

E. ATLAS HISTORIES

169 Brown, Ernest F.
    THE WAR IN MAPS: AN ATLAS OF THE NEW YORK TIMES MAPS. London and New York, Oxford University Press, 1946. 197 p.

170 Horrabin, James F.
    AN ATLAS-HISTORY OF THE SECOND GREAT WAR. London and New York, Nelson, 1942-46. 10 v.

171 Stembridge, Jasper H.
    THE OXFORD WAR ATLAS. New York, Oxford University Press, 1941-46. 4 v.

172 U.S. War Dept. General Staff.
    ATLAS OF THE WORLD BATTLE FRONTS IN SEMI-MONTHLY PHASES, TO AUGUST 15, 1945: SUPPLEMENT TO BIENNIAL REPORT OF CHIEF OF STAFF OF THE U.S. ARMY, JULY 1, 1943 TO JUNE 30, 1945, TO SECRETARY OF WAR. Washington, 1945. 101 p.

F. HISTORIOGRAPHY

173 Eremenko, Andrei I.
    FALSE WITNESSES: AN EXPOSURE OF FALSIFIED SECOND WORLD WAR HISTORIES. Translated from Russian by Vic Schneierson. Moscow. Foreign Languages Publishing House, 1962. 144 p.

174 Gallagher, Matthew P.
    THE SOVIET HISTORY OF WORLD WAR II: MYTHS, MEMORIES, AND REALITIES. London and New York, Praeger, 1963. 205 p. (Praeger Publications in Russian History and World Communism)

175 Greenfield, Kent R.
    THE HISTORIAN AND THE ARMY. New Brunswick, Rutgers University Press, 1954. 93 p. (Brown and Haley Lectures, 1953)

176 Russia. Sovetskoe Informatsionnoe Biuro.
    FALSIFIERS OF HISTORY: HISTORICAL SURVEY. Moscow, Foreign Languages Publishing House, 1951. 110 p.

G. LINGUISTIC STUDIES

177 Partridge, Eric (ed.).
    A DICTIONARY OF FORCES' SLANG, 1939-1945. Naval slang by Wilfred Granville; Army slang by Frank Roberts; Air Force slang by Eric Partridge. London, Secker and Warburg, 1948. 212 p.

178 Taylor, Anna M. (comp.).
    THE LANGUAGE OF WORLD WAR II: ABBREVIATIONS, CAPTIONS, QUOTATIONS, SLOGANS, TITLES, AND OTHER TERMS AND PHRASES. Rev. ed. New York, Wilson, 1948. 265 p.

179 Zandvoort, Reinard W., and others.
    WARTIME ENGLISH: MATERIALS FOR A LINGUISTIC HISTORY OF WORLD WAR II. Groningen, Wolters, 1957. 254 p. (Groningen Studies in English)

II. PRELUDE TO THE WAR: ORIGINS AND OUTBREAK (see also IV.B)

A. GENERAL

180 Beard, Charles A.
PRESIDENT ROOSEVELT AND THE COMING OF THE WAR, 1941: A STUDY IN APPEARANCES AND REALITIES. New Haven, Conn., Yale University Press, 1948. 614 p.

181 Cave, Floyd A.
THE ORIGINS AND CONSEQUENCES OF WORLD WAR II. New York, Dryden, 1948. 820 p.

182 Divine, Robert A.
THE RELUCTANT BELLIGERENT: AMERICAN ENTRY INTO WORLD WAR II. New York, Wiley, 1965. 172 p. (America in Crisis)

183 Drummond, Donald F.
THE PASSING OF AMERICAN NEUTRALITY, 1937-1941. Ann Arbor, University of Michigan Press; London, Oxford University Press, 1955. 409 p. (History and Political Science)

184 Freeman, Kathleen.
WHAT THEY SAID AT THE TIME: A SURVEY OF THE CAUSES OF THE SECOND WORLD WAR AND THE HOPES FOR A LASTING PEACE, AS EXHIBITED IN THE UTTERANCES OF THE WORLD'S LEADERS AND SOME OTHERS FROM 1917-1944. London, Muller, 1945. 470 p.

185 Gantenbein, James W.
DOCUMENTARY BACKGROUND OF WORLD WAR II, 1931-1941. New York, Columbia University Press, 1948. 1112 p.

186 Germany. Auswärtiges Amt.
DOCUMENTS AND MATERIALS RELATING TO THE EVE OF THE SECOND WORLD WAR. New York, International Publishers, 1948. 2 v.

187 Haines, C. Grove, and Ross J. S. Hoffman.
THE ORIGINS AND BACKGROUND OF THE SECOND WORLD WAR. London and New York, Oxford University Press, 1943. 659 p.

Other edition:
New York, Oxford University Press, 1947. 729 p.

188 Heller, Bernard.
DAWN OR DUSK? Foreword by George N. Shuster. New York, Bookman's, Inc., 1961. 314 p.

189 Hofer, Walther.
WAR PREMEDITATED, 1939. Translated by Stanley Godman. London, Thames and Hudson, 1955. 227 p.

190 Neilson, Francis.
THE MAKERS OF WAR. Appleton, Wis., Nelson, 1950. 240 p.

191 Rowse, Alfred L.
APPEASEMENT: A STUDY IN POLITICAL DECLINE, 1933-1939. New York, Norton, 1961. 123 p.

192 Salvemini, Gaetano.
PRELUDE TO WORLD WAR II. Translated from Italian by Helene Cantarella. London, Gollancz, 1953. 519 p.

Other edition:
Garden City, N. Y., Doubleday, 1954.

193 Sanborn, Frederic R.
DESIGN FOR WAR: A STUDY OF SECRET POWER POLITICS, 1937-1941. New York, Devin-Adair, 1951. 607 p.

194 Schroeder, Paul W.
THE AXIS ALLIANCE AND JAPANESE-AMERICAN RELATIONS, 1941. Ithaca, N. Y., Cornell University Press, 1958. 246 p.

195 Snell, John L. (ed.).
THE OUTBREAK OF THE SECOND WORLD WAR: DESIGN OR BLUNDER? Boston, Heath, 1962. 107 p. (Problems in European Civilization)

196 Taylor, Alan J. P.
THE ORIGINS OF THE SECOND WORLD WAR. London, Hamilton, 1961. 296 p.

Other editions:
New York, Atheneum, 1962.

Harmondsworth, Eng., Hamilton, 1964. 357 p.

197 Trefousse, Hans L.
GERMANY AND AMERICAN NEUTRALITY, 1939-1941. New York, Bookman Associates, 1951. 247 p.

B. EUROPE

198 Ball, Adrian.
THE LAST DAY OF THE OLD WORLD: 3RD SEPTEMBER, 1939. London, Muller, 1963. 291 p.

Other edition:
Garden City, N. Y., Doubleday, 1963. 278 p.

199 Colvin, Ian G.
VANSITTART IN OFFICE: AN HISTORICAL SURVEY OF THE ORIGINS OF THE SECOND WORLD WAR BASED ON THE PAPERS OF SIR ROBERT VANSITTART, PERMANENT UNDER-SECRETARY OF STATE FOR FOREIGN AFFAIRS, 1930-38. London, Gollancz, 1965. 360 p.

Other edition:
NONE SO BLIND. New York, Harcourt, Brace and World, 1965. 360 p.

200 Eubank, Keith.
MUNICH. Norman, University of Oklahoma Press, 1963. 322 p.

201 Furnia, Arthur H.
THE DIPLOMACY OF APPEASEMENT: ANGLO-FRENCH RELATIONS AND THE PRELUDE TO WORLD WAR II, 1931-1938. Washington, University Press of Washington, 1960. 454 p.

202 Gafencu, Grigory.
THE LAST DAYS OF EUROPE: A DIPLOMATIC JOURNEY IN 1939. Translated by E. Fletcher-Allen. New Haven, Conn., Yale University Press, 1948. 239 p.

203 Loewenheim, Francis L. (ed.).
PEACE OR APPEASEMENT? HITLER, CHAMBERLAIN, AND THE MUNICH CRISIS. Boston, Houghton Mifflin, 1965. 204 p.

204 Namier, Lewis B.
DIPLOMATIC PRELUDE, 1938-1939. London, Macmillan, 1948. 502 p.

205 Namier, Lewis B.
EUROPE IN DECAY: A STUDY IN DISINTEGRATION, 1936-1940. London, Macmillan, 1950. 329 p.

206 Noguères, Henri.
MUNICH: PEACE FOR OUR TIME. Translated from French by Patrick O'Brian. New York, McGraw-Hill, 1965. 423 p.

207 Preuss, Ernst G.
MERCHANTS OF DEATH. London and New York, Hutchinson, 1945. 80 p.

208 Rothstein, Andrew.
MUNICH CONSPIRACY. London, Lawrence and Wishart, 1958. 320 p.

209 Seth, Ronald S.
THE DAY WAR BROKE OUT: THE STORY OF THE 3RD OF SEPTEMBER, 1939. London, Spearman, 1963. 175 p.

210 Wheeler-Bennett, John W.
MUNICH: PROLOGUE TO TRAGEDY. New York, Duell, Sloan and Pearce; London, Macmillan, 1948. 507 p.

C. FAR EAST

211 Burtness, Paul S., and Warren V. Ober (eds.).
THE PUZZLE OF PEARL HARBOR. Evanston, Ill., Row, Peterson, 1962. 244 p.

212 Butow, Robert J. C.
TOJO AND THE COMING OF THE WAR. Princeton, N.J., Princeton University Press, 1961. 584 p.

213 Feis, Herbert.
THE ROAD TO PEARL HARBOR: THE COMING OF THE WAR BETWEEN THE UNITED STATES AND JAPAN. Princeton, N.J., Princeton University Press, 1950. 356 p.

214 Hoehling, Adolph A.
THE WEEK BEFORE PEARL HARBOR. New York, Norton, 1963. 238 p.

Other edition:
London, Hale, 1964. 189 p.

215 Kimmel, Husband E.
ADMIRAL KIMMEL'S STORY. Chicago, Regnery, 1955. 206 p.

216 Lord, Walter.
DAY OF INFAMY. New York, Holt, 1957. 254 p.

Other editions:
London, Longmans, Green, 1957. 243 p.

London, Transworld, 1959. 254 p. (Corgi Books)

217 Millis, Walter.
THIS IS PEARL! THE UNITED STATES AND JAPAN, 1941. New York, Morrow, 1947. 384 p.

218 Morgenstern, George E.
PEARL HARBOR: THE STORY OF THE SECRET WAR. New York, Devin-Adair, 1947. 425 p.

219 Sakamaki, Kazuo.
I ATTACKED PEARL HARBOR. Translated by Toru Matsumoto; Introduced by Tsutae Nara. New York, Association Press, 1949. 133 p.

220 Theobald, Robert A.
THE FINAL SECRET OF PEARL HARBOR: THE WASHINGTON CONTRIBUTION TO THE JAPANESE ATTACK. Forewords by Husband E. Kimmel and William F. Halsey. New York, Devin-Adair, 1954. 202 p.

Other edition:
London, Holborn, 1959. 204 p.

221 Transill, Charles C.
BACKDOOR TO WAR: THE ROOSEVELT FOREIGN POLICY, 1933-1941. Chicago, Regnery, 1952. 609 p.

222 Trefousse, Hans L. (ed.).
WHAT HAPPENED TO PEARL HARBOR? DOCUMENTS PERTAINING TO THE JAPANESE ATTACK OF DECEMBER 7, 1941, AND ITS BACKGROUND. New York, Twayne, 1958. 324 p.

223 U.S. Congress. Joint Committee on the Investigation of the Pearl Harbor Attack.
PEARL HARBOR ATTACK: HEARINGS BEFORE THE JOINT COMMITTEE ON THE INVESTIGATION OF THE PEARL HARBOR ATTACK. Washington, U.S. Government Printing Office, 1946. 39 v.

224 Waller, George M. (ed.).
PEARL HARBOR: ROOSEVELT AND THE COMING OF THE WAR. Boston, Heath, 1953. 112 p. (Problems in American Civilization)

Other edition:
1965. 111 p.

225 Wohlstetter, Roberta.
PEARL HARBOR: WARNING AND DECISION. Stanford, Calif., Stanford University Press, 1962. 426 p.

III. MILITARY ASPECTS OF THE WAR

A. GENERAL ACCOUNTS

226   Augé, J. N. (ed.).
        WITH THE BRITISH AND U.S. FORCES AT WAR: A MILITARY READER. Paris, Didier, 1948. 2 v.

227   Australian War Memorial.
        THE ARMY CHRISTMAS BOOKS. Canberra, Australian War Memorial, 1941-45. 5 v.

228   Australian War Memorial.
        STAND EASY. Canberra, Australian War Memorial, 1945. 208 p.

229   Beith, John H. (Ian Hay, pseud.).
        ARMS AND THE MEN. London, H. M. Stationery Office, 1950. 330 p. (The Second World War, 1939-1945: A Popular Military History)

230   Brent, Rafer (ed.).
        GREAT WAR STORIES: TRUE ADVENTURES OF FIGHTING MEN IN TWO WORLD WARS. New York, Bartholomew House, 1957. 188 p.

231   Brodrick, Alan H.
        BEYOND THE BURMA ROAD. London and New York, Hutchison, 1945. 112 p.

232   Canada. Dept. of National Defence. General Staff.
        THE CANADIAN ARMY AT WAR. Ottawa, King's Printer, 1945-46. 3 v.

233   Canada. Dept. of National Defence. General Staff.
        OFFICIAL HISTORY OF THE CANADIAN ARMY IN THE SECOND WORLD WAR. Ottawa, Queen's Printer, 1955-60. 3 v.

234   Cant, Gilbert.
        WAR ON JAPAN. New York, American Council, Institute of Pacific Relations, 1945. 64 p.

235   Carroll, Gordon (ed.).
        HISTORY IN THE WRITING, BY THE FOREIGN CORRESPONDENTS OF TIME, LIFE AND FORTUNE. New York, Duell, Sloan and Pearce, 1945. 401 p.

236   Chaphekar, Shankarrao G.
        WAR IN THE WEST. Poona, Maharashtra Militarisation Board, 1958. 157 p.

237   Cohn, David L.
        THIS IS THE STORY. Boston, Houghton Mifflin, 1947. 563 p.

238   Congdon, Don (ed.).
        COMBAT: EUROPEAN THEATRE, WORLD WAR II. Introduction by Merle Miller. New York, Dell, 1958. 380 p.

Other edition:
New York, Dell, 1959. 382 p.

239   Congdon, Don (ed.).
        COMBAT: THE WAR WITH JAPAN. Introduction by Richard Tregaskis. New York, Dell, 1962. 384 p. (Dell First Edition)

Other editions:
London, Mayflower, 1963.
        COMBAT: WAR IN THE PACIFIC. London, Mayflower, 1965. 382 p. (Mayflower Dell Paperbacks)

240   Conn, Stetson, and Byron Fairchild.
        THE FRAMEWORK OF HEMISPHERE DEFENSE. Washington, Office of Chief of Military History, Dept. of Army, 1960. (U. S. Army in World War II: The Western Hemisphere)

241   Cooper, Herston.
        OVER MY SHOULDER. Philadelphia, Dorrance, 1948. 145 p.

242   Dupuy, Trevor N.
        ASIATIC LAND BATTLES: THE EXPANSION OF JAPAN IN ASIA. London, Ward, 1965. 68 p. (Illustrated History of World War II)

Originally published:
New York, Watts, 1963.

243   Dziuban, Stanley W.
        MILITARY RELATIONS BETWEEN THE UNITED STATES AND CANADA, 1939-1945. Washington, Office of Chief of Military History, Dept. of Army, 1959. 432 p. (U. S. Army in World War II: Special Studies)

244   Dziuban, Stanley W.
        UNITED STATES MILITARY COLLABORATION WITH CANADA IN WORLD WAR II. Washington, Office of Chief of Military History, Dept. of Army, 1954. 830 p.

245   Fuller, John F. C.
        THE SECOND WORLD WAR, 1939-45: A STRATEGICAL AND TACTICAL HISTORY. London, Eyre and Spottiswoode, 1948. 431 p.

Other editions:
New York, Duell, Sloan and Pearce, 1949; 1954; 1962.

246   Gallagher, O'Dowd.
        RETREAT IN THE EAST: A WAR BOOK. London, World Distributors, 1956. 192 p. (Viking Books)

Originally published:
London, Harrap, 1942. 190 p.

247   Gardner, Brian.
        THE YEAR THAT CHANGED THE WORLD: 1945. New York, Coward-McCann, 1964. 356 p.

248   Gleeson, James J., and Thomas J. Waldron.
        NOW IT CAN BE TOLD. Foreword by Sir Colin Gubbins. London, Elek; New York, Philosophical Library, 1952. 188 p.

249 Holles, Everett.
UNCONDITIONAL SURRENDER. New York, Howell, Soskin, 1945.

250 Hunter, Kenneth E., and Margaret E. Tackley (comps.).
THE WAR AGAINST JAPAN. Edited by Mary Ann Bacon. Washington, Office of Chief of Military History, Dept. of Army, 1952. 471 p. (U.S. Army in World War II: Pictorial Record)

251 Jacobsen, Hans A., and Jürgen Rohwer (eds.).
DECISIVE BATTLES OF WORLD WAR II: THE GERMAN VIEW. Introduction by Cyril Falls; translated by Edward Fitzgerald. London, Deutsch; New York, Putnam, 1965. 509 p. (Arbeitskreis für Wehrforschung Publications)

252 Kirby, Stanley W., with C. T. Addis and others.
THE WAR AGAINST JAPAN. London, H.M. Stationery Office, 1957-. 4 v. published.

253 Leitgeber, Witold (comp.).
IT SPEAKS FOR ITSELF: WHAT BRITISH WAR LEADERS SAID ABOUT THE POLISH ARMED FORCES, 1936-1946; SELECTIONS FROM COMMUNIQUES, SPEECHES, MESSAGES AND PRESS REPORTS. n.p., 1946. 163 p.

254 Loomis, William.
FIGHTING FIRSTS. New York, Vantage Press, 1958. 343 p.

255 New Zealand. Prime Minister's Dept. Information Section.
WAR RECORD. Wellington, Paul, Government Printer, 1946. 60 p.

256 Oleck, Howard L. (comp.).
HEROIC BATTLES OF WORLD WAR II. New York, Belmont Books, 1962. 189 p.

257 Olsson, Carl.
FROM HELL TO BREAKFAST: EPIC OPERATIONS OF THE LAST WAR. London, Brown, Watson, 1959. 157 p. (Digit Books)

258 THE 100 BEST TRUE STORIES OF WORLD WAR II, WITH THIRTY-TWO ILLUSTRATIONS. New York, Wise, 1945. 896 p.

259 O'Neill, Herbert C. (Strategicus, pseud.).
FOOTHOLD IN EUROPE: THE CAMPAIGNS IN SICILY, ITALY, THE FAR EAST AND RUSSIA BETWEEN JULY 1943 AND MAY 1944. London, Faber and Faber, 1945. 243 p.

260 Pratt, Fletcher.
WAR FOR THE WORLD: A CHRONICLE OF OUR FIGHTING FORCES IN WORLD WAR II. New Haven, Conn., Yale University Press, 1950. 364 p. (Chronicles of America Series)

261 Pringle, Patrick.
FIGHTING MEN. London, Evans, 1964. 191 p.

262 Ramsey, Guy H. W. (comp.).
EPIC STORIES OF THE SECOND WORLD WAR. Preface by Guy Ramsey. London, Odhams Press, 1957. 318 p.

263 Rooney, Andrew A.
THE FORTUNES OF WAR: FOUR GREAT BATTLES OF WORLD WAR II. Boston, Little, Brown, 1962. 236 p.

264 Rowan-Robinson, Henry.
FROM TUNISIA TO NORMANDY. London and New York, Hutchinson, 1945. 176 p.

265 Saturday Evening Post.
BATTLE: TRUE STORIES OF COMBAT IN WORLD WAR II FROM THE SATURDAY EVENING POST. New York, Curtis Books, 1965. 310 p.

266 Scott, Jay (pseud.).
AMERICA'S WAR HEROES: DRAMATIC TRUE TALES OF COURAGEOUS MARINES, ARMY, AIR FORCE, AND NAVY MEN WHOSE EXPLOITS WON THEM THE CONGRESSIONAL MEDAL OF HONOR. Derby, Conn., Monarch Books, 1961. 143 p. (Monarch Americana Series)

267 70 TRUE STORIES OF THE SECOND WORLD WAR. London, Odhams Press, 1958. 320 p. (Beacon Books)

268 Sheppard, Eric W., and Francis C. C. Yeats-Brown.
THE ARMY: A COMPLETE RECORD IN TEXT AND PICTURES. London, Hutchinson, 1941-47. 5 v. (Britain at War)

269 Silvera, John D.
THE NEGRO IN WORLD WAR II. Baton Rouge, Military Press, 1946. 1 v. (unpaged)

270 Smyth, Sir John George.
BEFORE THE DAWN: A STORY OF TWO HISTORIC RETREATS. 2d ed. London, Cassell, 1957. 220 p.

271 Steinbeck, John.
ONCE THERE WAS A WAR. New York, Viking Press, 1958. 233 p.

Other editions:
London, Heinemann, 1959. 233 p.

London, Transworld, 1961. 222 p. (Corgi Books)

272 Sterling, Dorothy (ed.).
I HAVE SEEN WAR: 25 STORIES FROM WORLD WAR II. New York, Hill and Wang, 1960. 273 p.

273 Stewart, George.
THESE MEN, MY FRIENDS. Caldwell, Idaho, Caxton Printers, 1954. 400 p.

274 True.
TRUE WAR STORIES: A CREST ANTHOLOGY, SELECTED BY BOB CONSIDINE FROM TRUE, THE MAN'S MAGAZINE. Greenwich, Conn., Fawcett Publications, 1961. 239 p. (Crest Book)

275 U.S. Military Academy, West Point. Dept. of Military Art and Engineering.
EARLY CAMPAIGNS OF WORLD WAR II. West Point, N.Y., 1950. 52 p.

Other edition:
1951. 136 p.

276 U.S. Military Academy, West Point. Dept. of Military Art and Engineering.
A MILITARY HISTORY OF WORLD WAR II. Edited by T. Dodson Stamps and Vincent J. Esposito. West Point, N.Y., 1953. 2 v.

277 U.S. Military Academy, West Point. Dept. of Military Art and Engineering.
THE WAR WITH JAPAN. West Point, N.Y., 1944-46. 3 pts.

278 Urquhart, Fred (ed.).
GREAT TRUE WAR ADVENTURES. London, Arco, 1957. 342 p.

279 Warner, Harold P.
FIRST AUTHENTIC MINIATURE V-MAIL PORTRAITS OF WORLD WAR II, AND SEVERAL SHORT STORIES. Raleigh, N.C., 1948. 84 p.

280 Westphal, Siegfried.
THE GERMAN ARMY IN THE WEST. Translated from the German. London, Cassell, 1952. 222 p.

281 Wigmore, Lionel.
THE JAPANESE THRUST. Canberra, Australian War Memorial, 1957. 715 p. (Australia in the War of 1939-1945. Series 1 [Army])

282 Yank, The Army Weekly.
YANK--THE G.I. STORY OF THE WAR, BY THE STAFF OF YANK, THE ARMY WEEKLY. Selected and edited by Debs Myers and others. New York, Duell, Sloan and Pearce, 1947. 319 p.

283 Ziemke, Earl F.
THE GERMAN NORTHERN THEATER OF OPERATIONS, 1940-1945. Washington, U.S. Government Printing Office, 1960. 342 p.

B. MEMOIRS AND BIOGRAPHIES

1. American

284 Allied Forces. Supreme Headquarters.
EISENHOWER'S OWN STORY OF THE WAR: THE COMPLETE RECORD BY THE SUPREME COMMANDER, GENERAL DWIGHT D. EISENHOWER, ON THE WAR IN EUROPE FROM THE DAY OF INVASION TO THE DAY OF VICTORY. New York, Arco, 1946. 122 p.

285 Arrington, Grady P.
INFANTRYMAN AT THE FRONT. New York, Vantage, 1959. 244 p.

286 Bradley, Omar N.
A SOLDIER'S STORY. New York, Holt; London, Eyre and Spottiswoode, 1951. 618 p.

287 Brown, David T.
LETTERS, 1941-45, OF DAVID TUCKER BROWN, JR., U.S. MARINE CORPS RESERVE, KILLED IN ACTION ON OKINAWA SHIMA, RYUKYU ISLANDS. n.p., 1946. 105 p.

Other edition:
MARINE FROM VIRGINIA. Chapel Hill, University of North Carolina Press, 1947. 105 p.

288 Brundage, Helen (ed.).
LETTERS TO HELEN. New York, Vantage, 1955. 108 p.

289 Butcher, Harry C.
MY THREE YEARS WITH EISENHOWER. New York, Simon and Schuster, 1946. 911 p.

290 Casey, Robert J.
THIS IS WHERE I CAME IN. Indianapolis, Bobbs-Merrill, 1945. 307 p.

291 Chennault, Claire L.
WAY OF A FIGHTER: THE MEMORIES OF CLAIRE LEE CHENNAULT. Edited by Robert Hotz. New York, Putnam, 1949. 375 p.

292 Clark, Mark W.
CALCULATED RISK. New York, Harper, 1950. 500 p.

Other editions:
London, Harrap, 1951. 478 p.

London, Hamilton, 1956. 448 p. (Panther Books)

293 Dickey, Charles W.
HERE WE GO AGAIN. New York, Pageant Press, 1951. 165 p.

294 Dye, John T.
GOLDEN LEAVES. Los Angeles, Ward Ritchie Press, 1962. 227 p.

295 Eisenhower, Dwight D.
CRUSADE IN EUROPE. Garden City, N.Y., Doubleday, 1948. 559 p.

Other edition:
Garden City, N.Y., Garden City Books, 1952. 573 p.

296 Farago, Ladislas.
PATTON: ORDEAL AND TRIUMPH. New York, Obolensky, 1964. 885 p.

297 Gray, Jesse G.
THE WARRIORS: REFLECTIONS ON MEN IN BATTLE. New York, Harcourt, Brace, 1959. 242 p.

298 Halsey, William F., and J. Bryan III.
ADMIRAL HALSEY'S STORY. New York, Whittlesey House, 1947. 310 p.

299 Hatch, Alden.
GEORGE PATTON: GENERAL IN SPURS. New York, Messner, 1950. 184 p.

300 Hirsch, Phil (ed.).
THE KENNEDY WAR HEROES. New York, Pyramid Books, 1962. 159 p.

301 Hogan, John J.
I AM NOT ALONE. Washington, Mackinac Press, 1947. 130 p.

302 Hovsepian, Aramais A.
YOUR SON AND MINE. Culver City, Calif., Murray and Gee; New York, Duell, Sloan and Pearce, 1950. 205 p.

303 Johnson, Franklyn A.
ONE MORE HILL. New York, Funk and Wagnalls, 1949. 181 p.

304 Joswick, Jerry J., with Lawrence A. Keating.
COMBAT CAMERAMAN. Foreword by John D. Craig. Philadelphia, Chilton Co., 1961. 200 p.

305 Kahn, Ely J.
McNAIR, EDUCATOR OF AN ARMY. Washington, Infantry Journal, 1945. 64 p.

306 Kennedy, Sir John.
THE BUSINESS OF WAR. Edited by Bernard Fergusson. London, Hutchinson, 1957. 370 p.

Other edition:
New York, Morrow, 1958. 370 p.

307 Kenney, George C.
GENERAL KENNEY REPORTS: A PERSONAL HISTORY OF THE PACIFIC WAR. New York, Duell, Sloan and Pearce, 1949. 594 p.

308 MacArthur, Douglas.
REMINISCENCES. New York, McGraw-Hill, 1964. 438 p.

309 MacArthur, Douglas.
A SOLDIER SPEAKS: PUBLIC PAPERS. New York, Praeger, 1965. 367 p.

310 McKeogh, Michael J., and Richard Lockridge.
SERGEANT MICKEY AND GENERAL IKE. New York, Putnam, 1946. 185 p.

311 McWane, Frederick W.
MEMOIRS. Lynchburg, Va., 1951. 150 p.

312 Marshall, George C.
SELECTED SPEECHES AND STATEMENTS OF GENERAL OF THE ARMY GEORGE C. MARSHALL. Edited by H. A. De Weerd. Washington, Infantry Journal Press, 1945. 263 p.

Other edition:
Washington, Infantry Journal Press, 1945. 324 p. (Fighting Forces Series)

313 Mauldin, William H.
UP FRONT. Cleveland and New York, World, 1945. 228 p.

314 Middleton, Drew.
OUR SHARE OF NIGHT: A PERSONAL NARRATIVE OF THE WAR YEARS. New York, Viking Press, 1946. 380 p.

315 Miller, Francis T.
GENERAL DOUGLAS MacARTHUR. Introduction by Lowell Thomas. Philadelphia, Winston, 1944. 280 p.

Other editions:
1945. 295 p.

GENERAL DOUGLAS MacARTHUR: SOLDIER-STATESMAN. 1951.

316 Patton, George S.
WAR AS I KNEW IT. Annotated by Paul D. Harkins; edited by Beatrice A. Patton. Boston, Houghton Mifflin, 1947. 425 p.

317 Pearl, Jack.
BLOOD-AND-GUTS PATTON: THE SWASHBUCKLING LIFE STORY OF AMERICA'S MOST DARING AND CONTROVERSIAL GENERAL. Derby, Conn., Monarch Books, 1961. 142 p. (Monarch Americana Book)

318 Reynolds, Bart.
PAISANO. Los Angeles, Gamma Delta Upsilon, 1957. 176 p.

319 Rontch, Isaac E.
JEWISH YOUTH AT WAR: LETTERS FROM AMERICAN SOLDIERS. New York, Marstin Press, 1945. 304 p.

320 Salisbury-Jones, Sir Guy.
SO FULL A GLORY: A BIOGRAPHY OF MARSHAL DE LATTRE DE TASSIGNY. Foreword by Viscount Norwich. London, Weidenfeld and Nicolson, 1954. 288 p.

321 Semmes, Harry H.
PORTRAIT OF PATTON. New York, 1955. 308 p.

322 Seramgard, Arthur K.
THE LOG OF THE OLD SARGE. Helena, Mont., 1950. 185 p.

323 Sevareid, A. Eric.
NOT SO WILD A DREAM. New York, Knopf, 1946. 516 p.

324 Sheean, Vincent.
THIS HOUSE AGAINST THIS HOUSE. New York, Random House, 1946. 420 p.

325 Stilwell, Joseph W.
THE STILWELL PAPERS. Arranged and edited by Theodore H. White. New York, Sloane, 1948. 357 p.

326 Summersby, Kathleen.
　　EISENHOWER WAS MY BOSS. Edited by Michael Kearns. New York, Prentice-Hall, 1948. 302 p.

327 Sykes, Christopher.
　　ORDE WINGATE. Cleveland, World, 1959. 575 p.

328 Taylor, Henry, Jr.
　　MEN AND POWER. New York, Dodd, Mead, 1946. 257 p.

329 Taylor, Theodore.
　　THE MAGNIFICENT MITSCHER. Foreword by Arthur W. Radford. New York, Norton, 1954. 364 p.

330 Truscott, Lucian K.
　　COMMAND MISSIONS: A PERSONAL STORY. New York, Dutton, 1954. 570 p.

331 Tumey, Ben.
　　G.I.'S VIEW OF WORLD WAR II: THE DIARY OF A COMBAT PRIVATE. New York, Exposition Press, 1959. 64 p.

332 Wainwright, Jonathan M.
　　GENERAL WAINWRIGHT'S STORY. Edited by Robert Considine. Garden City, N.Y., Doubleday, 1946. 314 p.

333 Wedemeyer, Albert C.
　　WEDEMEYER REPORTS! New York, Holt, 1958. 497 p.

334 Welch, Robert H. W.
　　THE LIFE OF JOHN BIRCH: IN THE STORY OF ONE AMERICAN BOY, THE ORDEAL OF HIS AGE. Chicago, Regnery, 1954. 118 p.

335 Welker, Robert H.
　　A DIFFERENT DRUMMER: THE ODYSSEY OF A HOME-GROWN REBEL. Boston, Beacon Press; London, Paterson, 1958. 404 p.

336 Whitney, Cornelius V.
　　LONE AND LEVEL SANDS. New York, Farrar, Straus and Young, 1951. 314 p.

337 Whitney, Courtney.
　　MacARTHUR: HIS RENDEZVOUS WITH HISTORY. New York, Knopf, 1956. 547 p.

　　　　2. British and Commonwealth

338 Alexander, Harold R. L. G. Alexander, 1st earl.
　　THE ALEXANDER MEMOIRS, 1940-1945. Edited by John North. London, Cassell, 1962. 209 p.

Other edition:
New York, McGraw-Hill, 1963. 209 p.

339 Allison, Errol S.
　　KIWI AT LARGE. London, Hale, 1961. 190 p.

340 Bramwell, James G. (James Byrom, pseud.).
　　THE UNFINISHED MAN. London, Chatto and Windus, 1957. 252 p.

341 Bryant, Sir Arthur.
　　THE TURN OF THE TIDE, 1939-1943: A STUDY BASED ON DIARIES AND AUTOBIOGRAPHICAL NOTES OF FIELD MARSHAL LORD ALANBROOKE, CHIEF OF IMPERIAL GENERAL STAFF. London, Collins, 1957. 706 p.

Other editions:
Garden City, N.Y., Doubleday, 1957. 624 p.

London, Collins, 1965. 637 p. (Fontana Books)

342 Bryant, Benjamin.
　　ONE MAN BAND: THE MEMOIRS OF A SUBMARINE C.O. London, Kimber, 1958. 238 p.

343 Calvert, Michael.
　　FIGHTING MAD. London, Jarrolds, 1964. 224 p.

344 Carew, John M. (Tim Carew, pseud.).
　　ALL THIS AND A MEDAL TOO. London, Constable, 1954. 252 p.

Other editions:
London, Transworld, 1957. 312 p. (Corgi Books)

London, Transworld, 1960. 319 p. (Corgi Books)

345 Chalmers, William S.
　　FULL CYCLE: THE BIOGRAPHY OF ADMIRAL SIR BERTRAM HOME RAMSAY. London, Hodder and Stoughton, 1950. 288 p.

346 Chalmers, William S.
　　MAX HORTON AND THE WESTERN APPROACHES: A BIOGRAPHY OF ADMIRAL SIR MAX KENNEDY HORTON. London, Hodder and Stoughton, 1954. 301 p.

347 Cunningham, Andrew B. Cunningham, 1st viscount.
　　A SAILOR'S ODYSSEY: THE AUTOBIOGRAPHY OF ADMIRAL OF THE FLEET, VISCOUNT CUNNINGHAM OF HYNDHOPE. London and New York, Hutchinson; New York, Dutton, 1951. 715 p.

348 De Guingand, Sir Francis W.
　　OPERATION VICTORY. London, Hodder and Stoughton; New York, Scribner, 1947. 488 p.

349 Dollmann, Eugen.
　　CALL ME COWARD. Introduction by Field-Marshal Kesselring; translated from German by Edward Fitzgerald. London, Kimber, 1956. 201 p.

350 Dyer, H. G.
　　LANDS OF ALADDIN: LETTERS FROM A NEW ZEALAND SOLDIER TO HIS SMALL SON. Ilfracombe, Eng., Stockwell, 1953. 80 p.

351 Embry, Sir Basil E.
　　WINGLESS VICTORY: THE STORY OF SIR BASIL EMBRY'S ESCAPE FROM OCCUPIED FRANCE IN THE SUMMER OF 1940. Related by Anthony Richardson. London, Odhams Press, 1950. 256 p.

Other edition:
　　ALONE HE WENT. New York, Norton, 1951. 248 p.

352 Fairfax, John.
DRIFT OF LEAVES. Edited by John Brennan. Sydney, U. Smith, 1952. 96 p.

353 Farran, Roy A.
WINGED DAGGER: ADVENTURES ON SPECIAL SERVICE. London, Collins, 1948. 384 p.

Other edition:
1956. 383 p.

354 Firbank, Thomas.
I BOUGHT A STAR. London, Harrap, 1951. 240 p.

355 Gander, Leonard M.
LONG ROAD TO LEROS. London, Macdonald, 1945. 215 p.

356 Goodbody, Ernest.
HOW I WON THE WAR. As told to Patrick Ryan. London, Muller, 1963. 255 p.

357 Graham, Cosmo M.
A SPACE FOR DELIGHT: LETTERS FROM THE LATE REAR-ADMIRAL COSMO GRAHAM TO HIS WIFE DURING THE YEARS 1939 TO 1942. London, Witherby, 1954. 191 p.

358 Henriques, L. Q. (comp.).
FRATRES: CLUB BOYS IN UNIFORM: AN ANTHOLOGY. London, Secker and Warburg, 1951. 216 p.

359 Hetherington, John A.
BLAMEY: THE BIOGRAPHY OF FIELD-MARSHAL SIR THOMAS BLAMEY. Melbourne, Cheshire, 1954. 257 p.

Other edition:
London, Angus and Robertson, 1955. 277 p.

360 Hillson, Norman.
ALEXANDER OF TUNIS: A BIOGRAPHICAL PORTRAIT. London, Allen, 1952. 252 p.

361 Holman, Dennis.
THE MAN THEY COULDN'T KILL. London, Heinemann, 1960. 232 p.

362 Horrocks, Sir Brian.
ESCAPE TO ACTION. London, Collins; New York, St. Martin's Press, 1961. 320 p.

363 Ismay, Hastings L. Ismay, baron.
MEMOIRS. New York, Viking Press, 1960. 488 p.

364 Keyes, Elizabeth.
GEOFFREY KEYES, V.C.M.C., CROIX DE GUERRE, ROYAL SCOTS GREYS, LIEUTENANT-COLONEL, 11TH SCOTTISH COMMANDO. London, Newnes, 1956. 278 p.

365 Kimmins, Anthony M.
HALF-TIME. London, Heinemann, 1947. 290 p.

366 King, Ernest J., and Walter M. Whitehall.
FLEET ADMIRAL KING: A NAVAL RECORD. New York, Norton, 1952. 674 p.

Other edition:
London, Eyre, 1953. 465 p.

367 Kinsella, Patrick.
LETTERS FROM PATRICK: LETTERS OF LIFE AND LOVE FROM AN R.A.F. PILOT BOMBARDIER TO THE AMERICAN ACTRESS, CLAIRE LUCE. Philadelphia, Chilton Books, 1965. 182 p.

368 Kippenberger, Sir Howard.
INFANTRY BRIGADIER. New York, Oxford University Press, 1949. 371 p.

369 Legg, Frank.
WAR CORRESPONDENT. Adelaide, Rigby, 1964. 265 p.

Other edition:
London, Angus, 1965.

370 Lodwick, John.
BID THE SOLDIERS SHOOT. London, Heinemann, 1958. 295 p.

Other edition:
London, Hamilton, 1960. 224 p. (Panther Books)

371 McGill, Michael C., and William D. Flackes.
MONTGOMERY, FIELD-MARSHAL: AN ULSTER TRIBUTE. Belfast, Quota Press, 1945. 99 p.

3rd edition:
1946. 122 p.

372 MacInnes, Colin.
TO THE VICTORS THE SPOILS. Macgibbon and Kee, 1950. 350 p.

373 Maclean, Fitzroy.
ESCAPE TO ADVENTURE. Boston, Little, Brown, 1950. 419 p.

374 Maule, Henry.
SPEARHEAD GENERAL: THE EPIC STORY OF GENERAL SIR FRANK MESSERVY AND HIS MEN IN ERITREA, NORTH AFRICA AND BURMA. London, Odhams Press, 1961. 383 p.

Other edition:
London, Transworld, 1963. (Corgi Books)

375 Montgomery, Bernard L. Montgomery, 1st viscount.
MEMOIRS. London, Collins, 1958. 574 p. (Fontana Books)

Other editions:
Cleveland, World Publishing Co., 1958. 508 p.

THE MEMOIRS OF FIELD-MARSHAL THE VISCOUNT-MONTGOMERY OF ALAMEIN, K.G. New York, New American Library, 1959. 508 p. (Signet Book)

376 Moxon, Oliver.
AFTER THE MONSOON. London, Hale, 1958. 160 p.

377 Mulgan, John.
REPORT ON EXPERIENCE. London and New York, Oxford University Press, 1947. 150 p.

378 Pereira, Jocelyn.
A DISTANT DRUM: WAR MEMORIES OF THE INTELLIGENCE OFFICER OF THE 5TH BN. COLDSTREAM GUARDS, 1944-45. Aldershot, Gale and Polden, 1948. 213 p.

379 THE PITCHER AND THE WELL. Hamilton, N.Z., Paul's Book Arcade, 1961. 224 p.

Other editions:
Boston, Houghton Mifflin, 1963. 308 p.

London, Oldbourne, 1963. 224 p.

380 Pleasants, Eric.
I KILLED TO LIVE: THE STORY OF ERIC PLEASANTS AS TOLD TO EDDIE CHAPMAN. London, Cassell, 1957. 223 p.

381 Robertson, John H. (John Connell, pseud.).
AUCHINLECK: A BIOGRAPHY OF FIELD-MARSHAL SIR CLAUDE AUCHINLECK. London, Cassell, 1959. 975 p.

382 Robson, Walter.
LETTERS FROM A SOLDIER. Introduction by Henry Williamson. London, Faber and Faber, 1960. 192 p.

383 Rowdon, Maurice.
OF SINS AND WINTER. London, Chatto and Windus, 1955. 182 p.

384 Samwell, H. P.
AN INFANTRY OFFICER WITH THE EIGHTH ARMY. Foreword by Sir Philip Gibbs. Edinburgh, Blackwood, 1945. 208 p.

385 Sandford, Kenneth.
MARK OF THE LION: THE STORY OF CAPT. CHARLES UPHAM, V.C. AND BAR. London, Hutchinson; New York, Washburn, 1962. 287 p.

Other edition:
London, Arrow, 1964. 320 p.

386 Schimanski, Stefan, and Henry Treece (eds.).
LEAVES IN THE STORM: A BOOK OF DIARIES. London, Drummond, 1947. 299 p.

387 Smeeton, Miles.
A CHANGE OF JUNGLES. London, Hart-Davis, 1962. 192 p.

388 Stevens, William G.
FREYBERG, V.C.: THE MAN, 1939-1945. London, Jenkins; Wellington, Reed, 1965. 130 p.

389 Strauss, Cyril A.
A SOLDIER LOOKS BACK: THE JOURNALS OF CYRIL ANTHONY STRAUSS. Edited and introduced by Derek Patmore. London, Falcon Press, 1951. 257 p.

390 Thompson, Reginald W.
AN ECHO OF TRUMPETS London, Allen and Unwin, 1964. 222 p.

391 Verney, John.
GOING TO THE WARS: A JOURNEY IN VARIOUS DIRECTIONS. London, Collins, 1955. 254 p.

Other editions:
New York, Dodd, Mead, 1955. 247 p.

Harmondsworth, Eng., Penguin, 1958. 238 p.

392 Wavell, Archibald P.
SPEAKING GENERALLY: BROADCASTS, ORDERS, AND ADDRESSES IN TIME OF WAR, 1939-43. London, Macmillan, 1946. 166 p.

393 West, Adam.
JUST AS THEY CAME. London and New York, Longmans, Green, 1946. 199 p.

394 Weygand, Maxime.
RECALLED TO SERVICE: THE MEMOIRS OF GENERAL MAXIME WEYGAND. Translated by E. W. Dickes. Garden City, N.Y., Doubleday; London, Heinemann, 1952. 454 p.

395 Weygand, Maxime.
THE ROLE OF GENERAL WEYGAND: CONVERSATIONS WITH HIS SON, COMMANDANT J. WEYGAND. Translated by J. H. F. McEwen; introduction by Cyril Falls. London, Eyre and Spottiswoode, 1948. 191 p.

396 Wicklow, W. C. J. P. J. P. H., 8th earl of.
FIRESIDE FUSILIER. Introduction by Evelyn Waugh. Dublin, Clonmore and Reynolds; London, Hollis and Carter, 1958. 145 p.

397 Wilson, Henry M. Wilson, baron.
EIGHT YEARS OVERSEAS, 1939-1947. Foreword by D. D. Eisenhower. London and New York, Hutchinson, 1950. 285 p.

398 Winant, John G.
OUR GREATEST HARVEST: SELECTED SPEECHES, 1941-46. London, Hodder and Stoughton. 1950. 228 p.

399 Woodward, David.
RAMSAY AT WAR: THE FIGHTING LIFE OF ADMIRAL SIR BERTRAM RAMSAY. London, Kimber, 1957. 204 p.

3. German

400 Abshagen, Karl H.
CANARIS. Translated by Alan H. Brodrick. London, Hutchinson, 1956. 264 p.

401 Bahnemann, Gunther.
I DESERTED ROMMEL. London, Jarrolds, 1961. 256 p.

Other edition:
London, Arrow, 1963. 256 p.

402 Blumentritt, Guenther.
VON RUNDSTEDT: THE SOLDIER AND THE MAN. Foreword by Field-Marshal von Rundstedt; translated from German by Cuthbert Reavely. London, Odhams, 1952. 288 p.

403 Dönitz, Karl.
MEMOIRS: TEN YEARS AND TWENTY DAYS. Translated by R. H. Stevens, with David Woodward. Cleveland, World Publishing Co.; London, Weidenfeld and Nicolson, 1959. 500 p.

404 Görlitz, Walter.
PAULUS AND STALINGRAD: A LIFE OF FIELD-MARSHAL FRIEDRICH PAULUS WITH NOTES, CORRESPONDENCE AND DOCUMENTS FROM HIS PAPERS. Preface by Ernst A. Paulus; translated by R. H. Stevens. New York, Citadel Press; London, Methuen, 1963. 301 p.

405 Guderian, Heinz.
PANZER LEADER. Foreword by B. H. Liddell Hart; translated from German by Constantine FitzGibbon. London, Joseph; New York, Dutton, 1952. 528 p.

Other edition:
London, Harborough, 1957. 223 p. (Ace Books)

406 Halder, Franz.
DIARY, COVERING THE PERIOD AUGUST 14, 1939 TO SEPTEMBER 24, 1942. Nuremberg, Office of Chief of Council for War Crimes, Office of Military Government for Germany (U. S.), 1946. 4 v.

Other edition:
THE HALDER DIARIES. Washington, Infantry Journal, 1950. 7 v.

407 Keitel, Wilhelm B. J. G.
THE MEMOIRS OF FIELD-MARSHAL KEITEL. Edited with introduction and epilogue by Walter Gorlitz; translated from German by David Irving. London, Kimber, 1965. 288 p.

408 Kesselring, Albert.
KESSELRING: A SOLDIER'S RECORD. Translated by Lynton Hudson. New York, Morrow, 1954. 381 p.

Other edition:
THE MEMOIRS OF FIELD-MARSHAL KESSELRING. London, Kimber, 1953. 319 p.

409 Mannerheim, Carl G. E.
MEMOIRS. Translated by Count Eric Lewenhaupt. London, Cassell; New York, Dutton, 1954. 540 p.

410 Paget, Reginald T.
MANSTEIN: HIS CAMPAIGNS AND HIS TRIAL. Foreword by Lord Hankey. London, Collins, 1951. 239 p.

411 Prüller, Wilhelm.
DIARY OF A GERMAN SOLDIER. Edited by H. C. Robbins Landon and Sebastian Leitner; introduction by Robert Leckie; English translation by H. C. Robbins Landon. London, Faber; New York, Coward-McCann, 1963. 200 p.

412 Rodenhauser, Reiner, and Ralph R. Napp, with H. R. Napp.
BREAKING DOWN THE BARRIER: A HUMAN DOCUMENT ON WAR. Durham, N. C., Seeman Printery, 1961. 148 p.

413 Rommel, Erwin.
THE ROMMEL PAPERS. Edited by B. H. Liddell Hart, with Lucie-Marie Rommel, Manfred Rommel, and Fritz Bayerlein; translated by Paul Findlay. London, Collins; New York, Harcourt, Brace, 1953. 545 p.

414 Senger und Etterlin, Fridolin von.
NEITHER FEAR NOR HOPE: THE WARTIME CAREER OF GENERAL FRIDO VON SENGER UND ETTERLIN, DEFENDER OF CASSINO. Translated from the German by George Malcolm; foreword by B. H. Liddell Hart. London, Macdonald, 1963. 368 p.

Other edition:
New York, Dutton, 1964.

415 Young, Desmond.
ROMMEL. Foreword by Sir Claude Auchinleck. London, Collins, 1950. 288 p.

Other edition:
New York, Harper, 1951. 264 p.

4. Japanese

416 Kodama, Yoshio.
I WAS DEFEATED. Translated from Japanese. Tokyo, Booth and Fukuda, 1951. 223 p.

Other edition:
Tokyo, 1959. 228 p.

417 Potter, John D.
A SOLDIER MUST HANG: A BIOGRAPHY OF AN ORIENTAL GENERAL. London, Muller, 1963. 210 p.

Other edition:
London, New English Library, 1964. 191 p. (Four Square Books)

418 Potter, John D.
YAMAMOTO: THE MAN WHO MENACED AMERICA. New York, Viking Press, 1965. 332 p.

Other edition:
ADMIRAL OF THE PACIFIC. London, Heinemann, 1965.

5. Others

419 Maugeri, Franco.
FROM THE ASHES OF DISGRACE. Edited by Victor Rosen. New York, Reynal and Hitchcock, 1948. 376 p.

420 Richardson, Anthony.
NO PLACE TO LAY MY HEAD. Foreword by Otto Heilbrunn. London, Odhams Press, 1957. 254 p.

421 Sosabowski, Stanislaw.
FREELY I SERVE. Foreword by Richard Gale. London, Kimber, 1960. 203 p.

Other edition:
PARACHUTE GENERAL. London, Kimber, 1961. 159 p.

422　Vaculik, Serge.
AIR COMMANDO. Translated from the French by Edward Fitzgerald. London and New York, Jarrolds, 1954. 303 p.

Other edition:
New York, Dutton, 1955. 320 p.

C. GENERAL ASPECTS

1. Strategy; High Command

423　Ansel, Walter.
HITLER CONFRONTS ENGLAND. Durham, N.C., Duke University Press; London, Cambridge University Press, 1960. 348 p.

424　Arnold, Ralph C. M.
A VERY QUIET WAR. London, Hart-Davis; New York, Macmillan, 1962. 176 p.

425　Barclay, Cyril N.
ON THEIR SHOULDERS: BRITISH GENERALSHIP IN THE LEAN YEARS, 1939-1942. London, Faber and Faber, 1964. 184 p.

426　Burne, Alfred H.
STRATEGY IN WORLD WAR II: A STRATEGICAL EXAMINATION OF LAND OPERATIONS. Harrisburg, Pa., Military Service Publishing Co., 1947. 91 p.

427　Butler, James R. M. (ed.).
GRAND STRATEGY. London, H. M. Stationery Office, 1956-. 4 v. published. (History of the Second World War: United Kingdom Military Series)

428　Chamberlain, Thomas H.
THE GENERALS AND THE ADMIRALS: SOME LEADERS OF THE UNITED STATES FORCES IN WORLD WAR II. New York, Devin-Adair, 1945-. 1 v. published.

429　Clarke, Comer.
IF THE NAZIS HAD COME. London, World Distributors, 1962. 160 p. (Consul Books)

430　Cline, Ray S.
WASHINGTON COMMAND POST: THE OPERATIONS DIVISION. Washington, Office of Chief of Military History, Dept. of Army, 1951. 413 p. (U.S. Army in World War II: The War Department)

431　Creswell, John.
GENERALS AND ADMIRALS: THE STORY OF THE AMPHIBIOUS COMMAND. London and New York, Longmans, Green, 1952. 192 p.

432　De Guingand, Sir Francis W.
GENERALS AT WAR. London, Hodder and Stoughton, 1964. 256 p.

433　Edwards, Kenneth.
SEVEN SAILORS. London, Collins, 1945. 255 p.

434　Eyre, James K.
THE ROOSEVELT-MacARTHUR CONFLICT. Chambersburg, Pa., Craft Press, 1950. 234 p.

435　Fleming, Peter.
INVASION 1940: AN ACCOUNT OF THE GERMAN PREPARATIONS AND THE BRITISH COUNTER-MEASURES. London, Hart-Davis, 1957. 323 p.

Other edition:
London, Hamilton, 1959. 285 p. (Panther Books)

436　Fleming, Peter.
OPERATION SEA LION. New York, Simon and Schuster, 1957. 323 p.

437　Germany. Kriegsmarine. Oberkommando.
FUEHRER CONFERENCES ON MATTERS DEALING WITH THE GERMAN NAVY, 1939-1945. London, British Admiralty; Washington, U.S. Navy Dept., 1947. 7 v. in 9.

438　Germany. Wehrmacht. Oberkommando.
HITLER DIRECTS HIS WAR: THE SECRET RECORDS OF HIS DAILY MILITARY CONFERENCES. Selected and annotated by Felix Gilbert from manuscript in the University of Pennsylvania Library. New York and London, Oxford University Press, 1951. 187 p.

439　Germany. Wehrmacht. Oberkommando.
HITLER'S WAR DIRECTIVES, 1939-1945. Edited by H. R. Trevor-Roper. London, Sidgwick and Jackson, 1964. 229 p.

Other edition:
BLITZKRIEG TO DEFEAT: HITLER'S WAR DIRECTIVES, 1939-1945. New York, Holt, Rinehart and Winston, 1965.

440　Greenfield, Kent R.
AMERICAN STRATEGY IN WORLD WAR II: A RECONSIDERATION. Baltimore, Johns Hopkins Press, 1963. 145 p.

441　Grinnell-Milne, Duncan W.
THE SILENT VICTORY, SEPTEMBER 1940. London, Lane; London, Bodley Head, 1958. 208 p.

442　Halder, Franz.
HITLER AS WAR LORD. Translated from German by Paul Findlay. London, Putnam, 1950. 70 p.

443　Hinsley, Francis H.
HITLER'S STRATEGY: THE NAVAL EVIDENCE. Cambridge, Eng., Cambridge University Press, 1951. 244 p.

444　Hitler, Adolf.
HITLER'S TABLE TALK 1941-1944. Translated by Norman Cameron and R. H. Stevens; introductory essay by H. R. Trevor-Roper. London, Weidenfeld and Nicolson, 1953. 746 p.

Other edition:
SECRET CONVERSATIONS, 1941-1944. New York, Farrar, Straus and Young, 1953.

445   Hollis, Sir Leslie.
      ONE MARINE'S TALE. Foreword by Lord Ismay. London, Deutsch, 1956. 188 p.

446   Kingston-McCloughry, Edgar J.
      THE DIRECTION OF WAR: A CRITIQUE OF THE POLITICAL DIRECTION AND HIGH COMMAND IN WAR. London, Cape, 1955. 261 p.

Other edition:
New York, Praeger, 1955. 261 p. (Books That Matter)

447   Kreipe, Werner, and others.
      THE FATAL DECISION. Edited by Seymour Freidin and William Richardson; commentary by Siegfried Westphal; foreword by S. L. A. Marshall; translated from the German by Constantine FitzGibbon. New York, Sloane, 1956. 302 p.

Other edition:
London, Joseph, 1956. 261 p.

448   Liddell Hart, Basil H.
      THE GERMAN GENERALS TALK. New York, Morrow, 1948. 308 p.

Other editions:
THE OTHER SIDE OF THE HILL: GERMANY'S GENERALS, THEIR RISE AND FALL, WITH THEIR OWN ACCOUNT OF MILITARY EVENTS, 1939-1945. London, Cassell, 1948. 320 p.

London, Cassell, 1951. 488 p.

449   Liddell Hart, Basil H.
      STRATEGY: THE INDIRECT APPROACH. New York, Praeger, 1954. 420 p.

450   Manstein, Erich von.
      LOST VICTORIES. Edited and translated by Anthony G. Powell; foreword by B. H. Liddell Hart. Chicago, Regnery; London, Methuen, 1958. 574 p.

451   Marshall, George C., H. H. Arnold, and Ernest J. King.
      THE WAR REPORTS OF GENERAL OF THE ARMY GEORGE C. MARSHALL, CHIEF OF STAFF, GENERAL OF THE ARMY H. H. ARNOLD, COMMANDING GENERAL, ARMY AIR FORCES AND FLEET ADMIRAL ERNEST J. KING, COMMANDER-IN-CHIEF, UNITED STATES FLEET AND CHIEF OF NAVAL OPERATIONS. Foreword by Walter Millis. Philadelphia, Lippincott, 1947. 801 p.

452   Martienssen, Anthony K.
      HITLER AND HIS ADMIRALS. London, Secker and Warburg, 1948. 275 p.

Other edition:
New York, Dutton, 1949. 275 p.

453   Matloff, Maurice, and Edwin M. Snell.
      STRATEGIC PLANNING FOR COALITION WARFARE, 1941-1942-1943-1944. Washington, Office of Chief of Military History, Dept. of Army, 1953-59. 2 v. (U.S. Army in World War II: The War Department)

454   Mellenthin, Friedrich W. von.
      PANZER BATTLES, 1939-1945: A STUDY OF THE EMPLOYMENT OF ARMOUR IN THE SECOND WORLD WAR. Translated by H. Betzler; edited by L. C. F. Turner. London, Cassell, 1955. 371 p.

Other edition:
Norman, University of Oklahoma Press, 1956. 383 p.

455   Morgan, Henry G.
      PLANNING THE DEFEAT OF JAPAN: A STUDY OF TOTAL WAR STRATEGY. Washington, Office of Chief of Military History, Dept. of Army, 1961. 197 p.

456   Morison, Samuel E.
      AMERICAN CONTRIBUTIONS TO THE STRATEGY OF WORLD WAR II. London, Oxford University Press, 1958. 79 p.

457   Morison, Samuel E.
      STRATEGY AND COMPROMISE. Boston, Little, Brown, 1958. 120 p.

458   Morton, Louis.
      STRATEGY AND COMMAND: THE FIRST TWO YEARS. Washington, Office of Chief of Military History, Dept. of Army, 1962. 761 p. (U.S. Army in World War II: The War in the Pacific)

459   Nickerson, Hoffman.
      ARMS AND POLICY, 1939-1944. New York, Putnam, 1945. 356 p.

460   Pogue, Forrest C.
      THE SUPREME COMMAND. Washington, Office of Chief of Military History, Dept. of Army, 1954. 607 p. (U.S. Army in World War II: The European Theater of Operations)

461   Romanus, Charles F., and Riley Sunderland.
      STILWELL'S COMMAND PROBLEMS. Washington, Office of Chief of Military History, Dept. of Army, 1956. 518 p. (U.S. Army in World War II: China-Burma-India Theater)

462   Smith, Walter B.
      EISENHOWER'S SIX GREAT DECISIONS: EUROPE, 1944-1945. New York, Longmans, Green, 1956. 237 p.

463   U.S. Dept. of the Army. Office of Military History.
      COMMAND DECISIONS. Edited by Kent R. Greenfield; introduction by Hanson W. Baldwin. New York, Harcourt, Brace, 1959. 481 p.

Other editions:
Washington, 1960. 565 p.

London, Methuen, 1960. 477 p.

464   U.S. Dept. of Defense.
      THE ENTRY OF THE SOVIET UNION INTO THE WAR AGAINST JAPAN, MILITARY PLANS, 1941-1945. Washington, 1955. 107 p.

465   Watson, Mark S.
      CHIEF OF STAFF: PREWAR PLANS AND PREPARA-

TIONS. Washington, Historical Division, Dept. of Army, 1950. 551 p. (U. S. Army in World War II: The War Department)

466 Wheatley, Dennis.
STRANGER THAN FICTION. Introduction by Lawrance Darvall. London, Hutchinson, 1959. 364 p.

Other edition:
London, Arrow, 1965. 414 p.

467 Wheatley, Ronald.
OPERATION SEA LION: GERMAN PLANS FOR THE INVASION OF ENGLAND, 1939-1942. Oxford, Clarendon Press, 1958. 201 p.

Other edition:
Oxford, Clarendon Press, 1962. (Oxford Paperbacks)

2. Techniques and Technology; Logistics; Administration; Psychological Warfare
(for the atomic bomb,
see also III. D. 3. c)

468 Allied Forces. Supreme Headquarters. Psychological Warfare Division.
THE PSYCHOLOGICAL WARFARE DIVISION, SUPREME HEADQUARTERS, ALLIED EXPEDITIONARY FORCE: AN ACCOUNT OF ITS OPERATIONS IN THE WESTERN EUROPEAN CAMPAIGN, 1944-1945. Bad Homburg, Ger., 1945. 243 plus 35 p.

469 Allied Forces. 21st Army Group.
BRIDGING NORMANDY TO BERLIN. [1945?] 193 p.

470 Amrine, Michael.
THE GREAT DECISION: THE SECRET HISTORY OF THE ATOMIC BOMB. New York, Putnam, 1959. 251 p.

Other edition:
London, Heinemann, 1960.

471 Armed Forces Chemical Association.
THE CHEMICAL WARFARE SERVICE IN WORLD WAR II: A REPORT OF ACCOMPLISHMENTS. New York, Reinhold, 1948. 222 p.

472 Ballantine, Duncan S.
U. S. NAVAL LOGISTICS IN THE SECOND WORLD WAR. Princeton, N. J., Princeton University Press, 1947. 308 p.

473 Barkas, Geoffrey, with Natalie Barkas.
THE CAMOUFLAGE STORY, FROM AINTREE TO ALAMEIN. London, Cassell, 1952. 216 p.

474 Barnes, Gladeon M.
WEAPONS OF WORLD WAR II. New York, Van Nostrand, 1947. 317 p.

475 Bates, P. W.
SUPPLY COMPANY. Wellington, War History Branch, Dept. of Internal Affairs, 1955. 371 p. (Official History of New Zealand in the Second World War, 1939-45)

476 Behan, John M.
DOGS OF THE WAR. New York, Scribner, 1946. 80 p.

477 Birkenhead, Frederick W. F. Smith, 2d earl of.
THE PROFESSOR AND THE PRIME MINISTER: THE OFFICIAL LIFE OF PROFESSOR F. A. LINDEMANN, VISCOUNT CHERWELL. Boston, Houghton Mifflin, 1962. 400 p.

478 Blore, Trevor.
COMMISSIONED BARGES: THE STORY OF THE LANDING CRAFT. London and New York, Hutchinson, 1946. 216 p.

479 Boles, Antoinette.
WOMEN IN KHAKI. New York, Vantage, 1953. 240 p.

480 Boswell, Rolfe.
MEDALS FOR MARINES. New York, Crowell, 1945. 211 p.

481 Bourne, Dorothea St. H.
THEY ALSO SERVE. London, Winchester, 1947. 226 p.

482 Bowman, Waldo G.
AMERICAN MILITARY ENGINEERING IN EUROPE FROM NORMANDY TO THE RHINE. New York, McGraw-Hill, 1945. 102 p.

483 Boyce, Joseph C. (ed.).
NEW WEAPONS FOR AIR WARFARE: FIRE-CONTROL EQUIPMENT, PROXIMITY FUZES, AND GUIDED MISSILES. Foreword by Richard C. Tolman. Boston, Little, Brown, 1947. 292 p. (Science in World War II: Office of Scientific Research and Development) (Atlantic Monthly Press Book)

484 Brophy, Leo P., Wyndham D. Miles, and Rexmond C. Cochrane.
THE CHEMICAL WARFARE SERVICE: FROM LABORATORY TO FIELD. Washington, Office of Chief of Military History, Dept. of Army, 1959. 496 p. (U. S. Army in World War II: The Technical Services)

485 Brophy, Leo P.
THE CHEMICAL WARFARE SERVICE: ORGANIZING FOR WAR. Washington, Office of Chief of Military History, Dept. of Army, 1959. 498 p. (U. S. Army in World War II: The Technical Services)

486 Burchard, John E. (ed.).
ROCKETS, GUNS AND TARGETS: ROCKETS, TARGET INFORMATION, EROSION INFORMATION AND HYPERVELOCITY GUNS DEVELOPED DURING WORLD WAR II BY THE OFFICE OF SCIENTIFIC RESEARCH AND DEVELOPMENT. Boston, Little, Brown, 1948. 482 p. (Science in World War II: Office of Scientific Research and Development)

487 Burton, Eli F.
CANADIAN NAVAL RADAR OFFICERS: THE STORY OF UNIVERSITY GRADUATES FOR WHOM PRELIMINARY TRAINING WAS GIVEN IN THE DEPARTMENT OF PHY-

SICS, UNIVERSITY OF TORONTO. Toronto, University of Toronto Press, 1946. 63 p.

488 Bykofsky, Joseph, and Harold Larson.
THE TRANSPORTATION CORPS: OPERATION OVERSEAS. Washington, Office of Chief of Military History, Dept. of Army, 1957. 671 p. (U.S. Army in World War II: The Technical Services)

489 Carter, Worrall R.
BEANS, BULLETS, AND BLACK OIL: THE STORY OF FLEET LOGISTICS AFLOAT IN THE PACIFIC DURING WORLD WAR II. Washington, Dept. of the Navy, 1953. 482 p.

490 Carter, Worrall R., and Elmer E. Duvall.
SHIPS, SALVAGE, AND SINEWS OF WAR: THE STORY OF FLEET LOGISTICS AFLOAT IN ATLANTIC AND MEDITERRANEAN WATERS DURING WORLD WAR II. Washington, Dept. of the Navy, 1954. 533 p.

491 Castillo, Edmund L.
THE SEABEES OF WORLD WAR II. New York, Random House, 1963. 190 p. (Landmark Books)

492 Clark, Ronald W.
THE BIRTH OF THE BOMB: THE UNTOLD STORY OF BRITAIN'S PART IN THE WEAPON THAT CHANGED THE WORLD. London, Phoenix House; New York, Horizon Press, 1961. 209 p.

493 Clark, Ronald W.
THE RISE OF THE BOFFINS. London, Phoenix House, 1962. 268 p.

494 Clark, Ronald W.
TIZARD. Cambridge, Mass., MIT Press, 1965. 458 p.

495 Cole, Howard N.
HERALDRY IN WAR: FORMATION BADGES, 1939-1945. Aldershot, Eng., Wellington Press, Gale and Polden, 1946. 143 p.

496 Coleman, John M.
THE DEVELOPMENT OF TACTICAL SERVICES IN THE ARMY AIR FORCE. New York, Columbia University Press, 1950. 298 p.

497 Coll, Blanche D., Jean E. Keith, and Herbert H. Rosenthal.
THE CORPS OF ENGINEERS: TROOPS AND EQUIPMENT. Washington, Office of Chief of Military History, Dept. of Army, 1958. 622 p. (U.S. Army in World War II: The Technical Services)

498 Condit, Kenneth W., Gerald Diamond, and Edwin T. Turnbladh.
MARINE CORPS GROUND TRAINING IN WORLD WAR II. Washington, Historical Branch, U.S. Marine Corps, 1956. 353 p.

499 Connell, Charles.
THE HIDDEN CATCH: BASED LARGELY UPON MATERIAL SUPPLIED BY AND ON THE EXPERIENCES OF MR. X. London, Elek, 1955. 176 p.

500 Cowie, J. S.
MINES, MINELAYERS AND MINELAYING. New York and London, Oxford University Press, 1949. 216 p.

501 Darwin, Bernard R. M.
WAR ON THE LINE: THE STORY OF THE SOUTHERN RAILWAY IN WARTIME. London, Southern Railway Co., 1946. 215 p.

502 Daugherty, William E., and Morris Janowitz.
A PSYCHOLOGICAL WARFARE CASEBOOK. Baltimore, Johns Hopkins Press; London, Oxford University Press, 1958. 880 p.

503 Downey, Fairfax D.
DOGS FOR DEFENSE: AMERICAN DOGS IN THE SECOND WORLD WAR, 1941-45. Edited and distributed by Daniel P. McDonald. New York, 1955. 159 p.

504 . FUEL RESEARCH, 1939-1946. London, H. M. Stationery Office, 1950. 76 p. (Fuel Research Station)

505 Furer, Julius A.
ADMINISTRATION OF THE NAVY DEPARTMENT IN WORLD WAR II. Foreword by Charles Edison; introduction by Ernest McN. Eller. Washington, U.S. Government Printing Office, 1959. 1042 p.

506 Gebler, Robert T.
PHILADELPHIA ORDNANCE DISTRICT IN WORLD WAR II: A RECORD OF THE PHILADELPHIA ORDNANCE DISTRICT AND INDUSTRY OF THE DISTRICT DURING THE WAR YEARS 1941-1945. Philadelphia, Westbrook, 1949. 284 p.

507 Godwin, George S.
MARCONI, 1939-1945: A WAR RECORD. London, Chatto and Windus, 1946. 125 p.

508 Goudsmit, Samuel.
ALSOS. New York, Schuman, 1947. 259 p.

509 Graves, Charles.
THE THIN RED LINES. London, Standard Art Book Co., 1946. 183 p.

510 Great Britain. Air Ministry.
ATLANTIC BRIDGE: THE OFFICIAL ACCOUNT OF R.A.F. TRANSPORT COMMAND'S OCEAN FERRY. Prepared by the Ministry of Information. London, H.M. Stationery Office, 1945. 75 p.

511 Great Britain. Air Ministry.
THE ORIGINS AND DEVELOPMENT OF OPERATIONAL RESEARCH IN THE ROYAL AIR FORCE. London, H.M. Stationery Office, 1963. 218 p.

512 Great Britain. Army. Corps of Royal Engineers.
BRIDGING NORMANDY TO BERLIN. n.p., 1945. 193 p.

513   Great Britain. Cabinet Office. Historical Section.
      ORDERS OF BATTLE: UNITED KINGDOM AND COLONIAL FORMATIONS AND UNITS IN THE SECOND WORLD WAR, 1939-1945. Prepared by Lieutenant-Colonel H. F. Joslen. London, H.M. Stationery Office, 1960. 2 v.

514   Great Britain. War Office.
      ILLUSTRATED RECORD OF GERMAN ARMY EQUIPMENT, 1939-1945. London, 1959-.

515   Green, Constance M.
      THE ORDNANCE DEPARTMENT. Washington, Office of Chief of Military History, Dept. of Army, 1955-. 2 v. published (U.S. Army in World War II: The Technical Services)

516   Greenfield, Kent R., Robert R. Palmer, and Bill I. Wiley.
      THE ORGANIZATION OF GROUND COMBAT TROOPS. Washington, Historical Division, Dept. of Army, 1947. 540 p. (U.S. Army in World War II: The Army Ground Forces)

517   Groves, Leslie R.
      NOW IT CAN BE TOLD: THE STORY OF THE MANHATTAN PROJECT. New York, Harper, 1962. 464 p.

518   Haarer, Alec E.
      A COLD-BLOODED BUSINESS. Foreword by Lord Tedder. London, Staples Press, 1958. 208 p.

      Other edition:
      London, Hamilton, 1960. 189 p. (Panther Books)

519   Hamilton, James W., and William J. Bolce, Jr.
      GATEWAY TO VICTORY. Stanford, Calif., Stanford University Press, 1946. 220 p.

520   Hare-Scott, Kenneth.
      FOR VALOUR. London, Garnett, 1949. 178 p.

521   Harris, Lionel H.
      SIGNAL VENTURE. Aldershot, Eng., Gale and Polden, 1951. 278 p.

522   Harrod, Roy F.
      THE PROF: A PERSONAL MEMOIR OF LORD CHERWELL. London, Macmillan, 1959. 281 p.

523   Hartley, Arthur B.
      UNEXPLODED BOMB: A HISTORY OF BOMB DISPOSAL. Foreword by Herbert Morrison. London, Cassell, 1958. 272 p.

      Other edition:
      New York, Norton, 1959.

524   Hewlett, Richard G., and Oscar E. Anderson, Jr.
      A HISTORY OF THE UNITED STATES ATOMIC ENERGY COMMISSION: Vol. I, THE NEW WORLD, 1939-1946. University Park, Pennsylvania State University Press, 1962. 766 p.

525   Huzel, Dieter.
      PEENEMUNDE TO CANAVERAL. Introduction by Werner von Braun. Englewood Cliffs, N.J., Prentice-Hall, 1962. 247 p.

526   Idriess, Ion L.
      HORRIE, THE WOG-DOG WITH THE A.I.F. IN EGYPT, GREECE, CRETE AND PALESTINE. Written from the diary of J. B. Moody, Private, VX13091, A.I.F. Sydney, Angus and Robertson, 1945. 232 p.

527   Japan. Hikiage Engochō. Fukuinkyoku.
      RAILWAY OPERATIONS RECORD. Tokyo, Military History Section, Japanese Research Division, Headquarters, Armed Forces, Far East, 1951. 208 l. (Japanese Monograph)

528   Joslen, H. F.
      ORDERS OF BATTLE: UNITED KINGDOM AND COLONIAL FORMATIONS AND UNITS IN THE SECOND WORLD WAR, 1939-1945. London, H.M. Stationery Office, 1960. 2 v. 628 p.

529   Joubert de la Ferté, Sir Philip B.
      ROCKET. London, Hutchinson; New York, Philosophical Library, 1957. 190 p.

530   Kemp, Norman.
      THE DEVICES OF WAR. London, Laurie, 1956. 232 p.

531   Kennedy, John de N.
      HISTORY OF THE DEPARTMENT OF MUNITIONS AND SUPPLY: CANADA IN THE SECOND WORLD WAR. Foreword by C. D. Howe; preface by G. K. Sheils. Ottawa, King's Printer, 1950. 2 v.

532   Kerr, George F.
      BUSINESS IN GREAT WATERS: THE WAR HISTORY OF THE P. and O., 1939-1945. London, Faber and Faber, 1951. 196 p.

533   Kirk, John, and Robert Young, Jr.
      GREAT WEAPONS OF WORLD WAR II. Introduction by Hanson W. Baldwin. New York, Walker, 1961. 347 p.

534   Klee, E., and O. Merke.
      THE BIRTH OF THE MISSILE. Translated by T. Schoeters. London, Harrap; New York, Dutton; Toronto, Clarke, Irwin, 1965. 126 p.

535   Knebel, Fletcher, and Charles W. Bailey.
      NO HIGH GROUND: THE INSIDE STORY OF THE MEN WHO PLANNED AND DROPPED THE FIRST ATOMIC BOMB. London, Weidenfeld and Nicolson, 1960. 272 p.

536   Lane, Frederic C., and others.
      SHIPS FOR VICTORY: A HISTORY OF SHIP-BUILDING UNDER THE U.S. MARITIME COMMISSION IN WORLD WAR II. Baltimore, Johns Hopkins Press, 1951. 881 p. (Historical Reports on War Administration)

537 Lawrence, William I.
DAWN OVER ZERO: THE STORY OF THE ATOMIC BOMB. New York, Knopf, 1947. 289 p.

Other edition:
London, Museum Press, 1947. 251 p.

538 Leigh, Randolph.
48 MILLION TONS TO EISENHOWER: THE ROLE OF THE SOS IN THE DEFEAT OF GERMANY. Washington Infantry Journal, 1945. 179 p.

Other edition:
AMERICAN ENTERPRISE IN EUROPE. Paris, Bellenand, 1945. 233 p.

539 Leighton, Richard M., and Robert W. Coakley.
GLOBAL LOGISTICS AND STRATEGY. Washington, Office of Chief of Military History, Dept. of Army, 1955-. 1 v. published. (U.S. Army in World War II: The War Department)

540 Lerner, Daniel.
SYKEWAR: PSYCHOLOGICAL WARFARE AGAINST GERMANY, D-DAY TO VE-DAY. Foreword by Robert A. McClure; supplementary essay by Richard H. S. Crossman. New York, Stewart, 1949. 463 p. (Library of Policy Sciences)

541 Linebarger, Paul M. A.
PSYCHOLOGICAL WARFARE. Washington, Infantry Journal Press, 1948. 259 p.

542 Lusar, Rudolf.
GERMAN SECRET WEAPONS OF THE SECOND WORLD WAR. Translated by R. P. Heller and M. Schindler. New York, Philosophical Library, 1959. 264 p.

543 Mansfield, Alan (comp.).
A BRIEF HISTORY OF THE NEW GUINEA AIR WARNING WIRELESS CO. (A.I.F.). Melbourne, James, 1961. 96 p.

544 Margolin, Leo J.
PAPER BULLETS: A BRIEF STORY OF PSYCHOLOGICAL WARFARE IN WORLD WAR II. New York, Froben, 1946. 149 p.

545 Martel, Giffard Le Q.
OUR ARMOURED FORCES. London, Faber and Faber, 1945. 406 p.

546 Maskelyne, Jasper.
MAGIC--TOP SECRET. London and New York, Paul, 1949. 191 p.

547 Mueller, Chester.
THE NEW YORK ORDNANCE DISTRICT IN WORLD WAR II. New York, New York Post, Army Ordnance Association, 1947. 243 p.

548 Nash, George C.
THE LMS AT WAR. Euston, London Midland and Scottish Railway, 1946. 87 p.

549 Noyes, William A. (ed.).
CHEMISTRY: A HISTORY OF THE CHEMISTRY COMPONENTS OF THE NATIONAL DEFENSE RESEARCH COMMITTEE, 1940-1946. By R. Connor and others; foreword by James B. Conant and Roger Adams. Boston, Little, Brown, 1948. 524 p. (Science in World War II: Office of Scientific Research and Development) (Atlantic Monthly Press Book)

550 Osman, W. H.
PIGEONS IN WORLD WAR II. London, Racing Pigeon Publishing Co., 1950. 146 p.

551 Palmer, Robert R., Bill I. Wiley, and William R. Keast.
THE ARMY GROUND FORCES: THE PROCUREMENT AND TRAINING OF GROUND COMBAT TROOPS. Washington, Historical Division, Dept. of Army, 1948. 696 p. (U.S. Army in World War II: The Army Ground Forces)

552 Patton, William.
THE SCRAP LOG OF AN ENGINEER. Ilfracombe, Stockwell, 1952. 206 p.

553 Pawle, Gerald.
THE SECRET WAR, 1939-45. Foreword by Nevil Shute. London, Harrap, 1956. 297 p.

Other edition:
New York, Sloane, 1957.

554 Postan, Michael M., D. Day, and J. D. Scott.
DESIGN AND DEVELOPMENT OF WEAPONS: STUDIES IN GOVERNMENT AND INDUSTRIAL ORGANIZATION. London, H.M. Stationery Office, 1964. 579 p. (History of the Second World War: United Kingdom Civil Series)

555 Prasad, Sri N.
EXPANSION OF THE ARMED FORCES AND DEFENSE ORGANIZATION, 1939-45. Edited by Bisheshwar Prasad. Delhi, Combined Inter-Services Historical Section (India and Pakistan), 1956. 546 p. (Official History of the Indian Armed Forces in the Second World War, 1939-45. General War Administration and Organisation)

556 Qualter, Terence H.
PROPAGANDA AND PSYCHOLOGICAL WARFARE. New York, Random House, 1962. 176 p. (Studies in Political Science)

557 Richardson, Eudora R., and Sherman Allan.
QUARTERMASTER SUPPLY IN THE EUROPEAN THEATER OF OPERATIONS IN WORLD WAR II. Camp Lee, Va., Quartermaster School, 1948-. 10 v. (v. 1, 3-8, 10 published)

558 Riddell, James.
DOG IN THE SNOW. London, Joseph, 1957. 143 p.

559 Robinson, Clinton F.
FOREIGN LOGISTICAL ORGANIZATIONS AND METHODS: A REPORT FOR THE SECRETARY OF THE ARMY. Washington, 1947. 210 p.

560 Rogers, Hugh C. B.
TANKS IN BATTLE. London, Seeley Service, 1965. 240 p. (Imperial Services Library)

561   Rose, Joseph R.
      AMERICAN WARTIME TRANSPORTATION. New York, Crowell, 1953. 290 p.

562   Rowe, Albert P.
      ONE STORY OF RADAR. Cambridge, Eng., Cambridge University Press, 1948. 207 p.

563   Ruppenthal, Roland G.
      LOGISTICAL SUPPORT OF THE ARMIES. Washington, Office of Chief of Military History, Dept. of Army, 1953-58. 2 v. (U.S. Army in World War II: The European Theater of Operations)

564   Savage, Christopher I.
      INLAND TRANSPORT. London, H.M. Stationery Office, 1957. 678 p. (History of the Second World War: United Kingdom Civil Series)

565   Sawicki, James A.
      NAZI DECORATIONS AND MEDALS, 1933-1945. Rochester, N.Y., Babin, 1958. 75 p.

566   Shomon, Joseph J.
      CROSSES IN THE WIND. New York, Stratford House, 1947. 191 p.

567   Sill, Van R.
      AMERICAN MIRACLE: THE STORY OF WAR CONSTRUCTION AROUND THE WORLD. New York, Odyssey Press, 1947. 301 p.

568   Simpson, Evan J. (Evan John, pseud.).
      TIME TABLE FOR VICTORY: A BRIEF AND POPULAR ACCOUNT OF THE RAILWAYS AND RAILWAY-OWNED DOCKYARDS OF GREAT BRITAIN AND NORTHERN IRELAND DURING THE SIX YEARS' WAR, 1939-45. London, British Railways, 1947. 268 p.

569   Smyth, Henry DeW.
      ATOMIC ENERGY FOR MILITARY PURPOSES: THE OFFICIAL REPORT ON THE DEVELOPMENT OF THE ATOMIC BOMB UNDER THE AUSPICES OF THE U.S. GOVERNMENT, 1940-1945. Princeton, N.J., Princeton University Press, 1945. 264 p.

570   South Africa. Director-General of Supplies.
      A RECORD OF THE ORGANIZATION OF THE DIRECTOR-GENERAL OF WAR SUPPLIES (1939-1943) AND DIRECTOR-GENERAL OF SUPPLIES (1943-1945). Johannesburg, Gray, 1946. 147 p.

571   South Africa. Railways and Harbours Board.
      WE FOUGHT THE MILES: THE HISTORY OF THE SOUTH AFRICAN RAILWAYS AT WAR, 1939-1945. Johannesburg, 1946. 120 p.

572   Southall, Ivan.
      SOFTLY TREAD THE BRAVE: A TRIUMPH OVER TERROR, DEVILRY, AND DEATH BY MINE DISPOSAL OFFICERS JOHN STUART MOULD AND HUGH RANDAL SYME. Sydney, Angus and Robertson, 1960. 293 p.

573   Sparrow, John C.
      HISTORY OF PERSONNEL DEMOBILIZATION IN THE UNITED STATES ARMY. Washington, Office of Chief of Military History, Dept. of Army, 1951. 525 p.

      Other edition:
Washington, Dept. of Army, 1952. 358 p.

574   Startup, Robin McG.
      THE MAILS WENT THROUGH: THE STORY OF NEW ZEALAND'S ARMED FORCES POSTAL SERVICES DURING THE WAR YEARS, 1939-1949. Masterton, N.Z., 1957. 169 p.

575   Stauffer, Alvin P.
      THE QUARTERMASTER CORPS: OPERATIONS IN THE WAR AGAINST JAPAN. Washington, Office of Chief of Military History, Dept. of Army, 1956. 358 p. (U.S. Army in World War II: The Technical Services)

576   Steere, Edward, and Thayer M. Boardman.
      FINAL DISPOSITION OF WORLD WAR II DEAD, 1945-51. Washington, Historical Branch, Office of Quartermaster General, 1957. 710 p. (QMC Historical Studies)

577   Stout, Wesley W.
      THE GREAT DETECTIVE. Detroit, Chrysler Corp., 1946. 98 p.

578   Stout, Wesley W.
      A WAR JOB "THOUGHT IMPOSSIBLE." Detroit, Chrysler Corp., 1945. 51 p.

579   Terrell, Edward.
      ADMIRALTY BRIEF: THE STORY OF INVENTIONS THAT CONTRIBUTED TO VICTORY IN THE BATTLE OF THE ATLANTIC. London, Harrap, 1958. 240 p.

580   Terret, Dulany.
      THE SIGNAL CORPS: THE EMERGENCY, TO DECEMBER 1941. Washington, Office of Military History, Dept. of Army, 1956. 383 p. (U.S. Army in World War II: The Technical Services)

581   Thiesmeyer, Lincoln R., and John F. Burchard.
      COMBAT SCIENTISTS. Edited by Alan T. Waterman; foreword by Karl T. Compton. Boston, Little, Brown, 1947. 412 p. (Science in World War II: Office of Scientific Research and Development) (Atlantic Monthly Press Book)

582   Thompson, Clary (ed.).
      UNSUNG HEROES! YOUR SERVICE FORCES IN ACTION: A PHOTOGRAPHIC EPIC OF ASF OPERATIONS OF WORLD WAR II. New York, Wise, 1949. 385 p.

583   Thompson, George R., and others.
      THE SIGNAL CORPS: THE TEST (DECEMBER 1941 TO JULY 1943). Washington, Office of Chief of Military History, Dept. of Army, 1957. 621 p. (U.S. Army in World War II: The Technical Services)

584   Turner, John F.
      HIGHLY EXPLOSIVE: THE EXPLOITS OF MAJOR BILL HARTLEY, M.B.E., G.M. OF BOMB DISPOSAL. London, Harrap, 1961. 208 p.

585 Turner, John F.
 V.C.'S OF THE ARMY, 1939-1951. London, Harrap, 1962. 222 p.

586 U.S. Army. Chemical Corps.
 REPORT OF ACTIVITIES OF THE TECHNICAL DIVISION DURING WORLD WAR II. Compiled by E. R. Baker. Washington, 1946. 222 p.

587 U.S. Army. European Theater of Operations.
 CONAD HISTORY, CONTINENTAL ADVANCE SECTION, COMMUNICATIONS ZONE, EUROPEAN THEATER OF OPERATIONS, UNITED STATES ARMY. Edited by Charles H. E. Scheer. Heidelberg, Gräf, 1945. 379 p.

588 U.S. Army. European Theater of Operations.
 WE BOUGHT THE EIFFEL TOWER: THE STORY OF THE GENERAL PURCHASING AGENT, EUROPEAN THEATER, 16TH MAY, 1942-1ST SEPTEMBER, 1945. Prepared by Samuel I. Katz and Jordan Y. Miller. Paris, 1949. 228 p.

589 U.S. Army Service Force. Information and Education Division.
 COMBAT DIVISIONS OF WORLD WAR II, ARMY OF THE UNITED STATES. Washington, 1946. 96 p.

590 U.S. Bureau of Ordnance (Navy Dept.).
 U.S. NAVY BUREAU OF ORDNANCE IN WORLD WAR II. By Buford Rowland and William B. Boyd. Washington, 1953. 539 p.

591 U.S. Bureau of Ships.
 AN ADMINISTRATIVE HISTORY OF THE BUREAU OF SHIPS DURING WORLD WAR II. Washington, 1952. 4 v.

592 U.S. Bureau of Yards and Docks.
 BUILDING THE NAVY'S BASES IN WORLD WAR II: HISTORY OF THE BUREAU OF YARDS AND DOCKS AND THE CIVIL ENGINEER CORPS, 1940-1946. Washington, U.S. Government Printing Office, 1947. 2 v.

593 U.S. Dept. of Army. Office of Military History.
 ORDER OF BATTLE OF THE UNITED STATES ARMY GROUND FORCES IN WORLD WAR II: PACIFIC THEATER OF OPERATIONS; ADMINISTRATIVE AND LOGISTICAL COMMANDS, ARMIES, CORPS, AND DIVISIONS. Washington, 1959. 697 p.

594 U.S. Naval Air Transport Service.
 THE ROLE OF THE NAVAL AIR TRANSPORT SERVICE IN THE PACIFIC WAR. Washington, 1945. 1 v.

595 U.S. Office of Defense Transportation.
 CIVILIAN WAR TRANSPORT: A RECORD OF CONTROL OF DOMESTIC TRAFFIC OPERATIONS, 1941-1946. Washington, U.S. Government Printing Office, 1948. 361 p.

596 U.S. Office of Scientific Research and Development.
 APPLIED PHYSICS. Boston, Little, Brown, 1948. 3 v. in 1. (Science in World War II)

597 U.S. Quartermaster Corps.
 THE QUARTERMASTER CORPS. Prepared under direction of Thomas M. Pitkin. Washington, Office of Chief of Military History, Dept. of Army, 1953-55. 2 v. (U.S. Army in World War II: The Technical Services)

598 U.S. Quartermaster School, Fort Lee, Va.
 STORAGE AND DISTRIBUTION OF QUARTERMASTER SUPPLIES IN THE EUROPEAN THEATER OF OPERATIONS IN WORLD WAR II. Fort Lee, 1962. 291 p.

599 U.S. War Dept. General Staff.
 THE GERMAN REPLACEMENT ARMY, ERSATZHEER. Washington, Military Intelligence Division, War Dept., 1945. 504 p.

600 U.S. War Dept. General Staff.
 LOGISTICAL HISTORY OF NATOUSA, MTOUSA. Naples, 1945. 486 p.

601 U.S. War Dept. General Staff. Military Intelligence Division.
 JAPANESE RECRUITING AND REPLACEMENT SYSTEM. Washington, Military Intelligence Division, War Dept., 1945. 366 p.

602 Vigneras, Marcel.
 REARMING THE FRENCH. Washington, Office of Chief of Military History, Dept. of Army, 1957. 444 p. (U.S. Army in World War II: Special Studies)

603 Wadge, D. Collett.
 WOMAN IN UNIFORM. London, Low, Marston, 1946. 386 p.

604 Warburg, James P.
 UNWRITTEN TREATY. New York, Harcourt, Brace, 1946. 186 p.

605 Wardlow, Chester.
 THE TRANSPORTATION CORPS: MOVEMENTS, TRAINING, AND SUPPLY. Washington, Office of Chief of Military History, Dept. of Army, 1956. 564 p. (U.S. Army in World War II: The Technical Services)

606 Watson-Watt, Sir Robert A.
 THE PULSE OF RADAR: THE AUTOBIOGRAPHY OF SIR ROBERT WATSON-WATT. New York, Dial Press, 1959. 438 p.

607 Watson-Watt, Sir Robert A.
 THREE STEPS TO VICTORY: A PERSONAL ACCOUNT BY RADAR'S GREATEST PIONEER. London, Odhams Press, 1957. 480 p.

608 Weaver, William G.
 YANKEE DOODLE DANDY. Ann Arbor, 1958. 370 p.

 Other edition:
 YANKEE DOODLE WENT TO TOWN. Ann Arbor, 1959. 432 p.

609 Weeks, Sir Ronald M.
 ORGANIZATION AND EQUIPMENT FOR WAR. Foreword by Viscount Montgomery. Cambridge, Eng., Cambridge University Press, 1950. 132 p.

610 Woodbury, David O.
BUILDERS FOR BATTLE: HOW THE PACIFIC NAVAL AIR BASES WERE CONSTRUCTED. Introduction by Vice Admiral B. Moreell. New York, Dutton, 1946. 415 p.

3. Medical Aspects

611 Ahrenfeldt, Robert H.
PSYCHIATRY IN THE BRITISH ARMY IN THE SECOND WORLD WAR. Foreword by Eli Ginzberg. New York, Columbia University Press; London, Routledge, 1958. 312 p.

612 Allen, Ted.
THE SCAPEL, THE SWORD: THE STORY OF DR. NORMAN BETHUNE. Boston, Little, Brown, 1952. 336 p.

613 Allied Forces. 21st Army Group. Medical Services.
PENICILLIN THERAPY AND CONTROL IN 21 ARMY GROUP. n.p., 1945. 365 p.

614 Anson, Thomas V.
THE NEW ZEALAND DENTAL SERVICES. Wellington, War History Branch, Dept. of Internal Affairs, 1960. 422 p. (Official History of New Zealand in the Second World War, 1939-45)

615 Archard, Theresa.
G.I. NIGHTINGALE: THE STORY OF AN AMERICAN ARMY NURSE. New York, Norton, 1945. 187 p.

616 Bartlett, Dorothy A.
NURSE IN WAR. London, Macmillan, 1961. 265 p.

617 Beebe, Gilbert W., and Michael E. DeBakey.
BATTLE CASUALTIES: INCIDENCE, MORTALITY, AND LOGISTIC CONSIDERATIONS. Springfield, Ill., Thomas, 1952. 277 p.

618 Beebe, Gilbert W., and John W. Appel.
VARIATION IN PSYCHOLOGICAL TOLERANCE TO GROUND COMBAT IN WORLD WAR II. Washington, National Academy of Science, 1958. 280 p.

619 Beecher, Henry K.
RESUSCITATION AND ANESTHESIA FOR WOUNDED MEN. Springfield, Ill., Thomas, 1949. 161 p.

620 Benedek, Therese.
INSIGHT AND PERSONALITY ADJUSTMENT: A STUDY OF THE PSYCHOLOGICAL AFFECTS OF WAR. New York, Ronald, 1948. 305 p.

621 Bonaparte, Marie.
MYTHS OF WAR. Translated by John Rodker. London, Imago, 1947. 161 p.

622 Borden, Mary.
JOURNEY DOWN A BLIND ALLEY. London and New York, Hutchinson, 1946. 296 p.

623 Bowden, Jean.
GREY TOUCHED WITH SCARLET: THE WAR EXPERIENCES OF THE ARMY NURSING SISTERS. London, Hale, 1959. 189 p.

624 Brashear, Alton D.
FROM LEE TO BARI: THE HISTORY OF THE FORTY-FIFTH GENERAL HOSPITAL, 1940-1945. Richmond, Whittet and Shipperson, 1957. 468 p.

625 Bright, Pamela.
LIFE IN OUR HANDS. London, MacGibbon and Kee, 1955. 208 p.

626 Bunnell, Sterling.
HAND SURGERY. Washington, Office of Surgeon General, Dept. of Army, 1955. 447 p. (U.S. Army Medical Service, The Medical Department of the U.S. Army in World War II: Surgery in World War II)

627 Coates, John B.
ENVIRONMENTAL HYGIENE. Washington, Office of Surgeon General, Dept. of Army, 1955. 404 p. (U.S. Army Medical Service. Preventive Medicine in World War II)

628 Coates, John B., and others (eds.).
GENERAL SURGERY. Washington, Office of Surgeon General, Dept. of Army, 1955. 417 p. (U.S. Army Medical Service. The Medical Dept. of the U.S. Army in World War II: Surgery in World War II)

629 Cocks, Edith M. S.
KIA KAHA: LIFE AT 3 NEW ZEALAND GENERAL HOSPITAL, 1940-1946. Christchurch, Caxton, 1958. 285 p.

630 Cole, Howard N.
ON WINGS OF HEALING: THE STORY OF THE AIRBORNE MEDICAL SERVICES, 1940-1960. Edinburgh and London, Blackwood, 1963. 227 p.

631 Cooke, Elliot D.
ALL BUT ME AND THEE: PSYCHIATRY AT THE FOXHOLE LEVEL. Washington, Infantry Journal Press, 1946. 215 p.

632 Cooper, Page.
NAVY NURSE. New York and London, Whittlesey House, McGraw-Hill, 1946. 226 p.

633 Cope, Sir Zachary.
SURGERY. London, H.M. Stationery Office, 1953. 772 p. (History of the Second World War: United Kingdom Medical Series)

634 Cope, Sir Zachary (ed.).
MEDICINE AND PATHOLOGY. London, H.M. Stationery Office, 1952. 565 p. (History of the Second World War: United Kingdom Medical Series)

635 Coulter, Jack L.
    THE ROYAL NAVAL MEDICAL SERVICE. London, H.M. Stationery Office, 1954-56. 2 v. (History of the Second World War: United Kingdom Medical Series)

636 Crew, Francis A. E.
    THE ARMY MEDICAL SERVICES: ADMINISTRATION. London, H.M. Stationery Office, 1953-55. 2 v. (History of the Second World War: United Kingdom Medical Series)

637 Crew, Francis A. E.
    THE ARMY MEDICAL SERVICES: CAMPAIGNS. London, H.M. Stationery Office, 1956-66. 5 v. (History of the Second World War: United Kingdom Medical Series)

638 Davies, Arfor T.
    FRIENDS AMBULANCE UNIT: THE STORY OF THE F.A.U. IN THE SECOND WORLD WAR, 1939-1946. London, Allen and Unwin, 1947. 494 p.

639 Dunn, Cuthbert L.
    THE EMERGENCY MEDICAL SERVICES. London, H.M. Stationery Office, 1952-53. 2 v. (History of the Second World War: United Kingdom Medical Series)

640 Edge, Geraldine, and Mary E. Johnston.
    THE SHIPS OF YOUTH: THE EXPERIENCES OF TWO ARMY NURSING SISTERS ON BOARD THE HOSPITAL CARRIER LEINSTER. London, Hodder and Stoughton, 1945. 124 p.

641 Elkin, Daniel C., and Michael E. DeBakey (eds.).
    VASCULAR SURGERY. Washington, Office of Surgeon General, Dept. of Army, 1955. 465 p. (Medical Dept., U.S. Army: Surgery in World War II)

642 Emmrich, Kurt (Peter Bamm, pseud.).
    THE INVISIBLE FLAG. Translated by Frank Hermann. New York, Day, 1956. 250 p.

    Other editions:
    London, Faber, 1956. 229 p.

    New York, New American Library; London, Muller, 1958. 189 p. (Signet Books)

    Harmondsworth, Eng., Penguin, 1962. 272 p.

643 Feasby, W. R. (ed.).
    OFFICIAL HISTORY OF THE CANADIAN MEDICAL SERVICES, 1939-1945. Ottawa, Queen's Printer, 1953-56. 2 v.

644 Fishbein, Morris (ed.).
    DOCTORS AT WAR. New York, Dutton, 1945. 418 p.

645 Flowers, Wilfred S.
    A SURGEON IN CHINA: VIVID PERSONAL EXPERIENCES OF DR. W. S. FLOWERS WITH A BRITISH RED CROSS UNIT. London, Carey Press, 1946. 52 p.

646 Great Britain. War Office.
    STATISTICAL REPORT ON THE HEALTH OF THE ARMY, 1943-1945. London, H.M. Stationery Office, 1948. 204 p.

647 Green, Francis H.K., and Sir Gordon Covell (eds.).
    MEDICAL RESEARCH. London, H.M. Stationery Office, 1953. 387 p. (History of the Second World War: United Kingdom Medical Series)

648 Griffin, Alexander R.
    OUT OF CARNAGE. New York, Howell, Soskin, 1945. 327 p.

649 Grygier, Tadeusz.
    OPPRESSION: A STUDY IN SOCIAL AND CRIMINAL PSYCHOLOGY. Foreword by Hermann Mannheim. London, Routledge and Paul, 1954. 362 p. (International Library of Sociology and Social Reconstruction)

650 Hamilton, Thomas.
    SOLDIER SURGEON IN MALAYA. Sydney, Angus and Robertson, 1957. 218 p.

    Other edition:
    London, World Distributors, 1959. 189 p.

651 Hampton, Oscar P.
    ORTHOPEDIC SURGERY IN THE MEDITERRANEAN THEATER OF OPERATIONS. Washington, Office of Surgeon General, Dept. of Army, 1957. 368 p. (Medical Dept., U.S. Army: Surgery in World War II)

652 Hardison, Irene.
    A NIGHTINGALE IN THE JUNGLE. Philadelphia, Dorrance, 1954. 133 p.

653 Ileana, Princess of Rumania.
    I LIVE AGAIN. London, Gollancz; New York, Rinehart, 1952. 374 p.

654 Inter-Allied Conferences on War Medicine, London.
    INTER-ALLIED CONFERENCES ON WAR MEDICINE, 1942-43, CONVENED BY THE ROYAL SOCIETY OF MEDICINE. Honorary editor, Henry L. Tidy; assistant editor, J. M. Browne Kutschbach. New York, Staples Press, 1947. 531 p.

655 Jeffcott, George F.
    UNITED STATES ARMY DENTAL SERVICE IN WORLD WAR II. Washington, Office of Surgeon General, Dept. of Army, 1955. 362 p. (Medical Dept., U.S. Army)

656 Leslie, Anita.
    TRAIN TO NOWHERE. Foreword by Viscount Alexander of Tunis. London and New York, Hutchinson, 1948. 192 p.

657 Link, Mae M., and Hubert A. Coleman.
    MEDICAL SUPPORT OF THE ARMY AIR FORCES IN WORLD WAR II. Washington, Office of Surgeon General, U.S. Air Force, 1955. 1027 p.

658 Long, Esmond R., and Seymour Jablon.
    TUBERCULOSIS IN THE ARMY OF THE UNITED STATES IN WORLD WAR II: AN EPIDEMIOLOGICAL STUDY WITH AN EVALUATION OF X-RAY SCREENING. Washington, U.S. Government Printing Office, 1955. 88 p. (VA Medical Monograph)

659 Maas, Henry (ed.).
ADVENTURE IS MENTAL HEALTH: PSYCHIATRIC SOCIAL WORK WITH THE ARMED FORCES IN WORLD WAR II. A symposium by Betty P. Broadhurst and others. New York, Columbia University Press, 1951. 334 p.

660 MacNalty, Arthur S. (ed.).
THE CIVILIAN HEALTH AND MEDICAL SERVICES. London, H.M. Stationery Office, 1953-55. 2 v. (History of the Second World War: United Kingdom Medical Services)

661 Marsden, Alexandrina.
RESISTANCE NURSE. London, Odhams Press, 1961. 208 p.

662 MEDICAL SCIENCE ABUSED: GERMAN MEDICAL SCIENCE AS PRACTISED IN CONCENTRATION CAMPS AND IN SO-CALLED PROTECTORATE, REPORTED BY CZECHOSLOVAK DOCTORS. Prague, Orbis, 1946. 91 p.

663 MEMOIRS OF AN ARMY SURGEON. Foreword by Sir Alexander Hood. Edinburgh, Blackwood, 1948. 354 p.

664 Milbourne, Andrew R.
LEASE OF LIFE. Introduction by Tom Driberg. London, Museum Press, 1952. 189 p.

665 Mitscherlich, Alexander, and Fred Mielke.
DOCTORS OF INFAMY: THE STORY OF THE NAZI MEDICAL CRIMES. New York, Schuman, 1949. 172 p.

666 Oughterson, Ashley W., and Shields Warren (eds.).
MEDICAL EFFECTS OF THE ATOMIC BOMB IN JAPAN. New York, McGraw-Hill, 1956. 477 p. (National Nuclear Energy Series. Manhattan Project Technical Section)

667 Parsons, Robert P.
MOB THREE: A NAVAL HOSPITAL IN A SOUTH SEA JUNGLE. Indianapolis, Bobbs-Merrill, 1945. 248 p.

668 Paul, Daniel (pseud.), with John St. John.
SURGEON AT ARMS. London, Heinemann, 1956. 227 p.

Other editions:
London, Landsborough, 1959. 192 p. (Four Square Books)

New York, Norton, 1959. 227 p.

669 Peto, Marjorie.
WOMEN WERE NOT EXPECTED: AN INFORMAL STORY OF THE NURSES OF 2ND GENERAL HOSPITAL IN THE ETO. West Englewood, N.J., 1947. 159 p.

670 Powell, Lyle S.
A SURGEON IN WARTIME CHINA. Lawrence, University of Kansas Press, 1946. 233 p.

671 Raina, Bishen L. (ed.).
PREVENTIVE MEDICINE (NUTRITION, MALARIA CONTROL AND PREVENTION OF DISEASES). Delhi, Combined Inter-Services Historical Section, India and Pakistan, 1961. 814 p. (Official History of the Indian Armed Forces in the Second World War, 1939-45. Medical Services)

672 Raina, Bishen L. (ed.).
STATISTICS. Director, Bisheshwar Prasad. Delhi, Combined Inter-Services Historical Section, India and Pakistan, 1962. 610 p. (Official History of the Indian Armed Forces in the Second World War, 1939-1945. Medical Services)

673 Rees, John R.
THE SHAPING OF PSYCHIATRY BY WAR. London, Chapman and Hall; New York, Norton, 1945. 158 p.

674 Rees, John R. (ed.).
THE CASE OF RUDOLF HESS: A PROBLEM IN DIAGNOSIS AND FORENSIC PSYCHIATRY. By the ... physicians ... concerned with him from 1941 to 1945: Henry V. Dicks and others. London, Heinemann, 1947. 224 p.

Other edition:
New York, Norton, 1948. 224 p.

675 Rexford-Welch, Samuel C. (ed.).
THE ROYAL AIR FORCE MEDICAL SERVICES. London, H.M. Stationery Office, 1954-58. 3 v. (History of the Second World War: United Kingdom Medical Series)

676 Rogers, Lindsay.
GUERRILLA SURGEON. Garden City, N.Y., Doubleday, 1957. 280 p.

Other editions:
London, Collins, 1957. 254 p.

London, Collins, 1959. 253 p. (Fontana Books)

677 Seagrave, Gordon S.
BURMA SURGEON. London, Transworld, 1958. 189 p. (Corgi Books)

678 Seagrave, Gordon S.
BURMA SURGEON RETURNS. New York, Norton, 1946. 268 p.

679 Sharon, Henrietta B.
IT'S GOOD TO BE ALIVE. New York, Dodd, Mead, 1945. 150 p.

680 Simpson, William.
I BURNED MY FINGERS. London, Putnam, 1955. 283 p.

681 Smith, Clarence McK.
THE MEDICAL DEPARTMENT: HOSPITALIZATION AND EVACUATION, ZONE OF INTERIOR. Washington, Office of Chief of Military History, Dept. of Army, 1956. 503 p. (U.S. Army in World War II: The Technical Services)

682 Smith, Dean A., and Michael F.A. Woodruff.
DEFICIENCY DISEASES IN JAPANESE PRISON CAMPS. Introduction by J. Bennet. London, H.M. Stationery Office, 1951. 209 p. (Medical Research Council. Special Report Series)

683 South, Oron P.
MEDICAL SUPPORT IN A COMBAT AIR FORCE: A STUDY OF MEDICAL LEADERSHIP IN WORLD WAR II.

Maxwell Air Force Base, Ala., Documentary Research Division, Research Studies Institute, Air University, 1956. 126 p. (U.S. Air University. Documentary Research Study)

684 Social Science Research Council.
STUDIES IN SOCIAL PSYCHOLOGY IN WORLD WAR II. Princeton, N.J., Princeton University Press, 1949-50. 4 v.

685 Stevenson, Eleanor, and Pete Martin.
I KNEW YOUR SOLDIER. Washington, Infantry Journal; New York, Penguin Books, 1945. 237 p.

686 Stout, Thomas D. M.
MEDICAL SERVICES IN NEW ZEALAND AND THE PACIFIC IN ROYAL NEW ZEALAND NAVY, ROYAL NEW ZEALAND AIR FORCE AND WITH PRISONERS OF WAR. Wellington, War History Branch, Dept. of Internal Affairs, 1958. 450 p. (Official History of New Zealand in the Second World War, 1939-1945)

687 Stout, Thomas D. M.
NEW ZEALAND MEDICAL SERVICES IN MIDDLE EAST AND ITALY. Wellington, War History Branch, Dept. of Internal Affairs, 1956. 721 p. (Official History of New Zealand in the Second World War, 1939-45)

688 Stout, Thomas D. M.
WAR SURGERY AND MEDICINE. Wellington, War History Branch, Dept. of Internal Affairs, 1954. 779 p. (Official History of New Zealand in the Second World War, 1939-45)

689 Trew, Cecil G.
WHAT ARE YOU DOING HERE? BEING THE ADVENTURES OF A SURGICAL ARTIST WITH THE B.L.A. Edinburgh, International Publishing Company, 1947. 128 p.

Other edition:
1950.

690 Tsuchida, William S.
WEAR IT PROUDLY: LETTERS. Berkeley, University of California Press, 1947. 147 p.

691 U.S. Air Force. School of Aviation Medicine.
GERMAN AVIATION MEDICINE, WORLD WAR II. Washington, Dept. of Air Force, 1950. 2 v. (1302 p.)

692 U.S. Army. 11th Field Hospital.
OPERATION SUCCESSFUL: THE STORY OF THE 11TH FIELD HOSPITAL IN THE U.S., ALGERIA, TUNISIA, SICILY, ITALY, FRANCE, ALSACE, GERMANY, AUSTRIA. Edited by Clifford W. Nyberg. n.p., n.d. 79 p.

693 U.S. Army. Evacuation Hospital No. 12.
HISTORY OF THE 12TH EVACUATION HOSPITAL, 25 AUGUST, 1945. Nuremberg, Sebaldus, 1945. 130 p.

694 U.S. Army. Evacuation Hospital No. 41.
A NARRATIVE STYLE REPORT OF THE ACTIVITIES OF THE 41ST EVACUATION HOSPITAL, SEMIMOBILE. Prepared by Albert W. Kuhlmann, Leroy Davis, and Elizabeth C. Hogan. n.p., 1945. 291 p.

695 U.S. Army. Evacuation Hospital No. 77.
MEDICINE UNDER CANVAS: A WAR JOURNAL OF THE 77TH EVACUATION HOSPITAL. Edited by Max S. Allen. Kansas City, Mo., Sosland Press, 1949. 196 p.

696 U.S. Army. Mediterranean Theater of Operations.
THE PHYSIOLOGIC EFFECTS OF WOUNDS. Washington, Office of the Surgeon General, Dept. of Army, 1952. 376 p. (Medical Dept., U.S. Army: Surgery in World War II)

697 U.S. Army Medical Service.
ACTIVITIES OF SURGICAL CONSULTANTS. Prepared and published under direction of Leonard D. Heaton with editors John B. Coates, Jr., B. Noland Carter, and Elizabeth M. McFetridge. Washington, Office of Surgeon General, Dept. of Army, 1962. 2 v. 621 p. (Medical Dept., U.S. Army: Surgery in World War II)

698 U.S. Army Medical Service.
BLOOD PROGRAM IN WORLD WAR II. By Douglas B. Kendrick; published under direction of Leonard D. Heaton, with editors John B. Coates, Jr., and Elizabeth M. McFetridge. Washington, Office of Surgeon General, Dept. of Army, 1964. 922 p. (Medical Dept., U.S. Army in World War II)

699 U.S. Army Medical Service.
INTERNAL MEDICINE IN WORLD WAR II. Edited by John B. Coates, Jr. Washington, Office of Surgeon General, Dept. of Army, 1961-. 2 v. published.

700 U.S. Army Medical Service.
NEUROSURGERY. Edited by R. Glen Spurling and Barnes Woodhall. Washington, Office of Surgeon General, Dept. of Army, 1958-59. 2 v. (Medical Dept., U.S. Army: Surgery in World War II)

701 U.S. Army Medical Service.
OPHTHALMOLOGY AND OTOLARYNGOLOGY. Edited by John B. Coates, Jr., with M. Elliott Randolph and Norton Canfield. Washington, Office of Surgeon General, Dept. of Army, 1957. 605 p. (Medical Dept., U.S. Army: Surgery in World War II)

702 U.S. Army Medical Service.
ORGANIZATION AND ADMINISTRATION IN WORLD WAR II. Published under direction of Leonard D. Heaton, with editors John B. Coates, Jr. and Charles M. Wiltse. Washington, Office of Surgeon General, Dept. of Army, 1963. 613 p. (Medical Dept., U.S. Army in World War II)

703 U.S. Army Medical Service.
ORTHOPEDIC SURGERY IN THE EUROPEAN THEATER OF OPERATIONS. Edited by John B. Coates, Jr., with Mather Cleveland. Washington, Office of Surgeon General, Dept. of Army, 1956. 397 p. (Medical Dept., U.S. Army: Surgery in World War II)

704 U.S. Army Medical Service.
PERSONNEL IN WORLD WAR II. By John H. McMinn and Max Levin; published under direction of Leonard D. Heaton;

edited by John B. Coates, Jr. and Charles M. Wiltse. Washington, Office of Surgeon General, Dept. of Army, 1963. 548 p. (Medical Dept., U.S. Army in World War II)

705 U.S. Army Medical Service.
PREVENTIVE MEDICINE IN WORLD WAR II. Edited by John B. Coates, Jr. Washington, Office of Surgeon General, Dept. of Army, 1955-. Vols. 2, 4, 5, 7 published. (Medical Dept., U.S. Army in World War II)

706 U.S. Army Medical Service.
RADIOLOGY IN WORLD WAR II. Edited by Arnold L. Ahnfeldt. Washington, Office of Surgeon General, Dept. of Army, 1966. 1087 p. (Medical Dept., U.S. Army in World War II)

707 U.S. Army Medical Service.
THORACIC SURGERY. Edited by John B. Coates, Jr. Washington, Office of Surgeon General. Dept. of Army, 1963-. 1 v. published. (Medical Dept., U.S. Army: Surgery in World War II)

708 U.S. Army Medical Service.
U.S. ARMY VETERINARY SERVICE IN WORLD WAR II. By Everett B. Miller; published under direction of Leonard D. Heaton; edited by John B. Coates, Jr. and George L. Caldwell. Washington, Office of Surgeon General, Dept. of Army, 1961. 779 p. (Medical Dept., U.S. Army in World War II)

709 U.S. Army Medical Services.
WOUND BALLISTICS. Edited by John B. Coates, Jr. Washington, Office of Surgeon General, Dept. of Army, 1962. 883 p. (Medical Dept., U.S. Army in World War II)

710 U.S. Bureau of Medicine and Surgery.
THE HISTORY OF THE MEDICAL DEPARTMENT OF THE U.S. NAVY IN WORLD WAR II. Washington, U.S. Government Printing Office, 1950-. 5 v. 2 v. published.

Other edition:
1953. 2 v. published.

711 U.S. Bureau of Medicine and Surgery.
U.S. NAVY MEDICAL DEPARTMENT ADMINISTRATIVE HISTORY, 1941-1945. Washington, 1946. 2 v. in 8.

712 U.S. Naval Special Hospital. Yosemite National Park, California.
HISTORY OF THE UNITED STATES NAVAL SPECIAL HOSPITAL, YOSEMITE NATIONAL PARK, CALIFORNIA. Yosemite National Park, Yosemite Park and Curry Co., 1946. 76 p.

713 U.S. Navy. Fleet Hospital No. 108.
THE STORY OF THE U.S. NAVAL MOBILE HOSPITAL NUMBER 8. By Captain William H. H. Turville. New York, Kelly, 1945. 161 p.

714 Walker, Allan S.
CLINICAL PROBLEMS OF WAR. Canberra, Australian War Memorial, 1952. 720 p. (Australia in the War of 1939-1945. Series 5 [Medical])

715 Walker, Allan S.
THE ISLAND CAMPAIGNS. Canberra, Australian War Memorial, 1957. 426 p. (Australia in the War of 1939-1945. Series 5 [Medical])

716 Walker, Allan S.
MIDDLE EAST AND FAR EAST. Canberra, Australian War Memorial, 1961. 701 p. (Australia in the War of 1939-1945. Series 5 [Medical])

717 Walker, Allan S., and others.
MEDICAL SERVICES OF THE R.A.N. AND R.A.A.F., WITH SECTION ON WOMEN IN THE ARMY MEDICAL SERVICES. Canberra, Australian War Memorial, 1961. 574 p. (Australia in the War of 1939-1945. Series 5 [Medical])

718 Walker, Arthur E., and Seymour Jackson.
A FOLLOW-UP STUDY OF HEAD WOUNDS IN WORLD WAR II. Washington, U.S. Government Printing Office, 1961. 202 p. (VA Medical Monograph)

719 Watts, John C.
SURGEON AT WAR. London, Allen and Unwin, 1955. 165 p.

Other edition:
London, Brown, 1959. 158 p. (Digit Books)

720 Whayne, Tom F., and Michael E. DeBakey.
COLD INJURY, GROUND TYPE. Washington, Office of Surgeon General, Dept. of Army, 1958. 579 p. (Medical Dept., U.S. Army in World War II)

721 Wheeler, Keith.
WE ARE THE WOUNDED. New York, Dutton, 1945. 224 p.

722 Wolfe, Don M. (ed.).
THE PURPLE TESTAMENT: LIFE STORIES BY DISABLED VETERANS. Preface by John Dos Passos. Harrisburg, Pa., Stackpole, 1946. 361 p.

Other edition:
Garden City, N.Y., Doubleday, 1947. 361 p.

723 Zachodnia Agencja Prasowa.
EXPERIMENTAL OPERATIONS ON PRISONERS OF RAVENSBRUCK CONCENTRATION CAMP. Edited by Wanda Machlejd. Poznan, Wydawn. Zachodnie, 1960. 58 p. (Studies and Monographs)

4. Espionage; Secret Services; Special Operations, Commando Operations (see also III. E)

724 Alcorn, Robert H.
NO BUGLES FOR SPIES: TALES OF THE OSS. New York, McKay, 1962. 209 p.

Other edition:
London, Jarrolds, 1963. 209 p.

725 Alsop, Stewart J. O., and Thomas Braden.
SUB ROSA: THE O.S.S. AND AMERICAN ESPIONAGE. New York, Reynal and Hitchcock, 1946. 237 p.

Other edition:
New York, Harcourt, Brace and World, 1964. 264 p. (Harvest Books)

726 Andersen, Hartvig.
THE DARK CITY: A TRUE ACCOUNT OF ADVENTURE OF A SECRET AGENT IN BERLIN. New York, Rinehart, 1954. 314 p.

Other edition:
London, Cresset, 1954.

727 Arnold, Richard.
THE TRUE BOOK ABOUT THE COMMANDOS. London, Muller, 1954. 144 p.

728 Astier De La Vigerie, Emmanuel D'.
SEVEN TIMES SEVEN DAYS. Translated from French by Humphrey Hare. London, MacGibbon and Kee, 1958. 221 p.

729 Babington-Smith, Constance.
AIR SPY: THE STORY OF PHOTO INTELLIGENCE IN WORLD WAR II. New York, Harper, 1957. 266 p.

Other editions:
EVIDENCE IN CAMERA. London, Chatto and Windus 1958. 256 p.

Harmondsworth, Eng., Penguin, with Chatto and Windus, 1961. 239 p.

730 Baker, Peter.
MY TESTAMENT. London, Calder, 1955. 288 p.

731 Bartz, Karl.
THE DOWNFALL OF THE GERMAN SECRET SERVICE. Introduction by Ian Colvin; translated from German by Edward Fitzgerald. London, Kimber, 1956. 202 p.

732 Bazna, Elyesa, with Hans Nogly.
I WAS CICERO. Translated by Eric Mosbacher. London, Deutsch, 1962. 192 p.

Other editions:
New York, Harper and Row, 1962. 212 p.

London, Pan, 1964. 192 p.

733 Bell, Leslie.
SABATAGE! THE STORY OF LT.-COL. J. ELDER WILLS. London, Laurie, 1957. 189 p.

Other edition:
London, Landsborough, 1959. 188 p. (Four Square Books)

734 Bergier, Jacques.
SECRET WEAPONS--SECRET AGENTS. Translated from French by Edward Fitzgerald. London, Hurst and Blackett, 1956. 184 p.

Other edition:
London, Hamilton, 1958. (Panther Books)

735 Best, Sigismund P.
THE VENLO INCIDENT. London and New York, Hutchinson, 1951. 260 p.

736 Bleicher, Hugo E.
COLONEL HENRI'S STORY: THE WAR MEMOIRS OF HUGO BLEICHER, FORMER GERMAN SECRET AGENT. Related to Erich Borchers; edited by Ian Colvin. 2d ed. London, Kimber, 1954. 200 p.

737 Braddon, Russell.
NANCY WAKE: THE STORY OF A VERY BRAVE WOMAN. London, Cassell, 1956. 273 p.

Other edition:
London, Pan Books, 1958. 223 p.

738 Buckmaster, Maurice J.
THEY FOUGHT ALONE: THE STORY OF BRITISH AGENTS IN FRANCE. London, Odhams Press; New York, Norton, 1958. 255 p.

Other edition:
London, Hamilton, 1960. 192 p. (Panther Books)

739 Butler, Ewan.
AMATEUR AGENT. London, Harrap, 1963. 240 p.

Other edition:
New York, Norton, 1964.

740 Cardif, Maurice (John Lincoln, pseud.).
ACHILLES AND THE TORTOISE: AN EASTERN AEGEAN EXPLOIT. London, Heinemann, 1958. 256 p.

741 Carre, Mathilde (Belard).
I WAS "THE CAT": THE TRUTH ABOUT THE MOST REMARKABLE WOMAN SPY SINCE MATA HARI. Translated by Mervyn Savill. London, Souvenir, 1960. 223 p.

Other edition:
London, Four Square, 1961. 190 p.

742 Chapman, Edward A.
THE EDDIE CHAPMAN STORY. As told to Frank Owen. London, Wingate, 1953. 258 p.

Other edition:
New York, Messner, 1954. 242 p.

743 Churchill, Peter.
DUEL OF WITS. London, Hodder and Stoughton, 1953. 319 p.

Other edition:
London, Transworld, 1955. 409 p. (Corgi Books)

744 Churchill, Peter.
OF THEIR OWN CHOICE. London, Hodder and Stoughton, 1952. 218 p.

Other edition:
London, Transworld, 1955. 255 p. (Corgi Books)

745 Clarke, Dudley.
SEVEN ASSIGNMENTS. London, Cape, 1948. 262 p.

746 Colvin, Ian G.
CHIEF OF INTELLIGENCE. London, Gollancz, 1951. 224 p.

Other editions:
MASTER SPY: THE INCREDIBLE STORY OF ADMIRAL WILHELM CANARIS, WHO, WHILE HITLER'S CHIEF OF INTELLIGENCE, WAS A SECRET ALLY OF THE BRITISH. New York, McGraw-Hill, 1952. 286 p.

HITLER'S SECRET ENEMY. London, Pan Books, 1957. 222 p.

747 Colvin, Ian G.
FLIGHT 777. London, Evans, 1957. 212 p.

748 Colvin, Ian G.
THE UNKNOWN COURIER. With a note on the situation confronting the Axis in the Mediterranean in the spring of 1943, by Field-Marshal Kesselring. London, Kimber, 1953. 208 p.

749 Cooper, Dick.
THE ADVENTURES OF A SECRET AGENT. London, Muller, 1957. 255 p.

750 Cowburn, Benjamin.
NO CLOAK, NO DAGGER. London, Jarrolds, 1960. 192 p.

Other edition:
London, Brown, Watson, 1961. 160 p. (Digit Books)

751 Dallin, David J.
SOVIET ESPIONAGE. New Haven, Conn., Yale University Press, 1956. 558 p.

752 Dasch, George J.
EIGHT SPIES AGAINST AMERICA. New York, McBride, 1959. 241 p.

753 Davidson-Houston, James V.
ARMED PILGRIMAGE. London, Hale, 1949. 313 p.

754 Denham, Elizabeth.
I LOOKED RIGHT. London, Cassell, 1956. 191 p.

755 Dourlein, Pieter.
INSIDE NORTH POLE: A SECRET AGENT'S STORY. Translated by F. G. Renier and Anne Cliff. London, Kimber, 1953. 206 p.

Other edition:
London, Kimber, 1954.

756 Downes, Donald C.
THE SCARLET THREAD: ADVENTURES IN WARTIME ESPIONAGE. London, Verschoyle, 1953. 207 p.

Other edition:
London, Hamilton, 1959. 190 p. (Panther Books)

757 Duke, Madelaine (pseud.).
SLIPSTREAM: THE STORY OF ANTHONY DUKE. Foreword by Lieutenant-Colonel A. P. Scotland. London, Evans, 1955. 243 p.

Other edition:
London, Odhams Press, 1957. 252 p. (Beacon Books)

758 Duncan, Sylvia, and Peter Duncan.
ANNE BRUSSELMANS, M.B.E. London, Benn, 1959. 207 p.

759 Durnford-Slater, John.
COMMANDO. London, Kimber, 1953. 222 p.

760 Durrani, Mahmood K.
THE SIXTH COLUMN: THE HEROIC PERSONAL STORY OF LT. COL. MAHMOOD KHAN DURRANI, G.C. London, Cassell, 1955. 367 p.

761 Edlmann, Edmund G.
WITH MY LITTLE EYE. London, Jarrolds, 1961. 240 p.

762 Eliscu, William.
COUNT FIVE AND DIE. Told to Barry Wynne. London, Souvenir Press, 1958. 179 p.

Other editions:
London, Transworld, 1959. 188 p.

New York, Ballantine Books, 1959. 152 p.

763 Evans, Jack.
CONFESSIONS OF A SPECIAL AGENT. As told to Ernest Dudley. London, Hale, 1957. 192 p.

Other editions:
THE FACE OF DEATH. New York, Morrow, 1958. 220 p.

London, Hamilton, 1959. 189 p. (Panther Books)

764 Farago, Ladislas.
BURN AFTER READING: THE ESPIONAGE HISTORY OF WORLD WAR II. New York, Walker, 1961. 319 p.

765 Farago, Ladislas.
THE WAR OF WITS: THE ANATOMY OF ESPIONAGE AND INTELLIGENCE. New York, Funk and Wagnalls, 1954. 379 p.

766 Feldt, Eric A.
THE COASTWATCHERS. New York, Oxford University Press, 1946. 264 p.

767 Firmin, Stanley.
THEY CAME TO SPY. London and New York, Hutchinson, 1946. 156 p.

768 Foley, Charles.
COMMANDO EXTRAORDINARY. Foreword by Sir Robert Laycock. London and New York, Longmans, Green, 1954. 231 p.

Other edition:
Foreword by Telford Taylor. New York, Putnam, 1955. 241 p.

769 Foote, Alexander.
HANDBOOK FOR SPIES. London, Museum Press, 1949. 223 p.

770 Ford, Corey, and Alastair MacBain.
CLOAK AND DAGGER: THE SECRET STORY OF O.S.S. New York, Random House, 1946. 216 p.

771 Fox, John.
AFGHAN ADVENTURE. As told to Roland Goodchild. London, Hale, 1958. 190 p.

772 Fuller, Jean O.
 DOUBLE WEBS: LIGHT ON THE SECRET AGENTS' WAR IN FRANCE. London and New York, Putnam, 1958. 256 p.

 Other edition:
 DOUBLE AGENT? London, Pan, 1961. 218 p.

773 Garby-Czerniawski, Roman.
 THE BIG NETWORK. London, Ronald, 1961. 248 p.

774 Gimpel, Erich, with Will Berthold.
 SPY FOR GERMANY. Translated from German by Eleanor Brockett. London, Hale, 1957. 238 p.

 Other edition:
 London, Hamilton, 1959. 224 p. (Panther Books)

775 Giskes, H. J.
 LONDON CALLING NORTH POLE. London, Kimber, 1953. 208 p.

776 Granovsky, Anatoli M.
 ALL PITY CHOKED: THE MEMOIRS OF A SOVIET SECRET AGENT. London, Kimber, 1955. 248 p.

777 Hall, Roger.
 YOU'RE STEPPING ON MY CLOAK AND DAGGER. New York, Norton, 1957. 219 p.

 Other edition:
 London, Kimber, 1958. 205 p.

778 Hauge, Eiliv O.
 SALT-WATER THIEF. Translated by Malcolm Munthe. London, Duckworth, 1958. 159 p.

779 Hearn, Cyril V.
 DESERT ASSIGNMENT. London, Hale, 1963. 192 p.

780 Hearn, Cyril V.
 FOREIGN ASSIGNMENT. London, Hale, 1961. 191 p.

781 Heilbrunn, Otto.
 THE SOVIET SECRET SERVICES. London, Allen and Unwin, 1956. 216 p.

 Other edition:
 New York, Praeger, 1956. 216 p. (Books That Matter)

782 Hernandez, Al.
 BAHÁLA NA, COME WHAT MAY: THE STORY OF MISSION ISRM (I SHALL RETURN MacARTHUR), AN ARMY-NAVY INTELLIGENCE MISSION IN THE PACIFIC. As told to Dixon Earle; foreword by General Douglas MacArthur. Berkeley, Calif., Howell-North, 1961. 315 p.

783 Hoettl, Wilhelm.
 HITLER'S PAPER WEAPON. Translated from German by Basil Creighton. London, Hart-Davis, 1955. 187 p.

784 Hoettl, Wilhelm.
 THE SECRET FRONT: THE STORY OF NAZI POLITICAL ESPIONAGE. Introduction by Ian Colvin; translated from German by R. H. Stevens. London, Weidenfeld and Nicolson, 1953.

 Other edition:
 New York, Praeger, 1954. 327 p.

785 Howarth, David A.
 WE DIE ALONE. New York, Macmillan, 1955. 231 p.

 Other editions:
 London, Collins, 1955. 254 p.

 ESCAPE ALONE. London, Collins, 1958. 190 p. (Fontana Books)

 London, Collins, 1962. 256 p. (Laurel and Gold Series)

 London, Collins, 1965. (Laurel and Gold Series)

786 Howarth, Patrick (ed.).
 SPECIAL OPERATIONS. By Peter Fleming and others. London, Routledge and Paul, 1955. 239 p.

787 Hyde, Harford M.
 CYNTHIA. New York, Farrar, Straus and Giroux, 1965. 240 p.

 Other edition:
 CYNTHIA: THE SPY WHO CHANGED THE COURSE OF THE WAR. London, Hamilton, 1966. 181 p.

788 Hyde, Harford M.
 THE QUIET CANADIAN: THE SECRET SERVICE STORY OF SIR WILLIAM STEPHENSON. Foreword by the Hon. David Bruce. London, Hamilton, 1962. 225 p.

 Other edition:
 ROOM 3603: THE STORY OF THE BRITISH INTELLIGENCE CENTER IN NEW YORK DURING WORLD WAR II. New York, Farrar, Straus, 1963. 257 p.

789 Icardi, Aldo.
 ALDO ICARDI: AMERICAN MASTER SPY; A TRUE STORY. Pittsburgh, Stalwart Enterprises, 1954. 275 p.

790 Ind, Allison.
 ALLIED INTELLIGENCE BUREAU: OUR SECRET WEAPON IN THE WAR AGAINST JAPAN. New York, McKay, 1958. 305 p.

 Other edition:
 SPY RING PACIFIC. London, Weidenfeld and Nicolson, 1958. 305 p.

791 James, Meyrich E. C.
 I WAS MONTY'S DOUBLE. London and New York, Rider, 1954. 192 p.

 Other edition:
 London, Hamilton, 1958. 192 p. (Panther Books)

792 Johnson, Chalmers A.
 AN INSTANCE OF TREASON: OZAKI HOTSUMI AND THE SORGE SPY RING. Stanford, Calif., Stanford University Press, 1964. 278 p.

793 Jong, Louis de.
 THE GERMAN FIFTH COLUMN IN THE SECOND WORLD WAR. Translated from Dutch by C. M. Geyl. Chicago, University of Chicago Press; London, Routledge and Paul, 1956. 308 p.

794 Kemp, Peter K.
    ALMS FOR OBLIVION. London, Cassell, 1961. 188 p.

795 Kemp, Peter K.
    NO COLOURS OR CREST. London, Cassell, 1958. 305 p.
    Other edition:
    London, Hamilton, 1960. 288 p. (Panther Books)

796 Kimche, Jon.
    SPYING FOR PEACE: GENERAL GUISAN AND SWISS NEUTRALITY. London, Weidenfeld and Nicolson, 1961. 168 p.

797 Klein, Alexander.
    THE COUNTERFEIT TRAITOR. New York, Holt, 1958. 301 p.
    Other editions:
    London, Muller, 1958. 258 p.
    London, Pan Books, 1961. 254 p.

798 Langelaan, George.
    KNIGHTS OF THE FLOATING SILK. London, Hutchinson; Garden City, N. Y., Doubleday, 1959. 284 p.

799 Laughlin, Austin.
    BOOTS AND ALL: THE INSIDE STORY OF THE SECRET WAR. Melbourne, Colorgravure Publication, 1951. 208 p.

800 Lepotier, Adolphe.
    RAIDERS FROM THE SEA. Translated from French by Mervyn Savill; foreword by Admiral the Earl Mountbatten of Burma. London, Kimber, 1954. 200 p.

801 Leverkuehn, Paul.
    GERMAN MILITARY INTELLIGENCE. Translated from German by R. H. Stevens and Constantine FitzGibbon. London, Weidenfeld and Nicolson; New York, Praeger, 1954. 209 p. (Books That Matter)

802 Listowel, Judith Hare, Countess of.
    CRUSADER IN THE SECRET WAR. London, Johnson, 1952. 287 p.

803 Lockhart, Sir Robert H. B.
    COMES THE RECKONING. London, Putnam, 1947. 384 p.

804 Lonsdale Bryans, James.
    BLIND VICTORY: SECRET COMMUNICATIONS, HALIFAX-HASSELL. London and New York, Skeffington, 1951. 191 p.

805 Lovell, Stanley P.
    OF SPIES AND STRATAGEMS. Englewood Cliffs, N.J., Prentice-Hall, 1963. 191 p.

806 MacDonald, Elizabeth P.
    UNDERCOVER GIRL. New York, Macmillan, 1947. 305 p.

807 McDougall, Murdoch C.
    SWIFTLY THEY STRUCK: THE STORY OF NO. 4 COMMANDO. Foreword by Brigadier the Lord Lovat. London, Odhams Press, 1954. 208 p.
    Other edition:
    London, Odhams Press, 1957. 224 p. (Beacon Books)

808 Martelli, George.
    AGENT EXTRAORDINARY: THE STORY OF MICHEL HOLLARD, D.S.O. CROIX DE GUERRE. London, Collins, 1960. 285 p.
    Other editions:
    THE MAN WHO SAVED LONDON. London, Collins, 1963. 253 p. (Fontana Books)
    Garden City, N.Y., Doubleday, 1961. 258 p.

809 Milkomane, George A. M. (George Borodin, pseud.).
    NO CROWN OF LAURELS. London, Laurie, 1950. 224 p.

810 Mills-Roberts, Derek.
    CLASH BY NIGHT: A COMMANDO CHRONICLE. London, Kimber, 1956. 204 p.

811 Minney, Rubeigh J.
    CARVE HER NAME WITH PRIDE. London, Newnes, 1956. 187 p.
    Other editions:
    London, Pan Books, 1958. 191 p.
    London, Collins, 1964.
    London, Collins, 1965. (Fontana Books)

812 Montagu, Ewin E. S.
    THE MAN WHO NEVER WAS. Foreword by Lord Ismay. London, Evans, 1953. 144 p.
    Other editions:
    Harmondsworth, Eng., Penguin, 1956. 122 p.
    London, Transworld, 1964. 116 p. (Corgi Books)
    London, Evans, 1965. 142 p.

813 Morgan, William J.
    THE O.S.S. AND I. New York, Norton, 1957. 281 p.

814 Morgan, William J.
    SPIES AND SABOTEURS. London, Gollancz, 1955. 183 p.

815 Mosley, Leonard O.
    THE CAT AND THE MICE. London, Barker, 1958. 160 p.
    Other edition:
    FOXHOLE IN CAIRO. London, Hamilton, 1960. 127 p. (Panther Books)

816 Moss, William S.
    A WAR OF SHADOWS. London and New York, Boardman, 1952. 240 p.

817 Moyzisch, L. C.
OPERATION CICERO. Postscript by Franz von Papen; translated by Constantine Fitzgibbon and Heinrich Fraenkel. London and New York, Wingate; New York, Coward-McCann, 1950. 208 p.

Other editions:
London, Wingate, 1952. 183 p. (News of the World Readers Circle Series)

London, Hamilton, 1956. 156 p. (Panther Books)

818 Neville, Ralph.
SURVEY BY STARLIGHT: A TRUE STORY OF RECONNAISSANCE WORK IN THE MEDITERRANEAN. London, Hodder and Stoughton, 1949. 206 p.

819 Nicholas, Elizabeth.
DEATH BE NOT PROUD. London, Cresset Press, 1958. 294 p.

820 O'Callaghan, Sean.
THE JACKBOOT IN IRELAND. London, Wingate; New York, Roy, 1958. 157 p.

821 Phillips, Norman C.
GUNS, DRUGS, AND DESERTERS: THE SPECIAL INVESTIGATION BRANCH IN THE MIDDLE EAST. London. Laurie, 1954. 176 p.

822 Pinto, Oreste.
FRIEND OR FOE? London, Laurie, 1953. 187 p.

Other editions:
New York, Putnam, 1954. 245 p.

London, Hamilton, 1957. 160 p. (Panther Books)

MORE EXPLOITS OF SPYCATCHER. London, Hamilton, 1961. 160 p. (Panther Books)

823 Pinto, Oreste.
SPYCATCHER. London, Laurie, 1952. 175 p.

Other editions:
London, Hamilton, 1961. 160 p. (Panther Books)

London, Nelson, 1964. 154 p. (Reading Today Series)

824 Pinto, Oreste.
SPYCATCHER 2. London, Landsborough, 1960. 160 p. (Four Square Books)

825 Pinto, Oreste.
SPYCATCHER 3. London, Four Square Books, 1960. 160 p.

826 Pinto, Oreste.
THE SPYCATCHER OMNIBUS: THE SPY AND COUNTER-SPY ADVENTURES OF LT.-COL ORESTE PINTO. London, Hodder and Stoughton, 1962. 479 p.

827 Piquet-Wicks, Eric.
FOUR IN THE SHADOWS: A TRUE STORY OF ESPIONAGE IN OCCUPIED FRANCE. London, Jarrolds, 1957. 206 p.

828 Pirie, Anthony.
OPERATION BERNHARD: THE GREATEST FORGERY OF ALL TIME. London, Cassell, 1961. 236 p.

829 Pitt, Roxane.
THE COURAGE OF FEAR. London, Jarrolds; New York, Duell, Sloan and Pearce, 1957. 242 p.

Other edition:
London, Brown, 1959. 190 p. (Digit Books)

830 Priest, Barbara.
A FAR BELL. Salisbury, 1951. 213 p.

831 Rachlis, Eugene.
THEY CAME TO KILL: THE STORY OF EIGHT NAZI SABOTEURS IN AMERICA. New York, Random House, 1961. 306 p.

Other edition:
London, Deutsch, 1962.

832 The Reader's Digest.
SECRETS AND SPIES: BEHIND-THE-SCENES STORIES OF WORLD WAR II. Pleasantville, N.Y., Reader's Digest Association, 1964. 576 p.

833 Renault-Roulier, Gilbert (Rémy, pseud.).
COURAGE AND FEAR. Translated from French by Lancelot C. Sheppard. London, Barker, 1950. 320 p.

834 Renault-Roulier, Gilbert (Rémy, pseud.).
PORTRAIT OF A SPY. Translated from French by Launcelot C. Sheppard. London, Barker; New York, Roy, 1955. 224 p.

835 Rendel, Alexander M.
APPOINTMENT IN CRETE: THE STORY OF A BRITISH AGENT. London, Wingate, 1953. 240 p.

836 Richardson, Hal.
ONE-MAN WAR: THE JOCK McLAREN STORY. Sydney and London, Angus and Robertson, 1957. 189 p.

Other edition:
London, Hamilton, 1958. (Panther Books)

837 Robinson, Georgette.
GREEN AVALANCHE: THE STORY OF AN ENGLISH GIRL'S ADVENTURES AS A COMBATANT IN WORLD WAR II. Translated from French by W. J. Tucker. London, Pythagorean Publications, 1960. 225 p.

838 Rowan, Richard W.
SPY SECRETS. New York, Buse Publications, 1946. 112 p.

839 Saelen, Frithjof.
NONE BUT THE BRAVE: THE STORY OF "SHETLANDS" LARSEN. Translated from Norwegian by Kate Austin Lund; adapted for English by Ronald Payne. London, Souvenir Press, 1955. 232 p.

Other edition:
London, Transworld, 1956. 252 p. (Corgi Books)

840 Saunders, Hilary A. St. G.
THE GREEN BERET: THE STORY OF THE COMMANDOS, 1940-1945. Foreword by the Earl Mountbatten of Burma. London, Joseph, 1949. 362 p.

Other edition:
London, Landsborough, 1959. 320 p. (Four Square Books)

841 Schellenberg, Walter.
THE SCHELLENBERG MEMOIRS. Edited and translated by Louis Hagen; introduction by Alan Bullock. London, Deutsch, 1956. 479 p.

Other editions:
London, Mayflower, 1965. 192 p.

THE LABYRINTH: MEMOIRS. New York, Harper, 1956. 423 p.

New York, Pyramid Books, 1958. 222 p. (Pyramid Royal Books) (Abridged from THE LABYRINTH)

842 Schofield, Stephen.
MUSKETOON: COMMANDO RAID, GLOMFJORD, 1942. London, Cape, 1964. 156 p.

843 Schuetz, Arthur (Tristan Busch, pseud.).
SECRET SERVICE UNMASKED. Foreword by Wickham Steen; translated from German by Antony V. Ireland. London and New York, Hutchinson, 1950. 272 p.

844 Schulze-Holthus, Bernhard.
DAYBREAK IN IRAN: A STORY OF THE GERMAN INTELLIGENCE SERVICE. Translated by Mervyn Savill. London, Staples Press, 1954. 319 p.

845 Schwarzwalder, John.
WE CAUGHT SPIES. New York, Duell, Sloan and Pearce, 1946. 296 p.

846 Scotland, A. P.
THE LONDON CAGE. London, Evans, 1957. 203 p.

847 Seth, Ronald.
A SPY HAS NO FRIENDS. London, Deutsch, 1952. 206 p.

Other edition:
New York, Library Publishers, 1954.

848 Seth, Ronald.
THE TRUE BOOK ABOUT THE SECRET SERVICE. London, Muller, 1958. 142 p.

849 Sinevirskii, Nikolai.
SMERSH. Edited by Kermal and Milt Hill; translated by Constantin W. Boldyreff. New York, Holt, 1950. 253 p.

850 Singer, Kurt D.
SPIES AND TRAITORS OF WORLD WAR II. New York, Prentice-Hall, 1945. 295 p.

851 Singer, Kurt D.
SPY STORIES FROM ASIA. New York, Funk, 1955. 336 p.

852 Skorzeny, Otto.
SECRET MISSIONS: WAR MEMOIRS OF THE MOST DANGEROUS MAN IN EUROPE. Translated from French by Jacques Le Clercq. New York, Dutton, 1950. 256 p.

853 Skorzeny, Otto.
SKORZENY'S SPECIAL MISSIONS. London, Hale, 1957. 221 p.

Other edition:
London Hamilton, 1959. (Panther Books)

854 Snow, John H.
THE CASE OF TYLER KENT. New York and Chicago, Domestic and Foreign Affairs and Citizens Press, 1946. 59 p.

855 Soltikow, Michael.
THE CAT: A TRUE STORY OF ESPIONAGE. Translated from German by Mervyn Savill. London, MacGibbon and Kee, 1957. 227 p.

856 Spiro, Edward (E. H. Cookridge, pseud.).
SECRETS OF THE BRITISH SECRET SERVICE: BEHIND THE SCENES OF THE WORK OF BRITISH COUNTERESPIONAGE DURING THE WAR. London, Low, Marston, 1948. 216 p.

857 Spiro, Edward (E. H. Cookridge, pseud.).
THEY CAME FROM THE SKY: THE STORIES OF LIEUTENANT-COLONEL FRANCIS CAMMAERTS, D.S.O., LEGION OF HONOUR AND CAPTAIN HARRY REE, D.S.O., O.B.E. Foreword by Colonel Maurice J. Buckmaster. London, Heinemann, 1965. 264 p.

858 Stead, Philip J.
SECOND BUREAU. London, Evans, 1959. 212 p.

859 Stephan, Enno.
SPIES IN IRELAND. Translated from German by Arthur Davidson. London, Macdonald, 1963. 311 p.

Other editions:
Harrisburg, Stackpole, 1965. 311 p.

London, New English Library, 1965. 286 p. (Four Square Books)

860 Strutton, Bill, and Michael Pearson.
THE SECRET INVADERS. London, Hodder and Stoughton, 1958. 286 p.

861 Sweet-Escott, Bickham A. C.
BAKER STREET IRREGULAR. London, Methuen, 1956. 278 p.

862 Teare, T. D. G.
EVADER. London, Hodder and Stoughton, 1954. 256 p.

863 Tickell, Jerrard.
MOON SQUADRON. London, Wingate, 1956. 204 p.

Other edition:
Garden City, N.Y., Doubleday, 1958.

864 Tickell, Jerrard.
ODETTE: THE STORY OF A BRITISH AGENT. London, Chapman, 1949. 334 p.

Other edition:
London, Pan Books, 1965. 286 p.

865 Tompkins, Peter.
A SPY IN ROME. New York, Simon and Schuster; London, Weidenfeld and Nicolson, 1962. 347 p.

Other edition:
London, Hamilton, 1964. 317 p. (Panther Books)

866 Toyne, John.
WIN TIME FOR US. Toronto, Longmans, 1962. 241 p.

867 U.S. Army. Forces in the Pacific.
HISTORY OF TECHNICAL INTELLIGENCE: SOUTHWEST AND WESTERN PACIFIC AREAS, 1942-1945. Tokyo, U.S. Army Technical Intelligence Center, 1945. 2 v.

868 U.S. Counter Intelligence Corps School, Baltimore.
HISTORY AND MISSION OF THE COUNTER INTELLIGENCE CORPS IN WORLD WAR II. Special text. Baltimore, CIC School, Counter Intelligence Corps Center, 1951. 83 p.

869 Walker, David E.
ADVENTURE IN DIAMONDS. London, Evans, 1955. 186 p.

Other editions:
London, World Distributors, 1957. 192 p. (Viking Books)

London, Evans, 1962.

870 Walker, David E.
LUNCH WITH A STRANGER. London, Wingate, 1957. 195 p.

Other editions:
New York, Norton, 1957. 223 p.

London, Hamilton, 1958. 160 p. (Panther Books)

871 White, John B.
THE BIG LIE. London, Evans; New York, Crowell, 1955. 220 p.

Other edition:
London, Pan Books, 1958. 191 p.

872 Wighton, Charles, and Gunter Peis.
HITLER'S SPIES AND SABOTEURS, BASED ON GERMAN SECRET SERVICE WAR DIARY OF GENERAL LAHOUSEN. New York, Holt, 1958. 285 p.

Other edition:
THEY SPIED ON ENGLAND. London, Odhams Press, 1958. 320 p.

873 Wighton, Charles.
PIN-STRIPE SABOTEUR: THE STORY OF "ROBIN," BRITISH AGENT AND FRENCH RESISTANCE LEADER. Foreword by Captain Peter Churchill. London, Odhams Press, 1959. 256 p.

874 Young, George G.
THE CAT WITH TWO FACES. London, Putnam; New York, Coward-McCann, 1957. 223 p.

Other edition:
London, Odhams Press, 1958. 222 p. (Beacon Books)

875 Young, Peter.
STORM FROM THE SEA. London, Kimber, 1958. 221 p.

876 Zacharias, Ellis M.
SECRET MISSIONS: THE STORY OF AN INTELLIGENCE OFFICER. New York, Putnam, 1946. 433 p.

5. Unit Histories

a. Australia

877 Aitken, Edward F.
THE STORY OF THE 2/2ND AUSTRALIAN PIONEER BATTALION. Melbourne, 2/2nd Pioneer Battalion Association, 1953. 288 p.

878 Alexander, Peter.
WE FIND AND DESTROY: HISTORY OF 458 SQUADRON. n.p., 458 Squadron Council, 1959. 232 p.

879 Allchin, Frank.
PURPLE AND BLUE: THE HISTORY OF THE 2/10TH BATTALION, A.I.F. (THE ADELAIDE RIFLES), 1939-1945. Adelaide, Griffin Press, 1958. 454 p.

880 Argent, Jack N. L. ("Silver John").
TARGET TANK: THE HISTORY OF THE 2/3RD AUSTRALIAN ANTI-TANK REGIMENT, 9TH DIVISION, A.I.F. Paramatta, Cumberland, 1957. 350 p.

881 Australia. Army. 2/13th Infantry Battalion.
BAYONETS ABROAD: A HISTORY OF THE 2/13TH BATTALION A.I.F. IN THE SECOND WORLD WAR. Edited by G. H. Fearnside. Sydney, Waite and Bull, 1953. 434 p.

882 Bellett, Aubrey C.
JOLLY GOOD COMPANY: MEMORIES OF SERVICE WITH "B" COMPANY NO. 2 (FREMANTLE) BATTALION, VOLUNTEER DEFENCE CORPS, DURING THE SECOND WORLD WAR, 1939-1945. n.p. [1947?] 57 p.

883 Benson, S. E.
THE STORY OF THE 42 AUSTRALIA INFANTRY BATTALION. Sydney, Dymock's Book Arcade, 1952. 220 p.

884 Boss-Walker, Geoffrey.
DESERT SAND AND JUNGLE GREEN: A PICTORIAL HISTORY OF THE 2/43RD AUSTRALIAN INFANTRY BATTALION (NINTH DIVISION) IN THE SECOND WORLD WAR, 1939-1945. Hobard, Oldham, Beddome and Meredith, 1948. 164 p.

885 Burns, John.
THE BROWN AND BLUE DIAMOND AT WAR: THE STORY OF THE 2/27TH BATTALION, A.I.F. Adelaide, 2/27th Battalion Ex-Servicemen's Association, Griffin Press, 1960. 259 p.

886 Callinan, Bernard J.
INDEPENDENT COMPANY: THE 2/2 AND 2/4 AUSTRALIAN INDEPENDENT COMPANIES IN PORTUGUESE TIMOR, 1941-1943. London, Heinemann, 1953. 235 p.

887 Charlott, Rupert.
THE UNOFFICIAL HISTORY OF THE 29/46TH AUSTRA-

LIAN INFANTRY BATTALION, A.I.F., SEPT. 1939-SEPT. 1945. Sydney, Halstead, 1952. 147 p.

888 THE CORPS OF ROYAL AUSTRALIAN ENGINEERS IN THE SECOND WORLD WAR, 1939-45. Compiled by Some Who Were There. Melbourne, Specialty Press, 1947. 54 p.

889 Cremor, W. E.
ACTION FRONT: THE HISTORY OF THE 2/2ND AUSTRALIAN FIELD REGIMENT ROYAL AUSTRALIAN ARTILLERY A.I.F. Melbourne, 2/2nd Field Regiment Association, 1961. 234 p.

890 Fairclough, H.
EQUAL TO THE TASK: PAR ONERI; THE HISTORY OF THE ROYAL AUSTRALIAN ARMY SERVICE CORPS. Melbourne, Cheshire, 1962. 310 p.

891 Fearnside, Geoffrey H. (ed.).
BAYONETS ABROAD: A HISTORY OF THE 2/13TH BATTALION, A.I.F., IN THE SECOND WORLD WAR, BY EX-MEMBERS OF THE 2/13TH BATTALION, A.I.F. Sydney, Waite and Bull, 1953. 434 p.

892 Firkins, Peter C.
STRIKE AND RETURN: THE STORY OF THE EXPLOITS OF NO. 460 R.A.A.F. HEAVY BOMBER SQUADRON, R.A.F. BOMBER COMMAND IN THE WORLD WAR. Perth, Paterson Brokensha Party, 1964. 200 p.

893 Glenn, John G.
TOBRUK TO TARAKAN: THE STORY OF A FIGHTING UNIT. Adelaide, Rigby, 1960. 209 p.

894 Goodhart, David.
THE HISTORY OF THE 2/7 AUSTRALIAN FIELD REGIMENT. Adelaide, Rigby, 1952. 380 p.

895 Hartley, Francis J.
SANANANDA INTERLUDE: THE 7TH AUSTRALIAN DIVISION CAVALRY REGIMENT. Melbourne, Book Depot, 1949. 101 p.

896 Haywood, E. V.
SIX YEARS IN SUPPORT: OFFICIAL HISTORY OF 2/1ST AUSTRALIAN FIELD REGIMENT. Edited by A. G. Hanson. Sydney, Angus and Robertson, 1959. 211 p.

897 Henry, R. L.
THE STORY OF THE 2/4TH FIELD REGIMENT: A HISTORY OF A ROYAL AUSTRALIAN ARTILLERY REGIMENT DURING THE SECOND WORLD WAR. Melbourne, Merrion Press, 1950. 410 p.

898 Jacobs, James W., and R. J. Bridgland (eds.).
THROUGH: THE STORY OF SIGNALS 8 AUSTRALIAN DIVISION AND SIGNALS A.I.F. MALAYA. Sydney, 8 Division Signals Association, 1949. 270 p.

899 Kerr, Colin G.
TANKS IN THE EAST: THE STORY OF AN AUSTRALIAN CAVALRY REGIMENT. Melbourne, Oxford University Press, 1945. 200 p.

900 THE LOGBOOK: COLLECTED RECORDS OF 2/7 AUSTRALIAN SERVICE BATTERY. R.A.A. A.I.F., 1940-1945. Sydney, Patterson, 1946. 76 p.

901 Mcfarlan, Graeme.
ETCHED IN GREEN: THE HISTORY OF THE 22ND AUSTRALIAN INFANTRY BATTALION, 1939-1946. Melbourne, 22nd Australian Infantry Battalion Association; Adelaide, Griffin Press, 1961. 262 p.

902 Marshall, Alan J.
NULLI SECUNDUS LOG. Published by the 2/2nd Australian Infantry Battalion, A.I.F. Sydney, Consolidated Press, 1946. 130 p.

903 Masel, Philip.
THE SECOND 28TH: THE STORY OF A FAMOUS BATTALION OF THE NINTH AUSTRALIAN DIVISION. Foreword by Lieutenant-General Sir Henry Wells. Perth, 2/28th Battalion and 24th Anti-Tank Company Association, 1961. 196 p.

904 Matthews, Russell.
MILITIA BATTALION AT WAR: THE HISTORY OF THE 58/59TH AUSTRALIAN INFANTRY BATTALION IN THE SECOND WORLD WAR. Melbourne, 58/59TH Battalion Association, 1961. 236 p.

905 O'Brien, John W.
GUNS AND GUNNERS: THE STORY OF THE 2/5TH AUSTRALIAN FIELD REGIMENT IN WORLD WAR II. Sydney and London, Angus and Robertson, 1950. 267 p.

906 Penfold, A. W., W. C. Bayliss, and K. E. Crispin.
GALLEGHAN'S GREYHOUNDS: THE STORY OF THE 2/30TH AUSTRALIAN INFANTRY BATTALION, 22ND NOVEMBER, 1940-10TH OCTOBER, 1945. Sydney, 2/30th Battalion A.I.F. Association, 1949. 404 p.

907 Russell, William B.
THE SECOND FOURTEENTH BATTALION: A HISTORY OF AN AUSTRALIAN INFANTRY BATTALION IN THE SECOND WORLD WAR. Sydney, Angus and Robertson, 1948. 336 p.

908 Serle, R. P. (ed.).
THE SECOND TWENTY-FOURTH AUSTRALIAN INFANTRY BATTALION OF THE 9TH AUSTRALIAN DIVISION: A HISTORY. Foreword by R. W. Tovell. Brisbane, Jacaranda Press, 1963. 378 p.

909 Uren Malcolm, John L.
A THOUSAND MEN AT WAR: THE STORY OF THE 2/16TH BATTALION A.I.F. Foreword by Major-General Sir Jack Stevens. Melbourne, Heinemann, 1959. 259 p.

910 Voss, Vivian.
THE STORY OF NO. 1 SQUADRON, S.A.A.F. Cape Town, Meshantile Atlas, 1952. 519 p.

911 Wiencke, James.
6TH DIVISION SKETCHES, AITAPE TO WEWAK: BEING A COLLECTION OF SKETCHES, DRAWINGS AND NOTES FROM THE SIXTH AUSTRALIAN DIVISION'S LAST NEW GUINEA CAMPAIGN THROUGH AITOPE, MAPRIK AND WEWAK, 1944-1945. Sydney, 1946. 60 p.

912 Yeates, James D., and W. G. Loh (eds.).
RED PLATYPUS: A RECORD OF THE ACHIEVEMENT OF THE 24TH AUSTRALIAN INFANTRY BRIGADE, NINTH AUSTRALIAN DIVISION, 1940-45. Perth, Imperial Printing Co., 1945. 83 p.

b. Canada

913 Canada. Army. 5th Canadian Light Anti-Aircraft Regiment.
REGIMENTAL HISTORY, WORLD WAR II (1 March 1941-8 MAY 1945. Groningen, De Waal, 1945. 64 p.

914 Canada. Army. Governor General's Horse Guards.
THE GOVERNOR GENERAL'S HORSE GUARDS, 1939-1945. Toronto, Canadian Military Journal, 1954. 243 p.

915 Cassidy, George L.
WARPATH: THE STORY OF THE ALGONQUIN REGIMENT, 1939-1945. Toronto, Ryerson, 1948. 372 p.

916 407 SQUADRON RCAF, OVERSEAS 1941-1945. n.p., 1945. 60 p.

917 Johnson, Charles M.
ACTION WITH THE SEAFORTHS. New York, Vantage Press, 1954. 342 p.

918 McAvity, J. M.
LORD STRATHCONA'S HORSE (ROYAL CANADIANS): A RECORD OF ACHIEVEMENT. Toronto, 1947. 280 p.

919 Mowat, Farley.
THE REGIMENT. Toronto, McClelland and Stewart, 1955. 312 p.

920 Pavey, Walter G.
AN HISTORICAL ACCOUNT OF THE 7TH CANADIAN RECONNAISSANCE REGIMENT (17TH DUKE OF YORK'S ROYAL CANADIAN HUSSARS) IN THE WORLD WAR, 1939-1945. Montreal, 1948. 139 p.

921 Queen-Hughes, R. W.
WHATEVER MEN DARE: A HISTORY OF THE QUEEN'S OWN CAMERON HIGHLANDERS OF CANADA, 1935-1960. Foreword by G. G. Simonds. Winnipeg, 1960. 247 p.

922 Spencer, Robert A.
HISTORY OF THE FIFTEENTH CANADIAN FIELD REGIMENT, ROYAL CANADIAN ARTILLERY, 1941 TO 1945. Amsterdam and New York, Elsevier, 1945. 302 p.

c. Great Britain

923 Anderson, Robert C. B.
THE HISTORY OF THE ARGYLL AND SUTHERLAND HIGHLANDERS 1ST BATTALION: Vol. II, 1939-1954. Stirling, Scotland, Argyll and Highlanders Depot, 1956. 520 p.

924 Barclay, Cyril N.
THE HISTORY OF THE CAMERONIANS (SCOTTISH RIFLES): Vol. III, 1933-1946. London, Sifton Praed, 1948. 280 p.

925 Barclay, Cyril N.
THE HISTORY OF THE 53RD (WELSH) DIVISION IN THE SECOND WORLD WAR. Foreword by C. F. C. Coleman. London, Clowes, 1956. 233 p.

926 Barclay, Cyril N.
THE HISTORY OF THE ROYAL NORTHUMBERLAND FUSILIERS IN THE SECOND WORLD WAR. London, Clowes, 1952. 241 p.

927 Barclay, Cyril N.
THE HISTORY OF THE SHERWOOD FORESTERS (NOTTINGHAMSHIRE AND DERBYSHIRE REGIMENT) 1919-1957. London, Clowes, 1959. 182 p.

928 Barclay, Cyril N.
THE LONDON SCOTTISH IN THE SECOND WORLD WAR: 1939 TO 1945. Foreword by R. J. L. Ogilby. London, Clowes, 1952. 459 p.

929 Barclay, Cyril N. (ed.).
THE HISTORY OF THE DUKE OF WELLINGTON'S REGIMENT, 1919-1952. London, Clowes, 1953. 387 p.

930 Barker, Frank R. P.
HISTORY OF THE ARGYLL AND SUTHERLAND HIGHLANDERS, 9TH BATTALION, 54TH LIGHT A.A. REGIMENT, 1939-45. London and New York, Nelson, 1950. 131 p.

931 Beddington, William R.
A HISTORY OF THE QUEEN'S BAYS (THE 2ND DRAGOON GUARDS) 1929-1945. Foreword by General Sir R. L. McCreery. Winchester, Warren, 1954. 271 p.

932 Bell, Archibald C.
HISTORY OF THE MANCHESTER REGIMENT: Vol. III, FIRST AND SECOND BATTALIONS, 1922-1948. Altrincham, Sherrati, 1954. 554 p.

933 Birdwood, Christopher B. B.
THE WORCESTERSHIRE REGIMENT, 1922-1950. Aldershot, Gale and Polden, 1952. 302 p.

934 Blake, George.
MOUNTAIN AND FLOOD: THE HISTORY OF THE 52ND (LOWLAND) DIVISION, 1939-1946. Glasgow, Jackson, 1950. 265 p.

935 Blight, Gordon.
THE HISTORY OF THE ROYAL BERKSHIRE REGIMENT, PRINCESS CHARLOTTE OF WALES'S, 1920-1947. Foreword by Sir Miles Dempsey. London and New York, Staples, 1953. 499 p.

936 Borthwick, James.
51ST HIGHLAND DIVISION IN NORTH AFRICA AND SICILY. Glasgow, MacKensie, 1945. 63 p.

937 Bouskell-Wade, George E.
    THERE IS HONOUR LIKEWISE . . . : THE STORY OF 154 (LEICESTERSHIRE YEOMANRY) FIELD REGIMENT. Leicester, Backus, 1948. 143 p.

938 Briant, Keith.
    FIGHTING WITH THE GUARDS. London, Evans, 1958. 224 p.

939 Bright, Joan.
    HISTORY OF THE NORTHUMBERLAND HUSSARS YEOMANRY, 1924-1949. Foreword by D. Clifton Brown. Newcastle upon Tyne, Mawson, Swan and Morgan, 1949. 406 p.

940 Bright, Joan (ed.).
    THE NINTH QUEEN'S ROYAL LANCERS, 1936-1945: THE STORY OF AN ARMOURED REGIMENT IN BATTLE. Aldershot, Gale and Polden, 1951. 359 p.

941 Bullen, Roy E.
    HISTORY OF THE 2/7TH BATTALION, THE QUEEN'S ROYAL REGIMENT, 1939-1946. Foreword by Lt.-Gen. Sir William Stratton. London, Neale, 1958. 161 p.

942 Cameron, Ian C.
    HISTORY OF THE ARGYLL AND SUTHERLAND HIGHLANDERS, 7TH BATTALION, FROM EL ALAMEIN TO GERMANY. London, Nelson, 1946. 242 p.

943 Capleton, Eric W.
    SHABASH-149: THE WAR STORY OF THE 149TH REGIMENT R. A., 1939-1945. London, 149th Regiment Royal Artillery, Old Comrades Association, 1963. 268 p.

944 Carver, Richard N. P.
    SECOND TO NONE: THE ROYAL SCOTS GREYS--1919-1945. Foreword by Field-Marshal Viscount Montgomery of Alamein. Glasgow, McCorquodale, 1954. 210 p.

945 Casper, Bernard M.
    WITH THE JEWISH BRIGADE. London, Goldstone, 1947. 128 p.

946 Chaplin, Howard D.
    THE QUEEN'S OWN ROYAL WEST KENT REGIMENT, 1920-1950. London, Joseph, 1954. 510 p.

947 Clabby, J.
    THE HISTORY OF THE ROYAL ARMY VETERINARY CORPS, 1919-1961. London, Allen, 1963. 244 p.

948 Clarke, Dudley.
    THE ELEVENTH AT WAR: BEING THE STORY OF THE XIth HUSSARS (PRINCE ALBERT'S OWN) THROUGH THE YEARS 1934-1945. London, Joseph, 1952. 504 p.

949 Clarke, Edward B. S.
    FROM KENT TO KOHIMA: BEING THE HISTORY OF THE 4TH BATTALION THE QUEEN'S OWN ROYAL WEST KENT REGIMENT (T. A.), 1939-1947. Aldershot, Gale and Polden, 1951. 259 p.

950 Clay, Ewart W.
    THE PATH OF THE 50TH: THE STORY OF THE 50TH (NORTHUMBRIAN) DIVISION IN THE SECOND WORLD WAR, 1939-1945. Aldershot, Gale and Polden, 1950. 327 p.

951 Crozier, Stephen F.
    THE HISTORY OF THE CORPS OF ROYAL MILITARY POLICE. Aldershot, Gale and Polden, 1951. 224 p.

952 Cunliffe, Marcus F.
    HISTORY OF THE ROYAL WARWICKSHIRE REGIMENT, 1919-1955. Foreword by Field-Marshal the Viscount Montgomery of Alamein. London, Clowes, 1956. 200 p.

953 Davy, George M. O.
    THE SEVENTH AND THREE ENEMIES: THE STORY OF WORLD WAR II AND THE 7TH QUEEN'S OWN HUSSARS. Cambridge, Eng., Heffer, 1953. 468 p.

954 Dean, Charles G. T.
    THE LOYAL REGIMENT (NORTH LANCASHIRE), 1919-1953. Preston, Loyal Regiment, 1955. 329 p.

955 De Courcy, John, and C. E. N. Lomax.
    THE HISTORY OF THE WELCH REGIMENT, 1919-1951. Cardiff, Western Mail, 1952. 337 p.

956 Drummond, John D.
    BLUE FOR A GIRL: THE STORY OF THE W. R. N. S. London, Allen, 1960. 207 p.

957 Duncan, William E. (ed.).
    THE ROYAL ARTILLERY COMMEMORATION BOOK, 1939-1945. London, Bell, 1950. 790 p.

958 Durand, Algernon T. M., and R. H. W. S. Hastings.
    THE LONDON RIFLE BRIGADE, 1919-1950. Aldershot, Gale and Polden, 1952. 320 p.

959 Eeles, Henry S.
    THE HISTORY OF THE 17TH LIGHT ANTI-AIRCRAFT REGIMENT, ROYAL ARTILLERY, 1938-1945. Tunbridge Wells, Courier, 1945. 251 p.

960 Ellenberger, G. F.
    HISTORY OF THE KING'S OWN YORKSHIRE LIGHT INFANTRY, 1939-1948. Aldershot, Gale and Polden, 1961. 184 p. (History of the King's Own Yorkshire Light Infantry Series)

961 Ellis, Lionel F.
    WELSH GUARDS AT WAR. Aldershot, Gale and Polden, 1946. 586 p.

962 Erskine, David H. (comp.).
    THE SCOTS GUARDS, 1919-1955. London, Clowes, 1956. 624 p.

963 Essame, Hubert.
    THE 43RD WESSEX DIVISION AT WAR, 1944-1945. London, Clowes, 1952. 292 p.

964 Evans, Sir Geoffrey C.
     THE JOHNNIES. London, Cassell, 1964. 231 p.

965 Fergusson, Bernard.
     THE BLACK WATCH AND THE KING'S ENEMIES. Foreword by Earl Wavell. London, Collins, 1950. 384 p.

966 Ffrench Blake, R. L. V.
     A HISTORY OF THE 17TH/21ST LANCERS, 1922-1959. Foreword by Lord Harding of Petherton. London, Macmillan; New York, St. Martin's Press, 1962. 283 p.

967 Finch, Peter.
     WARMEN COURAGEOUS: THE STORY OF THE ESSEX HOME GUARD, 1940-1945. Southend-on-Sea, Burrows, 1951. 351 p.

968 THE 1ST AND 2ND NORTHAMPTONSHIRE YEOMANRY, 1939-1946. Brunswick, Ger., 1946. 141 p.

969 Fitzgerald, Desmond J. L.
     HISTORY OF THE IRISH GUARDS IN THE SECOND WORLD WAR. Foreword by Viscount Alexander of Tunis. Aldershot, Gale and Polden, 1949. 615 p.

970 Fitzroy, Olivia.
     MEN OF VALOUR: THE THIRD VOLUME OF THE HISTORY OF THE VIII KING'S ROYAL IRISH HUSSARS, 1927-1958. Foreword by H. R. H. the Duke of Edinburgh. Gyrn Castle, Llanasa, Lydywells, Sir Geoffrey V. Bates, 1961. 375 p.

971 Flower, Desmond.
     HISTORY OF THE ARGYLL AND SUTHERLAND HIGHLANDERS 5TH BATTALION, 91ST ANTI-TANK REGIMENT, 1939-45. London and New York, Nelson, 1950. 395 p.

972 Forbes, Patrick.
     6TH GUARDS TANK BRIGADE: THE STORY OF GUARDSMEN IN CHURCHILL TANKS. London, Low, Marston, 1946. 244 p.

973 Fox, Sir Frank.
     THE ROYAL INNISKILLING FUSILIERS IN THE SECOND WORLD WAR: A RECORD OF THE WAR AS SEEN BY THE ROYAL INNISKILLING FUSILIERS, THREE BATTALIONS OF WHICH SERVED. Aldershot, Gale and Polden, 1951. 204 p.

974 Gates, Lionel C. (comp.).
     THE HISTORY OF THE TENTH FOOT, 1919-1950. Edited by Major-General J. A. A. Griffin. Aldershot, Gale and Polden, 1953. 355 p.

975 Gilchrist, R. T.
     MALTA STRIKES BACK: THE STORY OF 231 INFANTRY BRIGADE. Aldershot, Gale and Polden, 1946. 136 p.

976 Graham, Andrew.
     SHARPSHOOTERS AT WAR: THE 3RD, THE 4TH AND THE 3RD/4TH COUNTY OF LONDON YEOMANRY, 1939 TO 1945. Foreword by Field-Marshal the Viscount Montgomery of Alamein. London, Sharpshooters Regimental Association, 1964. 252 p.

977 Graham, Frederick C. C.
     HISTORY OF THE ARGYLL AND SUTHERLAND HIGHLANDERS 1ST BATTALION (PRINCESS LOUISE'S) 1939-1945. Foreword by G. H. A. MacMillan. London and New York, Nelson, 1948. 247 p.

978 Great Britain. Air Ministry.
     BY AIR TO BATTLE: THE OFFICIAL ACCOUNT OF THE BRITISH FIRST AND SIXTH AIRBORNE DIVISIONS. London, H.M. Stationery Office, 1945. 144 p.

979 Great Britain. Army. East Lancashire Regiment.
     HISTORY OF THE EAST LANCASHIRE REGIMENT IN THE WAR, 1939-1945. Manchester, Rawson, 1953. 331 p.

980 Great Britain. Army. Grenadier Guards.
     THE GRENADIER GUARDS, 1939-1945. Aldershot, Gale and Polden, 1946. 79 p.

981 Great Britain. Army. Princess Louise's Kensington Regiment. Regimental Old Comrades' Association.
     THE KENSINGTONS: PRINCESS LOUISE'S KENSINGTON REGIMENT, SECOND WORLD WAR. London, Kensington Old Comrades' Association, 1952. 392 p.

982 Great Britain. Army. Royal Army Service Corps.
     THE STORY OF THE ROYAL ARMY SERVICE CORPS, 1939-1945. London, Bell, 1955. 720 p.

983 Great Britain. Army. Royal Artillery. 7th Medium Regiment. Historical Committee.
     THE HISTORY OF THE 7TH MEDIUM REGIMENT, ROYAL ARTILLERY (NOW 32ND MEDIUM REGIMENT R. A.) DURING WORLD WAR II, 1939-1945. London, Langrishe, 1951. 222 p.

984 Great Britain. Army. 79th Armoured Division.
     THE STORY OF 79TH ARMOURED DIVISION, OCTOBER 1942-JUNE 1945. Hamburg, 1945. 314 p.

985 Gunning, Hugh.
     THE BORDERERS IN BATTLE: THE WAR STORY OF THE KING'S OWN SCOTTISH BORDERERS, 1939-1945. Berwick-upon-Tweed, 1948. 287 p.

986 Guttery, David R.
     THE QUEEN'S OWN WORCESTERSHIRE HUSSARS, 1922-1956. Stourbridge, Mark and Moddy, 1958. 159 p.

987 Hastings, Robin H. W. S.
     THE RIFLE BRIGADE IN THE SECOND WORLD WAR, 1939-1945. Foreword by Duke of Gloucester. Aldershot, Gale and Polden, 1950. 475 p.

988 Hills, Reginald J. T.
     PHANTOM WAS THERE. London, Arnold, 1951. 344 p.

989 Hingston, Walter G.
     NEVER GIVE UP: THE HISTORY OF THE KING'S OWN YORKSHIRE LIGHT INFANTRY, 1919-1942. London, 1950. 243 p. (History of the King's Own Yorkshire Light Infantry)

990   HISTORY OF THE CHESHIRE HOME GUARD FROM L. D. V. FORMATION TO STAND-DOWN, 1940-1944. Aldershot, Gale and Polden, 1950. 158 p.

991   A HISTORY OF THE 44TH ROYAL TANK REGIMENT IN THE WAR OF 1939-45. Brighton, 44th Royal Tank Regiment Association, 1965. 214 p.

992   Howard, Michael E. and John H. A. Sparrow.
        THE COLDSTREAM GUARDS, 1920-1946. London, Oxford University Press, 1951. 593 p.

993   Jervois, Wilfrid J.
        THE HISTORY OF THE NORTHAMPTONSHIRE REGIMENT: 1934-1948. Northampton, Northamptonshire Regiment, 1953. 448 p.

994   Johnson, Roy F.
        REGIMENTAL FIRE: THE HONOURABLE ARTILLERY COMPANY IN WORLD WAR II, 1939-1945. London, Honourable Artillery Company, 1958. 440 p.

995   Jolly, Alan.
        BLUE FLASH: THE STORY OF AN ARMOURED REGIMENT. Foreword by Sir John T. Crocker. London, 1952. 168 p.

996   Jones, Arthur J.
        THE SECOND DERBYSHIRE YEOMANRY: AN ACCOUNT OF THE REGIMENT DURING WORLD WAR, 1939-45. Bristol, White Swan Press, 1949. 134 p.

997   Jones, Ira.
        TIGER SQUADRON: THE STORY OF THE 74 SQUADRON, R. A. F. IN TWO WORLD WARS. London, Allen, 1954. 295 p.

998   Karaka, Dosoo F.
        WITH THE 14TH ARMY. London, Crisp, 1945. 85 p.

999   Kemp, James C.
        THE HISTORY OF THE ROYAL SCOTS FUSILIERS, 1919-1959. Foreword by Field-Marshal Sir Francis W. Festing. Glasgow, House of Grant, 1963. 423 p.

1000   Kemp, Peter K., and John Graves.
        THE RED DRAGON: THE STORY OF THE ROYAL WELCH FUSILIERS, 1919-1945. Foreword by Hugh Stockwell. Aldershot, Gale and Polden, 1960. 414 p.

1001   Kemp, Peter K.
        THE STAFFORDSHIRE YEOMANRY, Q. O. R. R. IN THE FIRST AND SECOND WORLD WARS, 1914-1918 AND 1939-1945. Aldershot, Gale and Polden, 1950. 168 p.

1002   Kemsley, Walter, and M. R. Riesco.
        THE SCOTTISH LION ON PATROL: BEING THE STORY OF THE 15TH SCOTTISH RECONNAISSANCE REGIMENT, 1943-1946. Bristol, White Swan Press, 1950. 232 p.

1003   Knight, Peter.
        THE 59TH DIVISION: ITS HISTORY. London, Muller, 1954. 110 p.

1004   Lawrence, W. J.
        NO. 5 BOMBER GROUP, R. A. F. (1939-1945). Preface by Air Chief Marshal Sir Ralph Cochrane. London, Faber, 1951. 253 p.

1005   Lewis, Peter J. (comp.), with I. R. English.
        8TH BATTALION: THE DURHAM LIGHT INFANTRY 1939-1945. Newcastle upon Tyne, J. and P. Bealls, 1949. 319 p.

1006   Lindsay, Martin.
        SO FEW GOT THROUGH: THE PERSONAL DIARY OF LIEUTENANT-COLONEL MARTIN LINDSAY WHO SERVED WITH THE GORDON HIGHLANDERS IN THE 51ST HIGHLAND DIVISION FROM JULY 1944 TO MAY 1945. London, Collins, 1946. 287 p.

1007   Lindsay, Thomas M.
        SHERWOOD RANGERS. London, Burrop, Mathieson, 1952. 182 p.

1008   Lockhart, Sir Robert H. B.
        THE MARINES WERE THERE: THE STORY OF THE ROYAL MARINES IN THE SECOND WORLD WAR. London, Putnam, 1950. 229 p.

1009   Lowry, M. A.
        AN INFANTRY COMPANY IN ARAKAN AND KOHIMA. Foreword by General Sir George Giffard. Aldershot, Gale and Polden, 1950. 132 p.

1010   McCorquodale, D., B. L. B. Hutchings, and A. D. Woozley.
        HISTORY OF THE KING'S DRAGOON GUARDS. Edited by A. D. Woozley; foreword by Sir Richard L. McCreery. Glasgow, 1950. 403 p.

1011   McElwee, William L.
        HISTORY OF THE ARGYLL AND SUTHERLAND HIGHLANDERS, 2ND BATTALION, RECONSTITUTED, EUROPEAN CAMPAIGN 1944-45. Foreword by G. H. A. MacMillan. London and New York, Nelson, 1949. 212 p.

1012   McGeoch, W. Percy.
        THE TRIUMPHS AND TRAGEDIES OF A HOME GUARD (FACTORY) COMPANY, B. COMPANY 41ST WARWICKSHIRE (BIRMINGHAM) BATTALION HOME GUARD. Foreword by J. Clive Piggott. Birmingham, Tuckey, 1946. 188 p.

1013   McMath, J. S.
        THE FIFTH BATTALION: THE WILTSHIRE REGIMENT IN NORTHWEST EUROPE, JUNE, 1944 TO MAY, 1945. London, n. d. 128 p.

1014   Madden, B. J. G.
        A HISTORY OF THE 6TH BATTALION, THE BLACK WATCH, ROYAL HIGHLAND REGIMENT, 1939-1945. Perth, Leslie, 1948. 143 p.

1015   Malcolm, Alec D.
        HISTORY OF THE ARGYLL AND SUTHERLAND HIGHLANDERS, 8TH BATTALION, 1939-47. Foreword by G. H. A. MacMillan. London and New York, Nelson, 1949. 284 p.

1016 Martin, Hugh G.
THE HISTORY OF THE FIFTEENTH SCOTTISH DIVISION, 1939-1945. Edinburgh, Blackwood, 1948. 383 p.

1017 Martin, Thomas A.
THE ESSEX REGIMENT, 1929-1950. London, Watson and Viney, 1951. 668 p.

Other edition:
London, Essex Regiment Association, 1952.

1018 Masters, David.
WITH PENNANTS FLYING: THE IMMORTAL DEEDS OF THE ROYAL ARMOURED CORPS. 2d ed., abridged. London, Spencer, 1957. 159 p. (Badger Books)

1019 Melling, Leonard.
WITH THE EIGHTH IN ITALY. Manchester, Eng., Torch Publishing Co., 1955. 172 p.

Other edition:
London, Brown, 1958. (Digit Books)

1020 Mepham, Clement R.
WITH THE EIGHTH ARMY IN ITALY. Ilfracombe, Eng., Stockwell, 1951. 117 p.

1021 Morris, Arthur H. M. (ed.).
THE FOUR-TWO: SCRAPS FROM THE HISTORY OF THE 42ND FIELD COMPANY, R.E. Aldershot, Gale and Polden, 1952. 68 p.

1022 Mottram, E. (ed.).
THE PIONEER: BRITISH ARMY OF THE RHINE, 1943-46. n.p., 1946. 60 p.

1023 Muir, Augustus.
THE FIRST OF FOOT: THE HISTORY OF THE ROYAL SCOTS (THE ROYAL REGIMENT). Foreword by H.R.H. the Princess Royal. Edinburgh, Royal Scots History Committee, 1961. 504 p.

1024 Nalder, Reginald F. H.
THE HISTORY OF BRITISH ARMY SIGNALS IN THE SECOND WORLD WAR: GENERAL SURVEY. Aldershot, Gale and Polden, 1953. 377 p.

1025 Neville, James E. H.
THE OXFORDSHIRE AND BUCKINGHAMSHIRE LIGHT INFANTRY CHRONICLE: THE RECORD OF THE 43RD, 52ND, 4TH, 5TH, AND 1ST BUCKINGHAMSHIRE BATTALIONS IN THE SECOND GERMAN WAR. Aldershot, Gale and Polden, 1949-54. 4 v.

1026 Nicholson, Walter N.
THE SUFFOLK REGIMENT, 1928 TO 1946. Ipswich, East Anglian Magazine, 1948. 374 p.

1027 Oglivy-Dalgleish, James W.
THE RUTLAND HOME GUARD OF 1940-44. Springfield, Oakham, 1955. 68 p.

1028 Orde, Roden.
THE HOUSEHOLD CAVALRY AT WAR: SECOND HOUSEHOLD CAVALRY REGIMENT. Aldershot, Gale and Polden, 1953. 624 p.

1029 Packe, Michael St. J.
FIRST AIRBORNE. London, Secker and Warburg, 1948. 252 p.

1030 Parkinson, Cyril N.
ALWAYS A FUSILIER: THE WAR HISTORY OF THE ROYAL FUSILIERS (CITY OF LONDON REGIMENT), 1939-1945. London, Low, 1949. 320 p.

1031 Parsons, Anthony D., D. I. M. Robbins, and D. C. Gilson (comps.).
THE MAROON SQUARE: A HISTORY OF THE 4TH BATTALION, THE WILTSHIRE REGIMENT (DUKE OF EDINBURGH'S) IN NORTH WEST EUROPE, 1939-46. London, Franey, 1955. 231 p.

1032 Parsons, Laurence M. H., and E. R. Hill.
THE STORY OF THE GUARDS ARMOURED DIVISION. London, Bles, 1956. 320 p.

1033 Paul, William P. (ed.).
HISTORY OF THE ARGYLL AND SUTHERLAND HIGHLANDERS 6TH BATTALION, 93RD ANTI-TANK REGIMENT, R.A. (A. AND S.H.). Foreword by G. H. A. MacMillan. London and New York, Nelson, 1949. 134 p.

1034 Pitman, Stuart.
SECOND ROYAL GLOUCESTERSHIRE HUSSARS: LIBYA-EGYPT, 1941-1942. Foreword by the Duke of Beaufort. London, Saint Catherine Press, 1950. 96 p.

1035 Pitt, P. W.
ROYAL WILTS: THE HISTORY OF THE ROYAL WILTSHIRE YEOMANRY, 1920-1945. London, Burrop, Mathieson, 1946. 234 p.

1036 Pitt-Rivers, Julian A. L.
THE STORY OF THE ROYAL DRAGOONS, 1938-1945: BEING THE HISTORY OF THE ROYAL DRAGOONS IN THE CAMPAIGNS OF NORTH AFRICA, THE MIDDLE EAST, ITALY AND NORTH-WEST EUROPE. London, Clowes, 1945. 160 p.

Other edition:
London, Clowes, 1956.

1037 Quilter, D. C. (comp.).
NO DISHONOURABLE NAME: THE 2ND AND 3RD BATTALIONS COLDSTREAM GUARDS IN FRANCE, NORTH AFRICA AND ITALY, 1939-1946. London, Clowes, 1947. 334 p.

1038 Ray, Cyril.
ALGIERS TO AUSTRIA: A HISTORY OF 78 DIVISION IN THE SECOND WORLD WAR. London, Eyre and Spottiswoode, 1952. 253 p.

1039 Rhodes-Wood, Edward H.
A WAR HISTORY OF THE ROYAL PIONEER CORPS, 1939-1945. Aldershot, Gale and Polden, 1960. 368 p.

1040 Rissik, David.
THE D. L. I. AT WAR: THE HISTORY OF THE DURHAM LIGHT INFANTRY, 1939-1945. Durham, Durham Light Infantry, 1953. 352 p.

1041 Rosse, Laurence M. H. Parsons, 6th earl of, and E. R. Hill.
THE STORY OF THE GUARDS ARMOURED DIVISION. London, Bles, 1956. 320 p.

1042 Salmond, James B.
THE HISTORY OF THE 51ST HIGHLAND DIVISION, 1939-1945. Edinburgh, Blackwood, 1953. 287 p.

1043 Sandes, Edward W. C.
FROM PYRAMID TO PAGODA: THE STORY OF WEST YORKSHIRE REGIMENT (THE PRINCE OF WALE'S OWN) IN THE WAR 1939-45 AND AFTERWARDS. York, West Yorkshire Regiment, 1952. 306 p.

1044 Saunders, Hilary A. St. G.
THE RED BERET: THE STORY OF THE PARACHUTE REGIMENT AT WAR, 1940-1945. Foreword by Field-Marshal the Viscount Montgomery of Alamein. London, Joseph, 1950. 336 p.

Other edition:
London, Odhams Press, 1958. 384 p.

1045 Sellar, Robert J. B.
THE FIFE AND FORFAR YEOMANRY, 1919-1956. Foreword by Brian Horrocks. Edinburgh, Blackwood, 1960. 288 p.

1046 Seth, Ronald S.
LION WITH BLUE WINGS: THE STORY OF THE GLIDER PILOT REGIMENT, 1942-1945. Foreword by Viscount Alanbrooke and Sir Leslie Hollinghurst. London, Gollancz, 1955. 245 p.

Other edition:
London, Hamilton, 1959. 188 p. (Panther Books)

1047 Shears, Philip J.
THE STORY OF THE BORDER REGIMENT, 1939-1945. Foreword by G. Hyde Harrison. London, Nisbet, 1948. 184 p.

1048 Stanley Clarke, Edward B., and A. T. Tillott.
FROM KENT TO KOHIMA: BEING THE HISTORY OF THE 4TH BATTALION THE QUEEN'S OWN ROYAL WEST KENT REGIMENT (R.A.). Aldershot, Gale and Polden, 1951. 259 p.

1049 Stewart, Ian M.
HISTORY OF THE ARGYLL AND SUTHERLAND HIGHLANDERS, 2ND BATTALION, THE THIN RED LINE, MALAYAN CAMPAIGN, 1941-42. Foreword by Earl Wavell. London and New York, Nelson, 1947. 171 p.

1050 Sutton, Harry T.
RAIDERS APPROACH! THE FIGHTING TRADITION OF THE ROYAL AIR FORCE STATION HORNCHURCH AND SUTTON'S FARM. Foreword by Marshal of the Royal Air Force, Sir John Slessor. Aldershot, Gale and Polden, 1956. 181 p.

1051 Synge, William A. T.
THE STORY OF THE GREEN HOWARDS, 1939-1945. Richmond, Yorkshire, Green Howards, 1952. 428 p.

1052 TAURUS PURSUANT: A HISTORY OF 11TH ARMOURED DIVISION. London, 1945. 118 p.

1053 Taylor, Jeremy L.
THIS BAND OF BROTHERS: A HISTORY OF THE RECONNAISSANCE CORPS OF THE BRITISH ARMY. Bristol, White Swan Press, 1947. 271 p.

1054 Taylor, Jeremy L. (ed.).
RECORD OF A RECONNAISSANCE REGIMENT: HISTORY OF THE 43RD RECONNAISSANCE REGIMENT (THE GLOUCESTERSHIRE REGIMENT), 1939-1945. Foreword by Sir Ivor Thomas. Bristol, White Swan Press, 1950. 252 p.

1055 Tuker, Sir Francis I. S.
APPROACH TO BATTLE, A COMMENTARY: EIGHTH ARMY, NOVEMBER 1941 TO MAY 1943. London, Cassell, 1963. 410 p.

1056 Underhill, William E. (ed.).
THE ROYAL LEICESTERSHIRE REGIMENT, 17TH FOOT: A HISTORY OF THE YEARS 1928 TO 1956. South Wigston, Royal Leicestershire Regiment, 1958. 277 p.

1057 Verney, Gerald L.
THE DESERT RATS. THE HISTORY OF THE 7TH ARMOURED DIVISION 1938-1945. Foreword by Field Marshal Sir John Harding. London, Hutchinson, 1954. 312 p.

1058 Verney, Gerald L.
THE GUARDS ARMOURED DIVISION: A SHORT HISTORY. London, Hutchinson, 1955. 184 p.

1059 Wake, Sir Hereward, and W. F. Deedes (eds.).
SWIFT AND BOLD: THE STORY OF THE KING'S ROYAL RIFLE CORPS IN THE SECOND WORLD WAR, 1939-1945. Aldershot, Gale and Polden, 1949. 416 p.

1060 Ward, Irene.
F.A.N.Y. INVICTA. Foreword by H.R.H. the Princess Alice, Countess of Athlone. London, Hutchinson, 1955. 348 p.

1061 Watkins, J. Harold, and Donald Leslie (eds.).
ON TARGET: A SOUVENIR OF "ACK-ACK", PRODUCED TO MARK THE DISBANDMENT OF ANTI-AIRCRAFT COMMAND IN WHICH ONE MILLION MEN AND WOMEN HAVE SERVED IN PEACE AND TWO WARS. London, Territorial Publications, 1955. 68 p.

1062 White, Oliver G. W.
STRAIGHT ON FOR TOKYO: THE WAR HISTORY OF THE 2ND BATTALION, THE DORSETSHIRE REGIMENT, 54TH FOOT, 1939-1948. Aldershot, Gale and Polden, 1948. 425 p.

1063   Whitty, H. Ramsden (comp.).
         OBSERVERS' TALE: THE STORY OF GROUP 17 OF THE R. O. C. London, Roland, 1950. 70, 51 p.

1064   Williamson, Hugh A. F.
         THE FOURTH DIVISION, 1939 TO 1945. London, Neame, 1951. 348 p.

1065   Willis, Anthony A. (Anthony Armstrong, pseud.).
         SAPPERS AT WAR. Aldershot, Gale and Polden, 1949. 98 p.

1066   Wilson, R. D.
         CORDON AND SEARCH: WITH 6TH AIRBORNE DIVISION IN PALESTINE. Foreword by Sir Hugh Stockwell. Aldershot, Gale and Polden, 1949. 275 p.

1067   Wilton, Eric.
         CENTRE CREW: A MEMORY OF THE ROYAL OBSERVER CORPS. Bromley, 1946. 84 p.

1068   Woollcombe, Robert.
         LION RAMPANT. London, Chatto and Windus, 1955. 223 p.
         Other edition:
         London, Brown, Watson, 1957. 219 p. (Digit Books)

1069   Wyndham, Hon. Humphrey.
         THE HOUSEHOLD CAVALRY AT WAR: FIRST HOUSEHOLD CAVALRY REGIMENT. Aldershot, Gale and Polden, 1952. 189 p.

d. India

1070   Brett-James, Anthony.
         BALL OF FIRE: THE FIFTH INDIAN DIVISION IN THE SECOND WORLD WAR. Foreword by Earl Mountbatten of Burma. Aldershot, Gale and Polden, 1951. 481 p.

1071   Brett-James, Antony.
         REPORT MY SIGNALS. London, Locke, 1948. 352 p.

1072   Doulton, Alfred J. F.
         THE FIGHTING COCK: BEING THE HISTORY OF THE 23RD INDIAN DIVISION, 1942-1947. Foreword by Sir Reginald Savory. Aldershot, Gale and Polden, 1951. 318 p.

1073   Elliott, James G.
         A ROLL OF HONOUR: THE STORY OF THE INDIAN ARMY, 1939-1945. Preface by Field-Marshal Sir Claude Auchinleck. London, Cassell, 1965. 392 p.

1074   Graham, Cuthbert A. L.
         THE HISTORY OF THE INDIAN MOUNTAIN ARTILLERY. Foreword by Viscount Alanbrooke. Aldershot, Gale and Polden, 1957. 470 p.

1075   Roberts, Michael R.
         GOLDEN ARROW: THE STORY OF THE 7TH INDIAN DIVISION IN THE SECOND WORLD WAR, 1939-1945. Aldershot, Gale and Polden, 1952. 304 p.

1076   Sandes, Edward W. C.
         THE INDIAN ENGINEERS, 1939-47. Kirkee, India, Institution of Military Engineers, 1956. 534 p.

1077   THE TIGER TRIUMPHS: THE STORY OF THE THREE GREAT INDIAN DIVISIONS IN ITALY. London, H. M. Stationery Office, 1946. 212 p.

e. New Zealand

1078   Borman, Clifford A.
         DIVISIONAL SIGNALS. Wellington, War History Branch, Dept. of Internal Affairs, 1954. 540 p. (Official History of New Zealand in the Second World War, 1939-45)

1079   Burdon, Randal M.
         24 BATTALION. Wellington, War History Branch, Dept. of Internal Affairs, 1953. 361 p. (Official History of New Zealand in the Second World War, 1939-45)

1080   Cody, Joseph F.
         21 BATTALION. Wellington, War History Branch, Dept. of Internal Affairs, 1953. 471 p. (Official History of New Zealand in the Second World War, 1939-45)

1081   Cody, Joseph F.
         28 (MAORI) BATTALION. Wellington, War History Branch, Dept. of Internal Affairs, 1956. 514 p. (Official History of New Zealand in the Second World War, 1939-45)

1082   Dawson, William D.
         18 BATTALION AND ARMOURED REGIMENT. Wellington, War History Branch, Dept. of Internal Affairs, 1961. 676 p. (Official History of New Zealand in the Second World War, 1939-45)

1083   Henderson, James H.
         RMT: OFFICIAL HISTORY OF THE 4TH AND 6TH RESERVE MECHANICAL TRANSPORT COMPANIES, 2 NZEF. Wellington, War History Branch, Dept. of Internal Affairs, 1954. 378 p. (Official History of New Zealand in the Second World War, 1939-45)

1084   Henderson, James H.
         22 BATTALION. Wellington, War History Branch, Dept. of Internal Affairs, 1958. 487 p. (Official History of New Zealand in the Second World War, 1939-45)

1085   Hunt, Leslie.
         DEFENCE UNTIL DAWN: THE STORY OF 488 N. Z. SQUADRON; CHURCH FENTON, 25TH JUNE, 1942 TO GILZE-RIJEN, HOLLAND, 26TH APRIL, 1945. Southend-on-Sea, Washburn, 1949. 104 p.

1086   Kay, Robin L.
         27TH MACHINE GUN BATTALION. Wellington, War History Branch, Dept. of Internal Affairs, 1958. 543 p.

1087   Kidson, Arthur L.
         PETROL COMPANY. Wellington, War History Branch, Dept. of Internal Affairs, 1961. 363 p. (Official History of New Zealand in the Second World War, 1939-45)

1088 New Zealand. Army. 3d Division. Histories Committee.
BASE WALLAHS: STORY OF THE UNITS OF THE BASE ORGANISATION, NEW ZEALAND EXPEDITIONARY FORCE IN THE PACIFIC. Dunedin, Reed, 1946. 256 p.

1089 New Zealand. Army. 3d Division. Histories Committee.
THE GUNNERS: AN INTIMATE RECORD OF UNITS OF THE 3RD NEW ZEALAND DIVISIONAL ARTILLERY IN THE PACIFIC FROM 1940 UNTIL 1945. Dunedin, Reed, 1948. 290 p.

1090 New Zealand. Army. 3d Division. Histories Committee.
HEADQUARTERS: A BRIEF OUTLINE OF THE ACTIVITIES OF THE HEADQUARTERS OF THE THIRD DIVISION AND THE 8TH AND 14TH BRIGADE DURING THEIR SERVICE IN THE PACIFIC. Dunedin, Reed, 1947. 278 p.

1091 New Zealand. Army. 3d Division. Histories Committee.
PACIFIC KIWIS: BEING THE STORY OF THE SERVICE IN THE PACIFIC OF THE 30TH BATTALION, THIRD DIVISION, SECOND NEW ZEALAND EXPEDITIONARY FORCE. Wellington, Reed, 1947. 150 p.

1092 New Zealand. Army. 3d Division. Histories Committee.
PACIFIC PIONEERS: THE STORY OF THE ENGINEERS OF THE NEW ZEALAND EXPEDITIONARY FORCE IN THE PACIFIC. Dunedin, Reed, 1945. 168 p.

1093 New Zealand. Army. 3d Division. Histories Committee.
PACIFIC SAGA: THE PERSONAL CHRONICLE OF THE 37TH BATTALION AND ITS PART IN THE THIRD DIVISION'S CAMPAIGN. Wellington, Reed, 1947. 114 p.

1094 New Zealand. Army. 3d Division. Histories Committee.
PACIFIC SERVICE: THE STORY OF THE NEW ZEALAND ARMY SERVICE CORPS UNITS WITH THE THIRD DIVISION IN THE PACIFIC. Wellington, Reed, 1948. 140 p.

1095 New Zealand. Army. 3d Division. Histories Committee.
SHOVEL, SWORD AND SCALPEL: A RECORD OF SERVICE OF MEDICAL UNITS OF THE SECOND NEW ZEALAND EXPEDITIONARY FORCE IN THE PACIFIC. Dunedin, n.p. 1945. 171 p.

1096 New Zealand. Army. 3d Division. Histories Committee.
STEPPING STONES TO THE SOLOMONS: THE UNOFFICIAL HISTORY OF THE 29TH BATTALION WITH THE SECOND NEW ZEALAND EXPEDITIONARY FORCE IN THE PACIFIC. Wellington, Reed, 1947. 121 p.

1097 New Zealand. Army. 3d Division. Histories Committee.
STORY OF THE 34TH: THE UNOFFICIAL HISTORY OF A NEW ZEALAND INFANTRY BATTALION WITH THE THIRD DIVISION IN THE PACIFIC. Wellington, Reed, 1947. 159 p.

1098 New Zealand. Army. 3d Division. Histories Committee.
THE TANKS: AN UNOFFICIAL HISTORY OF THE ACTIVITIES OF THE THIRD NEW ZEALAND DIVISION, TANK SQUADRON IN THE PACIFIC. Dunedin, Reed, 1947. 227 p.

1099 New Zealand. Army. 3d Division. Histories Committee.
THE 35TH BATTALION: A RECORD OF SERVICE OF THE 35TH BATTALION WITH THE THIRD DIVISION IN THE PACIFIC. Wellington, Reed, 1947. 143 p.

1100 New Zealand. Army. 3d Division. Histories Committee.
THE 36TH BATTALION: A RECORD OF SERVICE OF THE 36TH BATTALION WITH THE THIRD DIVISION IN THE PACIFIC. Wellington, Reed, 1948. 129 p.

1101 Norton, Frazer D.
26 BATTALION. Wellington, War History Branch, Dept. of Internal Affairs, 1952. 554 p. (Official History of New Zealand in the Second World War, 1939-45)

1102 Pringle, Dave J. C., and W. A. Glue.
20 BATTALION AND ARMOURED REGIMENT. Wellington, War History Branch, Dept. of Internal Affairs 1957. 631 p. (Official History of New Zealand in the Second World War, 1939-45)

1103 Ross, Angus.
23 BATTALION. Wellington, War History Branch, Dept. of Internal Affairs, 1959. 506 p. (Official History of New Zealand in the Second World War, 1939-45)

1104 Sinclair, Donald W.
19 BATTALION AND ARMOURED REGIMENT. Wellington, War History Branch, Dept. of Internal Affairs, 1954. 559 p. (Official History of New Zealand in the Second World War, 1939-45)

1105 Stevens, William G.
PROBLEMS OF 2 NZEF. Wellington, War History Branch, Dept. of Internal Affairs, 1958. 331 p. (Official History of New Zealand in the Second World War, 1939-45)

f. United States

1106 Abbott, Harry P.
THE NAZI "88" MADE BELIEVERS. Dayton, Ohio, Otterbein, 1946. 150 p.

1107 AIR GROUP 20: AN UNOFFICIAL PORTRAYAL OF CARRIER AIR GROUP TWENTY, U.S. PACIFIC FLEET, FROM COMMISSIONING TO COMPLETION OF COMBAT CRUISE, 1943-1945. n.p., 1949. 84 p.

1108 Allen, Robert S.
LUCKY FORWARD: THE HISTORY OF PATTON'S THIRD U.S. ARMY. New York, Vanguard, 1947. 424 p.

1109 Allied Forces. 15th Army Group.
15TH ARMY GROUP HISTORY, 16 DECEMBER 1944-2 MAY 1945. n.p., 1946. 214 p.

1110 Altieri, James.
THE SPEARHEADERS. Indianapolis, Bobbs-Merrill, 1960. 318 p.

1111 Amory, Robert (ed.).
SURF AND SAND: THE SAGA OF THE 53RD ENGINEER BOAT AND SHORE REGIMENT AND 1461ST ENGINEER MAINTENANCE COMPANY, 1942-1945. ANDOVER, 1947. 408 p.

1112 Anderson, Trezzvant W.
COME OUT FIGHTING: THE EPIC TALE OF THE 761ST TANK BATTALION, 1942-1945. Salzburg, Salzburger Druckerei und Verlag, 1945. 135 p.

1113 Army Air Forces Aid Society.
THE NINTH AIR FORCE SERVICE COMMAND IN THE EUROPEAN THEATRE OF OPERATIONS: A PICTORIAL REVIEW. Philadelphia, 1945. 96 p.

1114 Army Times.
COMBAT DIVISIONS OF WORLD WAR II, ARMY OF UNITED STATES. Washington, Army Times, 1946. 96 p.

1115 Augspurger, Owen B. (comp.).
WORLD WAR II HISTORY OF THE 102ND ANTIAIRCRAFT BATTALION (AW), NEW YORK NATIONAL GUARD OF BUFFALO, N.Y. Buffalo, Buffalo and Erie County Historical Society, 1961. 115 p.

1116 Aurthur, Robert A., and Kenneth Cohlmia.
THE THIRD MARINE DIVISION. Edited by Robert T. Vance. Washington, Infantry Journal Press, 1948. 385 p.

1117 Baer, Alfred E.
"D-FOR-DOG": THE STORY OF A RANGER COMPANY. Memphis, 1946. 119 p.

1118 Barker, John S. (ed.).
THE FLIGHT OF THE LIBERATORS: THE STORY OF THE FOUR HUNDRED FIFTY-FOURTH BOMBARDMENT GROUP. n.p., Flight of the Liberators Association, 1946. 172 p.

1119 Beck, Henry C.
THE 397TH BOMB GROUP (M): A PICTORIAL HISTORY. Cleveland, Howard, 1946. 122 p.

1120 Bell, Frank F.
THE 373RD ENGINEER GENERAL SERVICE REGIMENT IN WORLD WAR II. Dallas [1947?] 281 p.

1121 Bennett, Edwin G.
COMING THROUGH: THE STORY OF THE THIRTY-FIRST SPECIAL NAVAL CONSTRUCTION BATTALION. Tokyo, Dai Nippon Printing Co., 1946. 64 p.

1122 Binkoski, Joseph, and Arthur Plant.
THE 115TH INFANTRY REGIMENT IN WORLD WAR II. Washington, Infantry Journal Press, 1948. 370 p.

1123 Boice, William S. (ed.).
HISTORY OF THE TWENTY-SECOND U.S. INFANTRY IN WORLD WAR II. n.p., 1959. 183 p.

1124 Boston, Bernard (ed.).
HISTORY OF THE 398TH INFANTRY REGIMENT IN WORLD WAR II. Washington, Infantry Journal, 1947. 204 p.

1125 Bove, Arthur P.
FIRST OVER GERMANY: A STORY OF THE 306TH BOMBARDMENT GROUP. San Angelo, Tex., Newsfoto, 1946. 148 p.

1126 Braman, Oscar, and others (eds.).
REMEMBER WHEN? n.p., 1945. 228 p.

1127 Briggs, Richard A.
BLACK HAWKS OVER THE DANUBE: THE HISTORY OF THE 86TH INFANTRY DIVISION IN WORLD WAR II. Louisville, 1954. 127 p.

1128 Brower, David R.
REMOUNT BLUE: THE COMBAT STORY OF THE 3RD BATTALION, 86TH MOUNTAIN INFANTRY. Berkeley, 1948. 112 p.

1129 Buckeridge, Justin P.
550 INFANTRY AIRBORN BATTALION: A BOLT FROM THE BLUE, 1941-1945. Nancy, 1945. 94 p.

1130 Bullard, Oral.
THE HOT LOOP: A HISTORY OF THE 383RD ANTI-AIRCRAFT ARTILLERY BATTALION: U.S. JANUARY 1943-NOVEMBER 1945, OVERSEAS NOVEMBER 1943-DECEMBER 1945. Waterloo, Iowa, 1950. 111 p.

1131 Burhans, Robert D.
THE FIRST SPECIAL SERVICE FORCE: A WAR HISTORY OF THE NORTH AMERICANS, 1942-1944. Washington, Infantry Journal, 1947. 376 p.

1132 Burwell, Lewis C.
SCRAPBOOK: A PICTORIAL AND HISTORICAL RECORD OF THE DEEDS, EXPLOITS, ADVENTURES, TRAVELS AND LIFE OF THE 27TH TROOP CARRIER SQUADRON FOR THE YEAR 1944. Charlotte, N.C., By the author, 1947. 130 p.

1133 Carter, Joseph.
THE HISTORY OF THE 14TH ARMOURED DIVISION. Atlanta, Love [1945?] 294 p.

1134 Carter, Ross S.
THOSE DEVILS IN BAGGY PANTS. New York, Appleton-Century-Crofts, 1951. 299 p.

1135 Casper, Jack A.
HISTORY AND PERSONNEL, 489TH, 340TH BOMB GROUP: COMBAT CAMPAIGN PARTICIPATED IN BY THE 489TH BOMB SQUADRON (M). Middletown, Ohio, 1947. 247 p.

1136 Cass, Bevan G. (ed.).
HISTORY OF THE SIXTH MARINE DIVISION. Washington, Infantry Journal Press, 1948. 262 p.

1137 Castagna, Edwin.
THE HISTORY OF THE 771ST TANK BATTALION. Berkeley, 1946. 110 p.

1138 Chapin, John C.
THE FOURTH MARINE DIVISION IN WORLD WAR II. Washington, Historical Division Headquarters, U. S. Marine Corps, 1945. 89 p.

1139 COMBAT HISTORY OF THE 6TH ARMOURED DIVISION IN THE EUROPEAN THEATER OF OPERATIONS 18 JULY, 1944-8 MAY 1945. With a statement by Major General Robert W. Grow. Yadkinville, N. C., Ripple, 194-. 176 p.

1140 Conner, Howard M.
THE SPEARHEAD: THE WORLD WAR II HISTORY OF THE 5TH MARINE DIVISION. Washington, Infantry Journal Press, 1950. 325 p.

1141 Cooper, John P.
THE HISTORY OF THE 110TH FIELD ARTILLERY, WITH SKETCHES OF RELATED UNITS. Baltimore, War Records Division, Maryland Historical Society, 1953. 318 p.

1142 Corbo, Dominick R.
ON YOUR FEET, SOLDIER! UNOFFICIAL HISTORY OF COMPANY G, 376TH INFANTRY REGIMENT. n.p., 1949. 80 p.

1143 Covington, Henry L.
A FIGHTING HEART: AN UNOFFICIAL STORY OF THE 82ND AIRBORNE DIVISION. Fayetteville, N. C., Davis, 1949. 75 p.

1144 Cronin, Francis D.
UNDER THE SOUTHERN CROSS: THE SAGA OF THE AMERICAL DIVISION. Washington, Combat Forces Press, 1951. 432 p.

1145 Davis, Albert H., and others (ed.).
THE 56TH FIGHTER GROUP IN WORLD WAR II. Washington, Infantry Journal Press, 1948. 222 p.

1146 Dawson, W. Forrest (ed.).
SAGA OF THE ALL AMERICAN. Atlanta, Love, 1946. unpaged.

1147 Delaney, John P.
THE BLUE DEVILS IN ITALY: A HISTORY OF THE 88TH INFANTRY DIVISION IN WORLD WAR II. Washington, Infantry Journal Press, 1947. 359 p.

1148 De Polo, Taber (ed.).
BRIDGING EUROPE. Munich, Bruckmann, 1945. 193 p.

1149 Deveikis, Casey.
THE EAGER BEAVER REGIMENT: THE REGIMENTAL HISTORY OF THE 1303 ENGINEERS. Chicago, 1952. 407 p.

1150 Draper, Theodore.
THE 84TH INFANTRY DIVISION IN THE BATTLE OF THE ARDENNES, DECEMBER 1944-JANUARY 1945. n.p., Historical Section, 84th Infantry Division, 1945. 55 p.

Other edition:
New York, Viking Press, 1946. 260 p.

1151 Duggan, Thomas V.
HISTORY OF 234TH ENGINEER COMBAT BATTALION. Long Island City, Duggan, 1947. 117 p.

1152 Dupuy, Richard E.
ST. VITH: LION IN THE WAY; 106TH INFANTRY DIVISION IN WORLD WAR II. Washington, Infantry Journal Press, 1949. 252 p.

1153 East, William, and William F. Gleason.
THE 409TH INFANTRY IN WORLD WAR II. Washington, Infantry Journal Press, 1947. 167 p.

1154 Edwards, L. R., and A. O. LeBlanc.
COMBAT DIARY; 357 INFANTRY. Tirschenreuth, Bayern, Bruck, A. Nickl, 1945. 105 p.

1155 Ewing, Joseph H.
29, LET'S GO! A HISTORY OF THE 29TH INFANTRY DIVISION IN WORLD WAR II. Washington, Infantry Journal Press, 1948. 315 p.

1156 Farnum, Sayward H.
THE FIVE BY FIVE: A HISTORY OF THE 555TH ANTI-AIRCRAFT ARTILLERY AUTOMATIC WEAPONS BATTALION (MOBILE). Boston, Athenaeum Press, 1946. 136 p.

1157 Farrell, Harry G.
RECON DIARY: COMBAT HISTORY OF THE 79TH CAVALRY RECONNAISSANCE TROOP. San Jose, Calif. 172 p.

1158 Finkelstein, Samuel M.
REGIMENT OF THE CENTURY: THE STORY OF THE 397TH INFANTRY REGIMENT. Stuttgart, 1945. 314 p.

1159 Flanagan, Edward M.
THE ANGELS: A HISTORY OF THE 11TH AIRBORNE DIVISION, 1943-1946. Washington, Infantry Journal Press, 1948. 176 p.

1160 Frankel, Stanley A.
THE 37TH INFANTRY DIVISION IN WORLD WAR II. Washington, Infantry Journal Press, 1949. 398 p.

1161 Fuermann, George M., and F. Edward Cranz.
NINETY-FIFTH INFANTRY DIVISION HISTORY, 1918-1946. Atlanta, Love, 1947. 1 v.

1162 Gillies, Frederick W.
THE STORY OF A SQUADRON: AN ILLUSTRATED OVERSEAS WAR DIARY-ALBUM, 1942-1945; 154TH (OBSERVATION, RECONNAISSANCE) WEATHER RECONNAISSANCE SQUADRON. Medford, Mass., 1946. 137 p.

1163 Gregory, Andrew G.
THE SAGA OF THE 708 RAILWAY GRAND DIVISION. Edited by Carroll Bateman. Baltimore, 1947. 73 p.

1164 Guild, Frank H.
    ACTION OF THE TIGER: THE SAGA OF THE 437TH TROOP CARRIER GROUP. Tyler, Tex., City Printing Co., 1950. 177 p.

1165 Gurley, Frank.
    399TH IN ACTION WITH THE 100TH INFANTRY DIVISION. n.p., 194-? 185 p.

1166 Hall, Grover C.
    1000 DESTROYED: THE LIFE AND TIMES OF THE 4TH FIGHTER GROUP. London, Putnam, 1962. 286 p.

1167 Hawkins, John, and Ward Hawkins.
    HISTORY OF THE 835TH SIGNAL SERVICE BATTALION, 1942-1946. n.p., 1946. 96 p.

1168 Heavey, William F.
    DOWN RAMP! THE STORY OF THE ARMY AMPHIBIAN ENGINEERS. Washington, Infantry Journal Press, 1947. 272 p.

    Other edition:
    1950.

1169 Heidenheimer, Arnold J.
    VANGUARD TO VICTORY: HISTORY OF THE 18TH INFANTRY. Aschaffenburg, Ger., 18th Infantry, 1954. 64 p.

1170 Hewitt, Robert L.
    WORK HORSE OF THE WESTERN FRONT: THE STORY OF THE 30TH INFANTRY DIVISION. Washington, Infantry Journal Press, 1946. 356 p.

1171 Hoegh, Leo A., and Howard J. Doyle.
    TIMBERWOLF TRACKS: THE HISTORY OF THE 104TH INFANTRY DIVISION, 1942-1945. Washington, Infantry Journal Press, 1946. 444 p.

1172 Hoge, Peyton (ed.).
    38TH INFANTRY DIVISION: "AVENGERS OF BATAAN," LUZON CAMPAIGN; BATTLE PICTURES; OVERSEAS PICTORIAL, DIVISION ROSTER. Atlanta, Love, 1947. 1 v.

1173 Hornsby, Henry H.
    THE TREY OF SEVENS. Dallas, Mathis, Van Nort, 1946. 126 p.

1174 Hougen, John H.
    THE STORY OF THE FAMOUS 34TH INFANTRY DIVISION. Arlington, 1949. 1 v.

1175 Houston, Karl H., and Newt Carpenter.
    66TH FIGHTER WING IN EUROPE. Cambridge, Eng., 1945. 1 v.

1176 Howe, George F.
    THE BATTLE HISTORY OF THE 1ST ARMORED DIVISION, "OLD IRONSIDES." Washington, Combat Forces Press, 1954. 471 p.

1177 Hurkala, John.
    THE FIGHTING FIRST DIVISION: A TRUE STORY. New York, Greenwich Book Co., 1957. 201 p.

1178 Huston, James A.
    BIOGRAPHY OF A BATTALION, 3D BATTALION, 134TH INFANTRY (35TH DIVISION): BEING THE LIFE AND TIMES OF AN INFANTRY BATTALION IN EUROPE IN WORLD WAR II. Gering, Neb., Courier Press, 1950. 306 p.

1179 Irwin, John G.
    HISTORY OF THE 389TH INFANTRY REGIMENT IN WORLD WAR II. New York, Hobson Book Press, 1946. 224 p.

1180 Johnson, Gerden F.
    HISTORY OF THE TWELFTH INFANTRY REGIMENT IN WORLD WAR II. Boston, 1948. 443 p.

1181 Johnston, Richard W.
    FOLLOW ME! THE STORY OF THE SECOND MARINE DIVISION OF WORLD WAR II. New York, Random House, 1948. 305 p.

1182 Jones, Ken.
    DESTROYER SQUADRON 23: COMBAT EXPLOITS OF ARLEIGH BURKE'S GALLANT FORCE. Philadelphia, Chilton Co., 1959. 283 p.

1183 Jones, William E., with Irene E. Jones.
    BUZZINGS OF COMPANY B; COMPANY B, 23RD ARMORED INFANTRY BATTALION OF THE 7TH ARMORED (LUCKY SEVENTH) DIVISION. Winston-Salem, Clay Printing Co., 1951. 59 p.

1184 Kadar, Alfred F. (ed.).
    305TH FIELD ARTILLERY BATTALION, 77TH INFANTRY DIVISION. Hakodate, Japan, Yuji Itagaki, 1946. 72 p.

1185 Kahn, Ely J., Jr., and Henry McLemore.
    FIGHTING DIVISION. Washington, Infantry Journal, 1945. 218 p.

1186 Koyen, Kenneth A.
    THE FOURTH ARMORED DIVISION: FROM THE BEACH TO BAVARIA. Munich, Herder-druck, 1946. 295 p.

1187 Krebs, Richard J. H. (Jan Valtin, pseud.).
    CHILDREN OF YESTERDAY. New York, Readers' Press, 1946. 429 p.

1188 Krueger, Walter.
    FROM DOWN UNDER TO NIPPON: THE STORY OF SIXTH ARMY IN WORLD WAR II. Washington, Combat Forces Press, 1953. 393 p.

1189 Lamensdorf, Rolland G.
    HISTORY OF THE 31ST FIGHTER GROUP. Washington, 1952. 79 p.

1190 Lauer, Walter E.
    BATTLE BABIES: THE STORY OF THE 99TH INFANTRY DIVISION IN WORLD WAR II. Baton Rouge, Military Press of Louisiana, 1951. 351 p.

1191 Lavender, Don E.
NUDGE BLUE: A CHRONICLE OF WORLD WAR II EXPERIENCE. n.p., 1964. 82 p.

1192 Leach, Charles R.
IN TORNADO'S WAKE: A HISTORY OF THE 8TH ARMORED DIVISION. Chicago, Eighth Armored Division Association, 1956. 232 p.

1193 Lockwood, Theodore.
MOUNTAINEERS. Denver, Artcraft Press, 1950. 65 p.

1194 Lord, William G.
HISTORY OF THE 508TH PARACHUTE INFANTRY. Washington, Infantry Journal Press, 1948. 120 p.

1195 Love, Edmund G.
THE HOURGLASS: A HISTORY OF THE 7TH INFANTRY DIVISION IN WORLD WAR II. Washington, Infantry Journal Press, 1950. 496 p.

1196 Love, Edmund G.
THE 27TH INFANTRY DIVISION IN WORLD WAR II. Washington, Infantry Journal Press, 1949. 677 p.

1197 McGrann, Roy T.
THE 610TH TANK DESTROYER BATTALION: APRIL 10, 1942-DECEMBER 7, 1945. Elizabeth, Pa., 1946. 146 p.

1198 MacGregor, Harold.
HISTORY OF THE 28TH INFANTRY REGIMENT. Washington, Infantry Journal Press, 1947. 104 p.

1199 McMillan, George.
THE OLD BREED: A HISTORY OF THE FIRST MARINE DIVISION IN WORLD WAR II. Washington, Infantry Journal Press, 1949. 483 p.

1200 Matson, Clifford H., Jr., and Elliot K. Stein.
WE WERE THE LINE: A HISTORY OF COMPANY G, 335TH INFANTRY, 84TH INFANTRY DIVISION. Fort Wayne, 1946. 219 p.

1201 Millett, John D.
THE ORGANIZATION AND ROLE OF THE ARMY SERVICE FORCES. Washington, Office of Chief of Military History, Dept. of Army, 1954. 494 p. (U.S. Army in World War II: The Army Service Forces)

1202 Mittelman, Joseph B.
EIGHT STARS TO VICTORY: A HISTORY OF THE VETERAN NINTH U.S. INFANTRY DIVISION. Washington, The 9th Infantry Association, 1948. 406 p.

1203 Morrison, Jack K. (ed.).
A HISTORY OF THE 274TH ARMORED FIELD ARTILLERY BATTALION, 15 APRIL 1943 TO 2 SEPTEMBER 1945. Chicago [Privately printed] 1946. 110 p.

1204 Morrison, Wilbur H.
THE INCREDIBLE 305TH: THE "CAN DO" BOMBERS OF WORLD WAR II. New York, Duell, Sloan and Pearce, 1962. 181 p.

1205 Moskop, Roy L.
ON THE WAY! THE STORY OF THE 91ST DIVISION ARTILLERY. n.p., 1947. 87 p.

1206 Mueller, Ralph, and Jerry Turk.
REPORT AFTER ACTION: THE STORY OF THE 103RD INFANTRY DIVISION. Innsbruck, Headquarters, 103d Infantry Division, U.S. Army, 1945. 165 p.

1207 Munsell, Warren P.
THE STORY OF A REGIMENT: A HISTORY OF THE 179TH REGIMENTAL COMBAT TEAM. New York, 1946. 152 p.

1208 Murphy, Thomas D.
AMBASSADORS IN ARMS: THE STORY OF HAWAII'S 100TH BATTALION. Honolulu, University of Hawaii Press, 1954. 315 p.

Special edition:
Honolulu, University of Hawaii Press, 1954. 339 p.

1209 Nichols, Lester M.
IMPACT: THE BATTLE STORY OF THE TENTH ARMORED DIVISION. New York, Bradbury, Sayles, O'Neill Co., 1954. 325 p.

1210 Nilsson, John R. (ed.).
THE STORY OF THE CENTURY. Beverly Hills, 1946. 222 p.

1211 19 DAYS FROM THE APENNINES TO THE ALPS: THE STORY OF THE PO VALLEY CAMPAIGN OF THE U.S. FIFTH ARMY. Milan, 1945. 90 p.

1212 Ogburn, Charlton.
THE MARAUDERS. New York, Harper, 1959. 307 p.

Other edition:
London, Hodder and Stoughton, 1960. 319 p.

1213 Oliver, Philip G.
HELLBIRD WAR BOOK. n.p., Kalberer, 194-. 117 p.

1214 ON THE WAY: COMBAT EXPERIENCES OF THE 693RD FIELD ARTILLERY BATTALION IN THE EUROPEAN THEATER OF OPERATIONS: NORMANDY, NORTHERN FRANCE, RHINELAND, CENTRAL EUROPE. Salzburg, Moller, 1945. 89 p.

1215 Owens, Walter E.
AS BRIEFED: A FAMILY HISTORY OF THE 384TH BOMBARDMENT GROUP. n.p., 1946. 210 p.

1216 Paddock, Robert H. (ed.).
THE 1876TH ENGINEERS IN WORLD WAR II: A HISTORY OF THE 1876TH ENGINEER AVIATION BATTALION FROM ITS ACTIVATION AT MARCH FIELD, CALIFORNIA, IN MARCH 1943 UNTIL ITS DEACTIVATION IN JAPAN IN MARCH, 1946. Madison, Wis., 1947. 147 p.

1217 Panther Veterans Organization.
40,000 BLACK PANTHERS OF THE 66TH DIVISION. n.p., 1946. 248 p.

1218 Pay, Don R.
THUNDER FROM HEAVEN: STORY OF THE 17TH AIRBORNE DIVISION 1943-1945. Birmingham, Mich., Boots, the Airborne Quarterly, 1947. 179 p.

1219 Pearson, Ralph E.
ENROUTE TO THE REDOUBT: A SOLDIER'S REPORT, AS A REGIMENT GOES TO WAR, TO THE MEMBERS OF THE 80TH INFANTRY DIVISION AND PARTICULARLY THOSE OF THE 318TH INFANTRY; A CHRONOLOGICAL ACCOUNT OF SOME OF THE ACTIVITIES OF THE 318TH IN EUROPE. Fort Bragg, N.C., 1957-59. 5 v.

1220 Peaslee, Budd J.
HERITAGE OF VALOR: THE EIGHTH AIR FORCE IN WORLD WAR II. Philadelphia, Lippincott, 1964. 288 p. (Airmen and Aircraft)

1221 Prince, Morris.
OVERSEAS AND THEN--OVER THE TOP. Washington, 1946. 57, 67, 70 p.

1222 Randolph, John H.
MARSMEN IN BURMA. Houston, Randolph, 1946. 229 p.

1223 Rapport, Leonard, and Arthur Norwood, Jr.
RENDEZVOUS WITH DESTINY: A HISTORY OF 101ST AIRBORNE DIVISION. Washington, Infantry Journal Press, 1948. 810 p.

1224 Rebert, Richard R.
IS THIS IT? A HISTORY OF THE 165TH ENGINEER COMBAT BATTALION IN WORLD WAR II FROM 5 MAY 1943 TO 19 OCTOBER 1945. Washington, 1946. 50 p.

1225 THE RECORD: THE ELEVENTH BOMBARDMENT SQUADRON (M). Richmond, Va., 1945. 103 p.

1226 Robbins, Robert A.
THE 91ST INFANTRY DIVISION IN WORLD WAR II. Washington, Infantry Journal Press, 1947. 423 p.

1227 Robinett, Paul M.
ARMOR COMMAND: THE PERSONAL STORY OF A COMMANDER OF THE 13TH ARMORED REGIMENT OF CCB, 1ST ARMORED DIVISION AND OF THE ARMORED SCHOOL DURING WORLD WAR II. Washington, 1958. 252 p.

1228 Rubel, George K.
DAREDEVIL TANKERS: THE STORY OF THE 740TH TANK BATTALION, UNITED STATES ARMY. Edited by Charles W. Edwards. Göttingen, 1945. 335 p.

1229 Ryan, Allen L.
ROUGH AND READY UNIT HISTORY: 276 ENGINEER COMBAT BATTALION. Edited by Clayton A. Rust. Fort Belvoir, Va., Engineer School, 1946. 206 p.

1230 Sargent, Frederic O. (comp.).
NIGHT FIGHTERS: AN UNOFFICIAL HISTORY OF THE 415TH NIGHT FIGHTER SQUADRON. Madison, Wis., 1946. 79 p.

1231 Savin, William A. (comp.).
THE NINTH AIR FORCE SERVICE COMMAND IN THE EUROPEAN THEATRE OF OPERATIONS: A PICTORIAL REVIEW. New York, Andrews, 1945. 96 p.

1232 Schultz, Paul L.
85TH INFANTRY DIVISION IN WORLD WAR II. Washington, Infantry Journal Press, 1949. 240 p.

1233 THE 727TH RAILWAY OPERATING BATTALION IN WORLD WAR II. New York, Simmons-Boardman, 1948. 102 p.

1234 Sheridan, Jack W.
THEY NEVER HAD IT SO GOOD: THE PERSONAL UNOFFICIAL STORY OF THE 350TH BOMBARDMENT SQUADRON H, 100TH BOMBARDMENT GROUP H, USAAF, 1942-1945. San Francisco, Stark-Rath, 1946. 165 p.

1235 Shirey, Orville C.
AMERICANS: THE STORY OF THE 442D COMBAT TEAM. Washington, Infantry Journal Press, 1947. 151 p.

1236 Sinton, Russell L. (comp.).
THE MENACE FROM MORESBY: A PICTORIAL HISTORY OF THE 5TH AIR FORCE IN WORLD WAR II. Narrative prepared by Leon Schloss. San Angelo, Tex., Newsfoto Publishing Co., 195-. 1 v.

1237 Smith, Frank E.
BATTLE DIARY: THE STORY OF THE 243RD FIELD ARTILLERY BATTALION IN COMBAT. New York, Hobson Book Press, 1946. 214 p.

1238 Snyder, Earl A.
GENERAL LEEMY'S CIRCUS: A NAVIGATOR'S STORY OF THE 20TH AIR FORCE IN WORLD WAR II. New York, Exposition Press, 1955. 175 p.

1239 Starr, Chester G. (ed.).
FROM SALERNO TO THE ALPS: A HISTORY OF THE FIFTH ARMY, 1943-1945. Washington, Infantry Journal Press, 1948. 529 p.

1240 Steele, Theodore M.
A PICTORIAL RECORD OF THE COMBAT DUTY OF PATROL BOMBING SQUADRON ONE HUNDRED NINE IN THE WESTERN PACIFIC, 20 APRIL 1945-15 AUGUST 1945. New York, General Offset Co., 1946. (unpaged)

1241 Strahl, Fred M.
THE MONUMENT, THE MOUNTAINS, AND THE TOWNS: A PICTORIAL RECORD OF THE CAMPAIGN FOR THE APENNINES. Glendale, Calif., 1946. 50 p.

1242 Straus, Jack M., and G. Friedberg.
WE SAW IT THROUGH: HISTORY OF THE 331ST COMBAT TEAM, TODAY, TOMORROW, FOREVER. Munich, Bruckmann, 1945. 239 p.

1243 Strootman, Ralph E.
HISTORY OF THE 363RD INFANTRY: ONE REGIMENT OF THE 91ST DIVISION IN WORLD WAR II. Washington, Infantry Journal Press, 1947. 354 p.

1244 Stussman, Morton J.
FOLLOW THRU. Stuttgart, 1946. 112 p.

1245 Templeton, Kenneth S. (comp.).
10TH MOUNTAIN DIVISION, AMERICA'S SKI TROOPS. Chicago [Privately printed] 1945. 208 p.

1246 Ter Braak, Harry F.
ACK ACK. Hamilton, Ohio, 1946. 103 l.

1247 Terrell, Edgar A.
THE TRAINING AND COMBAT HISTORY OF COMPANY D, 19TH TANK BATTALION, FROM MAY, 1943 TO JULY, 1945. Charlotte, N.C., 1945. 94 p.

1248 Trahan, E. A. (ed.).
A HISTORY OF THE SECOND UNITED STATES ARMORED DIVISION, 1940 TO 1946. Atlanta, Love, 1947. 1 v.

1249 Treadwell, Mattie E.
THE WOMEN'S ARMY CORPS. Washington, Office of Chief of Military History, Dept. of Army, 1954. 841 p. (U.S. Army in World War II: Special Studies)

1250 Trice, Frasia D., and Thurlow B. Simons (eds.).
THIRTY-FOURTH U.S. NAVAL CONSTRUCTION BATTALION. Arlington, Marx, 1946. 81 p.

1251 U.S. Air Force. 20th Fighter Bomber Wing.
20TH FIGHTER BOMBER WING. Weathersfield, Eng., New York and London, Montgomery Enterprises, 1953. 95 p.

1252 U.S. Army. Corps of Engineers. Great Lakes Division.
GLD IN WORLD WAR II. Edited by Alden D. Walker. n.p., Corps of Engineers, 1946. 180 p.

1253 U.S. Army. Corps of Engineers. 2d Combat Battalion.
SECOND ENGINEER COMBAT BATTALION, OCTOBER 1943-MAY 1945, WORLD WAR II, EUROPEAN THEATRE OF OPERATIONS. Omaha, 1945. 196 p.

1254 U.S. Army. Corps of Engineers. 2d Special Brigade.
HISTORY OF THE SECOND ENGINEER SPECIAL BRIGADE, UNITED STATES ARMY, WORLD WAR II. Harrisburg, Pa., Telegraph Press, 1946. 269 p.

1255 U.S. Army. Corps of Engineers. 9th Command.
THE HISTORY OF IX ENGINEER COMMAND, FROM ITS BEGINNING TO V-E DAY. Wiesbaden, 1945. 213 p.

1256 U.S. Army. Corps of Engineers. 48th Combat Battalion.
WE THE 48TH. Heidelberg, Brausdruck, 1945. 352 p.

1257 U.S. Army. Corps of Engineers. 155th Combat Battalion.
HISTORY OF THE 155TH ENGINEER COMBAT BATTALION FROM ACTIVATION APRIL 15, 1943 TO DEACTIVATION APRIL, 1946. Edited by James F. Ristig. Portland, Ore., 1946. 1 v.

1258 U.S. Army. Corps of Engineers. 187th Combat Battalion.
STORY OF THE 187TH ENGINEER COMBAT BATTALION, CENTRAL EUROPE, ARDENNES, RHINELAND. Prepared by Melvin L. Epstein and others. n.p., 1945. 113 p.

1259 U.S. Army. Corps of Engineers. 256th Combat Battalion.
256TH ENGINEER BATTALION. n.p., 194-. 176 p.

1260 U.S. Army. Corps of Engineers. 291st Combat Battalion.
BATTALION 291 ENGINEER COMBAT BATTALION HISTORY. Edited by William L. McKinsey. n.p., 194-. 115 p.

1261 U.S. Army. Corps of Engineers. 320th Battalion.
320TH ENGINEER BATTALION, 1942-1945. n.p., 1946. 96 p.

1262 U.S. Army. Corps of Engineers. 373d Regiment.
THE 373RD ENGINEER GENERAL SERVICE REGIMENT IN WORLD WAR II. Dallas, 1945. 281 p.

1263 U.S. Army. Corps of Engineers. 654th Topographic Battalion.
654 ENGINEER TOPOGRAPHIC BATTALION. n.p., 1945. 248 p.

1264 U.S. Army. Corps of Engineers. 816th Aviation Battalion.
816TH ENGINEER AVIATION BATTALION PASSES IN REVIEW. Munich, Bruckmann, 1945. 176 p.

1265 U.S. Army. Corps of Engineers. 1374th Petroleum Distribution Co.
HISTORY OF THE 1374TH EPD CO. n.p., 1946. 133 p.

1266 U.S. Army. Corps of Engineers. 1629th Construction Battalion.
ENGINEERING IN THE PACIFIC THEATER WITH THE 1629TH ENGINEER CONSTRUCTION BATTALION. n.p., 1946. 52 p.

1267 U.S. Army. Corps of Engineers. 1880th Aviation Battalion.
SITUATION CBI: THE STORY OF THE 1880TH ENGINEER AVIATION BATTALION IN WORLD WAR II, MARCH 1943-DECEMBER 1945. Edited by Charles R. Rowley. n.p., 1946. 237 p.

1268 U.S. Army. Forces in the European Theater.
THE THIRTEENTH ARMORED DIVISION: A HISTORY OF THE BLACK CATS FROM TEXAS TO FRANCE, GERMANY, AND AUSTRIA, AND BACK TO CALIFORNIA. Baton Rouge, Army and Navy Publishing Co., 1945. 145 p.

1269 U.S. Army. Military Government Detachment F-13.
HISTORY OF MILITARY GOVERNMENT DETACHMENT F-13, CITY AND COUNTY, OFFENBACH AM MAIN, GERMANY. Written by Max Leive and Paul Bergman. Offenbach am Main, 1945. 54 p.

1270 U.S. Army. Signal Corps. 43d Battalion.
HISTORY OF THE 43D SIGNAL HEAVY CONSTRUCTION BATTALION FROM ACTIVATION TO V-J DAY, 7 FEBRUARY 1944 TO 2 SEPTEMBER 1945. Frankfurt am Main-Schwanheim, Henrich, 1945. 114 p.

1271 U.S. Army. Signal Corps. 116th Signal Radio Intelligence Company.
HISTORY FROM DATE OF ACTIVATION, 18 MAY, 1942 UNTIL V-J DAY, 2 SEPTEMBER, 1945. Munich, Oldenbourg, 1945. 128 p.

1272 U.S. Army. Signal Corps. 439th Battalion.
A BRIEF HISTORY OF THE 439TH SIGNAL HEAVY CONSTRUCTION BATTALION FROM ACTIVATION TO V-E DAY. n.p., 1945. 64 p.

1273 U.S. Army. Signal Corps. 803d Training Regiment.
803D SIGNAL TRAINING REGIMENT. Long Beach, N.J., Monmouth County Publishing Co., 1946. (unpaged)

1274 U.S. Army. Tank Corps. 81st Battalion.
HISTORY OF THE 81ST TANK BATTALION. n.p., 81st Tank Battalion Association, 1947. 117 p.

1275 U.S. Army. Tank Corps. 601st Destroyer Battalion.
AN INFORMAL HISTORY OF THE 601ST TANK DESTROYER BATTALION. Compiled and written by Edward L. Josowitz. Salzburg, 1945. 95 p.

1276 U.S. Army. Tank Corps. 628th Destroyer Battalion.
VICTORY T.D.: THE HISTORY OF THE 628TH TANK DESTROYER BN. IN TRAINING AND COMBAT. Prepared by and for the men who saw action with the battalion in France, Belgium, Luxembourg, Holland and Germany. Göttingen, 1945. 291 p.

1277 U.S. Army. Tank Corps. 644th Destroyer Battalion.
644TH TANK DESTROYER BATTALION. n.p., 1946. 92 p.

1278 U.S. Army. Tank Corps. 701st Battalion.
701ST TANK BATTALION, MARCH 1943, CAMP CAMPBELL, KENTUCKY, JUNE 1945, GOTHA, GERMANY. Edited by Edward C. Hassett. Nuremberg, 1946. 239 p.

1279 U.S. Army. Tank Corps. 717th Battalion.
717TH TANK BATTALION RECORD. San Angelo, Tex., Newsfoto Publishing Co., 1946. 69 p.

1280 U.S. Army. Transportation Corps. 13th Port.
THE 13TH PORT, 1943-1946. n.p., n.d. 62 p.

1281 U.S. Army. 2d Chemical Mortar Battalion.
HISTORY OF SECOND CHEMICAL MORTAR BATTALION. Salzburg, 1946. 63 p.

1282 U.S. Army. 2d Military Government Regiment.
OFFICIAL HISTORY OF THE SECOND MILITARY GOVERNMENT REGIMENT. n.p., 1945. 67 p.

1283 U.S. Army. 2d Mobile Radio Broadcasting Company.
HISTORY, SECOND MOBILE RADIO BROADCASTING COMPANY, DECEMBER 1943-MAY 1945. n.p., 1945. 80 p.

1284 U.S. Army. 3d Armored Division.
SPEARHEAD IN THE WEST, 1941-45: THE THIRD ARMORED DIVISION. Frankfurt am Main-Schwanheim, Henrich, 1945. 260 p.

1285 U.S. Army. Third Army.
AFTER ACTION REPORT: 1 AUGUST 1944-9 MAY 1945. n.p., 1945. 3 v.

1286 U.S. Army. Third Army.
MISSION ACCOMPLISHED: THIRD UNITED STATES ARMY OCCUPATION OF GERMANY, 9 MAY 1945-15 FEB. 1947. n.p., Engr. Repro. Plant, 1947. 69 p.

1287 U.S. Army. Third Army.
A SOUVENIR BOOKLET FOR THE OFFICERS, ENLISTED MEN AND CIVILIANS WHO MADE HISTORY WITH THE THIRD U.S. ARMY IN THE EUROPEAN THEATER OF OPERATIONS, 1944-1945. Bad Tolz, Ger., 1945. 1 v. (unpaged)

1288 U.S. Army. 3d Division.
HISTORY OF THE 3RD INFANTRY DIVISION IN WORLD WAR II. Washington, Infantry Journal Press, 1947. 574 p.

1289 U.S. Army. Fifth Army.
ENGINEER HISTORY: FIFTH ARMY, MEDITERRANEAN THEATER. n.p., 1945. 2 v.

1290 U.S. Army. 5th Division.
THE FIFTH INFANTRY DIVISION IN THE ETO. Atlanta, Love, 1945. (unpaged)

1291 U.S. Army. Sixth Army.
THE SIXTH ARMY IN ACTION: A PHOTO HISTORY, JANUARY 1943-JUNE 1945. Kyoto, Japan, 1945. 68 p.

1292 U.S. Army. 6th Division.
THE 6TH INFANTRY DIVISION IN WORLD WAR II, 1939-1945. Washington, Infantry Journal Press, 1947. 179 p.

1293 U.S. Army. Eighth Army.
THE AMPHIBIOUS EIGHTH. n.p., AG Printing Plant, 1946. 64 p.

1294 U.S. Army. Ninth Army.
CONQUER: THE STORY OF THE NINTH ARMY, 1944-1945. Washington, Infantry Journal Press, 1947. 404 p.

1295 U.S. Army. 9th Division.
THE FINAL THRUST: THE NINTH INFANTRY DIVISION IN GERMANY, SEPTEMBER 1944 TO MAY 1945; A HISTORY. Munich, 1945. 73 p.

1296   U.S. Army. 9th Engineer Command.
       THE HISTORY OF IX ENGINEER COMMAND, FROM ITS BEGINNING TO V-E DAY. Wiesbaden, 1945. 213 p.

1297   U.S. Army. 10th Infantry.
       HISTORY OF TENTH INFANTRY REGIMENT, U.S. ARMY. n.p., 1946. 165 p.

1298   U.S. Army. 11th Cavalry.
       THE ELEVENTH CAVALRY FROM THE ROER TO THE ELBE, 1944-1945. Prepared by George L. Haynes, Jr., with James C. Williams. Erlangen, 1945. 95 p.

1299   U.S. Army. Twelfth Army.
       REPORT OF OPERATIONS: FINAL AFTER ACTION REPORT. n.p., 1945. 14 v.

1300   U.S. Army. Fifteenth Army.
       HISTORY OF THE FIFTEENTH U.S. ARMY, 21ST AUGUST 1944 TO JULY 1945. n.p., 1946. 146 p.

1301   U.S. Army. II Corps.
       A BRIEF HISTORY, II CORPS. n.p., Editoriale Domus, 1946. 83 p.

1302   U.S. Army. III Corps.
       THE PHANTOM CORPS. Camp Polk, La., 1945. 53 p.

1303   U.S. Army. IV Corps.
       THE FINAL CAMPAIGN ACROSS NORTHWEST ITALY, 14 APRIL-2 MAY 1945. Edited by Curtis H. Nance. Milan, 1945. 119 p.

1304   U.S. Army. XI Corps.
       HISTORY OF XI CORPS, 15 JUNE 1942-15 MARCH 1946. n.p., 1946. 124 p.

1305   U.S. Army. XII Corps.
       XII CORPS ARTILLERY IN COMBAT: A RECORD AND STUDY OF ITS OPERATIONAL METHODS, PROCEDURES AND EXPERIENCES, IN COMBAT 13 AUG. 1944 TO 8 MAY 1945 IN FRANCE, LUXEMBOURG, GERMANY, CZECHOSLOVAKIA, AND AUSTRIA. Regensburg, 1945. 1 v.

1306   U.S. Army. XII Corps.
       XII CORPS: SPEARHEAD OF PATTON'S THIRD ARMY. Prepared by Lt. Col. George Dyer. Baton Rouge, Military Press of Louisiana, 1947. 560 p.

1307   U.S. Army. XVI Corps.
       HISTORY OF THE XVI CORPS FROM ITS ACTIVATION TO THE END OF THE WAR IN EUROPE. Washington, Infantry Journal Press, 1947. 111 p.

1308   U.S. Army. XX Corps.
       AN OPERATIONAL REPORT. n.p., 1945. 6 v.

1309   U.S. Army. XX Corps.
       THE XX CORPS: ITS HISTORY AND SERVICE IN WORLD WAR II. n.p., XX Corps Association, 194-. 406 p.

1310   U.S. Army. 25th Division.
       THE 25TH DIVISION AND WORLD WAR II. Edited by Robert F. Karolevitz. Baton Rouge, Army and Navy Publishing Co., 1946. 202 p.

1311   U.S. Army. 29th Infantry.
       WE LEAD THE WAY: THE TWENTY NINTH INFANTRY REGIMENT IN WORLD WAR II, 1941-1946. Edited by Byron O. Bush, Jr. Frankfurt am Main, 1946. 125 p.

1312   U.S. Army. 30th Division.
       30TH SIGNAL COMPANY, THIRTEENTH INFANTRY DIVISION. Hof, Ger., Kleemeier, 1945. 206 p.

1313   U.S. Army. 31st Division.
       HISTORY OF THE 31ST INFANTRY DIVISION IN TRAINING AND COMBAT, 1940-1945. Baton Rouge, Army and Navy Publishing Co., 1946. 188 p.

1314   U.S. Army. 33d Division.
       THE GOLDEN CROSS: A HISTORY OF THE 33RD INFANTRY DIVISION IN WORLD WAR II. Washington, Infantry Journal Press, 1948. 404 p.

1315   U.S. Army. 34th Division.
       THE STORY OF THE 34TH INFANTRY DIVISION, LOUISIANA TO PISA. n.p., Information and Education Section, MTOUSA, 1945. 89 p.

1316   U.S. Army. 35th Division.
       PRESENTING THE 35TH INFANTRY DIVISION IN WORLD WAR II, 1941-1945. Atlanta, Love, 1946. 244 p.

1317   U.S. Army. 40th Division.
       40TH INFANTRY DIVISION: THE YEARS OF WORLD WAR II, 7 DECEMBER 1941-7 APRIL 1946. Baton Rouge, Army and Navy Publishing Co., 1947. 180 p.

1318   U.S. Army. 42d Division.
       42ND "RAINBOW" INFANTRY DIVISION: A COMBAT HISTORY OF WORLD WAR II. Written and edited by Hugh C. Daly. Baton Rouge, Army and Navy Publishing Co., 1946. 105 p.

1319   U.S. Army. 43d Signal Battalion.
       HISTORY OF THE 43D SIGNAL HEAVY CONSTRUCTION BATTALION FROM ACTIVATION TO V-J DAY, 7 FEBRUARY 1944 TO 2 SEPTEMBER 1945. Frankfurt am Main-Schwanheim, 1945. 114 p.

1320   U.S. Army. 45th Division.
       THE FIGHTING FORTY-FIFTH: THE COMBAT REPORT OF AN INFANTRY DIVISION. Compiled and edited under supervision of Historical Board: Leo V. Bishop, Frank J. Glasgow, and George A. Fisher. Baton Rouge, Army and Navy Publishing Co., 1946. 200 p.

1321   U.S. Army. 47th Infantry Regiment.
       HISTORY OF THE 47TH INFANTRY REGIMENT. n.p., 1946. 175 p.

1322   U.S. Army. 56th Antiaircraft Artillery Brigade.
       HISTORY OF THE 56TH ANTIAIRCRAFT ARTILLERY BRIGADE, 10 APRIL 1943-15 SEPTEMBER 1945. Augsburg, Ger., 56th Brigade Rhine Valley News, 1945. (unpaged)

1323   U.S. Army. 65th Armored Field Artillery Battalion.
       THE THUNDERBOLT BATTALION, 1941-1945. Philadelphia, 1947. 215 p.

1324   U.S. Army. 67th Armored Regiment.
       HISTORY 67TH ARMORED REGIMENT. Brunswick, Ger., Westermann, 1945. 407, 39 p.

1325   U.S. Army. 71st Division.
       THE HISTORY OF THE 71ST INFANTRY DIVISION. Prepared by Fred Clinger, Arthur Johnston, and Vincent Masel. n.p., 1946. 117 p.

1326   U.S. Army. 75th Division.
       PHOTOGRAPHIC CAVALCADE: PICTORIAL HISTORY OF THE 75 INFANTRY DIVISION, 1944-1945. Baton Rouge, 1946. 1 v. published.

1327   U.S. Army. 76th Division.
       WE RIPENED FAST: THE UNOFFICIAL HISTORY OF THE SEVENTY-SIXTH INFANTRY DIVISION. Edited by Joseph J. Hutnik and Leonard Kobrick. Frankfurt, 1946. 248 p.

1328   U.S. Army. 78th Division.
       LIGHTNING: THE HISTORY OF THE 78TH INFANTRY DIVISION. Washington, Infantry Journal Press, 1947. 301 p.

1329   U.S. Army. 81st Chemical Mortar Battalion.
       THE EIGHTY-FIRST CHEMICAL MORTAR BATTALION. n.p., 1945. 107 p.

1330   U.S. Army. 81st Division.
       THE 81ST INFANTRY WILDCAT DIVISION IN WORLD WAR II. Washington, Infantry Journal Press, 1948. 324 p.

1331   U.S. Army. 81st Tank Battalion.
       HISTORY OF THE 81ST TANK BATTALION. n.p., 1947. 117 p.

1332   U.S. Army. 83d Division.
       THE THUNDERBOLT ACROSS EUROPE: A HISTORY OF THE 83D INFANTRY DIVISION, 1942-1945. Munich, Bruckmann, 1946. 119 p.

1333   U.S. Army. 85th Division.
       MINTURNO TO APPENNINES: 85TH INFANTRY DIVISION. Prepared by John Arthos. n.p., Information and Education Section, MTOUSA, 1945. 87 p.

1334   U.S. Army. 88th Division.
       WITH THE 88TH IN ITALY. n.p., Information and Education Section, MTOUSA, 1945. 95 p.

1335   U.S. Army. 89th Division.
       THE 89TH INFANTRY DIVISION, 1942-1945. Washington, Infantry Journal Press, 1947. 270 p.

1336   U.S. Army. 90th Division.
       A HISTORY OF THE 90TH DIVISION IN WORLD WAR II, 6 JUNE 1944 TO 9 MAY 1945. Baton Rouge, Army and Navy Publishing Co., 1946. 89 p.

1337   U.S. Army. 92d Division.
       OCTOBER 1942-JUNE 1945, WITH THE 92D INFANTRY DIVISION. n.p., Information and Education Section, MTOUSA, 1945. 95 p.

1338   U.S. Army. 94th Division.
       HISTORY OF THE 94TH INFANTRY DIVISION IN WORLD WAR II. Edited by Laurence G. Byrnes. Washington, Infantry Journal Press, 1948. 527 p.

1339   U.S. Army. 95th Armored Field Artillery Battalion.
       AVENGERS: THE STORY OF THE 95TH ARMORED FIELD ARTILLERY BATTALION OF THE 5TH ARMORED DIVISION. Edited by William Hardy and John Caulfield. n.p., 1946. 76 p.

1340   U.S. Army. 100th Division.
       33 MONTHS WITH THE ONE HUNDREDTH SIGNAL COMPANY, 100TH INFANTRY DIVISION. Stuttgart, 1945. 100 p.

1341   U.S. Army. 101st Cavalry Group.
       WINGFOOT, RHINELAND AND CENTRAL EUROPE CAMPAIGNS: OFFICIAL HISTORY, 101ST CAVALRY GROUP, MECHANIZED. Weinheim, Diesvach, 1945. 112 p.

1342   U.S. Army. 102d Division.
       WITH THE 102D INFANTRY DIVISION THROUGH GERMANY. Edited by Major Allan H. Mick. Washington, Infantry Journal Press, 1947. 541 p.

1343   U.S. Army. 106th Cavalry Group.
       THE 106TH CAVALRY GROUP IN EUROPE, 1944-1945. Augsburg, Himmer, 1945. 254 p.

1344   U.S. Army. 114th Infantry.
       WITH THE 114TH IN THE ETO: A COMBAT HISTORY, FRANCE, GERMANY, AUSTRIA, AS COMPILED FROM OFFICIAL HISTORICAL RECORDS, STAFF REPORTS, DAILY JOURNALS, AND INTERVIEWS OF THE MEN INVOLVED. Historian, Joseph S. Hasson. Baton Rouge, Army and Navy Publishing Co., 1945. 192 p.

1345   U.S. Army. 119th Field Artillery Group.
       THE 119TH FIELD ARTILLERY GROUP, WORLD WAR II, EUROPEAN THEATRE OF OPERATIONS. Offenbach, Ger., Gross-Steinheim, 1945. 213 p.

1346   U.S. Army. 129th Infantry.
       THE 129TH INFANTRY IN WORLD WAR II. Washington, Infantry Journal Press, 1947. 250 p.

1347   U.S. Army. 133d Anti-Aircraft Artillery Battalion.
       THE 133D AAA GUN BATTALION. Edited by George Braziller. Munich, Oldenbourg, 1945. 109 p.

1348   U.S. Army. 155th Engineer Combat Battalion.
       HISTORY OF THE 155TH ENGINEER COMBAT BATTALION FROM ACTIVATION APRIL 15, 1943, TO DEACTIVATION APRIL, 1946. Edited by James F. Ristig. Portland, Ore., 1946. 1 v. (unpaged)

1349   U.S. Army. 174th Field Artillery Group.
       174TH FIELD ARTILLERY GROUP, HISTORY AND OPERATIONS, EUROPEAN THEATRE OF OPERATIONS. n.p., 1945. 64 p.

1350   U.S. Army. 184th Anti-Aircraft Artillery Battalion.
       184TH AAA GUN BATTALION, ICELAND, ENGLAND, FRANCE, BELGIUM, HOLLAND, GERMANY. Fulda, Ger., 1945. 66 p.

1351   U.S. Army. 187th Engineer Combat Battalion.
       STORY OF THE 187TH ENGINEER COMBAT BATTALION, CENTRAL EUROPE, ARDENNES, RHINELAND. Prepared by Melvin L. Epstein and others. n.p., 1945. 113 p.

1352   U.S. Army. 194th Field Artillery Battalion.
       SHOOT, MOVE AND COMMUNICATE. Compiled by Peter T. Scott, 34th Special Service Company, from historical data and photographs gathered from Major Gordon B. Patton. Munich, 1946. 152 p.

1353   U.S. Army. 195th Anti-Aircraft Artillery Battalion.
       THE TRACER, A RECORD OF THE 195TH AAA AW BN (SP) MOJAVE TO BERLIN. Edited by Sid Klemow. Halle, 1945. 1 v. (unpaged)

1354   U.S. Army. 271st Infantry.
       TRESPASS AGAINST THEM, A HISTORY OF THE 271ST INFANTRY REGIMENT, 15 MAY 1943-25 MAY 1945. Prepared by John F. Higgins. Naumburg, Saale, 1945. 91 p.

1355   U.S. Army. 291st Engineer Combat Battalion.
       BATTALION 291 ENGINEER C BN HISTORY. Edited by William L. McKinsey. n.p., 194-. 115 p.

1356   U.S. Army. 305th Field Artillery Battalion.
       305 FIELD ARTILLERY BATTALION, 77TH INFANTRY DIVISION. Edited by Alfred F. Kadar. Hakodate, Japan, Itagaki, 1946. 72 p.

1357   U.S. Army. 305th Infantry.
       SECOND TO NONE! THE STORY OF THE 305TH INFANTRY IN WORLD WAR II. Edited by Charles O. West and others. Washington, Infantry Journal Press, 1949. 243 p.

1358   U.S. Army. 320th Engineer Battalion.
       320TH ENGINEER BATTALION, 1942-1945. n.p., 1946. 96 p.

1359   U.S. Army. 324th Infantry.
       COMBAT HISTORY OF THE 324TH INFANTRY REGIMENT, 44TH INFANTRY DIVISION. Baton Rouge, Army and Navy Publishing Co., 1946. 132 p.

1360   U.S. Army. 345th Field Artillery Battalion.
       345TH FIELD ARTILLERY BATTALION, 90TH INFANTRY DIVISION, THIRD U.S. ARMY. Munich, Bruckman, 1945. 77 p.

1361   U.S. Army. 350th Infantry.
       350TH INFANTRY, BATTLE MOUNTAIN, IN OCCUPATION, WITH THE 88TH "BLUE DEVIL" DIVISION IN ITALY. Prepared by the Information and Education Section of the Black Mountain Regt. n.p., 194-. 77 p.

1362   U.S. Army. 355th Anti-Aircraft Searchlight Battalion.
       CARTHAGINIANS, ROMANS AND AMERICANS, OVERSEAS WITH THE 355TH AAA SLT BN. Edited by Chaplain Karl W. Scheufler. Cincinnati, Gibson and Perin, 1946. 276 p.

1363   U.S. Army. 358th Infantry.
       PERAGIMUS, "WE ACCOMPLISH": A BRIEF HISTORY OF THE 358TH INFANTRY. n.p., 1945. 56 p.

1364   U.S. Army. 375th Field Artillery Battalion.
       THE HISTORY OF 375 F.A. BN. Stuttgart, 1945. 174 p.

1365   U.S. Army. 376th Infantry.
       HISTORY OF THE 376TH INFANTRY REGIMENT BETWEEN THE YEARS OF 1921-1945. Compiled, edited, and printed by the Regimental Historical Committee, Information and Education Office, Wuppertal-Barmen, 1945. 202 p.

1366   U.S. Army. 387th Anti-Aircraft Artillery Battalion.
       OUR STORY, 387TH AAA. AW. BN. (SP). Narrative by Irving Gerstein and others. Göttingen, 1945. 199 p.

1367   U.S. Army. 413th Infantry.
       HISTORY OF THE 413TH INFANTRY REGIMENT. Los Angeles, Lewis, 1946. 171 p.

1368   U.S. Army. 457th Anti-Aircraft Artillery Battalion.
       FROM TEXAS TO TEISNACH WITH THE 457 AAA AW BATTALION. Nancy, Humblot, 1945. 223 p.

1369   U.S. Army. 506th Infantry.
       SCRAPBOOK, 20 JULY 1942-4 JULY 1945. n.p., 1945. 1 v. (unpaged)

1370   U.S. Army. 536th Anti-Aircraft Artillery Battalion.
       WAR HISTORY OF THE 536TH AAA AW BN. (M), 1942-1944. Baton Rouge, Army and Navy Pictorial Publishers, 1947. 107 p.

1371   U.S. Army. 573rd Anti-Aircraft Battalion.
       HISTORY OF 573RD AAA (AW) BN. S/P, JUNE 10, 1943 TO SEPTEMBER 2, 1945. Edited by Arthur W. Stetson. Mannheim, Waldkirch, 1945. 63 p.

1372   U.S. Army. 611th Ordnance Base Armament Maintenance Battalion.
THE ODYSSEY OF COMPANY G, A UNIT OF THE 611TH O.B.A.M. BATTALION: HISTORY FROM NOVEMBER 16, 1942 TO AUGUST 17, 1945. Frankfurt am Main, Henrich, 1945. 96 p.

1373   U.S. Army. 612th Ordnance Base Armament Maintenance Battalion.
612TH ORDNANCE BASE ARMAMENT MAINTENANCE BATTALION, A BRIEF HISTORY. Edited by Robert S. Howseman. Le Mans, France, Information and Education Center, 1945. 1 v. (unpaged)

1374   U.S. Army. 628th Tank Destroyer Battalion.
VICTORY TD: THE HISTORY OF THE 628TH TANK DESTROYER BN. IN TRAINING AND COMBAT. Prepared by and for the men who saw action with the battalion in France, Belgium, Luxembourg, Holland and Germany. Gottingen, "Muster-Schmidt," 1945. 201 p.

1375   U.S. Army. 644th Tank Destroyer Battalion.
644TH TANK DESTROYER BATTALION. n.p., 1946. 92 p.

1376   U.S. Army. 693d Field Artillery Battalion.
ON THE WAY: COMBAT EXPERIENCE OF THE 693RD FA BN. IN THE EUROPEAN THEATER OF OPERATIONS, NORMANDY, NORTHERN FRANCE, RHINELAND, CENTRAL EUROPE. Salzburg, 1945. 89 p.

1377   U.S. Army. 701st Tank Battalion.
701ST TANK BATTALION: MARCH 1943, CAMP CAMPBELL, KENTUCKY--JUNE 1945, GOTHA, GERMANY. Edited by Edward C. Hassett. Nuremberg, 1946. 239 p.

1378   U.S. Army. 716th Railway Operation Battalion.
THE SOLDIER-RAILROADERS' STORY OF THE 716TH RAILWAY OPERATING BATTALION. Stuttgart, 1945. 120 p.

1379   U.S. Army. 778th Anti-Aircraft Artillery Battalion.
778 AAA AW BN (SP) FROM ACTIVATION TO VICTORY. Edited by Tom Lowery. Munich, 1945. 121 p.

1380   U.S. Army. 790th Field Artillery Battalion.
THUNDERING THUNDERBOLT: STORY OF THE 790TH FIELD ARTILLERY BATTALION, BY THE MEN WHO LIVED THE STORY. Laon, France, 1945. 72 p.

1381   U.S. Army. 834th Engineer Aviation Battalion.
THUS WE SERVED: THE DEEDS AND ACCOMPLISHMENTS FROM ACTIVATION TO DEMOBILIZATION. Nuremberg, 1945. 1 v. (unpaged)

1382   U.S. Army. 863d Anti-Aircraft Artillery Battalion.
ON TARGET: A HISTORY OF THE 862D AAA-AW-BN IN THE SECOND WORLD WAR. Edited by Benjamin Gise and Van Ness Richards. New York, Marbridge Printing Co., 194-. 168 p.

1383   U S. Army. 951st Field Artillery Battalion.
951ST F. A. BN. HISTORY. By Carl Isenberg, Bernard Silver, and Ernest M. Chamberlain. n.p., 1946. 131 p.

1384   U.S. Army. 1629th Engineer Construction Battalion.
ENGINEERING IN THE PACIFIC THEATER WITH THE 1629TH ENGINEER CONSTRUCTION BATTALION. n.p., 1946. 52 p.

1385   U.S. Army Air Forces. 8th Photo Squadron.
THE DIARY OF 8TH PHOTO SQUADRON, NEW GUINEA. New York, Ad Press, 1945. 217 p.

1386   U.S. Army Air Forces. IX Air Defense Command.
IX AIR DEFENSE COMMAND, HISTORICAL AND STATISTICAL SUMMARY, 1 JANUARY 1944-1 JUNE 1945. n.p., 194-. 95 p.

1387   U.S. Army Air Forces. 9th Air Force.
THE BATTLE OF FRANCE: A PHOTO-HISTORY OF THE NINTH AIR FORCE TACTICAL OPERATIONS DURING THE DRIVE FROM THE BEACH-HEADS TO THE SIEGFRIED LINE: CHERBOURG, ST. LO, BREST, ST. MALO, FALAISE GAP, PARIS, METZ. n.p., 1945. 54 photos.

1388   U.S. Army Air Forces. 9th Air Force.
NINTH AIR FORCE, USAAF. n.p., Executive Liaison Section, 1945. 50 p. of col. illus.

1389   U.S. Army Air Forces. 9th Air Force.
RHINE TO VICTORY: A PHOTO-HISTORY OF THE NINTH AIR FORCE OPERATIONS DURING THE FINAL PHASE OF THE WAR IN EUROPE. n.p., 1945. 54 photos.

1390   U.S. Army Air Forces. 13th Air Force.
FROM FIJI THROUGH THE PHILIPPINES WITH THE THIRTEENTH AIR FORCE. Prepared by Benjamin E. Lippincott and others. San Angelo, Tex., Newsfoto, 1948. 193 p.

1391   U.S. Army Air Forces. 14th Air Force.
AN ORIENTATION BOOKLET FOR UNITED STATES MILITARY PERSONNEL IN CHINA: BACKGROUND OF THE WAR IN THE AIR, 1943-1944. Washington, 1945. 89 p.

1392   U.S. Army Air Forces. 15th Air Force.
FIFTEENTH AIR FORCE OPERATIONS IN SOUTHEASTERN EUROPE, 23 DECEMBER 1944-18 MARCH 1945. n.p., 1945. 1 v. (unpaged)

1393   U.S. Army Air Forces. XIX Tactical Air Command.
SIGNALS, THE STORY OF COMMUNICATIONS IN THE XIX TACTICAL AIR COMMAND UP TO V-E DAY. Prepared by Eugene M. Greenberg. n.p., 1945. 155 p.

1394   U.S. Army Air Forces. 34th Bombardment Group.
HISTORY OF THE ARMY AIR FORCES 34TH BOMBARDMENT GROUP. 2d ed. Written and compiled by Edwin S. Smith, Jr. San Angelo, Tex., Newsfoto, 1947. 1 v. (unpaged)

1395   U.S. Army Air Forces. 42d Bombardment Group.
THE CRUSADERS: A HISTORY OF THE 42D BOMBARDMENT GROUP M. Baton Rouge, Army and Navy Pictorial Publishers, 1946. 204 p.

1396   U. S. Army Air Forces. 44th Bombardment Group.
LIBERATORS OVER EUROPE, 44TH BOMB GROUP. Written and compiled by Ursel P. Harvell. San Angelo, Tex., Newsfoto, 194-. 1 v. (unpaged)

1397   U. S. Army Air Forces. 61st Service Squadron.
61ST SERVICE SQUADRON. Edited by James E. Morrow. Ottumwa, Iowa, Messenger Printing, 1946. 120 p.

1398   U. S. Army Air Forces. 67th Troop Carrier Squadron.
SKY TRAIN, ADVENTURES OF A TROOP CARRIER SQUADRON, FEBRUARY 10, 1943-AUGUST 10, 1944. Prepared by Bill C. Birdzell. Sydney, Angus and Robertson, 1945. 217 p.

1399   U. S. Army Air Forces. 79th Fighter Group.
THE FALCON: COMBAT HISTORY OF THE 79TH FIGHTER GROUP, UNITED STATES ARMY AIR FORCES, 1942-1945. Edited by Ragnar G. Lind. Munich, 1946. 286 p.

1400   U. S. Army Air Forces. 95th Bombardment Group.
THE 95TH BOMBARDMENT GROUP H, UNITED STATES ARMY AIR FORCES. Edited by John P. Dwyer. n.p., 95th Group Photographic Section, 1945. 1 v. (unpaged)

1401   U. S. Army Air Forces. 100th Bombardment Group.
CONTRAILS, MY WAR RECORD: A HISTORY OF WORLD WAR II AS RECORDED AT U. S. ARMY AIR FORCE STATION NO. 139, THORPE ABBOTS, NEAR DISS, COUNTRY OF NORFOLK, ENGLAND. New York, Callahan, 1947. 284 p.

1402   U. S. Army Air Forces. 308th Bombardment Wing Heavy.
FROM DOBODURA TO OKINAWA: HISTORY OF THE 308TH BOMBARDMENT WING. Edited by Robert R. Herring. San Angelo, Tex., Newsfoto, 194-. 1 v. (unpaged)

1403   U. S. Army Air Forces. 326th Service Group.
TEAM B, 326TH AIR SERVICE GROUP: A PICTORIAL HISTORY OF THE UNSUNG HEROES WHO KEPT 'EM FLYING IN WORLD WAR II. Los Angeles, Wetzel, 1946. 137 p.

1404   U. S. Army Air Forces. 345th Bombardment Group.
WARPATH OF THE AIR APACHES. San Angelo, Tex., 1946. 277 p.

1405   U. S. Army Air Forces. 386th Bombardment Group.
THE HISTORY OF A BOMBING OUTFIT, THE 386TH BOMB GROUP. Written by T. B. Haire. St. Truiden, Ger., 1945. 72 p.

1406   U. S. Army Air Forces. 435th Troop Carrier Group.
HISTORY, 435TH TROOP CARRIER GROUP, NINTH TROOP CARRIER COMMAND. n.p., 1946. 1 v. (unpaged)

1407   U. S. Army Air Forces. 440th Troop Carrier Group.
DZ EUROPE: THE STORY OF THE 440TH TROOP CARRIER GROUP. n.p., 194-. 203 p.

1408   U. S. Army Air Forces. 444th Bombardment Group.
THE PICTORIAL HISTORY OF THE 444TH BOMBARDMENT GROUP, VERY HEAVY SPECIAL. n.p., 1947. 1 v. (unpaged)

1409   U. S. Army Air Forces. 446th Bombardment Group.
THE STORY OF THE 446TH BOMB GROUP. Edited by Edward H. Castens. San Angelo, Tex., Newsfoto, 194-. 1 v. (unpaged)

1410   U. S. Army Air Forces. 487th Bombardment Group.
THE HISTORY OF THE 487TH BOMBARDMENT GROUP, 22 SEPTEMBER 1943 TO 7 NOVEMBER 1945. n.p., 194-. 1 v. (unpaged)

1411   U. S. Army Air Forces. 493d Bombardment Group.
493D BOMBARDMENT GROUP: A PICTORIAL REVIEW OF OPERATIONS IN THE ETO. n.p., 194-. 1 v. (unpaged)

1412   U. S. Army Air Forces. 497th Bombardment Group.
THE LONG HAUL: THE STORY OF THE 497TH BOMB GROUP VH. n.p., 1947. 1 v. (unpaged)

1413   U. S. Coast Guard Reserve.
REMINISCENCES OF YOUR "HITCH" IN THE UNITED STATES COAST GUARD DURING WORLD WAR II: A PICTORIAL RECORD OF U.S.C.G. TEMPORARY RESERVE ACTIVITIES IN DIVISION 5A, FIRST NAVAL DISTRICT, 1941-1945. Boston, Division 5A Committee, 1946. 96 p.

1414   U. S. Dept. of the Army. Office of Military History.
COMBAT CHRONICLE, AN OUTLINE HISTORY OF U. S. ARMY DIVISIONS. Washington, 1948. 109 l. (Order of Battle Series)

1415   U. S. Marine Corps. 9th Regiment.
THE NINTH MARINES: A BRIEF HISTORY OF THE NINTH MARINE REGIMENT, WITH LISTS OF THE OFFICERS AND MEN WHO SERVED FROM ORGANIZATION TO DISBANDMENT, 1942-1945. Washington, Infantry Journal Press, 1946. 375 p.

1416   U. S. Navy. Air Group 86.
CARRIER AIR GROUP 86. n.p., 1946. 280 p.

1417   U. S. Navy. 4th Construction Battalion.
LIL' SHORT RUNNER PRESENTS THE FOURTH U. S. NAVAL CONSTRUCTION BATTALION PENGUIN, 1944-45. Baton Rouge, Army and Navy Pictorial Publishers, 1945. 171 p.

1418   U. S. Navy. 6th Construction Battalion.
SAGA OF THE SIXTH, A HISTORY, 1942-1945. n.p., 194-. 97 p.

1419   U. S. Navy. 7th Amphibious Force.
SEVENTH AMPHIBIOUS FORCE, COMMAND HISTORY, 10TH JANUARY 1943-23D DECEMBER 1945. n.p., 1945. 208 p.

1420 U.S. Navy. 8th Construction Battalion.
PIECES OF EIGHTS, PUBLISHED BY AND FOR THE MEN OF THE EIGHTH U.S. NAVAL CONSTRUCTION BATTALION, 1942-1945. Allentown, Pa., 194-. 1 v. (unpaged)

1421 U.S. Navy. 18th Construction Battalion.
THE ODYSSEY, EIGHTEENTH U.S. NAVAL CONSTRUCTION BATTALION. San Francisco, 1946. 94 p.

1422 U.S. Navy. 21st Construction Battalion.
THE BLACKJACK, 1944-1945: A STORY ABOUT AND PUBLISHED BY THE 21ST U.S. NAVAL CONSTRUCTION BATTALION. Baton Rouge, 1946. 190 p.

1423 U.S. Navy. 24th Construction Battalion.
THE TWENTY-FOURTH UNITED STATES NAVAL CONSTRUCTION BATTALION. Baton Rouge, 1946. 244 p.

1424 U.S. Navy. 25th Construction Battalion.
PACIFIC DIARY. n.p., Whelan, 1946. 125 p.

1425 U.S. Navy. 30th Construction Battalion. Special.
THE BOMB-DOZER, 30TH SPECIAL NAVAL CONSTRUCTION BATTALION. n.p., 1948. 144 p.

1426 U.S. Navy. 34th Construction Battalion. Special.
BATTALION REVIEW, SPECIAL 34TH BATTALION, USN, 1944-1945. Baton Rouge, Army and Navy Pictorial Publishers, 1946. 100 p.

1427 U.S. Navy. 42d Construction Battalion.
YEAR BOOK, 1944-1945. Edited by Thomas L. Hogan with W. Stone and others. Milwaukee, 194-. 155 p.

1428 U.S. Navy. 43d Construction Battalion.
THE LOG, 1942-1946. Baton Rouge, 1946. 153 p.

1429 U.S. Navy. 50th Construction Battalion.
THE FIFTIETH SEABEES. San Francisco, 1945. 108 p.

1430 U.S. Navy. 55th Construction Battalion.
THE 55 SEABEES, 1942-1945. Text by Delmas W. Abbott. Baton Rouge, Army and Navy Publishing Co., 1945. 169 p.

1431 U.S. Navy. 57th Construction Battalion.
SOPAC SAGA: 57TH SEABEES, 1942-1945. Edited by Lieutenant Lawrence J. Brodd. Arlington, Marx, 1946. 182 p.

1432 U.S. Navy. 58th Construction Battalion.
HISTORY OF THE 58TH SEABEES. Edited by C. Edward Gideon, with Miguel Gasco. Brooklyn, Foxcroft Commercial Press, 1950. 252 p.

1433 U.S. Navy. 62d Construction Battalion.
"WE DID": THE STORY OF THE 62ND NCB, DECEMBER 7, 1942 TO SEPTEMBER 15, 1945. Baton Rouge, Army and Navy Pictorial Publishers, 1946. 191 p.

1434 U.S. Navy. 82d Construction Battalion.
EIGHTY-SECOND U.S. NAVAL CONSTRUCTION BATTALION, 1943-1945. Greensburg, Pa., Henry, 1946. 178 p.

1435 U.S. Navy. 85th Construction Battalion.
THE EIGHTY-FIFTH U.S. NAVAL CONSTRUCTION BATTALION. Edited by Charles Scifres. n.p., 1946. 78 p.

1436 U.S. Navy. 90th Construction Battalion.
90TH USN CONSTRUCTION BATTALION: ITS HISTORY AND ACCOMPLISHMENTS, 1943-1945. n.p., 1946. 1 v. (unpaged)

1437 U.S. Navy. 91st Construction Battalion.
A HISTORY OF THE NINETY-FIRST NAVAL CONSTRUCTION BATTALION, 1943-1945. n.p., 1945. 164 p.

1438 U.S. Navy. 94th Construction Battalion.
PACIFIC DUTY, 94TH, AN OFFICIAL STORY OF THE WORK AND TRAVELS OF THE 94TH NAVAL CONSTRUCTION BATTALION IN TRAINING AND IN THE PACIFIC OCEAN AREAS, MAY 1943-July 1945. n.p., 1945. 155 p.

1439 U.S. Navy. 96th Construction Battalion.
96TH SEABEOGRAPHY. Baton Rouge, Army and Navy Pictorial Publishers, 1946. 150 p.

1440 U.S. Navy. 102d Construction Battalion.
102 CONSTRUCTION BATTALION, "SECOND TO NONE." Baton Rouge, Army and Navy Pictorial Publishers, 1946. 186 p.

1441 U.S. Navy. 105th Construction Battalion.
105 NAVAL CONSTRUCTION BATTALION. n.p., 194-. 1 v. (unpaged)

1442 U.S. Navy, 107th Construction Battalion.
THE LOG, 1943-1945, A STORY OF A SEABEE BATTALION CONCEIVED IN WAR, DEDICATED TO PEACE. Baton Rouge, 1946. 208 p.

1443 U.S. Navy, 116th Construction Battalion.
WORK AND WEAPONS, THE STORY OF THE ONE HUNDRED SIXTEENTH NAVAL CONSTRUCTION BATTALION. Portland, Ore., 1946. 111 p.

1444 U.S. Navy. 121st Construction Battalion.
BATTALION HISTORY, MAY 10, 1943-AUGUST 15, 1945. Edited by Mac McKerracher and others. Baton Rouge, Army and Navy Pictorial Publishers, 1946. 91 p.

1445 U.S. Navy. 130TH CONSTRUCTION BATTALION.
ONE HUNDRED AND THIRTIETH U.S. NAVAL CONSTRUCTION BATTALION. Baton Rouge, 1945. 209 p.

1446 U.S. Navy. 135th Construction Battalion.
135TH U.S. NAVAL CONSTRUCTION BATTALION REVIEW. Edited by F. P. Organ. n.p., 1946. 1 v. (unpaged)

1447 U. S. Navy. 136th Construction Battalion.
PHOTO-MEMORIES OF A SEABEE BATTALION. Published by and for the men of 136. Yokosuka, Japan, 1945. 1 v. (unpaged)

1448 U. S. Navy. 143d Construction Battalion.
143RD NAVAL CONSTRUCTION BATTALION, ADVANCE BASE CONSTRUCTION DEPOT: A BATTALION BIOGRAPHY. New York, 1946. 254 p.

1449 U. S. Navy. Construction Battalion Maintenance Unit 635.
CBMU 635. Baton Rouge, Army and Navy Pictorial Publishers, 1946. 143 p.

1450 U. S. Navy. Construction Battalion Detachment No. 1050.
THIS IS CBD 1050. Baton Rouge, Army and Navy Pictorial Publishers, 1946. 138 p.

1451 U. S. 62d Quartermaster Base Depot.
HISTORY OF THE 62d Q. M. BASE DEPOT, 1944-1945. n. p., 1945. 73 p.

1452 Von Roeder, George (comp.).
REGIMENTAL HISTORY OF THE 357TH INFANTRY. Weiden, Bavaria, F. Nickl Buchdruckerei, 1945. 74 p.

1453 Wardlow, Chester.
THE TRANSPORTATION CORPS: RESPONSIBILITIES ORGANIZATION, AND OPERATIONS. Washington, Office of Chief of Military History, U. S. Army, 1951. 454 p. (U. S. Army in World War II: The Technical Services)

1454 White, Nathan W.
FROM FEDALA TO BERCHTESGADEN: A HISTORY OF THE SEVENTH U. S. INFANTRY IN WORLD WAR II. Essex, Mass., 1947. 320 p.

1455 Williams, Jack J.
494TH GROUP HISTORY. Philadelphia, Peck, 1947. 147 p.

1456 Wilson, Robert E.
THE EARTHQUAKERS: OVERSEAS HISTORY OF THE 12TH BOMB GROUP. Tacoma, Wash., Dammeier, 1947. 147 p.

1457 Wolff, Perry S.
A HISTORY OF THE 334TH INFANTRY, 84TH DIVISION. Mannheim, Mannheimer Grossdruckerei, 1945. 230 p.

1458 Wood, Sterling A., and others.
HISTORY OF THE 313TH INFANTRY IN WORLD WAR II. Washington, Infantry Journal Press, 1947. 203 p.

1459 Wright, Bertram C.
THE 1ST CAVALRY DIVISION IN WORLD WAR II. Tokyo, Toppan, 1947. 245 p.

1460 Ziegler, Junior G.
BRIDGE BUSTERS, THE STORY OF THE 394TH BOMB GROUP OF THE 98TH BOMB WING, 9TH BOMB DIVISION, 9TH AIR FORCE. New York, 1949. 213 p.

1461 Zufelt, Edwin J. H.
THE ODYSSEY OF THE 411TH ENGINEER BASE SHOP BATTALION, 1943-1944: A PICTORIAL NARRATIVE OF THE 411TH ENGINEER BASE SHOP BATTALION IN AUSTRALIA AND NEW GUINEA. Sheboygan, Wis., 1946. 85 p.

g. Others

1462 Anders, Wladyslaw.
AN ARMY IN EXILE: THE STORY OF THE 2ND POLISH CORPS. London, Macmillan, 1949. 319 p.

1463 Bent, Rowland A. R.
TEN THOUSAND MEN OF AFRICA: THE STORY OF THE BECHUANALAND PIONEERS AND GUNNERS, 1941-1946. London, Published for the Bechuanaland Government by H. M. Stationery Office, 1952. 128 p.

1464 Brelsford, William V. (ed.).
THE STORY OF THE NORTHERN RHODESIA REGIMENT. Lusaka, Government Printer, 1954. 134 p.

1465 Cowin, John N. (comp.)
THE STORY OF THE NINTH: A RECORD OF THE 9TH FIELD COMPANY, SOUTH AFRICAN ENGINEER CORPS, JULY 1939-JULY 1943, COMPILED FROM COMPANY AND OTHER RECORDS. Johannesburg, Gover, Dande, 1948. 161 p.

1466 Fielding, W. L.
WITH THE 6TH DIVISION: AN ACCOUNT OF THE ACTIVITIES OF THE 6TH SOUTH AFRICAN ARMOURED DIVISION IN WORLD WAR II. Pietermaritzburg, Shuter and Shooter, 1946. 191 p.

1467 Gray, Brian.
BASUTO SOLDIERS IN HITLER'S WAR. Maseru, Basutoland Government, 1953. 97 p.

1468 Jamar, K.
WITH THE TANKS OF THE 1ST POLISH ARMOURED DIVISION. Translated from Polish by M. C. Slomczanka. Hengelo (O.), Holland, H. L. Smith, 1946. 332 p.

1469 Jameson, K., and D. Ashburner.
SOUTH AFRICAN W. A. A. F. Foreword by J. C. Smuts. Pietermaritzburg, Shuter and Shooter, 1948. 68 p.

1470 Kurcz, F. S.
THE BLACK BRIGADE: Vol. I, BETWEEN THE RIVERS RABA AND PRUT; Vol. II, ARMOURED ADVENTURE. Translated by Peter Jordan. Harrow, Middlesex, Eng., Atlantis, 1943. 232 p.

1471 Lattre de Tassigny, Jean de.
THE HISTORY OF THE FRENCH FIRST ARMY. Translated by Malcolm Barnes; with a preface by General Eisenhower and an appreciation by B. H. Liddell Hart. London, Allen and Unwin, 1952. 532 p.

Other edition:
New York, Macmillan, 1953.

1472 Tungay, Ronald W.
THE FIGHTING THIRD. Cape Town, Unie-Volkspers Beperk, 1948. 410 p.

1473 Wood, A. Mervyn.
MEN OF THE MIDLANDS, THE STORY OF WEENEN-KLIP RIVER NATIONAL RESERVE VOLUNTEERS. Pietermaritzburg, Natal Witness, 1946. 63 p.

D. CAMPAIGNS AND OPERATIONS
(see also III. A and B)

1. Land Campaigns: European Theater

a. German-Polish
(see also III. E. h and IV. D. 1. a)

1474 Berg, Mary.
WARSAW GHETTO: A DIARY. New York, Fischer, 1945. 253 p.

1475 Bryan, Julien H.
WARSAW: 1939 SIEGE; 1959 WARSAW REVISITED. Warsaw, Polonia Publishing House; distributed by International Film Foundation, New York, 1960. 177 p.

1476 Dynowska, Wanda (ed.) (Umadevi, pseud.).
ALL FOR FREEDOM: THE WARSAW EPIC. Swatantrapur, Aundh, M. Frydman; sole distributors for India, Padma Publications, Bombay, 1946. 217 p. (Indo-Polish Library)

1477 Friedman, Philip (ed.).
MARTYRS AND FIGHTERS: THE EPIC OF THE WARSAW GHETTO. New York, Praeger, 1954. 325 p.

Other edition:
London, Routledge, 1954. 227 p.

1478 Kennedy, Robert M.
THE GERMAN CAMPAIGN IN POLAND, 1939. Washington, Department of Army, 1956. 141 p. (German Report Series)

1479 Korwin-Rhodes, Marta.
THE MASK OF WARRIORS: THE SIEGE OF WARSAW, SEPTEMBER 1939. New York, Libra, 1964. 191 p.

1480 Peis, Gunter.
THE MAN WHO STARTED THE WAR. London, Odhams Press, 1960. 223 p.

b. War in the West, 1939-40

1481 Adamson, Hans C., and Per Klem.
BLOOD ON THE MIDNIGHT SUN. New York, Norton, 1964. 282 p.

1482 Ash, Bernard.
NORWAY, 1940. London, Cassell, 1964. 340 p.

1483 Benoist-Méchin, Jacques G. P. M.
SIXTY DAYS THAT SHOOK THE WEST: THE FALL OF FRANCE, 1940. Edited and with a preface by Cyril Falls; translated from French by Peter Wiles. London, Cape; New York, Putnam, 1963. 559 p.

1484 Bloch, Marc L. B.
STRANGE DEFEAT: A STATEMENT OF EVIDENCE WRITTEN IN 1940. Translated from French by Gerard Hopkins. London and New York, Oxford University Press, 1949. 178 p.

1485 Buckley, Christopher.
NORWAY; THE COMMANDOS; DIEPPE. London, H.M. Stationery Office, 1951 [i.e., 1952]. 276 p. (The Second World War, 1939-1945; A Popular Military History)

1486 Butler, Ewan, and J. Selby Bradford.
KEEP THE MEMORY GREEN: THE FIRST OF THE MANY, FRANCE 1939-40. London and New York, Hutchinson, 1950. 179 p.

Other edition:
THE STORY OF DUNKIRK. London, Hutchinson, 1955. 192 p.

1487 Clarke, Comer.
ENGLAND UNDER HITLER. New York, Ballantine, 1961. 143 p. (Ballantine Books)

1488 Collier, Richard.
THE SANDS OF DUNKIRK. London, Collins; New York, Dutton, 1961. 319 p.

1489 Derry, Kingston.
THE CAMPAIGN IN NORWAY. London, H.M. Stationery Office, 1952. 289 p. (History of the Second World War: United Kingdom Military Series)

1490 Dewey, Albert P.
AS THEY WERE. New York, Beechhurst Press, 1946. 283 p.

1491 Divine, Arthur D.
DUNKIRK. London, Faber and Faber, 1945. 307 p.

1492 Divine, David.
THE NINE DAYS OF DUNKIRK. London, Faber; New York, Norton, 1959. 308 p.

Other edition:
London, Pan, 1964. 320 p.

1493 Downing, Rupert.
IF I LAUGH: THE CHRONICLE OF MY STRANGE ADVENTURES IN THE GREAT PARIS EXODUS-JUNE 1940. London, Barker, 1959. 191 p. (Dragon Books)

1494 Draper, Theodore.
THE SIX WEEKS' WAR: FRANCE, MAY 10 TO JUNE 25, 1940. London, Methuen, 1946. 322 p.

1495 Ellis, Lionel F.
THE WAR IN FRANCE AND FLANDERS, 1939-1940. London, H.M. Stationery Office, 1953. 425 p. (History of the Second World War: United Kingdom Military Series)

1496 Goutard, Adolphe.
THE BATTLE OF FRANCE, 1940. Translated from French by Captain A. R. P. Burgess; foreword by Captain B. H. Liddell Hart. London, Muller, 1958. 280 p.

Other edition:
New York, Washburn, 1959. 280 p.

1497 Greenwall, Harry J.
WHEN FRANCE FELL. London, Wingate, 1958. 188 p.

1498 Haukelid, Knut.
SKIS AGAINST THE ATOM. Translated from Norwegian by F. H. Lyon; introduction by Major-General Colin Gubbins. London, Kimber, 1954. 201 p.

1499 Johnson, Amanda.
NORWAY, HER INVASION AND OCCUPATION. Brooklyn, Nordisk Tidende; Decatur, Ga., Bowen Press, 1948. 372 p.

1500 Macintyre, Donald G. F. W.
NARVIK. London, Evans, 1959. 224 p.

Other editions:
New York, Norton, 1960.

London, Pan, 1962. 238 p.

1501 Mann, Edna.
FLIGHT FROM FEAR. New York, Pageant Press, 1964. 127 p.

1502 Michie, Allan A., and Walter Graebner (eds.).
THEIR FINEST HOUR. London, Brown, Watson, 1959. 159 p. (Digit Books)

1503 Reoch, Ernest.
THE ST. VALERY STORY. Edinburgh, Reoch, 1965. 227 p.

1504 Rowe, Vivian.
THE GREAT WALL OF FRANCE: THE TRIUMPH OF THE MAGINOT LINE. London, Putnam, 1959. 328 p.

Other edition:
New York, Putnam, 1961.

1505 Taylor, Telford.
THE MARCH OF CONQUEST: THE GERMAN VICTORIES IN WESTERN EUROPE, 1940. New York, Simon and Schuster, 1958. 460 p.

Other editions:
London, Hulton, 1959. 462 p.

New York, Simon and Schuster, 1965.

1506 U. S. Military Academy, West Point. Dept. of Military Art and Engineering.
THE CAMPAIGN IN THE WEST, 1940. West Point, N. Y., 1945. 69 p.

Other editions:
1947, 1950. 55 p.

1507 Waage, Johan.
THE NARVIK CAMPAIGN. Translated from Norwegian by Ewan Butler. London, Harrap, 1964. 190 p.

Other edition:
London, Transworld, 1965. 190 p. (Corgi Books)

Battle of Britain
(see also III. D. 3. b and IV. E. 4. a)

1508 Bishop, Edward.
THE BATTLE OF BRITAIN. London, Allen and Unwin, 1960. 235 p.

Other edition:
London, Transworld, 1961. 254 p. (Corgi Books)

1509 Boorman, Henry R. P., and Howard L. Rusk.
RECALLING THE BATTLE OF BRITAIN: A PHOTOGRAPHIC ESSAY BASED UPON THE RECORDS OF THE "KENT MESSENGER" AND OTHER CONTEMPORARY SOURCES OF WORLD WAR 2. Maidstone, Kent Messenger, 1965. 71 p.

1510 Clark, Ronald W.
BATTLE FOR BRITAIN: SIXTEEN WEEKS THAT CHANGED THE COURSE OF HISTORY. London, Harrap, 1965. 175 p.

1511 Collier, Basil.
THE BATTLE OF BRITAIN. London, Batsford; New York, Macmillan, 1962. 183 p.

1512 Collier, Richard.
THE CITY THAT WOULDN'T DIE: LONDON, MAY 10-11, 1941. London, Collins, 1959. 256 p.

Other editions:
New York, Dutton, 1960. 280 p.

London, Transworld, 1961. 285 p. (Corgi Books)

1513 FitzGibbon, Constantine.
THE BLITZ. London, Wingate, 1957. 272 p.

Other edition:
THE WINTER OF THE BOMBS: THE STORY OF THE BLITZ OF LONDON. New York, Norton, 1958. 271 p.

1514 Hatchette, Antonio A.
THE BATTLE OF LONDON, AUGUST-SEPTEMBER 1940, AND BRIEF ACCOUNT OF THE FIFTEEN DECISIVE BATTLES OF THE WORLD. Santurce, P. R., 1949. 110 p.

1515 Henrey, Mrs. Robert (Robert Henrey, pseud.).
THE SIEGE OF LONDON. London, Dent, 1946. 200 p.

1516 Howard-Williams, Ernest L.
IMMORTAL MEMORY: DRAFTED DURING THE BATTLE OF BRITAIN FROM THE COMBAT REPORTS OF THOSE WHO TOOK PART. London, Bamber, 1947. 62 p.

1517 Lee, Asher.
BLITZ ON BRITAIN. London, Four Square Books, 1960. 160 p.

1518 McKee, Alexander.
STRIKE FROM THE SKY: THE STORY OF THE BATTLE OF BRITAIN. London, Souvenir Press; Boston, Little, Brown, 1960. 288 p.

Other edition:
London, New English Library, 1962. 272 p. (Four Square Books)

1519 Middleton, Drew.
THE SKY SUSPENDED: THE BATTLE OF BRITAIN. London, Secker and Warburg, 1960. 255 p.

Other editions:
New York, Longmans, 1960. 282 p.

London, Pan, 1963. 189 p.

1520 Narracott, Arthur H.
IN PRAISE OF THE FEW: A BATTLE OF BRITAIN ANTHOLOGY. London, Muller, 1947. 64 p.

1521 Newman, Bernard.
THEY SAVED LONDON. London, Laurie, 1952. 192 p.

Other edition:
London, Hamilton, 1955. (Panther Books)

1522 Pile, Sir Frederick A.
ACK-ACK: BRITAIN'S DEFENCE AGAINST AIR ATTACK DURING THE SECOND WORLD WAR. London, Harrap, 1949. 410 p.

Other edition:
London, Hamilton, 1956. 352 p. (Panther Books)

1523 Reynolds, Quentin J.
ALL ABOUT THE BATTLE OF BRITAIN. New York, Random House, 1953. 182 p. (World Landmark Books)

Other edition:
London, Allen, 1960. 118 p.

1524 Smith, Norman D.
THE BATTLE OF BRITAIN. London, Faber, 1962. 127 p. (Man and Events Series)

c. Russo-Finnish War

1525 Jakobson, Max.
THE DIPLOMACY OF THE WINTER WAR: AN ACCOUNT OF THE RUSSO-FINNISH WAR, 1939-1940. Cambridge, Mass., Harvard University Press; London, Oxford University Press, 1961. 281 p.

1526 Luukkanen, Eino A.
FIGHTER OVER FINLAND: THE MEMOIRS OF A FIGHTER PILOT. Translated from Finnish by Mauno A. Salo; Edited by William Green. London, Macdonald, 1963. 254 p.

1527 Tanner, Väinö A.
THE WINTER WAR: FINLAND AGAINST RUSSIA, 1939-1940. Stanford, Calif., Stanford University Press; London, Oxford University Press, 1957. 274 p.

1528 Upton, Anthony F.
FINLAND IN CRISIS, 1940-1941: A STUDY IN SMALL-POWER POLITICS. Ithaca, N.Y., Cornell University Press, 1965. 318 p.

Other edition:
London, Faber, 1964. 318 p.

d. Mediterranean

1529 Clark, Alan.
THE FALL OF CRETE. London, Blond; New York, Morrow, 1962. 206 p.

Other edition:
London, New English Library, 1964. 205 p. (Four Square Books)

1530 Comeau, Marcel G.
OPERATION MERCURY: AN AIRMAN IN THE BATTLE OF CRETE. London, Kimber, 1961. 160 p.

1531 Davin, Daniel M.
CRETE. Wellington, War History Branch, Dept. of Internal Affairs; London, Oxford University Press, 1953. 547 p. (Official History of New Zealand in the Second World War, 1939-45)

1532 Heydte, Friedrich A., Baron von der.
DAEDALUS RETURNED: CRETE, 1941. Translated from German by W. Stanley Moss. London, Hutchinson, 1958. 186 p.

Other edition:
London, World Distributors, 1959. 159 p.

1533 Lloyd, Sir Hugh P.
BRIEFED TO ATTACK: MALTA'S PART IN AFRICAN VICTORY. Foreword by Lord Tedder. London, Hodder and Stoughton, 1949. 230 p.

1534 Moss, William S.
ILL MET BY MOONLIGHT. London, Harrap: New York, Macmillan, 1950. 192 p.

Other editions:
London, Harrap, 1952. (Guild Books Series)

London, Transworld, 1956. 184 p. (Corgi Books)

1535 Norman, Kathleen.
FOR GALLANTRY: MALTA'S STORY BY A NAVAL WIFE. Ilfracombe, Stockwell, 1956. 208 p.

1536 Peniakoff, Vladimir.
POPSKI'S PRIVATE ARMY. New York, Crowell, 1950. 369 p.

Other editions:
PRIVATE ARMY. London, Cape, 1950. 512 p.

London, Pan, 1957. 437 p.

London, Transworld, 1965. 477 p. (Corgi Books)

1537 Playfair, Ian S. O.
THE MEDITERRANEAN AND MIDDLE EAST. London, H.M. Stationery Office, 1954-. 4 v. published. (History of the Second World War: United Kingdom Military Series)

1538 Spencer, John H.
BATTLE FOR CRETE. London, Heinemann, 1962. 306 p.

1539 Stephanides, Theodore.
CLIMAX IN CRETE. London, Faber and Faber, 1946. 166 p.

e. Africa and the Near East

1540 Agar-Hamilton, John A. I., and Leonard C. F. Turner (eds.).
CRISIS IN THE DESERT, MAY-JULY 1942. London, Oxford University Press, 1952. 368 p.

1541 Agar-Hamilton, John A. I., and Leonard C. F. Turner (eds.).
THE SIDI REZEG BATTLES. Cape Town and London, Oxford University Press, 1957. 505 p.

1542 Barber, Donald H.
AFRICANS IN KHAKI. London, Edinburgh House, 1948. 120 p.

1543 Barclay, Cyril N.
AGAINST GREAT ODDS: THE STORY OF THE FIRST OFFENSIVE IN LIBYA IN 1940-41, THE FIRST BRITISH VICTORY IN THE SECOND WORLD WAR. Including many extracts from the personal account of Sir Richard N. O'Connor, and with a foreword by Sir John Harding. London, Sifton Praed, 1955. 112 p.

1544 Barnett, Correlli D.
THE BATTLE OF EL ALAMEIN: DECISION IN THE DESERT. New York, Macmillan; London, Collier-Macmillan, 1964. 90 p. (Battle Books)

1545 Barnett, Correlli D.
THE DESERT GENERALS. London, Kimber, 1960. 320 p.

Other editions:
New York, Viking, 1961. 320 p.

London, Pan, 1962. 336 p.

1546 Bharucha, P. C.
THE NORTH AFRICAN CAMPAIGN, 1940-43. Edited by Bisheshwar Prasad. [Delhi?] Combined Inter-Services Historical Section (India and Pakistan), 1956. 567 p. (Official History of the Indian Armed Forces in the Second World War, 1939-45. Campaigns in the Western Theatre)

1547 Blamey, Arthur E. (Chooks Blamey, pseud.).
A COMPANY COMMANDER REMEMBERS, FROM EL YIBO TO EL ALAMEIN. [Pietermaritzburg?] 1963. 199 p.

1548 Braddock, David W.
THE CAMPAIGNS IN EGYPT AND LIBYA, 1940-1942. Foreword by N. H. Gibbs. Aldershot, Gale and Polden, 1964. 184 p.

1549 Buckley, Christopher.
FIVE VENTURES: IRAQ, SYRIA, PERSIA, MADAGASCAR, DODECANESE. London, H.M. Stationery Office, 1954. 257 p. (The Second World War, 1939-1945; A Popular Military History)

1550 Burman, Ben L.
THE GENERALS WEAR CORK HATS: AN AMAZING ADVENTURE THAT MADE WORLD HISTORY. New York, Taplinger, 1963. 257 p.

Other edition:
London, Harrap, 1965. 203 p.

1551 Carell, Paul.
THE FOXES OF THE DESERT. Translated from German by Mervyn Savill. London, Macdonald, 1960. 370 p.

Other editions:
New York, Dutton, 1961.

London, New English Library, 1961. 416 p. (Four Square Books)

1552 Carver, Michael.
EL ALAMEIN. London, Batsford; New York, Macmillan, 1962. 216 p. (British Battle Series)

1553 Carver, Michael.
TOBRUK. London, Batsford; Philadelphia, Dufour Editions, 1964. 271 p. (British Battle Series)

1554 Cody, Joseph F.
NEW ZEALAND ENGINEERS, MIDDLE EAST. Wellington, War History Branch, Dept. of Internal Affairs, 1961. 774 p. (Official History of New Zealand in the Second World War, 1939-45)

1555 Cowles, Virginia S.
THE PHANTOM MAJOR: THE STORY OF DAVID STIRLING AND THE S.A.S. REGIMENT. London, Collins; New York, Harper, 1958. 320 p.

Other edition:
London, Collins, 1960. 319 p. (Fontana Books)

Original title:
WHO DARES, WINS.

1556 Crichton-Stuart, Michael.
G PATROL. London, Kimber, 1958. 206 p.

1557 Crisp, Robert.
BRAZEN CHARIOTS: AN ACCOUNT OF TANK WARFARE IN THE WESTERN DESERT, NOVEMBER-DECEMBER, 1941. London, Muller, 1959. 223 p.

Other editions:
London, Transworld, 1960. 284 p.

New York, Norton, 1960.

1558 Croft-Cooke, Rupert.
THE BLOOD-RED ISLAND. London and New York, Staples, 1953. 248 p.

1559 Doody, John.
THE BURNING COAST. London, Joseph, 1955. 255 p.

1560 Ellsberg, Edward.
NO BANNERS, NO BUGLES. New York, Dodd, 1949. 370 p.

1561 Ellsberg, Edward.
UNDER THE RED SEA SUN. New York, Dodd, 1949. 500 p.

1562 Evans, Sir Geoffrey C.
THE DESERT AND THE JUNGLE. London, Kimber, 1959. 206 p.

1563 Gandar Dower, Kenneth C. (ed.).
ABYSSINIAN PATCHWORK: AN ANTHOLOGY. London, Muller, 1949. 289 p.

1564 Goodhart, David W.
WE OF THE TURNING TIDE. Adelaide, Preece, 1947. 260 p.

1565 Gosset, Renée P.
ALGIERS, 1941-1943: A TEMPORARY EXPEDIENT. Translated from French by Nancy Hecksher. London, Cape, 1945. 260 p.

1566 Gosset, Renée P.
CONSPIRACY IN ALGIERS, 1942-1943. Translated from French by Nancy Hecksher. New York, The Nation, 1945. 248 p.

1567 Great Britain. Central Office of Information.
PAIFORCE: THE OFFICIAL STORY OF THE PERSI AND IRAQ COMMAND, 1941-1946. London, H.M. Stationery Office, 1948. 137 p.

1568 Heckstall-Smith, Anthony.
TOBRUK. London, Blond, 1959. 255 p.

Other editions:
New York, Norton, 1960. 255 p.

London, Transworld, 1961. 282 p. (Corgi Books)

1569 Houart, Victor.
DESERT SQUADRON. Translated from French. London, Souvenir Press, 1959. 167 p.

Other edition:
London, Transworld 1960. 157 p. (Corgi Books)

1570 Howe, George F.
NORTHWEST AFRICA: SEIZING THE INITIATIVE IN THE WEST. Washington, Office of Chief of Military History, Dept. of Army, 1957. 748 p. (U.S. Army in World War II: The Mediterranean Theater of Operations)

1571 Hughes, Pennethorne.
WHILE SHEPHEARD'S WATCHED. London, Chatto and Windus, 1949. 207 p.

1572 Jackson, Henry C.
THE FIGHTING SUDANESE. Foreword by Sir William Platt. London, Macmillan; New York, St. Martin's Press, 1954. 84 p.

1573 Johnston, Denis.
NINE RIVERS FROM JORDAN: THE CHRONICLE OF A JOURNEY AND A SEARCH. London, Verschoyle, 1953. 458 p.

Other edition:
Boston, Little Brown, 1955. 496 p.

1574 Keogh, E. G.
MIDDLE EAST, 1939-1943. Melbourne, Wilke, 1959. 302 p.

1575 Laffin, John.
MIDDLE EAST JOURNEY. Sydney, Angus and Robertson, 1958. 193 p.

1576 Landsborough, Gordon.
TOBRUK COMMANDO. London, Cassell, 1956. 216 p.

Other edition:
London, Transworld, 1957. 256 p. (Corgi Books)

1577 Lloyd Owen, David.
THE DESERT MY DWELLING PLACE. Foreword by Sir Gerald Templer. London, Cassell, 1957. 271 p.

Other edition:
London, Hamilton, 1958. 224 p. (Panther Books)

1578 Long, Gavin M.
TO BENGHAZI. Canberra, Australian War Memorial, 1952. 336 p. (Australia in the War of 1939-1945. Series 1 [Army])

1579 Lugol, Jean.
EGYPT AND WORLD WAR II: THE ANTI-AXIS CAMPAIGNS IN THE MIDDLE EAST. Translated from French by A. G. Mitchell. Cairo, Société Orientale de Publicité, 1945. 402 p.

1580 MacDonald, John F.
ABYSSINIAN ADVENTURE. London, Cassell, 1957. 213 p.

1581 Majdalany, Fred.
THE BATTLE OF EL ALAMEIN: FORTRESS IN THE SAND. Philadelphia, Lippincott; London, Weidenfeld and Nicolson, 1965. 168 p. (Great Battles of History)

1582 Maugham, Robin.
COME TO DUST. London, Chapman and Hall, 1945. 191 p.

Other edition:
London, Transworld, 1957. (Corgi Books)

1583 Montgomery, Bernard L. Montgomery, 1st viscount.
EL ALAMEIN TO THE RIVER SANGRO. London, Hutchinson; New York, Dutton, 1948. 192 p.

Other edition:
London, Arrow Books, 1960. (Grey Arrow Books)

1584 Moorehead, Alan McC.
AFRICAN TRILOGY. London, Landsborough, 1959. 414 p. (Four Square Books)

Other editions:
London, Hamilton, 1965. 592 p.

    THE DESERT WAR. London, Hamilton, 1965. 250 p. (abridged ed.)

1585 Mosenson, Moshe.
    LETTERS FROM THE DESERT. Translated from Hebrew by Hilda Auerbach; edited with introduction by Shlomo Grodzensky. New York, Sharon Books, 1945. 222 p.

1586 Motter, Thomas H. V.
    THE PERSIAN CORRIDOR AND AID TO RUSSIA. Washington, Office of Chief of Military History, Dept. of Army, 1952. 545 p. (U.S. Army in World War II: The Middle East Theater)

1587 Murphy, W. E.
    THE RELIEF OF TOBRUK. Wellington, War History Branch, Dept. of Internal Affairs, 1961. 566 p. (Official History of New Zealand in the Second World War, 1939-45)

1588 Onslow, William A. B. Onslow, 6th earl of.
    MEN AND SAND. Foreword by General Sir H. L. McCreery. London, Saint Catherine Press, 1961. 140 p.

1589 Pal, Dharm.
    CAMPAIGN IN WESTERN ASIA. Edited by Bisheshwar Prasad. New Delhi, Combined Inter-services Historical Section. (India and Pakistan), 1957. 570 p. (Official History of the Indian Armed Forces in the Second World War, 1939-45. Campaigns in the Western Theatre)

1590 Phillips, Cecil E. L.
    ALAMEIN. London, Heinemann, 1962. 434 p.

Other editions:
Boston, Little, Brown, 1963. 434 p. (Atlantic Monthly Press Book)

London, Pan, 1965. 350 p.

1591 Potts, Charles.
    SOLDIERS IN THE SAND. London, P.R.M. Publishers, 1962. 201 p.

1592 Rabinowitz, Louis I.
    SOLDIERS FROM JUDEA: PALESTINIAN JEWISH UNITS IN THE MIDDLE EAST, 1941-1943. London, Gollancz, 1944. 79 p.

Other edition:
New York, American Zionist Emergency Council, 1945. 84 p.

1593 Rainier, Peter W.
    PIPELINE TO BATTLE. London, Hamilton, 1955. 192 p. (Panther Books)

1594 Ritchie, Lewis A. da Costa (Bartimus, pseud.).
    THE TURN OF THE ROAD: BEING THE STORY OF THE PART PLAYED BY THE ROYAL NAVY AND MERCHANT NAVY IN THE LANDINGS IN ALGERIA AND FRENCH MOROCCO OF COMBINED BRITISH AND UNITED STATES FORCES ON 8TH NOVEMBER 1942, AND THE FINAL DESTRUCTION OF THE AXIS FORCES IN NORTH AFRICA. London, Chatto and Windus, 1946. 122 p.

1595 Saber, Clifford.
    DESERT RAT SKETCH BOOK. Forewords by Tom Lea and Stephen Galatti. New York, Sketchbook Press, 1959. 187 p.

1596 Sayre, Joel.
    PERSIAN GULF COMMAND: SOME MARVELS ON THE ROAD TO KAZVIN. New York, Random House, 1945. 140 p.

1597 Schmidt, Heinz W.
    WITH ROMMEL IN THE DESERT. London, Harrap, 1951. 240 p.

Other edition:
London, Hamilton, 1955. (Panther Books)

1598 Scoullar, J. L.
    BATTLE FOR EGYPT, THE SUMMER OF 1942. Wellington, War History Branch, Dept. of Internal Affairs, 1955. 400 p. (Official History of New Zealand in the Second World War, 1939-45)

1599 Shaw, William B. K.
    LONG RANGE DESERT GROUP, THE STORY OF ITS WORK IN LIBYA 1940-1943. London, Collins, 1945. 256 p.

Other edition:
London, Landsborough, 1959. 192 p. (Four Square Books)

1600 Simpson, Evan J. (Evan John, pseud.).
    TIME IN THE EAST: AN ENTERTAINMENT. London and Toronto, Heinemann, 1946. 230 p.

1601 Skrine, Clarmont P.
    WORLD WAR IN IRAN. London, Constable, 1962. 267 p.

1602 South Africa. Prime Minister's Dept. Union War Histories Section.
    THE SIDI REZEG BATTLES, 1941. Edited by J.A.I. Agar-Hamilton and L.C.F. Turner. Capetown and New York, Oxford University Press, 1957. 506 p.

1603 Stark, Freya.
    EAST IS WEST. London, Murray, 1945. 218 p.

1604 Stevens, William G.
    BARDIA TO ENFIDAVILLE. Wellington, War History Branch, Dept. of Internal Affairs, 1962. 416 p. (Official History of New Zealand in the Second World War, 1939-45)

1605 Strathern, Robert F.
    LEST I FORGET: BEING THE RECORD OF A TOUR THROUGH NORTHERN AFRICA AND PART OF THE MIDDLE EAST. Durban, Church, 1947. 120 p.

1606 Thomas, Robert C. W.
    THE BATTLES OF ALAM HALFA AND EL ALAMEIN. London, Clowes, 1952. 56 p.

1607 Tunnell, James M.
MILITARY INSTALLATIONS IN NORTH AFRICA AND THE MIDDLE EAST. Washington, U.S. Government Printing Office, 1945. 66 p.

1608 U.S. Military Academy, West Point. Dept. of Military Art and Engineering.
THE WAR IN NORTH AFRICA. West Point, N.Y., 1945. 2 pts.

Other edition:
1951.

1609 U.S. War Department. General Staff.
TO BIZERTE WITH THE II CORPS, 23 APRIL 1943-13 MAY 1943. Washington, 1946. 80 p. (American Forces in Action)

1610 Walker, K. A.
MONTGOMERY'S SAND BLAST. Cairo, Schindler, 1945. 111 p.

1611 Willison, Arthur C.
THE RELIEF OF TOBRUK: A TRIBUTE TO THE BRITISH SOLDIER. Parracombe, Eng., Willison, 1951. 52 p.

1612 Woollcombe, Robert.
THE CAMPAIGNS OF WAVELL, 1939-1943. Foreword by Field-Marshal Viscount Alanbrooke of Brookeborough. London, Cassell, 1959. 227 p.

1613 Yeats-Brown, Francis C. C.
MARTIAL INDIA. London, Eyre and Spottiswoode, 1945. 200 p.

1614 Yindrich, Jan H.
FORTRESS TOBRUK. Foreword by H. L. Birks; epilogue by Hans von Ravenstein. London, Benn, 1951. 214 p.

Other edition:
London, Hamilton, 1956. 160 p. (Panther Books)

1615 Yunnie, Park.
WARRIORS ON WHEELS. London, Hutchinson, 1959. 383 p.

Other edition:
London, Arrow, 1961. 384 p.

f. The Balkans

1616 Agrafiotis, Cris J. (comp.).
WAS CHURCHILL RIGHT IN GREECE? Manchester, N.H., Granite, 1945. 152 p.

1617 Buckley, Christopher.
GREECE AND CRETE, 1941. London, H.M. Stationery Office, 1952. 311 p. (The Second World War, 1939-1945: A Popular Military History)

1618 Crisp, Robert.
THE GODS WERE NEUTRAL. London, Muller, 1960. 220 p.

Other edition:
New York, Norton, 1961.

1619 Davies, Edmund F. ("Trotsky" Davies, pseud.).
ILLYRIAN VENTURE: THE STORY OF THE BRITISH MILITARY MISSION TO ENEMY-OCCUPIED ALBANIA. London, Bodley Head, 1952. 246 p.

1620 Demetriades, Phokion.
SHADOW OVER ATHENS. New York and Toronto, Rinehart, 1946. 155 p.

1621 GERMAN ANTIGUERRILLA OPERATIONS IN THE BALKANS, 1941-1944: HISTORICAL STUDY. Washington, Dept. of Army. 1954. 82 p. (German Report Series)

1622 THE GERMAN CAMPAIGNS IN THE BALKANS; SPRING, 1941; HISTORICAL STUDY. Washington, Dept. of Army, 1953. 161 p. (German Report Series)

1623 Hamson, Denys.
WE FELL AMONG GREEKS. London, Cape, 1947. 221 p.

1624 Heckstall-Smith, Anthony, and H. T. Baillie-Grohman.
GREEK TRAGEDY, 1941. New York, Norton, 1961. 238 p. (Norton Books on Modern Warfare)

Other edition:
London, Blond, 1961. 240 p.

1625 Howell, Edward.
ESCAPE TO LIVE. London and New York, Longmans Green 1947. 230 p.

Other edition:
1952. 178 p.

1626 Long, Gavin M.
GREECE, CRETE, AND SYRIA. Canberra, Australian War Memorial, 1953. 587 p. (Australia in the War of 1939-1945. Series 1 [Army])

1627 McClymont, W. G.
TO GREECE. Wellington, War History Branch, Dept. of Internal Affairs, 1959. 538 p. (Official History of New Zealand in the Second World War, 1939-45)

1628 Papagos, Alexandros.
THE BATTLE OF GREECE, 1940-1941. Translated by Pat. Eliascos. Athens, Scazikis, 1949. 406 p.

1629 Psychoundakis, George.
THE CRETAN RUNNER: HIS STORY OF THE GERMAN OCCUPATION. Translated with introduction by Patrick L. Fermor; annotated by the translator and Xan Fielding. London, Murray, 1955. 242 p.

Other edition:
London, Hamilton, 1957. 160 p. (Panther Books)

1630 Reid, Francis.
I WAS IN NOAH'S ARK. London, Chambers, 1957. 143 p.

Other edition:
    RESISTANCE FIGHTER. London, Brown, 1961. 156 p. (Digit Books)

1631 St. John, Robert.
    FROM THE LAND OF SILENT PEOPLE. London, Hamilton, 1955. 318 p. (Panther Books)

1632 Thomas, Walter B.
    DARE TO BE FREE. London, Wingate, 1952. 256 p.

1633 Wheeler, Charles M.
    KALIMERA, KIWI, TO OLYMPUS WITH THE NEW ZEALAND ENGINEERS. Wellington, Reed, 1946. 203 p.

g. German-Russian

1634 Allen, William E. D., and Paul Maratoff.
    THE RUSSIAN CAMPAIGNS OF 1944-45. Harmondsworth, Eng., and New York, Penguin Books, 1946. 332 p.

1635 Anders, Wladyslaw.
    HITLER'S DEFEAT IN RUSSIA. Foreword by Truman Smith. Chicago, Regnery, 1953. 267 p.

1636 Arbing, Børge W. (Sven Hassel, pseud.).
    THE LEGION OF THE DAMNED. Translated from Danish by Maurice Michael. London, Allen and Unwin, 1957. 298 p.

Other edition:
London, Pan Books, 1959. 250 p.

1637 Arbing, Børge W. (Sven Hassel, pseud.).
    WHEELS OF TERROR. Translated from Danish by I. O'Hanlon. London, Souvenir Press, 1960. 278 p.

Other edition:
London, Transworld, 1961. 351 p. (Corgi Books)

1638 Baurdzham, Momysh-Uly.
    VOLOKOLANISH HIGHWAY. Translated from Russian. Moscow, Foreign Languages Publishing House, 195-?. 329 p.

1639 Blau, George E.
    THE GERMAN CAMPAIGN IN RUSSIA: PLANNING AND OPERATIONS, 1940-1942. Washington, Dept. of Army, 1955. 187 p. (U.S. Dept. of Army Pamphlet)

1640 Bongartz, Heinz.
    FLIGHT IN WINTER: RUSSIA CONQUERS, JANUARY TO MAY, 1945. Edited and translated by Fred Wieck. New York, Pantheon, 1951. 318 p.

1641 Carell, Paul.
    HITLER'S WAR ON RUSSIA: THE STORY OF THE GERMAN DEFEAT IN THE EAST. Translated from German by Ewald Osers. London, Harrap, 1964. 640 p.

Other edition:
HITLER MOVES EAST, 1941-1943. Boston, Little, Brown, 1965. 640 p.

1642 Chuikov, Vasilii I.
    THE BEGINNING OF THE ROAD. Translated from Russian by Harold Silver. London, MacGibbon and Kee, 1963. 388 p.

Other edition:
    THE BATTLE FOR STALINGRAD. New York, Holt, Rinehart and Winston, 1964. 364 p.

1643 Clark, Alan.
    BARBAROSSA: THE RUSSIAN-GERMAN CONFLICT, 1941-45. New York, Morrow, 1965. 522 p.

Other edition:
London, Hutchinson, 1965. 444 p.

1644 Devilliers, Catherine.
    LIEUTENANT KATIA. Translated from French by Charlotte Haldane. London, Constable, 1964. 256 p.

1645 Dibold, Hans.
    DOCTOR AT STALINGRAD: THE PASSION OF A CAPTIVITY. Translated from German by H. C. Stevens. London, Hutchinson, 1958. 190 p.

1646   EFFECTS OF CLIMATE ON COMBAT IN EUROPEAN RUSSIA. Washington, Dept. of Army, 1952. 81 p. (German Report Series)

1647 Ehrenburg, Il'ia G.
    THE WAR: 1941-1945. Translated by Tatiana Shebunina, with Yvonne Kapp. Cleveland, World Publishing Co., 1964. 198 p.

1648 Fadeev, Aleksandr A.
    LENINGRAD IN THE DAYS OF THE BLOCKADE. Translated from Russian by R. D. Charques. London and New York, Hutchinson, 1946. 104 p.

1649 Fernau, Joachim.
    CAPTAIN PAX: A REPORT ON THE TERRIBLENESS AND GREATNESS OF MEN. Translated from German by Robert Kee. London, Constable, 1960. 134 p.

1650   GERMAN DEFENSE TACTICS AGAINST RUSSIAN BREAK-THROUGHS: HISTORICAL STUDY. Washington, Dept. of Army, 1951. 80 p. (German Report Series)

1651 Gouré, Leon, and Herbert S. Dinerstein.
    POLITICAL VULNERABILITY OF MOSCOW, A CASE STUDY OF THE OCTOBER 1941 ATTACK. Santa Monica, Calif., Rand Corp., 1952. 131 l. (Project Rand Research Memorandum)

1652 Gouré, Leon.
    THE SIEGE OF LENINGRAD. Stanford, Calif., Stanford University Press, 1962. 363 p.

1653 Gouré, Leon.
    SOVIET ADMINISTRATIVE CONTROLS DURING THE SIEGE OF LENINGRAD. Santa Monica, Calif., Rand Corp., 1957. 73 p.

1654 Grossman, Vasilii S.
WITH THE RED ARMY IN POLAND AND BYELORUSSIA. Translated from Russian by Helen Altschuler. London, Hutchinson, 1945. 52 p.

1655 Guillaume, Augustin L.
SOVIET ARMS AND SOVIET POWER, THE SECRETS OF RUSSIA'S MIGHT. Washington, Infantry Journal Press, 1949. 212 p.

1656 Haape, Heinrich, with Dennis Henshaw.
MOSCOW TRAM STOP: A DOCTOR'S EXPERIENCES WITH THE GERMAN SPEARHEAD IN RUSSIA. London, Collins, 1957. 384 p.

Other edition:
London, Hamilton, 1959. 320 p. (Panther Books)

1657 Heisler, J. B.
RUSSIA'S FIGHTING MEN. London, New Europe, 1945. 95 p.

1658 Kernmayr, Erich (Erich Kern, pseud.).
DANCE OF DEATH. Translated by Paul Findlay, London, Collins; New York, Scribner, 1951. 255 p.

1659 Kournakoff, Sergei N.
WHAT RUSSIA DID FOR VICTORY. New York, New Century Publishers, 1945. 63 p.

1660 Kovpak, Sydir A.
OUR PARTISAN COURSE. Translated from Russian by Ernst and Mira Lesser. London and New York, Hutchinson, 1947. 126 p.

1661 Kriger, Evgenii G.
FROM MOSCOW TO THE PRUSSIAN FRONTIER. London and New York, Hutchinson, 1945. 136 p.

1662 Krylov, Ivan N. (pseud.).
SOVIET STAFF OFFICER. Translated by Edward Fitzgerald. London, Falcon Press; New York, Philosophical Library, 1951. 298 p.

1663 LAST LETTERS FROM STALINGRAD. Translated from German by John E. Vetter. McLean, Va., Coronet Press, 1955. 60 p.

Other editions:
London, Methuen, 1956. 70 p.

New York, Morrow, 1962. 127 p.

1664 LETTERS FROM THE DEAD: LAST LETTERS FROM SOVIET MEN AND WOMEN WHO DIED FIGHTING THE NAZIS 1941-1945. Moscow, Progress Publishers, 1965. 236 p.

1665 Malaparte, Curzio (pseud.).
THE VOLGA RISES IN EUROPE. Translated from Italian by David Moore. London, Redman, 1957. 281 p.

1666 MEN OF THE STALIN BREED: TRUE STORIES OF THE SOVIET YOUTH IN THE GREAT PATRIOTIC WAR. Moscow, Foreign Languages Publishing House, 1945. 186 p.

1667 MILITARY IMPROVISATIONS DURING RUSSIAN CAMPAIGN: HISTORICAL STUDY. Washington, Dept. of Army, 1951. 110 p. (German Report Series)

1668 Neumann, Peter.
OTHER MEN'S GRAVES. Translated from French by Constantine FitzGibbon. London, Weidenfeld and Nicolson, 1958. 286 p.

Other editions:
London, World Distributors, 1959.

London, World, 1965. (Consul Books)

1669 OPERATIONS OF ENCIRCLED FORCES: GERMAN EXPERIENCES IN RUSSIA; HISTORICAL STUDY. Washington, Dept. of Army, 1952. 74 p. (German Report Series)

1670 Pabst, Helmut.
THE OUTERMOST FRONTIER: A GERMAN SOLDIER IN THE RUSSIAN CAMPAIGN. Translated from German by Andrew and Eva Wilson. London, Kimber, 1957. 204 p.

1671 Pavlov, Dimitrii V.
LENINGRAD 1941, THE BLOCKADE. Translated by John C. Adams; foreword by Harrison E. Salisbury. Chicago, University of Chicago Press, 1965. 186 p.

1672 Polevoi, Boris N.
FROM BELGOROD TO THE CARPATHIANS, FROM A SOVIET WAR CORRESPONDENT'S NOTEBOOK. London and New York, Hutchinson, 1945. 164 p.

1673 Polevoi, Boris N.
WE ARE SOVIET PEOPLE: SHORT STORIES. Moscow, Foreign Languages Publishing House, 1949. 589 p. (Library of Selected Soviet Literature)

1674 Rigoni Stern, Mario.
THE SERGEANT IN THE SNOW. Translated by Archibald Colquhoun. London, MacGibbon and Kee, 1954. 158 p.

1675 THE ROAD OF BATTLE AND GLORY. Compiled by I. Danishevsky; translated from Russian by David Skvirsky. Moscow, Foreign Languages Publishing House, 1964. 306 p.

1676 RUSSIAN COMBAT METHODS IN WORLD WAR II: HISTORICAL STUDY. Washington, Dept. of Army, 1950. 116 p. (German Report Series)

1677 Schröter, Heinz.
STALINGRAD. Translated from German by Constantine FitzGibbon. London, Joseph; New York, Dutton, 1958. 263 p.

Other edition:
London, Pan Books, 1960. 317 p.

1678 Seth, Ronald S.
OPERATION BARBAROSSA; THE BATTLE FOR MOSCOW. London, Blond, 1964. 191 p.

Other edition:
London, World, 1965.

1679 Seth, Ronald S.
STALINGRAD--POINT OF RETURN: THE STORY OF THE BATTLE, AUGUST 1942-FEBRUARY 1943. London, Gollancz; New York, Coward-McCann, 1959. 254 p.

1680 SMALL UNIT ACTIONS DURING THE GERMAN CAMPAIGN IN RUSSIA: HISTORICAL STUDY. Washington, Dept. of Army, 1953. 289 p. (German Report Series)

1681 Smirnov, Sergei S.
HEROES OF BREST FORTRESS. Translated by R. Daglish. Moscow, Foreign Languages Publishing House, 1957. 211 p.

1682 TERRAIN FACTORS IN THE RUSSIAN CAMPAIGN. Washington, Office of Chief of Military History, Dept. of Army, 1950. 104 p. (German Report Series)

1683 Thorwald, Jürgen.
FLIGHT IN THE WINTER: RUSSIA CONQUERS, JANUARY TO MAY 1945. Edited and translated by Fred Wieck. New York, Pantheon, 1951. 318 p.

Other edition:
London, Hutchinson, 1953. 255 p.

1684 TRUE TO TYPE: A SELECTION FROM LETTERS AND DIARIES OF GERMAN SOLDIERS AND CIVILIANS, COLLECTED ON THE SOVIET-GERMAN FRONT. London and New York, Hutchinson, 1945. 160 p.

1685 U.S. Military Academy, West Point. Dept. of Military Art and Engineering.
OPERATIONS OF THE RUSSIAN FRONT. West Point, N.Y., 1945-46. 3 v. in 1.

1686 Virski, Fred.
MY LIFE IN THE RED ARMY. New York, Macmillan, 1949. 260 p.

1687 Werth, Alexander.
THE YEAR OF STALINGRAD: AN HISTORICAL RECORD AND A STUDY OF RUSSIAN MENTALITY, METHODS, AND POLICIES. London, Hamilton, 1946. 478 p.

Other edition:
New York, Knopf, 1947. 475 p.

1688 Zieser, Benno.
IN THEIR SHALLOW GRAVES. Translated from German by Alec Brown. London, Elek Books, 1956. 208 p.

Other edition:
London, World, 1957. 255 p. (Viking Books)

1689 Zieser, Benno.
THE ROAD TO STALINGRAD. Translated from German by Alec Brown. London, Elek Books, 1956. 208 p.

Other edition:
New York, Ballantine Books, 1956. 152 p.

h. European Theater, 1941-45

1690 Allied Forces.
FINITO! THE PO VALLEY CAMPAIGN, 1945, HEADQUARTERS, 15TH ARMY GROUP, ITALY. Milano, Rizzola, 1945. 62 p.

1691 Allied Forces. Mediterranean Theatre.
REPORT BY THE SUPREME ALLIED COMMANDER, MEDITERRANEAN, FIELD-MARSHAL THE VISCOUNT ALEXANDER OF TUNIS, TO THE COMBINED CHIEFS OF STAFF ON THE ITALIAN CAMPAIGN, 12TH DECEMBER 1944 TO 2ND MAY 1945. London, H.M. Stationery Office, 1951. 66 p.

1692 Allied Forces. Mediterranean Theatre.
REPORT BY THE SUPREME ALLIED COMMANDER, MEDITERRANEAN, TO THE COMBINED CHIEFS OF STAFF ON THE ITALIAN CAMPAIGN. London, H.M. Stationery Office, 1946-48. 2 v.

1693 Allied Forces. Supreme Headquarters.
REPORT BY THE SUPREME COMMANDER TO THE COMBINED CHIEFS OF STAFF ON THE OPERATIONS IN EUROPE OF THE ALLIED EXPEDITIONARY FORCE, 6 JUNE 1944 TO 8 MAY 1945. Washington, U.S. Government Printing Office, 1946. 123 p.

1694 Allied Forces. Supreme Headquarters. Mission to Norway.
THE ALLIES IN NORWAY. Oslo, Tanum, 1946. (unpaged)

1695 Angier, John C.
MOS 1542: A DRAMATIC TRUE STORY OF COMBAT IN WORLD WAR TWO. New York, Greenwich Book Publishers, 1959. 59 p.

1696 Aron, Robert.
DE GAULLE TRIUMPHANT: THE LIBERATION OF FRANCE, AUGUST 1944-MAY 1945. Translated by Humphrey Hare. London, Putnam, 1964. 360 p.

1697 Atwell, Lester.
PRIVATE. New York, Simon and Schuster, 1958. 499 p.

Other edition:
London, Transworld, 1961. 444 p. (Corgi Books)

1698 Aurén, Sven A. G.
THE TRICOLOUR FLIES AGAIN. Translated by Evelyn Ramsden. London, Hammond and Hammond, 1946. 200 p.

1699 Austin, Alexander B.
WE LANDED AT DAWN. London, Brown, Watson, 1958. 158 p. (Digit Books)

Original edition:
London, Gollancz; New York, Harcourt, Brace, 1943. 217 p.

1700 Bagnall, Stephen.
THE ATTACK. London, Hamilton, 1947. 200 p.

1701 Baker, Peter.
CONFESSION OF FAITH. London, Falcon, 1946, 233 p.

1702 Baker, Richard B.
  THE YEAR OF THE BUZZ BOMB: A JOURNAL OF LONDON, 1944. New York, Exposition Press, 1952. 118 p.

1703 Ball, Edmund F.
  STAFF OFFICER WITH THE FIFTH ARMY: SICILY, SALERNO AND ANZIO. Foreword by General Mark W. Clark. New York, Exposition Press, 1958. 365 p.

1704 Belfield, Eversley M. G., and Hubert Essame.
  THE BATTLE FOR NORMANDY. London, Batsford; Philadelphia, Dufour Editions, 1965. 239 p.

1705 Bellini delle Stelle, Pier L., and Urbano Lazzaro.
  DONGO, THE LAST ACT. Translated by W. C. Darwell. London, Macdonald, 1964. 187 p.

1706 Berlin, Sven.
  I AM LAZARUS. London, Galley Press; New York, Norton, 1961. 209 p.

1707 Bernstein, Walter S.
  KEEP YOUR HEAD DOWN. New York, Viking, 1945. 243 p.

1708 Blumenson, Martin.
  ANZIO: THE GAMBLE THAT FAILED. London, Weidenfeld and Nicolson, 1963. 204 p. (Great Battles of History Series)

  Other edition:
  Philadelphia, Lippincott, 1963. 212 p. (Great Battles of History).

1709 Blumenson, Martin.
  BREAKOUT AND PURSUIT. Washington, Office of Chief of Military History, Dept. of Army, 1961. 748 p. (U.S. Army in World War II: The European Theater of Operations).

1710 Blumenson, Martin.
  THE DUEL FOR FRANCE, 1944. Boston, Houghton Mifflin, 1963. 422 p.

1711 Boesch, Paul.
  ROAD TO HUERTGEN: FOREST IN HELL. Houston, Gulf, 1962. 254 p.

1712 Bohmler, Rudolf.
  MONTE CASSINO. Translated from German by Lt.-Col. R. H. Stevens. London, Cassell, 1964. 314 p.

1713 Bond, Harold L.
  RETURN TO CASSINO: A MEMOIR OF THE FIGHT FOR ROME. London, Dent; Garden City, N.Y., Doubleday, 1964. 208 p.

1714 Boussel, Patrice.
  D-DAY BEACHES POCKET GUIDE. London, Macdonald, 1965. 222 p.

  Other edition:
  Garden City, N.Y., Doubleday, 1966. 218 p.

1715 Briggs, Richard A.
  THE BATTLE OF THE RUHR POCKET: A COMBAT NARRATIVE. West Point, Ky., Tioga Book Press, 1957. 84 p.

1716 Bryant, Sir Arthur.
  TRIUMPH IN THE WEST, 1943-1946: BASED ON DIARIES AND AUTOBIOGRAPHICAL NOTES OF FIELD-MARSHAL THE VISCOUNT ALANBROOKE. London, Collins, 1959. 576 p.

  Other editions:
  Garden City, N.Y., Doubleday. 438 p.

  London, Collins, 1965. 447 p. (Fontana Books)

1717 Buckley, Christopher.
  ROAD TO ROME. London, Hodder and Stoughton, 1945. 333 p.

1718 Callison, Talmadge P.
  HIT THE SILK! New York, Comet, 1954. 91 p.

1719 Capa, Robert.
  SLIGHTLY OUT OF FOCUS. New York, Holt, 1947. 243 p.

1720 Carell, Paul.
  INVASION--THEY'RE COMING! THE GERMAN ACCOUNT OF THE ALLIED LANDINGS AND THE 80 DAYS' BATTLE FOR FRANCE. Translated from German by E. Osers. London, Harrap, 1962. 288 p.

  Other editions:
  New York, Dutton, 1963.

  London, Transworld, 1963. 317 p. (Corgi Books)

1721 Carlisle, John M.
  RED ARROW MEN: STORIES ABOUT THE 32ND DIVISION ON THE VILLA VERDE. Detroit, Powers, 1946. 215 p.

1722 Carpenter, Iris.
  NO WOMAN'S WORLD. Boston, Houghton Mifflin, 1946. 338 p.

1723 Caverhill, William M. (Alan Melville, pseud.).
  FIRST TIDE: "D" DAY INVASION, JUNE 6TH, 1944. London, Skeffington, 1945. 140 p.

1724 Celt, Marek.
  BY PARACHUTE TO WARSAW. London, Crisp, 1945. 88 p.

1725 Codman, Charles R.
  DRIVE. Boston, Little, Brown, 1957. 335 p.

1726 Cole, Hugh M.
  THE ARDENNES: BATTLE OF THE BULGE. Washington, Office of Chief of Military History, Dept. of Army, 1965. 720 p. (U.S. Army in World War II: The European Theater of Operations)

1727 Cole, Hugh M.
THE LORRAINE CAMPAIGN. Washington, Historical Division, Dept. of Army, 1950. 657 p. (U.S. Army in World War II: The European Theater of Operations)

1728 Collier, Basil.
THE BATTLE OF THE V-WEAPONS, 1944-45. London, Hodder and Stoughton, 1964. 191 p.

Other edition:
New York, Morrow, 1965. 191 p.

1729 Collins, Larry, and Dominique Lapierre.
IS PARIS BURNING? New York, Simon and Schuster; London, Gollancz, 1965. 376 p.

1730 Columbia Broadcasting System.
FROM D-DAY THROUGH VICTORY IN EUROPE: THE EYE-WITNESS STORY AS TOLD BY WAR CORRESPONDENTS ON THE AIR. New York, Columbia Broadcasting System, 1945. 314 p.

1731 Connell, Charles.
MONTE CASSINO, THE HISTORIC BATTLE. London, Elek, 1963. 206 p.

1732 Cooper, John St. J.
INVASION! THE D-DAY STORY, JUNE 6, 1944. London, Beaverbrook, 1954. 122 p.

1733 Cox, Geoffrey.
THE ROAD TO TRIESTE. London, Heinemann, 1947. 249 p.

1734 Cras, Hervé (Jacques Mordal, pseud.).
DIEPPE: THE DAWN OF DECISION. Translated by Mervyn Savill. London, Souvenir Press, 1963. 285 p.

Other edition:
London, Hamilton, 1964. 288 p. (Panther Books)

1735 Dalgleish, John.
WE PLANNED THE SECOND FRONT. London, Gollancz, 1945. 108 p.

1736 Darby, Hugh, and Marcus F. Cunliffe.
A SHORT STORY OF 21 ARMY GROUP: THE BRITISH AND CANADIAN ARMIES IN THE CAMPAIGNS IN NORTH-WEST EUROPE, 1944-1945. Aldershot, Gale and Polden, 1949. 147 p.

1737 D'Arcy-Dawson, John.
EUROPEAN VICTORY. London, Macdonald, 1945. 299 p.

1738 Davis, Franklin M.
BREAKTHROUGH: THE EPIC STORY OF THE BATTLE OF THE BULGE. Derby, Conn., Monarch Books, 1961. 159 p.

1739 Dupuy, Richard E., and Herbert L. Bregstein (comps.).
SOLDIER'S ALBUM. Boston, Houghton Mifflin, 1946. 173 p.

1740 Edwards, Kenneth.
OPERATION NEPTUNE. London, Collins, 1946. 319 p.

1741 Ellis, Lionel F., and others.
VICTORY IN THE WEST. London, H.M. Stationery Office, 1962-. 1 v. published. (History of the Second World War: United Kingdom Military Series)

1742 Ellsberg, Edward.
THE FAR SHORE. London, Gibbs and Phillips, 1961. 381 p.

Other edition:
London, Hamilton, 1964. 318 p. (Panther Books)

1743 Essame, Hubert, and Eversley M. G. Belfield.
THE NORTH-WEST EUROPE CAMPAIGN, 1944-1945. Foreword by Michael Howard. Aldershot, Gale and Polden, 1962. 111 p.

1744 Farran, Roy A.
OPERATION TOMBOLA. London, Collins, 1960. 256 p.

Other edition:
London, New English Library, 1964. 191 p. (Four Square Books)

1745 Fehrenbach, T. R.
THE BATTLE OF ANZIO: THE DRAMATIC STORY OF ONE OF THE MAJOR ENGAGEMENTS OF WORLD WAR II. Foreword by William H Simpson. Derby, Conn., Monarch Books, 1962. 160 p. (Monarch Americana Series)

1746 Florentin, Eddy.
BATTLE OF THE FALAISE GAP. Translated from French by Mervyn Savill. London, Elek, 1965. 336 p.

1747 Foley, Cedric J.
MAILED FIST. London, Hamilton, 1957. 190 p. (Panther Books)

1748 Galantai, Maria.
THE CHANGING OF THE GUARD: THE SIEGE OF BUDAPEST, 1944-45. London, Pall Mall Press, 1961. 224 p.

1749 Gallagher, Richard.
THE MALMEDY MASSACRE. New York, Paperback Library, 1964. 158 p.

1750 Gibson, Ronald.
NINE DAYS, 17TH TO 25TH SEPTEMBER, 1944. Ilfracombe, Eng., Stockwell, 1956. 95 p.

Other edition:
CLOUD OVER ARNHEM. London, Wingate, 1959. 63 p.

1751 Giles, Henry E.
THE G.I. JOURNAL OF SERGEANT GILES. Compiled and edited by Janice Holt Giles. Boston, Houghton Mifflin, 1965. 399 p.

1752 Graves, Charles.
PRIDE OF THE MORNING. London and New York, Hutchinson, 1945. 182 p.

1753 Hagen, Louis E.
ARNHEM LIFT: DIARY OF A GLIDER PILOT. London, Pilot Press; New York and Toronto, Farrar and Rinehart, 1945. 96 p.

Other edition:
London, Hammond and Hammond, 1953. 119 p.

1754 Hammond, Ralph C.
MY GI ACHING BACK. New York, Hobson Book Press, 1946. 169 p.

1755 Harr, Bill.
COMBAT BOOTS: TALES OF FIGHTING MEN, INCLUDING THE ANZIO DERBY. New York, Exposition Press, 1952. 232 p.

1756 Harrison, Gordon A.
CROSS-CHANNEL ATTACK. Washington, Office of Chief of Military History, Dept. of Army, 1951. 519 p. (U.S. Army in World War II: The European Theater of Operations)

1757 Harrison, Michael.
MULBERRY: THE RETURN IN TRIUMPH. London, Allen, 1965. 286 p.

1758 Hawkins, Desmond (ed.).
WAR REPORT: A RECORD OF DISPATCHES BROADCAST BY THE BBC'S WAR CORRESPONDENTS WITH THE ALLIED EXPEDITIONARY FORCE, 6 JUNE 1944 - 5 MAY 1945. London and New York, Oxford University Press, 1946. 452 p.

1759 Heaps, Leo.
ESCAPE FROM ARNHEM: A CANADIAN AMONG THE LOST PARATROOPS. Toronto, Macmillan of Canada, 1945. 159 p.

1760 Hechler, Kenneth W.
THE BRIDGE AT REMAGEN. Foreword by S. L. A. Marshall. New York, Ballantine Books, 1957. 238 p.

Other edition:
London, Hamilton, 1961. 172 p. (Panther Books)

1761 Henn, Peter.
THE LAST BATTLE. Translated from German by Mervyn Savill; introduction by Jules Roy. London, Kimber, 1954. 214 p.

1762 Hibbert, Christopher.
THE BATTLE OF ARNHEM. London, Batsford; New York, Macmillan, 1962. 224 p. (British Battles Series)

1763 Hine, Al.
D-DAY: THE INVASION OF EUROPE. Consultant: S. L. A. Marshall. New York, American Heritage Publishing Co.; book trade distribution by Meredith Press; institutional distribution by Harper and Roy, 1962. 153 p. (American Heritage Junior Library)

1764 Hobbs, Leslie.
KIWI DOWN THE STRADA. Christchurch, Whitcombe and Tombs, 1963. 122 p.

1765 Horst, Kate A.
CLOUD OVER ARNHEM: SEPTEMBER 17TH-26TH 1944. London, Wingate, 1959. 63 p.

1766 Howarth, David A.
D-DAY, THE SIXTH OF JUNE, 1944. New York, McGraw-Hill; London, Collins, 1959. 255 p.

Other edition:
London, Collins, 1961. 256 p. (Fontana Books)

1767 Hugill, J. A. C.
THE HAZARD MESH. London and New York, Hurst and Blackett, 1946. 128 p.

1768 Hunter, Kenneth E.
THE WAR AGAINST GERMANY: EUROPE AND ADJACENT AREAS. Washington, Office of Chief of Military History, Dept. of Army, 1951. 448 p. (U.S. Army in World War II: Pictorial Record)

1769 Huston, James A.
ACROSS THE FACE OF FRANCE: LIBERATION AND RECOVERY 1944-63. West Lafayette, Ind., Purdue University Studies, 1963. 251 p.

1770 Ingersoll, Ralph McA.
TOP SECRET. New York, Harcourt, Brace; London, Partridge Publications, 1946. 343 p.

1771 Irgang, Frank J.
ETCHED IN PURPLE. Caldwell, Idaho, Caxton Printers, 1949. 241 p.

1772 Johns, Glover S.
THE CLAY PIGEONS OF ST. LO. Harrisburg, Pa., Military Service Publishing Co., 1958. 257 p.

Other edition:
London, Hamilton, 1959. 224 p. (Panther Books)

1773 Liebling, Abbott J.
NORMANDY REVISITED. New York, Simon and Schuster, 1958. 243 p.

Other edition:
London, Gollancz, 1959.

1774 Linklater, Eric R. R.
THE CAMPAIGN IN ITALY. London, H.M. Stationery Office, 1951. 480 p. (Second World War, 1939-1945, Series)

2d impression:
1959.

1775 Lyon, Allan.
TOWARD AN UNKNOWN STATION. New York, Macmillan, 1948. 286 p.

1776 McCallum, Neil.
　　　JOURNEY WITH A PISTOL. London, Gollancz, 1959. 160 p.
　　Other edition:
　　London, Transworld, 1961. 156 p. (Corgi Books)

1777 MacDonald, Charles B.
　　　THE BATTLE OF HUERTGEN FOREST. Philadelphia, Lippincott, 1963. 215 p. (Great Battles of History)

1778 MacDonald, Charles B.
　　　COMPANY COMMANDER. Washington, Infantry Journal, 1947. 278 p.

1779 MacDonald, Charles B.
　　　THE SIEGFRIED LINE CAMPAIGN. Washington, Office of Chief of Military History, Dept. of Army, 1963. 670 p. (U.S. Army in World War II: The European Theater of Operations)

1780 MacDonald, Charles B., and Sidney T. Mathews.
　　　THREE BATTLES: ARNAVILLE, ALTUZZO, AND SCHMIDT. Washington, Office of Chief of Military History, Dept. of Army, 1952. 443 p. (U.S. Army in World War II: Special Studies)

1781 McElwee, William L.
　　　THE BATTLE OF D-DAY. London, Faber, 1965. 132 p. (Men and Events Series)

1782 McGovern, James.
　　　CROSSBOW AND OVERCAST. New York, Morrow, 1964. 279 p.
　　Other edition:
　　London, Hutchinson, 1965.

1783 McKee, Alexander.
　　　CAEN, ANVIL OF VICTORY. London, Souvenir Press, 1964. 368 p.

1784 McMillan, Richard.
　　　TWENTY ANGELS OVER ROME: THE STORY OF FASCIST ITALY'S FALL. London and New York, Jarrolds, 1945. 160 p.

1785 Maguire, Eric.
　　　DIEPPE, AUGUST 19. London, Cape, 1963. 205 p.

1786 Majdalany, Fred.
　　　CASSINO: PORTRAIT OF A BATTLE. London, Longmans, Green, 1957. 270 p.
　　Other editions:
　　　THE BATTLE OF CASSINO. Boston, Houghton Mifflin, 1957. 309 p.
　　London, Transworld, 1959. 282 p. (Corgi Books)

1787 Majdalany, Fred.
　　　THE MONASTERY. London, Lane, 1945. 115 p.
　　Other editions:
　　Boston, Houghton Mifflin, 1946. 148 p.
　　London, Transworld, 1957. 176 p. (Corgi Books)

1788 Marshall, Samuel L. A., with J. G. Westover and A. J. Webber.
　　　BASTOGNE, THE STORY OF THE FIRST EIGHT DAYS IN WHICH THE 101ST AIRBORNE DIVISION WAS CLOSED WITHIN THE RING OF GERMAN FORCES. Washington, Infantry Journal Press, 1946. 261 p.

1789 Marshall, Samuel L. A.
　　　NIGHT DROP: THE AMERICAN AIRBORNE INVASION OF NORMANDY. Preface by Carl Sandburg. Boston, Little, Brown; London, Macmillan, 1962. 425 p.

1790 Mayo, Andrew R.
　　　NO TIME FOR GLORY. New York, Pageant Press, 1955. 69 p.

1791 Merriam, Robert E.
　　　DARK DECEMBER: THE FULL ACCOUNT OF THE BATTLE OF THE BULGE. Chicago, Ziff-Davis, 1947. 234 p.
　　Other editions:
　　New York, Ballantine, 1957. 192 p.
　　　THE BATTLE OF THE ARDENNES. London, Souvenir Press, 1958. 233 p.
　　London, Hamilton, 1959. 192 p. (Panther Books)

1792 Michie, Allan A.
　　　HONOUR FOR ALL. London, Allen and Unwin, 1946. 218 p.

1793 Michie, Allan A.
　　　THE INVASION OF EUROPE: THE STORY BEHIND D-DAY. New York, Dodd, Mead, 1964. 203 p.

1794 Millin, Sarah G.
　　　FIRE OUT OF HEAVEN. London, Faber, 1947. 316 p.

1795 Millin, Sarah G.
　　　THE PIT OF THE ABYSS. London, Faber, 1946. 304 p.

1796 Millin, Sarah G.
　　　THE REELING EARTH. London, Faber, 1945. 305 p.

1797 Millin, Sarah G.
　　　THE SEVEN THUNDERS. London, Faber, 1948. 335 p.

1798 Millin, Sarah G.
　　　THE SOUND OF THE TRUMPET. London, Faber, 1947. 269 p.

1799 Millis, Walter.
　　　THE LAST PHASE, ALLIED VICTORY IN WESTERN EUROPE. Washington, Interim International Information Service, 1945. 91 p.
　　Other edition:
　　Boston, Houghton Mifflin, 1946. 130 p.

1800 Minott, Rodney G.
THE FORTRESS THAT NEVER WAS: THE MYTH OF THE NAZI ALPINE REDOUBT. London, Longmans, 1965. 208 p.

1801 Montgomery, Bernard L. Montgomery, 1st viscount.
NORMANDY TO THE BALTIC. London, Hutchinson, 1947. 226 p.

Other editions:
Boston, Houghton Mifflin, 1948. 351 p.

London, Arrow, 1961. 224 p. (Grey Arrow Books)

1802 Moorehead, Alan McC.
ECLIPSE. New York, Coward-McCann, 1945. 309 p.

Other edition:
London, Hamilton, 1946. 255 p.

1803 Morgan, Sir Frederick E.
OVERTURE TO OVERLORD. Foreword by Dwight D. Eisenhower. Garden City, N.Y., Doubleday, 1950. 302 p.

Other editions:
London, Hodder and Stoughton, 1950. 296 p.

London, Mayflower, 1962. 287 p.

1804 Moulton, James L.
HASTE TO THE BATTLE: A MARINE COMMANDO AT WAR. Preface by General Sir Richard Gale. London, Cassell, 1963. 210 p.

1805 Munro, Ross.
GAUNTLET TO OVERLORD: THE STORY OF THE CANADIAN ARMY. Toronto, Macmillan Co. of Canada, 1945. 477 p.

Other edition:
Cambridge and New York, Cambridge University Press, 1946. 477 p.

1806 Murphy, Audie.
TO HELL AND BACK. New York, Holt, 1949. 274 p.

Other edition:
London, Hammond and Hammond, 1950. 282 p.

1807 National Broadcasting Company.
THIS IS THE STORY OF THE LIBERATION OF EUROPE FROM THE FALL OF ROME TO VICTORY--AS NBC NEWSMEN RELAYED IT BY RADIO TO AMERICAN LISTENERS. New York, National Broadcasting Company, Inc., 1945. 50 p.

1808 Newton, Don, and Arthur C. Hampshire.
TARANTO. London, Kimber, 1959. 204 p.

Other edition:
London, Kimber, 1961. 159 p.

1809 Norman, Albert.
OPERATION OVERLOAD, DESIGN AND REALITY: THE ALLIED INVASION OF WESTERN EUROPE. Harrisburg, Pa., Military Service Publishing Co., 1952. 230 p.

1810 North, John.
NORTH-WEST EUROPE, 1944-5: THE ACHIEVEMENT OF 21ST ARMY GROUP. London, H.M Stationery Office, 1953. 270 p. (The Second World War, 1939-1945: A Popular Military History)

1811 O'Neill, Herbert C. (Strategicus, pseud.).
THE VICTORY CAMPAIGN, MAY 1944-AUGUST 1945. London, Faber and Faber, 1947. 282 p.

1812 Perrault, Gilles.
THE SECRETS OF D-DAY. Translated from French by Len Ortzen. London, Barker; Boston, Little, Brown, 1965. 249 p.

1813 Phillips, Cecil E. L., with H. G. Hasler.
COCKLESHELL HEROES. Foreword by Admiral the Earl Mountbatten of Burma. London, Heinemann, 1956. 252 p.

Other edition:
London, Pan Books, 1957. 256 p. (Great Pan Books)

1814 Phillips, Cecil E. L.
THE GREATEST RAID OF ALL. Foreword by Admiral the Earl Mountbatten of Burma. London, Heinemann, 1958. 288 p.

Other editions:
Boston, Little, Brown, 1960. 270 p.

London, Pan, 1961. 316 p.

1815 Phillips, Neville C.
ITALY. Wellington, War History Branch, Dept. of Internal Affairs, 1957. 1 v. published. (Official History of New Zealand in the Second World War, 1939-45)

1816 Pond, Hugh.
SALERNO. London, Kimber, 1961. 256 p.

Other editions:
Boston, Little, Brown, 1961. 269 p.

London, Pan, 1964. 270 p.

1817 Pond, Hugh.
SICILY. London, Kimber, 1962. 224 p.

1818 Pyle, Ernest T.
BRAVE MEN. New York, Grosset and Dunlap; London, Holt, 1945. 328 p.

Original edition:
New York, Holt, 1944.

1819 Randall, Howard M.
DIRT AND DOUGHFEET: COMBAT EXPERIENCES OF A RIFLE-PLATOON LEADER. New York, Exposition Press, 1955. 113 p.

1820 Renaud, Alexandre.
SAINTE-MERE-EGLISE: FIRST AMERICAN BRIDGEHEAD IN FRANCE, 6TH OF JUNE 1944. Monaco, Pathé, 1964. 198 p.

1821 Reyburn, Wallace.
DAWN LANDING. London, Brown, Watson, 1958. 160 p. (Digit Books)

1822 Robertson, Terence.
THE SHAME AND THE GLORY: DIEPPE. Toronto, McClelland and Stewart, 1962. 432 p.

Other edition:
DIEPPE: THE SHAME AND THE GLORY. London, Hutchinson, 1963. 508 p.

1823 Rowan-Robinson, Henry.
ONWARD FROM D-DAY. New York and London, Hutchinson, 1946. 175 p.

1824 Roy, Claude.
EIGHT DAYS THAT FREED PARIS. London, Pilot, 1945. 95 p.

1825 Ryan, Cornelius.
THE LONGEST DAY: JUNE 6, 1944. New York, Simon and Schuster, 1959. 350 p.

Other editions:
London, Gollancz, 1960. 256 p.

London, New English Library, 1962. (Four Square Books)

1826 Ryder, Robert E. D.
THE ATTACK ON ST. NAZAIRE, 28TH MARCH, 1942. Introduction by Admiral Sir Charles Forbes. London, Murray, 1947. 118 p.

1827 Samain, Bryan.
COMMANDO MEN: THE STORY OF A ROYAL MARINE COMMANDO IN NORTH-WEST EUROPE. London, Stevens, 1948. 188 p.

1828 Sawyer, John.
D-DAY. London, Landsborough, 1960. 160 p. (Four Square Books)

1829 Scrivener, Jane (pseud.).
INSIDE ROME WITH THE GERMANS. New York, Macmillan, 1945. 204 p.

1830 Shapiro, Lionel S. B.
THEY LEFT THE BACK DOOR OPEN: A CHRONICLE OF THE ALLIED CAMPAIGN IN SICILY AND ITALY. London, Jarrolds, 1945. 191 p.

1831 Sheehan, Fred.
ANZIO, EPIC OF BRAVERY. Norman, University of Oklahoma Press, 1964. 239 p.

1832 Shennan, Alexander F.
THE BACKDOOR GANG. Brooklyn, 1950. 90 p.

1833 Shulman, Milton.
DEFEAT IN THE WEST. New York, Dutton; London, Secker and Warburg, 1948. 336 p.

Other edition:
London, Heinemann, 1963. (Mercury Books)

1834 Simonds, Peter.
MAPLE LEAF UP, MAPLE LEAF DOWN: THE STORY OF THE CANADIANS IN THE SECOND WORLD WAR. New York, Island Press, 1947. 356 p.

1835 Speidel, Hans.
INVASION 1944: ROMMEL AND THE NORMANDY CAMPAIGN. Introduction by Truman Smith. Chicago, Regnery, 1950. 176 p.

1836 Speidel, Hans.
WE DEFENDED NORMANDY. Translated by Ian Colvin. London, Jenkins, 1951. 182 p.

1837 Stacey, Charles P.
CANADA'S BATTLE IN NORMANDY. Ottawa, King's Printer, 1946. 159 p.

1838 Stanford, Alfred B.
FORCE MULBERRY: THE PLANNING AND INSTALLATION OF THE ARTIFICIAL HARBOR OFF U.S. NORMANDY BEACHES IN WORLD WAR II. Introduction by Samuel E. Morison. New York, Morrow, 1951. 240 p.

1839 Studnitz, Hans-Georg von.
WHILE BERLIN BURNS: THE DIARY OF HANS-GEORG VON STUDNITZ, 1943-1945. Translated from German by R. H. Stevens. London, Weidenfeld and Nicolson, 1964. 290 p.

Other edition:
Englewood Cliffs, N.J., Prentice-Hall, 1965.

1840 Swiecicki, Marek.
SEVEN RIVERS TO BOLOGNA. London, Rolls, 1946. 115 p.

1841 Swiecicki, Marek.
WITH THE RED DEVILS AT ARNHEM. London, Love, 1945. 92 p.

1842 Thompson, Reginald W.
THE BATTLE FOR THE RHINELAND. London, Hutchinson, 1958. 241 p.

Other edition:
THE BATTLE FOR THE RHINE. New York, Ballantine Books, 1959. 207 p.

1843 Thompson, Reginald W.
DIEPPE AT DAWN: THE STORY OF THE DIEPPE RAID. London, Hutchinson, 1956. 215 p.

Other edition:
AT WHATEVER COST: THE STORY OF THE DIEPPE RAID. New York, Coward-McCann, 1957.

1844 Thompson, Reginald W.
THE EIGHTY-FIVE DAYS: THE STORY OF THE BATTLE OF THE SCHELDT. London, Hutchinson, 1957. 235 p.

Other edition:
New York, Ballantine Books, 1957. 220 p.

1845 Thompson, Reginald W.
MEN UNDER FIRE. London, Macdonald, 1946. 160 p.

1846 Thompson, Reginald W.
THE PRICE OF VICTORY. London, Constable, 1960. 279 p.

1847 Thornton, Willis.
THE LIBERATION OF PARIS. New York, Harcourt, Brace and World, 1962. 231 p.

Other edition:
London, Hart-Davis, 1963.

1848 Timothy, Patrick H.
THE RHINE CROSSING, TWELFTH ARMY GROUP ENGINEER OPERATIONS. Fort Belvoir, 1946. 57 p.

1849 Toland, John.
BATTLE: THE STORY OF THE BULGE. New York, Random House, 1959. 400 p.

Other edition:
London, Muller, 1960. 335 p.

1850 Trevelyan, Raleigh.
THE FORTRESS: A DIARY OF ANZIO AND AFTER. London, Collins, 1956. 221 p.

Other editions:
New York, St. Martin's Press, 1957.

Harmondsworth, Eng., Penguin, 1958. 184 p.

1851 Tully, Andrew.
BERLIN, STORY OF A BATTLE. New York, Simon and Schuster, 1963. 304 p.

1852 Turner, John F.
INVASION '44: THE FIRST FULL STORY OF D-DAY IN NORMANDY. New York, Putnam, 1959. 248 p.

Other editions:
London, Harrap, 1959. 253 p.

London, Transworld, 1960. 254 p.

1853 U.S. Congress. House. Committee on Veterans' Affairs.
D-DAY PLUS 20 YEARS, JUNE 6, 1944-JUNE 6, 1964. Washington, U.S. Government Printing Office, 1964. 58 p.

1854 U.S. Dept. of the Army. Office of Military History.
ANZIO BEACHHEAD, 22 JANUARY-25 MAY, 1944. Washington, U.S. Government Printing Office, 1948. 122 p. (American Forces in Action)

1855 U.S. Dept. of the Army. Office of Military History.
UTAH BEACH TO CHERBOURG, 6 JUNE-27 JUNE, 1944. Washington, U.S. Government Printing Office, 1948. 213 p. (American Forces in Action)

1856 U.S. Military Academy, West Point. Dept. of Military Art and Engineering.
THE INVASION OF WESTERN EUROPE. West Point, N.Y., 1946. 2 v.

1857 U.S. Military Academy, West Point, Dept. of Military Art and Engineering.
OPERATIONS IN SICILY AND ITALY, JULY 1943 TO DECEMBER, 1944. West Point, N.Y., 1945. 85 p.

Other edition:
1950. 102 p.

1858 U.S. Military Academy, West Point. Dept. of Military Art and Engineering.
THE WAR IN WESTERN EUROPE. West Point, N.Y., 1952. 2 pts.

1859 U.S. Office of War Information.
THE AMERICAN ARMY IN EUROPE. Washington, 1945. 117 p.

1860 U.S. War Dept. General Staff.
FIFTH ARMY AT THE WINTER LINE, 15 NOVEMBER 1943-15 JANUARY 1944. Washington, 1945. 117 p.

1861 U.S. War Dept. General Staff.
FROM THE VOLTURNO TO THE WINTER LINE, 6 OCTOBER-15 NOVEMBER 1943. Washington, 1945. 119 p.

1862 U.S. War Dept. General Staff.
OMAHA BEACHHEAD, 6 JUNE-13 JUNE 1944. Washington, Historical Division, War Dept., 1945. 167 p.

1863 U.S. War Dept. General Staff.
SMALL UNIT ACTIONS, FRANCE: 2D RANGER BATTALION AT POINTE DE HOE; SAIPAN: 27TH DIVISION ON TANAPAY PLAIN; ITALY: 351ST INFANTRY AT SANTE MARIA INFANTE; FRANCE: 4TH ARMOURED DIVISION AT SINGLING. Washington, Historical Division, War Dept., 1946. 212 p.

1864 U.S. War Dept. General Staff.
ST-LO, 7 JULY-19 JULY 1944. Washington, Historical Division, War Dept., 1947. 128 p. (American Forces in Action)

1865 Urquhart, Robert E., with Wilfred Greatorex.
ARNHEM. London, Cassell; New York, Norton, 1958. 238 p.

Other edition:
London, Pan Books, 1960. 221 p.

1866 Vaughan-Thomas, L. J. Wynford.
ANZIO. London, Longmans, Green; New York, Holt, Rinehart and Winston, 1961. 243 p.

Other edition:
London, Pan, 1963. 267 p.

1867 Villari, Luigi.
THE LIBERATION OF ITALY, 1943-1947. Appleton, Wis., Nelson, 1959. 265 p.

1868 Wallace, Brenton G.
PATTON AND HIS THIRD ARMY. Harrisburg, Pa., Military Service Publishing Co., 1946. 232 p.

1869 WAR REPORT: A RECORD OF DISPATCHES BROADCAST BY THE BBC'S WAR CORRESPONDENTS WITH THE ALLIED EXPEDITIONARY FORCE, 6 JUNE 1944 - 5 MAY 1945. London and New York, Oxford University Press, 1946. 452 p.

1870 Werstein, Irving.
    THE BATTLE OF AACHEN. New York, Crowell, 1962. 146 p.

1871 Werstein, Irving.
    THE BATTLE OF SALERNO. New York, Crowell, 1965. 152 p.

1872 White, Walter F.
    A RISING WIND. Garden City, N.Y., Doubleday, Doran, 1945. 155 p.

1873 Wilson, Andrew.
    FLAME THROWER. London, Kimber, 1956. 202 p.

1874 Wilson, Michael C. D., and A. S. L. Robinson.
    COASTAL COMMAND LEADS THE INVASION. London, Jarrolds, 1945. 160 p.

1875 Wingfield, Rex M.
    THE ONLY WAY OUT: AN INFANTRYMAN'S AUTOBIOGRAPHY OF THE NORTH-WEST EUROPE CAMPAIGN AUGUST 1944-FEBRUARY 1945. Foreword by G. L. Verney. London, Hutchinson, 1955. 190 p.

      2. Land Campaigns: Far Eastern Theater

            a. China

1876 Adamson, Iain.
    THE FORGOTTEN MEN. London, Bell, 1965. 195 p.

1877 Band, Claire, and William Band.
    TWO YEARS WITH THE CHINESE COMMUNISTS. New Haven, Conn., Yale University Press, 1948. 347 p.

    Other edition:
    DRAGON FANGS. London, Allen, 1947.

1878 Burr, Samuel E.
    CHINA A.P.O., MORE THAN EXPERIENCE: A STORY OF THE CHINA THEATER, 1944-1945. Washington, 1952.

1879 Carew, John M. (Tim Carew, pseud.).
    FALL OF HONG KONG. London, Blond, 1960. 228 p.

    Other edition:
    London, Pan, 1963. 235 p.

1880 Chu Tê.
    THE BATTLE FRONT OF THE LIBERATED AREAS. 3d ed. Peking, Foreign Languages Press, 1962. 79 p.

1881 Lee Kung-sam.
    THE SECRETS OF CHINA'S VICTORY. Shanghai, 1946. 169 p.

1882 Mao Tse-tung.
    ASPECTS OF CHINA'S ANTI-JAPANESE STRUGGLE. Bombay, People's Publishing House, 1948. 80 p.

1883 Morris, David E.
    CHINA CHANGED MY MIND. London, Cassell, 1948. 202 p.

1884 Noonan, William.
    THE SURPRISING BATTALION: AUSTRALIAN COMMANDOS IN CHINA. Sydney, Bookstall Co., 1945. 194 p.

1885 Romanus, Charles F., and Riley Sunderland.
    STILWELL'S MISSION TO CHINA. Washington, Office of Chief of Military History, Dept. of Army, 1953. 441 p. (U.S. Army in World War II: China-Burma-India Theater)

1886 Samson, Gerald.
    THE FAR EAST ABLAZE. London, Joseph, 1945. 183 p.

1887 Stuart, Gilbert, with Alan Levy.
    KIND-HEARTED TIGER. Boston, Little, Brown, 1964. 375 p.

1888 Tennien, Mark A.
    CHUNGKING LISTENING POST. New York, Creative Age Press, 1945. 201 p.

1889 Tipton, Laurance.
    CHINESE ESCAPADE. London, Macmillan, 1949. 247 p.

1890 U.S. Army. Forces in the Far East.
    ARMOR OPERATIONS. Prepared by Headquarters, U.S.A.F.F.E. and Eighth U.S. Army, Rear. n.p., Distributed by Office of Chief of Military History. Dept of Army, 1957. 154 p. (Japanese Studies on Manchuria)

1891 U.S. Army. Forces in the Far East.
    ARMY OPERATIONS IN CHINA. Prepared by Headquarters, U.S.A.F.F.E. and Eighth U.S. Army, Rear. Tokyo, Distributed by Office of Chief of Military History, Dept. of Army, 1956 or 1957. 2 v. (Japanese Monograph)

1892 U.S. Army. Forces in the Far East.
    INFANTRY OPERATIONS. Prepared by Headquarters, U.S.A.F.F.E. and Eighth U.S. Army, Rear. n.p., Distributed by Office of Chief of Military History, Dept. of Army, 1956. 122 p. (Japanese Studies on Manchuria)

1893 U.S. Army. Forces in the Far East.
    SOUTH CHINA AREA OPERATIONS RECORD, 1937-1941. Prepared by Military History Section. n.p., Distributed by Office of Chief of Military History, Dept. of Army, 1956. 139 p. (Japanese Monograph)

            b. Philippines

1894 Baclagon, Uldarico S.
    PHILIPPINE CAMPAIGNS. Manila, Graphic House, 1952. 388 p.

1895 Buenafe, Manuel E.
    WARTIME PHILIPPINES. Manila, Philippine Education Foundation, 1950. 248 p.

1896 Cannon, M. Hamlin.
LEYTE: THE RETURN TO THE PHILIPPINES. Washington, Office of Chief of Military History, Dept. of Army, 1954. 420 p. (U.S. Army in World War II: The War in the Pacific)

1897 Klestadt, Albert.
THE SEA GOD WAS KIND. London, Constable, 1959. 208 p.

Other edition:
New York, McKay, 1960.

1898 McGee, John H.
RICE AND SALT: A HISTORY OF THE DEFENSE AND OCCUPATION OF MINDANAO DURING WORLD WAR II. San Antonio, Naylor, 1962. 242 p.

1899 Marquez, Adalia.
BLOOD ON THE RISING SUN: A FACTUAL STORY OF THE JAPANESE INVASION OF THE PHILIPPINES. New York, DeTanko Publishers, 1957. 253 p.

1900 Morton, Louis.
THE FALL OF THE PHILIPPINES. Washington, Office of Chief of Military History, Dept. of Army, 1953. 626 p. (U.S. Army in World War II: The War in the Pacific)

1901 Phillips, Claire, and Myron B. Goldsmith.
MANILA ESPIONAGE. Portland, Ore., Binfords and Mort, 1947. 226 p.

1902 Smith, Robert R.
TRIUMPH IN THE PHILIPPINES. Washington, Office of Chief of Military History, Dept. of Army, 1963. 756 p. (U.S. Army in World War II: The War in the Pacific)

1903 U.S. Army. Sixth Army.
REPORT OF THE LUZON CAMPAIGN, 9 JANUARY 1945-30 JUNE 1945. n.p., 1945. 4 v.

c. Malaya: Singapore

1904 Attiwill, Kenneth.
THE SINGAPORE STORY. London, Muller, 1959. 253 p.

Other editions:
FORTRESS: THE STORY OF THE SIEGE AND FALL OF SINGAPORE. Garden City, N.Y., Doubleday, 1960. 243 p.

London, Transworld, 1961. 288 p. (Corgi Books)

1905 Chaphekar, Shankarrao G.
A BRIEF STUDY OF THE MALAYAN CAMPAIGN 1941-42. 2d and rev. ed. Poona, Maharashtra Militarisation Board; London, Bailey and Swinfen, 1960. 121 p.

1906 Chapman, Frederick S.
THE JUNGLE IS NEUTRAL. New York, Norton, 1949. 384 p.

Other editions:
London, Chatto and Windus, 1949. 435 p.

London, Transworld, 1957. 351 p. (Corgi Books)

1907 Chin Kee Onn.
MALAYA UPSIDE DOWN. Singapore, Jitts, 1946. 208 p.

1908 Coombes, J. H. H.
BANPONG EXPRESS: BEING AN ACCOUNT OF THE MALAYAN CAMPAIGN, WITH SOME SUBSEQUENT EXPERIENCES AS A GUEST OF THE IMPERIAL JAPANESE ARMY. Darlington, 1948. 153 p.

1909 Eyre, Donald C., with Douglas Bowler.
THE SOUL AND THE SEA. London, Hale, 1959. 192 p.

Other edition:
ORDEAL BY ENDURANCE. London, Hamilton, 1960. 192 p. (Panther Books)

1910 Glover, Edwin M.
IN 70 DAYS: THE STORY OF THE JAPANESE CAMPAIGN IN BRITISH MALAYA. London, Muller, 1946. 244 p.

Other edition:
1949. 249 p.

1911 Hill, Anthony.
DIVERSION IN MALAYA: AN INCIDENTAL ACCOUNT OF FIVE YEARS' RESIDENCE IN THE FEDERATED MALAY STATES, 1937-1942. London, Collins, 1948. 186 p.

1912 Holman, Dennis.
NOONE OF THE ULU. Foreword by Gerald Templer. London, Heinemann, 1958. 253 p.

1913 Low, N. I., and H. M. Cheng.
THIS SINGAPORE: OUR CITY OF DREADFUL NIGHT. Singapore, City Book Store (sole distributors), 194-. 173 p.

1914 Mant, Gilbert.
GRIM GLORY. Foreword by H. Gordon Bennett. New and expanded ed. Sydney, Currawong Publishing Co., 1955. 95 p.

1915 Owen, Frank.
THE FALL OF SINGAPORE. London, Joseph, 1960. 216 p.

Other edition:
London, Pan, 1962. 206 p.

1916 Percival, Arthur E.
THE WAR IN MALAYA. London, Eyre and Spottiswoode, 1949. 336 p.

1917 Russell-Roberts, Denis.
SPOTLIGHT ON SINGAPORE. Douglas, Isle of Man, Times Press; London, Gibbs and Phillips, 1965. 301 p.

1918 Sim, Katharine.
MALAYAN LANDSCAPE. London, Joseph, 1946. 248 p.

1919 Thatcher, Dorothy, and Robert Cross.
PAI NAA: THE STORY OF NONA BAKER. London, Constable, 1959. 184 p.

1920 Tsuji, Masanobu.
SINGAPORE, THE JAPANESE VERSION. Translated by Margaret E. Lake; edited by H. V. Howe; introduction by H. Gordon Bennett. Sydney, Smith; New York, St. Martin's Press, 1960. 358 p.

Other edition:
London, Constable, 1962. 358 p.

d. Dutch East Indies

1921 Coast, John.
RECRUIT TO REVOLUTION: ADVENTURE AND POLITICS IN INDONESIA. London, Christophers, 1952. 308 p.

1922 Droste, Chris B.
TILL BETTER DAYS. London and New York, Hurst and Blackett, 1946. 104 p.

1923 Harrisson, Thomas H.
WORLD WITHIN: A BORNEO STORY. London, Grosset Press, 1959. 349 p.

1924 Ryan, Peter.
FEAR DRIVE MY FEET. Sydney, Angus and Robertson, 1959. 251 p.

Other edition:
London, Cambridge University Press, 1961.

1925 U. S. Army. Japan. Headquarters.
BORNEO OPERATIONS, 1941-1945. Tokyo, Distributed by Office of Chief of Military History, Dept. of Army, 1957. 101 p. (Japanese Monograph)

e. Burma

1926 Allied Forces.
THE CAMPAIGN IN BURMA. London, H.M. Stationery Office, 1946. 175 p.

1927 Allied Forces. Southeast Asia Command.
REPORT TO THE COMBINED CHIEFS OF STAFF BY THE SUPREME ALLIED COMMANDER, SOUTH-EAST ASIA 1943-1945, VICE-ADMIRAL THE EARL OF MOUNTBATTEN OF BURMA. London, H.M. Stationery Office, 1951. 280 p.

1928 Allied Forces. Southeast Asia Command. Women's Auxiliary Service (Burma).
THE WASBIES: THE STORY OF THE WOMEN'S AUXILIARY SERVICE (BURMA). London, War Facts Press [1946?]. 79 p.

1929 Anders, Leslie.
THE LEDO ROAD: GENERAL JOSEPH W. STILWELL'S HIGHWAY TO CHINA. Norman, University of Oklahoma, 1965. 255 p.

1930 Baggaley, James.
A CHINDIT STORY. London, Souvenir, 1954. 163 p.

1931 Barker, A. J.
THE MARCH ON DELHI. London, Faber, 1963. 302 p.

1932 Barnard, Jack.
THE HUMP: THE GREATEST UNTOLD STORY OF THE WAR. London, Souvenir Press, 1960. 192 p.

Other edition:
London, Transworld, 1961. 188 p. (Corgi Books)

1933 Barrett, Neil H.
CHINGHPAW. New York, Vantage, 1962. 173 p.

1934 Beamish, John.
BURMA DROP. London, Elek, 1958. 222 p.

Other edition:
London, Elek, 1960. (Bestseller Library)

1935 Bickersteth, Anthony C.
ODTAA: BEING EXTRACTS FROM THE DIARY OF AN OFFICER WHO SERVED WITH THE 4/10TH GURKHA RIFLES IN MANIPUR AND BURMA. Foreword by General Sir Douglas Gracey. Aberdeen, Professor G. L. Bickersteth [private circulation] 1953. 258 p.

1936 Boyle, Patrick R.
JUNGLE, JUNGLE, LITTLE CHINDIT. London, Hollis and Carter, 1946. 97 p.

1937 Burchett, Wilfred G.
WINGATE'S PHANTOM ARMY. London, Muller, 1946. 195 p.

1938 Calvert, Michael.
PRISONERS OF HOPE. London, Cape, 1952. 303 p.

Other edition:
London, Hamilton, 1960. 205 p.

1939 Campbell, Arthur F.
THE SIEGE: A STORY FROM KOHIMA. London, Allen and Unwin, 1956. 213 p.

Other editions:
London, Transworld, 1957. 251 p. (Corgi Books)

New York, Macmillan, 1956. 211 p.

1940 Chaphekar, Shankarrao G.
A BRIEF STUDY OF THE BURMA CAMPAIGN, 1943-45. Poona, Maharashtra Militarisation Board, 1955. 100 p.

1941 Christian, John L.
BURMA AND THE JAPANESE INVADER. Bombay, Thacker, 1945. 418 p.

1942 Collis, Maurice.
LAST AND FIRST IN BURMA (1941-1948). London, Faber and Faber, 1956. 303 p.

1943 Denny, John H.
       CHINDIT INDISCRETION. London, Johnson, 1956. 256 p.

   Other edition:
   London, Hamilton, 1959. 187 p. (Panther Books)

1944 Dupuy, Trevor N.
       ASIATIC LAND BATTLES: ALLIED VICTORIES IN CHINA AND BURMA. London, Ward, 1965. 66 p. (Illustrated History of World War II)

1945 Eldridge, Fred.
       WRATH IN BURMA: THE UNCENSORED STORY OF GENERAL STILWELL AND INTERNATIONAL MANEUVERS IN THE FAR EAST. Garden City, N.Y., Doubleday, 1946. 320 p.

1946 Evans, Sir Geoffrey C., and Anthony Brett-James.
       IMPHAL: A FLOWER ON LOFTY HEIGHTS. London, Macmillan; New York, St. Martin's Press, 1962. 348 p.

   Other edition:
   1965.

1947 Fellowes-Gordon, Ian.
       AMIABLE ASSASSINS: THE STORY OF THE KACHIN GUERRILLAS OF NORTH BURMA. London, Hale, 1957. 159 p.

   Other edition:
   London, Hamilton, 1958. 160 p. (Panther Books)

1948 Fergusson, Bernard E.
       BEYOND THE CHINDWIN: BEING AN ACCOUNT OF THE ADVENTURES OF NUMBER FIVE COLUMN OF THE WINGATE EXPEDITION IN BURMA, 1943. London, Collins, 1951. 256 p. (St. James's Library Series)

   Other editions:
   London, Collins, 1955. 252 p. (Fontana Books)
   London, Collins, 1962. 256 p.

1949 Fergusson, Bernard E.
       RETURN TO BURMA. London, Collins, 1962. 256 p.

1950 Fergusson, Bernard E.
       THE WILD GREEN EARTH. London, Collins, 1946. 288 p.

   Other edition:
   London, Collins, 1956. 254 p. (Fontana Books)

1951 Friend, John F.
       THE LONG TREK. London, Muller, 1957. 187 p.

   Other edition:
   London, Transworld, 1958. 189 p. (Corgi Books)

1952 Halley, David.
       WITH WINGATE IN BURMA: BEING THE STORY OF THE ADVENTURES OF SGT. TONY AUBREY OF THE KING'S LIVERPOOL REGIMENT DURING THE 1943 WINGATE EXPEDITION INTO BURMA. Glasgow and London, Hodge, 1945. 189 p.

   Other edition:
   1946. 196 p.

1953 Hanley, Gerald.
       MONSOON VICTORY. London, Collins, 1946. 211 p.

1954 Ho Yung-chi.
       THE BIG CIRCLE. New York, Exposition Press, 1948. 152 p.

1955 Hunt, Gordon.
       ONE MORE RIVER. London, Collins, 1965. 255 p.

1956 Hunter, Charles N.
       GALAHAD. San Antonio, Naylor, 1963. 233 p.

1957 India. War Dept. Director of Public Relations.
       ON TO RANGOON. Bombay, Claridge, 1945. 64 p.

1958 Irvin, Anthony S.
       BURMESE OUTPOST. London, Collins, 1945. 160 p.

1959 Jeffrey, William F.
       SUNBEAMS LIKE SWORDS. London, Hodder and Stoughton, 1951. 176 p.

1960 MacHorton, Ian, with Henry Maule.
       THE HUNDRED DAYS OF LT. MacHORTON. New York, McKay, 1962. 224 p.

1961 MacHorton, Ian, with Henry Maule.
       SAFER THAN A KNOWN WAY: ONE MAN'S EPIC STRUGGLE AGAINST JAPANESE AND JUNGLE. London, Odhams Press, 1958. 224 p.

   Other edition:
   London, Transworld, 1961. 287 p. (Corgi Books)

1962 McKelvie, Roy.
       THE WAR IN BURMA. London, Methuen, 1948. 306 p.

1963 McLintock, James D.
       THE MANIPUR ROAD: STORY OF THE MANDALAY CAMPAIGN. Westport, Conn., Associated Bookseller, 1959. 158 p.

   Other editions:
   London, Brown, Watson, 195-. 158 p. (Digit Books)
   ROAD TO HELL. London, Brown, 1964. 158 p. (Digit Books)

1964 Madan, N. N.
       THE ARAKAN OPERATIONS, 1942-1945. Edited by Bisheshwar Prasad. Delhi, Combined Inter-Services Historical Section (India and Pakistan), 1954. 371 p. (Official History of the Indian Armed Forces in the Second World War, 1939-45: Campaigns in the Eastern Theatre)

1965 Matthews, Geoffrey F.
       THE RE-CONQUEST OF BURMA, 1943-1945. Foreword by Piers Mackesy. Aldershot, Gale and Polden, 1966. 104 p.

1966 Morrison, Ian.
       GRANDFATHER LONGLEGS: THE LIFE AND GALLANT DEATH OF MAJOR H. P. SEAGRIM. London, Faber and Faber, 1947. 239 p.

1967 Oatts, Lewis B.
THE JUNGLE IN ARMS. London, Kimber, 1962. 207 p.

1968 Owen, Frank.
THE CAMPAIGN IN BURMA. Prepared for South-East Asia Command by the Central Office of Information. London, H.M. Stationery Office, 1946. 175 p.

1969 Page, Robert C.
AIR COMMANDER DOC. As told to Lieutenant Alfred Aiken. New York, Ackerman, 1945. 186 p.

1970 Peacock, Geraldine.
THE LIFE OF A JUNGLE WALLA: REMINISCENCES IN THE LIFE OF LT.-COL. E. H. PEACOCK, D.S.O., M.C. Ilfracombe, Eng., Stockwell, 1958. 134 p.

1971 Peers, William R., and Dean Brelis.
BEHIND THE BURMA ROAD: THE STORY OF AMERICA'S MOST SUCCESSFUL GUERRILLA FORCE. Boston, Little, Brown, 1963. 246 p.

Other edition:
London, Hale, 1964. 194 p.

1972 Prasad, Bisheshwar (ed.).
THE RECONQUEST OF BURMA. Calcutta, Combined Inter-Services Historical Section (India and Pakistan); distributors: Orient Longmans, Bombay, 1958-. 2 v. published. (Official History of the Indian Armed Forces in the Second World War, 1939-45: Campaigns in the Eastern Theatre)

1973 Prasad, Bisheshwar (ed.).
THE RETREAT FROM BURMA, 1941-42. Delhi, Combined Inter-Services Historical Section, (India and Pakistan), 1952. 501 p. (Official History of the Indian Armed Forces in the Second World War, 1939-45: Campaigns in the Eastern Theatre)

Other edition:
1959.

1974 Rolo, Charles J.
WINGATE'S RAIDERS: AN ACCOUNT OF THE INCREDIBLE ADVENTURE THAT RAISED THE CURTAIN ON THE BATTLE OF BURMA. London, Harrap, 1944. 129 p.

Other edition:
New York, Viking Press, 1945. 200 p.

1975 Romanus, Charles F., and Riley Sunderland.
TIME RUNS OUT IN CBI. Washington, Office of Chief of Military History, Dept. of Army, 1959. 428 p. (U.S. Army in World War II: China-Burma-India Theater)

1976 Shaw, James.
THE MARCH OUT: THE END OF THE CHINDIT ADVENTURE. Introduced by Bernard Fergusson. London, Hart-Davis, 1953. 206 p.

Other edition:
London, Hamilton, 1956. 190 p. (Panther Books)

1977 Short, Stanley W.
ON BURMA'S EASTERN FRONTIER. Foreword by Lt.-Col. S. H. Middleton West. London and Edinburgh, Marshall, Morgan and Scott, 1945. 144 p.

1978 Singh, Bishan.
BURMA RETREAT. Kanpur, Vasudev Sing, 1949. 100 p.

1979 Slim, William Slim, 1st viscount.
DEFEAT INTO VICTORY. 2d ed. London, Cassell, 1956. 576 p.

Other editions:
London, Landsborough, 1958. 448 p. (Four Square Books)

New York, McKay, 1961. 468 p.

London, Cassell, 1962.

London, New English Library, 1965. (Four Square Books)

1980 Tainsh, Alsadair R.
AND SOME FELL BY THE WAYSIDE: AN ACCOUNT OF THE NORTH BURMA EVACUATION. Bombay, Orient Longmans; London, Longmans, Green, 1948. 175 p.

1981 Taylor, Joe G.
AIR SUPPLY IN THE BURMA CAMPAIGNS. Maxwell Air Force Base, Ala., USAF Historical Division, Research Studies Institute, Air University, 1957. 163 p. (USAF Historical Studies)

1982 Tyson, Geoffrey W.
FORGOTTEN FRONTIER. Calcutta, Targett, 1945. 146 p.

1983 U.S. War Department. General Staff.
MERRILL'S MARAUDERS, FEBRUARY-MAY 1944. Washington, 1945. 117 p. (American Forces in Action)

1984 Wilcox, W. A.
CHINDIT COLUMN 76. London, Longmans, Green, 1945. 137 p.

1985 Wilson, Richard C.
THE IMPHAL SHRIMPS, FROM "HIGH APPRECIATION: RECOLLECTIONS OF A CAPTAIN." Chester, Tug Books, 1962. 53 p.

3. Aerial Operations

a. General

1986 Air Force and Space Digest.
AIR FORCE DIARY: 111 STORIES FROM THE OFFICIAL SERVICE JOURNAL OF THE USAAF. Selected and edited by James H. Straubel. New York, Simon and Schuster, 1947. 492 p.

1987 Arnold, Henry H.
GLOBAL MISSION. New York, Harper, 1949. 626 p.

1988 Australia. Royal Australian Air Force.
VICTORY ROLL: THE ROYAL AUSTRALIAN AIR FORCE IN ITS SIXTH YEAR OF WAR. Canberra, Australian War Memorial 1945. 200 p.

1989 Aviation History Unit.
THE NAVY'S AIR WAR: A MISSION COMPLETED. Edited by A. R. Buchanan. New York, Harper, 1946. 432 p.

1990 Baker, Edgar C. R.
THE FIGHTER ACES OF THE R.A.F., 1939-1945. London, Kimber, 1962. 208 p.

1991 Blond, Georges.
BORN TO FLY: EXPLOITS OF THE WAR'S GREAT FIGHTER ACES. Translated from French by Mervyn Savill. London, Souvenir Press, 1956. 208 p.

Other edition:
London, Hamilton, 1957. 192 p. (Panther Books)

1992 Bowman, Gerald.
WAR IN THE AIR: BY ARRANGEMENT WITH THE B.B.C. AND BASED ON THE SERIES OF FIFTEEN TELEVISION FILMS "WAR IN THE AIR" MADE BY B.B.C. TELEVISION. Foreword by Air Chief Marshal Sir Philip Joubert. London, Evans, 1956. 224 p.

Other edition:
London, Pan Books, 1958. 185 p.

1993 Brereton, Lewis H.
THE BRERETON DIARIES: THE WAR IN THE AIR IN THE PACIFIC, MIDDLE EAST AND EUROPE, 3 OCTOBER 1941-8 MAY 1945. New York, Morrow, 1946. 450 p.

1994 Calmel, Jean.
NIGHT PILOT. London, Kimber, 1955. 200 p.

1995 Canada. Royal Canadian Air Force.
THE R.C.A.F. OVERSEAS: THE FIFTH YEAR. Foreword by Colonel the Honourable Colin Gibson. Toronto, Oxford University Press, 1945. 404 p.

1996 Canada. Royal Canadian Air Force.
THE R.C.A.F. OVERSEAS: THE SIXTH YEAR. London and Toronto, Oxford University Press, 1949. 537 p.

1997 Cave, Hugh B.
WINGS ACROSS THE WORLD: THE STORY OF THE AIR TRANSPORT COMMAND. New York, Dodd, Mead, 1945. 175 p.

1998 Charlton, Lionel E. O.
THE ROYAL AIR FORCE AND U.S.A.A.F.: A COMPLETE RECORD IN TEXT AND PICTURES, SEPT. 1939/DEC. 1940 - OCT. 1944/SEPT. 1945. London, Hutchinson, 1941-47. 5 v.

1999 Clarke, D. H.
WHAT WERE THEY LIKE TO FLY? London, Allen, 1964. 128 p.

2000 Cleveland, Reginald M.
AIR TRANSPORT AT WAR. Foreword by Lt. Gen. Harold L. George. New York and London, Harper, 1946. 324 p.

2001 Cosgrove, Edmund.
CANADA'S FIGHTING PILOTS. Toronto, Clarke, Irwin, 1965. 190 p. (Canadian Portraits)

2002 De Chant, John A.
DEVILBIRDS: THE STORY OF THE UNITED STATES MARINE CORPS AVIATION IN WORLD WAR II. New York, Harper, 1947. 265 p.

2003 Duke, Neville, with Alan W. Mitchell.
TEST PILOT. London, Wingate, 1953. 215 p.

2004 Embry, Sir Basil E.
MISSION COMPLETED. London, Methuen, 1957. 350 p.

2005 Forbes, Alexander.
QUEST FOR A NORTHERN AIR ROUTE. Cambridge, Mass., Harvard University Press; London, Oxford University Press, 1953. 141 p.

2006 Ford, Corey, and Alastair MacBain.
THE LAST TIME I SAW THEM. New York, Scribner, 1946. 244 p.

2007 Francis, Charles E.
THE TUSKEGEE AIRMEN: THE STORY OF THE NEGRO IN THE U.S. AIR FORCE. Boston, Bruce Humphries, 1956. 225 p.

2008 Genovese, Joseph G.
WE FLEW WITHOUT GUNS. Philadelphia, Winston, 1945. 304 p.

2009 Gibbs, Sir Gerald.
SURVIVOR'S STORY. London, Hutchinson, 1956. 182 p.

2010 Gillison, Douglas.
ROYAL AUSTRALIAN AIR FORCE, 1939-1942. Canberra, Australian War Memorial, 1962. 786 p. (Australia in the War of 1939-1945. Series 3 [Air])

2011 Glines, Carroll V., Jr., and Wendell F. Moseley.
GRAND OLD LADY: STORY OF THE DC-3. Cleveland, Pennington Press, 1959. 250 p.

Other editions:
PROUD OLD LADY. Cleveland, Pennington Press, 1959. 250 p.

THE DC-3: THE STORY OF A FABULOUS AIRPLANE. Philadelphia, Lippincott, 1966. 203 p. (Airmen and Aircraft)

2012 Goyal, S. N.
AIR POWER IN MODERN WARFARE. Bombay, Thackery, 1952. 131 p.

2013 Green, William.
FAMOUS BOMBERS OF THE SECOND WORLD WAR. 1st-2d series. London, Macdonald, 1959-60. 2 v.

Other edition:
Garden City, N.Y., Hanover House, 1960-61.

2014 Green, William.
FAMOUS FIGHTERS OF THE SECOND WORLD WAR. 1st-2d series. London, Macdonald, 1947-62. 2 v.

2015 Gribble, Leonard R.
BATTLE STORIES OF THE R.A.F. London, Burke, 1945. 96 p.

2016 Gupta, S. C.
HISTORY OF THE INDIAN AIR FORCE, 1933-45. Edited by Bisheshwar Prasad. Delhi, Combined Interservices Historical Section (India and Pakistan); distributors: Orient Longmans, 1961. 194 p. (Official History of the Indian Armed Forces in the Second World War, 1939-45. General War Administration and Organization)

2017 Gurney, Gene.
FIVE DOWN AND GLORY: A HISTORY OF THE AMERICAN AIR ACE. Edited by Mark P. Friedlander, Jr. New York, Putnam, 1958. 302 p.

2018 Gurney, Gene.
JOURNEY OF THE GIANTS. New York, Coward-McCann, 1961. 280 p.

Other edition:
B-29 STORY: THE PLANE THAT WON THE WAR. Greenwich, Conn., Fawcett Publications, 1963. 112 p. (Fawcett Book)

2019 Gurney, Gene.
THE WAR IN THE AIR: A PICTORIAL HISTORY OF WORLD WAR II AIR FORCES IN COMBAT. Foreword by Curtis E. LeMay. New York, Crown Publishers, 1962. 352 p.

2020 Hirsch, Phil (ed.).
FIGHTING ACES. New York, Pyramid Books, 1965. 173 p.

2021 Horsley, Terence.
FIND, FIX AND STRIKE: THE WORK OF THE FLEET AIR ARM. London, Eyre and Spottiswoode, 1945. 144 p.

2022 Jablonski, Edward.
FLYING FORTRESS. Garden City, N. Y., Doubleday, 1965. 362 p.

2023 Johnson, James E.
FULL CIRCLE: THE STORY OF AIR FIGHTING. London, Chatto and Windus, 1964. 290 p.

2024 Joubert de la Ferté, Philip B.
THE FORGOTTEN ONES: THE STORY OF THE GROUND CREWS. London, Hutchinson, 1961. 255 p.

2025 Kaplan, Chaim A.
SCROLL OF AGONY. New York, Macmillan, 1965. 350 p.

2026 La Farge, Oliver.
THE EAGLE IN THE EGG. Boston, Houghton Mifflin, 1949. 320 p.

2027 Lee, Arthur S. G.
SPECIAL DUTIES: REMINISCENCES OF A ROYAL AIR FORCE STAFF OFFICER IN THE BALKANS, TURKEY AND THE MIDDLE EAST. London, Low, Marston, 1946. 308 p.

2028 Lee, Asher.
AIR POWER. London, Duckworth; New York, Praeger, 1955. 200 p.

2029 Lee, James.
OPERATION LIFELINE: THE HISTORY AND DEVELOPMENT OF THE NAVAL AIR TRANSPORT SERVICE. Chicago, Ziff-Davis, 1946. 171 p.

2030 Loomis, Robert D.
GREAT AMERICAN FIGHTER PILOTS OF WORLD WAR II. New York, Random House, 1961. 208 p. (Landmark Books)

2031 Macintyre, Donald G. F. W.
WINGS OF NEPTUNE: THE STORY OF NAVAL AVIATION. London, Davies, 1963. 269 p.

Other edition:
New York, Norton, 1964.

2032 McKee, Philip.
WARRIORS WITH WINGS. New York, Crowell, 1947. 266 p.

2033 Macmillan, Norman.
THE ROYAL AIR FORCE IN THE WORLD WAR. London, Harrap, 1942-50. 4 v.

2034 Mason, Francis K.
THE HAWKER HURRICANE. London, Macdonald, 1962. 175 p. (Macdonald Aircraft Monographs)

2035 Munson, Kenneth G.
ABC BRITISH AIRCRAFT OF WORLD WAR II. London, Allen, 1961. 64 p.

2036 Munson, Kenneth G.
AIRCRAFT OF WORLD WAR TWO. London, I. Allan, 1962. 256 p.

2037 Narracott, Arthur H.
AIR POWER IN WAR. Foreword by Air Chief Marshal Sir Arthur Tedder. London, Muller, 1945. 168 p.

2038 Neprud, Robert E.
FLYING MINUTE MEN: THE STORY OF THE CIVIL AIR PATROL. New York, Duell, Sloan and Pearce, 1948. 243 p.

2039 Payne, Donald G. (Ian Cameron, pseud.).
WINGS OF THE MORNING: THE BRITISH FLEET AIR ARM IN WORLD WAR II. New York, Morrow, 1963. 288 p.

2040 Pearl, Jack.
AERIAL DOGFIGHTS OF WORLD WAR II. Derby, Conn., Monarch Books, 1962. 138 p. (Monarch Americana Book)

2041 Poolman, Kenneth.
FLYING BOAT: THE STORY OF THE SUNDERLAND. London, Kimber, 1962. 208 p.

2042 Pringle, Patrick.
FIGHTING PILOTS. London, Evans, 1961. 207 p.

2043 Quinterley, Esmond.
MY AIRMAN DAYS. London, Fortune Press, 1948. 262 p.

2044 R.A.F. Flying Review.
HEROES OF THE R.A.F.: THE BEST ADVENTURE STORIES FROM THE R.A.F. FLYING REVIEW. London, Jenkins, 1960. 142 p.

2045 R.A.F. Flying Review.
THE SKY THEIR BATTLEGROUND: TRUE ADVENTURE STORIES FROM R.A.F. FLYING REVIEW. London, Jenkins, 1962. 143 p.

2046 Reid, John P. M.
SOME OF THE FEW. Foreword by Hector McGregor. London, Macdonald, 1960. 60 p.

2047 Richards, Denis, and Hilary St. G. Saunders.
ROYAL AIR FORCE, 1939-1945. London, H.M. Stationery Office, 1953-54. 3 v.

2048 Robertson, Bruce.
LANCASTER: THE STORY OF A FAMOUS BOMBER. Los Angeles, Aero Publishers, 1964. 216 p.

2049 Robertson, Bruce.
SPITFIRE--THE STORY OF A FAMOUS FIGHTER. Letchworth, Harleyford Publications, 1960. 211 p.

2050 Ross, John M. S.
ROYAL NEW ZEALAND AIR FORCE. Wellington, War History Branch, Dept. of Internal Affairs, 1955. 343 p. (Official History of New Zealand in the Second World War, 1939-45)

2051 Royal Air Force Journal.
SLIPSTREAM: A ROYAL AIR FORCE ANTHOLOGY. Edited by R. Raymond and David Langdon. London, Eyre and Spottiswoode, 1946. 260 p.

2052 Saundby, Sir Robert H. M. S.
AIR BOMBARDMENT: THE STORY OF ITS DEVELOPMENT. London, Chatto and Windus, 1961. 276 p.

Other edition:
New York, Harper, 1961. 259 p.

2053 Sherrod, Robert L.
HISTORY OF MARINE CORPS AVIATION IN WORLD WAR II. Washington, Combat Forces Press, 1952. 496 p.

2054 Shores, Louis.
HIGHWAYS IN THE SKY: THE STORY OF THE AACS. New York, Barnes and Noble, 1947. 269 p.

2055 Sims, Edward H.
AMERICAN ACES IN GREAT FIGHTER BATTLES OF WORLD WAR II. Foreword by Nathan F. Twining. New York, Harper, 1958. 256 p.

Other edition:
AMERICAN ACES OF WORLD WAR II. London, MacDonald, 1958. 318 p.

2056 Sims, Edward H.
GREATEST FIGHTER MISSIONS OF THE TOP NAVY AND MARINE ACES OF WORLD WAR II. Foreword by Arleigh Burke. New York, Harper, 1962. 250 p.

2057 Southall, Ivan.
BLUEY TRUSCOTT: SQUADRON LEADER KEITH WILLIAM TRUSCOTT, R.A.F., D.F.C. AND BAR. Sydney, Angus and Robertson, 1958. 202 p.

2058 Spaight, James M.
AIR POWER CAN DISARM: A SEQUEL TO AIR POWER AND THE CITIES, 1930. London, Air League of the British Empire in association with I. Pitman, 1948. 173 p.

2059 Stanford Research Institute, Stanford University.
IMPACT OF AIR ATTACK IN WORLD WAR II: SELECTED DATA FOR CIVIL DEFENSE PLANNING. Prepared for Federal Civil Defense Administration. Washington, U.S. Government Printing Office, 1953. 3 v.

2060 Sunderman, James F. (ed.).
WORLD WAR II IN THE AIR. New York, Watts, 1962-63. 2 v. (Watts Aerospace Library)

2061 Tedder, Arthur W.
AIR POWER IN WAR. London, Hodder and Stoughton, 1948. 124 p. (Lees Knowles Lectures)

2062 Tempest, Victor (pseud.).
NEAR THE SUN: THE IMPRESSIONS OF A MEDICAL OFFICER OF BOMBER COMMAND. Foreword by Sir Archibald Sinclair. Brighton, Eng., Crabtree Press, 1946. 84 p.

2063 Thompson, Henry L.
NEW ZEALANDERS WITH THE ROYAL AIR FORCE. Wellington, War History Branch, Dept. of Internal Affairs, 1953-59. 3 v. (Official History of New Zealand in the Second World War, 1939-45)

2064 Turner, John F.
FAMOUS AIR BATTLES. London, Barker, 1963. 215 p.

2065 Turner, John F.
V.C.'S OF THE AIR. London, Harrap, 1960. 187 p.

2066 Ulanoff, Stanley M. (ed.).
FIGHTER PILOT. Garden City, N.Y., Doubleday, 1962. 430 p.

2067 U.S. Aerospace Studies Institute. Concepts Division.
THE ROLE OF AIRPOWER IN GUERRILLA WARFARE, WORLD WAR II. Maxwell Air Force Base, Ala., 1962. 264 p.

2068 U.S. Air Force. USAF Historical Division.
AIR FORCE COMBAT UNITS OF WORLD WAR II. Edited by Maurer Maurer. Washington, U.S. Government Printing Office, 1961. 506 p.

Other edition:
New York, Watts, 196-. (Watts Aerospace Library)

2069 U.S. Air Force. USAF Historical Division.
THE ARMY AIR FORCES IN WORLD WAR II. Edited by Wesley F. Craven and James L. Cate. Chicago, University of Chicago Press, 1948-58. 7 v.

2070 U.S. Air Force. USAF Historical Division.
USAF AIRBORNE OPERATIONS: WORLD WAR II AND KOREAN WAR. Washington, Liaison Office, 1962. 119 p.

2071 U.S. Air Force. USAF Historical Division.
USAF TACTICAL OPERATIONS: WORLD WAR II AND KOREAN WAR. Prepared by Joseph W. Angell, Jr., and others. Washington, Liaison Office, 1962. 178 p.

2072 U.S. Army Air Forces. Office of Statistical Control.
ARMY AIR FORCES STATISTICAL DIGEST, WORLD WAR II. Washington, 1945. 313 p.

2073 U.S. Army Air Forces. Personnel Narratives Division.
COMBAT AIR FORCES OF WORLD WAR II, ARMY OF UNITED STATES. Washington, Army Times, 1945. 95 p.

2074 U.S. Bureau of Aeronautics. (Navy Dept.).
OPERATIONAL HISTORY OF THE FLYING BOAT, OPEN-SEA AND SEADROME ASPECTS, SELECTED CAMPAIGNS, WORLD WAR II. Prepared by Michael G. Kammen. Washington, 1959. 133 p.

2075 U.S. Naval Air Station, Lakehurst, N.J.
THEY WERE DEPENDABLE: AIRSHIP OPERATION, WORLD WAR II, 7 DECEMBER 1941 TO SEPTEMBER 1945. Trenton, N.J., 1946. 56 p.

2076 U.S. Office of Air Force History.
THE ARMY AIR FORCES IN WORLD WAR II. Edited by Wesley F. Craven and James L. Cate. Chicago, University of Chicago Press, 1948-58. 7 v.

2077 U.S. Office of Naval Operations.
THE NAVY'S AIR WAR: A MISSION COMPLETED. Edited by A. R. Buchanan; foreword by Admiral Marc A. Mitscher. New York and London, Harper, 1946. 432 p.

2078 Waters, John C. A.
VALIANT YOUTH: THE MEN OF THE R.A.A.F. Sydney, Johnston, 1945. 103 p.

2079 Whitehouse, Arthur G. J.
THE YEARS OF THE WAR BIRDS. Garden City, N.Y., Doubleday, 1960. 384 p.

2080 Wilber, Edwin L., and E. R. Schoenholtz.
SILVER WINGS: TRUE ACTION STORIES OF THE U.S. AIR FORCE. New York and London, Appleton, 1948. 281 p.

2081 Wood, Winifred.
WE WERE WASPS. Coral Gables, Fla., Glade House, 1946. 195 p.

        b. European Theater
       (see also III. D. 1. b)

2082 Anderson, William.
PATHFINDERS. New York, Jarrolds, 1946. 111 p.

2083 Australia. Royal Australian Air Force.
R.A.A.F. OVER EUROPE. Edited by Frank Johnston. London, Eyre and Spottiswoode, 1946. 189 p.

2084 Bailey, James.
THE SKY SUSPENDED. Foreword by Peter Townsend. London, Hodder and Stoughton, 1965. 166 p.

2085 Baker, Edgar C. R.
PATTLE--SUPREME FIGHTER IN THE AIR. London, Kimber, 1965. 207 p.

2086 Barker, Ralph.
DOWN IN THE DRINK: TRUE STORIES OF THE GOLDFISH CLUB. London, Chatto and Windus, 1955. 253 p.

Other edition:
London, Pan Books, 1958. 206 p.

2087 Barker, Ralph.
THE SHIP-BUSTERS: THE STORY OF THE R.A.F. TORPEDO-BOMBERS. London, Chatto and Windus, 1957. 272 p.

Other edition:
London, Pan Books, 1959. 254 p.

2088 Barker, Ralph.
STRIKE HARD, STRIKE SURE: EPICS OF THE BOMBERS. London, Chatto and Windus, 1963. 210 p.

2089 Barker, Ralph.
THE THOUSAND PLAN: THE STORY OF THE FIRST THOUSAND BOMBER RAID ON COLOGNE. London, Chatto and Windus, 1965. 260 p.

2090 Bartz, Karl.
SWASTIKA IN THE AIR: THE STRUGGLE AND DEFEAT OF THE GERMAN AIR FORCE 1939-1945. 2d ed. Translated from German by Edward Fitzgerald. London, Kimber, 1956. 204 p.

2091 Baumbach, Werner.
BROKEN SWASTIKA: THE DEFEAT OF THE LUFTWAFFE. Translated by Frederick Holt. London, Hale, 1960. 224 p.

Other edition:
THE LIFE AND DEATH OF THE LUFTWAFFE. New York, Coward-McCann, 1960.

2092 Beck, Levitt C.
FIGHTER PILOT. Huntington Park, Calif., 1946. 200 p.

2093 Bennett, Donald C. T.
PATHFINDER: A WAR AUTOBIOGRAPHY. London, Muller, 1958. 287 p.
Other editions:
London, Muller, 1960.

London, Hamilton, 1960. 208 p. (Panther Books)

2094 Bennett, John M.
LETTERS FROM ENGLAND. San Antonio, 1945. 132 p.

2095 Bickers, Richard T.
GINGER LACEY, FIGHTER PILOT: BATTLE OF BRITAIN TOP SCORER. London, Hale, 1962. 189 p.

2096 Binder, Jenane (Patterson).
ONE CROWDED HOUR, THE SAGA OF AN AMERICAN BOY. New York, William-Frederick Press, 1946. 171 p.

2097 Bishop, Edward.
THE WOODEN WONDER: THE STORY OF THE DE HAVILLAND MOSQUITO. London, Parrish, 1959. 168 p.

2098 Bledsoe, Marvin V.
FIGHTER PILOT, A TRUE STORY (THUNDERBOLT PILOT). Riverside, Calif., 1948. 563 l.

2099 Block, Geoffrey.
THE WINGS OF WARFARE: AN INTRODUCTION TO THE MILITARY AIRCRAFT ENGAGED IN THE WESTERN THEATRE OF WAR. London, Hutchinson, 1945. 133 p.

2100 Bloemertz, Gunther.
HEAVEN NEXT STOP: IMPRESSIONS OF A GERMAN FIGHTER PILOT. Translated from German. London, Kimber, 1953. 189 p.

2101 Bolitho, Hector.
COMMAND PERFORMANCE: THE AUTHENTIC STORY OF THE LAST BATTLE OF THE COASTAL COMMAND, R.A.F. New York, Howell and Soskin, 1946. 262 p.

2102 Bolitho, Hector.
A PENGUIN IN THE EYRIE: AN R.A.F. DIARY, 1939-1945. London, Hutchinson, 1955. 254 p.

2103 Bolitho, Hector.
TASK FOR THE COASTAL COMMAND: THE STORY OF THE BATTLE OF THE SOUTH-WEST APPROACHES. London and New York, Hutchinson, 1946. 141 p.

2104 Braddon, Russell.
NEW WINGS FOR A WARRIOR: STORY OF GROUP-CAPTAIN LEONARD CHESHIRE. New York, Rinehart, 1955. 240 p.

2105 Braham, John R. D.
NIGHT FIGHTER. New York, Norton, 1962. 255 p.

2106 Braham, John R. D.
SCRAMBLE! London, Muller, 1961. 255 p.
Other edition:
London Pan, 1963. 189 p.

2107 Brandon, Lewis.
NIGHT FLYER. London, Kimber, 1961. 208 p.

2108 Brickhill, Paul.
THE DAM BUSTERS. London, Evans, 1951. 269 p.
Other editions:
New York, Ballantine, 1955. 185 p.

London, Evans, 1959. 191 p.

London, Evans, 1964. 269 p.

New York, Norton, 1966. 190 p.

2109 Brickhill, Paul.
REACH FOR THE SKY: THE STORY OF DOUGLAS BADER, LEGLESS ACE OF THE BATTLE OF BRITAIN. New York, Norton, 1954. 312 p.
Other editions:
London, Collins, 1954. 384 p.

London, Collins, 1956. 288 p. (Laurel and Gold Series)

London, Collins, 1957. 382 p.

London, Collins, 1964. 382 p. (Fontana Books)

2110 Bullmore, Francis T. K.
THE DARK HAVEN. Foreword by John Salmond. London, Cape, 1956. 192 p.

2111 Burke, Edmund.
GUY GIBSON V.C. London, Arco, 1961. 128 p.

2112 Caidin, Martin.
BLACK THURSDAY. New York, Dutton, 1960. 320 p.

2113 Caidin, Martin.
THE NIGHT HAMBURG DIED. New York, Ballantine Books, 1960. 158 p.

2114 Cameron, Ian.
WINGS OF THE MORNING: THE STORY OF THE FLEET AIR ARM IN THE SECOND WORLD WAR. London, Hodder and Stoughton, 1962. 288 p.

2115 Capka, Joseph.
RED SKY AT NIGHT: THE STORY OF JO CAPKA, D.F.M.. As told to Kendall McDonald; foreword by Archibald McIndoe. London, Blond; New York, Roy, 1958. 191 p.
Other edition:
London, Hamilton, 1959. 190 p. (Panther Books)

2116 Carne, Daphne.
THE EYES OF THE FEW. London, P.R. Macmillan, 1960. 238 p.

2117 Chance, John N.
YELLOW BELLY. London, Hale, 1959. 191 p.

2118 Charlwood, Donald E.
NO MOON TONIGHT. London, Angus and Robertson, 1956. 221 p.
Other edition:
London, Hamilton, 1958. 192 p. (Panther Books)

2119 Chatterton, George J. S.
THE WINGS OF PEGASUS. London, Macdonald, 1962. 282 p.

2120 Cheesman, E. C.
BRIEF GLORY: THE STORY OF A.T.A. Leicester, Harborough, 1946. 248 p.

2121 Chisholm, Roderick.
COVER OF DARKNESS. Foreword by Air Chief Marshal Sir William Elliot. London, Chatto and Windus, 1953. 222 p.
Other edition:
London, Odhams, 1958. 192 p. (Beacon Books)

2122 Clostermann, Pierre.
THE BIG SHOW: SOME EXPERIENCES OF A FRENCH FIGHTER PILOT IN THE R.A.F. Translated by Oliver Berthoud. New York, Random House, 1951. 242 p.
Other editions:
London, Chatto and Windus, 1951. 256 p.
London, Chatto and Windus with Heinemann, 1953. 244 p. (Vanguard Library Series)
Harmondsworth, Eng., Penguin with Chatto and Windus, 1958. 251 p.
London, Transworld, 1965. 254 p. (Corgi Books)

2123 Clostermann, Pierre.
FLAMES IN THE SKY. Translated by Oliver Berthoud. London, Chatto and Windus, 1952. 200 p.
Other editions:
London, Chatto and Windus with Heinemann, 1955. 248 p. (Vanguard Library)
London, Penguin with Chatto and Windus, 1957. 175 p.
London, Chatto and Windus, 1960. 151 p. (Beaver Books)

2124 Cumming, Michael.
PATHFINDER CRANSWICK. London, Kimber, 1962. 208 p.

2125 Deere, Alan C.
NINE LIVES. Foreword by Lord Dowding. London, Hodder and Stoughton, 1959. 262 p.

2126 DESTINY CAN WAIT: THE POLISH AIR FORCE IN THE SECOND WORLD WAR. Foreword by Viscount Portal of Hungerford; edited by M. Lisiewicz. London, Heinemann, 1949. 402 p.

2127 Dornberger, Walter.
V2. Translated from German by James Cleugh and Geoffrey Halliday. London, Hurst and Blackett; New York, Viking Press, 1954. 264 p.

2128 Drum, Karl.
AIRPOWER AND RUSSIAN PARTISAN WARFARE. Edited by Littleton B. Atkinson, Noel F. Parrish, and Albert F. Simpson. Maxwell Air Force Base, Ala., USAF Historical Division, Research Studies Institute, Air University, 1962. 63 p. (USAF Historical Studies)

2129 Dugan, James, and Carroll Stewart.
PLOESTI: THE GREAT GROUND-AIR BATTLE OF 1 AUGUST 1943. New York, Random House, 1962. 407 p.
Other edition:
London, Cape, 1963. 309 p.

2130 Dupuy, Trevor N.
THE AIR WAR IN THE WEST: JUNE 1941-APRIL 1945. London, Ward, 1965. 66 p. (Illustrated History of World War 2)
Original edition:
New York, Watts, 1963.

2131 Francis, Devon E.
FLAK BAIT: THE STORY OF THE MEN WHO FLEW THE MARTIN MARAUDERS. New York, Duell, Sloan and Pearce, 1948. 331 p.

2132 Frankland, Noble.
THE BOMBING OFFENSIVE AGAINST GERMANY: OUTLINES AND PERSPECTIVES. Foreword by Sir James Butler. London, Faber, 1965. 128 p.

2133 Friedheim, Eric, and Samuel W. Taylor.
FIGHTERS UP: THE STORY OF AMERICAN FIGHTER PILOTS IN THE BATTLE OF EUROPE. Edited by Arthur Gordon. Philadelphia, Macrae-Smith, 1945. 275 p.

2134 Galland, Adolf.
THE FIRST AND THE LAST: THE RISE AND FALL OF THE GERMAN FIGHTER FORCES, 1938-1945. Translated by Mervyn Savill. London, Methuen, 1955. 368 p.
Other editions:
New York, Ballantine Books, 1957. 280 p.
London, Transworld, 1957. 415 p. (Corgi Books)

2135 Gallico, Paul.
THE HURRICANE STORY. London, Joseph, 1959. 143 p.
Other edition:
Garden City, N.Y., Doubleday, 1960. 165 p.

2136 Gavin, James M.
AIRBORNE WARFARE. Washington, Infantry Journal, 1947. 186 p.

2137 Gerahty, Leslie M. (Gary Marsh, pseud.).
SAND IN MY SPINACH. London, Barker, 1958. 192 p.

2138 Gibson, Guy P.
ENEMY COAST AHEAD. London, Joseph, 1946. 302 p.

Other edition:
London, Four Square Books, 1961. 288 p.

2139 Godfrey, John T.
THE LOOK OF EAGLES. Foreword by Thomas D. White. New York, Random House, 1958. 245 p.

2140 Harris, Arthur T.
BOMBER OFFENSIVE. London, Collins; New York, Macmillan, 1947. 288 p.

2141 Harrison, Derrick I.
THESE MEN ARE DANGEROUS: THE SPECIAL AIR SERVICE AT WAR. 2d ed. London, Cassell, 1957. 240 p.

Other edition:
London, Transworld, 1958. 255 p. (Corgi Books)

2142 Heilmann, Will.
ALERT IN THE WEST. Translated by Mervyn Savill. London, Kimber, 1955. 202 p.

2143 Henry, Frank M. (Mike Henry, pseud.).
AIR GUNNER. London, Foulis, 1964. 239 p.

2144 Herington, John.
AIR WAR AGAINST GERMANY AND ITALY, 1939-1943. Canberra, Australian War Memorial, 1954. 731 p. (Australia in the War of 1939-1945. Series 3 [Air])

2145 Hichens, Robert P.
WE FOUGHT THEM IN GUNBOATS. Edited and with a preface and epilogue by David James; foreword by Rear-Admiral Hugh H. Rogers. London, Spencer, 1957. 191 p. (Badger Books)

2146 Hillary, Richard.
THE LAST ENEMY. London, Macmillan, 1952. 253 p.

Other edition:
London, Macmillan, 1961. 253 p. (St. Martin's Library)

2147 Irving, David J. C.
THE DESTRUCTION OF DRESDEN. Foreword by Robert Saundby. London, Kimber, 1963. 255 p.

Other edition:
New York, Holt, Rinehart and Winston, 1964.

2148 Irving, David J. C.
THE MARE'S NEST. London, Kimber, 1964. 320 p.

2149 Johnen, Wilhelm.
DUEL UNDER THE STARS: A GERMAN NIGHT FIGHTER PILOT IN THE SECOND WORLD WAR. 2d ed. London, Kimber, 1957. 202 p.

2150 Johnson, Frank (ed.).
R.A.F. OVER EUROPE. London, Eyre, 1946. 189 p.

2151 Johnson, James E.
WING LEADER. Foreword by Douglas Bader. London, Chatto and Windus, 1956. 320 p.

Other editions:
New York, Ballantine Books, 1957. 292 p. (Ballantine War Books)

Harmondsworth, Eng., Penguin, 1959. 304 p.

2152 Johnson, Robert S., with Martin Caidin.
THUNDERBOLT. New York, Rinehart, 1958. 305 p.

2153 Jubelin, Andre.
THE FLYING SAILOR. Translated from French by James Cleugh. London, Hurst and Blackett, 1953. 276 p.

2154 King, Alison.
GOLDEN WINGS: THE STORY OF SOME OF THE WOMEN FERRY PILOTS OF THE AIR TRANSPORT AUXILIARY. London, Pearson, 1956. 191 p.

2155 Knoke, Heinz.
I FLEW FOR THE FUEHRER: THE STORY OF A GERMAN AIRMAN. Translated by John Ewing; introduction by E. R. Quesada. London, Evans, 1953. 187 p.

Other editions:
New York, Holt, 1954. 213 p.

London, Transworld, 1956. 192 p. (Corgi Books)

2156 Lallemant, Raymond.
RENDEZVOUS WITH FATE. Edited and translated from French by Frank Ziegler. London, Macdonald, 1964. 192 p.

2157 Lambermont, Paul M.
LORRAINE SQUADRON. Translated from French by Anthony Pirie; with a letter to author from M. Pierre Mendès-France and a foreword by Air Chief Marshal Sir Basil Embry. London, Cassell, 1956. 196 p.

2158 Lanchbery, Edward.
AGAINST THE GUN: THE STORY OF WING COMMANDER ROLAND BEAUMONT, PILOT OF THE CANBERRA AND THE P.I. Foreword by Sir Hugh Saunders. London, Cassell, 1955. 270 p.

2159 Landau, Rom.
THE WING: CONFESSIONS OF AN R.A.F. OFFICER. London, Faber and Faber, 1945. 331 p.

2160 Lee, Asher.
THE GERMAN AIR FORCE. London, Duckworth, 1946. 284 p.

Other edition:
New York, Harper, 1946. 310 p.

2161 Livry-Level, Philippe, and Rémy (pseud.).
THE GATES BURST OPEN. Translated from French by Pamela Search; foreword by Air Chief Marshal Sir Basil E. Embry. London, Arco, 1955. 192 p.

Other edition:
BOMBS AWAY! London, Brown, Watson, 1957. 160 p. (Digit Books)

2162 McClendon, Dennis E.
THE LADY BE GOOD: MYSTERY BOMBER OF WORLD WAR II. New York, Day, 1962. 192 p.

2163 McLuskey, James F.
PARACHUTE PADRE. Foreword by F. Llewelyn Hughes. London, SCM Press, 1951. 175 p.

2164 Masters, David.
SO FEW: THE IMMORTAL RECORD OF THE ROYAL AIR FORCE. London, Transworld, 1956. 352 p. (Corgi Books)

2165 Meissner, Janusz (Flight Lieutenant Herbert, pseud.).
L FOR LUCY. Edinburgh, Skladneca Ksugarska, 1945. 140 p.

2166 Millington, Geoffrey.
THE UNSEEN EYE. Foreword by William F. Dickson; introduction by Gerald Templer. London, Gibbs and Phillips, 1961. 192 p.

Other edition:
London, Panther Books, 1965.

2167 Mitchell, Alan W.
NEW ZEALANDERS IN THE AIR WAR. Forewords by Right Honorable Sir Archibald Sinclair and W. J. Jordan. London, Harrap, 1945. 192 p.

2168 Morzik, Fritz.
GERMAN AIR FORCE AIRLIFT OPERATIONS. Maxwell Air Force Base, Ala., USAF Historical Division, Research Studies Institute, Air University, 1961. 417 p. (USAF Historical Studies)

2169 Mouchette, René.
THE MOUCHETTE DIARIES, 1940-1943. Edited by André Dezarrois: translated from French by Philip J. Stead. London, Staples Press, 1956. 221 p.

Other edition:
London, Hamilton, 1957. 205 p. (Panther Books)

2170 Munson, Kenneth G.
ABC ENEMY AIRCRAFT, GERMAN AND ITALIAN, OF WORLD WAR II. London, Allen, 1961. 64 p.

2171 Nicholas, M. and N. Nicholas (trs.).
THE FAME OF THE FALCON; AND OTHER STORIES. Translated from Russian. London and New York, Hutchinson, 1946. 104 p.

2172 Offenberg, Jean.
LONELY WARRIOR: THE JOURNAL OF BATTLE OF BRITAIN FIGHTER PILOT JEAN OFFENBERG. Edited by Victor Houart; preface by Peter Townsend; translated by Mervyn Savill. London, Souvenir Press, 1956. 239 p.

Other editions:
London, Transworld, 1957. 252 p. (Corgi Books)

London, World, 1965. (Consul Books)

2173 Owen, Roderic.
THE DESERT AIR FORCE. An authoritative history published in aid of the Royal Air Force Benevolent Fund; with a foreword by Lord Tedder. London and New York, Hutchinson, 1948. 274 p.

2174 Parham, Hetman J., and E. M. G. Belfield.
UNARMED INTO BATTLE: THE STORY OF THE AIR OBSERVATION POST. Foreword by Viscount Alanbrooke. Winchester, Eng., Published for the Air O. P. Officers' Association by Warren, 1956. 168 p.

2175 Plocher, Hermann.
THE GERMAN AIR FORCE VERSUS RUSSIA, 1941. Edited by Harry R. Fletcher. Maxwell Air Force Base, Ala., USAF Historical Division, Aerospace Studies Institute, Air University, 1965. 335 p.

2176 Pokryshkin, Aleksandr I.
RED AIR ACE. London, Soviet War News, 1945. 55 p.

2177 Poolman, Kenneth.
FAITH, HOPE, AND CHARITY: THREE PLANES AGAINST AN AIR FORCE. London, Kimber, 1954. 200 p.

2178 Popham, Hugh.
SEA FLIGHT: A FLEET AIR ARM PILOT'S STORY. London, Kimber, 1954. 200 p.

2179 Pudney, John.
WORLD STILL THERE. London, Hollis and Carter, 1945. 104 p.

2180 Rawnsley, Cecil F., and Robert Wright.
NIGHT FIGHTER. Foreword by John Cunningham. London, Collins; New York, Holt, 1957. 382 p.

2181 Reichers, Louis.
THE FLYING YEARS. New York, Holt, 1956. 384 p.

2182 Rivaz, Richard C.
TAIL GUNNER TAKES OVER. London and New York, Jarrolds, 1945. 112 p.

2183 Roy, Jules.
RETURN FROM HELL. Translated by Mervyn Savill. London, Kimber, 1954. 229 p.

2184 Rudel, Hans U.
STUKA PILOT. Translated by Lynton Hudson; foreword by Douglas Bader. Dublin, Euphorion Books, 1952. 259 p.

Other editions:
London, Transworld, 1957. 319 p.

New York, Ballantine Books, 1958. 239 p.

2185 Rumpf, Hans.
THE BOMBING OF GERMANY. Translated from German by Edward Fitzgerald. London, Muller; New York, Holt, Rinehart and Winston, 1963. 256 p.

2186 Sampson, Francis L.
    LOOK OUT BELOW! A STORY OF THE AIRBORNE BY A PARATROOPER PADRE. Washington, Catholic University of America Press, 1958. 234 p.

2187 Sampson, Francis L.
    PARATROOPER PADRE. Washington, Catholic University of America Press, 1948. 137 p.

2188 Saunders, Hilary A. St. G.
    VALIANT VOYAGING: A SHORT HISTORY OF THE BRITISH INDIA STEAM NAVIGATION COMPANY IN THE SECOND WORLD WAR, 1939-1945. London, Faber, 1949. 216 p.

2189 Saward, Dudley.
    THE BOMBER'S EYE. Foreword by Sir Robert Renwick. London, Cassell, 1959. 264 p.

2190 Schertl, Alfons (Peter Henn, pseud.).
    THE LAST BATTLE. Introduction by Jules Roy; translated by Mervyn Savill. London, Kimber, 1954. 214 p.

2191 Schwabedissen, Walter.
    THE RUSSIAN AIR FORCE IN THE EYES OF GERMAN COMMANDERS. Translated by Helmut Heitman and George E. Blau. n.p., USAF Historical Division, Research Studies Institute, Air University, 1960. 434 p. (USAF Historical Studies)

2192 Sherbrooke-Walker, Ronald.
    KHAKI AND BLUE. London, Saint Catherine Press, 1952. 135 p.

2193 Southall, Ivan.
    THEY SHALL NOT PASS UNSEEN. Sydney, Angus and Robertson, 1966. 216 p. (Pacific Books)

2194 Spooner, Anthony.
    IN FULL FLIGHT. London, Macdonald, 1965. 272 p.

2195 Stainforth, Peter.
    WINGS OF THE WIND. London, Falcon Press, 1952. 263 p.

Other edition:
London, World Distributors, 1956. 253 p. (Viking Books)

2196 Stiles, Bert.
    SERENADE TO THE BIG BIRD. New York, Norton, 1952. 216 p.

2197 Suchenwirth, Richard.
    HISTORICAL TURNING POINTS IN THE GERMAN AIR FORCE WAR EFFORT. Translated by Patricia Klamerth. Maxwell Air Force Base, Ala., USAF Historical Division, Research Studies Institute, Air University, 1959. 143 p. (USAF Historical Studies)

2198 Taylor, John W. R., and Maurice F. Allward.
    SPITFIRE. Leicester, Drysdale Press, 1946. 119 p.

2199 Tickell, Jerrard.
    ASCALON: THE STORY OF SIR WINSTON CHURCHILL'S WARTIME FLIGHTS FROM 1943 TO 1945. Based on records of John Mitchell. London, Hodder and Stoughton, 1964. 128 p.

2200 Tischer, Werner.
    AND SO WE BOMBED MOSCOW ALONE: THE EXCITING PERSONAL STORY OF ONE MAN'S EXPERIENCES IN THE GERMAN LUFTWAFFE. New York, Greenwich Book Publishers, 1960. 94 p.

2201 U.S. Army Air Forces. Mediterranean Theater of Operations.
    DEFEAT. Washington, Headquarters Army Air Forces, Office of the Assistant Chief of Air Staff-2, 1946. 80 p.

2202 Wallace, Graham.
    R.A.F. BIGGIN HILL. London, Putnam, 1957. 288 p.

2203 Warren, John C.
    AIRBORNE MISSIONS IN THE MEDITERRANEAN, 1942-1945. Maxwell Air Force Base, Ala., USAF Historical Division, Research Studies Institute, Air University, 1955. 137 p. (U.S.A.F. Historical Studies)

2204 Warren, John C.
    AIRBORNE OPERATIONS IN WORLD WAR II, EUROPEAN THEATER. Maxwell Air Force Base, Ala., USAF Historical Division, Research Studies Institute, Air University, 1956. 239 p. (USAF Historical Studies)

2205 Watt, Sholto.
    I'LL TAKE THE HIGH ROAD: A HISTORY OF THE BEGINNING OF THE ATLANTIC AIR FERRY IN WARTIME. Fredericton, Brunswick Press, 1960. 169 p.

2206 Webster, Sir Charles K., and Noble Frankland.
    THE STRATEGIC AIR OFFENSIVE AGAINST GERMANY, 1939-45. London, H.M. Stationery Office, 1961. 4 v. (History of the Second World War: United Kingdom Military Series)

2207 Whitnell, Lewis.
    ENGINES OVER LONDON. London, Carroll and Nicolson, 1949. 164 p.

2208 Wolff, Leon.
    LOW LEVEL MISSION. Introduction by John R. Kane. Garden City, N.Y., Doubleday, 1957. 240 p.

Other editions:
London, Longmans, 1958.

London, Hamilton, 1960. 159 p. (Panther Books)

2209 Wood, Derek, and Derek Dempster.
    THE NARROW MARGIN: THE BATTLE OF BRITAIN AND THE RISE OF AIR POWER, 1930-40. Foreword by Sir Thomas Pike. London, Hutchinson; New York, McGraw-Hill, 1961. 536 p.

2210 Wooldridge, John de L.
    LOW ATTACK: THE STORY OF TWO ROYAL AIR FORCE SQUADRONS FROM MAY, 1940 UNTIL MAY, 1943. London, Low, Marston, 1946. 176 p.

2211   Wykeham, Peter.
         FIGHTER COMMAND: A STUDY OF AIR DEFENCE 1914-1960. London, Putnam, 1960. 320 p.

          c. Pacific and Far Eastern Theater

2212   Bailey, James R. A.
         ESKIMO NEL. Foreword by Peter Townsend. Cape Town, Timmins, 1964. 166 p.

2213   Boyington, Gregory ("Pappy" Boyington, pseud.).
         BAA BAA, BLACK SHEEP. New York, Putnam, 1958. 384 p.

       Other edition:
       London, Putnam, 1960. 384 p.

2214   Bryan, Joseph, and Philip Reed.
         MISSION BEYOND DARKNESS. New York, Duell, 1945. 133 p.

2215   Caidin, Martin.
         A TORCH TO THE ENEMY: THE FIRE RAID ON TOKYO. New York, Ballantine; Leicester, Thorne and Porter, 1960. 160 p.

2216   Carter, Percy V.
         SIXTEEN AND FIVE. Roxbury, Mass., 1945. 113 p.

2217   Edmonds, Walter D.
         THEY FOUGHT WITH WHAT THEY HAD: THE STORY OF THE ARMY AIR FORCES IN THE SOUTHWEST PACIFIC, 1941-1942. Introduction by George C. Kenney. Boston, Little, Brown, 1951. 532 p.

2218   Foster, John M.
         HELL IN THE HEAVENS. New York, Putnam, 1961. 320 p.

2219   Glines, Carroll V.
         DOOLITTLE'S TOKYO RAIDERS. London and Princeton, N.J., Van Nostrand, 1964. 447 p.

2220   Graham, Burton, and Frank Smyth.
         A NATION GREW WINGS: THE GRAPHIC STORY OF THE AUSTRALIAN-BUILT BEAUFORTS OF THE ROYAL AUSTRALIAN AIR FORCE IN NEW GUINEA. Melbourne, Winterset House, 1946. 277 p.

2221   Great Britain. Air Ministry.
         WINGS OF THE PHOENIX: THE OFFICIAL STORY OF THE AIR WAR IN BURMA. Prepared by the Air Ministry and the Central Office of Information. London, H.M. Stationery Office, 1949. 143 p.

2222   Green, Alex.
         WE WERE THE (RIFF) R.A.A.F. Perth, Western Australia, Petersons Printing Press, 194-. 87 p.

2223   Hager, Alice.
         WINGS FOR THE DRAGON: THE AIR WAR IN ASIA. New York, Dodd, Mead, 1945. 307 p.

2224   Hastings, Robert P.
         PRIVATEER IN THE COCONUT NAVY. Los Angeles, 1946. 105 p.

2225   Haugland, Vern.
         THE AAF AGAINST JAPAN. New York, Harper, 1948. 515 p.

2226   Hough, Donald, and Elliott Arnold.
         BIG DISTANCE. New York, Duell, Sloan and Pearce, 1945. 255 p.

2227   Howard, Clive, and Joe Whitley.
         ONE DAMNED ISLAND AFTER ANOTHER. Chapel Hill, University of North Carolina Press, 1946. 403 p.

2228   Inoguchi, Rikihei, and Tadashi Nakajima, with Roger Pineau.
         THE DIVINE WIND: JAPAN'S KAMIKAZE FORCE IN WORLD WAR II. Foreword by Vice-Admiral C. R. Brown. London, Hutchinson, 1959. 224 p.

       Other edition:
       London, Four Square Books, 1961. 190 p.

2229   James, Stefan (pseud.).
         BITTER MONSOON: THE MEMOIRS OF A FIGHTER PILOT. Edited by Oliver Moxon. London, Hale, 1955. 192 p.

2230   Johnston, Stanley F.
         THE GRIM REAPERS. London and New York, Jarrolds, 1945. 108 p.

2231   Kenney, George C.
         THE SAGA OF PAPPY GUNN. New York, Duell, Sloan and Pearce, 1959. 133 p.

2232   Larteguy, Jean (ed.).
         THE SUN GOES DOWN: LAST LETTERS FROM JAPANESE SUICIDE-PILOTS AND SOLDIERS. Translated from French by Nora Wydenbruck. London, Kimber, 1956. 183 p.

2233   Lawson, J. H. W.
         FOUR FIVE FIVE: THE STORY OF 455 (R.A.A.F.) SQUADRON. Melbourne, Wilke, 1951. 207 p.

2234   Lawson, Ted W.
         THIRTY SECONDS OVER TOKYO. Edited by Bob Considine. New York, Random House, 1953. 186 p. (Landmark Books)

       Other edition:
       London, Brown, 1958. 160 p. (Digit Books)

2235   Merrill, James M.
         TARGET TOKYO: THE HALSEY-DOOLITTLE RAID. Chicago, Rand McNally, 1964. 208 p.

2236   Midlam, Don S.
         FLIGHT OF THE LUCKY LADY. Portland, Ore., Binfords and Mort, 1954. 208 p.

2237 Miller, Norman M.
I TOOK THE SKY ROAD. As told to Hugh B. Cove. New York, Dodd, Meade, 1945. 212 p.

2238 Morrison, Wilbur H.
HELLBIRDS: THE STORY OF THE B-29s IN COMBAT. Foreword by Curtis E. LeMay. New York, Duell, Sloan and Pearce, 1960. 181 p.

2239 Moxon, Oliver.
THE LAST MONSOON. London, Hale, 1957. 174 p.

2240 Odgers, George.
AIR WAR AGAINST JAPAN, 1943-1945. Canberra, Australian War Memorial, 1957. 533 p. (Australia in the War of 1939-1945. Series 3 [Air])

2241 Okumiya, Masatake, and Jiro Horikoshi, with Martin Caidin.
ZERO! New York, Dutton, 1956. 424 p.

Other editions:
London, Cassell, 1957. 364 p.

London, Transworld, 1958. 412 p. (Corgi Books)

2242 THE ROYAL INDIAN AIR FORCE AT WAR: AN ACCOUNT OF AIR OPERATIONS AGAINST THE JAPANESE IN SOUTH EAST ASIA. New Delhi, Sabharwall at Roxy Printing Press, 1945. 120 p.

2243 Russell, Wilfrid W.
FORGOTTEN SKIES: THE STORY OF THE AIR FORCES IN INDIA AND BURMA. Foreword by Air Chief Marshal Sir Richard Peirse. London and New York, Hutchinson, 1946. 128 p.

2244 Sakai, Saburo, with Martin Caidin and Fred Saito.
SAMURAI! New York, Dutton, 1957. 382 p.

Other edition:
London, Kimber, 1959. 206 p.

2245 Scott, Robert L.
FLYING TINGER: CHENNAULT OF CHINA. Garden City, N.Y., Doubleday, 1959. 285 p.

2246 Sinclair, William B.
JUMP TO THE LAND OF GOD: THE ADVENTURES OF A UNITED STATES AIR FORCE CREW IN TIBET. Based on interviews with Robert E. Crozier. Caldwell, Idaho, Caxton Printers, 1965. 313 p.

2247 Southall, Ivan.
THEY SHALL NOT PASS UNSEEN. London, Hamilton, 1958. 191 p. (Panther Books)

Other edition:
Sydney, Angus and Robertson, 1966. 216 p. (Pacific Books)

2248 Sutton, Barry.
JUNGLE PILOT. London, Macmillan, 1946. 127 p.

2249 Thomas, Lowell J.
BACK TO MANDALAY. New York, Greystone Press, 1951. 320 p.

Other edition:
London, Muller, 1952. 255 p.

2250 Thorburn, Lois and Don Thorburn.
NO TUMULT, NO SHOUTING: STORY OF THE PBY. New York, Holt, 1945. 148 p.

2251 Thorne, Bliss K.
THE HUMP, THE GREAT MILITARY AIRLIFT OF WORLD WAR II. Philadelphia, Lippincott, 1965. 188 p. (Airmen and Aircraft)

2252 Toland, John.
THE FLYING TIGERS. New York, Random House, 1963. 170 p. (Landmark Books)

2253 U.S. Army. Forces in the Far East.
AIR DEFENSE OF THE HOMELAND. Prepared by Headquarters, USAFFE and Eighth U.S. Army Rear. n.p., Distributed by Office of Chief of Military History, Dept. of Army, 1956. 91 p. (Japanese Monograph)

2254 U.S. Army Air Forces. Historical Office.
ARMY AIR FORCES IN THE WAR AGAINST JAPAN, 1941-1942. Washington, U.S. Government Printing Office, 1945. 171 p.

2255 U.S. Marine Corps.
MARINE AVIATION IN THE PHILIPPINES. By Charles W. Boggs, Jr. Washington, Historical Division, Headquarters, U.S. Marine Corps, 1951. 166 p.

2256 U.S. Office of Naval Operations.
U.S. NAVAL AVIATION IN THE PACIFIC. Washington, 1947. 56 p.

2257 Wandrey, Ralph H.
FIGHTER PILOT. Mason City, Iowa, 1950. 82 p.

2258 Wertenbaker, Green P. (Green Peyton, pseud.).
5,000 MILES TOWARDS TOKYO. Norman, University of Oklahoma Press, 1945. 173 p.

2259 Winston, Robert A.
FIGHTING SQUADRON: A SEQUEL TO DIVE BOMBER; A VETERAN SQUADRON LEADER'S FIRST-HAND ACCOUNT OF CARRIER COMBAT WITH TASK FORCE 58. New York, Holiday House, 1946. 182 p.

2260 Wistrand, R. B. (ed.).
PACIFIC SWEEP: A PICTORIAL HISTORY OF THE FIFTH AIR FORCE FIGHTER COMMAND. Sydney, Published for the Fifth Air Force Fighter Command by Johnston, 1946. 112 p.

The Atomic Bombing of Hiroshima and Nagasaki
(see also III. C. 2)

2261 Gensuibaku Kinshi Nihon Nyōgikai.
HIROSHIMA-NAGASAKI, DOCUMENT 1961. Edited by Bunichiro Sano and others; preface by Hideki Yukawa; photographed by Juichi Nagano and others; explanatory notes by Kiyoshi Sakuma and others. Tokyo, Japan Council Against Atomic and Hydrogen Bombs, 1961. 1 v. (chiefly illus.).

2262 Gigon, Fernand.
FORMULA FOR DEATH, $E=MC^2$: THE ATOM BOMBS AND AFTER. Translated from French by Constantine FitzGibbon. New York, Roy Publishers; London, Wingate, 1958. 223 p.

2263 Hachiya, Michihiko.
HIROSHIMA DIARY; THE JOURNAL OF A JAPANESE PHYSICIAN, AUGUST 6-SEPTEMBER 30, 1945. Translated and edited by Warner Wells. Chapel Hill, University of North Carolina Press; London, Gollancz, 1955. 256 p.

2264 Hersey, John R.
HIROSHIMA. New York, Knopf, 1946. 117 p.

Other edition:
Harmondsworth, Eng., Penguin Books, 1958. 127 p.

2265 Hiroshima Gembaku Shōgai Kenkyūkai.
PHYSICAL AND MEDICAL EFFECTS OF THE ATOMIC BOMB IN HIROSHIMA. Prepared by Hiroshima Research Group of Atomic Bomb Casualty. Tokyo, Maruzen Co., 1958. 117 p.

2266 Huie, William B.
THE HIROSHIMA PILOT. New York, Putnam, 1964. 318 p.

2267 Merton, Thomas.
ORIGINAL CHILD BOMB: POINTS FOR MEDITATION TO BE SCRATCHED ON THE WALLS OF A CAVE. New York, New Directions, 1962. (unpaged)

2268 Miller, Merle, and Abe Spitzer.
WE DROPPED THE A-BOMB. New York, Crowell, 1946. 152 p.

2269 Nagai, Takashi.
WE OF NAGASAKI: THE STORY OF SURVIVORS IN AN ATOMIC WASTELAND. Translated by Ichiro Shirato and Herbert B. L. Silverman. New York, Duell, Sloan and Pearce; London, Gollancz, 1951. 207 p.

2270 Osada, Arata (comp.).
CHILDREN OF THE A-BOMB; TESTAMENT OF THE BOYS AND GIRLS OF HIROSHIMA. Translated by Jean Dan and Ruth Sieben-Morgen. Tokyo, Uchida Rokakuho Publishing House, 1959. 437 p.

Other edition:
London, Owen; New York, Putnam, 1963. 256 p.

2271 Trumbull, Robert.
NINE WHO SURVIVED HIROSHIMA AND NAGASAKI: PERSONAL EXPERIENCES OF NINE MEN WHO LIVED THROUGH THE ATOMIC BOMBINGS. New York, Dutton, 1957. 148 p.

4. Naval Operations and Battles, Including Aircraft Carriers, Amphibious Operations, the Merchant Marine, and Submarines

a. General

2272 Auphan, G. A. J. Paul, and Jacques Mordal (pseud.).
THE FRENCH NAVY IN WORLD WAR II. Translated by A. C. J. Sabalot. Annapolis, U.S. Naval Institute, 1959. 413 p.

2273 Aylin, Robert N.
THE U.S.S. GENERAL W. H. GORDON: A PHOTO-STORY OF DUTY ABOARD NAVY TROOP TRANSPORT AP-117 MANNED BY THE U.S. COAST GUARD. New York, 1945. 223 p.

2274 Balison, Howard J.
NEWPORT NEWS SHIPS: THEIR HISTORY IN TWO WORLD WARS. Edited for the Museum by George C. Mason. Newport News, Va., Mariners Museum, 1954. 372 p. (Mariner's Museum [Warwick Co., Va.] Museum Publication)

2275 Bates, Joan (Joan Grosvenor, pseud.), and Leonard Bates.
OPEN THE PORTS: THE STORY OF HUMAN MINE-SWEEPERS. London, Kimber, 1956. 199 p.

2276 BATTLE STATIONS! YOUR NAVY IN ACTION: A PHOTOGRAPHIC EPIC OF THE NAVAL OPERATIONS OF WORLD WAR II, TOLD BY THE GREAT ADMIRALS WHO SAILED THE FLEET FROM NORFOLK TO NORMANDY AND FROM THE GOLDEN GATE TO THE INLAND SEA. New York, Wise, 1946. 402 p.

2277 Behrens, Catherine B. A.
MERCHANT SHIPPING AND THE DEMANDS OF WAR. London, H.M. Stationery Office, 1955. 494 p. (History of the Second World War: United Kingdom Civil Series)

2278 Ben Line Steamers, Ltd.
THE BEN LINE: THE STORY OF A MERCHANT FLEET AT WAR, 1939-1943. London and New York, Nelson, 1946. 107 p.

2279 Bennett, William E. (Warren Armstrong, pseud.).
H.M. SMALL SHIPS. Written with the authority and assistance of the Admiralty. London, Muller, 1958. 199 p.

Other edition:
London, Hamilton, 1961. 160 p. (Panther Books)

2280 Bone, Sir David W.
MERCHANTMEN REARMED. London, Chatto and Windus, 1949. 331 p.

2281 Bowen, Frank C.
THE FLAG OF THE SOURTHERN CROSS, 1939-1945. London, Shaw, Savill and Albion [1947?]. 71 p.

2282 Bragadin, Marc' A.
THE ITALIAN NAVY IN WORLD WAR II. Edited by

Giuseppe Fioravanzo; translated by Gale Hoffman. Annapolis, U.S. Naval Institute, 1957. 380 p.

2283 Brookes, Ewart.
DESTROYER. London, Jarrolds, 1962. 212 p.

2284 Brookes, Ewart.
GLORY PASSED THEM BY. London, Jarrolds, 1958. 175 p.

2285 Brou, Willy C.
COMBAT BENEATH THE SEA. Translated from French by Edward Fitzgerald. New York, Crowell, 1957. 240 p.

Other edition:
THE WAR BENEATH THE SEA. London, Muller, 1958. 239 p.

2286 Bulkley, Robert J.
AT CLOSE QUARTERS: PT BOATS IN THE U.S. NAVY. Foreword by John F. Kennedy; introduction by Ernest McN. Eller. Washington, Naval History Division, Office of Naval Operations, Dept. of Defense, 1962 (published 1963).

2287 Bushell, Thomas A.
EIGHT BELLS: ROYAL MAIL LINES WAR STORY, 1939-1945. London, Trade and Travel Publications, 1950. 207 p.

2288 Campbell, Archibald B.
SALUTE THE RED DUSTER. Foreword by Lord Mountevans. London, Johnson, 1952. 207 p.

Other edition:
London, Brown, Watson, 1957. 157 p. (Digit Books)

2289 Cant, Gilbert.
AMERICA'S NAVY IN WORLD WAR II. New York, Day, 1945. 279 p.

2290 Casey, Robert J.
BATTLE BELOW: THE WAR OF THE SUBMARINE. Indianapolis, Bobbs-Merrill, 1945. 380 p.

2291 Charles, Roland W.
TROOPSHIPS OF WORLD WAR II. Washington, Army Transportation Association, 1947. 374 p.

2292 Chatterton, Edward K., and Kenneth Edwards.
THE ROYAL NAVY: FROM SEPTEMBER 1939 TO SEPTEMBER 1945. London, Hutchinson, 1942-47. 5 v. (Britain at War)

2293 Cope, Harley F., and Walter Karig.
BATTLE SUBMERGED: SUBMARINE FIGHTERS OF WORLD WAR II. New York, Norton, 1951. 244 p.

2294 Corbett, Edmund V. (comp.).
WAVES OF BATTLE. London, Arco, 1959. 280 p.

2295 Creighton, Sir Kenelm.
CONVOY COMMODORE. 2d ed. London, Kimber, 1956. 205 p.

2296 Creswell, John.
SEA WARFARE, 1939-1945: A SHORT HISTORY. London and New York, Longmans, Green, 1950. 344 p.

2297 Cross, Wilbur.
CHALLENGERS OF THE DEEP: THE STORY OF SUBMARINES. New York, Sloane, 1959. 258 p.

2298 Dickson, Robert K.
NAVAL BROADCASTS. London, Allen and Unwin, 1946. 91 p.

2299 Drummond, John D.
H.M. U-BOAT. London, Allen, 1958. 227 p.

Other edition:
London, Hamilton, 1960. 189 p. (Panther Books)

2300 Fane, Francis D., and Don Moore.
THE NAKED WARRIORS. Foreword by Richmond K. Turner. New York, Appleton-Century-Crofts, 1956. 308 p.

Other editions:
London, Wingate, 1957. 223 p.

London, Hamilton, 1958. 189 p. (Panther Books)

2301 Farago, Ladislas.
THE TENTH FLEET. New York, Obolensky, 1962. 366 p.

2302 Fergusson, Bernard E.
THE WATERY MAZE: THE STORY OF COMBINED OPERATIONS. London, Collins; New York, Holt, Rinehart and Winston, 1961. 445 p.

2303 Formidable (aircraft carrier).
A "FORMIDABLE" COMMISSION. Written by the Wardroom Officers of the H.M. Aircraft-Carrier Formidable. London, Seeley, 1948. 158 p.

2304 Frank, Wolfgang.
ENEMY SUBMARINE: THE STORY OF GUNTHER PRIEN, CAPTAIN OF U47, WRITTEN FROM PRIEN'S DIARIES AND FROM SAILING WITH HIM IN ACTION. London, Kimber, 1954. 200 p.

2305 Gallery, Daniel V.
CLEAR THE DECKS! New York, Morrow, 1951. 242 p.

Other editions:
London, Harrap, 1952. 215 p.

London, Hamilton, 1958. 192 p. (Panther Books)

2306 Gallery, Daniel V.
TWENTY MILLION TONS UNDER THE SEA. Chicago, Regnery, 1956. 344 p.

2307 Great Britain. Admiralty.
HIS MAJESTY'S SUBMARINES. London, H.M. Stationery Office, 1945. 64 p.

2308   Great Britain. British Information Services.
THE BRITISH MERCHANT NAVY. New York, 1945. 55 p.

2309   Great Britain. Ministry of War Transport.
BRITISH MERCHANTMEN AT WAR: OFFICIAL STORY OF THE MERCHANT NAVY: 1939-1945. Prepared by J. L. Hodson. London, H. M. Stationery Office; Chicago, Ziff-Davis, 1945. 142 p.

2310   Grider, George.
WAR FISH. As told to Lydel Sims. Boston, Little, Brown, 1958. 282 p.

2311   Hampshire, Arthur C.
THE PHANTOM FLEET. London, Kimber, 1960. 208 p.

2312   Hardy, Alfred C.
EVERYMAN'S HISTORY OF THE SEA WAR. London, Nicholson and Watson, 1948-55. 3 v.

2313   Hart, Sydney G.
DISCHARGED DEAD: A TRUE STORY OF BRITAIN'S SUBMARINES AT WAR. London, Odhams Press, 1956. 208 p.

Other edition:
London, Odhams Press, 1958. 191 p. (Beacon Books)

2314   Heckstall-Smith, Anthony.
THE FLEET THAT FACED BOTH WAYS. London, Blond, 1963. 232 p.

2315   Hinsley, Francis H.
COMMAND OF THE SEA: THE NAVAL SIDE OF BRITISH HISTORY FROM 1918 TO THE END OF THE SECOND WORLD WAR. Foreword by Lord Fraser of North Cape, London. Christophers, 1950. 104 p.

2316   Holman, Gordon.
IN DANGER'S HOUR. London, Hodder and Stoughton, 1948. 217 p.

2317   Holman, Gordon.
THE KING'S CRUISERS. London, Hodder and Stoughton, 1947. 263 p.

2318   Hough, Richard A.
DEATH OF THE BATTLESHIP. New York, Macmillan, 1963. 216 p.

Other editions:
THE HUNTING OF FORCE Z. London, Collins, 1963. 255 p.

London, Collins, 1964. 189 p. (Fontana Books)

2319   Icenhower, Joseph B. (ed.).
SUBMARINE IN COMBAT. New York, Watts, 1964. 180 p. (Watts Seapower Library)

2320   Isakov, Ivan S.
THE RED FLEET IN THE SECOND WORLD WAR. Translated by Jack Hural. London and New York, Hutchinson, 1947. 124 p.

2321   James, Sir William M.
THE BRITISH NAVIES IN THE SECOND WORLD WAR. London, Longmans, 1946. 255 p.

2322   James, Sir William M.
THE PORTSMOUTH LETTERS. London, Macmillan, 1946. 285 p.

2323   Jameson, Sir William S.
SUBMARINERS V.C. Foreword by Rear-Admiral G.W.G. Simpson. London, Davies, 1962. 208 p.

2324   Karig, Walter, and others.
BATTLE REPORT. Prepared from official sources. New York, Published for the Council on Books in Wartime by Farrar and Rinehart, 1944-52. 6 v.

2325   Kauffman, Russell W.
FIFTY THOUSAND HUMAN CORKS. Philadelphia, Dorrance, 1957. 163 p.

2326   Keating, Bern.
THE MOSQUITO FLEET. New York, Putnam, 1963. 244 p.

2327   Keeble, L. A. J.
ORDEAL BY WATER. Foreword by Bernard Rawlings. London and New York, Longmans, Green, 1957. 216 p.

Other editions:
Garden City, N.Y., Doubleday, 1958.

London, Pan, 1959. 206 p.

2328   Kemp, Peter K.
VICTORY AT SEA, 1939-1945. Foreword by Viscount Cunningham of Hyndhope. London, Muller, 1957. 382 p.

Other edition:
KEY TO VICTORY: THE TRIUMPH OF BRITISH SEA POWER IN WORLD WAR II. Boston, Little, Brown, 1957. 382 p.

2329   Kerr, James L. (ed.).
TOUCHING THE ADVENTURES OF MERCHANTMEN IN THE SECOND WORLD WAR. Foreword by John Masefield. London, Harrap, 1953. 256 p.

2330   Kroese, A.
THE DUTCH NAVY AT WAR. London, Allen and Unwin, 1945. 131 p.

2331   Land, Emory.
WINNING THE WAR WITH SHIPS: LAND, SEA, AND AIR, MOSTLY LAND. New York, McBride, 1958. 310 p.

2332   Langmaid, Kenneth J. R.
THE APPROACHES ARE MINED! London, Jarrolds, 1965. 256 p.

2333   Lee, Norman.
LANDLUBBER'S LOG: 25,000 MILES WITH THE MERCHANT NAVY. London, Quality Press Ltd., 1945. 98 p.

2334   Lenton, H. T., and J. J. Colledge.
WARSHIP LOSSES OF WORLD WAR II: BRITISH AND DOMINION FLEETS. London, Allan, 1965. 64 p.

2335   Lincoln, Fredman A.
SECRET NAVAL INVESTIGATOR. London, Kimber, 1961. 207 p.

2336   Lott, Arnold S.
MOST DANGEROUS SEA: A HISTORY OF MINE WARFARE AND AN ACCOUNT OF U.S. NAVY MINE WARFARE OPERATIONS IN WORLD WAR II AND KOREA. Annapolis, U.S. Naval Institute, 1959. 322 p.

2337   Macdonnell, James E.
VALIANT OCCASIONS. Foreword by John Collins. London, Constable, 1952. 261 p.

2338   Macintyre, Donald G. F. W.
FIGHTING SHIPS AND SEAMEN. London, Evans, 1963. 192 p.

2339   Macintyre, Donald G. F. W.
FIGHTING UNDER THE SEA. London, Evans, 1965. 174 p.

2340   Masters, David.
EPICS OF SALVAGE: WARTIME FEATS OF THE MARINE SALVAGE MEN IN WORLD WAR II. London, Cassell, 1953. 264 p.

Other edition:
Boston, Little, Brown, 1954. 234 p.

2341   Masters, David.
IN PERIL ON THE SEA: WAR EXPLOITS OF ALLIED SEAMEN. London, Cresset Press, 1960. 255 p.

2342   Maund, Loben E. H.
ASSAULT FROM THE SEA. London, Methuen, 1950. 311 p.

2343   Mercey, Arch A., and Lee Grove (eds.).
SEA, SURF AND HELL: THE U.S. COAST GUARD IN WORLD WAR II. New York, Prentice-Hall, 1945. 352 p.

2344   Morison, Samuel E.
HISTORY OF UNITED STATES NAVAL OPERATIONS IN WORLD WAR II. Boston, Little, Brown, 1947-62. 15 v.

2345   Morison, Samuel E.
THE TWO-OCEAN WAR: A SHORT HISTORY OF THE UNITED STATES NAVY IN THE SECOND WORLD WAR. Boston, Little, Brown, 1963. 611 p.

2346   Ommanney, Francis D.
FLAT-TOP, THE STORY OF AN ESCORT CARRIER. London and New York, Longmans, Green, 1945. 63 p.

2347   Parrish, Thomas D.
VICTORY AT SEA: THE SUBMARINE. New York, Published for Scholastic Book Services by Ridge Press, 1959. 60 p. (Rutledge Book)

2348   Poolman, Kenneth.
ILLUSTRIOUS. London, Kimber, 1955. 246 p.

2349   Potter, Elmer B., and Chester W. Nimitz.
THE GREAT SEA WAR: THE STORY OF NAVAL ACTION IN WORLD WAR II. Englewood Cliffs, N.J., Prentice-Hall, 1960. 468 p.

Other edition:
London, Harrap, 1962.

2350   Pugh, Marshall.
COMMANDER CRABB. London, Macmillan, 1956. 166 p.

Other editions:
London, World Distributors, 1957. 160 p.
FROGMAN: COMMANDER CRABB'S STORY. New York, Scribner, 1956. 208 p.

2351   Pugsley, A. F., with Donald Macintyre.
DESTROYER MAN. London, Weidenfeld and Nicolson, 1957. 224 p.

2352   Puleston, William D.
THE INFLUENCE OF SEA POWER IN WORLD WAR II. New Haven, Conn., Yale University Press, 1947. 310 p.

Other edition:
London, Oxford University Press, 1947. 284 p.

2353   Rasmussen, Albert H.
RETURN TO THE SEA. London, Constable, 1956. 207 p.

2354   Riesenberg, Felix.
SEA WAR: THE STORY OF THE U.S. MERCHANT MARINE IN WORLD WAR II. New York, Rinehart, 1956. 320 p.

2355   Roscoe, Theodore.
UNITED STATES DESTROYER OPERATIONS IN WORLD WAR II. Research and technical editing by Thomas L. Wattles. Annapolis, U.S. Naval Institute, 1953. 581 p.

2356   Roscoe, Theodore.
UNITED STATES SUBMARINE OPERATIONS IN WORLD WAR II. Written for the Bureau of Naval Personnel from material prepared by R. G. Voge and others. Annapolis, U.S. Naval Institute, 1949. 577 p.

Other edition:
PIG BOATS: THE TRUE STORY OF THE FIGHTING SUBMARINERS OF WORLD WAR II. New York, Bantam Books, 1958. 450 p. (authorized abridgement)

2357   Roskill, Stephen W.
A MERCHANT FLEET IN WAR: ALFRED HOLT AND CO., 1939-1945. London, Collins, 1962. 352 p.

2358   Roskill, Stephen W.
THE NAVY AT WAR, 1939-1945. London, Collins, 1960. 480 p.

Other edition:
WHITE ENSIGN: THE BRITISH NAVY AT WAR, 1939-1945. Annapolis, U.S. Naval Institute, 1960. 480 p.

2359   Roskill, Stephen W.
THE WAR AT SEA, 1939-1945. London, H. M. Stationery Office, 1954-61. 3 v. in 4 pts. (History of the Second World War: United Kingdom Military Series)

2360   Ruge, Friedrich.
SEA WARFARE, 1939-1945: A GERMAN VIEWPOINT. Translated by M. G. Saunders. London, Cassell, 1957. 337 p.

2361   Salomon, Henry.
VICTORY AT SEA. Text by Richard Hanser. Garden City, N.Y., Doubleday, 1959. 256 p.

2362   Schull, Joseph.
THE FAR DISTANT SHIPS: AN OFFICIAL ACCOUNT OF CANADIAN NAVAL OPERATIONS IN THE SECOND WORLD WAR. Ottawa, Cloutier, 1952. 527 p.

2363   Schull, Joseph.
SHIPS OF THE GREAT DAYS: CANADA'S NAVY IN WORLD WAR II. London, Macmillan, 1963. 156 p. (Great Stories of Canada)

2364   Seabrook, William C.
IN THE WAR AT SEA: A RECORD OF ROTTERDAM'S LARGEST MERCHANT FLEET AND ITS GALLANT CREWS FROM 1940 TO 1945. [New York? 1946?] 64 p.

2365   Sellwood, Arthur V.
STAND BY TO DIE. London, New English Library, 1961. 128 p. (Four Square Books)

2366   Shaw, Frank H.
EPIC NAVAL FIGHTS. London, Laurie, 1955. 208 p.

2367   Shaw, Frank H.
UNDER THE RED ENSIGN. Foreword by Rear-Admiral C. G. Brodie. London, Lane, 1958. 207 p.

2368   Silverstone, Paul H.
U.S. WARSHIPS OF WORLD WAR II. Garden City, N.Y., Doubleday, 1965. 442 p.

2369   South Africa. Prime Minister's Dept. Union War Histories Section.
WAR IN THE SOUTHERN OCEANS, 1939-45. Prepared by L. C. Turner, H. R. Gordon-Cumming, and J. E. Betzler. Cape Town and New York, Oxford University Press, 1961. 288 p.

2370   Standard Oil Company.
SHIPS OF THE ESSO FLEET IN WORLD WAR II. New York, Standard Oil Co. [of] New Jersey, 1946. 530 p.

2371   Taylor, Theodore.
FIRE ON THE BEACHES. New York, Norton, 1958. 248 p.

2372   Thomas, David A.
SUBMARINE VICTORY: THE STORY OF BRITISH SUBMARINES IN WORLD WAR II. London, Kimber, 1961. 224 p.

2373   Thomas, David A.
WITH ENSIGNS FLYING: THE STORY OF HER MAJESTY'S DESTROYERS AT WAR, 1939-1945. London, Kimber, 1958. 216 p.

2374   Turner, John F.
BATTLE STATIONS: THE U.S. NAVY'S WAR. New York, Putnam, 1960. 192 p.

2375   Turner, John F.
SERVICE MOST SILENT: THE NAVY'S FIGHT AGAINST ENEMY MINES. London, Harrap, 1955. 200 p.

Other edition:
London, Woeld, 1956. (Viking Books)

2376   Turner, John F.
V.C.'S OF THE ROYAL NAVY. London, Harrap, 1956. 192 p.

Other edition:
London, World, 1957.

2377   U.S. Office of Naval Operations. Naval History Division.
UNITED STATES SUBMARINE LOSSES, WORLD WAR II. Reissued with appendix of Axis submarine losses, fully indexed. Washington, 1963. 244 p.

2378   Vian, Sir Philip.
ACTION THIS DAY: A WAR MEMOIR. London, Muller, 1960. 223 p.

2379   Waldron, Thomas J., and James J. Gleeson.
THE FROGMEN: THE STORY OF THE WARTIME UNDERWATER OPERATORS. London, Evans, 1950. 191 p.

Other edition:
New York, Berkley, 1963. 173 p. (Berkley Highland Book)

2380   Warren, Charles E. T., and James Benson.
ABOVE US THE WAVES: THE STORY OF MIDGET SUBMARINES AND HUMAN TORPEDOES. Foreword by Sir George Creasy. London, Harrap, 1953. 256 p.

Other editions:
London, Transworld, 1955. 332 p. (Corgi Books)

London, Harrap, 1964. 176 p.

THE MIDGET RAIDERS. New York, Sloane, 1954. 318 p.

2381   Waters, Sydney D.
ORDEAL BY SEA: THE NEW ZEALAND SHIPPING COMPANY IN THE SECOND WORLD WAR, 1939-1945. London, New Zealand Shipping Co., 1949. 263 p.

2382 Waters, Sydney D.
THE ROYAL NEW ZEALAND NAVY. Wellington, War History Branch, Dept. of Internal Affairs, 1956. 570 p. (Official History of New Zealand in the Second World War, 1939-45)

2383 Whitehouse, Arthur G. J.
SQUADRONS OF THE SEA. Garden City, N.Y., Doubleday, 1962. 383 p.

2384 Whitehouse, Arthur G. J.
SUBS AND SUBMARINERS. Garden City, N.Y., Doubleday, 1961. 335 p.

Other edition:
London, Muller, 1963. 416 p.

2385 Wilkinson, Burke.
BY SEA AND BY STEALTH. New York, Coward-McCann, 1956. 218 p.

Other editions:
London, Davies, 1957. 224 p.

London, Hamilton, 1958. 156 p. (Panther Books)

2386 Willoughby, Malcolm F.
THE U.S. COAST GUARD IN WORLD WAR II. Annapolis, U.S. Naval Institute, 1957. 347 p.

2387 Young, Edward P.
ONE OF OUR SUBMARINES. London, Hart-Davis, 1952. 316 p.

Other editions:
London, Penguin Books, 1954. 311 p.

London, Hart-Davis, 1957. 252 p. (Adventure Library)

2388 Young, Edward P.
UNDERSEA PATROL. New York, McGraw-Hill, 1953. 298 p.

    b. Atlantic, Mediterranean, and the Arctic

2389 Anscomb, Charles.
SUBMARINER. Foreword by Sydney Raw. London, Kimber, 1957. 203 p.

2390 Beecher, John.
ALL BRAVE SAILORS: THE STORY OF THE S.S. BOOKER T. WASHINGTON. New York, Fisher, 1945. 208 p.

2391 Belot, Raymond de.
THE STRUGGLE FOR THE MEDITERRANEAN, 1939-1945. Translated by James A. Field, Jr. Princeton, N.J., Princeton University Press, 1951. 287 p.

2392 Benyon-Tinker, W. E.
DUST UPON THE SEA. London, Hodder and Stoughton, 1947. 215 p.

2393 Berenbrok, Hans D. (Cajus D. Bekker, pseud.).
K-MEN: THE STORY OF THE GERMAN FROGMEN AND MIDGET SUBMARINES. Preface by Hellmuth Heye; translated from German by George Malcolm. London, Kimber, 1955. 202 p.

Other edition:
London, Kimber, 1961. 157 p.

2394 Berenbrok, Hans D. (C. D. Bekker, pseud.).
SWASTIKA AT SEA: THE STRUGGLE AND DESTRUCTION OF THE GERMAN NAVY, 1939-1945. London, Kimber, 1953. 207 p.

Other edition:
DEFEAT AT SEA. New York, Holt, 1955. 222 p.

2395 Berthold, Will.
THE SINKING OF THE "BISMARCK." Translated from German by Michael Bullock. London, Longmans, Green. 1958. 191 p.

Other edition:
London, Transworld, 1960. 287 p. (Corgi Books)

2396 Blond, Georges.
ORDEAL BELOW ZERO: THE HEROIC STORY OF THE ARCTIC CONVOYS IN WORLD WAR II. London, Souvenir Press, 1956. 199 p.

Other editions:
London, Transworld, 1957. 224 p. (Corgi Books)

London, Mayflower, 1965. 189 p. (Mayflower-Dell Paperbacks)

2397 Blore, Trevor.
TURNING POINT--1943. London and New York, Hutchinson, 1945. 128 p.

2398 Bond, Geoffrey.
LANCASTRIA. London, Oldbourne, 1959. 256 p.

2399 Borghese, Junio V.
SEA DEVILS. Translated from Italian "Decima Flottiglia Mas" by James Clugh and adapted by author. London, Melrose, 1952. 263 p.

Other edition:
Chicago, Regnery, 1954. 261 p.

2400 Bradford, Ernle.
THE MIGHTY HOOD. London, Hodder, 1959. 224 p.

Other edition:
Cleveland, World, 1960. 239 p.

2401 Brennand, Frank.
SINK THE BISMARCK! London, Landsborough, 1960. 160 p. (Four Square Books)

2402 Brennecke, Hans J.
GHOST CRUISER H.K. 33. Written with the co-operation of survivors, including Lieut. Helmut Hanefeld, Assistant Ship's Surgeon Dr. Hasselmann and Chief Quartermaster Ernst Neumeister. Translated by Edward Fitzgerald. London, Kimber, 1954. 208 p.

Other edition:
CRUISE OF THE RAIDER H K-33. New York, Crowell, 1955. 241 p.

2403 Brennecke, Hans J.
   THE HUNTERS AND THE HUNTED. Translated by R. H. Stevens. New York, Norton; London, Burke, 1958. 320 p.
   Other edition:
   London, Transworld, 1960. 383 p. (Corgi Books)

2404 Brennecke, Hans J.
   THE TIRPITZ: THE DRAMA OF THE "LONE QUEEN OF THE NORTH." Translated from German by Frederick Holt. London, Hale, 1963. 187 p.

2405 Bridges, Antony.
   SCAPA FERRY. London, Davies, 1957. 231 p.

2406 Brookes, Ewart.
   THE GATES OF HELL. London, Jarrolds, 1960. 144 p.
   Other edition:
   London, Arrow, 1962. 191 p.

2407 Brown, Winifred.
   NO DISTRESS SIGNALS. London, Davies, 1952. 248 p.

2408 Bull, Peter.
   TO SEA IN A SIEVE. London, Davies, 1956. 224 p.
   Other edition:
   London, Odhams Press, 1958. 223 p. (Beacon Books)

2409 Busch, Fritz O.
   THE DRAMA OF THE SCHARNHORST: A FACTUAL ACCOUNT FROM THE GERMAN VIEWPOINT. Translated from German by Eleanor Brockett and Anton Ehrenzweig. London, Hale, 1956. 186 p.
   Other editions:
   New York, Rinehart, 1956. 182 p.
   London, Hamilton, 1957. 154 p. (Panther Books)

2410 Busch, Fritz O.
   THE STORY OF THE "PRINCE EUGEN." Translated from German by Eleanor Brockett. London, Hale, 1960. 190 p.

2411 Busch, Harold.
   U-BOATS AT WAR. Translated from German by L. P. R. Wilson. New York, Ballantine, 1955. 176 p.
   Other editions:
   London, Putnam, 1955. 288 p.
   London, Hamilton, 1956. 189 p. (Panther Books)

2412 Cain, T. J.
   H.M.S. ELECTRA. As told to A. V. Sellwood. London, Muller, 1959. 282 p.

2413 Cameron, Ian.
   RED DUSTER, WHITE ENSIGN: THE STORY OF THE MALTA CONVOYS. London, Muller, 1959. 218 p.
   Other edition:
   FIVE DAYS TO HELL. London, Hamilton, 1961. 176 p. (Panther Books)

2414 Campbell, Sir Ian, and Donald Macintyre.
   THE KOLA RUN: A RECORD OF ARCTIC CONVOYS, 1941-1945. London, Muller, 1958. 254 p.
   Other edition:
   London, Hamilton, 1960. 190 p. (Panther Books)

2415 Caulfield, Malachy F. (Max Caulfield, pseud.).
   A NIGHT OF TERROR: THE STORY OF THE ATHENIA AFFAIR. London, Muller, 1958. 222 p.
   Other edition:
   TOMORROW NEVER CAME. New York, Norton, 1959. 223 p.

2416 Chell, Randolph A.
   TROOPSHIP. Aldershot, Gale and Polden, 1948. 88 p.

2417 Cherry, Alex H.
   YANKEE R.N.: BEING THE STORY OF A WALL STREET BANKER WHO VOLUNTEERED FOR ACTIVE DUTY IN THE ROYAL NAVY BEFORE AMERICA CAME INTO THE WAR. London and New York, Jarrolds, 1951. 544 p.

2418 Cocchia, Aldo.
   THE HUNTERS AND THE HUNTED: ADVENTURES OF ITALIAN NAVAL FORCES. Translated by Margaret Gwyer. Annapolis, U. S. Naval Institute, 1958. 179 p.

2419 Cocchia, Aldo.
   SUBMARINES ATTACKING: ADVENTURES OF ITALIAN NAVAL FORCES. Translated from Italian by Margaret Gwyer. London, Kimber, 1956. 204 p.

2420 Cooke, Kenneth.
   WHAT CARES THE SEA? London, Hutchinson, 1960. 168 p.
   Other edition:
   New York, McGraw-Hill, 1960. 210 p.

2421 Davies, John.
   LOWER DECK. Introduction by Admiral Sir James Somerville. New York and London, Macmillan, 1945. 186 p.
   Other edition:
   London, Hamilton, 1956. 159 p. (Panther Books)

2422 Davies, John.
   THE STONE FRIGATE. London, Macmillan, 1947. 178 p.

2423 Detmers, Theodor.
   THE RAIDER KORMORAN. Translated from German by Edward Fitzgerald. London, Kimber, 1959. 206 p.
   Other edition:
   London, Kimber, 1961. 159 p.

2424 Di Phillip, John.
   GUNNER'S DIARY. Boston, Meador Publishing Co., 1946. 111 p.

2425 Donald William.
STAND BY FOR ACTION: A SAILOR'S STORY. London, Kimber, 1956. 200 p.

2426 Dorling, Henry T. (Traffrail, pseud.).
WESTERN MEDITERRANEAN, 1942-1945. London, Hodder and Stoughton, 1947. 461 p.

2427 Dove, Patrick G. G.
I WAS GRAF SPEE'S PRISONER! Manchester and London, World Distributors, 1957. 160 p. (Viking Press)

2428 Drummond, John D.
A RIVER RUNS TO WAR. London, Allen, 1960. 208 p.

2429 Dupuy, Trevor N.
THE NAVAL WAR IN THE WEST: THE WOLF PACKS. London, Ward, 1965. 62 p. (Illustrated History of World War 2)

Other edition:
New York, Watts, 1963.

2430 Easton, Alan.
50 NORTH: AN ATLANTIC BATTLEGROUND. Foreword by Rear-Admiral R. L. Dyer. London, Eyre and Spottiswoode, 1963. 287 p.

2431 Fehler, Hein.
DYNAMITE FOR HIRE: THE STORY OF HEIN FEHLER. As told to A. V. Sellwood. London, Laurie, 1956. 264 p.

Other edition:
London, Hamilton, 1958. 192 p. (Panther Books)

2432 Fiedler, Arkady.
THANK YOU, CAPTAIN, THANK YOU! London, Love, 1945. 145 p.

2433 Fisher, Richard.
WITH THE FRENCH MINESWEEPERS. London and New York, Selwyn and Blount, 1945. 175 p.

2434 Forbes, Donald.
TWO SMALL SHIPS. London, Hutchinson, 1957. 208 p.

Other edition:
London, Arrow Books, 1959. 255 p. (Grey Arrow Books)

2435 Forester, Cecil S.
HUNTING THE BISMARCK. London, Joseph, 1959. 110 p.

2436 Forester, Cecil S.
THE LAST NINE DAYS OF THE BISMARCK. Boston, Little, Brown, 1959. 138 p.

2437 Forester, Cecil S.
SINK THE BISMARCK! New York, Bantam Books, 1959. 118 p.

2438 Frank, Wolfgang.
THE SEA WOLVES: THE STORY OF GERMAN U-BOATS AT WAR. Translated by R. O. B. Long; foreword by Leland P. Lovette. New York, Rinehart, 1955. 340 p.

Other editions:
London, Weidenfeld and Nicolson, 1955. 252 p.

London, World Distributors, 1957. 256 p. (Viking Books)

2439 Fraser, Ian E.
FROGMEN V. C. London, Angus and Robertson, 1957.

Other edition:
London, Odhams Press, 1958. 224 p. (Beacon Books)

2440 Frischauer, Willi, and Robert Jackson.
THE ALTMARK AFFAIR. New York, Macmillan, 1955. 255 p.

Other editions:
"THE NAVY'S HERE!" London, Gollancz, 1955.

London, Pan Books, 1957.

2441 Gallery, Daniel V.
WE CAPTURED A U-BOAT. Introduction by Commander Edward Young. London, Sidgwick and Jackson, 1957. 268 p.

Other edition:
London, Landsborough, 1959. 224 p. (Four Square Books)

2442 Gibson, Charles E.
THE SHIP WITH FIVE NAMES. London and New York, Abelard-Schuman, 1965. 159 p.

2443 Gibson, John F.
DARK SEAS ABOVE. Edinburgh, Blackwood, 1947. 286 p.

2444 Glasfurd, Alexander L.
VOYAGE TO BERBERA. London, Sheppard Press, 1947. 133 p.

2445 Golovko, Arsenii G.
WITH THE RED FLEET: THE WAR MEMOIRS OF THE LATE ADMIRAL ARSENII G. GOLOVKO. Translated from Russian by Peter Broomfield; edited with introduction by Sir Aubrey Mansergh. London, Putnam, 1965. 248 p.

2446 Granville, Wilfred, and Robin A. Kelly.
INSHORE HEROES: THE STORY OF H. M. MOTOR LAUNCHES IN TWO WORLD WARS. London, Allen, 1961. 320 p.

2447 Great Britain. Central Office of Information.
THE BATTLE OF THE ATLANTIC: THE OFFICIAL ACCOUNT OF THE FIGHT AGAINST THE U-BOATS, 1939-1945. Prepared for the Admiralty and the Air Ministry. London, H.M. Stationery Office, 1946. 108 p.

2448 Grenfell, Russell.
THE BISMARCK EPISODE. London, Faber, 1948. 219 p.

Other editions:
New York, Macmillan, 1949.

London, Hamilton, 1957. 176 p. (Panther Books)

London, Faber, 1964. 204 p.

2449   Gretton, Sir Peter W.
          CONVOY ESCORT COMMANDER. London, Cassell, 1964. 223 p.

2450   Griffiths, Bernard.
          MACNAMARA'S BAND. London, Kimber, 1960. 192 p.

2451   Hampshire, Arthur C.
          LILIPUT FLEET: THE STORY OF THE ROYAL NAVAL PATROL SERVICE. London, Kimber, 1957. 204 p.

2452   Harling, Robert.
          AMATEUR SAILOR. London, Chatto and Windus, 1952. 291 p. (New Phoenix Library Series)

2453   Harling, Robert.
          THE STEEP ATLANTICK STREAM. London, Chatto and Windus, 1946. 231 p.

2454   Hart, Sydney.
          SUBMARINE UPHOLDER. London, Oldbourne, 1960. 208 p.

2455   Hauge, Eiliv O., and Vera Hartmann.
          FLIGHT FROM DAKAR. Translated by F. H. Lyon. New York, Dutton; London, Allen and Unwin, 1954. 200 p.

2456   Healiss, Ronald.
          ADVENTURE GLORIOUS. London, Muller, 1955. 144 p.

2457   Howarth, David A.
          ACROSS TO NORWAY. New York, Sloane, 1952. 286 p.

2458   Howarth, David A.
          THE SHETLAND BUS. London and New York, Nelson, 1951. 220 p.
       Other edition:
       1957. 228 p.

2459   Howarth, David A.
          THE SLEDGE PATROL. London, Collins; New York, Macmillan, 1957. 233 p.
       Other edition:
       London, Collins, 1959. 189 p. (Fontana Books)

2460   Hughes, Robert.
          THROUGH THE WATERS: A GUNNERY OFFICER IN H.M.S. SCYLLA, 1942-43. Foreword by Robert Burnett. London, Kimber, 1956. 202 p.
       Other edition:
          FLAGSHIP TO MURMANSK. London, Kimber, 1961. 159 p.

2461   Jameson, William.
          ARK ROYAL, 1939-1941. London, Hart-Davis, 1957. 371 p.

2462   Jewell, Norman L. A.
          SECRET MISSION SUBMARINE. As told to Cecil Carnes. Chicago, Ziff-Davis, 1945. 159 p.

2463   Joubert de la Ferté, Philip B.
          BIRDS AND FISHES: THE STORY OF COASTAL COMMAND. London, Hutchinson, 1960. 224 p.

2464   Jullian, Marcel.
          H.M.S. FIDELITY. Told to Marcel Jullian by Lt. Cmdr. Pat O'Leary and Lt. George Archibald. Translated from French by Mervyn Savill. London, Souvenir Press, 1957. 204 p.
       Other editions:
       New York, Norton, 1958. 223 p.
       London, Transworld, 1958. 190 p. (Corgi Books)

2465   Kerr, James L., and David James (eds.).
          WAVY NAVY BY SOME WHO SERVED. Foreword by Lord Cunningham of Hyndhope, London, Harrap, 1950. 263 p.

2466   Kerwin, Paschal E.
          BIG MEN IN THE LITTLE NAVY: THE AMPHIBIOUS FORCE IN THE MEDITERRANEAN, 1943-1944. Paterson, N.J., St. Anthony Guild Press, 1946. 129 p.

2467   King, William.
          THE STICK AND THE STARS. London, Hutchinson; New York, Norton, 1958. 192 p.
       Other edition:
       London, Arrow, 1961.

2468   Krancke, Theodor, and H. J. Brennecke.
          THE BATTLESHIP SCHEER. Translated from German by Edward Fitzgerald. London, Kimber, 1956. 200 p.
       Other edition:
          POCKET BATTLESHIP: THE STORY OF THE ADMIRAL SCHEER. New York, Norton, 1958. 239 p.

2469   Landsborough, Gordon.
          THE BATTLE OF THE RIVER PLATE. London, Hamilton, 1956. 160 p. (Panther Books)

2470   Langmaid, Rowland.
          "THE MED": THE ROYAL NAVY IN THE MEDITERRANEAN, 1939-45. London, Batchworth Press, 1945. 130 p.

2471   Lassen, Suzanne.
          ANDERS LASSEN, V.C. Translated from Danish by Inge Hack. London, Muller, 1965. 244 p.

2472   Lewis, David D.
          THE FIGHT FOR THE SEA: THE PAST, PRESENT, AND FUTURE OF SUBMARINE WARFARE IN THE ATLANTIC. Cleveland, World Publishing Co., 1961. 350 p.

2473   L'Herminier, Jean.
          CASABIANCA: THE SECRET MISSIONS OF A FAMOUS SUBMARINE. Translated from French by Edward Fitzgerald. London, Muller, 1953. 243 p.

2474 Lipscombe, Frank W.
THE BRITISH SUBMARINE. London, Black, 1954. 269 p.

2475 Liversidge, Douglas.
THE THIRD FRONT: THE STRANGE STORY OF THE SECRET WAR IN THE ARTIC. London, Souvenir Press, 1960. 219 p.

Other edition:
London, Four Square Books, 1961. 160 p.

2476 Lodwick, John.
THE FILIBUSTERS: THE STORY OF THE SPECIAL BOAT SERVICE. London, Methuen, 1947. 188 p.

2477 Macintyre, Donald G. F. W.
THE BATTLE OF THE ATLANTIC. London, Batsford; New York, Macmillan, 1961. 208 p.

2478 Macintyre, Donald G. F. W.
THE BATTLE FOR THE MEDITERRANEAN. London, Batsford, 1964. 216 p. (British Battles Series)

Other edition:
New York, Norton, 1965.

2479 Macintyre, Donald G. F. W.
U-BOAT KILLER. Foreword by R. B. Carney. London, Weidenfeld and Nicolson, 1956. 179 p.

Other editions:
New York, Norton, 1957. 239 p.

London, World Distributors, 1957. 188 p.

2480 McKee, Alexander.
BLACK SATURDAY: THE TRAGEDY OF THE "ROYAL OAK." London, Souvenir Press, 1959. 220 p.

Other editions:
London, Transworld, 1960. 252 p. (Corgi Books)

New York, Holt, 1960. 211 p.

2481 McKee, Alexander.
THE COAL-SCUTTLE BRIGADE. London, Souvenir Press, 1957. 223 p.

Other edition:
London, Transworld, 1958. 252 p. (Corgi Books)

2482 Macneil, Calum.
SAN DEMETRIO. Sydney, Angus and Robertson, 1957. 127 p.

Other edition:
London, Transworld, 1958. 157 p. (Corgi Books)

2483 Mars, Alastair.
H.M.S. THULE INTERCEPTS. London, Elek, 1956. 242 p.

Other edition:
London, Pan Books, 1958. 221 p.

2484 Mars, Alastair.
UNBROKEN: THE STORY OF A SUBMARINE. London, Muller, 1953. 223 p.

Other edition:
Edinburgh and London, Oliver, 1962. 146 p. (Coromandel Library)

2485 Metzler, Jost.
THE LAUGHING COW: A U-BOAT CAPTAIN'S STORY. Translated from German by Mervyn Savill. London, Kimber, 1955. 217 p.

2486 Miller, Max.
ALWAYS THE MEDITERRANEAN. Foreword by Walter Karig. New York, Dutton, 1952. 256 p.

2487 Miller, Max.
THE FAR SHORE: WITH OFFICIAL U.S. NAVY AND COAST GUARD PHOTOGRAPHS. New York and London, Whittlesey House, McGraw-Hill, 1945. 173 p.

2488 Millington-Drake, Sir Eugen J. H. V. (comp.).
THE DRAMA OF GRAF SPEE AND THE BATTLE OF THE PLATE: A DOCUMENTARY ANTHOLOGY, 1914-1964. Foreword by Earl Mountbatten of Burma; preface by Sir Philip Vian. London, Davies, 1965. 510 p.

2489 Mohr, Ulrich.
ATLANTIC: THE STORY OF A GERMAN SURFACE RAIDER. As told to A. V. Sellwood. London, Laurie, 1955. 246 p.

Other editions:
New York, Day, 1956. 255 p.

London, Hamilton, 1956. 224 p. (Panther Books)

2490 Monks, Noel.
THAT DAY AT GIBRALTAR. London, Muller, 1957. 192 p.

2491 Monsarrat, Nicholas.
THREE CORVETTES: COMPRISING H.M. CORVETTE, EAST COAST CORVETTE, CORVETTE COMMAND. 2d ed. London, Cassell, 1953. 248 p.

Other edition:
London, Hamilton, 1957. 224 p. (Panther Books)

2492 Norway. Norske Regjerings Informasjonskontor.
ARCTIC WAR, NORWAY'S ROLE IN THE NORTHERN FRONT. London, H.M. Stationery Office on behalf of the Royal Norwegian Government Information Office, 1945. 64 p.

2493 Ogden, Graeme.
MY SEA LADY: THE STORY OF H.M.S. LADY MADELEIN FROM FEBRUARY 1941 TO FEBRUARY 1943. London, Hutchinson, 1963. 201 p.

2494 Ogden, Michael.
THE BATTLE OF NORTH CAPE. London, Kimber, 1962. 207 p.

2495 Pack, Stanley W. C.
THE BATTLE OF MATAPAN. London, Batsford, 1961. 183 p. (British Battles Series)

2496 Payne, Donald G. (Ian Cameron, pseud.).
RED DUSTER, WHITE ENSIGN: THE STORY OF MALTA AND THE MALTA CONVOYS. London, Muller, 1959. 218 p.

Other edition:
Garden City, N.Y., Doubleday, 1960. 260 p.

2497 Peillard, Léonce.
U-BOATS TO THE RESCUE: THE "LACONIA" INCIDENT. Translated from French by Oliver Coburn. London, Cape, 1963. 270 p.

Other edition:
THE LACONIA AFFAIR. New York, Putnam, 1963. 270 p.

2498 Pocock, Arthur.
RED FLANNEL AND GREEN ICE. London, Jenkins, 1951. 254 p.

2499 Pollock, George.
THE JERVIS BAY. London, Kimber, 1958. 206 p.

Other edition:
1961. 160 p.

2500 Poolman Kenneth.
ARK ROYAL. 3d ed. London, Kimber, 1956. 202 p.

2501 Poolman, Kenneth.
THE BATTLE OF SIXTY NORTH. London, Cassell, 1958. 191 p.

2502 Poolman, Kenneth.
THE KELLY. Foreword by Earl Mountbatten of Burma. London, Kimber, 1954. 219 p.

2503 Pope, Dudley.
THE BATTLE OF THE RIVER PLATE. Foreword by Sir Edward Parry. London, Kimber, 1956. 259 p.

Other edition:
GRAF SPEE: THE LIFE AND DEATH OF A RAIDER. Philadelphia, Lippincott, 1957. 256 p.

2504 Pope, Dudley.
FLAT 4: THE BATTLE OF COASTAL FORCES IN THE MEDITERRANEAN. Foreword by Rhoderick R. McGrigor. London, Kimber, 1954. 300 p.

2505 Pope, Dudley.
73 NORTH: THE BATTLE OF THE BARENTS SEA. Foreword by Lord Tovey. London, Weidenfeld and Nicolson. 1958. 320 p.

Other edition:
Philadelphia, Lippincott, 1958. 288 p.

2506 Powell, Michael.
GRAF SPEE. London, Hodder and Stoughton, 1956. 224 p.

Other edition:
DEATH IN THE SOUTH ATLANTIC: THE LAST VOYAGE OF THE GRAF SPEE. New York, Rinehart, 1957. 247 p.

2507 Raeder, Eric.
STRUGGLE FOR THE SEA. Translated from German by Edward Fitzgerald. London, Kimber, 1959. 270 p.

2508 Rayner, Denys A.
ESCORT: THE BATTLE OF THE ATLANTIC. Edited by S. W. Roskill. London, Kimber, 1955. 250 p.

2509 Reynolds, Leonard C.
GUNBOAT 658: THE STORY OF THE OPERATIONS OF A MOTOR GUNBOAT IN THE MEDITERRANEAN FROM THE FALL OF TUNISIA UNTIL THE GERMAN SURRENDER. London, Kimber, 1955. 246 p.

2510 Robertson, Terence.
CHANNEL DASH: THE DRAMA OF TWENTY-FOUR HOURS OF WAR. London, Evans; New York, Dutton, 1958. 208 p.

Other edition:
London, Panther Books, 1959. 189 p.

2511 Robertson, Terence.
THE GOLDEN HORSESHOE. Preface by Sir George Creasy. London, Evans, 1955. 210 p.

Other editions:
New York, Dutton, 1956. 256 p.

London, Pan, 1957. 192 p.

2512 Robertson Terence.
THE SHIP WITH TWO CAPTAINS. Foreword by the American captain, Jerauld Wright, and by the British captain, N. L. A. Jewell. New York, Dutton, 1957. 256 p.

Other editions:
London, Evans, 1957. 192 p.

London, Pan, 1959. 189 p.

2513 Robertson, Terence.
WALKER, R.N.: THE STORY OF CAPTAIN FREDERIC JOHN WALKER. London, Evans, 1956. 216 p.

Other editions:
London, Pan, 1958. 205 p.

London, Evans, 1958. 192 p.

2514 Rogge, Bernhard, and Wolfgang Frank.
THE GERMAN RAIDER ATLANTIS. Translated by R. O. R. Long. New York, Ballantine Books, 1956. 154 p.

Other editions:
UNDER TEN FLAGS: THE STORY OF THE GERMAN COMMERCE RAIDER ATLANTIS. By Bernhard Rogge as told to Wolfgang Frank. London, Weidenfeld and Nicolson, 1957. 185 p.

London, Landsborough, 1960. 160 p. (Four Square Books)

2515 Roskill, Stephen W.
THE SECRET CAPTURE. London, Collins, 1959. 161 p.

2516 Sanders, Jacquin.
THE NIGHT BEFORE CHRISTMAS. New York, Putnam, 1963. 320 p.

2517 Schaeffer, Heinz.
U-BOAT 977. Preface by Earl of Cork and Orrery; foreword by Nicholas Monsarrat. London, Kimber, 1952. 207 p.

Other edition:
New York, Norton, 1953. 260 p.

2518 Schofield, Brian B.
THE RUSSIAN CONVOYS. London, Batsford, 1964. 224 p.

2519 Schofield, William G.
EASTWARD THE CONVOYS. Chicago, Rand McNally, 1965. 239 p.

2520 Sclater, William.
HAIDA. Introduction by Right Honorable A. V. Alexander. Toronto, Oxford University Press, 1947. 221 p.

2521 Scott, Peter T.
THE BATTLE OF THE NARROW SEAS: A HISTORY OF THE LIGHT COASTAL FORCES IN THE CHANNEL AND NORTH SEA, 1939-1945. London, Country Life, 1945. 228 p.

Other edition:
New York, Scribner, 1946. 228 p.

2522 Seligman, Adrian C. C.
NO STARS TO GUIDE. London, Hodder and Stoughton, 1947. 332 p.

Other edition:
London, Pan Books, 1958. 255 p. (slightly abridged)

2523 Sellwood, Arthur V.
DYNAMITE FOR HIRE: THE STORY OF HEIN FEHLER. London, Laurie, 1956. 264 p.

2524 Seth, Ronald S.
THE FIERCEST BATTLE: THE STORY OF NORTH ATLANTIC CONVOY ONS 5, 22ND APRIL-7TH MAY 1943. Foreword by P. W. Gretton. London, Hutchinson, 1961. 208 p.

Other edition:
New York, Norton, 1962.

2525 Seth, Ronald S.
TWO FLEETS SURPRISED: THE STORY OF THE BATTLE OF CAPE MATAPAN, MEDITERRANEAN, MARCH, 1941. Forewords by His Excellency Admiral Angelo Iachino, Commander-in-Chief of the Italian Fleet at Matapan, and Admiral Sir William James. London, Bles, 1960. 201 p.

2526 Shankland, Peter, and Anthony Hunter.
MALTA CONVOY. New York, Washburn; London, Collins, 1961. 256 p.

Other editions:
London, Collins, 1963. 192 p. (Fontana Books)

London, Collins, 1965.

2527 Shirer, William L.
THE SINKING OF THE BISMARCK. New York, Random House, 1962. 178 p.

Other edition:
ALL ABOUT THE SINKING OF THE BISMARCK. London, Allen, 1963. 136 p.

2528 Shropshire (cruiser).
PORTHOLE: BEING A CHRONICLE OF THE OPERATIONS, EXPERIENCES AND PEREGRINATIONS OF H.M.A.S. SHROPSHIRE IN THE SECOND WORLD WAR, 1939-1945; WITH SOME ANIMADVERSIONS THEREON BY MEMBERS OF THE SHIP'S COMPANY. Sydney, Sands, 1946. 95 p.

2529 Sired, Ronald.
ENEMY ENGAGED: A NAVAL RATING WITH THE MEDITERRANEAN FLEET, 1942-44. Edited by F. C. Flynn. London, Kimber, 1957. 205 p.

2530 Taylor, John E. S. R.
THE LAST PASSAGE. London, Allen and Unwin, 1946. 137 p.

2531 Taylor, John E. S. R.
NORTHERN ESCORT. London, Allen and Unwin, 1945. 127 p.

2532 Texas (battleship).
THE U. S. SHIP TEXAS IN WORLD WAR II: A PICTORIAL REVIEW OF THE ACCOMPLISHMENTS OF THE THIRTY-ONE YEAR OLD BATTLESHIP, PUBLISHED FOR THE OFFICERS AND MEN WHO SERVED IN HER DURING THE SECOND WORLD WAR. New York, Publishers Printing Co., 1946. 111 p.

2533 Thomas, Charles W.
ICE IS WHERE YOU FIND IT. Indianapolis, Bobbs-Merrill, 1951. 378 p.

2534 Thompson, Kenneth, and others.
H.M.S. "RODNEY" AT WAR: BEING AN ACCOUNT OF THE PART PLAYED IN THE WAR BY H.M.S. "RODNEY" FROM 1939 TO 1945. London, Hollis and Carter, 1946. 180 p.

2535 Tuleja, Thaddeus V.
TWILIGHT OF THE SEA GODS. New York, Norton, 1958. 284 p.

Other edition:
ECLIPSE OF THE GERMAN NAVY. London, Dent, 1959.

2536 Turner, John F.
A GIRL CALLED JOHNNIE: THREE WEEKS IN AN OPEN BOAT. London, Harrap, 1963. 185 p.

2537 Turner, John F.
PERISCOPE PATROL: THE SAGA OF MALTA SUBMARINES. London, Harrap, 1957. 218 p.

Other edition:
London, Hamilton, 1958. 160 p. (Panther Books)

2538 Vulliez, Albert, and Jacques Mordal (pseud.).
BATTLESHIP SCHARNHORST. Translated from French by George Malcolm. Fair Lawn, N.J., Essential Books; London, Hutchinson, 1958. 255 p.

2539 Warren, Charles E. T., and James Benson.
"THE ADMIRALTY REGRETS...": THE STORY OF HIS MAJESTY'S SUBMARINES "THETIS" AND "THUNDERBOLT." London, Harrap, 1958. 223 p.

2540 Warren, Charles E. T., and James Benson.
WILL NOT WE FEAR: THE STORY OF HIS MAJESTY'S SUBMARINE "SEAL" AND OF LIEUTENANT-COMMANDER RUPERT LONSDALE. Foreword by R. P. Lonsdale. London, Harrap, 1961. 228 p.

Other editions:
New York, Sloane, 1962. 228 p.

London, Collins, 1964. 220 p. (Panther Books)

2541 Wemyas, David E. G.
WALKER'S GROUPS IN THE WESTERN APPROACHES. Liverpool, Liverpool Daily Post and Echo, 1948. 167 p.

Other edition:
RELENTLESS PURSUIT. London, Kimber, 1955. 167 p.

2542 Weyher, Kurt, and Hans J. Ehrlich.
THE BLACK RAIDER. Translated from German by Paul Dinnage. London, Elek Books, 1955. 200 p.

2543 Woodroofe, Thomas.
THE BATTLE OF THE ATLANTIC. London, Faber and Faber, 1965. 120 p. (Men and Events)

2544 Woodrooffe, Thomas.
IN GOOD COMPANY. London, Faber and Faber, 1947. 229 p.

2545 Woodward, David.
THE SECRET RAIDERS: THE STORY OF THE OPERATIONS OF THE GERMAN ARMED MERCHANT RAIDERS IN THE SECOND WORLD WAR. London, Kimber; New York, Norton, 1955. 288 p.

2546 Woodward, David.
THE TIRPITZ; THE STORY, INCLUDING THE DESTRUCTION OF THE CHARNHORST, OF THE CAMPAIGNS AGAINST THE GERMAN BATTLESHIP. London, Kimber; New York, Norton, 1953. 223 p.

c. The War in the Pacific

2547 Andrieu d'Albas, Emmanuel M. A.
DEATH OF A NAVY: JAPANESE NAVAL ACTION IN WORLD WAR II. Translated from French by Anthony Rippon; introduction, notes and maps by Robert A. Theobold. New York, Devin-Adair 1957. 362 p.

Other editions:
London, Hale, 1957. 224 p.

London, Hamilton, 1959. (Panther Books)

2548 Appleman, Roy E., and others.
OKINAWA: THE LAST BATTLE. Washington, Historical Division, Dept. of Army, 1948. 529 p.

Other edition:
London, Paterson, 1960. 527 p.

2549 Ash, Bernard.
SOMEONE HAD BLUNDERED: THE STORY OF THE "REPULSE" AND THE "PRINCE OF WALES." London, Joseph, 1960. 267 p.

Other edition:
Garden City, N.Y., Doubleday, 1961. 305 p.

2550 Babcock, Myles S.
A GUY WHO KNOWS...: A DIARY OF STAFF SERGEANT MYLES S. BABCOCK, COMPANY K, 129TH INFANTRY, 37TH DIVISION. Bemidji, Minn., By the author, 1946. 123 p.

2551 Barns-Graham, John W.
UP AND OVER THE HILL. Oxford, Ronald, 1952. 166 p.

2552 Beach, Edward L.
SUBMARINE! New York, Holt, 1952. 301 p.

Other editions:
London, Heinemann, 1953. 274 p.

London, Brown, 1958. 318 p. (Digit Books)

2553 Belleau Wood (aircraft carrier).
FLIGHT QUARTERS: THE WAR STORY OF THE U.S.S. BELLEAU WOOD, AIRCRAFT CARRIER. Los Angeles, Cole-Holmquist, 1946. 192 p.

2554 Bliven, Bruce.
FROM PEARL HARBOR TO OKINAWA: THE WAR IN THE PACIFIC, 1941-1945. New York, Random House, 1960. 192 p. (Landmark Books)

2555 Bryan, Joseph.
AIRCRAFT CARRIER. New York, Ballantine Books, 1954. 206 p.

2556 Buggy, Hugh.
PACIFIC VICTORY: A SHORT HISTORY OF AUSTRALIA'S PART IN THE WAR AGAINST JAPAN. Issued under the direction and by authority of Australian Minister for Information. North Melbourne, Victorian Railway Print Works, 1945. 301 p.

2557 Cant, Gilbert.
THE GREAT PACIFIC VICTORY FROM THE SOLOMONS TO TOKYO. New York, Day, 1946. 422 p.

2558 Carmer, Carl L.
THE JESSE JAMES OF THE JAVA SEA. New York, Farrar and Rinehart, 1945. 119 p.

2559 Chambliss, William C.
THE SILENT SERVICE. London, Muller; New York, New American Library, 1959. 158 p. (Signet Book)

2560 Chenango (U.S. aircraft carrier).
THE CHENANIGAN, VICTORY EDITION, 1942-1945. Los Angeles, Kater, 1945. 64 p.

2561 Clifford, L. E.
     THE LEADER OF THE CROOKS. Melbourne, Cheshire, 1945. 221 p.

2562 Columbia Broadcasting System.
     FROM PEARL HARBOR INTO TOKYO: THE STORY AS TOLD BY WAR CORRESPONDENTS ON THE AIR. New York, Columbia Broadcasting System, 1945. 312 p.

2563 Connell, Brian.
     RETURN OF THE TIGER. London, Evans, 1960. 207 p.

Other editions:
Garden City, N.Y., Doubleday, 1961. 282 p.

London, Brown, 1961. 160 p. (Digit Books)

London, Evans, 1965. 158 p.

2564 Crowl, Philip A.
     CAMPAIGN IN THE MARIANAS. Washington, Office of Chief of Military History, Dept. of Army, 1960. 505 p. (U.S. Army in World War II: The War in the Pacific)

2565 Crowl, Philip A., and Edmund G. Love.
     SEIZURE OF THE GILBERTS AND MARSHALLS. Washington, Office of the Chief of Military History, Dept. of Army, 1955. 414 p. (U.S. Army in World War II: The War in the Pacific)

2566 Cunningham, Winfield S., with Lydel Sims.
     WAKE ISLAND COMMAND. Boston, Little, Brown, 1961. 300 p.

2567 Davis, Russell G.
     MARINE AT WAR. Boston, Little, Brown, 1961. 258 p.

2568 Devereux, James P. S.
     THE STORY OF WAKE ISLAND. Preface by Robert E. Sherwood. Philadelphia, Lippincott, 1947. 252 p.

Other edition:
London, Hamilton, 1959. 160 p. (Panther Books)

2569 Dexter, David.
     THE NEW GUINEA OFFENSIVES. Canberra, Australian War Memorial, 1961. 851 p. (Australia in the War of 1939-1945. Series 1 [Army])

2570 Donovan, Robert J.
     PT109: JOHN F. KENNEDY IN WORLD WAR II. New York, McGraw-Hill, 1961. 247 p.

2571 Donovan, Robert J.
     THE WAR-TIME ADVENTURES OF PRESIDENT JOHN F. KENNEDY. London, Gibbs and Phillips, 1962. 160 p.

2572 Dos Passos, John.
     TOUR OF DUTY. Boston, Houghton Mifflin, 1946. 336 p.

2573 Dupuy, Trevor N.
     ASIATIC LAND BATTLES: JAPANESE AMBITIONS IN THE PACIFIC. London, Ward, 1965. 116 p. (Illustrated History of World War 2)

Other edition:
New York, Watts, 1963. 116 p. (Military History of World War II)

2574 Edgar, Louise E.
     OUT OF BOUNDS. Philadelphia, Dorrance, 1950. 227 p.

2575 Eichelberger, Robert L., with Milton Mackaye.
     OUR JUNGLE ROAD TO TOKYO. New York, Viking Press, 1950. 306 p.

Other editions:
London, Odhams Press, 1951. 287 p.

London, Odhams Press, 1957. 320 p. (Beacon Books)

2576 Ellis, Albert F.
     MID-PACIFIC OUTPOSTS. Auckland, Brown and Stewart, 1946. 303 p.

2577 Ellsworth, Lyman R.
     GUYS ON ICE. New York, McKay, 1952. 277 p.

2578 Essex (aircraft carrier).
     SAGA OF THE ESSEX. Baton Rouge, Army and Navy Pictorial Publishers, 1946. 141 p.

2579 Fahey, James J.
     PACIFIC WAR DIARY, 1942-1945. Boston, Houghton Mifflin, 1963. 404 p.

2580 Farley, Edward I.
     PT PATROL: WARTIME ADVENTURES IN THE PACIFIC AND THE STORY OF PT'S IN WORLD WAR II. Foreword by Thomas C. Kinkaid. New York, Exposition Press, 1957. 108 p. (Banner Book)

2581 Feakes, Henry J.
     WHITE ENSIGN--SOUTHERN CROSS: A STORY OF THE KING'S SHIPS OF AUSTRALIA'S NAVY. Sydney, Smith, 1952. 246 p.

2582 Feis, Herbert.
     JAPAN SUBDUED: THE ATOMIC BOMB AND THE END OF THE WAR IN THE PACIFIC. Princeton, N.J., Princeton University Press, 1961. 199 p.

2583 Field, James A.
     THE JAPANESE AT LEYTE GULF: THE SHO-OPERATION. Princeton, N.J., Princeton University Press, 1947. 162 p.

2584 Frank, Gerold, and James D. Horan, with J. M. Eckberg.
     U.S.S. SEAWOLF: SUBMARINE RAIDER OF PACIFIC. New York, Putnam, 1945. 197 p.

2585 Fuchida, Mitsuo, and Masatake Okumiya.
     MIDWAY: THE BATTLE THAT DOOMED JAPAN. Translated by Masataka Ohihaya. Annapolis, U.S. Naval Institute, 1955. 263 p.

Other editions:
London, Hutchinson, 1957. 263 p.

Annapolis, U.S. Naval Institute, 1959. 266 p.

London, Arrow, 1961. 255 p.

2586 Gallant, Thomas G.
ON VALOR'S SIDE. Garden City, N.Y., Doubleday, 1963. 364 p.

2587 George, John B.
SHOTS FIRED IN ANGER: A RIFLEMAN'S EYE-VIEW OF THE ACTIVITIES ON THE ISLAND OF GUADALCANAL, IN THE SOLOMONS, DURING THE ELIMINATION OF THE JAPANESE FORCES THERE BY THE AMERICAN ARMY UNDER GENERAL PATCH. Plantersville, S.C., Small Arms Technical Publishing Co., 1947. 421 p. (Samworth Book on Firearms)

2588 Gill, George H.
ROYAL AUSTRALIAN NAVY, 1939-1942. Canberra, Australian War Memorial, 1957. 686 p. (Australia in the War of 1939-1945. Series 2 [Navy])

2589 Gillespie, Oliver A.
THE PACIFIC. Wellington, War History Branch, Dept. of Internal Affairs, 1952. 395 p. (Official History of New Zealand in the Second World War, 1939-45)

2590 Gilroy, Maxwell L.
SOLDIER OF MISFORTUNE. Portland, Ore., 1945. 205 p.

2591 Gordon, Oliver L.
FIGHT IT OUT. London, Kimber, 1957. 238 p.
Other edition:
1961. 160 p. (abridged)

2592 Great Britain. Colonial Office.
AMONG THOSE PRESENT: THE OFFICIAL STORY OF THE PACIFIC ISLANDS AT WAR. London, H.M. Stationery Office, 1946. 95 p.

2593 Great Britain. Ministry of Information.
OCEAN FRONT: THE STORY OF THE WAR IN THE PACIFIC, 1941-44. London, H.M. Stationery Office, 1945. 65 p.

2594 Grenfell, Russell.
MAIN FLEET TO SINGAPORE. London, Faber and Faber, 1951. 238 p.
Other edition:
New York, Macmillan, 1952.

2595 Griffith, Samuel B.
THE BATTLE FOR GUADALCANAL. Philadelphia, Lippincott, 1963. 282 p. (Great Battles of History)

2596 Hammer, David H.
LION SIX. Annapolis, U.S. Naval Institute, 1947. 107 p.

2597 Hara, Tameichi, Fred Saito, and Roger Pineau.
JAPANESE DESTROYER CAPTAIN. Translated and expanded from Japanese. New York, Ballantine; Leicester, Thorpe and Porter, 1961. 312 p.

2598 Hashimoto, Mochitsura.
SUNK: THE STORY OF THE JAPANESE SUBMARINE FLEET, 1941-1945. Translated by E.H.M. Colegrave; introduction by Edward L. Beach. New York, Holt, 1954. 276 p.
Other edition:
London, Cassell, 1954. 218 p.

2599 Hawkins, Maxwell.
TORPEDOES AWAY, SIR! OUR SUBMARINE NAVY IN THE PACIFIC. New York, Holt, 1946. 268 p.

2600 Hayashi, S., and A.D. Coox.
KOGUN: THE JAPANESE ARMY IN THE PACIFIC WAR. Quantico, Va., Marine Corps Association, 1959. 249 p.

2601 Helm, Thomas.
ORDEAL BY SEA: THE TRAGEDY OF THE U.S.S. INDIANAPOLIS. New York, Dodd, Mead, 1963. 243 p.

2602 Henri, Raymond.
IWO JIMA: SPRINGBOARD TO FINAL VICTORY. New York, U.S. Camera, 1945. 95 p.

2603 Henri, Raymond, and others.
THE U.S. MARINES ON IWO JIMA. Washington, Infantry Journal, 1945. 312 p.
Other edition:
New York, Dial Press. 1945, 294 p.

2604 Higgins, Edward T., with Dean Phillips.
WEBFOOTED WARRIORS: THE STORY OF A "FROGMAN" IN THE NAVY DURING WORLD WAR II. New York, Exposition Press, 1955. 172 p. (Banner Book)

2605 Hines, Eugene G.
THE FIGHTING HANNAH: A WAR HISTORY OF THE U.S.S. HANCOCK CV-19. n.p., 1946. 1 v.

2606 Hines, Eugene G.
SHANGRI-LA TO BIKINI. n.p., 1946. 127 p.

2607 Hopkins, Harold.
NICE TO HAVE YOU ABOARD. London, Allen and Unwin, 1964. 217 p.

2608 Horan, James D.
ACTION TONIGHT: THE STORY OF THE DESTROYER O'BARNNON IN THE PACIFIC. New York, Putnam, 1945. 171 p.

2609 Hough, Frank O.
THE ASSAULT ON PELELIU. Washington, Historical Division Headquarters, U.S. Marine Corps, 1950. 209 p.

2610 Hough, Frank O.
THE ISLAND WAR: THE UNITED STATES MARINE CORPS IN THE PACIFIC. Philadelphia and New York, Lippincott, 1947. 413 p.

2611 Howard, Richard A.
999 SURVIVED: AN ANALYSIS OF SURVIVAL EXPERIENCES IN THE SOUTHWEST PACIFIC. Maxwell Air Force Base, Ala., Arctic, Desert, Tropic Information Center, Air University, 1953. 60 p. (ADTIC Publications)

2612 Howlett, R. A. (comp.).
THE HISTORY OF THE FIJI MILITARY FORCES, 1939-1945, COMPILED FROM OFFICIAL RECORDS AND DIARIES. Historical Committee: A. H. Stafford and others. London, Published by the Crown Agents for the Colonies on behalf of the Government of Fiji, 1948. 267 p.

2613 Huie, William B.
FROM OMAHA TO OKINAWA: THE STORY OF THE SEABEES. New York, Dutton, 1945. 257 p.

2614 Hunt, George P.
CORAL COMES HIGH. New York, Harper, 1946. 147 p.

Other edition:
New York, New American Library; London, Muller, 1958. 127 p. (Signet Books)

2615 Isely, Jeter A., and Philip A. Crowl.
THE U.S. MARINES AND AMPHIBIOUS WAR: ITS THEORY, AND ITS PRACTICE IN THE PACIFIC. Princeton, N.J., Princeton University Press, 1951. 636 p.

2616 Ito, Masanori, and Roger Pineau.
THE END OF THE IMPERIAL JAPANESE NAVY. Translated by Andrew Y. Kuroda and Roger Pineau. New York, Norton, 1962. 240 p.

Other edition:
London, Weidenfeld and Nicolson, 1963.

2617 Japan. Hikiage Engochō. Fukuinkyoku. Dai 2 Fukuinkyoku Zammu Shoribu.
OKINAWA AREA NAVAL OPERATIONS, JAN.-JUNE 1945. Compiled by Welfare Ministry Demobilization Bureau, 2d Demobilization Bureau, Liquidation Dept. Tokyo, Allied Translator and Interpreter Section, General Staff, Military Intelligence Section, General Headquarters, Far East Command, 1948. 1 v. (Japanese Monograph)

2618 Japan. Second Demobilization Bureau.
JAPANESE NAVAL VESSELS AT THE END OF THE WAR. Compiled by Shizuo Fakui. Tokyo, 1947. 225 l.

2619 Jensen, Oliver O.
CARRIER WAR. New York, Simon and Schuster; New York, Pocket Books, 1945. 172 p.

2620 Kahn, Ely J.
THE STRAGGLERS. New York, Random House, 1962. 176 p.

2621 Larsen, Colin R.
PACIFIC COMMANDOS: NEW ZEALANDERS AND FIJIANS IN ACTION: A HISTORY OF SOUTHERN INDEPENDENT COMMANDO AND FIRST COMMANDO FIJI GUERRILLAS. Wellington, Reed, 1946. 161 p.

2622 Leckie, Robert.
CHALLENGE FOR THE PACIFIC: GUADALCANAL, THE TURNING POINT OF THE WAR. Garden City, N.Y., Doubleday, 1965. 372 p. (Crossroads of World History Series)

2623 Leckie, Robert.
HELMET FOR MY PILLOW. New York, Random House, 1957. 311 p.

2624 Leckie, Robert.
STRONG MEN ARMED: THE UNITED STATES MARINES AGAINST JAPAN. New York, Random House, 1962. 563 p.

2625 Little, Eric H.
ACTION PACIFIC. London, Spencer, 1956. 189 p. (Badger Books)

2626 Lockwood, Charles A., and Hans C. Adamson.
HELLCATS OF THE SEA. Foreword by Chester W. Nimitz. New York, Greenberg, 1955. 335 p.

2627 Lockwood, Charles A.
SINK 'EM ALL: SUBMARINE WARFARE IN THE PACIFIC. Foreword by Chester W. Nimitz. New York, Dutton, 1951. 416 p.

2628 Lockwood, Charles A., and Hans C. Adamson.
THROUGH HELL AND DEEP WATER: THE STIRRING STORY OF THE NAVY'S DEADLY SUBMARINE, THE U.S.S. HARDER, UNDER THE COMMAND OF SAM DEALEY, DESTROYER KILLER! Foreword by Thomas C. Kinkaid. New York, Greenberg, 1956. 317 p.

2629 Lockwood, Charles A., and Hans C. Adamson.
ZOOMIES, SUBS, AND ZEROES. Foreword by C. A. Pownall and Curtis E. LeMay. New York, Greenberg, 1956. 301 p.

2630 Lott, Arnold S.
BRAVE SHIP, BRAVE MEN. Indianapolis, Bobbs-Merrill, 1964. 272 p.

2631 Louisville (U.S. heavy cruiser).
MAN OF WAR: LOG OF THE UNITED STATES HEAVY CRUISER LOUISVILLE. Philadelphia, Dunlap, 1946. 212 p.

2632 Love, Edmund G.
WAR IS A PRIVATE AFFAIR. New York, Harcourt, Brace, 1959. 192 p.

2633 Luey, Allen T., and H. P. Bruvold.
THE "MINNIE"; OR THE WAR CRUISE OF THE U.S.S. MINNEAPOLIS. Elkhart, Ind., 1946. 126 p.

2634 McCarthy, Dudley.
SOUTH-WEST PACIFIC AREA--FIRST YEAR: KOKODA TO WAU. Canberra, Australian War Memorial, 1959. 656 p. (Australia in the War of 1939-1945. Series 1 [Army])

2635 Macdonnell, James E.
FLEET DESTROYER. Melbourne, The Book Depot, 1945. 102 p.

2636 McKie, Ronald C. H.
THE HEROES. Sydney and London, Angus and Robertson, 1960. 285 p.

Other edition:
London, Hamilton (Panther Books); New York, Harcourt, 1961. 307 p.

2637 McKie, Ronald C. H.
THE SURVIVORS Indianapolis, Bobbs-Merrill, 1953. 246 p.

Other editions:
PROUD ECHO. Sydney and London, Angus and Robertson, 1953. 158 p.

London, Hamilton, 1958. (Panther Books)

2638 McMillan, George, and others.
UNCOMMON VALOR, MARINE DIVISIONS IN ACTION. Washington, Infantry Journal Press, 1946. 256 p.

2639 Markey, Morris.
WELL DONE! AN AIRCRAFT CARRIER IN BATTLE ACTION. Foreword by Ralph A. Ofstie. New York and London, Appleton-Century, 1945. 223 p.

2640 Martin, Ralph G.
BOY FROM NEBRASKA, THE STORY OF BEN KUROKI. New York and London, Harper, 1946. 208 p.

2641 Maruyama, Michirō.
ANATAHAN. Translated, with a foreword by Younghill Kang. New York, Hermitage House; London, Weidenfeld and Nicolson, 1954. 206 p.

2642 Matthews, Allen R.
THE ASSAULT. New York, Simon and Schuster, 1947. 216 p. (Venture Press Book)

2643 Miller, Ernest B.
BATAAN UNCENSORED. Long Prairie, Minn., Hart Publications, 1949. 403 p.

2644 Miller, John.
CARTWHEEL: THE REDUCTION OF RABAUL. Washington, Office of Chief of Military History, Dept. of Army, 1959. 418 p. (U.S. Army in World War II: The War in the Pacific)

2645 Miller, John.
GUADALCANAL: THE FIRST OFFENSIVE. Washington, Historical Division, Dept. of Army, 1949. 413 p. (U.S. Army in World War II: The War in the Pacific)

2646 Miller, Max.
IT'S TOMORROW OUT HERE. New York and London, Whittlesey House, McGraw-Hill, 1945. 186 p.

2647 Milner, Samuel.
VICTORY IN PAPUA. Washington, Office of Chief of Military History, Dept. of Army, 1957. 409 p. (U.S. Army in World War II: The War in the Pacific)

2648 Monks, John, Jr.
A RIBBON AND A STAR: THE THIRD MARINES AT BOUGAINVILLE. New York, Holt, 1945. 242 p.

2649 Moody, Dallas D.
AERIAL GUNNER FROM VIRGINIA: THE LETTERS OF DON MOODY TO HIS FAMILY DURING 1944. Edited by William E. Hemphill. Richmond, Virginia State Library, 1950. 366 p.

2650 Morgan, Murray C.
BRIDGE TO RUSSIA: THOSE AMAZING ALEUTIANS. New York, Dutton, 1947. 222 p.

2651 Napa (attack transport).
NAPALOGUE. Berkeley, Calif., 1946. 107 p.

2652 Newcomb, Richard F.
ABANDON SHIP! New York, Holt, 1958. 316 p.

Other editions:
London, Constable, 1960. 215 p.

London, Transworld, 1961. 252 p. (Corgi Books)

2653 Newcomb, Richard F.
SAVO: THE INCREDIBLE NAVAL DEBACLE OFF GUADALCANAL. Foreword by Captain S. W. Roskill. New York, Holt, 1961. 278 p.

Other edition:
London, Constable, 1963. 237 p.

2654 Norton-Taylor, Duncan.
I WENT TO SEE FOR MYSELF. London and Toronto, Heinemann, 1945. 156 p.

Other edition:
WITH MY HEART IN MY MOUTH. New York, Coward-McCann, 1944.

2655 Noyes, John H.
SAGA SHANNON: THE STORY OF THE USS SHANNON DM25 IN ACTION, 1944-1945. Brooklyn, 1948. 80 p.

2656 O'Callahan, Joseph T.
I WAS CHAPLAIN ON THE FRANKLIN. New York, Macmillan, 1956. 153 p.

Other edition:
1961.

2657 O'Sheel, Patrick, and Gene Cook (eds.).
SEMPER FIDELIS, THE U.S. MARINES IN THE PACIFIC, 1942-1945. New York, Sloane, 1947. 360 p.

2658 Parkin, Ray.
OUT OF THE SMOKE. Introduction by Laurens van der Post. London, Hogarth Press; New York, Morrow, 1960. 311 p.

2659 Paull, Raymond.
  RETREAT FROM KOKODA. Foreword by Sydney Rowell. Melbourne, Heinemann, 1958. 319 p.

  Other edition:
  London, Hamilton, 1960. (Panther Books)

2660 Pensacola (cruiser).
  A HISTORY OF THE U.S.S. PENSACOLA, WITH EMPHASIS ON THE YEARS SHE SERVED IN THE PACIFIC AGAINST THE JAPANESE DURING WORLD WAR II. San Francisco, Phillips and Van Orden, 1946. 108 p.

2661 Pondera (transport).
  U.S.S. PONDERA (APA-191). San Diego, Frye and Smith, 1946. 115 p.

2662 Potter, Elmer B., and Chester W. Nimitz (eds.).
  TRIUMPH IN THE PACIFIC: THE NAVY'S STRUGGLE AGAINST JAPAN. Englewood Cliffs, N.J., Prentice-Hall, 1963. 186 p. (Spectrum Book)

2663 Pratt, Fletcher.
  FLEET AGAINST JAPAN. New York and Longon, Harper, 1946. 263 p.

2664 Pratt, Fletcher.
  THE MARINES' WAR: AN ACCOUNT OF THE STRUGGLE FOR THE PACIFIC FROM BOTH AMERICAN AND JAPANESE SOURCES. New York, Sloane, 1948. 456 p.

2665 Pratt, Fletcher.
  NIGHT WORK: THE STORY OF TASK FORCE 39. New York, Holt, 1946. 267 p.

2666 Pyle, Ernest T.
  LAST CHAPTER. New York, Holt, 1946. 150 p.

2667 Reading, Geoffrey.
  PAPUAN STORY. Sydney and London, Angus and Robertson, 1946. 198 p.

2668 Reinhold, William J.
  THE BULLDOG WAU ROAD. Brisbane, University of Queensland Press, 1946. 53 p.

2669 Reynolds, Quentin J.
  70,000 TO 1: THE STORY OF LIEUTENANT GORDON MANUEL. New York, Random House, 1946. 148 p.

  Other editions:
  London, Cassell, 1947.

  London, Brown, 1957. 156 p. (Digit Books)

2670 Rhys, Lloyd.
  MY SHIP IS SO SMALL. Melbourne, Georgian House, 1946. 127 p.

2671 Richards, Benjam J. (ed.).
  SARA, THE STORY OF THE U.S.S. SARATOGA. n.p., 1945. 173 p.

2672 Riegelman, Harold.
  CAVES OF BIAK: AN AMERICAN OFFICER'S EXPERIENCES IN THE SOUTHWEST PACIFIC. Prefatory notes by Robert L. Eichelberger and Hu Shih. New York, Dial Press, 1955. 278 p.

2673 St. George, Thomas R.
  PROCEED WITHOUT DELAY. New York, Crowell, 1945. 181 p.

2674 St. John, Joseph F.
  LEYTE CALLING. New York, Vanguard Press, 1945. 220 p.

2675 Savo Island (aircraft carrier).
  BATTLE BABY: A PICTORIAL HISTORY OF THE ESCORT CARRIER U.S.S. SAVO ISLAND (CVE 78) BORN FEBRUARY 3, 1944 AT ASTORIA, OREGON, LIVED, FOUGHT AND RAISED HELL UNTIL V-J DAY. SHE WILL NEVER DIE! Edited by Lieutenant Brantford B. Benton; photographed by Howard F. Reser and others. Baton Rouge, Army and Navy Publishing Co., 1946. 132 p.

2676 Schubart, William H.
  FROM THE LETTERS OF WILLIAM HOWARD SCHUBART, JR., LIEUTENANT, UNITED STATES NAVAL RESERVE. Stamford, Conn., Overbrook Press, 1946. 108 p.

2677 Seasholes, Henry C.
  ADRIFT IN THE SOUTH PACIFIC; OR SIX NIGHTS IN THE CORAL SEA. Boston, Baker, 1951. 55 p.

2678 Selby, David.
  HELL AND HIGH FEVER. Sydney, Currawong Publishing Co., 1956. 198 p.

  Other edition:
  London, Angus, 1957. 198 p.

2679 Sheridan, Martin.
  OVERDUE AND PRESUMED LOST: THE STORY OF THE U.S.S. BULLHEAD. Francistown, N.H., Jones, 1947. 143 p.

2680 Sherman, Frederick C.
  COMBAT COMMAND: THE AMERICAN AIRCRAFT CARRIERS IN THE PACIFIC WAR. Preface by William F. Halsey. New York, Dutton, 1950. 427 p.

2681 Sherrod, Robert L.
  ON TO WESTWARD! WAR IN THE CENTRAL PACIFIC. New York, Duell, Sloan and Pearce, 1945. 333 p.

2682 Sherrod, Robert L.
  TARAWA: THE STORY OF A BATTLE. 10th anniversary ed. New York, Duell, Sloan and Pearce, 1954. 164 p.

2683 Smith, Chester L.
  MIDWAY, 4 JUNE 1942. London, Regency Press, 1962. 67 p.

2684 Smith, Holland M., and Percy Finch.
  CORAL AND BRASS. New York, Scribner, 1949. 289 p.

2685 Smith, Robert R.
THE APPROACH TO THE PHILIPPINES. Washington, Office of Chief of Military History, Dept. of Army, 1953. 623 p. (U.S. Army in World War II: The War in the Pacific)

2686 Smith, Stanley E.
THE BATTLE OF LEYTE GULF. Preface by William H. Brockman. New York, Belmont Books, 1961. 174 p.

2687 Smith, Stanley E.
THE BATTLE OF SAVO. New York, Macfadden-Bartell, 1962. 152 p.

2688 Smith, Stanley E.
13 AGAINST THE RISING SUN. New York, Belmont Books, 1961. 140 p. (Belmont Books)

2689 Stafford, Edward P.
THE BIG E: THE STORY OF THE USS ENTERPRISE. Foreword by Arthur W. Radford. New York, Random House, 1962. 499 p.

2690 Steichen, Edward.
THE BLUE GHOST: A PHOTOGRAPHIC LOG AND PERSONAL NARRATIVE OF THE AIRCRAFT CARRIER U.S.S. LEXINGTON IN COMBAT OPERATION. New York, Harcourt, Brace, 1947. 149 p.

2691 Sterling, Forest J.
WAKE OF THE WAHOO. Foreword by Charles A. Lockwood. Philadelphia, Chilton Co., Book Division, 1960. 210 p.

2692 THE STORY OF THE BENNION. n.p., 1947. 110 p.

2693 Stratton, Roy O.
SACO, THE RICE PADDY NAVY. Pleasantville, N.Y., Palmer, 1950. 408 p.

2694 Thompson, James A.
ONLY THE SUN REMEMBERS. London, Dakers, 1950. 276 p.

2695 Toland, John.
BUT NOT IN SHAME: THE SIX MONTHS AFTER PEARL HARBOR. New York, Random House, 1961. 427 p.

Other editions:
London, Gibbs, 1962. 443 p.

London, Hamilton, 1964. (Panther Books)

2696 Tomlinson, Henry M.
MALAY WATERS: THE STORY OF LITTLE SHIPS COASTING OUT OF SINGAPORE AND PENANG IN PEACE AND WAR. London, Hodder and Stoughton, 1950. 199 p.

2697 Tregaskis, Richard W.
GUADALCANAL DIARY. New York, Random House, 1955. 180 p. (Landmark Books)

2698 Trumbull, Robert.
SILVERSIDES. New York, Holt, 1945. 217 p.

2699 Tuleja, Thaddeus V.
CLIMAX AT MIDWAY. New York, Norton, 1950. 248 p.

Other edition:
London, Dent, 1960.

2700 Tweed, George R.
ROBINSON CRUSOE, U.S.N.: THE ADVENTURES OF GEORGE R; TWEED ON JAP-HELD GUAM. As told to Blake Clark. New York and London, Whittlesey House, McGraw-Hill, 1945. 267 p.

2701 U.S. Army. Eighth Army.
REPORT OF THE COMMANDING GENERAL, EIGHTH ARMY, ON THE LUZON MOP-UP OPERATION. n.p., 1945. 57 l.

2702 U.S. Army. Eighth Army.
REPORT OF THE COMMANDING GENERAL, EIGHTH ARMY, ON THE MINDANAO OPERATION, VICTOR V. n.p., 1945. 210 l.

2703 U.S. Army. Eighth Army.
REPORT OF THE COMMANDING GENERAL, EIGHTH ARMY, ON THE NASUGBU AND BATAAN OPERATIONS, MIKE SIX AND MIKE SEVEN. n.p., 1946. 125 l.

2704 U.S. Army. Eighth Army.
REPORT OF THE COMMANDING GENERAL, EIGHTH ARMY, ON THE PALAWAN AND ZAMBOANGA OPERATIONS, VICTOR III AND IV. n.p., 1946. 176 l.

2705 U.S. Army. Eighth Army.
REPORT OF THE COMMANDING GENERAL, EIGHTH ARMY, ON THE PANAY-NEGROS AND CEBU OPERATIONS, VICTOR I AND II. n.p., 1946. 179 l.

2706 U.S. Army. Far East Command.
THE IMPERIAL JAPANESE NAVY IN WORLD WAR II: A GRAPHIC PRESENTATION OF THE JAPANESE NAVAL ORGANIZATION AND LIST OF COMBATANT AND NON-COMBATANT VESSELS LOST OR DAMAGED IN THE WAR. Prepared by Military History Section, Special Staff, General Headquarters, Far East Command, Tokyo, 1952. 279 p. (Japanese Operational Monograph)

2707 U.S. Army. Forces in the Pacific.
ENGINEERS OF THE SOUTHWEST PACIFIC, 1941-1945. Reports of Operations of the U.S. Army Forces in the Far East, Southwest Pacific area, Army Forces, Pacific. Washington, U.S. Government Printing Office, 1947, 1948-. 8 v. V. 1-4, 6-8 published.

2708 U.S. Joint Army-Navy Assessment Committee.
JAPANESE NAVAL AND MERCHANT MARINE SHIPPING LOSSES DURING WORLD WAR II BY ALL CAUSES. Washington, 1947. 1 v. (various pagings)

2709 U.S. Marine Corps.
THE ASSAULT ON PELELIU. Prepared by Frank O. Hough. Washington, Historical Division, Headquarters, U.S. Marine Corps, 1950. 209 p.

2710   U.S. Marine Corps.
THE BATTLE FOR TARAWA. Prepared by Capt. James R. Stockman. Washington, Historical Section, Division of Public Information, Headquarters, U.S. Marine Corps, 1947. 86 p.

2711   U.S. Marine Corps.
BOUGAINVILLE AND THE NORTHERN SOLOMONS. Prepared by John N. Rentz. Washington, Historical Section, Division of Public Information, Headquarters, U.S. Marine Corps, 1948. 166 p.

2712   U.S. Marine Corps.
THE CAMPAIGN ON NEW BRITAIN. Prepared by Frank O. Hough and John A. Crown. Washington, Historical Division, Headquarters, U.S. Marine Corps, 1952. 220 p.

2713   U.S. Marine Corps.
DEFENSE AT WAKE. Prepared by Lt. Col. Robert D. Heinl, Jr. Washington, Historical Section, Division of Public Information, U.S. Marine Corps, 1947. 75 p.

2714   U.S. Marine Corps.
THE GUADALCANAL CAMPAIGN, AUGUST 1942 TO FEBRUARY 1943. Washington, Historical Division, Headquarters, U.S. Marine Corps, 1945. 96 p.

2715   U.S. Marine Corps.
THE GUADALCANAL CAMPAIGN. Prepared by John L. Zimmerman. Washington, Historical Division, Headquarters, U.S. Marine Corps, 1949. 189 p.

2716   U.S. Marine Corps.
HISTORY OF THE U.S. MARINE CORPS OPERATIONS IN WORLD WAR II. Washington, Historical Branch, G-3 Division, Headquarters, U.S. Marine Corps, 1958-. 1 v. published.

2717   U.S. Marine Corps.
HIT THE BEACH! YOUR MARINE CORPS IN ACTION: A PHOTOGRAPHIC EPIC OF MARINE CORPS OPERATIONS IN WORLD WAR II, TOLD BY THE INTREPID LEADERS WHO LAUNCHED THE INITIAL OFFENSIVE AT GUADALCANAL, SWEPT THE PACIFIC, AND SPEARHEADED THE OCCUPATION OF THE JAPANESE EMPIRE. New York, Wise, 1948. 386 p.

2718   U.S. Marine Corps.
IWO JIMA, AMPHIBIOUS EPIC. Prepared by Whitman S. Bartley. Washington, Historical Branch, G-3 Division, Headquarters, U.S. Marine Corps, 1954. 253 p.

2719   U.S. Marine Corps.
MARINES IN THE CENTRAL SOLOMONS. Prepared by John N. Rentz. Washington, Historical Branch, Headquarters, U.S. Marine Corps, 1952. 186 p.

2720   U.S. Marine Corps.
MARINES AT MIDWAY. Prepared by Lt. Col. Robert D. Heinl, Jr. Washington, Historical Section, Division of Public Information, Headquarters, U.S. Marine Corps, 1948. 56 p.

2721   U.S. Marine Corps.
THE MARSHALLS, INCREASING THE TEMPO. Prepared by Lt. Col. Robert D. Heinl, Jr., and John A. Crown. Washington, Historical Branch, G-3 Division, Headquarters, U.S. Marine Corps, 1954. 188 p.

2722   U.S. Marine Corps.
OKINAWA: VICTORY IN THE PACIFIC. Prepared by Charles S. Nichols, Jr., and Henry I. Shaw. Washington, Historical Branch, G-3 Division, Headquarters, U.S. Marine Corps, 1955. 332 p.

Other edition:
Rutland, Vt., Tuttle, 1965. 332 p.

2723   U.S. Marine Corps.
THE RECAPTURE OF GUAM. Prepared by O. R. Lodge. Washington, Historical Branch, G-3 Division, Headquarters, U.S. Marine Corps, 1954. 214 p.

2724   U.S. Marine Corps.
SAIPAN, THE BEGINNING OF THE END. Prepared by Carl W. Hoffman. Washington, Historical Division, U.S. Marine Corps, 1950. 286 p.

2725   U.S. Marine Corps.
THE SEIZURE OF TINIAN. Prepared by Carl W. Hoffman. Washington, Historical Division, Headquarters, U.S. Marine Corps, 1951. 169 p.

2726   U.S. Marine Corps Institute, Washington, D.C.
MARINES IN ACTION: A REVIEW OF THE U.S. MARINE CORPS' OPERATIONS IN THE PACIFIC PHASE OF WORLD WAR II, FROM SAMOA TO PELELIU. Washington, 1945. 61 p.

2727   U.S. Navy.
POWER IN THE PACIFIC: OFFICIAL U.S. NAVY MARINE CORPS AND COAST GUARD PHOTOGRAPHS EXHIBITED AT THE MUSEUM OF MODERN ART, NEW YORK, A PICTORIAL RECORD OF NAVY COMBAT OPERATIONS ON LAND, SEA AND IN THE SKY. Compiled by Captain Edward Steichen. New York, U.S. Camera, 1945. 144 p.

2728   U.S. Navy.
U.S. NAVY WAR PHOTOGRAPHS, PEARL HARBOR TO TOKYO HARBOR: A COLLECTION OF OFFICIAL U.S. NAVY, MARINE CORPS, AND COAST GUARD PHOTOGRAPHS. Compiled by Captain Edward Steichen, New York, U.S. Camera, 1946. 108 p.

2729   U.S. Navy. Escort Carrier Force.
THE ESCORT CARRIERS IN ACTION: THE STORY IN PICTURES OF THE ESCORT CARRIER FORCE, U.S. PACIFIC FLEET, 1945, WITH A SUPPLEMENT FOR THE FLAGSHIP U.S.S. MAKIN ISLAND. Compiled and edited by Price Gilbert, Jr. Atlanta, Ruralist Press, 1946. 228 p.

2730   U.S. Navy. Pacific Fleet and Pacific Ocean Areas.
PHIBSTRAPAC: THE STORY OF THE AMPHIBIOUS TRAINEE, TRAINING COMMAND, AMPHIBIOUS FORCES, PACIFIC FLEET. Atlanta, Love, 194-. 1 v. (unpaged)

2731   U.S. Office of Naval Intelligence.
THE JAPANESE STORY OF THE BATTLE OF MIDWAY. A translation. Washington, 1947. 68 p.

2732　U.S. War Dept. General Staff.
THE CAPTURE OF MAKIN, 20 NOVEMBER-24 NOVEMBER 1943. Washington, Historical Division, War Dept., 1946. 136 p. (American Forces in Action)

2733　U.S. War Dept. General Staff.
GUAM: OPERATORS OF THE 77TH DIVISION, 21 JULY-10 AUG. 1944. Washington, Historical Division, War Dept., 1946. 136 p.

2734　Washington (battleship).
HISTORY OF THE USS WASHINGTON, 1941-1946. Lieutenant Commander R. W. Baker, USN, editor and photographic officer. New York, Kelly, 1946. 116 p.

2735　Wasp (aircraft carrier, 2d of the name).
THE AIRCRAFT CARRIER USS WASP, CV-18. Edited by Lieutenant James S. Ferris. Boston, Crosby, 1946. 105 p.

2736　Wasp (aircraft carrier, 2d of the name).
PREP CHARLIE: A HISTORY OF THE PEREGRINATIONS OF OUR FIGHTING LADY USS WASP WHILE MOTHERING AIR GROUP EIGHTY-ONE. New York, Personnel of the USS Wasp and Air Group 81, 1945. 206 p.

2737　Werstein, Irving.
THE BATTLE OF MIDWAY. New York, Crowell, 1961. 145 p.

2738　Werstein, Irving.
GUADALCANAL. New York, Crowell, 1963. 186 p.

2739　Werstein, Irving.
TARAWA: A BATTLE REPORT. New York, Crowell, 1965. 146 p.

2740　Werstein, Irving.
WAKE: THE STORY OF A BATTLE. New York, Crowell, 1964. 145 p.

2741　Wheeler, Keith.
THE PACIFIC IS MY BEAT. London and New York, Robinson, 1945. 192 p.

2742　Wheeler, Richard.
THE BLOODY BATTLE FOR SURIBACHI. New York, Crowell, 1965. 148 p.

2743　Whipple, Chandler.
LT. JOHN F. KENNEDY--EXPENDABLE! New York, Universal Publishing and Distributing Corp., 1962. 160 p. (Envoy Book)

2744　White, Osmar E. D.
GREEN ARMOUR. Sydney, Angus and Robertson, 1945. 246 p.

Other edition:
New York, Norton, 1945. 288 p.

2745　Willoughby, Charles A., and John Chamberlain.
MacARTHUR: 1941-1951: VICTORY IN THE PACIFIC. London, Heinemann, 1956. 414 p.

2746　Wilson, Earl J.
BATIO BEACHHEAD: U.S. MARINES' OWN STORY OF THE BATTLE FOR TARAWA: AN ACCOUNT DOCUMENTED AND WRITTEN BY FOUR MARINES WHO WENT THROUGH THE BATTLE. New York, Putnam, 1945. 160 p.

2747　Woodward, Gomer V.
THE BATTLE OF LEYTE GULF. New York, Macmillan, 1947. 244 p.

Other editions:
New York, Ballantine, 1957. 190 p.

London, Landsborough, 1958. 192 p. (Four Square Books)

2748　Yokota, Yutaka, with Joseph D. Harrington.
THE KAITEN WEAPON. New York, Ballantine Books, 1962. 255 p. (Ballantine Original)

E. UNDERGROUND AND RESISTANCE, INCLUDING THE GERMAN ANTI-NAZI MOVEMENT (see also III. C. 4)

1. General

2749　International Conference on the History of the Resistance Movements, 1st, Liège, 1958.
EUROPEAN RESISTANCE MOVEMENTS, 1939-1945. London and New York, Pergamon Press, 1960. 410 p.

2750　International Conference on the History of the Resistance Movements, 2d, Milan, 1961.
EUROPEAN RESISTANCE MOVEMENTS, 1939-45: PROCEEDINGS. New York, Macmillan, 1964. 663 p. (Pergamon Press Book)

2751　Levi, Maxine.
THE COMMUNISTS AND THE LIBERATION OF EUROPE. New York, New Century Publishers, 1945. 63 p.

2752　Miksche, F. O.
SECRET FORCES, THE TECHNIQUE OF UNDERGROUND MOVEMENTS. London, Faber, 1950. 181 p.

2753　Novitch, Marian.
THE JEWISH RESISTANCE AND THE ALLIES. Milan, Museu della Scienza e della Tecnica, 1961. 66 l.

2754　Orbaan, Albert.
DUEL IN THE SHADOWS: TRUE ACCOUNTS OF ANTI-NAZI UNDERGROUND WARFARE DURING WORLD WAR II. Garden City, N.Y., Doubleday, 1965. 229 p.

2755　Sanderson, James D.
BEHIND ENEMY LINES. Princeton, N.J., Van Nostrand, 1959. 322 p.

2756　Seth, Ronald S.
HOW THE RESISTANCE WORKED. London, Bles, 1961. 157 p.

2757 Seth, Ronald S.
 THE UNDAUNTED: THE STORY OF RESISTANCE IN WESTERN EUROPE. London, Muller, 1956. 327 p.

Other edition:
London, Hamilton, 1958. 288 p. (Panther Books)

2758 Syrkin, Marie.
 BLESSED IS THE MATCH: THE STORY OF JEWISH RESISTANCE. New York, Knopf, 1947. 361 p.

2759 Thorne, Charles B.
 ST. GEORGE AND THE OCTOPUS. London, Love, 1945. 158 p.

2760 Tilman, Harold W.
 WHEN MAN AND MOUNTAINS MEET. Cambridge, Eng., University Press, 1946. 232 p.

  2. Europe (by country)

   a. Albania

2761 Amery, Julian.
 SONS OF THE EAGLE: A STUDY IN GUERILLA WAR. London, Macmillan, 1948. 354 p.

   b. Belgium and the Netherlands

2762 Boas, J. H.
 RELIGIOUS RESISTANCE IN HOLLAND. London, Allen and Unwin for the Netherlands Government Information Bureau, 1945. 64 p.

2763 Brusselmans, Anne.
 RENDEZ-VOUS 127: THE DIARY OF MADAM BRUSSELMANS, M.B.E., SEPTEMBER 1940-SEPTEMBER 1944. Transcribed by Denis Hornsey; forewords by Sir Basil Embry and Carl Spaatz. London, Benn, 1954. 172 p.

2764 Doneaux, Jacques.
 THEY ARRIVED BY MOONLIGHT. London, Odhams Press, 1956. 230 p.

Other edition:
London, World Distributors, 1959. 222 p.

2765 Duren, Theo van.
 ORANGE ABOVE. London, Staples Press, 1956. 221 p.

2766 Eloy, Victor.
 THE FIGHT IN THE FOREST. Translated from French by N. C. Hunter. London, Hale, 1949. 192 p.

2767 Graaf, Klaas de (A. J. Noel de Gaulle, pseud.).
 DESPERATE CARNIVAL. Translated from Dutch, London, Muller, 1955. 288 p.

2768 Martens, Allard, with Daphne Dunlop.
 THE SILENT WAR: GLIMPSES OF THE DUTCH UNDERGROUND AND VIEWS ON THE BATTLE OF ARNHEM. London, Hodder and Stoughton, 1961. 318 p.

2769 Neave, Airey.
 LITTLE CYCLONE. London, Hodder and Stoughton, 1954. 189 p.

Other edition:
London, Hamilton, 1957. 160 p. (Panther Books)

2770 Rigby, Francoise L.
 IN DEFIANCE. Introduced by Christopher Chataway. London, Elek Books, 1960. 224 p.

2771 Van Woerdan, Peter.
 IN THE SECRET PLACE: A STORY OF THE DUTCH UNDERGROUND. Wheaton, Ill., Van Kampen Press, 1954. 64 p.

   c. France

2772 Bird, Michael J.
 THE SECRET BATTALION. New York, Holt, Rinehart and Winston, 1964. 189 p.

Other edition:
London, Muller, 1965. 189 p.

2773 Bird, William R.
 THE TWO JACKS: THE AMAZING ADVENTURES OF MAJOR JACK M. VENESS AND MAJOR JACK L. FAIRWEATHER. Toronto, Ryerson, 1954. 209 p.

Other edition:
London, Kimber, 1955. 205 p.

2774 Braddon, Russell.
 THE WHITE MOUSE. New York, Norton, 1957. 255 p.

2775 Bromme, Vincent.
 THE WAY BACK: THE STORY OF LIEUT. COMMANDER PAT O'LEARY, G.C., D.S.O., R.N. 2d ed. London, Cassell, 1957. 267 p.

Other editions:
New York, Norton, 1958. 249 p.

London, Panther, 1959. 256 p.

2776 Buckmaster, Maurice J.
 SPECIALLY EMPLOYED: THE STORY OF BRITISH AID TO FRENCH PATRIOTS OF THE RESISTANCE. London, Batchworth, 1952. 200 p.

2777 Collier, Richard.
 TEN THOUSAND EYES. London, Collins; New York, Dutton, 1958. 320 p.

Other edition:
London, Transworld, 1960. 349 p. (Corgi Books)

2778 Ehrlich, Blake.
 RESISTANCE: FRANCE 1940-1945. Boston, Little, Brown, 1965. 278 p.

2779 Fuller, Jean O.
MADELEINE: THE STORY OF NOOR INAYAT KHAN, GEORGE CROSS, M.B.E., CROIX DE GUERRE WITH GOLD STAR. Foreword by Selwyn Jepson. London, Gollancz, 1952. 192 p.

Other edition:
BORN FOR SACRIFICE (MADELEINE); London, Pan Books, 1957. 255 p.

2780 Fuller, Jean O.
NO. 13, BOB. Boston, Little, Brown, 1954. 240 p.

2781 Fuller, Jean O.
THE STARR AFFAIR. London, Gollancz, 1954. 222 p.

Other edition:
London, Hamilton, 1957. 188 p. (Panther Books)

2782 Guillain de Bénouville, Pierre.
THE UNKNOWN WARRIORS: A PERSONAL ACCOUNT OF THE FRENCH RESISTANCE. Translated by Lawrence G. Blackman. New York, Simon and Schuster, 1949. 372 p.

2783 Instone, Gordon.
FREEDOM THE SPUR. London, Burke, 1953. 256 p.

2784 Liebling, Abbot J.
THE REPUBLIC OF SILENCE. New York, Harcourt, Brace, 1947. 522 p.

2785 Marshall, Bruce.
THE WHITE RABBIT. From the story told by F. F. E. Yeo-Thomas. London, Evans, 1952. 262 p.

Other edition:
Boston, Houghton Mifflin, 1953.

2786 Millar, George R.
MAQUIS. London, Heinemann, 1945. 364 p.

Other editions:
London, Pan Books, 1956. 286 p.

London, New English Library, 1965. 383 p. (Four Square Books)

WAITING IN THE NIGHT. Garden City, N.Y., Doubleday, 1946. 377 p.

2787 Prosser, David G.
JOURNEY UNDERGROUND. New York, Dutton, 1945. 347 p.

2788 Renault-Roulier, Gilbert (Rémy, pseud.).
THE SILENT COMPANY. Translated by Lancelot C. Shepherd. London, Barker, 1948. 406 p.

2789 Scott, Lionel.
I DROPPED IN. London, Barrie and Rockliff, 1959. 224 p.

2790 Tartière, Dorothy, and Morris R. Werner.
THE HOUSE NEAR PARIS: AN AMERICAN WOMAN'S STORY OF TRAFFIC IN PATRIOTS. New York, Simon and Schuster, 1946. 326 p.

2791 Tchok, Ivan M.
THE FIRST TO RESIST: THE STORY OF THE FIRST UNDERGROUND MOVEMENT IN THIS WAR. London, New Europe Publishing Co., 1945. 64 p.

2792 Thomas, John.
NO BANNERS: THE STORY OF ALFRED AND HENRY NEWTON. London, Allen, 1955. 346 p.

Other edition:
London, Transworld, 1957. 364 p. (Corgi Books)

2793 Vomécourt, Philippe de.
WHO LIVED TO SEE THE DAY: FRANCE IN ARMS, 1940-1945. Foreword by Lord Tedder. London, Hutchinson, 1961. 288 p.

Other edition:
AN ARMY OF AMATEURS. Garden City, N.Y., Doubleday, 1961. 307 p.

2794 Waldheim-Emmerick, Ragnhild Schurer von.
IN THE FOOTSTEPS OF JOAN OF ARC: TRUE STORIES OF HEROINES OF THE FRENCH RESISTANCE IN WORLD WAR II. Translated from French by Frank Gaynor. New York, Exposition Press, 1959. 153 p. (Exposition-Banner Book)

2795 Walters, Anne M.
MOONDROP TO GASCONY. London, Macmillan, 1946. 296 p.

Other editions:
London, Macmillan, 1951. 296 p

London, Pan Books, 1951. 239 p.

2796 Wynne, Barry.
THE EMPTY COFFIN: THE STORY OF ALAIN ROMANS. London, Souvenir Press, 1959. 196 p.

Other edition:
London, Transworld, 1960. 188 p. (Corgi Books)

2797 Wynne, Barry.
NO DRUMS...NO TRUMPETS: THE STORY OF MARY LINDELL. London, Barker, 1961. 277 p.

2798 Young, George G.
IN TRUST AND TREASON: THE STRANGE STORY OF SUZANNE WARREN. London, Hulton, 1959. 198 p.

Other edition:
London, Studio Vista, 1965. 199 p.

d. Germany and Austria

2799 Almond, Gabriel A. (ed.).
THE STRUGGLE FOR DEMOCRACY IN GERMANY. New York, Russell and Russell, 1965. 345 p.

2800 Andreas-Friedrich, Ruth.
BERLIN UNDERGROUND, 1939-1945. Translated by Barrows Mussey. New York, Holt, 1945. 312 p.

Other edition:
London, Latimer House, 1948. 254 p.

2801 Bayles, William D.
SEVEN WERE HANGED: AN AUTHENTIC ACCOUNT OF THE STUDENT REVOLT IN MUNICH UNIVERSITY. London, Gollancz, 1945. 80 p.

2802 Boehm, Eric H. (ed.).
WE SURVIVED: THE STORIES OF FOURTEEN OF THE HIDDEN AND HUNTED OF NAZI GERMANY. New Haven, Conn., Yale University Press, 1949. 308 p.

2803 Buttinger, Joseph.
IN THE TWILIGHT OF SOCIALISM: A HISTORY OF THE REVOLUTIONARY SOCIALISTS OF AUSTRIA. Translated from German by E. B. Ashton. New York, Praeger, 1953. 577 p.

2804 Donohoe, James.
HITLER'S CONSERVATIVE OPPONENTS IN BAVARIA, 1939-1945: A STUDY OF CATHOLIC, MONARCHIST, AND SEPARATIST ANTI-NAZI ACTIVITIES. Leiden, Brill, 1961. 348 p.

2805 Dulles, Allen W.
GERMANY'S UNDERGROUND. New York and London, Macmillan, 1947. 207 p.

2806 FitzGibbon, Constantine.
20 JULY. New York, Norton, 1956. 285 p.

Other edition:
THE SHIRT OF NESSUS. London, Cassell, 1956. 288 p.

2807 Gallin, Mary A.
ETHICAL AND RELIGIOUS FACTORS IN THE GERMAN RESISTANCE TO HITLER. Washington, Catholic University of America Press, 1955. 231 p.

Other edition:
GERMAN RESISTANCE TO HITLER: ETHICAL AND RELIGIOUS FACTORS. Washington, Catholic University of America Press, 1962. 259 p.

2808 Gisevius, Hans B.
TO THE BITTER END. Translated by Richard and Clara Winstone. Boston, Houghton Mifflin, 1947. 600 p.

Other edition:
London, Cape, 1948.

2809 Gollwitzer, Helmut, Kathe Kuhn, and Reinhold Schneider, (eds.).
DYING WE LIVE: THE FINAL MESSAGES AND RECORDS OF THE RESISTANCE. Edited by Helmut Gollwitzer; translated by Reinhard C. Kuhn. New York, Pantheon, 1956. 285 p.

2810 Izbicki, John.
THE NAKED HEROINE: THE STORY OF LYDIA LOVE. London, Spearman, 1963. 189 p.

2811 Leber, Annedore (comp.), assisted by Willy Brandt and Karl Dietrich Bracher.
CONSCIENCE IN REVOLT: SIXTY-FOUR STORIES OF RESISTANCE IN GERMANY, 1933-45. With contributions from Hilde Walter, Wolfgang Steglich and Harald Poelchau; introduction by Robert Birley; translated from the German by Rosemary O'Neill. London, Vallentine, Mitchell, 1957. 270 p.

2812 Manvell, Roger, and Heinrich Fraenkel.
THE JULY PLOT: THE ATTEMPT IN 1944 ON HITLER'S LIFE AND THE MEN BEHIND IT. London, Bodley Head, 1964. 272 p.

Other edition:
THE MEN WHO TRIED TO KILL HITLER. New York, Coward-McCann, 1964. 272 p.

2813 Prittie, Terence C. F.
GERMANS AGAINST HITLER. Foreword by Hugh Trevor-Roper. London, Hutchinson, New York, Little, Brown, 1964. 291 p.

2814 Ritter, Gerhard.
THE GERMAN RESISTANCE: CARL GOERDELER'S STRUGGLE AGAINST TYRANNY. Translated by R. T. Clark. London, Allen and Unwin, 1958. 330 p.

Other edition:
New York, Praeger, 1959. 330 p.

2815 Rothfels, Hans.
THE GERMAN OPPOSITION TO HITLER: AN APPRAISAL. Hinsdale, Ill., Regnery, 1948. 166 p.

Other editions:
New York, Wheelwright and Regnery, 1948. 172 p. (Humanist Library)

London, Wolff, 1961. 166 p.

Chicago, Regnery, 1962. 166 p. (Foundation for Foreign Affairs Series)

2816 Royce, Hans (ed.).
GERMANS AGAINST HITLER, JULY 20, 1944. 4th ed., newly compiled and supplemented by Erich Zimmermann and Hans-Adolf Jacobsen. English translation by Allan and Lieselotte Yahraes. Bonn, Press and Information Office of the Federal German Government, 1964. 360 p.

2817 Schlabrendorff, Fabian von.
REVOLT AGAINST HITLER: THE PERSONAL ACCOUNT OF FABIAN VON SCHLABRENDORFF. Prepared and edited by Gero V. S. Gaevernitz. London, Eyre and Spottiswoode, 1948. 176 p.

2818 Schlabrendorff, Fabian von.
THE SECRET WAR AGAINST HITLER. Translated by Hilda Simon; foreword by John J. McCloy. New York, Pitman, 1965. 438 p.

2819 Schlotterbeck, Friedrich.
THE DARKER THE NIGHT, THE BRIGHTER THE STARS: A GERMAN WORKER REMEMBERS 1933-1945. Translated by Edward Fitzgerald. London, Gollancz, 1947. 250 p.

2820 Schramm, Wilhelm.
CONSPIRACY AMONG GENERALS. Translated and edited by R. T. Clark. London, Allen and Unwin, 1956. 215 p.

Other edition:
New York, Scribner, 1957. 215 p.

2821 Wetzel, Friedrich.
THEY CALLED ME ALFRED. London, Ronald, 1959. 237 p.

e. Greece

2822 American University, Washington D. C. Special Warfare Research Division.
CASE STUDY IN GUERRILLA WAR: GREECE DURING WORLD WAR II. Prepared by D. M. Condit. Washington, 1961. 338 p.

2823 Byford-Jones, W.
THE GREEK TRILOGY (RESISTANCE-LIBERATION-REVOLUTION). London and New York, Hutchinson, 1945. 270 p.

2824 Fielding, Xan.
HIDE AND SEEK: THE STORY OF A WAR-TIME AGENT. London, Secker and Warburg, 1954. 255 p.

Other edition:
London, World Distributors, 1957. 253 p.

2825 Jecchinis, Chris.
BEYOND OLYMPUS: THE THRILLING STORY OF THE "TRAIN-BUSTERS" IN NAZI-OCCUPIED GREECE. Foreword by C. M. Woodhouse. London, Harrap, 1960. 218 p.

2826 Saraphēs, Stephanos.
GREEK RESISTANCE ARMY: THE STORY OF ELAS. Foreword by Compton Mackenzie. English edition translated and abridged by Marion Pascoe. London, Birch Books, 1951. 324 p.

f. Hungary

2827 Boldizsár, Iván.
THE OTHER HUNGARY. Edited by "New Hungary." Budapest, 1946. 76 p.

g. Italy

2828 Battaglia, Roberto.
THE STORY OF THE ITALIAN RESISTANCE. Translated and edited by P. D. Cummins. Lond Acre, London, Odhams Press, 1957. 287 p.

2829 Delzell, Charles F.
MUSSOLINI'S ENEMIES: THE ITALIAN ANTI-FASCIST RESISTANCE. Princeton, N.J., Princeton University Press, 1961. 620 p.

2830 Hood, Stuart.
PEBBLES FROM MY SKULL. New York, Dutton; London, Hutchinson, 1963. 153 p.

2831 Lett, Gordon.
ROSSANO: AN ADVENTURE OF THE ITALIAN RESISTANCE. Foreword by Freya Stark. London, Hodder and Stoughton, 1955. 223 p.

Other edition:
London, Hamilton, 1956. 224 p. (Panther Books)

2832 Luzzatto, Riccardo.
UNKNOWN WAR IN ITALY. Preface by Vernon Bartlett. London, New Europe Publishing Co., 1946. 135 p.

h. Poland

2833 Gazel, Stefan.
TO LIVE AND KILL. London, Jarrolds, 1958. 215 p.

Other edition:
London, Arrow, 1960. 224 p. (Grey Arrow Books)

2834 Kaminski, Aleksander (J. Gorecki, pseud.).
STONES FOR THE RAMPART: THE STORY OF TWO LADS IN THE POLISH UNDERGROUND MOVEMENT. Foreword by Percy H. B. Lyon. London, Polish Boy Scouts' and Girl Guides' Association, 1945. 68 p. (Polish Boy Scouts' and Girl Guides' Library)

2835 Komorowski, Tadeusz.
THE SECRET ARMY. London, Gollancz, 1950. 407 p.

Other edition:
New York, Macmillan, 1951.

2836 Korbonski, Stefan.
FIGHTING WARSAW: THE STORY OF THE POLISH UNDERGROUND STATE, 1939-1945. Translated from Polish by F. B. Czarnomski. London, Allen and Unwin, 1956. 495 p.

Other edition:
New York, Macmillan, 1957.

2837 Maks, Leon.
RUSSIA BY THE BACK DOOR. Translated from Polish by Rosamond Batchelor. London and New York, Sheed and Ward, 1954. 264 p.

2838 Nirenstein, Albert (ed.).
A TOWER FROM THE ENEMY: CONTRIBUTIONS TO A HISTORY OF JEWISH RESISTANCE IN POLAND. Translated from the Polish, Yiddish, and Hebrew by David Neiman; from the Italian by Mervyn Savill. New York, Orion Press, 1959. 372 p.

2839 Poland. Polskie Sily Zbrojne Armia Krajowa.
THE UNSEEN AND SILENT: ADVENTURES FROM THE UNDERGROUND MOVEMENT NARRATED BY PARATROOPS OF THE POLISH HOME ARMY. Translated from Polish by George Iranek-Osmecki. London and New York, Sheed and Ward, 1954. 350 p.

2840 Tenenbaum, Joseph.
UNDERGROUND: THE STORY OF A PEOPLE. New York, Philosophical Library, 1952. 532 p.

i. Russia

2841 Armstrong, John A. (ed.)
SOVIET PARTISANS IN WORLD WAR II. Foreword by Philip E. Mosely. Madison, University of Wisconsin Press, 1964. 792 p.

2842 Armstrong, John A.
UKRAINIAN NATIONALISM. 2d ed. New York, Columbia University Press, 1963. 361 p. (Studies of the Russian Institute, Columbia University)

Other edition:
1955. 322 p.

2843 BEHIND THE FRONT LINES: BEING AN ACCOUNT OF THE MILITARY ACTIVITIES, EXPLOITS, ADVENTURES, AND DAY TO DAY LIFE OF THE SOVIET GUERILLAS OPERATING BEHIND GERMAN LINES FROM THE FINNISH-KARELIAN FRONT TO THE CRIMEA. Prepared by Lieutenant-General Ponomarenko and others. London and New York, Hutchinson, 1945. 160 p.

2844 Dallin, Alexander.
THE KAMINSKY BRIGADE, 1941-1944: A CASE STUDY OF GERMAN MILITARY EXPLOITATION OF SOVIET DISAFFECTION. Maxwell Air Force Base, Ala., Human Resources Research Institute, Air University, 1952. 96 l.

Other edition:
Cambridge, Mass., Russian Research Center, Harvard University, 1956. 122 l.

2845 Dixon, C. Aubrey, and Otto Heilbrunn.
COMMUNIST GUERILLA WARFARE. Foreword by Sir Reginald F. S. Denning. London, Allen and Unwin, 1954. 229 p.

2846 Fedorov, Aleksei F.
THE UNDERGROUND COMMITTEE CARRIES ON. Translation edited by L. Stoklitsky. Moscow, Foreign Languages Publishing House, 1952. 517 p.

2847 Howell, Edgar M.
THE SOVIET PARTISAN MOVEMENT, 1941-1944. Washington, Dept. of Army, 1956. 217 p. (U.S. Dept. of Army. Pamphlet)

2848 Ignatov, Petr K.
PARTISANS OF THE KUBAN. Translated from Russian by J. Fineberg. London and New York, Hutchinson, 1945. 212 p.

2849 Martovych, Oleh (pseud.).
UKRAINIAN LIBERATION MOVEMENT IN MODERN TIMES. Introduction by John F. Stewart. Edinburgh, Scottish League for European Freedom, 1951. 176 p. (Today's World: Handbooks of Current World Affairs)

2850 Medvedev, Dmitrii N.
STOUT HEARTS (THIS HAPPENED NEAR ROVNO). Translated from Russian by David Skvirsky. Moscow, Foreign Languages Publishing House [195-?]. 237 p.

j. Scandinavia and the Baltic States

2851 Astrup, Helen, and B. L. Jacot.
NIGHT HAS A THOUSAND EYES. London, Macdonald, 1953. 221 p.

Other edition:
London, Landsborough, 1958. 192 p. (Four Square Books)

2852 Astrup, Helen, and B. L. Jacot.
OSLO INTRIGUE: A WOMAN'S MEMOIR OF THE NORWEGIAN RESISTANCE. New York, McGraw-Hill 1954. 237 p.

2853 Drummond, John D.
BUT FOR THESE MEN: HOW ELEVEN COMMANDOS SAVED WESTERN CIVILIZATION. London, Allen, 1962. 205 p.

2854 Flender, Harold.
RESCUE IN DENMARK. New York, Simon and Schuster, 1963. 281 p.

Other edition:
London, Allen, 1963. 224 p.

2855 Hovelsen, Leif.
OUT OF THE EVIL NIGHT. Translated from Norwegian by John Morrison. London, Blandford Press, 1959. 160 p.

2856 Klefos, Brede.
THEY CAME IN THE NIGHT: WARTIME EXPERIENCES OF A NORWEGIAN AMERICAN. Introduction by Styles Bridges. Greenlawn, N.Y., Harian Publications; trade distributor: Crown Publishers, 1959. 206 p.

Other edition:
London, Davies, 1960. 215 p.

2857 Lampe, David.
THE SAVAGE CANARY: THE STORY OF RESISTANCE IN DENMARK. Foreword by Basil Embry. London, Cassell, 1957. 236 p.

Other editions:
London, Transworld, 1959. 284 p. (Corgi Books)

THE DANISH RESISTANCE. New York, Ballantine, 1960. 179 p.

2858 Malthe-Bruun, Kim.
HEROIC HEART: THE DIARY AND LETTERS OF KIM MALTHE-BRUUN, 1941-1945. Edited by Vibeko Malthe-Bruun; translated by Gerry Bothmer. New York, Random House, 1955. 177 p.

2859 Manus, Max, with Dorothy Giles.
9 LIVES BEFORE THIRTY. Garden City, N.Y., Doubleday, 1947. 328 p.

2860 Manus, Max.
UNDERWATER SABOTEUR. Translated from Norwegian by F. H. Lyon. London, Kimber, 1953. 239 p.

2861 Mercer, Asja, with Robert Jackson.
ONE WOMAN'S WAR. London, Wingate, 1958. 220 p.

Other edition:
London, Hamilton, 1960. 192 p. (Panther Books)

2862 Munthe, Malcolm.
SWEET IS WAR. London, Duckworth, 1954. 185 p.

2863 Muus, Flemming B.
THE SPARK AND THE FLAME. Translated from Danish and edited by Varinka Muus and J. F. Burke. London, Museum Press, 1956. 172 p.

2864 Olsen, Oluf R.
TWO EGGS ON MY PLATE. Translated from Norwegian by F. H. Lyon. London, Allen and Unwin, 1952. 208 p.

Other edition:
Chicago, Rand McNally, 1953. 365 p.

2865 Tauras, K. V. (pseud.).
GUERILLA WARFARE ON THE AMBER COAST. New York, Voyages Press, 1962. 110 p.

k. Yugoslavia

2866 Caffin, James.
PARTISAN. Auckland, N. Z., Collins, 1945. 186 p.

2867 Colaković, Rodoljub.
WINNING FREEDOM. Translated by Alec Brown. London, Lincolns-Prager, 1962. 430 p.

2868 Davidson, Basil.
PARTISAN PICTURE. New York, Universal Distributors, 1945. 351 p.

Other edition:
Bedford, Eng., Bedford Books, 1946. 351 p.

2869 Dedijer, Vladimir.
WITH TITO THROUGH THE WAR: PARTISAN DIARY, 1941-1944. London, Hamilton, 1951. 403 p.

2870 GENERAL MIHAILOVICH, THE WORLD'S VERDICT: A SELECTION OF ARTICLES ON THE FIRST RESISTANCE LEADER IN EUROPE PUBLISHED IN THE WORLD PRESS. Introduction by the General's friends; foreword by F. A. Voigt. Gloucester, Eng., Bellows, 1947. 223 p.

2871 Jones, Major W.
TWELVE MONTHS WITH TITO'S PARTISANS. Bedford, Eng., Bedford Books, 1946. 128 p.

2872 Kapetanović, Nikola.
TITO AND HIS PARTISANS: WHAT REALLY HAPPENED IN YUGOSLAVIA FROM 1941 TO 1945. Belgrade, Jugoslovenska Knjiga, 195-. 50 p. (Facts about Yugoslavia)

2873 Lawrence, Christie N.
IRREGULAR ADVENTURE. Introduction by Evelyn Waugh. London, Faber and Faber, 1947. 276 p.

2874 Neil, Roy S.
ONCE ONLY. London, Cape, 1947. 285 p.

2875 Rootham, Jasper.
MISS FIRE: THE CHRONICLE OF A BRITISH MISSION TO MIHAILOVICH, 1943-1944. London, Chatto and Windus, 1946. 224 p.

2876 Strutton, Bill.
ISLAND OF TERRIBLE FRIENDS. London, Hodder and Stoughton, 1961. 192 p.

Other edition:
New York, Norton, 1962.

3. Far East

2877 Allied Forces. Southwest Pacific Area.
GUERRILLA RESISTANCE MOVEMENTS IN THE PHILIPPINES. [Melbourne?] 1945. 143 l.

2878 Burchett, Wilfred G.
DEMOCRACY WITH A TOMMYGUN. Melbourne, Cheshire, 1946. 291 p.

2879 Cross, John.
RED JUNGLE. London, Hale, 1957. 244 p.

Other edition:
THE THREE THEY COULDN'T KILL. London, Transworld, 1959. 288 p. (Corgi Books)

2880 Doromal, Jose D.
THE WAR IN PANAY: A DOCUMENTARY HISTORY OF THE RESISTANCE MOVEMENT IN PANAY DURING WORLD WAR II. Manila, Diamond Historical Publications, 1952. 313 p.

2881 Harkins, Philip.
BLACKBURN'S HEADHUNTERS. New York, Norton, 1955. 326 p.

Other edition:
London, Cassell, 1956.

2882 Holman, Dennis.
THE GREEN TORTURE: THE ORDEAL OF ROBERT CHRYSTAL. London, Hale, 1962. 190 p.

2883 Ingham, Travis.
RENDEZVOUS BY SUBMARINE: THE STORY OF CHARLES PARSONS AND THE GUERILLA SOLDIERS IN THE PHILIPPINES. Garden City, N. Y., Doubleday, 1945. 255 p.

2884 Kathigasu, Sybil D.
NO DRAM OF MERCY. Introduction by Sir Richard Winstedt. London, Spearman, 1954. 237 p.

Other edition:
London, Harborough, 1957. 205 p. (Ace Books)

2885 Keats, John.
THEY FOUGHT ALONE. Philadelphia, Lippincott, 1963. 425 p.

Other editions:
London, Secker and Warburg, 1964. 400 p.

New York, Pocket Books, 1965. 450 p.

2886 Loo Pin-fei.
IT IS DARK UNDERGROUND. New York, Putnam, 1946. 200 p.

2887 Panlilio, Yay.
THE CRUCIBLE: AN AUTOBIOGRAPHY. New York, Macmillan, 1950. 348 p.

2888 Singh, Gurchan.
SINGA, THE LION OF MALAYA: BEING THE MEMOIRS OF GURCHAN SINGH. Edited by Hugh Barnes. London, Quality Press, 1949. 255 p.

2889 Smith, Nicol, and Thomas B. Clark.
INTO SIAM, UNDERGROUND KINGDOM. Indianapolis, Bobbs-Merrill, 1946. 315 p.

2890 Spencer, Louis R.
GUERRILLA WIFE. New York, Crowell, 1945. 209 p.

2891 Volckmann, Russell W.
WE REMAINED: THREE YEARS BEHIND THE ENEMY LINES IN THE PHILIPPINES. New York, Norton, 1954. 244 p.

2892 Wolfert, Ira.
AMERICAN GUERRILLA IN THE PHILIPPINES. New York, Simon and Schuster, 1945. 301 p.

Other edition:
GUERRILLA. London, Transworld, 1958. 152 p. (Corgi Books)

IV. POLITICAL ASPECTS OF THE WAR

A. GENERAL ACCOUNTS

2893 Baldwin, Hanson W.
GREAT MISTAKES OF THE WAR. New York, Harper, 1950. 114 p.

Other edition:
London, Redman, 1950. 105 p.

2894 Berneri, Marie L.
NEITHER EAST NOR WEST: SELECTED WRITINGS. London, Published for the Marie Louise Berneri Memorial Committee by Freedom Press, 1952. 192 p.

2895 Borsody, Stephen.
THE TRIUMPH OF TYRANNY: THE NAZI AND SOVIET CONQUEST OF CENTRAL EUROPE. London, Cape, 1960. 285 p.

2896 Dahlerus, Johan B. E.
THE LAST ATTEMPT. Translated from the Swedish by A. Dick. London, Hutchinson, 1948. 134 p.

2897 Fischer, Louis.
THE GREAT CHALLENGE. New York, Duell, Sloan and Pearce, 1946. 346 p.

Other edition:
London, Cape, 1947. 358 p.

2898 Fox, Annette B.
THE POWER OF SMALL STATES: DIPLOMACY IN WORLD WAR II. Chicago, University of Chicago Press, 1959. 211 p.

2899 Gardner, Brian.
THE WASTED HOUR: THE TRAGEDY OF 1945. London, Cassell, 1963. 356 p.

Other edition:
New York, Coward-McCann, 1964.

2900 Germany. Auswärtiges Amt.
NAZI-SOVIET RELATIONS, 1939-1941, FROM THE ARCHIVES OF THE GERMAN FOREIGN OFFICE. Edited by Raymond J. Sontag and James S. Beddie. Washington, Dept. of State, 1948. 362 p.

2901 Graham-Murray, James.
THE SWORD AND THE UMBRELLA. Douglas, Isle of Man, Times Press; London, Gibbs and Phillips, 1964. 254 p.

2902 Hankey, Maurice P. A. Hankey, baron.
POLITICS, TRIALS AND ERRORS. Oxford, Pen-in-Hand; Chicago, Regnery, 1950. 150 p.

2903 Kalyanasundaram, V.
WORLD WAR II: INSIDE STORY OF A GREAT CONSPIRACY. Nellore, Murthi, 1949. 263 p.

2904 Kase, Toshikazu.
JOURNEY TO THE MISSOURI. Edited with a foreword by David N. Rowe. New Haven, Conn., Yale University Press, 1950. 282 p.

2905 Kecskemeti, Paul.
STRATEGIC SURRENDER: THE POLITICS OF VICTORY AND DEFEAT. Stanford, Calif., Stanford University Press, 1958. 287 p.

2906 Kleist, Peter.
THE EUROPEAN TRAGEDY. Douglas, Isle of Man, Times Press; London, Gibbs and Phillips, 1965. 201 p.

2907 Kogan, Norman.
ITALY AND THE ALLIES. Cambridge, Mass., Harvard University Press, 1956. 246 p.

2908 Langer, William L., and S. Everett Gleason.
THE CHALLENGE TO ISOLATION. New York, Harper, 1952. 794 p. (The World Crisis and American Foreign Policy)

Other edition:
New York, Harper and Row, 1964. 2 v. (794 p.)
(Harper Torchbooks. The University Library)

2909 Langer, William L.
OUR VICHY GAMBLE. London, Knopf, 1947. 412 p.

Other edition:
Hamden, Conn., Archon Books, 1965. 412 p.

2910 Langer, William L., and S. Everett Gleason.
THE UNDECLARED WAR, 1940-1941. New York, Published for the Council on Foreign Relations by Harper, 1953. 963 p. (The World Crisis and American Foreign Policy)

2911 Launay, Jacques de.
SECRET DIPLOMACY OF WORLD WAR II. Translated by Edouard Nadier. New York, Simmons-Boardman, 1963. 175 p.

2912 League of Nations.
REPORT ON THE WORK OF THE LEAGUE DURING THE WAR. Geneva, League of Nations Paper, League of Nations, 1945. 167 p.

Other edition:
New York, Columbia University Press; London, Allen, 1946.

2913 Leasor, James.
WAR AT THE TOP: BASED ON THE EXPERIENCES OF GENERAL SIR LESLIE HOLLIS. London, Joseph, 1959. 306 p.

Other editions:
THE CLOCK WITH FOUR HANDS: BASED ON THE EXPERIENCES OF GENERAL SIR LESLIE HOLLIS. New York, Reynal, 1959. 314 p.

London, Hamilton, 1961. 252 p. (Panther Books)

2914 London. Instytut Historyczny imienia Generala Sikorskiego.
DOCUMENTS ON POLISH-SOVIET RELATIONS, 1939-1945. London, Heinemann, 1961. 625 p.

2915 Maiskii, Ivan Mikhailovich.
WHO HELPED HITLER? Translated from Russian by Andrew Rothstein. London, Hutchinson, 1964. 216 p.

2916 Meyer, Hershel D.
MUST WE PERISH? THE LOGIC OF 20TH CENTURY BARBARISM. New York, New Century Publishers, 1949. 171 p.

2917 Newman, Bernard.
THE CAPTURED ARCHIVES: THE STORY OF THE NAZI-SOVIET DOCUMENTS. London, Latimer House, 1948. 222 p.

2918 Newsome, Noël F., and Alan Bullock (eds.).
EUROPE LIBERATED. London, Staples Press, 1945. 91 p.

2919 Newsweek.
THE MONTH THAT MADE HISTORY: A NEWSWEEK REPORT. New York, Newsweek, 1945. 64 p.

2920 O'Neill, Herbert C.
MAN OF DESTINY: BEING STUDIES OF THE FOUR WHO RODE THE WAR AND MADE THIS PRECARIOUS LANDFALL. London, Phoenix House, 1953. 240 p.

2921 Pritt, Denis N.
THE STATE DEPARTMENT AND THE COLD WAR: COMMENTARY ON ITS PUBLICATION "NAZI-SOVIET RELATIONS, 1939-1941." New York, International Publishers, 1948. 96 p.

2922 Reed, Douglas.
FROM SMOKE TO SMOTHER, 1938-1948: A SEQUEL TO INSANITY FAIR. London, Cape, 1948. 317 p.

2923 Rei, August (comp.).
NAZI-SOVIET CONSPIRACY AND THE BALTIC STATES: DIPLOMATIC DOCUMENTS AND OTHER EVIDENCE. London, Boreas, 1948. 61 p.

2924 Root, Waverly L.
THE SECRET HISTORY OF THE WAR. New York, Scribner, 1945-46. 3 v.

2925 Rossi, Angelo (pseud.).
THE RUSSO-GERMAN ALLIANCE, AUGUST 1939-JUNE 1941. Translated from French by John and Micheline Cullen. London, Chapman and Hall, 1950. 218 p.

Other edition:
Boston, Beacon Press, 1951.

2926 Shelton, John B.
A NIGHT IN LITTLE PARK STREET. London, Britannicus Liber, 1950. 31 p.

2927 Snell, John L.
ILLUSION AND NECESSITY: THE DIPLOMACY OF GLOBAL WAR, 1939-1945. Boston, Houghton Mifflin, 1963. 229 p.

2928 Snow, Edgar.
GLORY AND BONDAGE. Sydney and London, Gollancz, 1945. 263 p.

Other edition:
Sydney and London, Angus and Robertson, 1946. 257 p.

2929 SOVIET-POLISH RELATIONS: A COLLECTION OF DOCUMENTS AND PRESS EXTRACTS 1944-1946. London, Soviet News, 1946. 51 p. (Illustrated Soviet Shilling Booklets)

2930 Survey of International Affairs.
THE WARTIME SERIES FOR 1939-46, edited by A. J. Toynbee, comprises the following volumes: [v. 1]: THE WORLD IN MARCH 1939, edited by A. J. Toynbee and F. T. Ashton-Gwatkin. [v. 2]: THE MIDDLE EAST IN THE WAR, by G. Kirk. [v. 3]: AMERICA, BRITAIN AND RUSSIA, THEIR CO-OPERATION AND CONFLICT, 1941-1946, by W. H. McNeill. [v. 4]: HITLER'S EUROPE, edited by A. J. Toynbee and V. M. Toynbee. [v. 5]: THE MIDDLE EAST, 1945-1950, by G. Kirk. [v. 6]: THE REALIGNMENT OF EUROPE, edited by A. J. Toynbee and V. M. Toynbee. [v. 7]: THE FAR EAST, 1942-1946, by F. C. Jones, H. Borton, and B. R. Pearn. London, Oxford University Press, 1952-.

2931 Tasca, Angelo (A. Rossi, pseud.).
THE RUSSO-GERMAN ALLIANCE, AUGUST 1939-JUNE 1941. Translated by John and Micheline Cullen. London, Chapman and Hall, 1950. 218 p.

Other edition:
Boston, Beacon Press, 1951.

2932 Umiastowski, Roman, with Joanna M. Aldridge.
POLAND, RUSSIA AND GREAT BRITAIN, 1941-1945: A STUDY OF EVIDENCE. London, Hollis and Carter, 1946. 544 p.

2933 Wandycz, Piotr S.
CZECHOSLOVAK-POLISH CONFEDERATION AND THE GREAT POWERS, 1940-43. Bloomington, Research Center in Anthropology, Folklore, and Linguistics, Indiana University, 1956. 152 p.

2934 Weinberg, Gerhard L.
GERMANY AND THE SOVIET UNION, 1939-1941. Leiden, Brill, 1954. 218 p. (Studies in East European History)

B. MEMOIRS AND BIOGRAPHIES

2935 Adamic, Louis.
DINNER AT THE WHITE HOUSE. New York and London, Harper, 1946. 276 p.

2936 Attlee, Clement R.
A PRIME MINISTER REMEMBERS: THE WAR AND POST-WAR MEMOIRS OF THE RT. HON. EARL ATTLEE. London, Heinemann, 1961. 264 p.

2937 Baudouin, Paul.
THE PRIVATE DIARIES (MARCH 1940 TO JANUARY 1941). Translated by Sir Charles Petrie. London, Eyre and Spottiswoode, 1948. 308 p.

2938 Beaton, Cecil W. H.
FAR EAST. London, Batsford, 1945. 110 p.

2939 Beaton, Cecil W. H.
THE YEARS BETWEEN: DIARIES, 1939-44. London, Weidenfeld and Nicolson, 1954. 352 p.

2940 Bell, Richard.
TRAVELER FROM WAR. n.p., 1949. 84 p.

2941 Beneš, Eduard.
MEMOIRS OF DR. EDUARD BENES: FROM MUNICH TO NEW WAR AND NEW VICTORY. Translated from Czech original by Godfrey Lias. London, Allen and Unwin, 1954. 346 p.

Other edition:
Boston, Houghton Mifflin, 1955. 346 p.

2942 Bentwich, Norman de M.
WANDERER IN WAR, 1939-45. London, Gollancz, 1946. 196 p.

2943 Bilainkin, George.
SECOND DIARY OF A DIPLOMATIC CORRESPONDENT. London, Low and Marston, 1947. 423 p.

2944 Blum, John M.
FROM THE MORGENTHAU DIARIES: YEARS OF DECISION, 1938-1941. Boston, Houghton Mifflin, 1964. 576 p.

2945 Bormann, Martin.
THE BORMANN LETTERS: THE PRIVATE CORRESPONDENCE BETWEEN MARTIN BORMANN AND HIS WIFE, FROM JANAURY 1943 TO APRIL 1945. Edited by H. R. Trevor-Roper; translated by R. H. Steven. London, Weidenfeld and Nicolson, 1954. 200 p.

2946 Byrnes, James F.
SPEAKING FRANKLY. New York, Harper, 1947. 324 p.

2947 Casey, Richard G.
PERSONAL EXPERIENCE, 1939-1946. London, Constable; New York, McKay, 1962. 256 p.

2948 Churchill, Sir Winston L. S.
MEMOIRS OF THE SECOND WORLD WAR. An abridgment of the six volumes of the Second World War, with an epilogue by the author on the postwar years written for this volume. London, Cassell; Boston, Houghton Mifflin, 1959. 1065 p.

2949 Churchill, Sir Winston L. S.
THE SECOND WORLD WAR. London, Cassell, 1948-54. 6 v.

Other edition:
London, Cassell, 1964. 12 v.

2950 Churchill, Sir Winston L. S., and the editors of Life.
THE SECOND WORLD WAR. New York, Time, Inc., 1959. 2 v. (615 p.)

2951 Ciano, Galeazzo, conte.
THE CIANO DIARIES, 1939-1943: THE COMPLETE UNABRIDGED DIARIES OF COUNT GALEAZZO CIANO, ITALIAN MINISTER FOR FOREIGN AFFAIRS, 1936-1943. Edited by Hugh Gibson; introduction by Sumner Welles. Garden City, N.Y., Doubleday, 1946. 584 p.

Other editions:
Garden City, N.Y., Doubleday, 1947.

CIANO'S DIARY, 1939-1943. Edited with introduction by Malcolm Muggeridge; foreword by Sumner Welles. London and Toronto, Heinemann, 1947. 575 p.

2952 Ciano, Geleazzo, conte.
HIDDEN DIARY, 1937-1938. Translated with notes by Andreas Meyer. New York, Dutton, 1953. 220 p.

2953 Cooper, Diana M., Viscountess Norwich.
TRUMPETS FROM THE STEEP. London, Hart-Davis, 1960. 253 p.

2954 Croce, Benedetto.
CROCE, THE KING AND THE ALLIES: EXTRACTS FROM A DIARY BY BENEDETTO CROCE, JULY 1943-JUNE 1944. Translated from Italian by Sylvia Sprigge. London, Allen and Unwin, 1950. 158 p.

2955 Eden, Sir Anthony.
FREEDOM AND ORDER: SELECTED SPEECHES, 1939-1946. Boston, Houghton Mifflin, 1948. 436 p.

2956 Eden, Sir Anthony.
THE RECKONING: THE EDEN MEMOIRS. London, Cassell; Boston, Houghton Mifflin, 1965. 623 p.

2957 Gaulle, Charles de.
THE COMPLETE WAR MEMOIRS. Translated by J. Griffin and R. Howard. London, Weidenfeld and Nicolson, 1959-60. 3 v.

Other editions:
London, Collins; New York, Viking Press, 1955-60. 3 v.

New York, Simon and Schuster, 1964. 3 v. in 1. (1048 p.)

2958 Goebbels, Joseph.
THE GOEBBELS DIARIES, 1942-1943. Edited, translated and with an introduction by Louis P. Lochner. Garden City, N.Y., Doubleday, 1948. 566 p.

Other edition:
London, Hamilton, 1948. 458 p.

2959 Grabowski, Zbigniew (Axel Heyst, pseud.).
THERE SHALL BE NO VICTORY: DIARY OF A EUROPEAN. London, Gollancz, 1947. 336 p.

2960 Hassell, Ulrich von.
THE VON HASSELL DIARIES, 1938-1944: THE STORY OF FORCES AGAINST HITLER INSIDE GERMANY. Introduction by Allen W. Dulles. Garden City, N.Y., Doubleday, 1947. 400 p.

Other edition:
London, Hamilton, 1948. 365 p.

2961 Henderson, Sir Neville.
WATER UNDER THE BRIDGE. London, Hodder and Stoughton, 1945. 228 p.

2962 Hodson, James L.
THE SEA AND THE LAND: BEING SOME ACCOUNT OF JOURNEYS, MEETINGS, AND WHAT WAS SAID TO ME IN BRITAIN, FRANCE, ITALY, GERMANY, AND HOLLAND BETWEEN MARCH 1943 AND MAY 1945. London, Gollancz, 1945. 369 p.

2963 Hugessen, Sir Hughe M. K.
DIPLOMAT IN PEACE AND WAR. London, Murray, 1949. 270 p.

2964 Hull, Cordell.
THE MEMOIRS OF CORDELL HULL. New York, Macmillan, 1948. 2 v. (1804 p.)

2965 Ickes, Harold L.
THE SECRET DIARY OF HAROLD L. ICKES. New York, Simon and Schuster, 1953-54. 3 v.

2966 Ironside, William E.
THE IRONSIDE DIARIES, 1937-1940. Edited by Colonel Roderick Macleod and Denis Kelly. London, Constable, 1962. 434 p.

Other edition:
TIME UNGUARDED: THE IRONSIDE DIARIES, 1937-1940. New York, McKay, 1963.

2967 Kersten, Felix.
THE KERSTEN MEMOIRS, 1940-1945. Introduction by H. R. Trevor-Roper; translated from German by Constantine FitzGibbon and James Oliver. New York, Macmillan, 1957. 314 p.

2968 Konoye, Fumimaro, Prince.
THE MEMOIRS OF PRINCE FUMIMARO KONOYE. Translated from the Asahi Shimbun, 1945. Tokyo, Okuyama Service, 195-. 62 l

2969 Kuncewiczowa, Maria S.
THE KEYS: A JOURNEY THROUGH EUROPE AT WAR. Translated from the Polish. London and New York, Hutchinson, 1945. 176 p.

2970 Leahy, William D.
I WAS THERE: THE PERSONAL STORY OF THE CHIEF OF STAFF TO PRESIDENTS ROOSEVELT AND TRUMAN, BASED ON HIS NOTES AND DIARIES MADE AT THE TIME. Foreword by President Truman. New York, Whittlesey House, 1950. 527 p.

2971 Lomax, Sir John G.
THE DIPLOMATIC SMUGGLER. London, Barker, 1965. 288 p.

2972 Maclean, Fitzroy.
EASTERN APPROACHES. London, Cape, 1949. 543 p.

Other editions:
London, New English Library, 1965. 447 p. (Four Square Books)

ESCAPE TO ADVENTURE. Boston, Little, Brown, 1950. 419 p.

2973 Maugham, Robin.
NOMAD. London, Chapman and Hall, 1947. 243 p.

Other edition:
New York, Viking Press, 1948. 183 p.

2974 Mitchell, Sir Harold P.
INTO PEACE. London and New York, Hutchinson, 1945. 124 p.

2975 Papen, Franz von.
MEMOIRS. Translated by Brian Connell. London, Deutsch, 1952. 630 p.

Other edition:
New York, Dutton, 1953. 634 p.

2976 Peter II, King of Yugoslavia.
A KING'S HERITAGE: THE MEMOIRS OF KING PETER II OF YUGOSLAVIA. London, Cassell, 1955. 214 p.

2977 Pickersgill, J. W.
THE MACKENZIE KING RECORD. Vol. I, 1939-1944. Toronto, University of Toronto Press, 1960. 723 p.

2978 Ribbentrop, Joachim von.
THE RIBBENTROP MEMOIRS. Translated by Oliver Watson; introduction by Alan Bullock. London, Weidenfeld and Nicolson, 1954. 216 p.

2979 Spears, Sir Edward L., baronet.
ASSIGNMENT TO CATASTROPHE. London, Heinemann, 1954; New York, Wyn, 1954-55. 2 v.

2980 Stark, Freya.
DUST IN THE LION'S PAW: AUTOBIOGRAPHY, 1939-1946. London, Murray, 1961. 296 p.

Other edition:
New York, Harcourt, Brace and World, 1962.

2981 Tabori, Paul.
RESTLESS SUMMER: A PERSONAL RECORD. London, Sylvan Press, 1946. 224 p.

2982 Thayer, Charles W.
HANDS ACROSS THE CAVIAR. Philadelphia, Lippincott, 1952. 251 p.

Other edition:
London, Joseph, 1953. 222 p.

2983 Truman, Harry S.
MEMOIRS: Vol. I, YEAR OF DECISIONS, 1945. London, Hodder and Stoughton, 1955. 526 p.

2984 Weizäcker, Ernst H.
MEMOIRS. Translated by John Andrews. London, Gollancz; Chicago, Regnery, 1951. 322 p.

2985 Williams, Francis.
A PRIME MINISTER REMEMBERS: THE WAR AND POST-WAR MEMOIRS OF THE RT. HON. EARL ATTLEE. Based on his private papers and on a series of recorded conversations. London, Heinemann, 1961. 264 p.

Other edition:
TWILIGHT OF EMPIRE: MEMOIRS OF PRIME MINISTER CLEMENT ATLEE. New York, Barnes, 1962. 264 p.

2986 Wilson, Hugh R.
A CAREER DIPLOMAT: THE THIRD CHAPTER: THE THIRD REICH. Edited by Hugh R. Wilson, Jr. New York, Vantage Press, 1961. 112 p.

2987 Winant, John G.
A LETTER FROM GROSVENER SQUARE: AN ACCOUNT OF A STEWARDSHIP. Boston, Houghton Mifflin; London, Hodder and Stoughton, 1947. 278 p.

2988 Wrench, Sir Evelyn.
IMMORTAL YEARS, 1937-1944, AS VIEWED FROM FIVE CONTINENTS. London and New York, Hutchinson, 1945. 232 p.

C. THE AXIS POWERS

1. General Diplomacy

2989 Alfieri, Dino.
DICTATORS FACE TO FACE. Translated from Italian by David Moore. London, Elek, 1954. 307 p.

Other edition:
New York, New York University Press, 1955.

2990 Ciano, Galeazzo, conte.
CIANO'S DIPLOMATIC PAPERS: BEING A RECORD OF NEARLY 200 CONVERSATIONS HELD DURING THE YEARS 1936-42 WITH HITLER, MUSSOLINI, FRANCO, GOERING, RIBBENTROP, CHAMBERLAIN, EDEN, SUMNER WELLS, SCHUSCHNEGG, LORD PERTH, FRANÇOIS-PONCET, AND MANY OTHER WORLD DIPLOMATIC AND POLITICAL FIGURES, TOGETHER WITH IMPORTANT MEMORANDA, LETTERS, TELEGRAMS, ETC. Edited by Malcolm Muggeridge; translated by Stuart Hood. London, Odhams Press, 1948. 490 p.

2991 Deakin, Frederick W.
THE BRUTAL FRIENDSHIP: MUSSOLINI, HITLER, AND THE FALL OF ITALIAN FASCISM. London, Weidenfeld and Nicolson; New York, Harper and Row, 1962. 806 p.

2992 Gafencu, Grigory.
PRELUDE TO THE RUSSIAN CAMPAIGN, FROM THE MOSCOW PACT (AUGUST 21, 1939) TO THE OPENING OF HOSTILITIES IN RUSSIA (JUNE 22, 1941). Translated by Fletcher-Allen. London, Muller, 1945. 348 p.

2993 Iklé, Frank W.
GERMAN-JAPANESE RELATIONS, 1936-1940. New York, Bookman, 1956. 243 p.

2994 Presseisen, Ernst L.
GERMANY AND JAPAN: A STUDY IN TOTALITARIAN DIPLOMACY, 1933-1941. The Hague, Nijhoff, 1958. 368 p. (International Scholars Forum: A Series of Books by American Scholars)

2995 Wiskemann, Elizabeth.
THE ROME-BERLIN AXIS: A HISTORY OF THE RELATIONS BETWEEN HITLER AND MUSSOLINI. London and New York, Oxford University Press, 1949. 376 p.

2. Individual Countries

a. Germany

2996 Allied Forces. Supreme Headquarters. Air Defense Division.
GERMAN CIVIL DEFENSE, WORLD WAR II. Prepared by Ivan B. Franks. Portland, Ore., Disaster Relief and Civil Defense [1955?] 108 l.

2997 Bannister, Sybil.
I LIVED UNDER HITLER: AN ENGLISH WOMAN'S STORY. London, Rockliff, 1957. 264 p.

2998 Bernadotte of Wisborg, Folke, greve.
THE CURTAIN FALLS: THE LAST DAYS OF THE THIRD REICH. Translated by Count Eric Lewenhaupt. New York, Knopf, 1945. 154 p.

2999 Bewley, Charles H.
HERMANN GÖRING AND THE THIRD REICH: A BIOGRAPHY BASED ON FAMILY AND OFFICIAL RECORDS. New York, Devin-Adair, 1962. 517 p.

3000 Blond, Georges.
THE DEATH OF HITLER'S GERMANY. Translated from French by Frances Frenaye. New York and London, Macmillan, 1954. 302 p.

Other edition:
New York, Pyramid Books, 1958. 240 p.

3001 Boldt, Gerhard.
IN THE SHELTER WITH HITLER. Edited by Ernst A. Hepp; translated by Edgar Stern-Rubarth. London, Citadel, 1948. 78 p.

3002 Buchheim, Hans.
THE THIRD REICH, ITS BEGINNING, ITS DEVELOPMENT, ITS END. Translated by Allan and Lieselotte Yahraes. London, Wolff, 1961. 98 p.

3003 Bullock, Alan L. C.
HITLER: A STUDY IN TYRANNY. London, Odhams Press, 1952. 776 p.

3004 Byford-Jones, W.
BERLIN TWILIGHT. London and New York, Hutchinson, 1947. 192 p.

3005 Crankshaw, Edward.
GESTAPO: INSTRUMENT OF TYRANNY. London, Putnam; New York, Viking Press, 1956. 275 p.

3006 David, Claude.
HITLER'S GERMANY. Translated by Anne-Marie Geoghegan. New York, Walker, 1963. 154 p. (Walker Sun Books)

3007 Delarue, Jacques.
THE GESTAPO: A HISTORY OF HORROR. Translated from the French by Mervyn Savill. New York, Morrow, 1964. 384 p.

3008 De Mendelssohn, Peter.
THE NUREMBERG DOCUMENTS: SOME ASPECTS OF GERMAN WAR POLICY, 1939-45. London, Allen and Unwin, 1946. 291 p.

3009 Dietrich, Otto.
HITLER. Translated by Richard and Clara Winston. Chicago, Regnery, 1955. 277 p.

Other edition:
THE HITLER I KNEW. London, Methuen, 1957. 277 p.

3010 Dirksen, Herbert von.
MOSCOW, TOKYO, LONDON: TWENTY YEARS OF GERMAN FOREIGN POLICY. London and New York, Hutchinson, 1951. 288 p.

Other edition:
Norman, University of Oklahoma Press, 1952. 276 p.

3011 Ebenstein, William
THE GERMAN RECORD: A POLITICAL PORTRAIT. New York and Toronto, Farrar and Rinehart, 1945. 334 p.

3012 Edinger, Lewis J.
GERMAN EXILE POLITICS: THE SOCIAL DEMOCRATIC EXECUTIVE COMMITTEE IN THE NAZI ERA. Berkeley, University of California Press, 1956. 329 p.

3013 Frischauer, Willi.
HIMMLER: THE EVIL GENIUS OF THE THIRD REICH. Boston, Beacon Press; London, Odhams Press, 1953. 269 p.

3014 Frischauer, Willi.
THE RISE AND FALL OF HERMANN GOERING. Boston, Houghton Mifflin, 1951. 309 p.

Other edition:
GOERING. London, Odhams Press, 1951. 303 p.

3015 Germany. Auswärtiges Amt.
DOCUMENTS ON GERMAN FOREIGN POLICY, 1918-1945, FROM THE ARCHIVES OF THE GERMAN FOREIGN MINISTRY. Washington, 1949-66. 13 v. published. Series D: 1934-1945.

3016 Germany. Auswärtiges Amt.
GERMAN FOREIGN OFFICE DOCUMENTS: GERMAN POLICY IN TURKEY, 1941-1943. Moscow, Foreign Languages Publishing House, 1948. 126 p.

3017 Hanser, Richard (comp.).
TRUE TALES OF HITLER'S REICH: A CREST ANTHOLOGY. Greenwich, Conn., Fawcett Publications, 1962. 192 p. (Crest Book)

3018 Hesse, Fritz.
HITLER AND THE ENGLISH. Edited and translated from German by F. A. Voigt. London, Wingate, 1954. 218 p.

3019 Hitler, Adolf.
THE TESTAMENT OF ADOLF HITLER: THE HITLER-BORMANN DOCUMENTS, FEBRUARY-APRIL 1945. Edited by François Genoud; translated from German by Colonel R. H. Stevens; with introduction by H. R. Trevor-Roper. London, Cassell, 1961. 115 p.

Other edition:
London, Icon Books, 1962. 127 p.

3020 Hoemberg, Elisabeth S.
THY PEOPLE, MY PEOPLE. New York, Crowell, 1950. 314 p.

3021 Hoffmann, Heinrich.
HITLER WAS MY FRIEND. Translated by R. H. Stevens. London, Burke, 1955. 256 p.

3022 Horstmann, Lali von S.
NOTHING FOR TEARS. Introduction by Harold Nicolson. London, Weidenfeld and Nicolson, 1953. 206 p.

3023 Horstmann, Lali von S.
WE CHOSE TO STAY. Introduction by Harold Nicolson. Boston, Houghton Mifflin, 1954. 206 p.

3024 Howe, Ellic.
NOSTRADAMUS AND THE NAZIS: A FOOTNOTE TO THE HISTORY OF THE THIRD REICH. London, Arborfield, 1965. 138 p.

3025 International Council for Philosophy and Humanistic Studies.
THE THIRD REICH. London, Weidenfeld and Nicolson; New York, Praeger, 1955. 910 p.

3026 Jarman, Thomas L.
THE RISE AND FALL OF NAZI GERMANY. London, Grosset Press, 1955. 388 p.

Other edition:
New York, New York University Press, 1956. 388 p.

3027 Kaps, Johannes (ed.).
THE MARTYRDOM AND HEROISM OF THE WOMEN OF EAST GERMANY: AN EXCERPT FROM THE SILESIAN PASSION, 1945-1946. Translated by Gladys H. Hartinger. Munich, "Christ Unterwegs," 1955. 155 p.

3028 Kaps, Johannes (ed.).
THE TRAGEDY OF SILESIA, 1945-46: A DOCUMENTARY ACCOUNT WITH A SPECIAL SURVEY OF THE ARCHDIOCESE OF BRESLAU. Translated by Gladys H. Hartinger. Munich, "Christ Unterwegs," 1952-53. 576 p.

3029 Kardorff, Ursula von.
DIARY OF A NIGHTMARE: BERLIN, 1942-1945. Translated from German by Ewan Butler. London, Hart-Davis, 1965. 224 p.

3030 Kessel, Joseph E.
THE MAGIC TOUCH. Translated from French by Denise Folliot; introduction by H. R. Trevor-Roper. London, Hart-Davis, 1961. 254 p.

Other edition:
London, Pan, 1963. 224 p.

3031 Koehl, Robert L.
RKFDV: GERMAN RESETTLEMENT AND POPULATION POLICY, 1939-1945; A HISTORY OF THE REICH COMMISSION FOR THE STRENGTHENING OF GERMANDOM. Cambridge, Mass., Harvard University Press, 1957. 263 p.

3032 Leasor, Thomas J.
RUDOLF HESS: THE UNINVITED ENVOY. London, Allen and Unwin, 1962. 239 p.

Other edition:
THE UNINVITED ENVOY. New York, McGraw-Hill, 1962. 249 p.

3033 Lerner, Daniel, with Ithiel de Sola Pool and George K. Schueller.
THE NAZI ELITE. Introduced by Franz L. Neumann. Stanford, Calif., Stanford University Press, 1951. 112 p. (Hoover Institute Studies. Series B: Elite Studies)

3034 McKee, Ilse.
TOMORROW THE WORLD. London, Dent, 1960. 199 p.

Other edition:
London, Brown, 1962. 160 p. (Digit Books)

3035 Manvell, Roger, and Heinrich Fraenkel.
DOCTOR GOEBBELS: HIS LIFE AND DEATH. London, Heinemann, 1960. 329 p.

Other edition:
New York, Simon and Schuster, 1960. 306 p.

3036 Manvell, Roger, and Heinrich Fraenkel.
GOERING. New York, Simon and Schuster, 1962. 442 p.

3037 Mau, Hermann, and Helmut Krausnick.
GERMAN HISTORY, 1933-45: AN ASSESSMENT BY GERMAN HISTORIANS. Translated from the German by Andrew and Eva Wilson. London, Wolff, 1959. 157 p.

Other edition:
New York, Ungar, 1963.

3038 Mayer, Milton S.
THEY THOUGHT THEY WERE FREE: THE GERMANS, 1933-45. Chicago, University of Chicago Press, 1955. 357 p.

3039 Meinecke, Friedrich.
THE GERMAN CATASTROPHE: REFLECTIONS AND RECOLLECTIONS. Translated by Sidney B. Fay. Cambridge, Mass., Harvard University Press, 1950. 121 p.

3040 Musmanno, Michael A.
TEN DAYS TO DIE. Garden City, N.Y., Doubleday, 1950. 276 p.

Other edition:
London, Davies, 1951.

3041 Neumann, Peter.
THE BLACK MARCH: THE PERSONAL STORY OF AN SS MAN. Translated from French by Constantine FitzGibbon. New York, Sloane, 1959. 312 p.

3042 Neumann, Robert, with Helga Koppel.
THE PICTORIAL HISTORY OF THE THIRD REICH. New York, Bantam Books, 1962. 224 p. (Bantam Books)

3043 Reitlinger, Gerald R.
THE S.S.: ALIBI OF A NATION, 1922-1945. Melbourne, London and Toronto, Heinemann, 1956. 502 p.

Other edition:
New York, Viking, 1957. 502 p.

3044 Riess, Curt.
JOSEPH GOEBBELS: A BIOGRAPHY. Preface by Louis P. Lochner. London, Hollis and Carter; Garden City, N.Y., Doubleday, 1949. 460 p.

3045 Riess, Curt.
THE NAZIS GO UNDERGROUND. London, Boardman, 1945. 224 p.

Other edition:
Garden City, N.Y., Doubleday, 1944. 210 p.

3046 Robertson, Esmonde M.
HITLER'S PRE-WAR POLICY AND MILITARY PLANS, 1933-1939. London, Longmans, 1963. 207 p.

3047 Sayers, Michael A. K.
PLOT AGAINST THE PEACE: NAZI GERMANY PLANS FOR FUTURE WARS. New York, Dial Press, 1945. 258 p.

3048 Schmidt, Paul.
HITLER'S INTERPRETER. Edited by R. H. C. Steed. London, Heinemann; New York, Macmillan, 1951. 286 p.

3049 Seabury, Paul.
THE WILHELMSTRASSE: A STUDY OF GERMAN DIPLOMATS UNDER THE NAZI REGIME. Berkeley, University of California Press, 1954. 217 p.

3050 Seger, Gerhart.
DICTATORSHIP, WAR, DISASTER: HISTORY OF THE NAZI REGIME. Oberaudorf, Bavaria, Schoenstein, 1957. 300 photos.

3051 Semmler, Rudolf.
GOEBBELS--THE MAN NEXT TO HITLER. Introduction by D. McLachlan; notes by G. S. Wagner. London, Westhouse, 1947. 234 p.

3052 Seydewitz, Max.
CIVIL LIFE IN WARTIME GERMANY: THE STORY OF THE HOME FRONT. New York, Viking, 1945. 448 p.

3053 Shirer, William L.
THE RISE AND FALL OF THE THIRD REICH: A HISTORY OF NAZI GERMANY. New York, Simon and Schuster; London, Secker and Warburg, 1960. 1245 p.

3054 Snyder, Louis L.
HITLER AND NAZISM. New York, Watts, 1961. 182 p.

3055 Stern, James.
THE HIDDEN DAMAGE. New York, Harcourt, Brace, 1947. 406 p.

3056 Taylor, Telford.
SWORD AND SWASTIKA: GENERALS AND NAZIS IN THE THIRD REICH. New York, Simon and Schuster, 1952. 431 p.

Other edition:
London, Gollancz, 1953.

3057 Trevor-Roper, Hugh R.
THE LAST DAYS OF HITLER. 3d ed. London, Macmillan; New York, St. Martin's Press, 1956. 283 p.

3058 TWO WOMEN AND A WAR: DIARY, BY GRETE PAQUIN; AND PILLAR OF FIRE, BY RENATE HAGEN. Philadelphia, Muhlenberg Press, 1953. 233 p.

3059 Vallance, Ute.
A GIRL SURVIVES. London, McGibbon and Kee, 1958. 298 p.

3060 Warlimont, Walter.
INSIDE HITLER'S HEADQUARTERS, 1939-45. Translated from the German by R. H. Barry. London, Weidenfeld and Nicolson; New York, Praeger, 1964. 658 p.

3061 Wendel, Else, with Eileen Winncroft.
HAUSFRAU AT WAR: A GERMAN WOMAN'S ACCOUNT OF LIFE IN HITLER'S REICH. London, Odhams Press, 1957. 255 p.

3062 WHAT WE SAW IN GERMANY: WITH THE RED ARMY TO BERLIN BY THIRTEEN LEADING SOVIET WAR CORRESPONDENTS. London, "Soviet News," 1945. 63 p.

3063 Wheeler-Bennett, Sir John W.
THE NEMESIS OF POWER: THE GERMAN ARMY IN POLITICS, 1918-1945. 2d ed. London, Macmillan; New York, St. Martin's Press, 1964. 831 p.

b. Italy

3064 Alessandro, Guilietta d'.
THE CHILD ACROSS THE RIVER. Translated from the Italian by Martha Bacon. New York, McDowell, Obolensky, 1958. 209 p.

3065 Badoglio, Pietro.
ITALY IN THE SECOND WORLD WAR: MEMORIES AND DOCUMENTS. Translated by Muriel Currey. London, Oxford University Press, 1948. 234 p.

3066 Carter, Barbara B.
ITALY SPEAKS. London, Gollancz, 1947. 195 p.

3067 Dąbrowski, Roman.
MUSSOLINI, TWILIGHT AND FALL. Translated and with a preface by H. C. Stevens. New York, Roy; London, Heinemann, 1956. 248 p.

3068 Giusti, Ernest H.
THE ITALIAN COUP AND ARMISTICE, 1943. Washington, 1949. 179 l.

3069 Hibbert, Christopher.
IL DUCE: THE LIFE OF BENITO MUSSOLINI. Boston, Little, Brown, 1962. 367 p.

Other edition:
BENITO MUSSOLINI. London, Longmans, 1962. 367 p.

3070 Lombroso, Silvia.
NO TIME FOR SILENCE. Introduction by Dorothy C. Fisher; translated by Adrienne W. Foulke. New York, Roy, 1945. 165 p.

3071 Maugeri, Franco.
FROM THE ASHES OF DISGRACE. Edited by Victor Rosen. New York, Reynal and Hitchcock, 1948. 376 p.

3072 Mussolini, Benito.
THE FALL OF MUSSOLINI: HIS OWN STORY. Translated from the Italian by Frances Frenaye; edited and with preface by May Ascoli. New York, Farrer, Straus, 1948. 212 p.

Other edition:
MEMOIRS, 1942-1943, WITH DOCUMENTS RELATING TO THE PERIOD. Translated by Frances Lobb; introduction by Cecil Sprigge; edited by Raymond Klibunsky. London, Weidenfeld and Nicolson, 1949. 320 p.

3073 Origo, Iris M.
WAR IN VAL D'ORCIA: A DIARY. London, Cape, 1947. 239 p.

Other editions:
London, Cape, 1951. 253 p. (Travellers' Library Series)

Harmondsworth, Eng., Penguin Books with Cape, 1956. 221 p.

3074 Quigley, Martin.
ROMAN NOTES: WAR AND PEACE IN THE ETERNAL CITY. New York, 1946. 71 p.

3075 Salerno, Attilio M.
THIS WAS OUR NIGHT. Translated from the Italian by Joseph N. Caputo. New Rochelle, N.Y., 1947. 117 p.

3076 Saporiti, Piero.
EMPTY BALCONY. Translated by D. F. L. Brown. London, Gollancz, 1947. 128 p.

3077 Wyss, M. de.
ROME UNDER THE TERROR. London, Hale, 1945. 218 p.

c. Japan

3078 Aikawa, Taksaki.
UNWILLING PATRIOT. Tokyo, Jordan Press, 1960. 150 p.

3079 Butow, Robert J. C.
JAPAN'S DECISION TO SURRENDER. Foreword by Edwin O. Reischauer. Stanford, Calif., Stanford University Press, 1954. 259 p. (The Hoover Library on War, Revolution and Peace. Publication)

3080 Dealey, Ted.
SUNSET IN THE EAST. Dallas, 1945. 65 p.

3081 Elsbree, Willard H.
JAPAN'S ROLE IN SOUTHEAST ASIAN NATIONALIST MOVEMENTS, 1940-1945. Cambridge, Mass., Harvard University Press for International Secretariat, Institute of Pacific Relations; London, Allen and Unwin, 1953. 182 p.

3082 Gordon, Gary.
THE RISE AND FALL OF THE JAPANESE EMPIRE. Derby, Conn., Monarch Books, 1962. 236 p. (Monarch Giants)

3083 James, David H.
THE RISE AND FALL OF THE JAPANESE EMPIRE. New York, Macmillan; London, Allen and Unwin, 1951. 409 p.

3084 Jones, Francis C.
JAPAN'S NEW ORDER IN EAST ASIA: ITS RISE AND FALL, 1937-1945. London and New York, Oxford University Press, 1954. 498 p.

3085 Kase, Toshikazu.
ECLIPSE OF THE RISING SUN. Edited by David N. Rowe. London, Cape, 1951. 282 p.

3086 Kato, Masuo.
THE LOST WAR: A JAPANESE REPORTER'S INSIDE STORY. New York, Knopf, 1946. 264 p.

3087 Kawai, Michi.
SLIDING DOORS. Tokyo, Keisen-jo-gaku-en, 1950. 201 p.

3088 Maxon, Yale C.
CONTROL OF JAPANESE FOREIGN POLICY: A STUDY OF CIVIL-MILITARY RIVALRY, 1930-1945. Berkeley, University of California Press; London, Cambridge University Press, 1957. 286 p.

3089 Misselwitz, Henry F.
JAPAN COMMITS HARI-KIRI: A SKETCHBOOK. San Mateo, Calif., Paulson, 1945. 151 p.

3090 Terasaki, Gwen H.
BRIDGE OF THE SUN. Chapel Hill, University of North Carolina Press, 1957. 260 p.

3091 Tōgō, Shigenori.
THE CAUSE OF JAPAN. Translated and edited by Togo Fumihiko and Ben B. Blakeney. New York, Simon and Schuster, 1956. 372 p.

3092 Tolischus, Otto D.
THROUGH JAPANESE EYES. New York, Reynal and Hitchcock, 1945. 182 p.

3093 Tsuji, Masanobu.
UNDERGROUND ESCAPE. Translated from Japanese. Tokyo, Booth and Fukuda, 1952. 298 p.

3094 U.S. Army Air Forces.
MISSION ACCOMPLISHED: INTERROGATIONS OF JAPANESE INDUSTRIAL, MILITARY AND CIVIL LEADERS OF WORLD WAR II. Washington, U.S. Government Printing Office, 1946. 110 p.

d. Others

3095 Arnothy, Christine.
I AM FIFTEEN AND I DON'T WANT TO DIE. Translated from French. New York, Dutton, 1956. 124 p.

Other editions:
London, Collins, 1956. 128 p.

London, Collins, 1958. 127 p.

3096 Bassett, George.
THIS ALSO HAPPENED. London, Epworth, 1947 126 p.

3097 Brewster, Ralph H.
WRONG PASSPORT. London, Cohen and West, 1954. 274 p.

3098 Burmetz, Paul.
OUR SHARE OF MORNING. Garden City, N.Y., Doubleday, 1961. 360 p.

Other edition:
London, Redman, 1962.

3099 Cretzianu, Alexandre.
THE LOST OPPORTUNITY. London, Cape, 1957. 188 p.

3100 Czebe, Jenő, and Tibor Pethö.
HUNGARY IN WORLD WAR II: A MILITARY HISTORY OF THE YEARS OF WAR. Edited by "New Hungary." Budapest, 1946. 74 p.

3101 FINLAND AND WORLD WAR II, 1939-1944. Edited by John H. Wuorinen; translated from an anonymous Finnish manuscript. New York, Ronald Press, 1948. 228 p.

3102 HUNGARY'S RESPONSIBILITY IN WORLD WAR II. Budapest [194-?] 86 l.

3103 Kállay, Miklós.
HUNGARIAN PREMIER: A PERSONAL ACCOUNT OF A NATION'S STRUGGLE IN THE SECOND WORLD WAR. Foreword by C. A. Macartney. New York, Columbia University Press, 1954. 518 p.

3104 Kertész, István.
DIPLOMACY IN A WHIRLPOOL: HUNGARY BETWEEN NAZI GERMANY AND SOVIET RUSSIA. Notre Dame, Ind., University of Notre Dame Press, 1953. 273 p. (International Studies of the Committee on International Relations, University of Notre Dame)

3105 Korbel, Josef.
THE COMMUNIST SUBVERSION OF CZECHOSLOVAKIA, 1938-1948: THE FAILURE OF COEXISTENCE. Princeton, N.J., Princeton University Press, 1959. 258 p.

3106 Lundin, Charles L.
FINLAND IN THE SECOND WORLD WAR. Bloomington, Indiana University Press, 1957. 303 p. (Indiana University Publications. Slavic and East European Series)

3107 Macartney, Carlile A.
A HISTORY OF HUNGARY, 1929-1945. New York, Praeger, 1956-57. 2 v.

Other editions:
OCTOBER FIFTEENTH: A HISTORY OF MODERN HUNGARY, 1929-1945. Edinburgh, Edinburgh University Press, 1945-57. 2 v.

Chicago, Aldine, 1962. 2 v.

3108 Paneth, Philip.
EDUARD BENES: A LEADER OF DEMOCRACY. London, Alliance Press, 1945. 127 p.

3109 THE STRUGGLE OF THE BULGARIAN PEOPLE AGAINST FASCISM. Sofia, 1946. 113 p.

3110 Wechsberg, Joseph.
HOMECOMING. New York, Knopf, 1946. 117 p.

Other edition:
London, Joseph, 1947. 104 p.

3. War Aims

3111 Bengtson, John R.
NAZI WAR AIMS: THE PLANS FOR THE THOUSAND YEAR REICH. Rock Island, Ill., Augustana, 1962. 155 p. (Augustana Library Publications)

3112 DeMendelssohn, Peter.
DESIGN FOR AGGRESSION: THE INSIDE STORY OF HITLER'S WAR PLANS. New York and London, Harper, 1946. 270 p.

Other edition:
THE NUREMBERG DOCUMENTS: SOME ASPECTS OF GERMAN WAR POLICY, 1939-45. London, Allen and Unwin, 1946. 291 p.

3113 Kamenetsky, Ihor.
SECRET NAZI PLANS FOR EASTERN EUROPE: A STUDY OF LEBENSRAUM POLICIES. New York, Bockman, 1961. 263 p.

3114 Stipp, John L. (ed.).
DEVIL'S DIARY: THE RECORD OF NAZI CONSPIRACY AND AGGRESSION. Preface by Kurt von Schuschnigg. Yellow Springs, Ohio, Antioch Press, 1955. 236 p.

4. Propaganda

3115 Bramsted, Ernest K.
GOEBBELS AND NATIONAL SOCIALIST PROPAGANDA, 1925-1945. East Lansing, Michigan State University Press, 1965. 488 p.

3116 Cole, John A.
LORD HAW-HAW-AND WILLIAM JOYCE: THE FULL STORY. London, Faber and Faber, 1964. 316 p.

Other edition:
New York, Farrar, Straus and Giroux, 1965. 316 p.

3117 George, Alexander L.
PROPAGANDA ANALYSIS: A STUDY OF INFERENCES MADE FROM NAZI PROPAGANDA IN WORLD WAR II. Evanston, Ill., Row, Peterson, 1959. 287 p.

3118 Gingerich, William F.
THE BERLIN PRESS AND THE WAR IN POLAND, 1939. Washington, 1947. 139 l.

3119 West, Rebecca.
THE MEANING OF TREASON. New York, Viking, 1947. 307 p.

Other edition:
THE NEW MEANING OF TREASON. New York, Viking, 1964. 374 p.

3120 Zeman, Z.A.B.
NAZI PROPAGANDA. London and New York, Published in association with the Weiner Library by Oxford University Press, 1964. 226 p.

D. AXIS-HELD COUNTRIES
(see also III. E and VI. A)

1. Europe

a. Poland

3121 Budish, Jacob M. (ed.).
WARSAW GHETTO UPRISING, APRIL 19TH, 10TH ANNIVERSARY. New York, United Committee to Commemorate the Tenth Anniversary of the Warsaw Ghetto, 1953. 53, 75 p.

3122 Bytniewska, Irena (Irena Orska, pseud.).
SILENT IS THE VISTULA: THE STORY OF THE WARSAW UPRISING. Translated by Marta Erdman. New York, Longmans, 1946. 275 p.

3123 Ciechanowski, Jan.
DEFEAT IN VICTORY. Garden City, N.Y., Doubleday, 1947. 397 p.

Other edition:
London, Gollancz, 1948.

3124 Cyprian, Tadeusz, and Jerzy Sawicki.
NAZI RULE IN POLAND, 1939-1945. Translated from Polish by Edward Rothbert. Warsaw, Polonia Publishing House; London, Collet's, 1961. 262 p.

3125 THE DARK SIDE OF THE MOON. Preface by T. S. Eliot. London, Faber, 1946. 232 p.

Other edition:
New York, Scribner, 1947. 299 p.

3126 Ginter, Maria.
LIFE IN BOTH HANDS. Translated from Polish by P. C. Blauth-Muszkowski. London, Hodder and Stoughton, 1964. 253 p.

3127 Hadar, Alizia R., with Aubrey Kaufman.
THE PRINCESS ELNASARI. London, Heinemann, 1963. 217 p.

3128 Hare, Judith, Countess Listowel.
CRUSADER IN THE SECRET WAR. London, Johnson, 1952. 287 p.

3129 Karski, Jan (pseud.).
STORY OF A SECRET STATE. Boston, Houghton Mifflin, 1944. 391 p.

Other edition:
London, Hodder and Stoughton, 1945. 319 p.

3130 Krzesinski, Andrew J.
POLAND'S RIGHTS TO JUSTICE. New York, Devin-Adair, 1946. 120 p.

3131 Lipschutz, Norman.
VICTORY THROUGH DARKNESS AND DESPAIR. New York, Vantage Press, 1960. 123 p.

3132 Mikolajczyk, Stanislaw.
THE RAPE OF POLAND: PATTERN OF SOVIET AGGRESSION. New York, Whittlesey House, 1948. 309 p.

3133 Orme, Alexandra.
FROM CHRISTMAS TO EASTER: A GUIDE TO A RUSSIAN OCCUPATION. Translated from the Polish by M. A. Michael and L. Meyer. London, Hodge, 1949. 343 p.

Other edition:
COMES THE COMRADE! New York, Morrow, 1950. 376 p.

3134 Pinkus, Oscar.
THE HOUSE OF ASHES. Cleveland, World Publishing Co., 1964. 243 p.

3135 Poland. Biuro Odszkodowań Wojennych.
STATEMENT ON WAR LOSSES AND DAMAGES OF POLAND IN 1939-1945. Warsaw, 1947. 88 p.

3136 Poland. Ministerstwo Informacji.
THE NAZI KULTUR IN POLAND. By several authors of necessity temporarily anonymous. London, Published for the Polish Ministry of Information by H. M. Stationery Office, 1945. 220 p.

3137 Pole, Aline.
ESCAPE. London, Temple, 1946. 158 p.

3138 Ranz, Jochanan.
IN NAZI CLAWS: BENDZIN, 1939-1944. New York, 1956. 91 p.

3139 Scaevola (pseud.).
A STUDY IN FORGERY. London, Rolls Book Co., 1945. 123 p.

3140 Sledziński, Waclaw.
GOVERNOR FRANK'S DARK HARVEST. Newtown, Mont., Mid-Wales, Montgomerys, 1946. 250 p.

3141 Super, Margaret L. (Stump) (Ann Su Cardwell, pseud.).
THE CASE FOR POLAND. Introduction by R. H. Markham. Ann Arbor, Mich., 1945. 92 p.

3142 Super, Margaret L. (Stump) (Ann Su Cardwell, pseud.).
POLAND, HERE IS THE RECORD: AN AMERICAN'S VIEW. Foreword by William H. Chamberlin. Ann Arbor, Michigan Committee of Americans for Poland, 1945. 64 p.

3143 Szymczyk, Norbert J.
THE DESTRUCTION OF THE LONDON POLISH GOVERNMENT, 17 SEPTEMBER 1939-5 JULY 1944. Oberammergau, Ger., 1962. 100 l.

3144 Tushnet, Leonard.
TO DIE WITH HONOR: THE UPRISING OF THE JEWS IN THE WARSAW GHETTO. New York, Citadel Press, 1965. 128 p.

3145 Warfield, Hania, and Gaither Warfield.
CALL US TO WITNESS: A POLISH CHRONICLE. New York, Ziff-Davis, 1945. 434 p.

3146 Zagórski, Waclaw.
SEVENTY DAYS. Translated from the Polish by John Welsh. London, Muller, 1957. 267 p.

Other edition:
London, Hamilton, 1959. 223 p. (Panther Books)

3147 Zajaczkowska, Anna.
POLAND: THE UNTOLD STORY. London, Brown, 1945. 54 p.

3148 Zwiazek Bojowników o Wolność i Demokracje.
WE HAVE NOT FORGOTTEN, 1939-1945. Collected and edited by Tadeusz Mazur, Jerzy Tomaszewski, and Stanislaw Wrzos-Glinka. 2d ed. Warsaw, Polonia Publishing House, 1960. 266 p.

b. Belgium and the Netherlands

3149 American Academy of Political and Social Science, Philadelphia.
THE NETHERLANDS DURING GERMAN OCCUPATION. Edited by H. W. Posthumus. Philadelphia, 1946. 231 p.

3150 Burgers, Nelly M. (comp. and trans.).
HOLLAND UNDER THE NAZI HEEL: LETTERS FROM HOLLANDERS TO THEIR COUNTRYMEN IN SOUTH AFRICA, WRITTEN AFTER THE WAR. Ilfracombe, Stockwell, 1958. 94 p.

3151 Donker, P. A.
...WINTER '44-'45 IN HOLLAND: A WINTER NEVER TO BE FORGOTTEN. Bilthoven and Antwerp, Donker, 1945. 72 p.

3152 Frank, Anne.
THE DIARY OF A YOUNG GIRL. Translated from Dutch by B. N. Mooyaart-Doubleday; introduction by Eleanor Roosevelt. Garden City, N. Y., Doubleday, 1952. 285 p.

Other editions:
New York, Modern Library, 1952. 285 p. (Modern Library of World's Best Books)

Foreword by Storm Jameson. London, Vallentine, Mitchell; London, Constellation Books, 1952. 281 p.

2d ed.: London, Vallentine, Mitchell, 1954. 224 p.

Edited by M. H. Lewittes. School ed. New York, Globe Book Co., 1958. 323 p.

London, Hutchinson, 1960. 224 p. (Unicorn Books)

3153 Goris, Jan A.
BELGIUM IN BONDAGE. New York, Fischer, 1943. 259 p.

Other edition:
Antwerp, Standaard-Bockhandel, 1946. 216 p.

3154 Goris, Jan A. (ed.).
BELGIUM UNDER OCCUPATION. Chapters by Fernand Baudhuin and others. New York, Moutus Press for the Belgian Government Information Center 1947. 240 p.

3155 Goris, Jan A.
STRANGERS SHOULD NOT WHISPER. New York, Fischer, 1945. 260 p.

3156 Kennedy, Joseph P., and James M. Landis.
THE SURRENDER OF KING LEOPOLD. With an Appendix containing the Keyes-Gort correspondence. New York, 1950. 61 p.

3157 Konijnenburg, Emile van.
ORGANISED ROBBERY. Prepared on the instructions of the Netherlands Ministry of Economic Affairs. The Hague, Netherlands Government Printing and Publishing Office, 1949. 242 p.

3158 MALNUTRITION AND STARVATION IN WESTERN NETHERLANDS, SEPTEMBER 1944-JULY 1945. The Hague, General State Printing Office, 1948. 2 v.

3159 Mason, Henry L.
THE PURGE OF DUTCH QUISLINGS: EMERGENCY JUSTICE IN THE NETHERLANDS. The Hague, Nijhoff, 1952. 199 p.

3160 Meerloo, Joost A. M.
TOTAL WAR AND THE HUMAN MIND: A PSYCHOLOGIST'S EXPERIENCES IN OCCUPIED HOLLAND. New York, International Universities Press, 1945. 78 p.

3161 Minco, Marga.
BITTER HERBS: A LITTLE CHRONICLE. Translated from Dutch by Roy Edwards. London and New York, Oxford University Press, 1960. 115 p.

3162 Schnabel, Ernst.
ANNE FRANK: A PORTRAIT IN COURAGE. Translated from the German by Richard and Clara Winston. New York, Harcourt, Brace, 1958. 192 p.

Other editions:
THE FOOTSTEPS OF ANNE FRANK. London, Longmans, Green, 1959. 160 p.

London, Pan, 1961. 158 p.

3163 Schreurs, Johannes J. M. H.
MY COUNTRY IN TROUBLE. New York, Carlton Press, 1962. 52 p.

3164 Somerhausen, Anne S.
WRITTEN IN DARKNESS: A BELGIAN WOMAN'S RECORD OF THE OCCUPATION, 1940-1945. New York, Knopf, 1946. 339 p.

3165 Van Paassen, Pierre.
EARTH COULD BE FAIR: A CHRONICLE. New York, Dial Press, 1946. 509 p.

3166 Walt, Harry P. van.
THE NIGHT IS FAR SPENT. Philadelphia, Dorrance, 1945. 221 p.

3167 Warmbrunn, Werner.
THE DUTCH UNDER GERMAN OCCUPATION, 1940-1945. Stanford, Calif., Stanford University Press; London, Oxford University Press, 1963. 338 p.

c. Denmark

3168 Bertelsen, Aage.
OCTOBER '43. Translated by Milly Lindholm and Willy Agtby; foreword by Sholem Asch. New York, Putnam, 1954. 246 p.

Other editions:
London, Museum Press, 1955. 160 p.

London, Spencer, 1956. 189 p. (Badger Books)

3169 Mentze, Ernst (ed.).
5 YEARS: THE OCCUPATION OF DENMARK IN PICTURES. Foreword by Poul N. Malmö. Sweden, Allhem; New York, Bonnier, 1946. 230 p.

3170   Michelsen, Kaj C. B.
        THEY DIED FOR US: IN MEMORY OF ALLIED AIRMEN WHO LOST THEIR LIVES IN DENMARK DURING THE SECOND WORLD WAR. Copenhagen and Chicago, Scandinavian Publishing Co., A. C. Christensen, 1946. 86 p.

3171   Outze, Børge (ed.).
        DENMARK DURING THE GERMAN OCCUPATION. Copenhagen and Chicago, Scandinavian Publishing Co., 1946. 155 p.

3172   TRIUMPH IN DISASTER: DENMARK'S FIGHT AGAINST GERMANY. London, H. M. Stationery Office for Danish Council in London, 1945. 64 p.

d. Norway

3173   Fjellbu, Arne.
        MEMOIRS FROM THE WAR YEARS. Translated from Norwegian by L. A. Vigness. Minneapolis, Augsburg Publishing House, 1947. 106 p.

3174   Lehmkuhl, Dik.
        JOURNEY TO LONDON: THE STORY OF THE NORWEGIAN GOVERNMENT AT WAR. London, Hutchinson, by the authority of the Norwegian State Information Office, 1946. 152 p.

3175   Walker, Roy.
        A PEOPLE WHO LOVED PEACE: THE NORWEGIAN STRUGGLE AGAINST NAZISM. London, Gollancz, 1946. 111 p.

3176   Warbey, William.
        LOOK TO NORWAY. London, Secker and Warburg, 1945. 242 p.

e. France

3177   Aron, Robert, with Georgette Elgey.
        THE VICHY REGIME, 1940-44. Translated by Humphrey Hare. New York, Macmillan, 1958. 536 p.

3178   De Polnay, Peter.
        DEATH AND TOMORROW. London, Hamilton, 1957. 320 p. (Panther Books)

        Other edition:
        London, Secker and Warburg, 1942. 299 p.

3179   Dutourd, Jean.
        THE TAXIS OF THE MARNE. Translated from the French by Harold King. New York, Simon and Schuster, 1957. 244 p.

3180   Farmer, Paul.
        VICHY: POLITICAL DILEMMA. London, Oxford University Press, 1955. 376 p.

3181   FRANCE DURING THE GERMAN OCCUPATION, 1940-1944: A COLLECTION OF 292 STATEMENTS ON THE GOVERNMENT OF MARECHAL PETAIN AND PIERRE LAVAL: Translated from French by Philip W. Whitcomb.
        Stanford, Calif., Stanford University Press for Hoover Institution on War, Revolution and Peace; London, Oxford University Press, 1959. 3 v. (Stanford University, Hoover Institution on War, Revolution and Peace, Documentary Series)

3182   French, Herbert E.
        MY YANKEE PARIS. New York, Vanguard Press, 1945. 260 p.

3183   Funk, Arthur L.
        CHARLES DE GAULLE: THE CRUCIAL YEARS, 1943-1944. Norman, University of Oklahoma Press, 1959. 336 p.

3184   Grinnell-Milne, Duncan W.
        THE TRIUMPH OF INTEGRITY: A PORTRAIT OF CHARLES DE GAULLE. London, Bodley Head, 1961. 320 p.

        Other edition:
        New York, Macmillan, 1962. 334 p.

3185   Groult, Benoîte, and Flora Groult.
        DIARY IN DUO. Translated from the French by Humphrey Hare. London, Barrie and Rockliff, 1965. 350 p.

3186   Henrey, Mrs. Robert.
        MADELEINE, YOUNG WIFE: THE AUTOBIOGRAPHY OF A FRENCH GIRL. New York, Dutton, 1954. 380 p.

3187   Henrey, Mrs. Robert (Robert Henrey, pseud.).
        THE RETURN TO THE FARM. London, Davies, 1947. 173 p.

        Other edition:
        A FARM IN NORMANDY AND THE RETURN TO THE FARM. London, Dent, 1952. 398 p.

3188   Huddleston, Sisley.
        FRANCE: THE TRAGIC YEARS; AN EYEWITNESS ACCOUNT OF WAR, OCCUPATION AND LIBERATION. New York, Devin-Adair, 1954. 384 p.

        Other edition:
        London, Holborn Publishing Co., 1958. 360 p.

3189   Huddleston, Sisley.
        PETAIN: PATRIOT OR TRAITOR? London, Dakus, 1951. 269 p.

3190   Hytier, Adrienne D.
        TWO YEARS OF FRENCH FOREIGN POLICY: VICHY, 1940-1942. Geneva, Droz, 1958. 402 p. (Etudes d'histoire économique, politique et sociale, 25)

        Other edition:
        New York, Loring, 1959. 402 p.

3191   Jucker, Ninetta.
        CURFEW IN PARIS: A RECORD OF THE GERMAN OCCUPATION. London, Hogarth Press, 1960. 206 p.

3192   Kerilles, Henri de.
        I ACCUSE DE GAULLE. Translated by Harold Rosenberg. New York, Harcourt, Brace, 1946. 270 p.

3193 Lorraine, Jacques.
THE GERMANS IN FRANCE. Translated by A. G. Cerisier-Duverney. London, Hutchinson, 1947. 192 p.

3194 Maritain, Jacques.
MESSAGES, 1941-1944. New York, Maison Française, 1945. 221 p. (Collection Civilisation)

3195 Odic, Charles J.
STEPCHILDREN OF FRANCE. Translated by Henry N. Hall. New York, Roy, 1945. 181 p.

3196 Pickles, Dorothy M.
FRANCE BETWEEN THE REPUBLICS. London. Contact Publications, 1946. 247 p.

3197 Reynaud, Paul.
IN THE THICK OF THE FIGHT, 1930-1945. Translated by James D. Lambert. New York, Simon and Schuster, 1955. 684 p.

3198 Rieber, Alfred.
STALIN AND THE FRENCH COMMUNIST PARTY, 1941-1947. New York, Columbia University Press, 1962. 395 p. (Studies of the Russian Institute, Columbia University)

3199 Saint Exupéry, Consuelo de.
KINGDOM OF THE ROCKS: MEMORIES OF OPPEDE. Translated from the French by Katherine Woods. New York, Random House, 1946. 305 p.

3200 Saliège, Jules Géraud, Cardinal.
WHO SHALL BEAR THE FLAME? Translated by Speer Strahan. South Bend, Fides Publishers, 1949. 191 p.

3201 Teissier du Cros, Janet.
DIVIDED LOYALTIES. Preface by D. E. Brogan. London, Hamilton, 1962. 329 p.

Other edition:
New York, Knopf, 1964. 350 p.

3202 Thomson, David.
TWO FRENCHMEN: PIERRE LAVAL AND CHARLES DE GAULLE. London, Cresset Press, 1951. 255 p.

3203 Tompkins, Peter.
THE MURDER OF ADMIRAL DARLAN: A STUDY IN CONSPIRACY. New York, Simon and Schuster; London, Weidenfeld and Nicolson, 1965. 287 p.

3204 Walter, Gérard.
PARIS UNDER THE OCCUPATION. Translated by Tony White. New York, Orion Press, 1960. 209 p.

f. Yugoslavia

3205 Armstrong, Hamilton F.
TITO AND GOLIATH. London, Gollancz, 1951. 318 p.

3206 Calder-Marshall, Arthur.
THE WATERSHED. London, Contact Publications, 1947. 216 p.

3207 Clissold, Stephen.
WHIRLWIND: AN ACCOUNT OF MARSHAL TITO'S RISE TO POWER. London, Cresset Press; New York, Philosophical Library, 1949. 245 p.

3208 Eton, Peter, and James Leasor.
WALL OF SILENCE. Indianapolis, Bobbs-Merrill, 1960. 268 p.

3209 Fotitch, Constantin.
THE WAR WE LOST: YUGOSLAVIA'S TRAGEDY AND THE FAILURE OF THE WEST. New York, Viking Press, 1948. 344 p.

3210 Huot, Louis.
GUNS FOR TITO. New York, Fischer, 1945. 273 p.

3211 Inks, James M.
EIGHT BAILED OUT. Edited by Lawrence Lingman. New York, Norton, 1954. 222 p.

Other editions:
London, Methuen, 1955. 162 p.

London, World Distributors, 1956. 159 p. (Viking Books)

3212 Jovichić, Lenka A.
WITHIN CLOSED FRONTIERS: A WOMAN IN WARTIME YUGOSLAVIA. London, Chambers, 1956. 253 p.

3213 THE LIBERATION STRUGGLE OF THE YUGOSLAV PEOPLES, 1941-1945. Translated from Serbo-Croatian by Zvonko Spaleta. Belgrade, 1961. 146 p.

3214 Markham, Reuben H.
TITO'S IMPERIAL COMMUNISM. Chapel Hill, University of North Carolina Press, 1947. 292 p.

3215 Martin, David.
ALLY BETRAYED: THE UNCENSORED STORY OF TITO AND MIHAILOVICH. Foreword by Rebecca West. New York, Prentice-Hall, 1946. 372 p.

3216 Mikes, George.
WE WERE THERE TO ESCAPE: THE TRUE STORY OF A JUGOSLAV OFFICER. London, Nicholson and Watson, 1945. 251 p.

3217 Morača, Pero, and Viktor Kučan.
THE WAR AND REVOLUTION OF THE PEOPLES OF YUGOSLAVIA, 1941-1945. Translated by Peter Mijušković. Belgrade, Mladost, 196-. 206 p.

3218 Radlovic, I. Monte.
TITO'S REPUBLIC. London, Coldharbour Press, 1948. 241 p.

3219 Rayner, Louisa.
WOMEN IN A VILLAGE: AN ENGLISHWOMAN'S EXPERIENCES AND IMPRESSIONS OF LIFE IN YUGOSLA-

VIA UNDER GERMAN OCCUPATION. London, Heinemann, 1957. 147 p.

3220 United Committee of South-Slavs in London.
THE EPIC OF YUGOSLAVIA, 1941-1944. London, 1945. 96 p.

3221 Yovitchitch, Lena A.
WITHIN CLOSED FRONTIERS: A WOMAN IN WAR-TIME YUGOSLAVIA. London, Chambers, 1956. 253 p.

g. Greece

3222 Gyalistras, Sergios A.
THE GREEK NATION ONCE MORE STEMS A BARBARIAN ONSLAUGHT. Translated from the Greek by G. H. Trypanis. Athens, 1950. 89 p.

3223 Kousoulas, Dimitrios G.
THE PRICE OF FREEDOM: GREECE IN WORLD AFFAIRS, 1939-1953. Syracuse, Syracuse University Press, 1953. 210 p.

3224 McNeill, William H.
THE GREEK DILEMMA: WAR AND AFTERMATH. Philadelphia, Lippincott, 1947. 291 p.

Other edition:
London, Gollancz, 1947. 240 p.

3225 Myers, Edmund C. W.
GREEK ENTANGLEMENT. London, Hart-Davis, 1955. 289 p.

3226 Noel-Baker, Francis E.
GREECE: THE WHOLE STORY London, New York, Melbourne, and Sydney, Hutchinson, 1946. 64 p.

3227 Paneth, Philip.
THE GLORY THAT IS GREECE. London, Alliance Press, 1945. 138 p.

3228 Pezas, Mikia.
THE PRICE OF LIBERTY. New York, Washburn, 1945. 261 p.

Other edition:
London, Gollancz, 1946. 235 p.

3229 Sweet-Escott, Bickham.
GREECE: A POLITICAL AND ECONOMIC SURVEY, 1939-1953. London and New York, Royal Institute of International Affairs, 1954. 206 p.

3230 Woodhouse, Christopher M.
APPLE OF DISCORD: A SURVEY OF RECENT GREEK POLITICS IN THEIR INTERNATIONAL SETTING. Foreword by Lord Altrincham. London and New York, Hutchinson, 1948. 320 p.

3231 Xydis, Stephen G.
GREECE AND THE GREAT POWERS, 1944-1947: PRELUDE TO THE "TRUMAN DOCTRINE." Thessaloniki, Institute for Balkan Studies, 1963. 758 p.

3232 Zitridou, Pipitsa C., and H. Psimeno.
WOMEN OF GREECE, WORLD WAR II, 1940-1944. Athens, Aetos, 1950. 199 p.

h. Baltic States

3233 Bīlmanis, Alfreds.
BALTIC STATES AND WORLD PEACE AND SECURITY ORGANIZATION, FACTS IN REVIEW. Washington, D.C., Latvian Legation, 1945. 67 p.

3234 Bīlmanis, Alfreds.
LATVIA, BETWEEN THE ANVIL AND THE HAMMER. Washington, D.C., Latvian Legation, 1945. 64 p.

3235 Collins, Charles.
LATVIAN-JEWISH RELATIONS: THE TRAGIC PLIGHT OF LATVIANS AND JEWS UNDER NAZI OCCUPATION IN LATVIA. n.p., 1946. 86 p.

3236 Feld, Mischa Jac (pseud.), and Ivan H. Peterman.
THE HUG OF THE BEAR. New York, Holt, Rinehart and Winston, 1961. 305 p.

3237 Harrison, Ernest J.
LITHUANIA'S FIGHT FOR FREEDOM. New York, Lithuanian American Information Center, 1952. 95 p.

3238 Oras, Arts.
BALTIC ECLIPSE. London, Gollancz, 1948. 307 p.

3239 Pakštas, Kazys.
LITHUANIA AND WORLD WAR II. Chicago, 1947. 80 p.

3240 Pelékis, K. (pseud.).
GENOCIDE: LITHUANIA'S THREEFOLD TRAGEDY. Edited by Rumsaitis (pseud.). n.p., "Venta," 1949. 286 p.

i. Channel Islands

3241 Cortvriend, V. V.
ISOLATED ISLAND: A HISTORY AND PERSONAL REMINISCENCES OF THE GERMAN OCCUPATION OF THE ISLAND OF GUERNSEY, JUNE 1940-MAY 1945. Guernsey, Guernsey Star and Gazette, 1949. 334 p.

3242 Durand, Ralph A.
GUERNSEY UNDER GERMAN RULE. London, Guernsey Society, 1946. 183 p.

3243 Hathaway, Dame Sibyl M. C. B.
DAME OF SAR: AN AUTOBIOGRAPHY. New York, Coward-McCann, 1962. 211 p.

3244 Higgs, Dorothy P.
GUERNSEY DIARY, 1940-1945: A HUMAN RECORD OF THE OCCUPATION YEARS. London, Linden, Lewis; distributors: Rolls House, 1947. 64 p.

3245　Mollet, Ralph.
　　　JERSEY UNDER THE SWASTIKA: AN ACCOUNT OF THE OCCUPATION OF THE ISLAND OF JERSEY BY THE GERMAN FORCES, 1ST JULY 1940 TO 12TH MAY 1945. London, Hyperion Press, 1945. 110 p.

3246　Pont-Alain, C. M. (Anthony M. Arrol, pseud.).
　　　THE BEST OF IT. Guernsey, Williams and Wardley, 1956. 67 p.

3247　Sinel, Leslie P.
　　　THE GERMAN OCCUPATION OF JERSEY: A COMPLETE DIARY OF EVENTS FROM JUNE 1940 TO JUNE 1945. Jersey, The Evening Post, 1946. 298 p.

3248　Wood, Alan, and Mary Wood.
　　　ISLANDS IN DANGER: THE STORY OF THE GERMAN OCCUPATION OF THE CHANNEL ISLANDS, 1940-1945. London, Evans, 1955. 255 p.

Other edition:
New York, Macmillan, 1956.

3249　Wyatt, Horace M.
　　　JERSEY IN JAIL, 1940-45. Jersey, Huelin, 1945. 92 p.

2. Far East

3250　Baker, Gilbert.
　　　THE CHANGING SCENE IN CHINA. London, S.C.M. Press, 1946. 139 p.

Other edition:
New York, Friendship Press, 1948. 152 p.

3251　Benda, Harry J.
　　　THE CRESCENT AND THE RISING SUN: INDONESIAN ISLAM UNDER THE JAPANESE OCCUPATION, 1942-1945. The Hague, W. van Hoeve, 1958. 320 p.

3252　Benda, Harry J., James K. Irikura, and Kōichi Kishi (eds.).
　　　JAPANESE MILITARY ADMINISTRATION IN INDONESIA: SELECTED DOCUMENTS. Translated by James K. Irikura, Margaret W. Broekhuysen, and Imam J. Pamoedjo. New Haven, Yale University Southeast Studies, 1965. 279 p. (Yale University. Southeast Asia Studies. Translation Series.)

3253　Briggs, Margaret Y. (Liang Yen, pseud.).
　　　DAUGHTER OF THE KHANS. New York, Norton, 1955. 285 p.

3254　Bustos, Felixberti G.
　　　AND NOW COMES HOXAS: A STORY OF THE OCCUPATION AND A LEADER. Manila, Bustos, 1945. 253 p.

3255　Caldwell, John C., and Mark Gayn.
　　　AMERICAN AGENT. New York, Holt, 1947. 220 p.

3256　Chaya, Prem, and Alethea (pseud.).
　　　THE PASSING HOURS: A RECORD OF FIVE AMAZING YEARS. Bangkok, Chatra Books, 1945. 95 p.

3257　Chiang Kai-shek.
　　　THE COLLECTED WARTIME MESSAGES OF GENERALISSIMO CHIANG KAI-CHEK, 1937-1945. New York, Day, 1946. 2 v.

3258　Clark, Thomas B.
　　　ROBINSON CRUSOE, USN: THE ADVENTURES OF GEORGE R. TWEED, ON JAP-HELD GUAM. New York, Whittlesey House, McGraw-Hill, 1945. 275 p.

3259　Feis, Herbert.
　　　THE CHINA TANGLE: THE AMERICAN EFFORT IN CHINA FROM PEARL HARBOR TO THE MARSHALL MISSION. Princeton, N.J., Princeton University Press, 1953. 445 p.

3260　Galang, Ricardo C.
　　　SECRET MISSION TO THE PHILIPPINES. Foreword by Carlos P. Romulo. Manila, University Publishing Co., 1948. 234 p.

3261　Gilmour, Oswald W.
　　　WITH FREEDOM TO SINGAPORE. London, Benn, 1950. 227 p.

3262　Gimenez, Pedro M.
　　　UNDER THE SHADOWS OF THE "KEMPI." Manila, Narvaez, 1946. 337 p.

3263　Lichauco, Marcial P.
　　　"DEAR MOTHER PUTNAM": A DIARY OF THE WAR IN THE PHILIPPINES. Manila, 1949. 219 p.

3264　Lin Yutang.
　　　BETWEEN TEARS AND LAUGHTER. London, Crisp, 1945. 234 p.

3265　Lin Yutang.
　　　THE VIGIL OF A NATION. Toronto, Longmans, Green, 1945. 262 p.

Other edition:
London, Heinemann, 1946. 324 p.

3266　Llewellyn, Bernard.
　　　I LEFT MY ROOTS IN CHINA. London, Allen and Unwin, 1953. 175 p.

3267　Monaghan, Forbes J.
　　　UNDER THE RED SUN: A LETTER FROM MANILA. New York, Declan X. McMullen Co., 1946. 279 p.

3268　Nu, U.
　　　BURMA UNDER THE JAPANESE. Edited and translated by J. S. Furnivall. London, Macmillan; New York, St. Martin's Press, 1954. 132 p.

3269 P'an Chao-ying.
CHINA FIGHTS ON, AN INSIDE STORY OF CHINA'S LONG STRUGGLE AGAINST OUR COMMON ENEMIES. New York and London, Revell, 1945. 188 p.

3270 Payne, Pierre S. R.
CHUNGKING DIARY. London and Toronto, Heinemann, 1945. 526 p.

Other edition:
FOREVER CHINA. New York, Dodd, Mead, 1945. 573 p.

3271 Peck, Graham.
TWO KINDS OF TIME. Boston, Houghton Mifflin, 1950. 725 p.

3272 Poppe, Janus.
POLITICAL DEVELOPMENT IN THE NETHERLANDS EAST-INDIES DURING AND IMMEDIATELY AFTER THE JAPANESE OCCUPATION. Washington, 1948. 339 l.

3273 Recto, Claro M.
THREE YEARS OF ENEMY OCCUPATION: THE ISSUE OF POLITICAL COLLABORATION IN THE PHILIPPINES. Manila, People's Publishers, 1946. 189 p.

3274 Rhys, Lloyd.
JUNGLE PIMPERNEL: THE STORY OF A DISTRICT OFFICER IN CENTRAL NETHERLANDS NEW GUINEA. London, Hodder and Stoughton, 1947. 239 p.

3275 Rosinger, Lawrence K.
CHINA'S CRISIS. New York, Knopf, 1945. 259 p.

3276 Rosinger, Lawrence K.
CHINA'S WARTIME POLITICS, 1937-1944. Princeton, N. J., Princeton University Press, 1945. 133 p.

3277 Savary, Gladys S.
OUTSIDE THE WALLS. New York, Vantage Press, 1954. 206 p.

3278 Tong, Hollington K.
CHINA AND THE WORLD PRESS. n. p., 1948. 282 p.

3279 Tun Pe, U.
SUN OVER BURMA. Rangoon, Rasika Ranjani Press, 1949. 114 p.

3280 U. S. Office of Strategic Services. Research and Analysis Branch.
WHO'S WHO IN THE NANKING PUPPET REGIME. Washington, 1945. 149 p. (R and A)

3281 Ward, Robert S.
ASIA FOR THE ASIATICS? THE TECHNIQUES OF JAPANESE OCCUPATION. Introduction by Laurence Salisbury. Chicago, University of Chicago Press, 1945. 204 p.

E. UNITED STATES COALITION

1. General Diplomacy

3282 Dallin, David J.
THE BIG THREE: THE UNITED STATES, BRITAIN, RUSSIA. New Haven, Conn., Yale University Press, 1945. 202 p.

3283 Dennett, Raymond, and Joseph E. Johnson (eds.).
NEGOTIATING WITH THE RUSSIANS. Boston, World Peace Foundation, 1951. 310 p.

3284 DeRoussy de Sales, Raoul J. J. F.
THE MAKING OF YESTERDAY. New York, Reynal and Hitchcock, 1947. 310 p.

3285 Feis, Herbert.
CHURCHILL, ROOSEVELT, STALIN: THE WAR THEY WAGED AND THE PEACE THEY SOUGHT. Princeton, N. J., Princeton University Press, 1957. 692 p.

3286 Goodhart, Philip.
FIFTY SHIPS THAT SAVED THE WORLD: THE FOUNDATION OF THE ANGLO-AMERICAN ALLIANCE. London, Heinemann; Garden City, N. Y., Doubleday, 1965. 267 p.

3287 Hamzavi, Abdol H.
PERSIA AND THE POWERS: AN ACCOUNT OF DIPLOMATIC RELATIONS, 1941-1946. London and New York, Hutchinson, 1946. 125 p.

3288 Rozek, Edward
ALLIED WARTIME DIPLOMACY: A PATTERN IN POLAND. New York, Wiley; London, Chapman and Hall, 1958. 481 p.

3289 Russia. Komissiia po Izdaniiu Diplomaticheskikh Dokumentov.
CORRESPONDENCE BETWEEN THE CHAIRMAN OF THE COUNCIL OF MINISTERS OF THE U.S.S.R. AND THE PRESIDENTS OF THE U.S.A. AND THE PRIME MINISTERS OF GREAT BRITAIN DURING THE GREAT PATRIOTIC WAR OF 1941-1945. Moscow, Foreign Languages Publishing House, 1957. 2 v.

Other editions:
STALIN'S CORRESPONDENCE WITH CHURCHILL, ATTLEE, ROOSEVELT AND TRUMAN, 1941-45. London, Lawrence and Wishart; New York, Dutton, 1958. 2 v. in 1.

3290 Schwartz, Andrew J.
AMERICA AND THE RUSSO-FINNISH WAR. Introduction by Quincy Wright. Washington, Public Affairs Press, 1960. 103 p.

3291 Snell, John L.
WARTIME ORIGINS OF THE EAST-WEST DILEMMA OVER GERMANY. New Orleans, Hauser Press, 1962. 268 p.

3292 Viorst, Milton.
HOSTILE ALLIES: FDR AND CHARLES DE GAULLE. New York, Macmillan; London, Collier-Macmillan, 1965. 280 p.

3293 VOICES OF HISTORY: GREAT SPEECHES AND PAPERS OF THE YEAR, 1941, 1942-43 TO 1945-46. Edited by Franklin Watts, Barbara E. Leighton, and Nathan Ausubel. New York, Gramercy Publishing Co., 1942-46. 5 v.

3294 Welles, Sumner.
SEVEN DECISIONS THAT SHAPED HISTORY. New York, Harper, 1951. 236 p.

Other edition:
SEVEN MAJOR DECISIONS. London, Hamilton, 1951. 224 p.

3295 White, Dorothy S.
SEED OF DISCORD: DE GAULLE, FREE FRANCE, AND THE ALLIES. Syracuse, Syracuse University Press, 1964. 471 p.

2. Big-Three Conferences

3296 Feis, Herbert.
BETWEEN WAR AND PEACE: THE POTSDAM CONFERENCE. Princeton, N.J., Princeton University Press; London, Oxford University Press, 1960. 367 p.

3297 Fenno, Richard F.
THE YALTA CONFERENCE. Boston, Heath, 1955. 112 p. (Problems in American Civilization)

3298 Iran. Ministry of Foreign Affairs.
THE TEHRAN CONFERENCE: THE THREE-POWER DECLARATION CONCERNING IRAN, DECEMBER 1943. Iran, 1945. 189 p.

3299 Keplicz, Klemens.
POTSDAM: TWENTY YEARS AFTER. Warsaw, Zachodnia Agencja Prasowa, 1965. 129 p.

3300 Kuter, Laurence S.
AIRMAN AT YALTA. New York, Duell, Sloan and Pearce, 1955. 180 p.

3301 Neumann, William L.
MAKING THE PEACE, 1941-1945: THE DIPLOMACY OF THE WARTIME CONFERENCES. Washington, Foundation for Foreign Affairs, 1950. 101 p.

3302 Pick, Frederick W.
PEACEMAKING IN PERSPECTIVE: FROM POTSDAM TO PARIS. Oxford, Pen-in-Hand, 1950. 251 p.

3303 Roosevelt, Elliott.
AS HE SAW IT. Foreword by Eleanor Roosevelt. New York, Duell, Sloan and Pearce, 1946. 270 p.

3304 Snell, John L.
THE MEANING OF YALTA: BIG THREE DIPLOMACY AND THE NEW BALANCE OF POWER. Foreword by Paul H. Clyde. Baton Rouge, Louisiana State University Press, 1956. 239 p.

3305 Stettinius, Edward R.
ROOSEVELT AND THE RUSSIANS: THE YALTA CONFERENCE. Edited by Walter Johnson. Garden City, N.Y., Doubleday, 1949. 367 p.

Other edition:
London, Cape, 1950. 320 p.

3306 Strauss, Harold.
THE DIVISION AND DISMEMBERMENT OF GERMANY, FROM THE CASABLANCA CONFERENCE (JANUARY 1943) TO THE ESTABLISHMENT OF THE EAST GERMAN REPUBLIC (OCTOBER 1949). Ambilly, Switz., Coopérative "Les Presses de Savoie," 1952. 240 p.

3307 U.S. Dept. of State.
THE CONFERENCE OF BERLIN (THE POTSDAM CONFERENCE), 1945. Washington, U.S. Government Printing Office, 1960. 2 v. (Foreign Relations of the U.S.: Diplomatic Papers)

3308 U.S. Dept. of State.
THE CONFERENCES AT CAIRO AND TEHRAN, 1943. Washington, U.S. Government Printing Office, 1961. 932 p. (Foreign Relations of the U.S.: Diplomatic Papers)

3309 U.S. Dept. of State.
THE CONFERENCES AT MALTA AND YALTA, 1945. Washington, U.S. Government Printing Office, 1955. 1032 p. (Foreign Relations of the U.S.: Diplomatic Papers)

3310 U.S. Dept. of State. Office of Public Affairs. Division of Historical Policy Research.
AGREEMENTS REACHED AT THE CAIRO, TEHRAN, YALTA, AND POTSDAM CONFERENCES, IMPLEMENTATION AND UNITED STATES POLICY. Washington, 1948. 51 p. (Research Project)

3311 Wittmer, Felix.
YALTA BETRAYAL: DATA ON THE DECLINE AND FALL OF FRANKLIN DELANO ROOSEVELT. Caldwell, Idaho, Caxton Printers, 1953. 136 p.

Territorial Questions

3312 Becker, George H.
THE DISPOSITION OF THE ITALIAN COLONIES, 1941-1951. Annemasse, 1952. 270 p.

3313 Boldizsár, Ivan.
...THIS NATION HAS ALREADY ATONED...A PAMPHLET ABOUT THE HUNGARIAN PEACE AND ABOUT THE DANUBE BASIN. Edited by "New Hungary." 1946. Budapest, 1946. 55 p. (Pamphlets of "New Hungary")

3314 Jordan, Z.
ODER-NEISSE LINE: A STUDY OF THE POLITICAL, ECONOMIC, AND EUROPEAN SIGNIFICANCE OF POLAND'S WESTERN FRONTIER. Prepared on the basis of the research and study group set up by the Polish Freedom Movement "Independence and Democracy." 2d ed. London, Polish Freedom Movement "Independence and Democracy," 1952. 141 p.

3315 Mihovilović, Ive.
ITALIAN EXPANSIONIST POLICY TOWARDS ISTRIA, RIJEKA AND DALMATIA (1945-1953): DOCUMENTS. Belgrade, Institute for International Politics and Economics, 1954. 222 p.

3316 Pankhurst, E. Sylvia, and Richard K. P. Pankhurst.
ETHOPIA AND ERITREA: THE LAST PHASE OF THE REUNION STRUGGLE, 1941-1952. Foreword by Lady Pethick Lawrence of Peaslake. Woodford Green, Essex, Lalibela House, 1953. 360 p.

3317 Rhode, Gotthold, and Wolfgang Wagner (comps. and eds.).
THE GENESIS OF THE ODER-NEISSE LINE IN THE DIPLOMATIC NEGOTIATIONS DURING WORLD WAR II: SOURCES AND DOCUMENTS. Stuttgart, Brentano-Verlag, 1959. 287 p.

3318 Sedmak, V., and J. Mejak.
TRIESTE: THE PROBLEM WHICH AGITATES THE WORLD. Belgrade, Edition "Jugoslavija," 1953. 79 p.

3319 Szaz, Zoltan M.
GERMANY'S EASTERN FRONTIERS: THE PROBLEM OF THE ODER-NEISSE LINE. Foreword by Harold Zink. Chicago, Regnery, 1960. 256 p. (Foundation for Foreign Affairs Series)

3320 Wagner, Wolfgang.
THE GENESIS OF THE ODER-NEISSE LINE: A STUDY IN DIPLOMATIC NEGOTIATIONS DURING WORLD WAR II. Stuttgart, Brentano-Verlag, 1957. 168 p.

3321 Wiskemann, Elizabeth.
GERMANY'S EASTERN NEIGHBORS: PROBLEMS RELATING TO THE ODER-NEISSE LINE AND THE CZECH FRONTIER REGIONS. Issued under the auspices of the Royal Institute of International Affairs. London, Oxford University Press, 1956. 309 p.

3322 Wojcik, Andrzej J.
THE TEHERAN CONFERENCE AND ODRA-NISA BOUNDARY. New York, Arlington, 1959. 70 p.

3. War Aims; United Nations Organization; Peace Treaties

3323 Abend, Hallett E.
RECONQUEST: ITS RESULTS AND RESPONSIBILITIES. Garden City, N.Y., Doubleday, 1946. 305 p.

3324 Armstrong, Anne.
UNCONDITIONAL SURRENDER: THE IMPACT OF THE CASABLANCA POLICY UPON WORLD WAR II. New Brunswick, N.J., Rutgers University Press, 1961. 304 p.

3325 Arne, Sigrid.
UNITED NATIONS PRIMER: THE KEY TO THE CONFERENCES. New York and Toronto, Rinehart, 1948. 266 p.

3326 Bentwich, Norman de M.
FROM GENEVA TO SAN FRANCISCO: AN ACCOUNT OF THE INTERNATIONAL ORGANIZATION OF THE NEW ORDER. London, Gollancz, 1946. 111 p.

3327 Brookings Institution, Washington D.C. International Studies Group.
THE SEARCH FOR PEACE SETTLEMENTS. Prepared by Redvers Opie and others. Washington, 1951. 366 p.

3328 Cohen, Bernard C.
THE POLITICAL PROCESS AND FOREIGN POLICY: THE MAKING OF THE JAPANESE PEACE SETTLEMENT. Princeton, N.J., Princeton University Press, 1957. 293 p.

3329 Dunn, Frederick S.
PEACE-MAKING AND THE SETTLEMENT WITH JAPAN. Principal collaborators: Annemarie Shimony, Percy E. Corbett, and Bernard C. Cohen. Princeton, N.J., Princeton University Press, 1963. 210 p.

3330 Goodrich, Leland M., and Edward Hambre.
CHARTER OF THE UNITED NATIONS: COMMENTARY AND DOCUMENTS. Boston, World Peace Foundation, 1946. 413 p.

3331 Holborn, Louise W.
WAR AND PEACE AIMS OF THE UNITED NATIONS. Boston, World Peace Foundation, 1943-48. 2 v. (1278 p.)

3332 Iványi-Grünwold, Béla, and Alan Bill.
ROUTE TO POTSDAM: THE STORY OF THE PEACE AIMS, 1939-1945. London, Wingate, 1945. 111 p.

3333 Leiss, Amelia C. (ed.), with Raymond Dennett.
EUROPEAN PEACE TREATIES AFTER WORLD WAR II: NEGOTIATIONS AND TEXTS OF TREATIES WITH ITALY, BULGARIA, HUNGARY, RUMANIA, AND FINLAND. Boston, World Peace Foundation, 1954. 341 p.

3334 Lytton, Victor A. G. R. Bulwer-Lytton, 2d earl of.
FIRST ASSEMBLY: THE BIRTH OF THE UNITED NATIONS ORGANIZATION. New York and London, Hutchinson, 1946. 96 p.

3335 Ratchford, Benjamin U., and William D. Ross.
BERLIN REPARATIONS ASSIGNMENT: ROUND ONE OF THE GERMAN PEACE SETTLEMENT. Chapel Hill, North Carolina University Press, 1947. 259 p.

3336 Raymond, Ernest, and Patrick Raymond.
BACK TO HUMANITY. London and Toronto, Cassell, 1945. 89 p.

3337 Royal Institute of International Affairs.
UNITED NATIONS DOCUMENTS, 1941-1945. London and New York, Royal Institute of International Affairs, 1946. 271 p.

3338 Russell, Ruth B.
A HISTORY OF THE U.N. CHARTER: THE ROLE OF THE U.S., 1940-1945. Washington, D.C., Brookings Institution, 1958. 1140 p.

3339 United Nations.
SURRENDER OF ITALY, GERMANY AND JAPAN, WORLD WAR II: INSTRUMENTS OF SURRENDER, PUBLIC PAPERS AND ADDRESSES OF THE PRESIDENT AND OF THE SUPREME COMMANDERS. Washington, U.S. Government Printing Office, 1946. 111 p.

3340 U.S. Armed Forces Information School, Carlisle Barracks, Pa.
PILLARS OF PEACE: DOCUMENTS PERTAINING TO AMERICAN INTEREST IN ESTABLISHING A LASTING WORLD PEACE, JANUARY 1941-FEBRUARY 1946. Carlisle Barracks, Pa., Book Dept., Army Information School, 1946. 166 p. (Pamphlets)

3341 U.S. Dept. of State.
MAKING THE PEACE TREATIES, 1941-1947: A HISTORY IN THE MAKING OF PEACE BEGINNING WITH THE ATLANTIC CHARTER, THE YALTA AND POTSDAM CONFERENCES, AND CULMINATING IN THE DRAFTING OF PEACE TREATIES WITH ITALY, BULGARIA, HUNGARY, RUMANIA, AND FINLAND. Washington, Dept. of State, 1947. 150 p. (Publication. European Series)

3342 World Peace Foundation, Boston.
THE UNITED NATIONS IN THE MAKING: BASIC DOCUMENTS. Boston, World Peace Foundation, 1945. 136 p.

4. Individual Countries

a. Great Britain

3343 Aberdeen. City Council.
ROLL OF HONOUR: A RECORD OF THOSE BELONGING TO THE CITY OF ABERDEEN WHO GAVE THEIR LIVES FOR THEIR COUNTRY IN THE SECOND WORLD WAR, 1939-1945. Aberdeen, City Assessor [private circulation] 1960. 252 p.

3344 Anderson, Verily (Bruce).
SPAM TOMORROW. London, Hart-Davis, 1956. 264 p.

3345 Arbib, Robert S.
HERE WE ARE TOGETHER: THE NOTEBOOK OF AN AMERICAN SOLDIER IN BRITAIN. New York, Longmans, Green, 1946. 211 p.

3346 Ballantine, W. M.
SCOTLAND'S RECORD. Edinburgh, Albyn Press, 1946. 184 p.

3347 Blake, John W.
NORTHERN IRELAND IN THE SECOND WORLD WAR. Belfast, H.M. Stationery Office, 1956. 569 p.

3348 Bloom, Ursula H.
WAR ISN'T WONDERFUL. London, Hutchinson, 1961. 222 p.

3349 Boorman, Henry R. P.
KENT UNCONQUERED. Maidstone, Eng., "Kent Messenger," 1951. 217 p.

3350 Burford and Fullbrook Women's Institute.
BURFORD IN THE WAR OF 1939-1945. Burford, Eng., 1947. 63 p.

3351 Charteris, John.
THE BRITISH ARMY TODAY. New York, British Information Service, 1945. 61 p.

3352 Churchill, Sir Winston L. S.
THE DAWN OF LIBERATION: WAR SPEECHES BY THE RIGHT HON. WINSTON S. CHURCHILL. Compiled by Charles Eade. Boston, Little, Brown, 1945. 417 p.

Other edition:
London, Cassell, 1945. 327 p.

3353 Churchill, Sir Winston L. S.
GREAT WAR SPEECHES BY SIR WINSTON CHURCHILL. London, Transworld Publishers, 1957. 384 p. (Corgi Books)

3354 Churchill, Sir Winston L. S.
SECRET SESSION SPEECHES BY THE RIGHT HON. WINSTON S. CHURCHILL. Compiled by Charles Eade. London, Cassell, 1946. 96 p.

Other edition:
New York, Simon and Schuster, 1946. 114 p.

3355 Churchill, Sir Winston L. S.
VICTORY SPEECHES BY THE RIGHT HON. WINSTON S. CHURCHILL. Compiled by Charles Eade. London, Cassell, 1945. 307 p.

3356 Churchill, Sir Winston L. S.
VICTORY; WAR SPEECHES BY THE RIGHT HON. WINSTON S. CHURCHILL, 1945. Compiled by Charles Eade. London, Cassell, 1946. 239 p.

3357 Churchill, Sir Winston L. S.
WAR SPEECHES. Compiled by Charles Eade. London, Cassell, 1951-52. 3 v.

Other edition:
Boston, Houghton Mifflin, 1953. 3 v.

3358 Cobb, Ivo G.
JOURNAL OF THE WAR YEARS...AND ONE YEAR LATER, INCLUDING THE UNAVOIDABLE SUBJECT, BY GEORGE BERNARD SHAW. Worcester, Eng., Littlebury, 1948. 2 v.

3359 Collier, Basil.
THE DEFENSE OF THE UNITED KINGDOM. London, H.M. Stationery Office, 1957. 557 p. (History of the Second World War: United Kingdom Military Series)

3360 Council of King George's Jubilee Trust.
THE ROYAL FAMILY IN WARTIME. London, Odhams Press, 1945. 128 p.

3361 Crisp, Dorothy.
THE DOMINANCE OF ENGLAND. London, Holborn, 1960. 299 p.

3362   Croydon Times.
       CROYDON COURAGEOUS: THE STORY OF CROYDON'S ORDEAL AND TRIUMPH, 1939-1945. Croydon, Eng., 1945. 92 p.

3363   THE DIARY OF A BRISTOL WOMAN, 1938-1945. By V. A. M. Ilfracombe (Devon), Stockwell, 1951. 248 p.

3364   Dimbleby, Richard.
       THE WAITING YEAR. London, Hodder and Stoughton, 1945. 186 p.

3365   DUXFORD DIARY, 1942-1945. Edited by Bowen I. Hosford and others. Cambridge, Eng., Printed by Heffer for American units stationed at Duxford, Eng., 1945. 151 p.

3366   Essex County Standard, Colchester, England.
       ESSEX AT WAR. Compiled by the editorial staff of the Essex County Standard; edited by Hervey Benham. Colchester, Benham, 1945. 154 p.

3367   Faviell, Frances.
       A CHELSEA CONCERTO. London, Cassell, 1959. 259 p.

3368   Grant, Douglas.
       THE FUEL OF THE FIRE. London, Cresset Press, 1950. 236 p.

3369   Grenfell, Russell.
       UNCONDITIONAL HATRED: GERMAN WAR GUILT AND THE FUTURE OF EUROPE. New York, Devin-Adair, 1953. 273 p.

       Other edition:
       New York, Devin-Adair, 1953. 273 p.

3370   Halifax, Edward F. L. Wood, 1st earl of.
       THE AMERICAN SPEECHES OF THE EARL OF HALIFAX. London and New York, Oxford University Press, 1947. 449 p.

3371   Higgins, Trumbull.
       WINSTON CHURCHILL AND THE SECOND FRONT, 1940-1943. London and New York, Oxford University Press, 1957. 281 p.

3372   Hislop, John.
       ANYTHING BUT A SOLDIER. London, Joseph, 1965. 189 p.

3373   Howgrave-Graham, Hamilton M.
       THE METROPOLITAN POLICE AT WAR. London, H.M. Stationery Office, 1947. 89 p.

3374   Jacob, Naomi E.
       ME AND THE MEDITERRANEAN. London and New York, Hutchinson, 1945. 156 p.

3375   James, Walter D. (ed.).
       HAMPTONIANS AT WAR: SOME WAR EXPERIENCES OF OLD BOYS OF HAMPTON GRAMMAR SCHOOL. Introduction by A. S. Mason. Denmead School, 1964. 201 p.

3376   Jedrzejewicz, Waclaw (ed.), with Pauline C. Ramsey.
       POLAND IN THE BRITISH PARLIAMENT, 1939-1945. New York, Józef Pilsudski Institute of America, 1946-1962. 3 v. (Józef Pilsudski Institute of America for Research in the Modern History of Poland, New York. Documents Series)

3377   Jenkins, Ford.
       PORT WAR: LOWESTOFT, 1939-1945. Ipswich and London, Cowell, 1946. 80 p.

3378   Kempe, A. B. C.
       MIDST BANDS AND BOMBS, BY THE TOP-HAT MAYOR OF RAMSGATE. Maidstone, Eng., "Kent Messenger," 1946. 135 p.

3379   Krabbe, Henning (ed.).
       BRITAIN AT WAR: GREAT DESCRIPTIONS AND SPEECHES FROM THE SECOND WORLD WAR. Copenhagen, Gyldendal, 1946. 288 p.

3380   Lehmann, John.
       I AM MY BROTHER: AUTOBIOGRAPHY II. London, Longmans; New York, Reynal, 1960. 326 p.

3381   Levy, Arnold.
       THIS I RECALL, 1939-1945. London, Saint Catherine Press, 1946. 311 p.

3382   Macinnes, Charles M.
       BRISTOL AT WAR. London, Museum Press, 1962. 202 p.

3383   THE "MAN IN THE STREET" (OF THE B.B.C.) TALKS TO EUROPE. Westminster (London), King and Staples, 1945. 260 p.

3384   Mersey Docks and Harbour Board, Liverpool.
       PORT AT WAR: BEING THE STORY OF THE PORT OF LIVERPOOL, ITS ORDEALS AND ACHIEVEMENTS, DURING THE WORLD WAR, 1939-1945. Liverpool, Mersey Docks and Harbour Board, 1946. 64 p.

3385   Pawle, Gerald.
       THE WAR AND COLONEL WARDEN: BASED ON RECOLLECTIONS OF C. R. THOMPSON, PERSONAL ASSISTANT TO THE PRIME MINISTER, 1940-1945. Foreword by W. Averell Harriman. New York, Knopf; London, Harrap, 1963. 422 p.

       Other edition:
       London, Transworld, 1965. 448 p. (Corgi Books)

3386   Sansom, William.
       WESTMINSTER IN WAR. London, Faber and Faber, 1947. 209 p.

3387   Sayers, William C. B. (ed.).
       CROYDON AND THE SECOND WORLD WAR: THE OFFICIAL HISTORY OF THE WAR WORK OF THE BOROUGH AND ITS CITIZENS FROM 1939 TO 1945; TOGETHER WITH THE CROYDON ROLL OF HONOUR. Croydon, Eng., Croydon Corp., 1949. 581 p.

3388 Shipley, S. Paul, and Howard Rankin (comps.).
BRISTOL'S BOMBED CHURCHES: A DESCRIPTIVE AND PICTORIAL RECORD OF THEIR HISTORIES AND DESTRUCTION. Bristol, Eng., Rankin, 1945. 68 p.

3389 Štĕdrý, Vladimír.
UNTIL OUR SUMMER COMES. Translated from Czechoslovakian by Dora Round. London, Allen and Unwin, 1945. 98 p.

3390 Street, Arthur G.
FROM DUSK TILL DAWN. London, Blandford Press, 1946. 138 p.

3391 Swanwick, Francis W.
A.R.P. (CIVIL DEFENCE) IN THE BOROUGH OF HESTON AND ISLEWORTH, 1938-1945. Hounslow, Eng., Swanwick, 1961. 65 p.

3392 Tabori, Paul (ed.).
TWENTY TREMENDOUS YEARS: WORLD WAR II AND AFTER. New York, McBride Books, 1962. 288 p.

3393 Thompson, Walter H.
I WAS CHURCHILL'S SHADOW. London, Johnson, 1951. 200 p.

3394 Tomlinson, Henry M.
THE TURN OF THE TIDE. London, Hodder and Stoughton, 1945. 179 p.

Other edition:
New York, Macmillan, 1947. 182 p.

3395 Turner, Ernest S.
THE PHONEY WAR ON THE HOME FRONT. London, Joseph, 1961. 311 p.

Other edition:
New York, St. Martin's Press, 1962.

3396 Varney, Joyce J.
A WELSH STORY. Indianapolis, Bobbs-Merrill, 1965. 313 p.

3397 Wanless, Alexander (comp.).
BRITISH PEOPLE AT WAR, 1939-1945. Compiled from the Daily Press. Cupar-Fife, Innes, 1956. 466 p.

3398 Watts, Stephen.
MOONLIGHT ON A LAKE IN BOND STREET. London, Bodley Head, 1961. 207 p.

Other edition:
New York, Norton, 1962.

3399 Weber, Wayne M.
MY WAR WITH THE U.S. ARMY. New York, Pageant Press, 1957. 148 p.

3400 Williamson, Catherine E.
THOUGH THE STREETS BURN. London, Headley Bros., 1949. 321 p.

3401 Woodward, Sir Ernest L.
BRITISH FOREIGN POLICY IN THE SECOND WORLD WAR. London, H.M. Stationery Office, 1962. 592 p.

Commonwealth Nations

3402 Ahluwalia, Gian C.
A WORLD IN CONFLICT: WORLD WAR II AND INDIA. Delhi, 1949. 227 p.

3403 Bickers, Emma P. (comp.).
PAKAI TARA TE KOPURU (TE KOPURU'S BAND OF WARRIORS). Dargaville, N.Z., North Auckland Times, 1947. 72 p.

3404 Blake, Alfred E. (Al Ethelred Blackeley, pseud.).
CONVOY TO INDIA. Brooklyn, Trilon Press, 1953. 214 p.

3405 Bose, Subhas C.
BLOOD BATH. Singapore, Publicity and Propaganda Department, Indian Independence League Headquarters at the Occasion of Netaji Week Celebration Lahore. Reproduced in India by Hero Publications, 1947. 134 p.

3406 Canadian Institute of International Affairs.
CANADA IN WORLD AFFAIRS. London and New York, Oxford University Press, for the Canadian Institute of International Affairs, 1941-51. Vols. 1-4.

3407 Canadian Jewish Congress.
CANADIAN JEWS IN WORLD WAR II. Edited by David Rome. Montreal, 1947-48. 2 v.

3408 Clare, Thomas H.
LOOKIN' EASTWARD, A G.I. SALAAM TO INDIA. As told to Irma M. Clare. New York, Macmillan, 1945. 321 p.

3409 Dawson, Robert M.
THE CONSCRIPTION CRISIS OF 1944. Toronto, University of Toronto Press, 1961. 136 p.

3410 Deb, J.N.
BLOOD AND TEARS. Bombay, Hind Kitabs, 1945. 244 p.

3411 Devanny, Jean.
BIRD OF PARADISE. Sydney, Johnson, 1945. 284 p.

3412 Duffus, Louis.
BEYOND THE LAAGER. Foreword by J.C. Smuts. London and New York, Hurst and Blackett, 1947. 168 p.

3413 Evatt, Herbert V.
FOREIGN POLICY OF AUSTRALIA. Sydney and London, Angus and Robertson, 1945. 266 p.

3414 Good, Mabel T.
MEN OF VALOUR. Toronto, Macmillan Co. of Canada, 1948. 137 p.

3415 Griffiths, Owen E.
DARWIN DRAMA. Sydney, Bloxham and Chambers, 1947. 218 p.

3416 Halton, Matthew H.
TEN YEARS TO ALAMEIN. Forest Hills, N.Y., Transatlantic Arts, 1945. 220 p.

3417 Hancock, Kenneth R.
NEW ZEALAND AT WAR: AN UNOFFICIAL ACCOUNT OF THE DOMINION'S WAR EFFORT OVERSEAS AND AT HOME, EMBRACING THE SERVICES IN ALL THEATRES AND THE INDUSTRIAL AND GENERAL DOMESTIC BACKGROUND DURING THE PERIOD OF HOSTILITIES, 1939-45. Wellington, Reed, 1946. 351 p.

3418 Hasluck, Paul.
THE GOVERNMENT AND THE PEOPLE. Canberra, Australian War Memorial, 1952-. 1 vol. published. (Australia in the War of 1939-1945. Series 4 [Civil])

3419 Jackson, C. O. Badham.
A STATE OF WAR: THE OFFICIAL HISTORY OF LORD MAYOR'S PATRIOTIC AND WAR FUND OF NEW SOUTH WALES, THE AUSTRALIAN COMFORTS FUND, N.S.W. DIVISION. Sydney, 1947. 144 p.

3420 Karaka, Dosoo F.
I'VE SHED MY TEARS: A CANDID VIEW OF RESURGENT INDIA. New York and London, Appleton-Century, 1947. 280 p.

3421 Khan, Shah N.
THE I.M.A. HEROES: AUTOBIOGRAPHIES OF MAJ. GEN. SHAHNAWAZ, COL. PREM K. SAHGAL AND COL. GURBAX SINGH DHILLON OF THE AZAD HIND FAUJ. Lahore, Hero Publications, 1946. 266 p.

3422 Khan, Shah N.
MY MEMORIES OF I.N.A. AND ITS NETAJI. Foreword by Pt. Jawahar L. Nehru. Delhi, Rajkamal Publications, 1946. 283 p.

3423 Long, Basil K.
IN SMUT'S CAMP. Preface by Sir Dougal O. Malcolm. London and New York, Oxford University Press, 1945. 162 p.

3424 MacDonald, John F.
THE WAR HISTORY OF SOUTHERN RHODESIA. Salisbury, Southern Rhodesia Government Stationery Office, 1947-50. 2 v.

3425 Mackenzie, Compton.
EASTERN EPIC. London, Chatto and Windus, 1951-. 1 vol. published.

3426 Malone, Richard S.
MISSING FROM THE RECORD. Toronto, Collins, 1946. 227 p.

3427 Masters, John.
THE ROAD PAST MANDALAY: A PERSONAL NARRATIVE. New York, Harper; London, Joseph, 1961. 344 p.

3428 Meadows, Maureen C.
I LOVED THOSE YANKS. Sydney, Dash, 1948. 336 p.

3429 Menon, Vapal P.
THE TRANSFER OF POWER IN INDIA. Princeton, N.J., Princeton University Press; London and New York, Longmans, Green, 1957. 543 p.

3430 Mukerji, Girija.
THIS EUROPE. Calcutta, Saraswaty Library, 1950. 215 p.

3431 New Zealand. Dept. of Internal Affairs. War History Branch.
DOCUMENTS RELATING TO NEW ZEALAND'S PARTICIPATION IN THE SECOND WORLD WAR, 1939-45. Wellington, 1949. 3 v.

3432 New Zealand. Dept. of Internal Affairs. War History Branch.
NEW ZEALAND IN THE SECOND WORLD WAR, 1939-1945: EPISODES AND STUDIES. Wellington, 1948-54. 2 v. (Official History of New Zealand in the Second World War, 1939-45)

3433 Nova Scotia.
NOVA SCOTIA HELPS THE FIGHTING MAN. Published by Authority of the Government of Nova Scotia. Halifax, King's Printer, 1945. 64 p.

3434 Palta, Krishan R.
MY ADVENTURES WITH THE I.N.A. Foreword by General Mohan Singh. Lahore, Lion Press, 1946. 215 p.

3435 Robertson, John H. (John Connell, pseud.).
THE HOUSE BY HEROD'S GATE. London, Low, Marston, 1947. 195 p.

3436 South African Jewish Board of Deputies.
SOUTH AFRICAN JEWS IN WORLD WAR II. Johannesburg, 1950. 189 p.

3437 United Party. South Africa.
SOUTH AFRICAN "NATIONALISM": ITS BLACK RECORD IN THE WAR, 1939-1945. Johannesburg, 1945. 104 p.

3438 Vaidya, Suresh.
OVER THERE. Bombay, Hind Kitabs, 1945. 102 p.

3439 Wade, Harry F.
FIVE MILES CLOSER TO HEAVEN: AN ADVENTURE BY PARACHUTE OVER THE JUNGLES OF INDIA. Oconomowoc, Wis., Liguorian Pamphlet Office, 1945. 60 p.

3440 Wood, Frederick L. W.
THE NEW ZEALAND PEOPLE AT WAR: POLITICAL AND EXTERNAL AFFAIRS. Wellington, War History Branch, Dept. of Internal Affairs, 1958. 395 p. (Official History of New Zealand in the Second World War, 1939-45)

b. Russia

3441 Carman, Ernest D.
SOVIET TERRITORIAL AGGRANDIZEMENT, 1939-1948: AN ANALYSIS OF CONCEPTS AND METHODS. Washington, Public Affairs Press, 1950.

3442 Dallin, Alexander.
GERMAN RULE IN RUSSIA, 1941-1945: A STUDY OF OCCUPATION POLICIES. London, Macmillan; New York, St. Martin's Press, 1957. 695 p.

3443 Dallin, Alexander.
ODESSA, 1941-1944: A CASE STUDY OF SOVIET TERRITORY UNDER FOREIGN RULE. Santa Monica, Rand Corp., 1957. 466 p. (Rand Corp. Research Memorandum)

3444 Davies, Raymond A.
INSIDE RUSSIA TODAY. Winnipeg, Contemporary Publishers, 1945. 92 p.

3445 Elvin, Harold.
A COCKNEY IN MOSCOW. London, Cresset Press, 1958. 222 p.

3446 Fainsod, Merle.
SMOLENSK UNDER SOVIET RULE. Cambridge, Mass., Harvard University Press, 1958. 484 p.

3447 Fischer, George.
SOVIET OPPOSITION TO STALIN: A CASE STUDY IN WORLD WAR 2. Cambridge, Mass., Harvard University Press; London, Oxford University Press, 1952. 230 p (Russian Research Center. Studies Series)

3448 Grossman, Vasilii S.
THE YEARS OF WAR, 1941-1945. Translated from the Russian by Elizabeth Donnelly and Rose Prokofiev. Moscow, Foreign Languages Publishing House, 1946. 451 p.

3449 Jacob, Alaric.
A WINDOW IN MOSCOW, 1944-45. London, Collins, 1946. 320 p.

3450 Kalinin, Mikhail I.
THE SOVIET PRESIDENT SPEAKS: SPEECHES, BROADCAST ADDRESS, AND ARTICLES ON THE GREAT PATRIOTIC WAR OF THE SOVIET UNION. London, Hutchinson, 1945. 79 p.

3451 Kamenetsky, Ihor.
HITLER'S OCCUPATION OF UKRAINE 1941-1944: A STUDY OF TOTALITARIAN IMPERIALISM. Milwaukee, Marquette University Press, 1956. 101 p.

3452 Lauterbach, Richard E.
THESE ARE THE RUSSIANS. New York, Harper, 1945. 368 p.

3453 McLane, Charles B.
SOVIET POLICY AND THE CHINESE COMMUNISTS, 1931-1946. New York, Columbia University Press, 1958. 310 p. (Studies of the Russian Institute, Columbia University)

3454 Mikhailov, Nikolai N.
THE RUSSIAN GLORY. London, Hutchinson, 1945. 142 p.

Other edition:
THE RUSSIAN STORY. New York, Sheridan House, 1945. 191 p.

3455 Moore, Harriet L.
SOVIET FAR EASTERN POLICY, 1931-1945. London, Geoffrey Cumberlege, Oxford University Press, 1945. 284 p.

Other edition:
Princeton, N.J., Princeton University Press, 1945. 284 p. (Institute of Pacific Relations. I.P.R. Inquiry Series)

3456 Petrov, Vladimir.
MY RETREAT FROM RUSSIA. Translated by David Chavchavadze. New Haven, Yale University Press, 1950. 357 p.

3457 Reitlinger, Gerald R.
THE HOUSE BUILT ON SAND: THE CONFLICTS OF GERMAN POLICY IN RUSSIA, 1939-1945. London, Weidenfeld and Nicolson; New York, Viking Press, 1960. 459 p.

3458 Rothstein, Andrew (trans.).
SOVIET FOREIGN POLICY DURING THE PATRIOTIC WAR: DOCUMENTS AND MATERIALS. London and New York, Hutchinson, 1946. 2 vols. published.

3459 Samarin, Vladimir D. (pseud.).
CIVILIAN LIFE UNDER THE GERMAN OCCUPATION, 1942-1944. New York, Research Program on the U.S.S.R., 1954. 90 p. (East European Fund. Mimeographed Series)

3460 Stalin, Iosif.
WAR SPEECHES, ORDERS OF THE DAY AND ANSWERS TO FOREIGN PRESS CORRESPONDENTS DURING THE GREAT PATRIOTIC WAR, 3 JULY 1941 TO 22 JUNE 1945. London and New York, Hutchinson, 1946. 140 p.

3461 Stevens, Edmund.
RUSSIA IS NO RIDDLE. New York, Greenburg, 1945. 300 p.

3462 Werth, Alexander.
RUSSIA AT WAR, 1941-1945. New York, Dutton; London, Barrie, 1964. 1100 p.

3463 Wettlin, Margaret.
RUSSIAN ROAD: THREE YEARS OF WAR IN RUSSIA AS LIVED THROUGH BY AN AMERICAN WOMAN. London and New York, Hutchinson, 1945. 126 p.

3464 White, William L.
REPORT ON THE RUSSIANS. New York, Harcourt, Brace, 1945. 309 p.

Other edition:
London, Eyre and Spottiswoode, 1946. 250 p.

3465 Winterton, Paul.
REPORT ON RUSSIA. London, Cresset Press, 1945. 138 p.

c. United States

General

3466 Allen, George E.
THE LIQUIDATION OF FEDERAL WAR AGENCIES: A STUDY. Washington, 1945. 79 l.

3467 Armenian General Benevolent Union of America.
ARMENIAN-AMERICAN VETERANS OF WORLD WAR II. Published and compiled by "Our Boys" Committee of Armenian General Benevolent Union of America, Inc. New York, 1951. 498 p.

3468 Buchanan, Albert R.
THE UNITED STATES AND WORLD WAR II. Edited by Henry Steele Commager and Richard B. Morris. New York and London, Harper and Row, 1964. 2 v. (635 p.)

3469 Catton, Bruce.
THE WAR LORDS OF WASHINGTON. New York, Harcourt, Brace, 1948. 313 p.

3470 Chamberlin, William H.
AMERICA'S SECOND CRUSADE. Chicago, Regnery, 1950. 372 p.

3471 Cole, Wayne S.
AMERICA FIRST: THE BATTLE AGAINST INTERVENTION, 1940-41. Madison, University of Wisconsin Press, 1953. 305 p.

3472 Conn, Stetson, Rose C. Engelman, and Byron Fairchild.
GUARDING THE UNITED STATES AND ITS OUTPOSTS. Washington, Office of Chief of Military History, Dept. of Army, 1964. 593 p. (U.S. Army in World War II: The Western Hemisphere)

3473 Crocker, George N.
ROOSEVELT'S ROAD TO RUSSIA. Chicago, Regnery; London, Bailey and Swinfen, 1959. 312 p.

3474 Current, Richard N.
SECRETARY STIMSON: A STUDY IN STATECRAFT. New Brunswick, N.J., Rutgers University Press, 1954. 272 p.

3475 Davis, Kenneth S.
EXPERIENCE OF WAR: THE UNITED STATES IN WORLD WAR II. Garden City, N.Y., Doubleday, 1965. 704 p. (Mainstream of America Series)

3476 Davis, Mac.
JEWS FIGHT TOO! New York, Jordan, 1945. 221 p.

3477 Dawson, Raymond H.
THE DECISION TO AID RUSSIA, 1941: FOREIGN POLICY AND DOMESTIC POLITICS. Chapel Hill, University of North Carolina Press, 1959. 315 p.

3478 Deane, John R.
THE STRANGE ALLIANCE: THE STORY OF AMERICAN EFFORTS AT WARTIME CO-OPERATION WITH RUSSIA. New York, Viking Press; London, Murray, 1947. 344 p.

3479 DOCUMENTS ON AMERICAN FOREIGN RELATIONS. Boston, World Peace Foundation, 1939-48. Vols. 1-8.

3480 Drury, Allen.
A SENATE JOURNAL, 1943-1945. New York, McGraw-Hill, 1963. 503 p.

3481 Furr, Arthur.
DEMOCRACY'S NEGROES: A BOOK OF FACTS CONCERNING THE ACTIVITIES OF NEGROES IN WORLD WAR II. Boston, House of Edinboro, 1947. 315 p.

3482 Gulick, Luther H.
ADMINISTRATIVE REFLECTIONS FROM WORLD WAR II. University, University of Alabama Press, 1948. 139 p.

3483 Hassett, William D.
OFF THE RECORD WITH F.D.R., 1942-1945. Introduced by Jonathan Daniels. New Brunswick, N.J., Rutgers University Press, 1958. 366 p.

3484 Hodson, James L.
AND YET I LIKE AMERICA: BEING SOME ACCOUNT OF A JOURNEY TO THE UNITED STATES OF AMERICA IN THE WINTER AND SPRING OF 1943-1944 AND OF MEETINGS THERE AND OF WHAT WAS SAID TO ME. London, Gollancz, 1945. 302 p.

3485 Huzar, Elias.
THE PURSE AND THE SWORD: CONTROL OF THE ARMY BY CONGRESS THROUGH MILITARY APPROPRIATIONS, 1933-50. Ithaca, N.Y., Cornell University Press, 1950. 417 p.

3486 Kammerer, Gladys M.
IMPACT OF WAR ON FEDERAL PERSONNEL ADMINISTRATION, 1939-1945. Lexington, University of Kentucky Press, 1951. 372 p.

3487 Kaufman, Isidor.
AMERICAN JEWS IN WORLD WAR II: THE STORY OF 550,000 FIGHTERS FOR FREEDOM. New York, Dial Press, 1947. 2 v.

3488 Kenney, William.
THE CRUCIAL YEARS, 1940-1945. New York, Macfadden-Bartell Corp., 1962. 207 p. (Macfadden Book)

3489 Knox, Robert S.
HIGH LEVEL PLANNING IN THE UNITED STATES REGARDING GERMANY, 1941-46. Washington, 1949. 167 l.

3490 Lawson, Don.
THE UNITED STATES IN WORLD WAR II: CRUSADE FOR WORLD FREEDOM. London and New York, Abelard-Schuman, 1963. 224 p.

3491 Lerner, Max.
PUBLIC JOURNAL: MARGINAL NOTES ON WARTIME AMERICA. New York, Viking, 1945. 414 p.

3492 Lombard, Helen C. C.
WHILE THEY FOUGHT: BEHIND THE SCENES IN WASHINGTON, 1941-1946. New York, Scribner, 1947. 322 p.

3493 McIntyre, Stuart H.
LEGAL EFFECT OF WORLD WAR II ON TREATIES OF THE UNITED STATES. The Hague, Nijhoff, 1958. 392 p.

3494 Martin, James J.
AMERICAN LIBERALISM AND WORLD POLITICS, 1931-1941: LIBERALISM'S PRESS AND SPOKESMEN ON THE ROAD BACK TO WAR BETWEEN MUKDEN AND PEARL HARBOR. Foreword by John Chamberlain. New York, Devin-Adair, 1964. 2 v. 1337 p.

3495 Misselwitz, Henry F.
THE MELTING POT BOILS OVER: A REPORT ON AMERICA AT WAR. Boston, Christopher, 1946. 242 p.

3496 Morin, Raul.
AMONG THE VALIANT: MEXICAN-AMERICANS IN WW II AND KOREA. Los Angeles, Borden Publishing Co., 1963. 290 p.

3497 Morris, Richard B., and James Woodress (eds.).
GLOBAL CONFLICT: THE UNITED STATES IN WORLD WAR II, 1937-1946. St. Louis, Webster Publishing Co., 1962. 58 p. (Voices from America's Past)

3498 Pendar, Kenneth W.
ADVENTURE IN DIPLOMACY: OUR FRENCH DILEMMA. New York, Dodd, Mead, 1945. 280 p.

3499 Pirinsky, George.
SLAVIC AMERICANS IN THE FIGHT FOR VICTORY AND PEACE. New York, American Slav Congress, 1946. 61 p.

3500 Polish American Congress.
SELECTED DOCUMENTS: A COMPILATION OF SELECTED RESOLUTIONS, DECLARATIONS, MEMORIALS, MEMORANDUMS, LETTERS, TELEGRAMS, PRESS STATEMENTS, ETC., IN CHRONOLOGICAL ORDER, SHOWING VARIOUS PHASES OF POLISH AMERICAN CONGRESS ACTIVITIES, 1944-1948. Chicago, 1948. 165 p.

3501 Rauch, Basil.
ROOSEVELT: FROM MUNICH TO PEARL HARBOR: A STUDY IN THE CREATION OF A FOREIGN POLICY. New York, Creative Age Press, 1950. 527 p.

3502 Roosevelt, Franklin D.
NOTHING TO FEAR: THE SELECTED ADDRESSES OF FRANKLIN DELANO ROOSEVELT, 1932-1945. Edited by B. D. Zwin. Boston, Houghton Mifflin, 1946. 470 p.

3503 Roosevelt, Franklin D.
WARTIME CORRESPONDENCE BETWEEN PRESIDENT ROOSEVELT AND POPE PIUS XII. New York, Macmillan, 1947. 127 p.

3504 Sherwood, Robert E.
ROOSEVELT AND HOPKINS: AN INTIMATE HISTORY. New York, Harper, 1948. 979 p.

Other edition:
New York, Harper, 1950. 1002 p.

3505 Smith, Gaddis.
AMERICAN DIPLOMACY DURING THE SECOND WORLD WAR, 1941-1945. New York, Wiley, 1965. 194 p. (America in Crisis)

3506 Sobel, Robert.
THE ORIGINS OF INTERVENTIONISM: THE UNITED STATES AND THE RUSSO-FINNISH WAR. New York, Bookman Associates, 1961. 204 p.

3507 Tashjian, James H.
THE ARMENIAN AMERICAN IN WORLD WAR II. With an appendix on the part played in the Korean conflict and prefatory statements by Louis F. Johnson and others. Boston, Hairenik Association, 1952. 511 p.

3508 Think.
DIARY OF U.S. PARTICIPATION IN WORLD WAR II. New York, International Business Machines Corp., 1950. 374 p.

3509 U.S. Bureau of the Budget.
THE U.S. AT WAR: DEVELOPMENT AND ADMINISTRATION OF WAR PROGRAM BY THE FEDERAL GOVERNMENT. Washington, Government Printing Office, 1946. 555 p. (Historical Reports on War Administration)

3510 U.S. Bureau of Indian Affairs.
INDIANS IN THE WAR. Chicago, Office of Indian Affairs, U.S. Dept. of Interior, 1945. 54 p.

3511 U.S. Congress. Senate. Committee on Foreign Relations.
A DECADE OF AMERICAN FOREIGN POLICY: BASIC DOCUMENTS (1941-1949). Prepared at the request of the Senate Committee on Foreign Relations by the staff of the Committee and the Dept. of State. Washington, Government Printing Office, 1950. 1381 p.

3512 U.S. Dept. of Agriculture. Graduate School.
WHAT WE LEARNED IN PUBLIC ADMINISTRATION DURING THE WAR. Lectures by J. Donald Kingsley and others. Washington, 1949. 131 p.

3513 U.S. Dept. of State.
THE AXIS IN DEFEAT: A COLLECTION OF DOCUMENTS ON AMERICAN POLICY TOWARD GERMANY AND JAPAN. Washington, 1945. 118 p.

3514 U.S. Dept. of State.
FOREIGN RELATIONS OF THE UNITED STATES: DIPLOMATIC PAPERS. Vols. for 1939-1944. Washington, U.S. Government Printing Office, 1956-67.

3515 U.S. Dept. of State.
UNITED STATES AND ITALY, 1936-1946, DOCUMENTARY RECORD. Washington, 1946. 236 p. (Publication. European Series)

3516 U.S. Office of Community War Services.
TEAMWORK IN COMMUNITY SERVICES, 1941-1946: A DEMONSTRATION IN FEDERAL, STATE AND LOCAL COOPERATION. Washington, 1946. 80 p.

3517 U.S. Office of Inter-American Affairs.
HISTORY OF THE OFFICE OF THE COORDINATOR OF INTER-AMERICAN AFFAIRS. Washington, U.S. Government Printing Office, 1947. 284 p. (Historical Reports on War Administration)

3518 Wilcox, Francis O., and Thorsten V. Kalijarvi.
RECENT AMERICAN FOREIGN POLICY: BASIC DOCUMENTS, 1941-1951. New York, Appleton-Century-Crofts, 1952. 927 p.

3519 Young, Roland A.
CONGRESSIONAL POLITICS IN THE SECOND WORLD WAR. New York, Columbia University Press, 1956. 281 p.

Local

3520 Albemarle County Historical Society. War History Committee.
PURSUITS OF WAR: THE PEOPLE OF CHARLOTTESVILLE AND ALBEMARLE COUNTY, VIRGINIA, IN THE SECOND WORLD WAR. Charlottesville, Va., Albemarle County Historical Society, 1948. 429 p.

3521 Allen, Gwenfread E.
HAWAII'S WAR YEARS, 1941-45. Honolulu, University of Hawaii Press, 1950. 418 p.

Other edition:
Notes and references. With complete bibliography. Honolulu, University of Hawaii Press, 1952. 1 v. (unpaged)

3522 Ashton, Dean H.
BE IT EVER SO HUMBLE: THE STORY OF HOPEWELL, NEW JERSEY, AND ITS SERVICEMEN DURING WORLD WAR II. Hopewell, N.J., 1947. 370 p.

3523 Chernoff, Howard L.
ANYBODY HERE FROM WEST VIRGINIA? Charleston, W. Va., Charleston Printing, 1945. 105 p.

3524 Delaware. Public Archives Commission.
DELAWARE'S ROLE IN WORLD WAR II, 1940-1946. Prepared by William H. Conner and Leon de Valinger, Jr. Dover, 1955. 2 v.

3525- Dryden, Clarence A.
3526 JEFFERSON COUNTY IN WORLD WAR II, 1941-1945. Madison, Ind., Jefferson County Historical Society, 1947. 282 p.

3527 Georgia. World War Historian.
GEORGIA IN WORLD WAR II: A STUDY OF THE MILITARY AND THE CIVILIAN EFFORT. Prepared by Lamar Q. Ball, with Mary L. Cobb. Vol. 1, 1939. Atlanta, 1946. 219 p.

3528 Griffin, Clarence W.
HISTORY OF RUTHERFORD COUNTY, 1937-1951. Asheville, N.C., Inland Press, 1952. 136 p.

3529 Guyol, Philip N.
DEMOCRACY FIGHTS: A HISTORY OF NEW HAMPSHIRE IN WORLD WAR II. Hanover, N.H., Dartmouth Publications, 1951. 309 p.

3530 Hall, George L.
SOMETIME AGAIN (E'LOT NEG-OO-SOO-LI). Seattle, Superior Publishing Co., 1945. 217 p.

3531 Hartzell, Karl D.
THE EMPIRE STATE AT WAR: WORLD WAR II. Compiled and written for the New York State War Council. Albany, N.Y., 1949. 423 p.

3532 Haverhill, Mass. War Records Committee.
HAVERHILL IN WORLD WAR II: AN ATTEMPT TO RECORD THE STORY OF ONE AMERICAN CITY, THE VALOR AND THE SACRIFICE OF ITS SONS AND DAUGHTERS IN THE ARMED FORCES, AND THE LABOR AND THE SACRIFICE OF ITS PEOPLE AT HOME IN THE PROTECTION OF THEIR OWN LIBERTIES AND THE LIBERTIES OF ALL GOOD MEN EVERYWHERE. Haverhill, 1946. 763 p.

3533 Hawaiian Sugar Planters' Association.
THE WAR RECORD OF CIVILIAN AND INDUSTRIAL HAWAII: A DOCUMENTARY HISTORY OF THE ASSISTANCE EXTENDED TO THE ARMED FORCES BY THE CIVILIAN COMMUNITY AND THE SUGAR PLANTATIONS. Honolulu, 1946. 133 l.

3534 Heller, Francis H.
VIRGINIA'S STATE GOVERNMENT DURING THE SECOND WORLD WAR: ITS CONSTITUTIONAL, LEGISLATIVE, AND ADMINISTRATIVE ADAPTATIONS, 1942-1945. Richmond, History Division, Virginia State Library, 1949. 203 p.

3535 Howell, Nathaniel R. (ed.).
ISLIP TOWN'S WORLD WAR II EFFORT. Islip, N.Y., Buys Bros., 1948. 768 p.

3536 Indiana. War History Commission.
INDIANA IN WORLD WAR II. Bloomington, 1948-. Vols. 1-7, 9 published.

3537 Irwin, Dudley M.
THE BUFFALO WAR COUNCIL 1942-1945: HOW ONE CITY MET THE CHALLENGE OF TOTAL WAR. Buffalo, Saxer and Pfeiffer Printing Co., 1945. 219 p.

3538 Karabatsos, Dick G., and others.
JEFFERSON COUNTY, NEBRASKA, IN WORLD WAR II, AN ILLUSTRATED HISTORICAL REPORT OF THE PEOPLE FROM JEFFERSON COUNTY, NEBRASKA, WHO PARTICIPATED IN WORLD WAR II, BOTH AT HOME AND ABROAD IN THE YEARS 1941, 42, 43, 44, 45 AND 46. Fairbury, Nebr., Stilwell Printery, 1946. 84 p.

3539 King, Spencer B.
SELECTIVE SERVICE IN NORTH CAROLINA IN WORLD WAR II. Chapel Hill, University of North Carolina Press, 1949. 451 p.

3540 Lanux, Pierre Combret de.
NEW YORK, 1939-1945. Paris, Hachette, 1947. 223 p.

3541 Larson, Taft A.
WYOMING'S WAR YEARS, 1941-1945. Laramie, University of Wyoming Press, 1954. 400 p.

3542 Leblanc, Cyrille, and Thomas F. Flynn.
GARDNER IN WORLD WAR II. Gardner, Mass., Hatton Press, 1947. 557 p.

3543 Lemon, Adele M.
TO YOU FROM HAWAII. Albany, Fort Orange Press, 1950. 377 p.

3544 Lind, Andrew W.
HAWAII'S JAPANESE: AN EXPERIMENT IN DEMOCRACY. Princeton, N.J., Princeton University Press, 1946. 264 p.

3545 Lutz, Francis E.
RICHMOND IN WORLD WAR II. Richmond, Va., Dietz Press, 1951. 623 p.

3546 McDermott, R. B.
WITHIN A STONE THROW: BENT COUNTY PEOPLE IN THE WAR; PEARL HARBOR, DECEMBER 7, 1941 TO V-J DAY, AUGUST 14, 1945. Las Animas, Colo., 1946. 163 p.

3547 Maryland Historical Society. War Records Division.
MARYLAND IN WORLD WAR II. Prepared for the State of Maryland. Baltimore, 1950-58. 4 v.

3548 Milford, N.H. War Memorial Book Committee.
MILFORD IN WORLD WAR II: THE RECORD OF ONE TOWN'S PART IN THE GREAT WAR WHICH ENGULFED HUMANITY FROM SEPTEMBER, 1939 TO AUGUST, 1945. Milford, 1949. (unpaged)

3549 Momeyer, William E. (ed.).
GREATER GREENSBURG SERVICE ALBUM, WORLD WAR II. Greensburg, Pa., Moschetti, 1946. 217 p.

3550 New Canaan, Connecticut. War Records Committee.
NEW CANAAN WAR VETERANS SPEAK. New Canaan, War Records Committee of the Town of New Canaan and the New Canaan Historical Society, 1946-51. 3 v.

3551 Newport News, Va. Historical Commission, World War II.
NEWPORT NEWS DURING THE SECOND WORLD WAR. Newport News, 1948. 174 p.

3552 Pennsylvania. Historical and Museum Commission.
PENNSYLVANIA AT WAR, 1941-1945. Harrisburg, Pennsylvania Historical and Museum Commission, 1946. 63 p.

3553 Pennsylvania. Historical and Museum Commission.
PENNSYLVANIA'S SECOND YEAR AT WAR, DECEMBER 7, 1942-DECEMBER 7, 1943. Prepared by S. K. Stevens, Marvin W. Schlegel, and Joseph T. Kingston. Harrisburg, Pennsylvania Historical and Museum Commission, 1945. 175 p.

3554 Rademaker, John A.
THESE ARE AMERICANS: THE JAPANESE AMERICANS IN HAWAII IN WORLD WAR II. Palo Alto, Calif., Pacific Books, 1951. 278 p.

3555 Schlegel, Marvin W.
CONSCRIPTED CITY: NORFOLK IN WORLD WAR II. Norfolk, Va., Norfolk War History Commission, 1951. 396 p.

3556 Schneider, Norris F.
MUSKINGUM COUNTY MEN AND WOMEN IN WORLD WAR II. Zanesville, Ohio, Times Recorder, 1947. 511 p.

3557 South Dakota. World War II History Commission.
SOUTH DAKOTA IN WORLD WAR II: AN ACCOUNT OF THE VARIOUS ACTIVITIES OF THE PEOPLE OF SOUTH DAKOTA DURING THE PERIOD OF WORLD WAR II, BOTH IN SOUTH DAKOTA AND WHERE SOUTH DAKOTANS AND SOUTH DAKOTA UNITS WERE ACTIVE THROUGHOUT THE WORLD. Pierre, 1947-. 1 vol. published.

3558 Temple Historical Society, Temple, N.H.
TEMPLE, NEW HAMPSHIRE, IN WORLD WAR II. Temple, 1951. 77 p.

3559 Union Club of the City of New York.
UNION CLUB WORLD WAR II RECORDS, 1940-1947. New York, 1947. 205 p.

3560 U.S. War Production Board.
UTAH MINUTE WOMEN, WORLD WAR II, 1942-1945. Salt Lake City, 1945. 64 p.

3561 Watters, Mary.
ILLINOIS IN THE SECOND WORLD WAR. Springfield, Illinois State Historical Library, 1951-52. 2 v.

3562 Wheeler, William R. (ed.).
THE ROAD TO VICTORY: A HISTORY OF HAMPTON ROADS PORT OF EMBARKATION IN WORLD WAR II. Foreword by Major General Charles P. Gross. Newport News, Va. [New Haven, Yale University Press] 1946. 2 v.

3563 William and Mary College, Williamsburg, Virginia. Hampton Roads-Peninsula War Studies Committee.
THE HAMPTON ROADS COMMUNITIES IN WORLD WAR II. Edited by Charles F. Marsh and others. Chapel Hill, University of North Carolina Press, 1951. 337 p.

3564 Willoughby, Malcolm F.
THE COAST GUARD'S TRS, FIRST NAVAL DISTRICT. Boston, Lauriat, 1945. 247 p.

3565 YOUNG AMERICAN PATRIOTS: THE YOUTH OF KENTUCKY IN WORLD WAR II. Richmond, Va., National Publishing Co., 1947. 163 p.

3566 YOUNG AMERICAN PATRIOTS: THE YOUTH OF OHIO IN WORLD WAR II. Richmond, Va., National Publishing Co., 1947. 1175 p.

3567 YOUNG AMERICAN PATRIOTS: THE YOUTH OF VIRGINIA IN WORLD WAR II. Richmond, Va., National Publishing Co., 1945. 713 p.

d. Others

3568 Woodward, Paul B.
BRAZIL'S PARTICIPATION IN THE SECOND WORLD WAR. n.p., 1951. 152 l.

5. Propaganda

3569 Carroll, Wallace.
PERSUADE OR PERISH. Boston, Houghton Mifflin, 1948. 392 p.

3570 Delmer, Sefton.
BLACK BOOMERANG. New York, Viking Press, 1962. 303 p.

3571 Delmer, Sefton.
TRAIL SINISTER. London, Secker and Warburg, 1961-. 1 v. published.

3572 Lerner, Daniel (ed.).
PROPAGANDA IN WAR AND CRISIS: MATERIALS FOR AMERICAN POLICY. New York, Stewart, 1951. 500 p. (Library of Policy Sciences)

3573 Merton, Robert K., with Marjorie Fiske and Alberta Curtis.
MASS PERSUASION: THE SOCIAL PSYCHOLOGY OF A WAR BOND DRIVE. New York and London, Harper, 1946. 210 p.

3574 Padover, Saul K.
EXPERIMENT IN GERMANY: THE STORY OF AN AMERICAN INTELLIGENCE OFFICER. New York, Duell, Sloan and Pearce, 1946. 400 p.

Other edition:
PSYCHOLOGIST IN GERMANY. London, Phoenix House, 1946. 320 p.

V. ECONOMIC AND LEGAL ASPECTS OF THE WAR

A. GENERAL

3575 Brunn, Geoffrey, and Dwight E. Lee.
THE SECOND WORLD WAR AND AFTER. Boston, Houghton Mifflin, 1964. 200 p.

3576 Gordon, David L., and Royden Dangerfield.
THE HIDDEN WEAPON: THE STORY OF ECONOMIC WARFARE. New York, Harper, 1947. 238 p.

3577 Lamer, Mirko.
THE WORLD FERTILIZER ECONOMY. Stanford, Calif., Stanford University Press, 1957. 715 p. (Food Research Institute. Studies on Food, Agriculture, and World War II)

3578 League of Nations.
MONEY AND BANKING, 1942/44. Geneva, League of Nations; London, Allen and Unwin, 1945. 224 p. (II Economic and Financial Series)

3579 League of Nations.
WORLD ECONOMIC SURVEY, 1931-44. Geneva, 1932-45. 11 v.

3580 League of Nations. Secretariat. Economic, Financial and Transit Dept.
FOOD, FAMINE AND RELIEF, 1940-1946. Geneva, League of Nations; London, Allen and Unwin, 1946. 162 p.

3581 Lloyd, Edward M. H.
FOOD AND INFLATION IN THE MIDDLE EAST, 1940-45. Stanford, Calif., Stanford University Press, 1956. 375 p. (Studies on Food, Agriculture, and World War II)

3582 Long, Clarence D.
THE LABOR FORCE IN WAR AND TRANSITION, FOUR COUNTRIES. New York, National Bureau of Economic Research, 1952. 61 p. (National Bureau of Economic Research. Occasional Paper)

3583 Medlicott, William N.
THE ECONOMIC BLOCKADE. London, H.M. Stationery Office, 1952-59. 2 v. (History of the Second World War: United Kingdom Civil Series)

3584 Paterson, Thomas T.
MORALE IN WAR AND WORK: AN EXPERIMENT IN THE MANAGEMENT OF MEN. London, Parrish, 1955. 256 p.

3585 Potiphar (pseud.).
THEY MUST NOT STARVE. London, Gollancz, 1945. 107 p.

3586 Prest, Alan R.
WAR ECONOMICS OF PRIMARY PRODUCING COUNTRIES. Cambridge, Eng., Cambridge University Press, 1948. 308 p.

3587 Smith, Herbert A.
THE CRISIS IN THE LAW OF NATIONS. London, Stevens, 1947. 102 p. (Library of World Affairs)

3588 Southard, Frank A.
THE FINANCES OF EUROPEAN LIBERATION, WITH SPECIAL REFERENCE TO ITALY. New York, Published for Carnegie Endowment for International Peace by King's Crown Press, 1946. 206 p.

3589 Wiener Library.
RESTITUTION; EUROPEAN LEGISLATION TO REDRESS THE CONSEQUENCES OF NAZI RULE: COMPENSATION, RETURN OF PROPERTY, RE-INSTATEMENT OF THE DISPOSSESSED, CONFISCATION OF GERMAN ASSETS IN NEUTRAL COUNTRIES, ETC. London, 1945. 106 p.

3590 Zagorov, Slavcho D., and others.
THE AGRICULTURAL ECONOMY OF THE DANUBIAN COUNTRIES, 1935-45. Stanford, Calif., Stanford University Press, 1955. 478 p. (Studies on Food, Agriculture, and World War II)

B. AXIS POWERS

3591 Bisson, Thomas A.
ASPECTS OF WARTIME ECONOMIC CONTROL IN JAPAN. Submitted by International Secretariat as a document for the Ninth Conference of the I.P.R. to be held in January 1945. New York, International Secretariat, Institute of Pacific Relations, 1945. 108 l. (Secretariat Paper)

3592 Bisson, Thomas A.
JAPAN'S WAR ECONOMY. New York, Macmillan, 1945. 267 p.

3593 Brandt, Karl, and others.
GERMANY'S AGRICULTURAL AND FOOD POLICIES IN WORLD WAR II. Stanford, Calif., 1953. 2 vols. published.

3594 Cohen, Jerome B.
THE JAPANESE WAR ECONOMY 1937-1945. Foreword by Sir George Sansom. Minneapolis, University of Minnesota Press, 1949. 545 p.

Other edition:
JAPAN'S ECONOMY IN WAR AND RECONSTRUCTION.

3595 Fried, John H. E.
THE EXPLOITATION OF FOREIGN LABOUR BY GERMANY. Montreal, 1945. 286 p. (International Labor Office Studies and Reports)

3596 GERMAN OCCUPIED GREAT BRITAIN: ORDINANCES OF THE MILITARY AUTHORITIES. Shoreham-by-Sea, Eng., Scutt-Dand, Foord, 196-. 94 p.

3597 Graham, Frank D., and J. J. Scanlon.
ECONOMIC PREPARATION AND CONDUCT OF WAR UNDER THE NAZI REGIME. Washington, Special Staff, Historical Division, War Dept., 1946. 53 l.

3598 Johnston, Bruce F., with Mosaburo Hosoda and Yoshio Kusumi.
JAPANESE FOOD MANAGEMENT IN WORLD WAR II. Stanford, Calif., Stanford University Press, 1953. 283 p. (Studies on Food, Agriculture, and World War II)

3599 Klein, Burton H.
GERMANY'S ECONOMIC PREPARATIONS FOR WAR. Cambridge, Mass., Harvard University Press, 1959. 272 p. (Harvard Economic Studies)

3600 Milward, Alan S.
THE GERMAN ECONOMY AT WAR. London, University of London, Athlone Press, 1965. 214 p.

3601 Moss, William S.
GOLD IS WHERE YOU HIDE IT: WHAT HAPPENED TO THE REICHSBANK TREASURE? London, Deutsch, 1956. 191 p.

3602 Shiomi, Saburo.
JAPANESE AND TAXATION, 1940-1956. New York, Columbia University Press, 1957. 190 p.

3603 U.S. Dept. of State. Interim Research and Intelligence Service. Research and Analysis Branch.
THE LABOR SUPPLY IN JAPAN. Washington, 1945. 2 v. in 1.

C. AXIS-HELD COUNTRIES

3604 Gross, Feliks.
THE POLISH WORKER: A STUDY OF A SOCIAL STRATUM. New York, Roy, 1945. 274 p.

3605 Maupin, Jere W.
GERMANY'S ECONOMIC EXPLOITATION OF FRANCE DURING THE WORLD WAR II OCCUPATION. Washington, 1950. 137 l.

3606 Netherlands. Departement van Financiën.
WHITE PAPER REGARDING THE MEASURES FOR THE CURRENCY REHABILITATION IN THE NETHERLANDS. The Hague, Government Publishers, 1947. 219 p.

3607 U.S. Dept. of State. Interim Research and Intelligence Service. Research and Analysis Branch.
JAPANESE USE OF BURMESE INDUSTRY. Washington, 1945. 65 p.

3608 Young, Arthur N.
CHINA AND THE HELPING HAND, 1937-1945. Cambridge, Mass., Harvard University Press, 1963. 502 p. (Harvard East Asian Series)

3609 Yugoslavia. War Reparations Commission.
HUMAN AND MATERIAL SACRIFICES OF YUGOSLAVIA IN HER WAR EFFORTS, 1941-1945. Belgrade, War Reparations Commission, The Federative People's Republic of Yugoslavia, 1946. 53 p.

D. UNITED NATIONS COALITION

1. General

3610 Combined Production and Resources Board (United States, Great Britain, and Canada).
THE IMPACT OF THE WAR ON CIVILIAN CONSUMPTION IN UNITED KINGDOM, UNITED STATES AND CANADA. Washington, U.S. Government Printing Office, 1945. 157 p.

3611 Hall, H. Duncan.
NORTH AMERICAN SUPPLY. London, H.M. Stationery Office, 1955. 559 p. (History of the Second World War: United Kingdom Civil Series; War Production Series)

3612 Hall, H. Duncan, and C. C. Wrigley.
STUDIES OF OVERSEAS SUPPLY. With a chapter by J. D. Scott. London, H.M. Stationery Office, 1956. 537 p. (History of the Second World War: United Kingdom Civil Series; War Production Series)

3613 James, Robert W.
WARTIME ECONOMIC CO-OPERATION: A STUDY OF RELATIONS BETWEEN CANADA AND THE UNITED STATES. Issued under the auspices of the Canadian Institute of International Affairs. Toronto, Ryerson Press, 1949. 415 p. (Studies in International Affairs)

3614 Jordan, George R., with Richard L. Stokes.
FROM MAJOR JORDAN'S DIARIES. New York, Harcourt, Brace, 1952. 284 p.

3615 Oxford University. Institute of Statistics.
STUDIES IN WAR ECONOMICS: A SELECTION OF ARTICLES REPRINTED FROM THE BULLETIN OF THE INSTITUTE OF STATISTICS AND OTHER PERIODICALS. Oxford, Blackwell, 1947. 410 p.

3616 Roll, Erich.
THE COMBINED FOOD BOARD: A STUDY IN WAR TIME INTERNATIONAL PLANNING. Stanford, Calif., Stanford University Press, 1956. 385 p. (Studies on Food, Agriculture, and World War II)

3617 Rosen, S. McKee.
THE COMBINED BOARDS OF THE SECOND WORLD WAR: AN EXPERIMENT IN INTERNATIONAL ADMINISTRATION. New York, Columbia University Press, 1951. 288 p.

3618 United Nations Monetary and Financial Conference, Bretton Woods, New Hampshire, 1944.
PROCEEDINGS AND DOCUMENTS. Washington, U.S. Government Printing Office, 1948. 2 v.

2. British Commonwealth

3619 Ashworth, William.
CONTRACTS AND FINANCE. London, H.M. Stationery Office, 1953. 309 p. (History of the Second World War United Kingdom Civil Series; War Production Series).

3620 Baker, Benjamin.
WARTIME FOOD PROCUREMENT AND PRODUCTION. New York, King's Crown Press, 1951. 219 p.

3621 Baker, John V. T.
THE NEW ZEALAND PEOPLE AT WAR: WAR ECONOMY. Wellington, Historical Publications Branch, Dept. of Internal Affairs, 1965. 660 p. (Official History of New Zealand in the Second World War, 1939-45)

3622 Barclays Bank (Dominion, Colonial and Overseas).
A BANK IN BATTLEDRESS: BEING THE STORY OF BARCLAYS BANK (DOMINION, COLONIAL, AND OVERSEAS) DURING THE SECOND WORLD WAR, 1939-45. London [for private circulation] 1948. 212 p.

3623 Beith, John H. (Ian Hay, pseud.).
THE POST OFFICE WENT TO WAR. London, H.M. Stationery Office, 1946. 94 p.

3624 Bell, Robert.
HISTORY OF THE BRITISH RAILWAYS DURING THE WAR, 1939-45. London, Railway Gazette, 1946. 291 p.

3625 British Iron and Steel Federation.
THE BATTLE OF STEEL: A RECORD OF THE BRITISH IRON AND STEEL INDUSTRY AT WAR. London, 1945. 52 p.

3626 Britnell, George E., and Vernon C. Fowke.
CANADIAN AGRICULTURE IN WAR AND PEACE, 1935-60. Stanford, Calif., Stanford University Press, 1962. 502 p.

3627 Butlin, Sydney J.
WAR ECONOMY. Canberra, Australian War Memorial, 1955-. 1 vol. published. (Australia in the War of 1939-1945. Series 4 [Civil])

3628 Canada. Dept. of Reconstruction.
LOCATION AND EFFECTS OF WARTIME INDUSTRIAL EXPANSION IN CANADA, 1939-1944. Prepared by Directorate of Economic Research of the Dept. of Reconstruction. Ottawa, Directorate of Economic Research, Dept. of Reconstruction and Supply, 1945. 65 l.

3629 Canadian Bank of Commerce.
WAR SERVICE RECORDS, 1939-1945: AN ACCOUNT OF THE WAR SERVICE OF MEMBERS OF THE STAFF DURING THE SECOND WORLD WAR. Toronto, 1947. 331 p.

3630 Ceylon. Ministry of Agriculture and Lands.
HOW LANKA FED HERSELF DURING THE WAR, 1939-1945. Colombo, 1947. 106 p.

3631 Chester, Daniel N. (ed.).
LESSONS OF THE BRITISH WAR ECONOMY. Cambridge, Eng., University Press, 1951. 260 p. (National Institute of Economic and Social Research. Economic and Social Studies)

3632 Court, William H. B.
COAL. London, H.M. Stationery Office, 1951. 422 p. (History of the Second World War: United Kingdom Civil Series)

3633 Crawford, John G., and others.
WARTIME AGRICULTURE IN AUSTRALIA AND NEW ZEALAND 1939-50. Stanford, Calif., Stanford University Press, 1954. 354 p. (Studies on Food, Agriculture, and World War II)

3634 Drawbell, James W.
THE LONG YEAR. London, Wingate, 1958. 242 p.

3635 Fairfax, Ernest.
CALLING ALL ARMS: THE STORY OF HOW A LOYAL COMPANY OF BRITISH MEN AND WOMEN LIVED THROUGH SIX HISTORIC YEARS. London and New York, Hutchinson, 1945. 159 p.

3636 Graves, Charles.
DRIVE FOR FREEDOM: HOW BRITAIN EQUIPPED HER FIGHTING SERVICES, SPEEDILY MADE GOOD HER LOSSES AFTER DUNKIRK, AND ACHIEVED ASTONISHING NEW RECORDS IN PRODUCTION FOR VICTORY. London, Hodder and Stoughton, 1945. 135 p.

3637 Great Britain. Central Statistical Office.
STATISTICAL DIGEST OF THE WAR. London, H.M. Stationery Office, 1951. 247 p. (History of the Second World War: United Kingdom Civil Series)

3638 Great Britain. Ministry of Food.
HOW BRITAIN WAS FED IN WAR TIME: FOOD CONTROL, 1939-1945. London, H.M. Stationery Office, 1946. 66 p.

3639 Hammond, Richard J.
FOOD. London, H.M. Stationery Office, 1951-62. 3 v. (History of the Second World War: United Kingdom Civil Series)

3640 Hammond, Richard J.
FOOD AND AGRICULTURE IN BRITAIN, 1939-45: ASPECTS OF WARTIME CONTROL. Stanford, Calif., Stanford University Press, 1954. 246 p. (Studies on Food, Agriculture, and World War II)

3641 Hancock, William K., and M. M. Gowing.
BRITISH WAR ECONOMY. London, H.M. Stationery Office, 1949. 583 p. (History of the Second World War: United Kingdom Civil Series)

3642 Hargreaves, Eric L., and M. M. Gowing.
CIVIL INDUSTRY AND TRADE. London, H.M. Stationery Office, 1952. 678 p. (History of the Second World War: United Kingdom Civil Series)

3643 Harkness, Sir Douglas.
A TRACT ON AGRICULTURAL POLICY. Westminster (London), King and Staples, 1945. 82 p.

3644 Higgins, Benjamin H.
LOMBARD STREET IN WAR AND RECONSTRUCTION. New York, Financial Research Program, National Bureau of Economic Research, 1949. 108 p. (National Bureau of Economic Research)

3645 Hornby, William.
FACTORIES AND PLANT. London, H.M. Stationery Office, 1958. 421 p. (History of the Second World War: United Kingdom Civil Series; War Production Series)

3646 Hurstfield, J.
THE CONTROL OF RAW MATERIALS. London, H.M. Stationery Office, 1953. 530 p. (History of the Second World War: United Kingdom Civil Series; War Production Series)

3647 Inman, Peggy.
LABOUR IN THE MUNITIONS INDUSTRIES. London, H.M. Stationery Office, 1957. 461 p. (History of the Second World War: United Kingdom Civil Series; War Production Series)

3648 Ker, Frederick I., and Wilfred H. Goodman.
PRESS PROMOTION OF WAR FINANCE. Toronto, Published jointly by the associations represented by the Canadian Publishers War Finance Publicity Committee, 1947. 106 p.

3649 Knight, Sir Henry.
FOOD ADMINISTRATION IN INDIA, 1939-47. Stanford, Calif., Stanford University Press, 1954. 323 p. (Studies on Food, Agriculture, and World War II)

3650 Kohan, C. M.
WORKS AND BUILDINGS. London, H.M. Stationery Office, 1952. 540 p. (History of the Second World War: United Kingdom Civil Series)

3651 Lancum, Frank H.
"PRESS OFFICER, PLEASE!" London, Lockwood, 1946. 144 p.

3652 Londerville, J. D.
THE PAY SERVICES OF THE CANADIAN ARMY OVERSEAS IN THE WAR OF 1939-45. Ottawa, Published by the Runge Press for the Royal Canadian Army Pay Corps Association, 1950. 315 p.

3653 McIvor, Russel C.
MONETARY EXPANSION IN CANADIAN WAR FINANCE, 1939-1945. Chicago, 1947. 247 l.

3654 McNair, Sir Arnold D.
LEGAL EFFECTS OF WAR. Cambridge, Eng., Cambridge University Press, 1948. 458 p.

3655 Meiggs, Russell.
HOME TIMBER PRODUCTION, 1939-1945. Foreword by Sir Gerald Lenanton. London, Lockwood, 1949. 277 p.

3656 Mellor, David P.
THE ROLE OF SCIENCE AND INDUSTRY. Canberra, Australian War Memorial, 1958. 738 p. (Australia in the War of 1939-1945. Series 4 [Civil])

3657 Muranjan, Sumant K.
ECONOMICS OF POST-WAR INDIA. Bombay, Hind Kitabs, 1945. 98 p.

Other edition:
1947. 208 p.

3658 Murray, Keith A. H.
AGRICULTURE. London, H.M. Stationery Office, 1955. 422 p. (History of the Second World War: United Kingdom Civil Series)

3659 Parker, Henry M. D.
MANPOWER: A STUDY OF WAR-TIME POLICY AND ADMINISTRATION. London, H.M. Stationery Office, 1957. 535 p. (History of the Second World War: United Kingdom Civil Series)

3660 Postan, Michael M.
BRITISH WAR PRODUCTION. London, H.M. Stationery Office, 1952. 512 p. (History of the Second World War: United Kingdom Civil Series)

3661 Price, John.
BRITISH TRADE UNIONS AND THE WAR. London, Ministry of Information, 1945. 55 p. (Half-title: BRITISH ACHIEVEMENTS OF THE WAR YEARS)

3662 Pumphrey, Bevan.
THE YEARS OF ENDURANCE, W. and M. PUMPHREY LTD., 1939-1945. West Hartlepool, Barlow, 1947. 55 p.

3663 Rao, Raghunath.
WARTIME LABOUR CONDITIONS AND RECONSTRUCTION PLANNING IN INDIA. Montreal, 1946. 113 p. (International Labor Office. Studies and Reports)

3664 Roberts, Eric S.
JUST AS IT CAME. Sheffield, Northend, 1945. 165 p.

3665 Saunders, Hilary A. St. G.
FORD AT WAR. London, 1946. 93 p.

3666 Sayers, Richard S.
FINANCIAL POLICY, 1939-45. London, H.M. Stationery Office, 1956. 608 p. (History of the Second World War: United Kingdom Civil Series)

3667 Scott, John D., and Richard Hughes.
THE ADMINISTRATION OF WAR PRODUCTION. London, H.M. Stationery Office, 1955. 544 p. (History of the Second World War: United Kingdom Civil Series; War Production Series)

3668 The Times, London.
BRITISH WAR PRODUCTION 1939-1945, A RECORD COMPILED BY THE TIMES. London, 1945. 240 p.

3669 Tinley, James M.
SOUTH AFRICAN FOOD AND AGRICULTURE IN WORLD WAR II. Stanford, Calif., Stanford University Press, 1954. 138 p. (Studies on Food, Agriculture, and World War II)

3670 Victoria, Australia. Forests Commission.
EMPIRE FORESTS AND THE WAR: STATEMENT

PREPARED FOR THE BRITISH EMPIRE FORESTRY CONFERENCE, LONDON, 1947. Melbourne, Gourley, Government Printer, 1946. 93 p.

3671 Walker, Edward R.
THE AUSTRALIAN ECONOMY IN WAR AND RECONSTRUCTION. Issued under the auspices of the Royal Institute of International Affairs. New York and London, Oxford University Press, 1947. 426 p.

3672 Weir, Sir Cecil McA.
CIVILIAN ASSIGNMENT. London, Methuen, 1953. 182 p.

3673 Woolton, Frederick J. Marquis, 1st earl of.
MEMOIRS. London, Cassell, 1959. 452 p.

3. Russia

3674 Voznesenskii, Nikolai A.
WAR ECONOMY OF THE U.S.S.R. IN THE PERIOD OF THE PATRIOTIC WAR. Moscow, Foreign Languages Publishing House, 1948. 150 p.

Other editions:
SOVIET ECONOMY DURING THE SECOND WORLD WAR. New York, International Publishers, 1949. 160 p.

THE ECONOMY OF THE USSR DURING WORLD WAR II. Washington, Public Affairs Press, 1948. 115 p.

4. United States

3675 Adams, Leonard P.
WARTIME MANPOWER MOBILIZATION: A STUDY OF WORLD WAR II EXPERIENCE IN THE BUFFALO-NIAGARA AREA. Ithaca, N.Y., Cornell University, 1951. 169 p. (Cornell Studies in Industrial and Labor Relations, v. 1)

3676 Allen, Ethan P.
HIDE AND LEATHER POLICIES OF THE WAR PRODUCTION BOARD AND PREDECESSOR AGENCIES, MAY 1940 TO DECEMBER 1943. Washington, 1946. 100 p. (Historical Reports on War Administration: War Production Board. Special Study)

3677 Allen, Ethan P.
POLICIES GOVERNING PRIVATE FINANCING OF EMERGENCY FACILITIES, MAY 1940 TO JUNE 1942. Washington, 1946. 95 p. (Historical Reports on War Administration: War Production Board. Special Study)

3678 Allen, Hugh.
GOODYEAR AIRCRAFT: WRITTEN AS A TYPICAL EXAMPLE OF HOW AMERICAN INDUSTRY AND AMERICAN MEN MET AN EMERGENCY AND WON A WAR. Akron, Ohio, 1947. 159 p.

3679 Anderson, Margaret K.
WOMEN'S WARTIME HOURS OF WORK: THE EFFECT ON THEIR FACTORY PERFORMANCE AND HOME LIFE. Washington, U.S. Government Printing Office, 1947. 187 p.

3680 Automobile Manufacturers Association.
FREEDOM'S ARSENAL: THE STORY OF THE AUTOMOBILE COUNCIL FOR WAR PRODUCTION. Detroit, 1950. 207 p.

3681 Baker, Botts, Andrews and Walne, Houston, Texas.
BAKER, BOTTS IN WORLD WAR II. Houston, 1947. 662 p.

3682 Bellamy, Francis R.
BLOOD MONEY: THE STORY OF U.S. TREASURY SECRET AGENTS. New York, Dutton, 1947. 257 p.

3683 Borth, Christy.
MASTERS OF MASS PRODUCTION. Indianapolis, Bobbs-Merrill, 1945. 290 p.

3684 Campbell, Levin H., Jr.
THE INDUSTRY-ORDNANCE TEAM. New York, Whittlesey House, McGraw-Hill, 1946. 461 p.

3685 Campbell, Robert F.
THE HISTORY OF BASIC METALS PRICE CONTROL IN WORLD WAR II. New York, Columbia University Press, 1948. 263 p.

3686 Chandler, Lester V.
INFLATION IN THE UNITED STATES, 1940-1948. New York, Harper, 1951. 402 p.

3687 Committee on Public Administration Cases, Washington, D.C.
THE FEASIBILITY DISPUTE: DETERMINATION OF WAR PRODUCTION OBJECTIVES FOR 1942 AND 1943. Washington, 1950. 116 p.

3688 Committee on Public Administration Cases, Washington, D.C.
THE RECONVERSION CONTROVERSY. Washington, 1950. 156 p.

3689 Connery, Robert H.
THE NAVY AND THE INDUSTRIAL MOBILIZATION IN WORLD WAR II. Princeton, N.J., Princeton University Press, 1951. 527 p.

3690 Craf, John R.
A SURVEY OF THE AMERICAN ECONOMY, 1940-1946. New York, North River Press, 1947. 217 p.

3691 Cunkle, Arthur L.
THE IMPACT OF WORLD WAR II ON STATE FINANCES. Charlottesville, Va., 1947. 312 l.

3692 De Schweinitz, Dorothea.
LABOR AND MANAGEMENT IN COMMON ENTERPRISE. Cambridge, Mass., Harvard University Press, 1949. 186 p. (Wertheim Fellowship Publications)

3693 Domke, Martin.
THE CONTROL OF ALIEN PROPERTY. New York, Central Book Co., 1947. 334 p.

Supplement to:
TRADING WITH THE ENEMY IN WORLD WAR II. New York, Central Book Co., 1943. 640 p.

3694 Dunlop, John T., and Arthur D. Hill.
THE WAGE ADJUSTMENT BOARD: WARTIME STABILIZATION IN THE BUILDING AND CONSTRUCTION INDUSTRY. Cambridge, Mass., Harvard University Press, 1950. 166 p.

3695 Fairchild, Byron, and Jonathan Grossman.
THE ARMY AND INDUSTRIAL MANPOWER. Washington, Office of Chief of Military History, Dept. of Army, 1959. 291 p. (U.S. Army in World War II: The War Dept.)

3696 Finnie, Richard (ed.).
MARINSHIP: THE HISTORY OF A WARTIME SHIPYARD, AS TOLD BY SOME OF THE PEOPLE WHO HELPED BUILD THE SHIPS, SAUSALITO, CALIF., 1942-1945. San Francisco, 1947. 403 p.

3697 First, Edythe W.
INDUSTRY AND LABOR ADVISORY COMMITTEES IN THE NATIONAL DEFENSE ADVISORY COMMISSION AND THE OFFICE OF PRODUCTION MANAGEMENT, MAY 1940 TO JANUARY 1942. Washington, 1946. 233 p. (Historical Reports on War Administration: War Production Board. Special Study)

3698 Fisher, Douglas A.
STEEL IN THE WAR. New York, U.S. Steel Corp., 1946. 164 p.

3699 Genung, Albert B.
FOOD POLICIES DURING WORLD WAR II: A HISTORICAL ACCOUNT OF AMERICAN FOOD PRODUCTION, PRICE, AND CONTROL OPERATIONS DURING THE SECOND WORLD WAR, 1941-1946. Ithaca, N.Y., Northeast Farm Foundation, 1951. 81 p.

3700 Gold, Bela.
WARTIME ECONOMIC PLANNING IN AGRICULTURE: A STUDY IN THE ALLOCATION OF RESOURCES. New York, 1949. 594 p.

3701 Hanson, Alice C.
FAMILY SPENDING AND SAVING IN WARTIME. Washington, Bureau of Labor Statistics, U.S. Dept. of Labor, 1945. 218 p. (U.S. Bureau of Labor Statistics Bulletin)

3702 Harris, Seymour E.
INFLATION AND THE AMERICAN ECONOMY. New York and London, McGraw-Hill, 1945. 559 p.

3703 Havighurst, Robert J., and H. Gerthon Morgan.
THE SOCIAL HISTORY OF A WAR-BOOM COMMUNITY. New York, Longmans, Green, 1951. 356 p.

3704 Holmaas, Arthur J.
AGRICULTURAL WAGE STABILIZATION IN WORLD WAR II. Washington, U.S. Bureau of Agricultural Economics, 1950. 140 p. (Agriculture Monograph)

3705 Hoover, Herbert C.
ADDRESSES UPON THE AMERICAN ROAD, WORLD WAR II, 1941-1945. New York, Van Nostrand, 1946. 442 p.

3706 Hungerford, Edward.
TIMKEN AT WAR. Canton, Ohio [private printer] 1945. 137 p.

3707 Inter-university Case Program.
THE FEASIBILITY DISPUTE: DETERMINATION OF WAR PRODUCTION OBJECTIVES FOR 1942 AND 1943. Washington, 1950. 116 p.

3708 Inter-university Case Program.
THE RECONVERSION CONTROVERSY. Washington, 1950. 156 p.

3709 Janeway, Eliot.
THE STRUGGLE FOR SURVIVAL: A CHRONICLE OF ECONOMIC MOBILIZATION IN WORLD WAR II. New Haven, Conn., Yale University Press, 1951. 382 p. (Chronicles of America Series)

3710 Jones, Drummond.
THE ROLE OF THE OFFICE OF CIVILIAN REQUIREMENTS IN THE OFFICE OF PRODUCTION MANAGEMENT AND WAR PRODUCTION BOARD, JANUARY 1941 TO NOVEMBER 1945. Washington, 1946. 351 p. (Historical Reports on War Administration: War Production Board. Special Study)

3711 Kinzie, George R.
COPPER POLICIES OF THE WAR PRODUCTION BOARD AND PREDECESSOR AGENCIES, MAY 1940 TO NOVEMBER 1945. Washington, 1947. 198 p. (Historical Reports on War Administration: War Production Board. Special Study)

3712 Kress, Andrew J.
CONTRACT PRICING, PRINCIPAL DEVELOPMENTS. Washington, Dept. of Research, Army Industrial College, 1946. 123 p. (Study of Experience in Industrial Mobilization in World War II)

3713 Kuznets, Simon S.
NATIONAL PRODUCT IN WARTIME. New York, National Bureau of Economic Research, 1945. 156 p.

3714 Lee, Alvin T. M.
ACQUISITION AND USE OF LAND FOR MILITARY AND WAR PRODUCTION PURPOSES, WORLD WAR II. Washington, 1947. 115 p. (U.S. Dept. of Agriculture. War Records Monograph)

3715 Lever, Harry, and Joseph Young.
WARTIME RACKETEERS. New York, Putnam, 1945. 226 p.

3716 Levitt, Theodore.
WORLD WAR II MANPOWER MOBILIZATION AND UTILIZATION IN A LOCAL LABOR MARKET: THE WARTIME MANPOWER EXPERIENCE IN THE COLUMBUS, OHIO AREA. Columbus, Ohio State University Research Foundation, 1951. 363 l.

3717   Liquor Store and Dispenser.
       THE RECORD OF THE ALCOHOLIC BEVERAGE INDUSTRY IN WORLD WAR II. New York, 1946. 50 p.

3718   Look, editors of.
       OIL FOR VICTORY: THE STORY OF PETROLEUM IN WAR AND PEACE. New York and London, Whittlesey House, McGraw-Hill, 1946. 287 p. (Look Picture Book)

3719   Louisiana. Dept. of Military Affairs.
       PROBLEMS OF WORLD WAR II: SELECTED ARTICLES. Compiled by Raymond H. Fleming. Baton Rouge, La., 194-? 1 v.

3720   Lumer, Hyman.
       WAR ECONOMY AND CRISIS. New York, International Publishers, 1954. 256 p.

3721   McAleer, James A.
       DOLLAR-A-YEAR AND WITHOUT COMPENSATION PERSONNEL POLICIES OF THE WAR PRODUCTION BOARD AND PREDECESSOR AGENCIES, AUGUST 1939 TO NOVEMBER 1945. Washington, 1947. 115 p. (Historical Reports on War Administration: War Production Board. Special Study)

3722   McAleer, James A.
       FARM MACHINERY AND EQUIPMENT POLICIES OF THE WAR PRODUCTION BOARD AND PREDECESSOR AGENCIES, MAY 1940 TO SEPTEMBER 1944. Washington, 1946. 191 p. (Historical Reports on War Administration: War Production Board. Special Study)

3723   McCauley, Maryclaire.
       CONCENTRATION OF CIVILIAN PRODUCTION BY THE WAR PRODUCTION BOARD, SEPTEMBER 1941 TO APRIL 1943. Washington, 1946. 131 p. (Historical Reports on War Administration: War Production Board. Special Study)

3724   McGrane, Reginald C.
       THE FACILITIES AND CONSTRUCTION PROGRAM OF THE WAR PRODUCTION BOARD AND PREDECESSOR AGENCIES, MAY 1940 TO MAY 1945. Washington, 1946. 246 p. (Historical Reports on War Administration: War Production Board. Special Study)

3725   Morgan, John D.
       THE DOMESTIC MINING INDUSTRY OF THE UNITED STATES IN WORLD WAR II: A CRITICAL STUDY OF THE ECONOMIC MOBILIZATION OF THE MINERAL BASE OF NATIONAL POWER. Washington, Government Printing Office, 1949. 500 p. (Pennsylvania, State College. Mineral Industries Experiment Station)

3726   Murphy, Henry C.
       THE NATIONAL DEBT IN WAR AND TRANSITION. New York, McGraw-Hill, 1950. 295 p.

3727   Musser, W. Daniel.
       VOCATIONAL TRAINING FOR WAR PRODUCTION WORKERS: FINAL REPORT. Washington, 1946. 290 p. (U.S. Office of Education)

3728   National Bureau for Industrial Protection.
       A HISTORY OF THE NATIONAL BUREAU FOR INDUSTRIAL PROTECTION, WASHINGTON, D.C., ORGANIZED FEBRUARY 3, 1941, DISBANDED SEPTEMBER 1, 1945. Washington, 1945. 157 p.

3729   Nelson, Donald M.
       ARSENAL OF DEMOCRACY: THE STORY OF AMERICAN WAR PRODUCTION. New York, Harcourt, 1946. 439 p.

3730   Nielander, William A.
       WARTIME FOOD RATIONING IN THE UNITED STATES. Baltimore, 1947. 318 p.

3731   Novick, David, Melvin Anshen, and W. C. Truppner.
       WARTIME PRODUCTION CONTROLS. New York, Columbia University Press, 1949. 441 p.

3732   Parnes, Herbert S.
       A STUDY OF THE DYNAMICS OF LOCAL LABOR FORCE EXPANSION: AN ANALYSIS OF THE WORLD WAR II INCREASE IN MANUFACTURING LABOR SUPPLY IN THE COLUMBUS, OHIO AREA. Columbus, Ohio State University Research Foundation, 1951. 201 l.

3733   Popple, Charles S.
       STANDARD OIL COMPANY, NEW JERSEY, IN WORLD WAR II. New York, Standard Oil Co., 1952. 340 p.

3734   Price, Harvey L.
       VIRGINIA FARMERS AT WAR: ESSAYS ON AGRICULTURAL PRODUCTION IN THE OLD DOMINION DURING THE SECOND WORLD WAR. Blacksburg, Va., 1950. 108 p. (Virginia Polytechnic Institute. Blacksburg. Agricultural Extension Service. Bulletin)

3735   Pubols, Ben H.
       CITRUS FRUIT DURING WORLD WAR II. Washington, U.S. Government Printing Office, 1950. 77 p. (U.S. Department of Agriculture. Agriculture Monograph)

3736   Purcell, Richard J.
       LABOR POLICIES OF THE NATIONAL DEFENSE ADVISORY COMMISSION AND THE OFFICE OF PRODUCTION MANAGEMENT, MAY 1940 TO APRIL 1942. Washington, 1946. 247 p. (Historical Reports on War Administration: War Production Board. Special Study)

3737   Riegelman, Carol.
       LABOUR-MANAGEMENT CO-OPERATION IN UNITED STATES WAR PRODUCTION: A STUDY OF METHODS AND PROCEDURE. Montreal, 1948. 405 p. (International Labor Office. Studies and Reports)

3738   Rundell, Walter.
       BLACK MARKET MONEY: THE COLLAPSE OF U.S. MILITARY CURRENCY CONTROL IN WORLD WAR II. Baton Rouge, Louisiana State University Press, 1964. 125 p.

3739   Russell, Judith, and Renée Fantin.
       STUDIES IN FOOD RATIONING. Washington, Office of Temporary Controls, Office of Price Administration, 1948. 404 p. (Historical Reports on War Administration)

3740 Seldman, Joel I.
AMERICAN LABOR FROM DEFENSE TO RECONVERSION. Chicago, University of Chicago Press, 1953. 307 p.

3741 Shaw, Carroll K.
FIELD ORGANIZATION AND ADMINISTRATION OF WAR PRODUCTION BOARD AND PREDECESSOR AGENCIES, MAY 1940 AND NOVEMBER 1945. Washington, 1947. 288 p. (Historical Reports on War Administration: War Production Board. Special Study)

3742 Sims, Grover J.
MEAT AND MEAT ANIMALS IN WORLD WAR TWO. Washington, Bureau of Agricultural Economics, U. S. Dept. of Agriculture, 1951. 149 p. (Agriculture Monograph)

3743 Small, Robert O.
ONE GOAL: THE HISTORY OF TRAINING WAR PRODUCTION WORKERS IN AND THROUGH THE VOCATIONAL SCHOOLS OF THE COMMONWEALTH OF MASSACHUSETTS, 1940-1945. Boston, Massachusetts Vocational Association, 1950. 371 p.

3744 Smaller War Plants Corporation.
ECONOMIC CONCENTRATION AND WORLD WAR II: REPORT TO THE SPECIAL COMMITTEE TO STUDY PROBLEMS OF AMERICAN SMALL BUSINESS, U. S. SENATE. Washington, U. S. Government Printing Office, 1946. 359 p.

3745 Smith, Ralph E.
THE ARMY AND ECONOMIC MOBILIZATION. Washington, Office of Chief of Military History, Dept. of Army, 1959. 749 p. (U. S. Army in World War II: The War Department)

3746 Somers, Herman M.
PRESIDENTIAL AGENCY OWMR, THE OFFICE OF WAR MOBILIZATION AND RECONVERSION. Cambridge, Mass., Harvard University Press, 1950. 238 p.

3747 Stoughton, Bradley.
HISTORY OF THE TOOLS DIVISION, WAR PRODUCTION BOARD. New York, McGraw-Hill, 1949. 154 p.

3748 Taylor, Frank J., and Lawton Wright.
DEMOCRACY'S AIR ARSENAL. New York, Duell, Sloan and Pearce, 1947. 208 p.

3749 Toulmin, Harry A., Jr.
DIARY OF DEMOCRACY: THE SENATE WAR INVESTIGATING COMMITTEE. Introduction by Harley M. Kilgore. New York, R. R. Smith, 1947. 277 p.

3750 U. S. Army Air Forces. Matériel Command.
SOURCE BOOK OF WORLD WAR II BASIC DATA, AIRFRAME INDUSTRY. Prepared by Industrial Mobilization Office, Research and Development, Procurement, and Industrial Mobilization T-3 Air Materiel Command, Army Air Forces, Wright Field. Dayton, Ohio, 1947-48. 2 v. (420 p.)

3751 U. S. Bureau of Agricultural Economics.
A CHRONOLOGY OF THE WAR FOOD ADMINISTRATION, INCLUDING PREDECESSOR AND SUCCESSOR AGENCIES, AUGUST 1939 TO DECEMBER 1946. Prepared by Gladys L. Baker and Wayne D. Rasmussen. Washington, 1950. 73 p.

3752 U. S. Bureau of Community Facilities.
HISTORY, DEVELOPMENT, AND PROGRESS OF WAR PUBLIC SERVICES DIVISION 2, BUREAU OF COMMUNITY FACILITIES, FEDERAL WORKS AGENCY 1941-1946, DEFENSE AND WAR YEARS. Prepared by the War Public Services Staff of Division 2. Washington, 1946. 1 v.

3753 U. S. Bureau of Foreign and Domestic Commerce. Office of Industry and Commerce.
WAR PRODUCTION BOARD'S STEEL DIVISION'S EXPERIENCE WITH WORLD WAR II CONTROLS, PARTICULARLY UNDER THE CONTROLLED MATERIALS PLAN. Prepared by Kenneth H. Hunter and Edward L. Hogan. Washington, Iron and Steel Division, Office of Industry and Commerce, Dept. of Commerce, 1950. 110 p.

3754 U. S. Bureau of Labor Statistics.
PROBLEMS AND POLICIES OF DISPUTE SETTLEMENT AND WAGE STABILIZATION DURING WORLD WAR II. Washington, U. S. Government Printing Office, 1950. 380 p. (Bulletin)

3755 U. S. Bureau of Labor Statistics.
WORKER MOBILITY AND SKILL UTILIZATION IN WORLD WAR II. Prepared by Willis C. Quant and Lily M. David. Washington, 1952. 106 p.

3756 U. S. Civilian Production Administration.
INDUSTRIAL MOBILIZATION FOR WAR, HISTORY OF THE WAR PRODUCTION BOARD AND PREDECESSOR AGENCIES, 1940-1945: Vol. I, PROGRAM AND ADMINISTRATION. Washington, 1947. 1010 p. (Historical Reports on War Administration)

3757 U. S. Dept. of Commerce.
WORLD WAR IN HISTORY OF THE DEPT. OF COMMERCE. Washington, 1945-. Pts. 5, 10 published.

3758 U. S. Office of Contract Settlement.
A HISTORY OF WAR CONTRACT TERMINATIONS AND SETTLEMENTS. Washington, U. S. Government Printing Office, 1947. 84 p.

3759 U. S. Office of Foreign Agricultural Relations.
COORDINATION OF INTERNATIONAL FOOD MANAGEMENT WITHIN THE U. S. GOVERNMENT, 1941-1948. Washington, 1948. 1 v.

3760 U. S. Office of Temporary Controls.
THE BEGINNINGS OF OPA. Washington, Office of Temporary Controls, Office of Price Administration, 1947. 246 p. (Historical Reports on War Administration)

3761 U. S. War Manpower Commission.
THE WAR MANPOWER COMMISSION IN INDIANA, 1943-1945. Indianapolis, 1946. 96 p.

3762 Walton, Francis.
MIRACLE OF WORLD WAR II: HOW AMERICAN INDUSTRY MADE VICTORY POSSIBLE. New York, Macmillan, 1956. 575 p.

3763 Walton, Frank L.
THREAD OF VICTORY: THE CONVERSION AND CONSERVATION OF TEXTILES, CLOTHING AND LEATHER FOR THE WORLD'S BIGGEST WAR PROGRAM. New York, Fairchild, 1945. 272 p.

3764 Wilcox, Walter W.
THE FARMER IN THE SECOND WORLD WAR. Ames, Iowa State College Press, 1947. 410 p.

3765 Wilson, Earl B.
SUGAR AND ITS WARTIME CONTROLS, 1941-1947. New York, 1948. 4 v. (1404 p.)

3766 Wiltse, Charles M.
LEAD AND ZINC POLICIES OF THE WAR PRODUCTION BOARD AND PREDECESSOR AGENCIES, MAY 1940 TO MARCH 1944. Washington, 1946. 130 p. (Historical Reports on War Administration: War Production Board. Special Study)

3767 Woodbury, David O.
BATTLEFRONTS OF INDUSTRY: WESTINGHOUSE IN WORLD WAR II. New York, Wiley, 1948. 342 p.

3768 Worsley, Thomas B.
WARTIME ECONOMIC STABILIZATION AND THE EFFICIENCY OF GOVERNMENT PROCUREMENT: A CRITICAL ANALYSIS OF CERTAIN EXPERIENCES OF THE UNITED STATES IN WORLD WAR II. Washington, National Security Resources Board, 1949. 422 p.

E. OTHER COUNTRIES

3769 Chamberlin, William C.
ECONOMIC DEVELOPMENT OF ICELAND THROUGH WORLD WAR II. New York, Columbia University Press, 1947. 141 p.

3770 Egoroff, Pavel P.
ARGENTINA'S AGRICULTURAL EXPORTS DURING WORLD WAR II. Stanford, Calif., Food Research Institute, Stanford University, 1945. 52 p. (War-Peace Pamphlets)

3771 Rosen, Josef.
WARTIME FOOD DEVELOPMENTS IN SWITZERLAND. Stanford, Calif., Food Research Institute, Stanford University, 1947. 104 p. (War-Peace Pamphlets)

VI. SOCIAL IMPACT OF THE WAR

A. PRISONER OF WAR CAMPS; CONCENTRATION CAMPS, RELOCATION CAMPS; ATROCITIES, "THE FINAL SOLUTION"; ESCAPE ACCOUNTS (see also VIII)

1. General

3772 Cohen, Bernard M., and Maurice Z. Cooper.
A FOLLOW-UP STUDY OF WORLD WAR II PRISONERS OF WAR. Washington, U.S. Government Printing Office, 1954. 81 p. (VA Medical Monograph)

3773 Cohen, Elie A.
HUMAN BEHAVIOR IN THE CONCENTRATION CAMP. Translated from Dutch by M. H. Braaksma. New York, Norton, 1953. 295 p.

Other edition:
London, Cape, 1954.

3774 Georgetown University, Washington, D.C. School of Foreign Service. Institute of World Policy.
PRISONERS OF WAR. Washington, 1948. 98 p.

3775 Mason, Walter W.
PRISONERS OF WAR. Wellington, War History Branch, Dept. of Internal Affairs, 1954. 546 p. (Official History of New Zealand in the Second World War, 1939-45)

2. Europe

a. General

3776 Burney, Christopher.
THE DUNGEON DEMOCRACY. London and Toronto, Heinemann, 1945. 100 p.

Other edition:
New York, Duell, Sloan and Pearce, 1946. 164 p.

3777 The Daily Mail. London.
LEST WE FORGET: THE HORRORS OF NAZI CONCENTRATION CAMPS REVEALED FOR ALL TIME IN THE MOST TERRIBLE PHOTOGRAPHS EVER PUBLISHED. London, Associated Newspapers, 1945. 79 p.

3778 Hajsman, Jan.
THE BROWN BEAST: THE CONCENTRATION CAMP, EUROPE UNDER THE RULE OF HITLER. Translated by L. H. Vydra and M. H. Levine. Prague, Orbis, 1948. 212 p.

3779 International Tracing Service.
CATALOGUE OF CAMPS AND PRISONS IN GERMANY AND GERMAN-OCCUPIED TERRITORIES, SEPTEMBER 1, 1939-MAY 8, 1945. Prepared by International Tracing Service, Records Branch, Documents Intelligence Section. Arolsen, Germany, 1949-50. 2 v.

3780 Kogon, Eugen.
THE THEORY AND PRACTICE OF HELL: THE GERMAN CONCENTRATION CAMPS AND THE SYSTEM BEHIND THEM. Translated by Heinz Norden. London, Secker and Warburg; New York, Farrar and Straus, 1950. 307 p.

b. Atrocities, "The Final Solution"

3781 Adler, Marta
MY LIFE WITH THE GIPSIES. London, Souvenir Press, 1960. 204 p.

3782 Allied Forces. 21st Army Group.
REPORT ON ATROCITIES COMMITTED BY THE GERMANS AGAINST THE CIVILIAN POPULATION OF BELGIUM. n.p., Headquarters 21 Army Group, 1945. 72 p.

3783 American Jewish Conference.
NAZI GERMANY'S WAR AGAINST THE JEWS. New York, American Jewish Conference, 1947. 857 p.

3784 Bar-Adon, Dorothy R.
SEVEN WHO FELL. Tel-Aviv, Lion the Printer for the Zionist Organization Youth Dept., 1947. 198 p.

3785 Berkowitz, Sarah B.
WHERE ARE MY BROTHERS? Foreword by Solomon Z. Ferziger. New York, Helios Books, 1965. 127 p.

3786 Board of Deputies of British Jews.
THE JEWS IN EUROPE, THEIR MARTYRDOM AND THEIR FUTURE. London, 1945. 64 p.

3787 Braham, Randolph L. (ed.).
THE DESTRUCTION OF HUNGARIAN JEWRY: A DOCUMENTARY ACCOUNT. New York, Pro Arte for World Federation of Hungarian Jews, 1963. 2 v. (969 p.)

3788 Brand, Joel.
DESPERATE MISSION: JOEL BRAND'S STORY AS TOLD BY ALEX WEISSBERG. Translated from the German by Constantine FitzGibbon and Andrew Foster-Milliar. New York, Criterion Books, 1958. 310 p.

Other editions:
ADVOCATE FOR THE DEAD. London, Deutsch, 1958. 255 p.

London, Landsborough, 1959. 190 p. (Four Square Books)

3789 Burgess, Alan.
SEVEN MEN AT DAYBREAK. London, Evans; New York, Dutton, 1960. 231 p.

Other edition:
London, Pan, 1962. 234 p.

3790 Central Commission for Investigation of German Crimes in Poland.
GERMAN CRIMES IN POLAND. London, The Reader, 1946. 276 p.

3791 Clarke, Comer.
EICHMANN: THE MAN AND HIS CRIMES. New York, Ballantine, 1960. 153 p. (Ballantine Books)

3792 Council of Polish Political Parties.
POLAND ACCUSES: AN INDICTMENT OF THE MAJOR GERMAN WAR CRIMINALS. London, 1946. 58 p.

3793	THE CRIME OF KATYN: FACTS AND DOCUMENTS. Foreword by General Wladyslaw Anders. London, Polish Cultural Foundation, 1965. 303 p.	3806	Jerusalem. Yad va-shem. BLACKBOOK OF LOCALITIES WHOSE JEWISH POPULATION WAS EXTERMINATED BY THE NAZIS. Jerusalem, 1965. 439 p.
3794	Czechoslovak Republic. Ministerstvo Zahranicnich Veci. HEROES AND VICTIMS. Preface by Jan Masaryk. London, Information Service, Czechoslovak Ministry of Foreign Affairs, 1945. 158 p.	3807	Jewish Black Book Committee. THE BLACK BOOK: THE NAZI CRIME AGAINST THE JEWISH PEOPLE. New York, Duell, Sloan and Pearce, 1946. 560 p.
3795	Dangerfield, Elma. BEYOND THE URALS. Preface by Rebecca West. London, British League for European Freedom, 1946. 94 p.	3808	Kinnaird, Clark. THIS MUST NOT HAPPEN AGAIN! THE BLACK BOOK OF FASCIST HORROR. New York, Distributors: Howell, Soskin, 1945. 157 p. (Pilot Press Book)
3796	Davies, Raymond A. ODYSSEY THROUGH HELL. New York, Fischer, 1946. 235 p.	3809	Král, Václav (ed.). LESSON FROM HISTORY: DOCUMENTS CONCERNING NAZI POLICIES FOR GERMANIZATION AND EXTERMINATION IN CZECHOSLOVAKIA. Translated by P. Eisler and K. Rotter. Prague, Orbis, 1961. 168 p.
3797	Donovan, John. EICHMANN, MAN OF SLAUGHTER. New York, Avon Book Division, Hearst Corp., 1960. 100 p.	3810	Kulkielko, Renya. ESCAPE FROM THE PIT. New York, Sharon Books, 1947. 189 p.
3798	Ehrenburg, Il'ia G. WE COME AS JUDGES. London, Soviet War News, 1945. 63 p.	3811	Latviešu Tautas Palidziba. THESE NAMES ACCUSE: NOMINAL LIST OF LATVIANS DEPORTED TO SOVIET RUSSIA IN 1940-41. Stockholm, Latvian National Fund in the Scandinavian Countries, 1951. 547 p.
3799	EXTERMINATION AND RESISTANCE: HISTORICAL RECORDS AND SOURCE MATERIAL. Edited by Zui Szner. Haifa, Ghetto Fighters' House, 1958. 1 vol. published.	3812	Lerner, Adolf R. THE MARCH OF EVIL: A HISTORY OF THE RISE AND FALL OF THE FASCIST EVIL. Foreword by James Sheldon and former Ambassador to Germany Hon. James W. Gerard. New York, F.F.F. Publishers, 1945. 79 p.
3800	Friedman, Philip. THE JEWISH GHETTOS OF THE NAZI ERA. New York, Conference on Jewish Relations, 1954. 88 p.	3813	Lestschinsky, Jacob. BALANCE SHEET OF EXTERMINATION. New York, Office of Jewish Information, 1946. 2 v. (Jewish Affairs)
3801	Friedmann, Tuvyah. THE HUNTER. Edited and translated by David G. Gross. Garden City, N.Y., Doubleday, 1961. 286 p.	3814	Lestschinsky, Jacob. CRISIS, CATASTROPHE AND SURVIVAL: A JEWISH BALANCE SHEET 1914-1948. New York, Institute of Jewish Affairs of the World Jewish Congress, 1948. 108 p.
3802	Goldstein, Bernard. THE STARS BEAR WITNESS. Translated and edited by Leonard Shatzkin. New York, Viking Press, 1949. 295 p. Other editions: London, Gollancz, 1950. FIVE YEARS IN THE WARSAW GHETTO. Garden City, N.Y., Doubleday, 1961. 275 p. (Dolphin Books)	3815	Lévai, Jeno (comp.). BLACK BOOK ON THE MARTYRDOM OF HUNGARIAN JEWRY. Edited by L. P. Davis. Zurich, Central European Times Publishing Co., 1948. 475 p.
3803	Hilberg, Raul. THE DESTRUCTION OF THE EUROPEAN JEWS. Chicago, Quadrangle Books; London, Allen, 1961. 788 p.	3816	Levy, Alan. WANTED: NAZI CRIMINALS AT LARGE. New York, Berkley Publishing Corp., 1962. 175 p. (Berkley Medallion Book)
3804	Hutak, Jakub B. WITH BLOOD AND WITH IRON: THE LIDICE STORY. London, Hale, 1957. 160 p. Other edition: London, Hamilton, 1958. 160 p. (Panther Books)	3817	Mackiewicz, Joseph. THE KATYN WOOD MURDERS. Foreword by Arthur B. Lane. London, Hollis and Carter, 1951. 252 p.
3805	Jaworski, Leon. AFTER FIFTEEN YEARS. Houston, Gulf Publishing Co., 1961. 154 p.	3818	Meier, Maurice. REFUGE. Translated by John W. Kurtz. New York, Norton, 1962. 241 p.

3819 Musmanno, Michael A.
THE EICHMANN KOMMANDOS. Philadelphia, Macrae Smith, 1961. 268 p.

3820 Nikitin, M. N., and P. I. Vagin.
THE CRIMES OF THE GERMAN FASCISTS IN THE LENINGRAD REGION: MATERIALS AND DOCUMENTS. London and New York, Hutchinson, 1946. 128 p.

3821 Paneth, Philip.
EICHMANN: TECHNICIAN OF DEATH. New York, Speller, 1960. 239 p.

3822 * Paris, Edmond.
GENOCIDE IN SATELLITE CROATIA, 1941-1945: A RECORD OF RACIAL AND RELIGIOUS PERSECUTIONS AND MASSACRES. Translated from French by Lois Perkins. Chicago, American Institute for Balkan Affairs, 1962. 306 p.

3823 Poland. Committee of Enquiry into the Question of the Polish Prisoners of War from the 1939 Campaign, Missing in the U.S.S.R.
FACTS AND DOCUMENTS CONCERNING POLISH PRISONERS OF WAR CAPTURED BY THE U.S.S.R. DURING THE 1939 CAMPAIGN. n.p., 1946. 454 p.

SUPPLEMENTARY REPORT OF FACTS AND DOCUMENTS CONCERNING THE KATYN MASSACRE. n.p., 1947. 70 l.

3824 Poliakov, Léon.
HARVEST OF HATE: THE NAZI PROGRAM FOR THE DESTRUCTION OF THE JEWS OF EUROPE. Foreword by Reinhold Niebuhr. Suracuse, Syracuse University Press, 1954. 338 p.

3825 Poliakov, Léon, and Jacques Sabrillo.
JEWS UNDER THE ITALIAN OCCUPATION. Paris, Editions du Centre, 1955. 207 p.

3826 Reitlinger, Gerald.
THE FINAL SOLUTION: THE ATTEMPT TO EXTERMINATE THE JEWS OF EUROPE, 1939-1945. London, Vallentine, Mitchell; New York, Beechhurst Press, 1953. 622 p.

3827 Reynolds, Quentin J., Ephraim Katz, and Zwy Aldouby.
MINISTER OF DEATH: THE ADOLF EICHMANN STORY. London, Cassell; New York, Viking, 1961. 246 p.

3828 Ringelblum, Emanuel.
NOTES FROM THE WARSAW GHETTO: THE JOURNAL OF EMANUEL RINGELBLUM. Edited and translated by Jacob Sloan. New York, McGraw-Hill, 1958. 369 p.

3829 Rohatyn Association of Israel.
THE ROHATYN JEWISH COMMUNITY: A TOWN THAT PERISHED. n.p., 1962. 362 p.

3830 Rudnicki, Adolf (ed.).
LEST WE FORGET. Warsaw, Polonia Foreign Languages Publishing House, 1955. 170 p.

3831 Russell, Edward F. L. Russell, 2d baron.
THE SCOURGE OF THE SWASTIKA: A SHORT HISTORY OF NAZI WAR CRIMES. London, Cassell; New York, Philosophical Library, 1954. 259 p.

3832 Schwarz, Leo W.
THE ROOT AND THE BOUGH: THE EPIC OF AN ENDURING PEOPLE. New York, Rinehart, 1949. 362 p.

3833 SOVIET GOVERNMENT STATEMENTS ON NAZI ATROCITIES. London and New York, Hutchinson, 1946. 320 p.

3834 Stroop, Jürgen.
THE REPORT OF JÜRGEN STROOP, CONCERNING THE UPRISING IN THE GHETTO OF WARSAW AND THE LIQUIDATION OF THE JEWISH RESIDENTIAL AREA. Warsaw, Jewish Historical Institute, 1958. 123 p.

3835 Svābe, Arveds.
GENOCIDE IN THE BALTIC STATES. Stockholm, Latvian National Fund in the Scandinavian Countries, 1952. 50 p.

3836 Svaz Protifašistických Bojovníků.
CRIMINALS ON THE BENCH: DOCUMENTS CONCERNING CRIMES COMMITTED ON THE OCCUPIED TERRITORY OF CZECHOSLOVAKIA BY TWO HUNDRED AND THIRTY NAZI JUDGES AND PUBLIC PROSECUTORS WHO TODAY HOLD LEGAL POSTS IN WESTERN GERMANY. Prague, Orbis, 1960. 138 p.

3837 Szende, Stefan.
THE PROMISE HITLER KEPT. Translated by Edward Fitzgerald. New York, Roy; London, Gollancz, 1945. 280 p.

3838 Szoskiis, Henryk J.
NO TRAVELER RETURNS. Edited with a prologue and an epilogue by Curt Reiss. Garden City, N.Y., Doubleday, Doran, 1945. 267 p.

3839 * Tenenbaum, Joseph L., with Sheila Tenenbaum.
IN SEARCH OF A LOST PEOPLE, THE OLD AND THE NEW POLAND. New York, Beechhurst Press, 1948. 312 p.

3840 Trinka, Z'dena.
A LITTLE VILLAGE CALLED LIDICE: STORY OF THE RETURN OF THE WOMEN AND CHILDREN OF LIDICE. Foreword by Joseph Auslander. Lidgerwood, N.D., International Book Publishers, 1947. 128 p.

3841 United Nations Relief and Rehabilitation Administration. Central Tracing Bureau. Documents Intelligence.
DEATH MARCHES. MARCHES DE LA MORT. ROUTES AND DISTANCES. Washington, 1946. 3 v.

3842 Veale, Frederick J. P.
CRIMES DISCREETLY VEILED. Foreword by Lord Hankey. London, Cooper Book Co., 1958. 240 p.

Other edition:
New York, Devin-Adair, 1959.

3843 Waren, Helen.
THE BURIED ARE SCREAMING. Foreword by Bartley Crum. New York, Beechhurst Press, 1948. 186 p.

3844 Wdowinski, David.
AND WE ARE NOT SAVED. New York, Philosophical Library, 1963. 123 p.

Other edition:
London, Allen, 1964. 124 p.

3845 Wells, Leon W.
THE JANOWSKA ROAD. New York, Macmillan, 1963. 305 p.

3846 Wiesel, Eliezer.
NIGHT. Foreword by François Mauriac; translated from the French by Stella Rodway. New York, Hill and Wang, 1960. 116 p.

3847 Wighton, Charles.
EICHMANN: HIS CAREER AND CRIMES. London, Odhams Press, 1961. 287 p.

3848 Wittlin, Tadeusz.
TIME STOPPED AT 6:30. Indianapolis, Bobbs-Merrill, 1965. 317 p.

3849 A WOMAN IN BERLIN, ANONYMOUS. Introduction by C. W. Ceram (pseud.); translated from German by James Stern. New York, Harcourt, Brace, 1954. 319 p.

3850 Yugoslavia. Jugoslavenski Informacione Kiro u Londonu.
ITALIAN CRIMES IN YUGOSLAVIA. London, Yugoslav Information Office, 1945. 82 p.

3851 Zawodney, Janusz K.
DEATH IN THE FOREST: THE STORY OF THE KATYN FOREST MASSACRES. Notre Dame, Ind., University of Notre Dame Press, 1962. 235 p.

3852 Zuckerman, Isaac (ed.).
THE FIGHTING GHETTOS. Translated and edited by Meyer Barkai. Philadelphia, Lippincott, 1962. 407 p.

c. Prisoners of War and Concentration Camps; Personal Accounts

3853 Allan, James.
NO CITATION. London, Angus and Robertson, 1955. 222 p.

3854 Ambrière, Francis.
THE EXILED. Translated from French by Erik de Mauny. London, Staples, 1951. 243 p.

3855 Ambrière, Francis.
THE LONG HOLIDAY. Translated by Elaine P. Halperin. Chicago, Ziff-Davis, 1948. 249 p.

3856 Armstrong, Colin N.
LIFE WITHOUT LADIES. Christchurch, Whitcombe and Tombs, 1947. 264 p.

3857 Aslanis, Anastasios.
THE MAN OF CONFIDENCE. New York, Vantage, 1963. 236 p.

3858 Beattie, Edward W.
DIARY OF A KRIEGIE. New York, Crowell, 1946. 312 p.

3859 Becker, Hans (pseud.).
DEVIL ON MY SHOULDER. Translated from German by Kennedy McWhirter and Jeremy Potter. London, Jarrolds, 1955. 216 p.

Other edition:
London, Landsborough, 1958. 192 p. (Four Square Books)

3860 Begin, Menahem.
WHITE NIGHTS: THE STORY OF A PRISONER IN RUSSIA. Translated from Hebrew by Katie Kaplan. London, Macdonald, 1957. 240 p.

3861 Bennett, Lowell.
PARACHUTE TO BERLIN. New York, Vanguard, 1945. 252 p.

3862 Benuzzi, Felice.
NO PICNIC ON MOUNT KENYA. 2d ed. London, Kimber, 1952. 230 p.

Other edition:
New York, Dutton, 1953. 238 p.

3863 Best, Sigismund P.
THE VENLO INCIDENT. London and New York, Hutchinson, 1950. 260 p.

3864 Blackman, Michael J. D'Arcy.
BY THE HUNTER'S MOON. London, Hodder and Stoughton, 1956. 191 p.

3865 Boom, Corrie ten.
A PRISONER AND YET.... London, Christian Literature Crusade, 1954. 160 p.

3866 Burney, Christopher.
SOLITARY CONFINEMENT. Foreword by Christopher Fry. London, Clerke and Cockeran, 1952. 152 p.

Other editions:
New York, Coward-McCann, 1953. 181 p.

London, Macmillan, 1961. 172 p.

New York, St. Martin's Press, 1961. 172 p.

3867 Caminada, Jerome.
MY PURPOSE HOLDS. London, Cape, 1952. 221 p.

Other edition:
London, Harborough, 1957. 206 p. (Ace Books)

3868 Caskie, Donald C.
THE TARTAN PIMPERNEL. London, Oldbourne, 1957. 270 p.

Other edition:
London, Collins, 1960. 256 p. (Fontana Books)

3869 Castle, John (pseud.).
THE PASSWORD IS COURAGE. London, Souvenir Press, 1954. 224 p.

Other edition:
New York, Norton, 1955. 287 p.

3870 Chambers, George W.
KEITH ARGRAVES, PARATROOPER: AN ACCOUNT OF THE SERVICE OF A CHRISTIAN MEDICAL CORPSMAN IN THE U.S. ARMY PARATROOPS DURING WORLD WAR II. Nashville, Tenn., Southern Publishing Association, 1946. 157 p.

3871 Chapman, Ivan.
DETAILS ENCLOSED. Sydney, Angus and Robertson, 1958. 233 p.

3872 Chiesl, Oliver M.
CLIPPED WINGS. Dayton, Kimball, 1948. 1 v.

3873 Chutter, James B.
CAPTIVITY CAPTIVE. London, Cape, 1954. 222 p.

3874 • Clifton, George.
THE HAPPY HUNTED. Foreword by Viscount Freyberg of Wellington. London, Cassell, 1952. 392 p.

Other edition:
London, Hamilton, 1955. 190 p. (Panther Books)

3875 • Czapski, Józef.
THE INHUMAN LAND. Translated from French by Gerard Hopkins. London, Chatto and Windus, 1951. 301 p.

Other edition:
New York, Sheed and Ward, 1952.

3876 Dalderup, Leo.
THE OTHER SIDE: THE STORY OF LEO DALDERUP. As told to John Murdoch. London, Hodder and Stoughton, 1954. 256 p.

3877 De Wet, Hugh W. A. O.
THE VALLEY OF THE SHADOW. London, Hamilton, 1956. 192 p. (Panther Books)

3878 Dobran, Edward A.
P.O.W.: THE STORY OF AN AMERICAN PRISONER OF WAR DURING WORLD WAR II. New York, Exposition Press, 1953. 123 p.

3879 Donat, Alexander.
THE HOLOCAUST KINGDOM: A MEMOIR. New York, Holt, Rinehart and Winston, 1965. 361 p.

3880 Dunning, George.
WHERE BLEED THE MANY. Foreword by Lt. Gen. Sir Brian G. Horrocks. London, Elek Books, 1955. 256 p.

Other edition:
London, Hamilton, 1956. 223 p. (Panther Books)

3881 Einsiedel, Heinrich, Graf von.
I JOINED THE RUSSIANS: A CAPTURED GERMAN FLIER'S DIARY OF THE COMMUNIST TEMPTATION. New Haven, Conn., Yale University Press, 1953. 306 p.

Other edition:
THE SHADOW OF STALINGRAD: BEING THE DIARY OF A TEMPTATION. Translated by Tania Alexander. London, Wingate, 1953. 254 p.

3882 Ekart, Antoni.
VANISHED WITHOUT TRACE: THE STORY OF SEVEN YEARS IN SOVIET RUSSIA. London, Parrish, 1954. 320 p.

3883 Emmens, Robert G.
GUESTS OF THE KREMLIN. New York, Macmillan, 1949. 291 p.

3884 Evstigneev, Georgii Vasil'evich.
FLIGHT TO FREEDOM. Translated from Russian by J. L. Vegoda. Moscow, Progress Publishers, 1965. 85 p.

3885 Faramus, Anthony C.
THE FARAMUS STORY: BEING THE EXPERIENCES OF ANTHONY CHARLES FARAMUS. Presented by Frank Owen; foreword by Eddie Chapman. London, Wingate, 1954. 178 p.

3886 Fauteux, Claire.
FANTASTIC INTERLUDE. New York, Vantage Press, 1962. 132 p.

3887 Fehling, Helmut M.
ONE GREAT PRISON: THE STORY BEHIND RUSSIA'S UNRELEASED P.O.W.'S. Translated by Charles R. Joy; foreword by Konrad Adenauer and Josef Cardinal Fings. With documents and official announcements concerning German and Japanese war prisoners in the Soviet Union, compiled by Charles R. Joy. Boston, Beacon Press, 1951. 175 p.

3888 Ferguson, Ion.
DOCTOR AT WAR. London, Johnson, 1955. 223 p.

Other edition:
London, Hamilton, 1957. 160 p. (Panther Books)

3889 Fittkau, Gerhard.
MY THIRTY-THIRD YEAR: A PRIEST'S EXPERIENCE IN A RUSSIAN WORK CAMP. New York, Farrar, Straus and Cudahy. 1958. 263 p.

3900 Fučik, Julius.
NOTES FROM THE GALLOWS. Sydney, Current Book Distributors, 1950. 75 p.

3901 • Furmanski, H. R. R.
LIFE CAN BE CRUEL. New York, Vantage Press, 1960. 61 p.

3902 Gallegos, Adrian.
FROM CAPRI INTO OBLIVION. London, Hodder and Stoughton, 1960. 256 p.

3903 Gant, Roland.
HOW LIKE A WILDERNESS. London, Gollancz, 1946. 160 p.

3904　Gerstel, Jan.
　　　THE WAR FOR YOU IS OVER. Chatswood, N.S.W., Adventure Publishing Co., 1960. 301 p.

3905　Gluck, Gemma La Guardia.
　　　MY STORY. Edited by S. L. Schneiderman. New York, McKay, 1961. 116 p.

3906　Gollwitzer, Helmut.
　　　UNWILLING JOURNEY: A DIARY FROM RUSSIA. Translated by E. M. Delacour. Philadelphia, Muhlenberg Press, 1953. 316 p.

3907　Grossman, Moishe.
　　　IN THE ENCHANTED LAND: MY SEVEN YEARS IN SOVIET RUSSIA. Translated from Yiddish by I. M. Lask. Tel-Aviv, Rachel, 1960-61. 383 p.

3908　Guareschi, Giovanni.
　　　MY SECRET DIARY. Translated from Italian by Frances Frenaye. London, Gollancz, 1958. 199 p.

Other edition:
New York, Farrar, 1958. 255 p.

3909　Guest, Francis H. (James Spenser, pseud.).
　　　THE AWKWARD MARINE. London, World Distributors, 1957. 251 p. (Viking Books)

Original edition:
London, Longmans, Green, 1948.

3910 • Gwiazdowski, Alexander P.
　　　I SURVIVED HITLER'S HELL. Boston, Meador Publishing Co., 1954. 182 p.

3911　Hadow, Maria.
　　　PAYING GUEST IN SIBERIA. London, Harvill Press, 1959. 189 p.

3912　Halley, David.
　　　WE MISSED THE BOAT. Glasgow and London, Hodge, 1946. 236 p.

3913　Hart, Kitty.
　　　I AM ALIVE. London and New York, Abelard-Schuman, 1962. 159 p.

3914 • Hecimovic, Joseph.
　　　IN TITO'S DEATH MARCHES AND EXTERMINATION CAMPS. Translated and edited by John Prcela. New York, Carlton, 1962. 209 p. (Reflection Book)

3915　Heimler, Eugene.
　　　NIGHT OF THE MIST. Translated from Hungarian by Andre Ungar. New York, Vanguard Press, 1959. 191 p.

3916　Henderson, James H.
　　　GUNNER INGLORIOUS, "NO HAUGHTY FEAT OF ARMS I TELL." Wellington, Tombs, 1945. 213 p.

3917　Hess, Rudolf.
　　　PRISONER OF PEACE. Translated from German of Ilse Hess by Meyrick Booth; edited by Georg Pele. London, Britons Publishing Co., 1954. 151 p.

3918　James, David.
　　　A PRISONER'S PROGRESS. Edinburgh, Blackwood, 1947. 164 p.

Other editions:
London, Hollis and Carter, 1954. 176 p.

　　　ESCAPER'S PROGRESS. New York, Norton, 1955. 205 p.

London, Brown, Watson, 1958. 159 p. (Digit Books)

3919　Janis, Charles G.
　　　BARBED BOREDOM: A SOUVENIR BOOK OF STALAG LUFT IV. Irvington, N.J., 1950. 109 p.

3920　Janta, Alexander.
　　　BOUND WITH TWO CHAINS. New York, Roy, 1945. 234 p.

3921　Jeanty, Ninette H.
　　　CERTIFIED SANE. Translated from French by R. C. Roberts. London, Sheppard Press, 1948. 243 p.

3922　Jones, Ewart C.
　　　GERMANS UNDER MY BED. London, Barker, 1957. 222 p.

Other edition:
London, Barker, 1959. 192 p. (Dragon Books)

3923　Jones, W. A.
　　　PRISONER OF THE KORMORAN. Told by W. A. Jones; written by James Taylor. London, Hamilton, 1955. 192 p. (Panther Books)

Original edition:
London, Harrap, 1945.

3924　Kelly, Frank.
　　　PRIVATE KELLY, BY HIMSELF. London, Evans, 1954. 224 p.

3925　Kennard, Coleridge.
　　　GESTAPO: FRANCE, 1943-1945. London, Richards, 1947. 206 p.

3926　Klein, Gerda W.
　　　ALL BUT MY LIFE. New York, Hill and Wang, 1957. 246 p.

3927 • Knapp, Stefan.
　　　THE SQUARE SUN. London, Museum Press, 1956. 172 p.

3928　Koestler, Arthur.
　　　SCUM OF THE EARTH. New ed. London, Collins with Hamish Hamilton, 1955. 255 p.

3929 Koriakov, Mikhail M.
I'LL NEVER GO BACK: A RED ARMY OFFICER TALKS. Translated from Russian by Nicolas Wreden. New York, Dutton, 1948. 248 p.

3930 Kospoth, B. J.
RED WINS. London, Macdonald, 1946. 220 p.

3931 Krasnov, Nikolai N.
THE HIDDEN RUSSIA: MY TEN YEARS AS A SLAVE LABORER. New York, Holt, 1960. 341 p.

3932 Larsen, Otto M.
NIGHTMARE OF THE INNOCENTS. London, Melrose, 1955. 240 p.

Other edition:
New York, Philosophical Library, 1957. 240 p.

3933 Lazar, Albert O. (pseud.).
INNOCENTS CONDEMNED TO DEATH: CHRONICLES OF SURVIVAL. New York, William-Frederick Press, 1961. 97 p.

3934 Leeming, John F.
ALWAYS TO-MORROW. London, Harrap, 1951. 188 p.

Other edition:
London, Hamilton, 1955. 190 p. (Panther Books)

3935 Leeming, John F.
THE NATIVES ARE FRIENDLY. New York, Dutton, 1952. 222 p.

3936 Legendre, Gertrude S.
THE SANDS CEASED TO RUN. New York, William-Frederick Press, 1947. 245 p.

3937 Levi, Primo.
THE REAWAKENING (LA TREGUA): A LIBERATED PRISONER'S LONG MARCH HOME THROUGH EAST EUROPE. Translated from Italian by Stuart Woolf. Boston, Little, Brown, 1965. 222 p. (Atlantic Monthly Press Book)

Other edition:
THE TRUCE. London, Bodley Head, 1965.

3938 Lias, Godfrey.
I SURVIVED. London, Evans Bros., 1954. 223 p.

Other editions:
New York, Day, 1954. 255 p.

London, Harborough, 1957. 159 p. (Ace Books)

3939 Lusseyran, Jacques.
AND THERE WAS LIGHT. Translated from French by Elizabeth R. Cameron. Boston, Little, Brown, 1963. 312 p.

Other edition:
London, Heinemann, 1964. 244 p.

3940 Lyle-Smythe, Alan (Alan Caillon, pseud.).
THE WORLD IS SIX FEET SQUARE. London, Davies, 1954. 214 p.

Other editions:
New York, Norton, 1955.

London, Hamilton, 1956. 186 p. (Panther Books)

3941 Magyar Harcosok Bajtársi Közössége. Hadifogolyszolgálat.
WHITE BOOK, CONCERNING THE STATUS OF HUNGARIAN PRISONERS OF WAR ILLEGALLY DETAINED BY THE SOVIET UNION AND OF HUNGARIAN CIVILIANS FORCEFULLY DEPORTED BY SOVIET AUTHORITIES. Published by the P.W. Service of Hungarian Veterans in cooperation with the weekly, HUNGARIA. Munich, Edition Hungaria, 1951. 116 p.

3942 Maurel, Micheline.
AN ORDINARY CAMP. Preface by François Mauriac; translated from French by Margaret S. Summers. New York, Simon and Schuster. 1958. 141 p.

3943 Mendès-France, Pierre.
THE PURSUIT OF FREEDOM. London and New York, Longmans, Green, 1956. 256 p.

3944 Millar, George R.
HORNED PIGEON. Garden City, N.Y., Doubleday, 1946. 434 p.

Other edition:
London, Heinemann, 1946. 443 p.

3945 Moen, Petter.
DIARY. Translated from Norwegian by Kate Austin-Lund. London, Faber and Faber, 1951. 146 p.

Other edition:
Translated by Bjorn Koefoed. New York, Creative Age Press, 1951. 176 p.

3946 Morgan, Guy.
ONLY GHOSTS CAN LIVE. London, Lockwood, 1945. 168 p.

Other editions:
London, Brown, Watson, 1957. 160 p. (Digit Books)

P.O.W. New York, Whittlesey House, McGraw-Hill, 1945. 226 p.

3947 Nabarro, Derrick.
WAIT FOR THE DAWN. London, Cassell, 1952. 207 p.

3948 Nansen, Odd.
FROM DAY TO DAY. Translated by Katherine John. New York, Putnam, 1949. 485 p.

3949 Newcomb, Alan H.
VACATION WITH PAY: BEING AN ACCOUNT OF MY STAY AT THE GERMAN REST CAMP FOR TIRED ALLIED AIRMEN AT BEAUTIFUL BARTH-ON-THE-BALTIC. Haverhill, Mass., Destiny Publishers, 1947. 198 p.

3950 Nork, Karl.
HELL IN SIBERIA. Translated from German by Eleanor Brockett. London, Hale, 1957. 222 p.

Other edition:
London, Spencer, 1959. 157 p. (Badger Books)

3951 Oliphant, Sir Lancelot.
AN AMBASSADOR IN BONDS. London, Putnam, 1946. 227 p.

3952 Pawlowicz, Sala K., with Kevin Klose.
I WILL SURVIVE. New York, Norton, 1962. 286 p.

3953 Percival, Winifred D.
NOT ONLY MUSIC, SIGNORA! Foreword by T. Edmund Harvey. Altrincham, Eng., Sherratt, 1947. 207 p.

3954 Perrin, Henri.
PRIEST-WORKMAN IN GERMANY. Translated by Rosemary Sheed. London, Sheed and Ward, 1947. 230 p.

3955 Philpot, Oliver L. S.
STOLEN JOURNEY. London, Hodder and Stoughton, 1950. 412 p.

Other editions:
New York, Dutton, 1952. 448 p.

London, Transworld, 1954. 440 p. (Corgi Books)

3956 Piliar, Iurii E.
IT ALL REALLY HAPPENED. Translated from Russian by Percy Ludwick. Moscow, Foreign Languages Publishing House, 1960. 187 p.

3957 Portway, Christopher.
JOURNEY TO DANA. London, Kimber, 1955. 248 p.

3958 Pryce, J. E.
HEELS IN LINE. London, Barker, 1958. 222 p.

Other edition:
London, Hamilton, 1960. 191 p. (Panther Books)

3959 Pury, Roland de.
JOURNAL FROM MY CELL. Translated by Barrows Musley; introduced by Paul Green. London and New York, Harper, 1946. 140 p.

3960 Raven, Hélène J.
WITHOUT FRONTIERS. London, Hutchinson, 1960. 221 p.

3961 Rawicz, Slavomir.
THE LONG WALK: A GAMBLE FOR LIFE. As told to Ronald Downing. New York, Harper; London, Constable, 1956. 239 p.

3962 Reiner, Ella L.
PRISONERS OF FEAR. London, Gollancz, 1948. 208 p.

3963 Reiners, Wilfred O.
SOVIET INDOCTRINATION OF GERMAN WAR PRISONERS, 1941-56. Cambridge, Center for International Studies, Massachusetts Institute of Technology, 1959. 80 l.

3964 Renault-Roulier, Gilbert (Rémy, pseud.).
TEN STEPS TO HOPE. Translated from French by Len Ortzen. London, Barker, 1960. 159 p.

3965 Rittenhouse, William H.
GOD'S P.O.W. 2d ed. New York, Greenwich Book Publishers, 1957. 91 p.

3966 Rofe, Cyril.
AGAINST THE WIND. London, Hodder and Stoughton, 1956. 319 p.

3967 Romilly, Giles, and Michael Alexander.
THE PRIVILEGED NIGHTMARE. London, Weidenfeld and Nicolson, 1954. 246 p.

3968 Roosenburg, Henriette.
THE WALLS CAME TUMBLING DOWN. New York, Viking Press, 1959. 248 p.

Other editions:
London, Secker, 1957. 222 p.

London, Pan, 1959. 185 p.

3969 Rosenfeld, Else R. B.
THE FOUR LIVES OF ELSBETH ROSENFELD, AS TOLD BY HER TO THE B.B.C. Foreword by James Parkes. London, Gollancz, 1964. 158 p.

3970 Rousset, David.
THE OTHER KINGDOM. Translated and with an introduction by Ramon Guthrie. New York, Reynal and Hitchcock, 1947. 173 p.

3971 • Rousset, David.
A WORLD APART. London, Secker and Warburg, 1951. 112 p.

3972 Sabey, Ian.
STALAG SCRAPBOOK. Melbourne, Cheshire, 1947. 136 p.

3973 Salvesen, Sylvia.
FORGIVE, BUT DO NOT FORGET. Translated from the Norwegian by Evelyn Ramsden; revised and edited by Lord Russell of Liverpool. London, Hutchinson, 1958. 234 p.

3974 Salwey, Ruth.
TWENTY-SEVEN STEPS OF HUMILIATION. Wimbledon, Eng., Ridgway Courcy, 1946. 101 p.

3975 Schrire, I.
STALAG DOCTOR. London, Wingate, 1956. 209 p.

Other edition:
London, Brown, Watson, 1958. 160 p. (Digit Books)

3976 Shrimpton, John A.
SOLDIERS IN BONDAGE. Maroubra, Messenger Print, 194-. 64 p.

3977 Simmons, Kenneth W.
KRIEGIE. New York, Nelson, 1960. 256 p.

3978   Sonnabend, H.
    ABOUT MYSELF AND OTHERS. Johannesburg, Eagle Press, 1951. 228 p.

3979   Soupault, Philippe.
    AGE OF ASSASSINS, THE STORY OF PRISONER NO. 1234. Translated from the French by Hannah Josephson. New York, Knopf, 1946. 315 p.

3980   Southon, Alfred.
    ALPINE PARTISAN. Edited by Vivian Milroy. London, Hammond and Hammond, 1957. 222 p.

    Other edition:
    London, Transworld, 1958. (Corgi Books)

3981   Spier, Eugen.
    THE PROTECTING POWER. London, Skeffington, 1951. 252 p.

3982   Stark, Flora.
    AN ITALIAN DIARY. Foreword by Freya Stark. London, Murray, 1945. 50 p.

3983   Stypulkowski, Zbigniew.
    INVITATION TO MOSCOW. Preface by H. R. Trevor-Roper. London, Thames and Hudson, 1951. 359 p.

    Other edition:
    New York, Walker, 1962.

3984   Tailliez, Philippe.
    AQUARIUS. Paris, Editions France-Empire, 1961. 366 p.

3985   Taylor, Geoff.
    PIECE OF CAKE. London, Davies, 1956. 273 p.

    Other edition:
    London, Odhams, 1957. 320 p. (Beacon Books)

3986   Thompson, Douglas W.
    CAPTIVES TO FREEDOM. London, Epworth Press, 1955. 188 p.

3987   Thomson, R. H.
    CAPTIVE KIWI. Christchurch, Whitcombe and Tombs, 1964. 196 p.

3988   Thorne, Leon.
    OUT OF THE ASHES: THE STORY OF A SURVIVOR. New York, Rosebern Press, 1961. 203 p.

3989   Turner, John F.
    PRISONER AT LARGE. London, Staples Press, 1957. 171 p.

    Other edition:
    London, Hamilton, 1958. 160 p. (Panther Books)

3990   Unsdorfer, S. B.
    THE YELLOW STAR. New York, Yoseloff, 1961. 205 p.

3991   Vaidya, Suresh.
    AN ENGLISH PRISON. Madras, Teachers' Publishing House, 1953. 207 p.

3992   Vincent, Adrian.
    THE LONG ROAD HOME. London, Allen and Unwin, 1956. 208 p.

    Other edition:
    London, World, 1957. 190 p. (Viking Books)

3993   Vrba, Rudolf, and Alan Bestic.
    I CANNOT FORGIVE. New York, Grove Press, 1964. 281 p.

3994   Ward, Edward.
    GIVE ME AIR. London, Lane, 1946. 253 p.

3995   Weiss, Reska.
    JOURNEY THROUGH HELL: A WOMAN'S ACCOUNT OF HER EXPERIENCES AT THE HANDS OF THE NAZIS. London, Vallentine, Mitchell, 1961. 255 p.

3996   Wigmans, Johan H.
    TEN YEARS IN RUSSIA AND SIBERIA. Translated by Arnout de Waal. London, Darton, Longmans and Todd, 1964. 234 p.

3997   Wittlin, Tadeusz.
    A RELUCTANT TRAVELLER IN RUSSIA. Translated from the Polish by Noel E. P. Clark. New York, Rinehart, 1952. 280 p.

    Other edition:
    London, Hodge, 1952. 236 p.

3998   Yamamoto, Tomomi.
    FOUR YEARS IN HELL: I WAS A PRISONER BEHIND THE IRON CURTAIN. Tokyo, Asian, 1952. 300 p.

3999   Young, Ramsay F. (Scotty Young, pseud.).
    DESCENT INTO DANGER. Presented by Gordon Thomas. London, Wingate, 1954. 240 p.

    Other edition:
    London, Hamilton, 1955. 190 p. (Panther Books)

4000   Younger, Calton.
    NO FLIGHT FROM THE CAGE. London, Muller, 1956. 254 p.

    Other edition:
    London, World, 1957. 255 p.

4001   Zammit, Romeo M.
    THEY WILL RISE AGAIN! Ilfracombe, Stockwell, 1954. 76 p.

d. Individual Camps

4002   Bernard, Jean-Jacques.
    THE CAMP OF SLOW DEATH. Translated by Edward O. Marsh. London, Gollancz, 1945. 132 p.

4003 Buber, Margarete.
UNDER TWO DICTATORS. Translated by Edward Fitzgerald. London, Gollancz, 1949. 331 p.

4004 Collis, W. Robert, and Han Hogerzeil.
STRAIGHT ON. London, Methuen, 1947. 178 p.

4005 Eggers, Reinhold.
COLDITZ: THE GERMAN SIDE OF THE STORY. Translated and edited by Howard Gee. New York, Norton; London, Hale, 1961. 190 p.

Other edition:
London, Pan, 1963. 220 p.

4006 Friedman, Filip.
THIS WAS OSWIECIM: THE STORY OF A MURDER CAMP. Translated by J. Leftwich London, United Jewish Appeal, 1946. 84 p.

4007 Geve, Thomas.
YOUTH IN CHAINS. Jerusalem, R. Mass, 1958. 262 p.

4008 Hardman, Leslie H., with Cecily Goodman.
THE SURVIVORS: THE STORY OF THE BELSEN REMNANT. Told by Leslie H. Hardman and written by Cecily Goodman. Foreword by Rt. Hon. Lord Russell of Liverpool. London, Vallentine, Mitchell, 1958. 113 p.

4009 Hoess, Rudolf.
COMMANDANT OF AUSCHWITZ: AUTOBIOGRAPHY. Translated by Constantine FitzGibbon. Cleveland, World Publishing Company, 1960. 285 p.

4010 Lengyel, Olga.
FIVE CHIMNEYS: THE STORY OF AUSCHWITZ. Chicago, Ziff-Davis, 1947. 213 p.

Other editions:
London, Hamilton, 1959. 221 p. (Panther Books)

I SURVIVED HITLER'S OVENS. New York, Avon, 1958. 189 p.

4011 Levi, Primo.
IF THIS IS A MAN. Translated from the Italian by Stuart Woolf. New York, Orion Press, 1959. 205 p.

Other editions:
London, Orion Press, 1961. 205 p.

London, Bodley Head, 1966. 206 p.

SURVIVAL IN AUSCHWITZ: THE NAZI ASSAULT ON HUMANITY. New York, Collier, 1966. 157 p.

4012 Ludden, Robert W.
BARBED WIRE INTERLUDE: A SOUVENIR OF KRIEGSGEFANGENENLAGER DER LUFTWAFFE NR. 4, DEUTSCHLAND, 1944. Baltimore, Photo-offset by the National Advertising Co., 1945. 77 p.

4013 • Newman, Judith S.
IN THE HELL OF AUSCHWITZ: THE WARTIME MEMOIRS OF JUDITH STERNBERG NEWMAN. New York, Exposition Press, 1964. 136 p.

4014 Niescior, Leon.
I SURVIVED HELL ON EARTH. n.p., 1956. 179 p.

4015 Nyiszli, Miklos.
AUSCHWITZ: A DOCTOR'S EYEWITNESS ACCOUNT. Translated by Tibere Kremer and Richard Seaver; foreword by Bruno Bettelheim. New York, Fell, 1960. 222 p.

4016 • Perl, Gisella.
I WAS A DOCTOR IN AUSCHWITZ. New York, International Universities Press, 1948. 189 p.

4017 Sington, Derrick.
BELSEN UNCOVERED. London, Duckworth, 1946. 208 p.

4018 Szalet, Leon.
EXPERIMENT "E": A REPORT FROM AN EXTERMINATION LABORATORY. Translated by Catharine B. Williams. New York, Didier, 1945. 284 p.

4019 Szmaglewska, Seweryne.
SMOKE OVER BIRKENAU. Translated by Indwiga Rynas. New York, Holt, 1947. 386 p.

4020 Vietor, John A.
TIME OUT: AMERICAN AIRMEN AT STALAG LUFT I. New York, Smith, 1951. 192 p.

4021 Weinstock, Eugene.
BEYOND THE LAST PATH. Foreword by Emil Lengyel. New York, Boni and Gaer, 1947. 281 p.

4022 Wood, Jerry E. R. (ed.).
DETOUR: THE STORY OF OFLAG IV C. London, Falcon Press, 1946. 308 p.

4023 Zywulska, Krystyna.
I CAME BACK. London, Dobson; New York, Roy, 1951. 246 p.

e. Escape Accounts

4024 Arkwright, Albert S. B.
RETURN JOURNEY: ESCAPE FROM OFLAG VI B. London, Seeley, 1948. 239 p.

4025 Aston, Walter H.
...NOR IRON BARS A CAGE. London, Macmillan, 1946. 160 p.

Other edition:
London, Brown, Watson, 1958. 160 p. (Digit Books)

4026 Barlow, Randle.
HIT OR MISS: BEING THE ADVENTURES OF DRIVER RANDLE BARLOW. As told by Francis S. Jones. London, Wingate, 1954. 223 p.

Other edition:
London, Brown, 1958. 160 p. (Digit Books)

4027 Bauer, Josef M.
AS FAR AS MY FEET WILL CARRY ME. Translated by Lawrence P. R. Wilson. New York, Random House, 1957. 347 p.

Other editions:
London, Deutsch, 1957. 254 p.

London, Landsborough, 1959. 223 p. (Four Square Books)

4028 Bellegarde, Carlo de.
AFRICAN ESCAPE. Translated from Italian by Muriel Currey; foreword by Lt. Col. R. W. Godson. London, Kimpton, 1957. 203 p.

4029 Billany, Dan, with David Dowie.
THE CAGE. London, Longmans, 1949. 189 p.

Other edition:
London, Hamilton, 1964. 189 p. (Panther Books)

4030 Brickhill, Paul.
ESCAPE OR DIE: AUTHENTIC STORIES OF THE R. A. F. ESCAPING SOCIETY. Commentary by H. E. Bates; foreword by Sir Basil Embry. London, Evans; New York, Norton, 1952. 248 p.

Other edition:
London, Evans, 1963. 192 p.

4031 Brickhill, Paul, and Conrad Norton.
ESCAPE TO DANGER. London, Faber, 1946. 341 p.

4032 Brickhill, Paul.
THE GREAT ESCAPE. New York, Norton, 1950. 264 p.

Other editions:
London, Faber and Faber, 1951. 263 p.

London, Faber, 1956. 168 p.

Harmondsworth, Penguin in association with Faber, 1957. 224 p.

London, Faber, 1963. 255 p.

4033 Brilhac, Jean.
THE ROAD TO LIBERTY: THE STORY OF 186 MEN WHO ESCAPED. London, Davies, 1945. 215 p.

4034 Broad, John E.
POOR PEOPLE, POOR US. Wellington, N. Z., Hitt, Tombs, 1946. 277 p.

4035 Burt, Kendal, and James Leasor.
THE ONE THAT GOT AWAY. London, Collins, 1956. 255 p.

Other editions:
New York, Random House, 1957. 292 p.

London, Collins, 1959. 256 p. (Fontana Books)

4036 Cardigan, Chandos S. C. Brudenell-Bruce, earl of.
I WALKED ALONE. London, Routledge and Paul, 1950. 206 p.

4037 Chrisp, John.
THE TUNNELLERS OF SANDBORSTAL. London, Hale, 1959. 172 p.

Other edition:
ESCAPE. London, Hamilton, 1960. 157 p. (Panther Books)

4038 Churchill, Peter.
THE SPIRIT IN THE CAGE. London, Hodder and Stoughton, 1954. 251 p.

Other editions:
New York, Putnam, 1955. 312 p.

London, Transworld, 1956. 320 p. (Corgi Books)

4039 Crawley, Aidan.
ESCAPE FROM GERMANY: A HISTORY OF R. A. F. ESCAPES DURING THE WAR. London, Collins, 1956. 318 p.

Other editions:
New York, Simon and Schuster, 1956. 291 p.

London, Collins, 1958. 255 p. (Fontana Books)

4040 Deane-Drummond, Anthony.
RETURN TICKET. London, Collins, 1953. 256 p.

Other edition:
Philadelphia, Lippincott, 1954.

4041 Delmayne, Anthony.
SAHARA DESERT ESCAPE. London, Jarrolds, 1958. 255 p.

4042 Derry, Sam.
THE ROME ESCAPE LINE: THE STORY OF THE BRITISH ORGANIZATION IN ROME FOR ASSISTING ESCAPED PRISONERS-OF-WAR, 1943-44. New York, Norton; London, Harrap, 1960. 239 p.

Other edition:
London, New English Library, 1962. 220 p. (Ace Books)

4043 Devigny, Andre.
ESCAPE FROM MONTLUC. Translated from the French by P. Green. London, Dobson, 1957. 223 p.

Other editions:
A MAN ESCAPED. New York, Norton, 1957. 207 p.

London, Landsborough, 1958. 191 p. (Four Square Books)

4044 Dunbar, John.
ESCAPE THROUGH THE PYRENEES. New York, Norton, 1955. 176 p.

Other edition:
London, Davis, 1956. 171 p.

4045 Duncan, Michael.
UNDERGROUND FROM POSEN. Foreword by Brigadier the Hon. Nigel Somerset. London, Kimber, 1954. 192 p.

Other edition:
1961. 158 p.

4046 Durnford, John.
BRANCH LINE TO BURMA. Foreword by Admiral of the Fleet, the Earl Mountbatten of Burma. London, Macdonald, 1958. 207 p.

Other edition:
London, World Distributors, 1959. 190 p.

4047　Embry, Sir Basil E.
　　　WINGLESS VICTORY: THE STORY OF SIR BASIL EMBRY'S ESCAPE FROM OCCUPIED FRANCE IN THE SUMMER OF 1940. Related by Anthony Richardson, London, Odhams Press, 1950. 256 p.

4048　Evans, Alfred J.
　　　ESCAPE AND LIBERATION, 1940-45. London, Hodder, 1945. 238 p.

4049　Fancy, John.
　　　TUNNELLING TO FREEDOM. London, Hamilton, 1957. 192 p. (Panther Books)

4050　Fowler, Elizabeth (comp.).
　　　WORLD-FAMOUS THRILLING EXPLOITS OF ESCAPE. New York, Hart, 1960. 191 p. (World-Famous Series)

4051　Furman, John.
　　　BE NOT FEARFUL. London, Blond, 1959. 224 p.

4052　Garrad-Cole, E.
　　　SINGLE TO ROME. London, Wingate, 1955. 143 p.

　　　Other edition:
　　　London, Brown, Watson, 1958. 160 p. (Digit Books)

4053　Gibbs, Patrick.
　　　IT'S FURTHER VIA GIBRALTAR. London, Faber and Faber, 1961. 144 p.

4054　Hargest, James.
　　　FAREWELL CAMPO 12. London, Joseph, 1945. 184 p.

4055　Harris, George H.
　　　PRISONER OF WAR AND FUGITIVE. Aldershot, Gale and Polden, 1947. 70 p.

4056　Heisler, J. B.
　　　ROUND THE WORLD TO BRITAIN. As told by Peter Toman. London, Trinity Press, 1946. 190 p.

4057　Hoare, Robert J. (comp.).
　　　TRUE STORIES OF CAPTURE AND RESCUE. London, Hamilton, 1960. 143 p. (Oak Tree Books)

　　　Other edition:
　　　London, Hamilton, 1961. 143 p. (Oak Tree Books)

4058　Hutton, Clayton.
　　　THE HIDDEN CATCH: BASED LARGELY UPON MATERIAL SUPPLIED BY AND ON THE EXPERIENCE OF MR. X. Edited by Charles Connell. London, Elek Books, 1955. 176 p.

　　　Other edition:
　　　London, Brown, Watson, 1958. (Digit Books)

4059　Hutton, Clayton.
　　　OFFICIAL SECRET: THE REMARKABLE STORY OF ESCAPE AIDS, THEIR INVENTION, PRODUCTION, AND THE SEQUEL. London, Parrish, 1960. 195 p.

　　　Other edition:
　　　New York, Crown, 1961. 212 p.

4060　Jackson, Robert.
　　　A TASTE OF FREEDOM: STORIES OF THE GERMAN AND ITALIAN PRISONERS WHO ESCAPED FROM CAMPS IN BRITAIN DURING WORLD WAR II. London, Barker, 1964. 207 p.

4061　Jolly, Cyril.
　　　THE VENGEANCE OF PRIVATE POOLEY. Foreword by Rt. Hon. the Lord Russell of Liverpool. London, Heinemann, 1956. 237 p.

4062　Jones, Francis S.
　　　ESCAPE TO NOWHERE. London, Bodley Head, 1952. 266 p.

　　　Other edition:
　　　London, Transworld, 1955. 254 p. (Corgi Books)

4063　Krige, Uys.
　　　THE WAY OUT. Rev. ed. Cape Town, Miller; London, Bailey and Swinfen, 1955. 260 p.

　　　Other edition:
　　　London, Collins, 1946. 384 p.

4064　Ljubljana. Znanstveni Institut.
　　　ALLIED AIRMEN AND PRISONERS OF WAR RESCUED BY THE SLOVENE PARTISANS. Compiled from the records of the Head-quarter of Slovenia. Ljubljana, 1946. 88 p.

4065　Medd, Peter N., with Frank Simms.
　　　THE LONG WALK HOME: AN ESCAPE THROUGH ITALY. Foreword by Anthony Kimmins. London, Lehmann, 1951. 176 p.

4066　Meynell, Laurence W.
　　　AIRMEN ON THE RUN: TRUE STORIES OF EVASION AND ESCAPE BY BRITISH AIRMEN OF WORLD WAR II. London, Odhams Press, 1963. 160 p.

4067　Monsey, Derek.
　　　THE HERO OBSERVED. London, Gollancz, 1960. 162 p.

4068　Neave, Airey.
　　　THEY HAVE THEIR EXITS. Foreword by Lord Justice Birkett. London, Hodder and Stoughton, 1953. 192 p.

　　　Other edition:
　　　Boston, Little, Brown, 1953. 275 p.

4069　Pape, Richard.
　　　BOLDNESS TO BE MY FRIEND. Foreword by Lord Tedder; introduced by Sir Archibald McIndoe. London and New York, Elek, 1953. 309 p.

　　　Other edition:
　　　Boston, Houghton Mifflin, 1954.

4070   Pape, Richard.
       SEQUEL TO BOLDNESS: THE ASTONISHING FOLLOW-ON STORY TO ONE OF THE GREATEST WAR BOOKS EVER WRITTEN. London, Odhams Press, 1959. 256 p.

   Other edition:
   London, Pan, 1961. 219 p.

4071   Prittie, Terence C. F., and W. Earle Edwards.
       ESCAPE TO FREEDOM. Foreword by Major-General Sir Victor Fortune. New ed. London, Hutchinson, 1953. 400 p.

4072   R. A. F. Flying Review.
       THEY GOT BACK: THE BEST ESCAPE STORIES FROM THE R. A. F. FLYING REVIEW. London, Jenkins, 1961. 143 p.

   Other editions:
   New York, Roy, 1963. 143 p.

   London, Brown, 1963. 155 p. (Digit Books)

4073   Reid, Ian D.
       PRISONER AT LARGE: THE STORY OF FIVE ESCAPES. London, Gollancz, 1947. 305 p.

4074   Reid, Patrick R.
       THE COLDITZ STORY. London, Hodder and Stoughton, 1952. 278 p.

   Other editions:
   Philadelphia, Lippincott, 1953. 288 p.

   London, University of London Press, 1958. 190 p. (Pilot Books)

4075   Reid, Patrick R.
       COLDITZ: THE TWO CLASSIC ESCAPE STORIES IN ONE VOLUME--THE COLDITZ STORY AND THE LATTER DAYS. London, Hodder and Stoughton, 1962. 622 p.

4076   Reid, Patrick R.
       THE LATTER DAYS. London, Hodder and Stoughton, 1953. 288 p.

4077   Reid, Patrick R.
       MEN OF COLDITZ. Philadelphia, Lippincott, 1954. 287 p.

   Other edition:
   London, Hodder, 1962. 253 p.

4078   Reynolds, Quentin J.
       OFFICIALLY DEAD. New York, Random House, 1945. 224 p.

   Other editions:
   London, Cassell, 1946. 186 p.

   London, Hamilton, 1955. 190 p. (Panther Books)

4079   Scott, Douglas.
       MY LUCK STILL HELD. Cape Town, South Africa, Unievolkspers Beperk, 1946. 143 p.

4080   Sexton, Winton K.
       WE FOUGHT FOR FREEDOM. Kansas City, Mo., Burton, 1948. 116 p.

4081   Warrack, Graeme.
       TRAVEL BY DARK AFTER ARNHEM. Foreword by H. R. H. Prince Bernhard of Netherlands. London, Harvill Press, 1963. 256 p.

4082   Wentzel, Fritz.
       SINGLE OR RETURN? THE STORY OF A GERMAN P.O.W. IN BRITISH CAMPS AND THE ESCAPE OF LIEUT. FRANZ VON WERRA. Translated from German by Edward Fitzgerald. London, Kimber, 1954. 172 p.

4083   Williams, Eric E.
       THE TUNNEL. London, Collins, 1951. 255 p.

   Other editions:
   New York, Coward-McCann, 1952. 245 p.

   London, Collins, 1955. 251 p. (Fontana Books)

   London, Collins; New York, Abelard-Schuman, 1961.

       THE TUNNEL ESCAPE. New York, Berkley, 1963. 190 p.

   London, Collins, 1964. 251 p. (Fontana Books)

4084   Williams, Eric E.
       THE WOODEN HORSE. New York, Harper, 1950. 255 p.

   Other editions:
   London, Collins, 1955.

   London, Longmans, Green, 1955. 137 p. (Simplified English Series)

   London, Collins, 1957. (Fontana Books)

   New York, Abelard-Schuman, 1958.

   London, Collins, 1964. (Fontana Books)

   London, Collins, 1965. 224 p. (Laurel and Gold Paperbacks)

4085   Williams, Eric E. (ed.).
       GREAT ESCAPE STORIES. London, Weidenfeld and Nicolson, 1958. 256 p. (Heirloom Library)

   Other editions:
   New York, McBride, 1959.

   Harmondsworth, Eng., Penguin, 1963. (Peacock Books)

3. Far East

4067   Allbury, Alfred G.
       BAMBOO AND BUSHIDE. London, Hale, 1955. 192 p.

   Other editions:
   London, World, 1956. 253 p. (Viking Books)

   London, World, 1965. 253 p. (Consul Book)

4087   Attiwill, Kenneth.
       THE RISING SUNSET. London, Hale, 1957. 206 p.

4088   Bank, Bertram.
       BACK FROM THE LIVING DEAD: AN ORIGINAL STORY DESCRIBING THE INFAMOUS MARCH OF DEATH, 33 MONTHS IN A JAPANESE PRISON AND LIBERATION BY THE RANGERS. Tuscaloosa, Ala., 1945. 108 p.

4089 Bernard, John T.
THE ENDLESS YEARS: A PERSONAL RECORD OF THE EXPERIENCES OF A BRITISH OFFICER AS A PRISONER OF WAR IN JAPANESE HANDS, FROM THE FALL OF SINGAPORE TO HIS LIBERATION; WRITTEN DURING HIS CAPTIVITY. Foreword by L. D. Stone. London, Chantry, 1950. 160 p.

Other edition:
London, Hamilton, 1957. 192 p. (Panther Books)

4090 Bell, Leslie.
DESTINED MEETING. London, Odhams, 1959. 256 p.

Other edition:
London, Hamilton, 1961. 192 p. (Panther Books)

4091 Benson, James.
PRISONER'S BASE AND HOME AGAIN: THE STORY OF A MISSIONARY P.O.W. London, Hale, 1957. 192 p.

4092 Bertram, James M.
BENEATH THE SHADOW: A NEW ZEALANDER IN THE FAR EAST, 1939-46. New York, Day, 1947. 308 p.

4093 Blackater, C. F.
GODS WITHOUT REASON. London, Eyre and Spottiswoode, 1948. 214 p.

4094 Boyle, Martin.
YANKS DON'T CRY. New York, Geis, 1963. 249 p.

4095 Braddon, Russell.
END OF A HATE: A SEQUEL TO "THE NAKED ISLANDS," WITH WHICH IS INCORPORATED SONG OF WAR, A SHORT STORY. London, Cassell, 1958. 201 p.

4096 Braddon, Russell.
THE NAKED ISLAND. With drawings made in Changi prison camp by Ronald Searle. London, Laurie, 1952. 266 p.

Other edition:
Garden City, N.Y., Doubleday, 1953. 286 p.

4097 Braly, William C.
THE HARD WAY HOME. Washington, Infantry Journal, 1947. 282 p.

4098 Broughton, Douglas G.
MONGOLIAN PLAINS AND JAPANESE PRISON. London, Pickering and Inglis, 1947. 71 p.

4099 Brown, Robert M. V., with Donald Permenter.
I SOLEMNLY SWEAR: THE STORY OF A GI NAMED BROWN. New York, Vantage Press, 1957. 203 p.

Other edition:
A G.I. NAMED BROWN. London, Brown, Watson, 1961. 160 p. (Digit Books)

4100 Bryan, John N. L.
THE CHURCHES OF THE CAPTIVITY IN MALAYA. London, Society for Promoting Christian Knowledge, 1946. 72 p.

4101 Bulcock, Roy.
OF DEATH BUT ONCE. Melbourne, Cheshire, 1947. 213 p.

4102 Burton, Reginald G.
THE ROAD TO THREE PAGODAS. London, Macdonald, 1963. 179 p.

4103 Bush, Lewis W.
CLUTCH OF CIRCUMSTANCE. Tokyo, Okuyama, 1956. 263 p.

4104 Bush, Lewis W.
THE ROAD TO INAMURA. London, Hale, 1961. 238 p.

4105 Caplan, Jack.
FROM GORBALS TO JUNGLE. Glasgow, MacLellan, 1960. 237 p.

Other edition:
London, Brown, 1961. 160 p. (Digit Books)

4106 Cates, Tressa R.
THE DRAINPIPE DIARY. New York, Vantage, 1957. 273 p.

4107 Clark, Russell S.
AN END TO TEARS. Sydney, Huston, 1946. 180 p.

4108 Coast, John.
RAILROAD TO DEATH. London, Commodore, 1946. 256 p.

Other edition:
London, Brown, 1957. 316 p. (Digit Books)

4109 Cooper, George T., with Dennis Holman.
ORDEAL IN THE SUN. London, Hale, 1963. 192 p.

Other edition:
London, Brown, Watson, 1964. 158 p. (Digit Books)

4110 Cornelius, Mary D.
CHANGI. Ilfracombe, Stockwell, 1953. 80 p.

4111 Corpe, Hilda R.
PRISONER BEYOND THE CHINDWIN. London, Barker, 1955. 158 p.

4112 Falk, Stanley L.
THE BATAAN DEATH MARCH. Washington, 1952. 169 l.

Other editions:
New York, Norton, 1962. 256 p.

THE MARCH OF DEATH. London, Hale, 1964. 192 p.

4113 Field, Ellen.
TWILIGHT IN HONG KONG. London, Muller, 1960. 232 p.

4114 Fitzgerald, Earl A.
VOICES IN THE NIGHT. Bellingham, Wash., Pioneer Printing Co., 1948. 203 p.

4115 Forbes, George K.
BORNEO BURLESQUE: COMIC TRAGEDY, TRAGIC COMEDY. n.p., 1947. 127 p.

4116 Gibson, Walter.
THE BOAT. London, Allen, 1952. 96 p.
Other edition:
Boston, Houghton Mifflin, 1953. 101 p.

4117 Goodwin, Ralph B.
HONGKONG ESCAPE. London, Barker, 1953. 223 p.
Other edition:
London, Barker, 1956. 191 p. (Dragon Books)

4118 Goodwin, Ralph B.
PASSPORT TO ETERNITY. London, Barker, 1956. 192 p.

4119 Gordon, Ernest.
MIRACLE ON THE RIVER KWAI. London, Collins, 1963. 255 p.
Other edition:
London, Collins, 1965. 190 p. (Fontana Books)

4120 Gordon, Ernest.
THROUGH THE VALLEY OF THE KWAI. New York, Harper and Row, 1962. 257 p.

4121 Guest, Freddie.
ESCAPE FROM THE BLOODIED SUN. London, Jarrolds, 1956. 192 p.
Other edition:
London, Landsborough, 1958. 188 p. (Four Square Books)

4122 Guirey, E. L.
LAUGHTER IN HELL: BEING THE TRUE EXPERIENCES OF LIEUTENANT E. L. GUIREY, U.S.N., AND TECHNICAL SERGEANT H. C. NIXON, U.S.M.C., AND THEIR COMRADES IN THE JAPANESE PRISON CAMPS IN OSAKA AND TSURUGA. As narrated to and written by Stephen Marek. Caldwell, Idaho, Caxton Printers, 1954. 256 p.

4123 Hartendorp, A. V. H.
THE SANTO TOMAS STORY. Edited by Frank H. Golay; foreword by Carlos P. Romulo. New York, McGraw-Hill, 1964. 446 p.

4124 Hartley, Peter G.
ESCAPE TO CAPTIVITY. London, Dent, 1952. 210 p.
Other edition:
London, Hamilton, 1956. 189 p. (Panther Books)

4125 Hastain, Ronald.
WHITE COOLIE. London, Transworld, 1956. 318 p. (Corgi Books)
Other edition:
London, Transworld, 1959. (Corgi Books)

4126 Hawkins, Jack.
NEVER SAY DIE. Philadelphia, Dorrance, 1961. 196 p.

4127 Hind, Robert R.
SPIRITS UNBROKEN: THE STORY OF THREE YEARS IN A CIVILIAN INTERNMENT CAMP, UNDER THE JAPANESE, AT BAGUIO AND AT OLD BILIBID PRISON IN THE PHILIPPINES FROM DECEMBER, 1941, TO FEBRUARY, 1945. San Francisco, Howell, 1946. 291 p.

4128 Jeffrey, Betty.
WHITE COOLIES. Sydney, Angus and Robertson, 1954. 204 p.
Other editions:
New York, Philosophical Library, 1955.

London, Hamilton, 1958. 192 p. (Panther Books)

4129 Jennings, Cyril O.
AN OCEAN WITHOUT SHORES. London, Hodder and Stoughton, 1950. 221 p.

4130 Johnston, Doris R.
BREAD AND RICE. Foreword by Carlos P. Romulo. New York, Thurston Macauley, 1947. 235 p.

4131 Keith, Agnes N.
THREE CAME HOME. Boston, Little, Brown, 1950. 316 p.
Other editions:
London, Joseph, 1948.

London, Pan Books, 1958. 253 p.

London, Transworld, 1964. 253 p. (Corgi Books)

4132 Kellett, Wanda L.
WINGS AS EAGLES. New York, Vantage Press, 1954. 105 p.

4133 Kent Hughes, Wilfrid S.
SLAVES OF THE SAMURAI: AN AUSTRALIAN ODYSSEY WHICH GIVES AN ACCOUNT OF LIFE AND THOUGHTS OF A SLAVE OF THE SAMURAI, DURING HIS THREE YEARS AND SEVEN MONTHS AS PRISONER OF WAR IN THE HANDS OF THE JAPANESE. Melbourne, Oxford University Press, 1947. 296 p.

4134 Kephart, Rodney.
WAKE, WAR AND WAITING. New York, Exposition Press, 1950. 84 p.

4135 Kopp, Hans.
HIMALAYA SHUTTLECOCK. Translated from German by H. C. Stevens. London, Hutchinson, 1957. 191 p.

4136 Lambert, Eric.
MacDOUGAL'S FARM. London, Muller, 1965. 154 p.

4137 Leffelaar, Hendrik L.
THROUGH A HARSH DAWN: A BOY GROWS UP IN A JAPANESE PRISON CAMP. Barre, Mass., Barre Publishing Co., 1963. 246 p.
Other edition:
London, Muller, 1964. 258 p.

4138 Levering, Robert W.
   HORROR TREK: A TRUE STORY OF BATAAN, THE DEATH MARCH AND THREE AND ONE-HALF YEARS IN JAPANESE PRISON CAMPS. Dayton, Ohio, 1948. 233 p.

4139 Lim, Janet.
   SOLD FOR SILVER: AN AUTOBIOGRAPHY. Cleveland, World Publishing Co.; London, Collins, 1958. 255 p.

4140 McCabe, Graeme.
   PACIFIC SUNSET. Hobart, Oldham, Beddome and Meredith, 1946. 108 p.

4141 McCormac, Charles.
   YOU'LL DIE IN SINGAPORE. London, Hale, 1954. 180 p.

   Other editions:
   New York, Dutton, 1955. 192 p.

   London, Pan, 1957.

4142 McDougall, William H.
   BY EASTERN WINDOWS: THE STORY OF A BATTLE OF SOULS AND MINDS IN THE PRISON CAMPS OF SUMATRA. New York, Scribner, 1949. 349 p.

   Other edition:
   London, Barker, 1951.

4143 McDougall, William H.
   SIX BELLS OFF JAVA: A NARRATIVE OF ONE MAN'S PRIVATE MIRACLE. New York, Scribner, 1948. 222 p.

   Other edition:
   Salt Lake City, Weller, 1955. 220 p.

4144 MacKenzie, Kenneth P.
   OPERATION RANGOON JAIL. Foreword by J. G. Smyth. London, Johnson, 1954. 201 p.

   Other edition:
   London, Hamilton, 1957. 159 p. (Panther Books)

4145 Magener, Rolf.
   PRISONERS' BLUFF. Translated from German by Basil Creighton. London, Hart-Davis, 1954. 239 p.

   Other editions:
   New York, Dutton, 1955. 250 p.

   London, Hamilton, 1956. 192 p. (Panther Books)

4146 Moody, Samuel B., and Maury Allen.
   REPRIEVE FROM HELL. Foreword by E. P. King, Jr. New York, Pageant Press, 1961. 213 p.

4147 Moule, William R.
   GOD'S ARMS AROUND US. New York, Vantage Press, 1960. 399 p.

4148 Murray, Mary.
   ESCAPE: A THOUSAND MILES TO FREEDOM. Adelaide, Rigby; San Francisco, Tri-Ocean Books; London, Angus, 1965. 260 p.

4149 Myers, Hugh H.
   PRISONER OF WAR, WORLD WAR II. Portland, Ore., Metropolitan Press, 1965. 200 p.

4150 Ogle Mary S.
   WORTH THE PRICE. Washington, D.C., Review and Herald Publishing Association, 1958. 319 p.

4151 O'Leary, Cedric P.
   A SHAMROCK UP A BAMBOO TREE: THE STORY OF EIGHT YEARS BEHIND THE 8-BALL IN SHANGHAI, 1941-49. New York, Exposition Press, 1956. 235 p. (Banner Books)

4152 Paget, Mrs. K. M.
   OUT OF THE HAND OF THE TERRIBLE. Melbourne, Bacon, 1945. 111 p.

4153 Parkin, Ray.
   INTO THE SMOTHER: A JOURNAL OF THE BURMA-SIAM RAILWAY. London, Hogarth Press, 1963. 290 p.

4154 Pavillard, Stanley S.
   BAMBOO DOCTOR. London, Macmillan; New York, St. Martin's Press, 1960. 206 p.

   Other edition:
   London, Pan, 1962. 156 p.

4155 Renne, Louis O.
   OUR DAY OF EMPIRE: WAR AND THE EXILE OF JAPANESE-AMERICANS. Glasgow, Strickland Press, 1954. 224 p.

4156 Reyes, José G.
   TERRORISM AND REDEMPTION: JAPANESE ATROCITIES IN THE PHILIPPINES. English version by José Garcia Insua. Manila, 1947. 91 p.

4157 Rivett, Rohan D.
   BEHIND BAMBOO: AN INSIDE STORY OF THE JAPANESE PRISON CAMPS. Sydney, Angus and Robertson, 1947. 335 p.

4158 Russell, Edward F. L. Russell, baron.
   THE KNIGHTS OF BUSHIDO: A SHORT HISTORY OF JAPANESE WAR CRIMES. London, Cassell; New York, Dutton, 1958. 334 p.

4159 Sewell, William G.
   STRANGE HARMONY. London, Edinburgh House Press, 1946. 192 p.

4160 Simons, Jessie E.
   WHILE HISTORY PASSED: THE STORY OF THE AUSTRALIAN NURSES WHO WERE PRISONERS OF THE JAPANESE FOR THREE AND A HALF YEARS. Foreword by A. M. Sage. London, Heinemann, 1954. 131 p.

   Other edition:
   IN THE ARMS OF THE JAPANESE. London, Hamilton, 1961. 160 p. (Panther Books)

4161 Smith, Donald.
   AND ALL THE TRUMPETS. London, Bles, 1954. 244 p.

   Other edition:
   London, Hamilton, 1958. 221 p. (Panther Books)

4162 Sneed, Bessie.
CAPTURED BY THE JAPANESE: BEING THE PERSONAL EXPERIENCES OF A MINER'S WIFE CAUGHT IN THE PHILIPPINES, AT THE OUTBREAK OF WORLD WAR II. Denver, Bradford-Robinson, 1946. 108 p.

4163 Stahl, Alfred J.
HOW WE TOOK IT: VIGNETTES OF JAPANESE INTERNMENT CAMPS IN THE PHILIPPINES. New York, Stahl, 1945. 118 p.

4164 Stericker, John.
A TEAR FOR THE DRAGON. London, Barker, 1958. 211 p.

4165 Stevens, Frederic H.
SANTO TOMAS INTERNMENT CAMP. Foreword by General Douglas MacArthur. New York, Stratford House, 1946. 569 p.

4166 Stewart, Sidney.
GIVE US THIS DAY. London, Staples, 1956. 246 p.

Other editions:
New York, Norton, 1957. 254 p.

London, Pan, 1958. 190 p.

4167 Stibbe, Philip.
RETURN VIA RANGOON. Foreword by Frank Owen. London, Wolsey, 1947. 224 p.

4168 Tantri, K'tut.
REVOLT IN PARADISE. New York, Harper, 1960. 308 p.

4169 Toschi, Elios.
NINTH TIME LUCKY. Translated from the Italian by James Cleugh. London, Kimber, 1955. 216 p.

4170 Van der Post, Laurens.
A BAR OF SHADOW. London, Hogarth Press, 1954. 58 p.

Other edition:
New York, Morrow, 1956. 61 p.

4171 Vaughan, Elizabeth H.
COMMUNITY UNDER STRESS: AN INTERNMENT CAMP CULTURE. Princeton, N.J., Princeton University Press, 1949. 160 p.

4172 Wallace, Walter.
ESCAPE FROM HELL: THE SANDAKAN STORY. London, Hale, 1958. 175 p.

Other edition:
London, World Distributors, 1959. 191 p.

4173 Weedon, Martin.
GUEST OF AN EMPEROR. London, Barker, 1948. 223 p.

4174 Wettern, Desmond.
THE LONELY BATTLE. Foreword by Geoffrey Layton. London, Allen, 1960. 223 p.

4175 Whitcomb, Edgar D.
ESCAPE FROM CORREGIDOR. Chicago, Regnery, 1958. 274 p.

Other editions:
London, Wingate, 1959.

London, Hamilton, 1960. 188 p. (Panther Books)

4176 Whitecross, Roy H.
SLAVES OF THE SON OF HEAVEN: THE PERSONAL STORY OF AN AUSTRALIAN PRISONER OF THE JAPANESE DURING THE YEARS 1942-1945. Sydney, Dymock's Book Arcade, 1951. 246 p.

Other edition:
London, Transworld, 1961. (Corgi Books)

4177 Whiting, George F.
JAPANESE BONDAGE. London, Brown, Watson, 1957. 160 p. (Digit Books)

4178 Whitney, Hans.
GUEST OF THE FALLEN SUN, IN THE PRISONER-OF-WAR CAMPS IN JAPAN AND CHINA. Edited by Dan Sterling. New York, Exposition Press, 1951. 69 p.

4179 Wright, Robert J.
I WAS A HELL CAMP PRISONER. London, Brown, Watson, 1963. 160 p. (Digit Books)

4. North America

4180 Boscolo, Armando.
FAME IN AMERICA. Milan, Ed. Europee, 1954. 204 p. (Uomini negli eventi, v. 7)

4181 Broom, Leonard, and John I. Kitsuse.
THE MANAGED CASUALTY: THE JAPANESE-AMERICAN FAMILY IN WORLD WAR II. Berkeley, University of California Press, 1956. 226 p. (University of California Publications in Culture and Society)

4182 Broom, Leonard, and Ruth Riemer.
REMOVAL AND RETURN: THE SOCIO-ECONOMIC EFFECTS OF THE WAR ON JAPANESE AMERICANS. Berkeley, University of California Press, 1949. 259 p. (University of California Publications in Culture and Society)

4183 Fisher, Anne M. R.
EXILE OF A RACE: A HISTORY OF THE FORCIBLE REMOVAL AND IMPRISONMENT BY THE ARMY OF THE 115,000 CITIZENS AND ALIEN JAPANESE WHO WERE LIVING ON THE WEST COAST IN THE SPRING OF 1942. Sydney, B.C., 1965. 245 p.

4184 Grodzins, Morton.
AMERICANS BETRAYED: POLITICS AND THE JAPANESE EVACUATION. Chicago, University of Chicago Press; London, Cambridge University Press, 1949. 445 p.

4185 Japanese American Citizen's League.
THE CASE FOR THE NISEI: BRIEF OF THE JAPANESE AMERICAN CITIZEN'S LEAGUE. Salt Lake City, 1945. 193 p.

4186 La Violette, Forrest E.
THE CANADIAN-JAPANESE AND WORLD WAR II: A SOCIOLOGICAL AND PSYCHOLOGICAL ACCOUNT. Issued under the auspices of Canadian Institute of International Affairs and Institute of Pacific Relations. Toronto, University of Toronto Press, 1948. 332 p.

4187 Leighton, Alexander H.
THE GOVERNING OF MEN: GENERAL PRINCIPLES AND RECOMMENDATIONS BASED ON EXPERIENCES AT A JAPANESE RELOCATION CAMP. Princeton, N.J., Princeton University Press, 1945. 404 p.

4188 Okubo, Miné.
CITIZEN 13660. New York, Columbia University Press, 1946. 209 p.

4189 Pabel, Reinhold.
ENEMIES ARE HUMAN. Philadelphia, Winston, 1955. 248 p.

4190 Thomas, Dorothy S.
JAPANESE AMERICAN EVACUATION AND RESETTLEMENT. Berkeley, University of California Press, 1946-54. 3 v.

4191 U.S. War Relocation Authority.
ADMINISTRATIVE HIGHLIGHTS OF THE WRA PROGRAM. Washington, U.S. Government Printing Office, 1946. 82 p.

4192 U.S. War Relocation Authority.
THE EVACUATED PEOPLE: A QUANTITATIVE DESCRIPTION. Washington, 1946. 200 p.

4193 U.S. War Relocation Authority.
WRA: A STORY OF HUMAN CONSERVATION. Washington, 1946. 212 p.

B. DEMOGRAPHIC CHANGES AND SHIFTS; DISPLACED PERSONS; CHILDREN

4194 American Council of Voluntary Agencies for Foreign Service, Survey Committee on Displaced Persons.
THE PROBLEM OF THE DISPLACED PERSONS: REPORT, JUNE 1946. New York, 1946. 80 l.

4195 Association of Jewish Refugees in Great Britain.
BRITAIN'S NEW CITIZENS: THE STORY OF THE REFUGEES FROM GERMANY AND AUSTRIA, 1941-1951. Tenth Anniversary publication. London, 1951. 75 p.

4196 Auerbach, Frank L.
THE ADMISSION AND RESETTLEMENT OF DISPLACED PERSONS IN THE UNITED STATES: A HANDBOOK OF LEGAL AND TECHNICAL INFORMATION FOR THE USE OF LOCAL SOCIAL AND CIVIC AGENCIES. Rev. ed. New York, Common Council for American Unity, 1950. 56 l.

4197 Baratinsky, Viacheslav (Victor Maritsky, pseud.).
MY PUPILS AND I: MEMORIES OF A TEACHER. New York, Comet, 1955. 78 p.

4198 Beith, John H. (Ian Hay, pseud.).
PEACEFUL INVASION. London, Hodder, 1946. 238 p.

4199 Bentwich, Norman de M.
I UNDERSTAND THE RISKS: THE STORY OF THE REFUGEES FROM NAZI OPPRESSION WHO FOUGHT IN THE BRITISH FORCES IN THE WORLD WAR. Foreword by the Marquis of Reading. London, Gollancz, 1950. 192 p.

4200 Bentwich, Norman de M.
THEY FOUND REFUGE: AN ACCOUNT OF BRITISH JEWRY'S WORK FOR VICTIMS OF OPPRESSION. London, Cresset, 1956. 227 p.

4201 Billingsley, Chris.
THE NAZIS CALLED ME TRAITOR: THE WARTIME MEMOIRS OF A TEEN-AGE REFUGEE. New York, Exposition Press, 1965. 232 p.

4202 Boder, David P.
I DID NOT INTERVIEW THE DEAD. Urbana, University of Illinois Press, 1949. 220 p.

4203 Carroll-Abbing, John P.
A CHANCE TO LIVE: THE STORY OF THE LOST CHILDREN OF THE WAR. Translated by Carol della Chiess. New York, Longmans, Green, 1952. 216 p.

4204 Collis, William R. F.
THE LOST AND THE FOUND: THE STORY OF EVA AND LASZLO, TWO CHILDREN OF WAR-TORN EUROPE. New York, Woman's Press, 1953. 181 p.

4205 Collis, William R. F.
THE ULTIMATE VALUE. London, Methuen, 1951. 183 p.

4206 Dembitzer, Salamon.
VISAS FOR AMERICA: A STORY OF AN ESCAPE. Translated by E. Baker; revised by E. Bell-Smith; foreword by Herbert V. Evatt. Sydney, Villon Press, 1952. 267 p.

4207 Forrest, Alec J.
BUT SOME THERE BE. London, Hale, 1957. 252 p.

4208 Friedman, Philip.
THEIR BROTHERS' KEEPERS. Foreword by John A. O'Brien. New York, Crown Publishers, 1957. 224 p.

4209 Frumkin, Grzegorz.
POPULATION CHANGES IN EUROPE SINCE 1939: A STUDY OF POPULATION CHANGES IN EUROPE DURING AND SINCE WORLD WAR II AS SHOWN BY THE BALANCE SHEETS OF TWENTY-FOUR EUROPEAN COUNTRIES. London, Allen and Unwin; New York, Kelley, 1951. 191 p.

4210 Harbinson, Robert.
SONG OF ERNE. London, Faber, 1960. 244 p.

4211 Hirschmann, Ira A.
LIFE LINE TO THE PROMISED LAND. New York, Vanguard Press, 1946. 214 p.

4212 Hungary. Külügyminiszterium.
HUNGARY AND THE CONFERENCE OF PARIS. Budapest, 1947. 5 v.

4213 Huxley-Blythe, Peter J.
THE EAST CAME WEST. Caldwell, Idaho, Caxton Printers, 1964. 225 p.

4214 IN THE NAME OF THE LITHUANIAN PEOPLE. Wolfberg, Austria, Perkunas, 1945. 71 p.

4215 International Social Service.
A REPORT ON THE DOCUMENTATION OF 9930 REFUGEES IN SWITZERLAND. Geneva, 1945. 63 l.

4216 International Tracing Service.
CATALOGUE OF RECORDS HELD BY THE INTERNATIONAL TRACING SERVICE OF THE ALLIED HIGH COMMISSION FOR GERMANY AT AROLSEN. Arolsen, Ger., 1954. 4 v.

4217 Kimche, Jon, and David Kimche.
THE SECRET ROADS: THE ILLEGAL MIGRATION OF A PEOPLE 1938-1948. London, Secker and Warburg, 1954. 223 p.

Other edition:
New York, Farrar, Straus and Cudahy, 1955. 223 p.

4218 Küchler-Silberman, Lena.
MY HUNDRED CHILDREN. London, Souvenir Press; Garden City, N.Y., Doubleday, 1961. 288 p.

4219 Lambert, D.
THE SHELTERED DAYS. London, Deutsch, 1965. 192 p.

4220 Lasker, Bruno.
ASIA ON THE MOVE: POPULATION PRESSURE, MIGRATION, AND RESETTLEMENT IN EASTERN ASIA UNDER THE INFLUENCE OF WANT AND WAR. New York, Holt, 1945. 207 p.

4221 Lowrie, Donald A.
THE HUNTED CHILDREN. New York, Norton, 1963. 256 p.

4222 Macardle, Dorothy.
CHILDREN OF EUROPE: A STUDY OF THE CHILDREN OF LIBERATED COUNTRIES; THEIR WAR-TIME EXPERIENCES, THEIR REACTIONS, AND THEIR NEEDS, WITH A NOTE ON GERMANY. London, Gollancz, 1949. 349 p.

4223 Murphy, Henry B. M.
FLIGHT AND RESETTLEMENT. With special contributions by Eduard Bakis and others; foreword by J. R. Rees. Paris, UNESCO, 1955. 231 p. (Population and Culture)

4224 Nadich, Judah.
EISENHOWER AND THE JEWS. New York, Twayne Publishers, 1953. 271 p.

4225 Noia, Joseph (ed.).
TWO YEARS WITH DISPLACED PERSONS. n.p., 1948. 97 p.

4226 O'Neill, Hester.
YOUNG PATRIOTS. New York, Nelson, 1948. 256 p.

4227 Peters, Clarence A. (comp.).
THE IMMIGRATION PROBLEM. New York, Wilson, 1948. 254 p. (Reference Shelf)

4228 Proudfoot, Malcolm J.
EUROPEAN REFUGEES: 1939-52: A STUDY IN FORCED POPULATION MOVEMENT. Evanston, Ill., Northwestern University Press, 1956. 542 p. (Northwestern University Studies. Social Sciences Series)

Other edition:
London, Faber and Faber, 1957.

4229 Schechtman, Joseph B.
EUROPEAN POPULATION TRANSFERS, 1939-1945. New York and London, Oxford University Press, 1946. 532 p. (Studies of the Institute of World Affairs)

4230 Schoenberner, Franz.
THE INSIDE STORY OF AN OUTSIDER. New York, Macmillan, 1949. 273 p.

4231 Sosnowski, Kiryl.
THE TRAGEDY OF CHILDREN UNDER NAZI RULE. Edited by Wanda Machlejd. Poznan, Zachodnia Agencja Prasowa, 1962. 470 p.

4232 Stone, Isidor F.
UNDERGROUND TO PALESTINE. New York, Boni and Gaer, 1946. 240 p.

4233 Travers, Pamela L.
I GO BY SEA, I GO BY LAND. New York, Norton, 1964. 233 p.

4234 U.S. Displaced Persons Commission.
MEMO TO AMERICA: THE DP STORY; THE FINAL REPORT OF THE U.S. DISPLACED PERSONS COMMISSION. Washington, U.S. Government Printing Office, 1952. 376 p.

4235 U.S. Provost Marshal General's School, Camp Gordon, Georgia.
DISPLACED PERSON, 1945-1946. Prepared by the Provost Marshal General's School, Military Government Dept. for ORC Units. Camp Gordon, 1951. 105 p. (Training Packet)

4236 Vanport City, Oregon. Schools.
6,000 KIDS FROM 46 STATES. Portland, Ore., 1946. 100 p.

4237 Warhaftig, Zorach.
UPROOTED: JEWISH REFUGEES AND DISPLACED PERSONS AFTER LIBERATION. New York, Institute of Jewish Affairs of the American Jewish Congress and the World Jewish Congress, 1946. 219 p.

4238 Zielinski, Henry K.
POPULATION CHANGES IN POLAND, 1939-50. New York, Mid-European Studies Center, National Committee for a Free Europe, 1954. 101 p.

C. RELIEF; MILITARY GOVERNMENT;
CIVIL AFFAIRS; RED CROSS, YMCA
USO, etc. (see also III. C. 3)

4239 Allied Commission.
A REVIEW OF ALLIED MILITARY GOVERNMENT AND OF THE ALLIED COMMISSION IN ITALY, JULY 10, 1942, D-DAY, SICILY TO MAY 2, 1945, GERMAN SURRENDER IN ITALY. Rome, Public Relations Branch, Allied Commission, U.S. Army, 1945. 125 p.

4240 American Academy of Political and Social Science, Philadelphia.
MILITARY GOVERNMENT. Edited by Sydney Connor and Carl J. Friedrich. Philadelphia, 1950. 261 p.

4241 Aye, Lillian.
IRAN CABOOSE. Hollywood, Calif., House-Warven, 1951. 190 p.

4242 Baker, Blanche E.
MRS. G.I. JOE. Goldsboro, N.C., 1951. 247 p.

4243 Baring, Norah.
A FRIENDLY HEARTH. Introduction by John A. Watson. London, Cape, 1946. 128 p.

4244 Barnett House, Oxford.
LONDON CHILDREN IN WARTIME OXFORD: A SURVEY OF SOCIAL AND EDUCATIONAL RESULTS OF EVACUATION. London, Oxford University Press, 1947. 113 p.

4245 Beardwell, M. F.
AFTERMATH. Ilfracombe, Stockwell, 1953. 72 p.

4246 Berenstein, Taliana, and Adam Rutkowski.
ASSISTANCE TO THE JEWS IN POLAND, 1939-1945. Translated by Edward Rothert. Warsaw, Polonia Publishing House, 1963. 82 p.

4247 Bernadotte of Wisborg, Folke, greve.
INSTEAD OF ARMS: AUTOBIOGRAPHICAL NOTES. Stockholm, Bonniers, 1948. 227 p.

4248 Bosanquet, Mary.
JOURNEY INTO A PICTURE. London, Hodder and Stoughton, 1947. 196 p.

4249 Briggs, David G.
ACTION AMID RUINS. New York, American Field Service, 1945. 174 p.

4250 Campbell, Alfred S.
GUADALCANAL ROUND-TRIP: THE STORY OF AN AMERICAN RED CROSS FIELD DIRECTOR IN THE PRESENT WAR. Lambertville, N.J., By the author, 1945. 112 p.

4251 Catholic Church.
CHARITY ABOUNDING: THE STORY OF PAPAL RELIEF WORK DURING THE WAR. London, Burns, Oates and Washbourne, 1945. 51 p.

4252 Contractors Pacific Naval Air Bases.
A REPORT TO RETURNED CPNAB PRISONER OF WAR HEROES AND THEIR DEPENDENTS. Boise, 1945. 51 p.

4253 Creedy, Brooks S.
WOMEN BEHIND THE LINES: YWCA PROGRAM WITH WAR PRODUCTION WORKERS, 1940-1947. New York, Woman's Press, 1949. 227 p.

4254 Donnison, Frank S. V.
BRITISH MILITARY ADMINISTRATION IN THE FAR EAST, 1943-46. London, H.M. Stationery Office, 1956. 483 p. (History of the Second World War: United Kingdom Military Series; Civil Affairs and Military Government Series)

4255 Donnison, Frank S. V.
CIVIL AFFAIRS AND MILITARY GOVERNMENT, NORTH-WEST EUROPE, 1944-1946. London, H.M. Stationery Office, 1961. 518 p. (History of the Second World War: United Kingdom Military Series)

4256 Douie, Vera.
DAUGHTERS OF BRITAIN. Oxford, 1949. 159 p.

4257 Egan, Eileen M., and Mary C. Reiss.
TRANSFIGURED NIGHT: THE CRALOG EXPERIENCE. Philadelphia, Livingston Publishing Co., 1964. 185 p.

4258 Ellis, Jean M.
FACE POWDER AND GUNPOWDER. Toronto, Saunders, 1947. 229 p.

4259 Ferguson, Sheila, and Hilde Fitzgerald.
STUDIES IN THE SOCIAL SERVICES. London, H.M. Stationery Office, 1954. 367 p. (History of the Second World War: United Kingdom Civil Series)

4260 FLIGHT OF THE SNOW GOOSE: HISTORY OF THE PRESQUE ISLE U.S.O. CLUB. Presque Isle, Me., 1946. 56 l.

4261 Fortescue, Winifred B.
BEAUTY FOR ASHES. Edinburgh, Blackwood, 1948. 318 p.

4262 Friedrich, Carl J., and others (eds.).
AMERICAN EXPERIENCES IN MILITARY GOVERNMENT IN WORLD WAR II. New York, Rinehart, 1948. 436 p.

4263 Gayre, George R.
ITALY IN TRANSITION; EXTRACTS FROM THE PRIVATE JOURNAL OF G. R. GAYRE. London, Faber and Faber, 1946. 254 p.

4264 Gerken, Mable R.
LADIES IN PANTS: A HOME FRONT DIARY. New York, Exposition Press, 1949. 96 p.

4265 Great Britain. Central Office of Information.
FRIENDS IN NEED: THE STORY OF BRITISH WAR RELIEF SOCIETY INC. OF THE UNITED STATES OF AMERICA, 1939-1945. London, H.M. Stationery Office, 1947. 75 p.

4266 Harris, Charles R. S.
ALLIED MILITARY ADMINISTRATION OF ITALY, 1943-1945. London, H.M. Stationery Office, 1957. 479 p. (History of the Second World War: United Kingdom Military Series; Civil Affairs and Military Government Series)

4267 Hinshaw, David.
AN EXPERIMENT IN FRIENDSHIP. New York, Putnam, 1947. 147 p.

4268 Holborn, Hajo.
AMERICAN MILITARY GOVERNMENT: ITS ORGANIZATION AND POLICIES. Washington, Infantry Journal Press, 1947. 243 p.

4269 Insh, George P.
THE WAR-TIME HISTORY OF THE SCOTTISH BRANCH, BRITISH RED CROSS SOCIETY. Glasgow, Jackson, 1952. 207 p.

4270 Isserman, Ferdinand M.
A RABBI WITH THE AMERICAN RED CROSS. New York, Whittier Books, 1958. 334 p.

4271 Jackson, C. O. Badham.
PROUD STORY: THE OFFICIAL HISTORY OF AUSTRALIAN COMFORTS FUND, A COMMONWEALTH-WIDE VOLUNTARY ORGANIZATION ACCREDITED TO ROYAL AUSTRALIAN NAVY, THE AUSTRALIAN MILITARY FORCES AND THE ROYAL AUSTRALIAN AIR FORCE AND CHARGED WITH THE DUTY OF CARING FOR ALL FIT AND WELL MEMBERS OF THE AUSTRALIAN FORCES DURING THE SECOND WORLD WAR, 1939-1945. Published by authority of Australian Comforts Fund. Sydney, F. H. Johnston Publishing Co., 1949. 336 p.

4272 Junod, Marcel.
WARRIOR WITHOUT WEAPONS. Preface by Max Huber; translated from the French by Edward Fitzgerald. London, Cape, 1951. 318 p.

Other edition:
New York, Macmillan, 1951. 283 p.

4273 Kershner, Howard E.
QUAKER SERVICE IN MODERN WAR. New York, Prentice-Hall, 1950. 195 p.

4274 Klemme, Marvin.
THE INSIDE STORY OF UNRRA, AN EXPERIENCE IN INTERNATIONALISM: A FIRST-HAND REPORT ON DISPLACED PEOPLE OF EUROPE. New York, Lifetime Editions, 1949. 307 p.

4275 Korson, George G.
AT HIS SIDE: THE STORY OF THE AMERICAN RED CROSS OVERSEAS IN WORLD WAR II. New York, Coward-McCann, 1945. 322 p.

4276 Lutz, Alma (comp. and ed.).
WITH LOVE, JANE: LETTERS FROM AMERICAN WOMEN ON THE WAR FRONTS. New York, Day, 1945. 199 p.

4277 McCloskey, Mark A., and Thomas H. Rickman, Jr.
PROFESSIONAL STUDY OF THE SERVICEMEN'S PIER, BRANCHES AND BRANCH SERVICES, APRIL 15, 1942-DECEMBER 1, 1945. Miami Beach, Fla., 1946. 105 p.

4278 MacDonald, Florence.
FOR GREECE A TEAR: THE STORY OF THE GREEK WAR RELIEF FUND OF CANADA. Fredericton, N.B., Brunswick Press, 1954. 193 p.

4279 McNalty, Sir Arthur S., and W. Franklin Mellor.
HEALTH RECOVERY IN EUROPE. London, Muller, 1946. 180 p.

4280 Morton, Gertrude B.
WOMANPOWER COMMITTEES DURING WORLD WAR II: UNITED STATES AND BRITISH EXPERIENCE. Washington, U.S. Government Printing Office, 1953. 73 p. U.S. Women's Bureau. Bulletin)

4281 New York City Committee for Service Men.
NEW YORK CITY'S RECREATION AND WELFARE PROGRAM FOR SERVICE MEN AND WOMEN, 1941-1948. New York, 1948. 53 p.

4282 O'Brien, Terence H.
CIVIL DEFENCE. London, H.M. Stationery Office, 1955. 729 p. (History of the Second World War: United Kingdom Civil Series)

4283 Ray, Jefferson F.
UNRRA IN CHINA: A CASE STUDY OF THE INTERPLAY OF INTERESTS IN A PROGRAM OF INTERNATIONAL AID TO AN UNDEVELOPED COUNTRY. New York, International Secretariat, Institute of Pacific Relations, 1947. 64 l. (Secretariat Paper)

4284 Red Cross. Finland. Finlands Röda Kors.
THE FINNISH RED CROSS: SOME FEATURES OF THE WORK OF THE SOCIETY. Helsinki, 1945. 63 p.

4285 Red Cross. International Committee, Geneva.
INTER ARMA CARITAS: THE WORK OF THE INTERNATIONAL COMMITTEE OF THE RED CROSS DURING THE SECOND WORLD WAR. Geneva, 1947. 135 p.

4286 Red Cross. International Committee, Geneva.
REPORT OF THE INTERNATIONAL COMMITTEE OF THE RED CROSS ON ITS ACTIVITIES DURING THE SECOND WORLD WAR, SEPTEMBER 1, 1939-JUNE 30, 1947. Geneva, 1948. 3 v.

4287 Red Cross. U.S. American National Red Cross.
THE AMERICAN RED CROSS WITH THE ARMED FORCES. Washington, 1945. 59 p. (ARC Circular)

4288 Red Cross. U.S. American National Red Cross.
THE GREATEST FREEWILL OFFERING IN HISTORY. Washington, 1947. 53 p. (ARC Circular)

4289 Red Cross. U.S. American National Red Cross.
RED CROSS SERVICE RECORD: ACCOMPLISHMENTS OF SEVEN YEARS: JULY 1, 1939-JUNE 30, 1946. Washington, 1946. 105 p. (ARC Circular)

4290 Red Cross. U.S. American National Red Cross. Hawaii Chapter.
HAWAII CHAPTER, AMERICAN RED CROSS, WAR RECORD OF VOLUNTEER SPECIAL SERVICES, BY THE SKIPPER AND THE TOP SERGEANT. Honolulu, 1947. 122 p.

4291 Rennel, Francis J. Rennel Rodd, baron.
BRITISH MILITARY ADMINISTRATION OF OCCUPIED TERRITORIES IN AFRICA DURING THE YEARS 1941-1947. London, H.M. Stationery Office, 1948. 637 p.

4292 Rosenman, Samuel I.
CIVILIAN SUPPLIES FOR THE LIBERATED AREAS OF NORTHWEST EUROPE: REPORT TO THE PRESIDENT OF THE UNITED STATES; PREPARED PURSUANT TO LETTER OF PRESIDENT FRANKLIN D. ROOSEVELT DATED JANUARY 20, 1945. Committee on Foreign Affairs, House of Representatives, 79th Cong., 1st sess. Washington, U.S. Government Printing Office, 1945. 242 p.

4293 Rygg, Andrew N.
AMERICAN RELIEF FOR NORWAY: A SURVEY OF AMERICAN RELIEF WORK FOR NORWAY DURING AND AFTER THE SECOND WORLD WAR. Chicago, 1947. 320 p.

4294 Saunders, Hilary A. St. G.
THE LEFT HANDSHAKE: THE BOY SCOUT MOVEMENT DURING THE WAR, 1939-1945. London, Collins, 1949. 256 p.

4295 Saunders, Hilary A. St. G.
THE RED CROSS AND THE WHITE: A SHORT HISTORY OF THE JOINT WAR ORGANIZATION OF THE BRITISH RED CROSS SOCIETY AND THE ORDER OF ST. JOHN OF JERUSALEM DURING THE WAR 1939-1945. Foreword by Lord Chetwode. London, Hollis and Carter, 1949. 195 p.

4296 Seymour, Harold J.
DESIGN FOR GIVING: THE STORY OF THE NATIONAL WAR FUND, INC., 1943-1947. New York, Harper, 1947. 182 p.

4297 Skimming, Sylvia.
SAND IN MY SHOES: THE TALE OF A RED CROSS WELFARE OFFICER WITH BRITISH HOSPITALS OVERSEAS IN THE SECOND WORLD WAR. Foreword by Sir Bertram N. Sergison-Brooke. Edinburgh, Oliver and Boyd, 1948. 182 p.

4298 Smith, Dudley G.
"THEY ALSO SERVED": THE STORY OF SUSSEX SCOUTS IN WAR. Foreword by Lt.-Col. W. J. Keen. Chichester, Sussex Scouts Association, 1945. 51 p.

4299 Spender, Stephen.
CITIZENS IN WAR, AND AFTER. Foreword by Herbert Morrison. London, Harrap, 1945. 112 p.

4300 Titmuss, Richard M.
PROBLEMS OF SOCIAL POLICY. London, H.M. Stationery Office, 1950. 596 p. (History of the Second World War: United Kingdom Civil Series)

4301 Trevelyan, Mary.
I'LL WALK BESIDE YOU: LETTERS FROM BELGIUM, SEPTEMBER 1944-MAY 1945. London and New York, Longmans, Green, 1946. 111 p.

4302 United Nations Relief and Rehabilitation Administration. Chief Historian.
U.N.R.R.A.: THE HISTORY OF THE UNITED NATIONS RELIEF AND REHABILITATION ADMINISTRATION. Prepared by a special staff under the direction of George Woodbridge. New York, Columbia University Press; London, Oxford University Press, 1950. 3 v.

4303 WAR ORGANIZATION OF THE BRITISH RED CROSS SOCIETY AND ORDER OF ST. JOHN OF JERUSALEM RED CROSS AND ST. JOHN: THE OFFICIAL RECORD OF THE HUMANITARIAN SERVICES OF THE WAR ORGANIZATION OF THE BRITISH RED CROSS SOCIETY. Compiled by P. G. Combray and G. G. B. Briggs. London, 1949. 723 p.

4304 Williams, Annabelle R.
OPERATION GREASE-PAINT. Hollywood, Calif., House-Warven, 1951. 240 p.

4305 Wilson, Roger C.
QUAKER RELIEF: AN ACCOUNT OF THE RELIEF WORK OF THE SOCIETY OF FRIENDS, 1940-48. London, Allen and Unwin, 1952. 373 p.

4306 Yoder, Samuel A.
MIDDLE-EAST SOJOURN. Scottdale, Pa., Herald Press, 1951. 310 p.

D. RELIGIOUS AND MORAL ASPECTS; MILITARY CHAPLAINS; CONSCIENTIOUS OBJECTORS; CHURCHES

4307   Amoury, Daisy.
FATHER CYCLONE. New York, Messner, 1958. 253 p.

4308   Bell, George K. A.
THE CHURCH AND HUMANITY, 1939-1946. London, Longmans, Green, 1946. 252 p.

4309   Bettelheim, Bruno.
DYNAMICS OF PREJUDICE: A PSYCHOLOGICAL AND SOCIOLOGICAL STUDY OF VETERANS. New York, Harper, 1950. 227 p.

4310   Braddon, Russell.
CHESHIRE, V.C.: A STORY OF WAR AND PEACE. London, Evans, 1954. 217 p.

4311   Bruckberger, Raymond L.
ONE SKY TO SHARE. Translated by Dorothy C. Howell. New York, Kenedy, 1952. 248 p.

4312   Caldwell, Daniel T., and Benjamin L. Bowman.
THEY ANSWERED THE CALL. Richmond, John Knox Press, 1952. 142 p.

4313   Carlson, Alvin O.
HE IS ABLE: FAITH OVERCOMES FEAR IN A FOXHOLE. Grand Rapids, Mich., Zondervan, 1945. 82 p.

4314   Catlin, George E. G., Vera Brittain, and Sheila Hodges.
ABOVE ALL NATIONS: AN ANTHOLOGY. Foreword by Victor Gollancz. London, Gollancz, 1945. 87 p.

4315   Chapman, Robert B.
TELL IT TO THE CHAPLAIN. New York, Exposition Press, 1952. 151 p.

4316   Christian Science Publishing Society.
THE STORY OF CHRISTIAN SCIENCE WARTIME ACTIVITIES, 1939-1946. Boston, 1947. 434 p.

4317   Connelly, Kenneth A.
CHAPLAIN'S ASSISTANT, FROM THE CORRESPONDENCE OF CORPORAL KENNETH A. CONNELLY, JR. Seattle, Craftsman Press, 1945. 103 p.

4318   Dennis, Clyde H. (ed.)
THESE LIVE ON: THE BEST OF TRUE STORIES UNVEILING THE POWER AND PRESENCE OF GOD IN WORLD WAR II. Chicago, Good Books, 1945. 204 p.

4319   Doward, Jan S.
OUT OF THE STORM. Mountain View, Calif., Pacific Press Publishing Association, 1954. 87 p.

4320   Eades, Prince Alvah.
THEY DID NOT MARCH ALONE. New York, Comet Press Books, 1956. 99 p. (Reflection Book)

4321   Friends, Society of. American Friends Service Committee.
THE EXPERIENCE OF THE AMERICAN FRIENDS SERVICE COMMITTEE IN CIVILIAN PUBLIC SERVICE UNDER THE SELECTIVE TRAINING AND SERVICE ACT OF 1940, 1941-1945. Philadelphia, 1945. 51 p.

4322   Garrenton, John S.
THE FLYING CHAPLAIN. New York, Vantage Press, 1957. 107 p.

4323   Glasser, Arthur F.
AND SOME BELIEVED: A CHAPLAIN'S EXPERIENCES WITH THE MARINES IN THE SOUTH PACIFIC. Chicago, Moody Press, 1946. 208 p.

4324   Goldmann, Gereon K.
THE SHADOW OF HIS WINGS. Translated by Benedict Leutenegger. Chicago, Franciscan Herald Press, 1964. 285 p.

4325   Hafer, Harold F.
THE EVANGELICAL AND REFORMED CHURCHES AND WORLD WAR II. Philadelphia, 1947. 137 p.

4326   Haggerty, James E.
GUERRILLA PADRE IN MINDANAO. New York and Toronto, Longmans, Green, 1946. 257 p.

4327   Hayes, Denis.
CHALLENGE OF CONSCIENCE. THE STORY OF THE CONSCIENTIOUS OBJECTORS OF 1939-1949. London, Allen and Unwin, 1949. 406 p.

4328   Hershberger, Guy F.
THE MENNONITE CHURCH IN THE SECOND WORLD WAR. Scottdale, Pa., Mennonite Publishing House, 1951. 308 p.

4329   Hickcox, Percy M.
MINE EYES HAVE SEEN. Boston, Mosher Press, 1950. 109 p.

4330   Hickey, Raymond M.
THE SCARLET DAWN. New York, Vantage Press, 1953. 222 p.

4331   Hough, Donald.
DARLING, I AM HOME. New York, Norton, 1946. 176 p.

4332   Hughes, William R. (comp. and trans.).
THOSE HUMAN RUSSIANS: A COLLECTION OF INCIDENTS RELATED BY GERMANS. Foreword by Victor Gollancz. London, Gollancz, 1950. 128 p.

4333   Kertzer, Morris N.
WITH AN H ON MY DOG TAG. New York, Behrman House, 1947. 197 p.

4334   Lehmann, Leo H.
VATICAN POLICY IN THE SECOND WORLD WAR. New York, Agora, 1946. 51 p.

4335 Leuschner, Martin L., Charles F. Zummach, and Walter E. Kohrs (eds. and comps.).
RELIGION IN THE RANKS. Cleveland, Roger Williams Press, 1946. 128 p.

4336 Lynip, G. Louise.
ON GOOD GROUND: MISSIONARY STORIES FROM THE PHILIPPINES. Grand Rapids, Mich., Eerdmans, 1946. 149 p.

4337 Lynn, Rita Le B.
THE NATIONAL CATHOLIC COMMUNITY SERVICE IN WORLD WAR II. Washington, Catholic University of America Press, 1952. 290 p.

4338 Maahs, Arnold M.
OUR EYES WERE OPENED. Columbus, Ohio, Wartburg Press, 1946. 110 p.

4339 McMillan, Archibald M.
FOR CHRIST IN CHINA. Nashville, Broadman Press, 1949. 141 p.

4340 Matsumoto, Toru.
BEYOND PREJUDICE: A STORY OF THE CHURCH AND JAPANESE AMERICANS. New York, Published for Home Missions Council of North America, Foreign Missions Conference of North America and Federal Council of Churches of Christ in America, by Friendship Press, 1946. 145 p.

4341 Matthews, Walter R.
SAINT PAUL'S CATHEDRAL IN WARTIME, 1939-1945. London, Hutchinson, 1946. 104 p.

4342 Metcalf, George R.
WITH CROSS AND SHOVEL: A CHAPLAIN'S LETTERS FROM ENGLAND, FRANCE, AND GERMANY, 1942-1945. Edited with commentary by Margaret C. Metcalf. Duxbury, Mass., 1960. 263 p.

4343 Methodist Church (U.S.). Commission on Chaplains.
CHAPLAINS OF THE METHODIST CHURCH IN WORLD WAR II: A PICTORIAL RECORD OF THEIR WORK. Washington, 1948. 156 p.

4344 Moellering, Ralph L.
MODERN WAR AND AMERICAN CHURCHES: A FACTUAL STUDY OF THE CHRISTIAN CONSCIENCE ON TRIAL FROM 1939 TO THE COLD WAR CRISIS OF TODAY. New York, American Press, 1947. 141 p.

4345 Moore, Edith.
NO FRIEND OF DEMOCRACY: A STUDY OF ROMAN CATHOLIC POLICIES, THEIR INFLUENCE ON THE COURSE OF THE WAR AND THE GROWTH OF FASCISM. 5th ed. London, International Publishing Co., 1945. 52 p.

4346 National Lutheran Council.
BY THEIR SIDE: A MEMORIAL; WAR SERVICE OF THE NATIONAL LUTHERAN COUNCIL, 1940-1948. n.p., 1949. 112 p.

4347 Nelson, Ralph W.
SOLDIER, YOU'RE IT! New York, Association Press, 1945. 132 p.

4348 Pollock, P. Hamilton.
WINGS ON THE CROSS: A PADRE WITH THE R.A.F. Dublin, Clonmore and Reynolds, 1954. 199 p.

4349 Ray, Samuel H.
A CHAPLAIN AFLOAT AND ASHORE. Salado, Tex., Jones Press, 1962. 122 p.

4350 Read, Frances W.
G.I. PARSON. New York, Morehouse and Gorham, 1945. 117 p.

4351 Rogers, Edward K.
DOUGHBOY CHAPLAIN. Boston, Meador, 1946. 230 p.

4352 ST. JOHN-ON-THE-HILL, PORT MORESBY, 1943-1944. Sydney, Penfold, 1945. 63 p.

4353 Satō, Tasuku, and Mark Tennien.
I REMEMBER FLORES. New York, Farrar, Straus, 1957. 129 p.

4354 Sholty, Alva H.
TWICE IN TWO THOUSAND YEARS. Foreword by Hon. Raymond E. Willis. Dayton, Ohio, Otterbein Press, 1946. 220 p.

4355 Sibley, Mulford Q., and Ada Wardlaw.
CONSCIENTIOUS OBJECTORS IN PRISON, 1940-45. Philadelphia, Pacifist Research Bureau, 1945. 68 p.

4356 Sibley, Mulford Q., and Philip E. Jacobs.
CONSCRIPTION OF CONSCIENCE: THE AMERICAN STATE AND THE CONSCIENTIOUS OBJECTOR, 1940-1947. Ithaca, N.Y., Cornell University Press, 1952. 580 p. (Cornell Studies in Civil Liberty)

4357 Sisters of Our Lady of the Sacred Heart.
RED GREW THE HARVEST: MISSIONARY EXPERIENCES DURING THE PACIFIC WAR OF 1941-45. Sydney, 1947. 185 p.

4358 Smith, Waldo E. L.
WHAT TIME THE TEMPEST: AN ARMY CHAPLAIN'S STORY. Toronto, Ryerson Press, 1953. 305 p.

4359 Snyder, Robert S.
AND WHEN MY TASK ON EARTH IS DONE: THE DAY BY DAY EXPERIENCES OF A CHRISTIAN GI, WRITTEN IN HIS DIARY WHICH WAS SENT HOME BY THE WAR DEPARTMENT. Kansas City, Mo., Graphic Laboratory, 1950. 160 p.

4360 Society for the Propagation of the Faith.
THE PRIEST GOES TO WAR: A PICTORIAL OUTLINE OF THE WORK OF THE CATHOLIC CHAPLAINS IN THE SECOND WORLD WAR. New York, Society for the Propagation of the Faith, 1946. 128 p.

4361 Spellman, Francis J.
NO GREATER LOVE: THE STORY OF OUR SOLDIERS. New York, Scribner, 1945. 147 p.

4362 Steven, Walter T.
IN THIS SIGN. Foreword by Charles Foulkes. Toronto, Ryerson Press, 1948. 182 p.

4363 THROUGH TOIL AND TRIBULATION: MISSIONARY EXPERIENCES IN CHINA DURING THE WAR OF 1937-1945 TOLD BY THE MISSIONARIES. London, Carey Press, 1947. 208 p.

4364 Underhill, M. L., and others.
NEW ZEALAND CHAPLAINS IN THE SECOND WORLD WAR. Wellington, War History Branch, Internal Affairs Dept., 1950. 188 p.

4365 U.S. Army. Chaplain Corps.
AMERICAN CHAPLAINS OF THE FIFTH ARMY. Milan, 1945. 86 p.

4366 U.S. Army. Forces in the Pacific.
HISTORY OF CHAPLAIN'S ACTIVITIES IN THE PACIFIC. Compiled by Chaplain Section, GHQ, AFPAC. n.p., 1946. 543 p.

4367 Van Dusen, Henry P.
THEY FOUND THE CHURCH THERE: THE ARMED FORCES DISCOVER CHRISTIAN MISSIONS. New York, Scribner, 1945. 148 p.

4368 Vansittart, Robert G.
BONES OF CONTENTION. New York, Knopf, 1945. 157 p.

4369 Walker, Reginald F.
PIUS OF PEACE: A STUDY OF THE PACIFIC WORK OF HIS HOLINESS POPE PIUS XII IN THE WORLD WAR, 1939-1945. Dublin, Gill; Westminster, Md., Newman Bookshop, 1946. 182 p.

4370 Wallace, Robert N. A. (ed.).
GOD'S WORKINGS IN WORLD WAR II; OR, PROPHECIES AND THEIR FULFILLMENTS, BOOK NO. 2. Placentia, Calif., Undenominational Church of the Lord, 1947. 115 p.

4371 Wuest, Karl A. (Padre, pseud.).
THEY TOLD IT TO THE CHAPLAIN. New York, Vantage Press, 1953. 138 p.

4372 Youell, George.
AFRICA MARCHES. London, S.P.C.K., 1949. 144 p.

4373 Yugoslavia. Poslanstvo, U.S.
THE CASE OF ARCHBISHOP STEPINAC. Washington, Information Officer, Embassy of the Federal People's Republic of Yugoslavia, 1947. 96 p.

4374 Zahn, Gordon C.
GERMAN CATHOLICS AND HITLER'S WARS: A STUDY IN SOCIAL CONTROL. New York, Sheed and Ward, 1962. 232 p.

E. THE ARTS AND THE WAR

4375 Allied Forces.
WORKS OF ART IN GREECE, THE GREEK ISLANDS AND THE DODECANESE, LOSSES AND SURVIVALS IN THE WAR. Compiled by the Monuments, Fine Arts and Archives Sub-commission of the C.M.F., and issued by the British Committee on the Preservation and Restitution of Works of Art, Archives, and Other Material in Enemy Hands. London, H.M. Stationery Office, 1946. 63 p.

4376 Bankson, Budd.
I SHOULD LIVE SO LONG. Philadelphia, Lippincott, 1952. 287 p.

4377 Colonna, Jerry.
WHO THREW THAT COCONUT! Foreword by Bob Hope. Garden City, N.Y., Distributed for McCombs Publishing Co. by Garden City Publishing Co., 1946. 94 p.

4378 Comfort, Charles F.
ARTIST AT WAR. Toronto, Ryerson Press, 1956. 187 p.

4379 Control Commission for Germany (British Element).
WORKS OF ART IN GERMANY (BRITISH ZONE OF OCCUPATION): LOSSES AND SURVIVALS IN THE WAR. Compiled by the Monuments, Fine Arts and Archives Branch of the Control Commission for Germany (British Element) and issued by the British Committee on the Preservation and Restitution of Works of Art, Archives, and Other Material in Enemy Hands. London, H.M. Stationery Office, 1946. 65 p.

4380 Dean, Basil.
THE THEATRE AT WAR. London, Harrap, 1956. 573 p.

4381 Fasola, Cesare.
THE FLORENCE GALLERIES AND THE WAR: HISTORY AND RECORDS, WITH A LIST OF MISSING WORKS OF ART. Florence, Casa Editrice Monsalvato, 1945. 112 p.

4382 Great Britain. Committee on the Preservation and Restitution of Works of Art, Archives, and Other Materials in Enemy Hands.
WORKS OF ART IN AUSTRIA (BRITISH ZONE OF OCCUPATION): LOSSES AND SURVIVALS IN THE WAR. Compiled from reports supplied by the Monuments, Fine Arts and Archives Branch of the Control Commission for Austria (British Element) and issued by the British Committee on the Preservation and Restoration of Works of Art, Archives, and Other Material in Enemy Hands. London, H.M. Stationery Office, 1946. 60 p.

4383 Great Britain. Committee on the Preservation and Restitution of Works of Art, Archives, and Other Materials in Enemy Hands.
WORKS OF ART IN ITALY: LOSSES AND SURVIVALS IN THE WAR. Compiled from War Office reports by the British Committee on the Preservation and Restitution of Works of Art, Archives, and Other Materials in Enemy Hands. London, H.M. Stationery Office, 1945-46. 2 v.

4384 Hartt, Frederick.
FLORENTINE ART UNDER FIRE. Princeton, N.J., Princeton University Press, 1949. 147 p.

4385 Howe, Thomas C.
SALT MINES AND CASTLES: THE DISCOVERY AND RESTITUTION OF LOOTED EUROPEAN ART. Indianapolis, Bobbs-Merrill, 1946. 334 p.

4386 Jenkinson, Hilary, and H. E. Bell (comps.).
ITALIAN ARCHIVES DURING THE WAR AND AT ITS CLOSE. Issued by the British Committee on the Preservation and Restitution of Works of Art, Archives, and Other Material in Enemy Hands. London, H.M. Stationery Office, 1947. 55 p.

4387 Kent, William.
THE LOST TREASURES OF LONDON. Introduction by Norman Brett-James. London, Phoenix House, 1947. 150 p.

4388 Lavagnino, Emilio.
FIFTY WAR-DAMAGED MONUMENTS OF ITALY. Foreword by Benedetto Croce and others; translated by Sara T. Morey. Rome, Instituto Poligrafico dello Stato, 1946. 132 p.

4389 Look, editors of.
MOVIE LOT TO BEACHHEAD: THE MOTION PICTURE GOES TO WAR AND PREPARES FOR THE FUTURE. Preface by Robert St. John. Garden City, N.Y., Doubleday, Doran, 1945. 291 p.

4390 Methuen, Paul A.
NORMANDY DIARY: BEING A RECORD OF SURVIVALS AND LOSSES OF HISTORICAL MONUMENTS IN NORTHWESTERN FRANCE, TOGETHER WITH THOSE IN THE ISLAND OF WALCHEREN AND IN THAT PART OF BELGIUM TRAVERSED BY 21ST ARMY GROUP IN 1944-45. London, Hale, 1952. 263 p.

4391 Richards, James M. (ed.).
THE BOMBED BUILDINGS OF BRITAIN: A RECORD OF THE ARCHITECTURAL CASUALTIES. London, Architectural Press, 1947. 202 p.

4392 Rorimer, James J., with Gilbert Rabin.
SURVIVAL: THE SALVAGE AND PROTECTION OF ART IN WAR. New York, Abelard Press, 1950. 291 p.

4393 Roxan, David, and Ken Wanstall.
THE JACKDAW OF LINZ: THE STORY OF HITLER'S ART THEFTS. London, Cassell, 1964. 195 p.

Other edition:
THE RAPE OF ART: THE STORY OF HITLER'S PLUNDER OF THE GREAT MASTERPIECES OF EUROPE. New York, Coward-McCann, 1965. 195 p.

4394 Schütz, William W.
PENS UNDER THE SWASTIKA: A STUDY IN RECENT GERMAN WRITING. London, Student Christian Movement Press, 1946. 110 p.

4395 Seddon, Richard.
A HAND UPLIFTED. London, Muller, 1963. 208 p.

4396 Woolley, Sir Charles L.
A RECORD OF THE WORK DONE BY THE MILITARY AUTHORITIES FOR THE PROTECTION OF THE TREASURES OF ART AND HISTORY IN WAR AREAS. London, H.M. Stationery Office, 1947. 71 p.

F. RADIO, PRESS, CENSORSHIP

4397 Allied Forces. Supreme Headquarters.
A HISTORY OF FIELD PRESS CENSORSHIP IN SHAEF, WORLD WAR II [COMPILED AS AN AFTER ACTION REPORT BY THE U.S. ARMY FIELD PRESS CENSORS AT SUPREME HEADQUARTERS, AEF]. Paramus, N.J., Reproduced by 201st Press Censorship Organization, n.d. 123 l.

4398 Carrigg, John J.
AMERICAN CATHOLIC PRESS OPINION WITH REFERENCE TO AMERICA'S INTERVENTION IN THE SECOND WORLD WAR. Washington, 1947. 161 l.

4399 Eide, Richard B.
NORWAY'S PRESS, 1940-1945, DURING THE OCCUPATION. Stillwater, Oklahoma A and M College, 1948. 54 l.

4400 Fletcher, Leonard.
THEY NEVER FAILED: THE STORY OF THE PROVINCIAL PRESS IN WARTIME. London, Newspaper Society, 1946. 80 p.

4401 Henslow, Miles.
THE MIRACLE OF RADIO: THE STORY OF RADIO'S DECISIVE CONTRIBUTION TO VICTORY. London, Evans, 1946. 127 p.

4402 Kirby, Edward M., and Jack W. Harris.
STAR-SPANGLED RADIO. Chicago, Ziff-Davis, 1948. 278 p.

4403 Koop, Theodore F.
WEAPON OF SILENCE. Chicago, University of Chicago Press, 1946. 304 p.

4404 Krabbe, Henning (ed.).
VOICES FROM BRITAIN: BROADCAST HISTORY, 1939-45. London, Allen and Unwin, 1947. 304 p.

4405 Legg, Frank.
THE EYES OF DAMIEN PARER. London, Angus and Robertson; Adelaide, Rigby, 1963. 54 p.

4406 Miller, Lee G.
THE STORY OF ERNIE PYLE. New York, Viking Press, 1950. 439 p.

4407 Monks, Noel.
EYE-WITNESS. London, Muller, 1956. 344 p.

Other edition:
London, Brown, Watson, 1959. 160 p. (Digit Books)

4408 Oldfield, Barney.
NEVER A SHOT IN ANGER. New York, Duell, Sloan and Pearce, 1956. 334 p.

4409 St. John, Robert.
FOREIGN CORRESPONDENT. Garden City, N.Y., Doubleday, 1957. 283 p.

Other edition:
London, Hutchinson, 1960. 240 p.

4410 Thomson, George P.
BLUE PENCIL ADMIRAL: THE INSIDE STORY OF PRESS CENSORSHIP. London, Low, Marston, 1947. 216 p.

G. SCIENCE, EDUCATION, LIBRARIES

4411 American Book Center for War Devastated Libraries.
THE AMERICAN BOOK CENTER FOR WAR DEVASTATED LIBRARIES, INC., 1944-1948, SPONSORED BY THE COUNCIL OF NATIONAL LIBRARY ASSOCIATIONS. New York, 1953. 60 p.

4412 Bawden, William T.
THE CONTRIBUTION OF KANSAS STATE TEACHERS COLLEGE TO THE WAR EFFORT, 1940-1945. Pittsburg, Kansas State Teachers College, 1950. 71 p.

4413 Bossing, Nelson L., and Leo J. Brueckner.
THE IMPACT OF THE WAR ON THE SCHOOLS OF RED WING. Minneapolis, University of Minnesota, 1945. 118 p.

4414 Brosse, Thérèse.
WAR-HANDICAPPED CHILDREN: REPORT ON THE EUROPEAN SITUATION. Paris, UNESCO, 1950. 142 p. (Problems in Education)

4415 Burchard, John E.
Q.E.D.: M.I.T. IN WORLD WAR II. New York, Wiley, 1948. 354 p.

4416 Butler, Pierce (ed.).
BOOKS AND LIBRARIES IN WARTIME. Chicago, University of Chicago Press, 1945. 159 p.

4417 Carnahan, Floyd L.
THE PENN SCHOOL OF CHEMISTRY AND PHYSICS IN WORLD WAR II. State College, Pennsylvania State College, 1948. 68 l.

4418 Clough, Wilson O.
THE UNIVERSITY OF WYOMING, 1939-1946, A LAND-GRANT COLLEGE IN WAR. n.p., 1951. 89 p.

4419 Council on Books in Wartime.
A HISTORY OF THE COUNCIL ON BOOKS IN WARTIME, 1942-1946. Written by Robert O. Ballou. New York, 1946. 126 p.

4420 Cowles, LeRoy E.
UNIVERSITY OF UTAH AND WORLD WAR II. Salt Lake City, Desert News Press, 1949. 236 p.

4421 Crowther, James G., and Richard Widdington.
SCIENCE AT WAR. London, H.M. Stationery Office, 1947. 185 p.

Other edition:
New York, Philosophical Library, 1948. 185 p.

4422 Cushing, Emory C.
HISTORY OF ENTOMOLOGY IN WORLD WAR II. Washington, Smithsonian Institution, 1957. 117 p. (Smithsonian Institution Publication)

4423 Duggan, Stephen, and Betty Drury.
THE RESCUE OF SCIENCE AND LEARNING: THE STORY OF THE EMERGENCY COMMITTEE IN AID OF DISPLACED FOREIGN SCHOLARS. New York, Macmillan, 1948. 214 p.

4424 Eggleston, Wilfrid.
SCIENTISTS AT WAR. Toronto and New York, Oxford University Press, 1950. 291 p.

4425 Gaunt, Howard C.A.
TWO EXILES: BEING A RECORD OF THE ADVENTURES OF MALVERN COLLEGE DURING THE WAR. London, Low, Marston, 1946. 86 p.

4426 Harvard University. Porcellian Club.
PORCELLIAN CLUB IN WORLD WAR II. Cambridge, Mass., Printed for the Club, 1948. 162 p.

4427 Herge, Henry C.
WARTIME COLLEGE TRAINING PROGRAMS OF THE ARMED SERVICES. With chapters on special phases by Sidney L. Pressey and others. Washington, D.C., American Council on Education, 1948. 214 p.

4428 James, Leonard F. (ed.).
PHILLIPS ACADEMY, ANDOVER, IN WORLD WAR II. Andover, Mass., Phillips Academy, 1948. 603 p.

4429 Jamieson, John A.
BOOKS FOR THE ARMY: THE ARMY LIBRARY SERVICES IN THE SECOND WORLD WAR. New York, Columbia University Press, 1950. 335 p.

4430 Lake Forest University, Lake Forest College.
WORLD WAR II MILITARY RECORDS. Edited by Francis Beidler II. Lake Forest, Ill., Lake Forest University Press, 1948. 199 p.

4431 Noyes, William A. (ed.).
CHEMISTRY: A HISTORY OF THE CHEMISTRY COMPONENTS OF THE NATIONAL DEFENSE RESEARCH COMMITTEE, 1940-1946. By R. Connor and others; foreword by James B. Conant and Roger Adams. Boston, Little, Brown, 1948. 524 p. (Science in World War II: Office of Scientific Research and Development)

4432 Purdue University.
A RECORD OF A UNIVERSITY IN THE WAR YEARS, 1941-1945. Edited by H.B. Knoll. Lafayette, Ind., 1947. 213 p. (Archives of Purdue)

4433 Purdue University.
THE ROLL OF HONOR OF PURDUE UNIVERSITY, 1941-1945. Edited by H. B. Knoll. Lafayette, Ind., 1947. 118 p. (Archives of Purdue)

4434 Simon, Leslie E.
GERMAN RESEARCH IN WORLD WAR II: AN ANALYSIS OF THE CONDUCT OF RESEARCH. New York, Wiley; London, Chapman and Hall, 1947. 218 p.

4435 Simon, Leslie E.
GERMAN SCIENTIFIC ESTABLISHMENTS: REPORT. Brooklyn, Reproduced by Mapleton House, 1947. 228 p.

4436 Snow, Sir Charles P.
A POSTSCRIPT TO "SCIENCE AND GOVERNMENT." Cambridge, Mass., Harvard University Press; London, Oxford University Press, 1962. 37 p.

4437 Snow, Sir Charles P.
SCIENCE AND GOVERNMENT. Cambridge, Mass., Harvard University Press, 1961. 88 p.

4438 Stewart, Irvin.
ORGANIZING SCIENTIFIC RESEARCH FOR WAR: THE ADMINISTRATIVE HISTORY OF THE OFFICE OF SCIENTIFIC RESEARCH AND DEVELOPMENT. Boston, Little, Brown, 1948. 358 p.

4439 Thiesmeyer, Lincoln R., and John E. Burchard.
COMBAT SCIENTISTS. Volume editor, Alan T. Waterman; foreword by Karl T. Compton. Boston, Little, Brown, 1947. 412 p. (Science in World War II: Office of Scientific Research and Development)

4440 U. S. Office of Education.
EDUCATION UNDER ENEMY OCCUPATION IN BELGIUM, CHINA, CZECHOSLOVAKIA, FRANCE, GREECE, LUXEMBOURG, NETHERLANDS, NORWAY, POLAND. Washington, 1945. 71 p.

4441 Vatican. Biblioteca Vaticana.
LIBRARIES GUESTS OF THE VATICANA DURING THE SECOND WORLD WAR, WITH THE CATALOGUE OF THE EXHIBITION. Vatican City, Apostolic Vatican Library, 1945. 70 p.

4442 Warmington, Eric H.
A HISTORY OF BIRKBECK COLLEGE, UNIVERSITY OF LONDON, DURING THE SECOND WORLD WAR, 1939-1945. London, Birkbeck College, 1954. 206 p.

4443 Watsonian Club, Edinburgh.
WATSONIAN WAR RECORD, 1939-1945. Edinburgh, 1951. 157 p.

4444 Wolf, Abraham.
HIGHER EDUCATION IN GERMAN-OCCUPIED COUNTRIES. London, Methuen, 1945. 133 p.

4445 World University Service.
WORLD STUDENT RELIEF 1940-1950: A STORY OF UNIVERSITY ENTERPRISE AND SOLIDARITY, AND OF THE COLLABORATION OF FIVE ORGANISATIONS TO GIVE COMMON EXPRESSION TO THE DESIRE OF TENS OF THOUSANDS OF PROFESSORS AND STUDENTS THROUGHOUT THE WORLD TO MAKE GOOD THE RAVAGES OF WAR. Geneva, 1951. 80 p.

VII. POSITION OF THE NEUTRAL COUNTRIES

4446   De Valera, Eamonn.
     IRELAND'S STAND: BEING A SELECTION OF SPEECHES OF EAMONN DE VALERA DURING THE WAR (1939-1945). Dublin, Gill, 1946. 102 p.

4447   Feis, Herbert.
     THE SPANISH STORY: FRANCO AND THE NATIONS AT WAR. New York, Knopf, 1948. 282 p.

4448   Haring, Clarence H.
     SUMMARY OF OPINION IN LATIN AMERICA: A CONFIDENTIAL REPORT. Princeton, N.J., 194-. 70 l.

4449   Hartmann, Frederick H.
     THE SWISS PRESS AND FOREIGN AFFAIRS IN WORLD WAR II. Gainesville, University of Florida Press, 1960. 87 p. (University of Florida Monographs. Social Sciences)

4450   Hayes, Carlton J. H.
     WARTIME MISSION IN SPAIN, 1942-1945. New York and London, Macmillan, 1945. 313 p.

4451   Ochsner, Charly R.
     NEUTRALITY IN WORLD WAR II, ITS ORIGIN, ITS APPLICATION AND ITS VALUE. Washington, 1946. 70 l.

4452   Templewood, Samuel J. G. Hoare, 1st viscount.
     AMBASSADOR ON SPECIAL MISSION. London, Collins, 1946. 320 p.

     Other edition:
     COMPLACENT DICTATOR. New York, Knopf, 1947. 318 p.

4453   Young, George G.
     OUTPOSTS OF PEACE. London, Hodder and Stoughton, 1945. 192 p.

VIII. WAR CRIMES TRIALS (see also I.A and VI.A)

A. GENERAL

4454 Appleman, John A.
MILITARY TRIBUNALS AND INTERNATIONAL CRIMES. Indianapolis, Bobbs-Merrill, 1954. 421 p.

4455 Keenan, Joseph B., and Brendan F. Brown.
CRIMES AGAINST INTERNATIONAL LAW. Washington, Public Affairs Press, 1950. 226 p.

4456 Lachs, Manfred.
WAR CRIMES: AN ATTEMPT TO DEFINE THE ISSUES. London, Stevens, 1945. 108 p.

4457 Maugham, Frederic H. M.
U.N.O. AND WAR CRIMES. With a postscript by Lord Hankey. London, Murray, 1951. 143 p.

4458 Pompe, Cornelia A.
AGGRESSIVE WAR: AN INTERNATIONAL CRIME. The Hague, Nijhoff, 1953. 382 p.

4459 United Nations War Crimes Commission.
HISTORY OF THE UNITED NATIONS WAR CRIMES COMMISSION AND THE DEVELOPMENT OF THE LAWS OF WAR. London, H.M. Stationery Office, 1948. 592 p.

B. GERMANY

4460 Alexander, Charles W.
JUSTICE AT NUERNBERG: A PICTORIAL RECORD OF THE TRIAL OF NAZI WAR CRIMINALS BY THE INTERNATIONAL TRIBUNAL, AT NUERNBERG, GERMANY, 1945-46. Photographed by Charles W. Alexander, director of photography for the trial; text by Anne Keeshan. Chicago, Marvel Press, 1946. 193 p.

4461 Arndt, Karl.
ALPHABETICAL INDEX OF ALL WITNESSES AND DEFENSE COUNSEL HEARD IN THE 12 NÜRNBERG WAR CRIMES TRIALS WITH PAGES OF THE OFFICIAL TRANSCRIPTS OF THE PROCEEDINGS. Bremen, 194-? 172 l.

4462 Belgion, Montgomery.
EPITAPH ON NUREMBERG: A LETTER INTENDED TO HAVE BEEN SENT TO A FRIEND TEMPORARILY ABROAD. London, Falcon Press, 1946. 96 p. (Forum Books)

4463 Belgion, Montgomery.
VICTOR'S JUSTICE: A LETTER INTENDED TO HAVE BEEN SENT TO A FRIEND RECENTLY IN GERMANY. Hinsdale, Ill., Regnery, 1949. 187 p. (Humanist Library)

(A rewriting of the author's EPITAPH ON NUREMBERG)

4464 Benton, Wilbourn E., and Georg Grimm (eds.).
NUREMBERG: GERMAN VIEWS OF THE WAR TRIALS. Dallas, Southern Methodist University Press, 1955. 232 p.

4465 Bernstein, Victor H.
FINAL JUDGEMENT: THE STORY OF NUREMBERG. New York, Boni and Gaer, 1947. 289 p.

Other edition:
London, Latimer House, 1947.

4466 Biddle, Francis B.
IN BRIEF AUTHORITY. Garden City, N.Y., Doubleday, 1962. 494 p.

4467 Brand, George (ed.).
THE VELPKE BABY HOME TRIAL: TRIAL OF HEINRICH GERIKE AND SEVEN OTHERS. London, Hodge, 1950. 356 p. (War Crimes Trials)

4468 Calvocoressi, Peter.
NUREMBERG: THE FACTS, THE LAW, AND THE CONSEQUENCES. London, Chatto and Windus, 1947. 176 p.

Other edition:
New York, Macmillan, 1948.

4469 Cameron, John (ed.).
THE "PELEUS" TRIAL: TRIAL OF KAPITANLEUTNANT ECK AND FOUR OTHERS. London, Hodge, 1948. 247 p. (War Crimes Trials)

4470 Cooper, B. W.
THE NUREMBERG TRIAL. Harmondsworth, Eng., and New York, Penguin Books, 1947. 301 p.

4471 Cuddon, Eric (ed.).
THE TRIAL OF ERICH KILLINGER, HEINZ JUNGE, OTTO BOEHRINGER, HEINRICH EBERGARDT, GUSTAV BAUER-SCHLICHTEGROLL (THE DULAG-LUFT TRIAL). London, Hodge, 1952. 255 p. (War Crimes Trials)

4472 Dubois, Josiah E., Jr., with Edward Johnson.
THE DEVIL'S CHEMISTS: 24 CONSPIRATORS OF THE INTERNATIONAL FARBEN CARTEL WHO MANUFACTURE WARS. Boston, Beacon Press, 1952. 374 p.

4473 Dubois, Josiah E., Jr., with Edward Johnson.
GENERALS IN GREY SUITS: THE DIRECTORS OF THE INTERNATIONAL "I. G. FARBEN" CARTEL, THEIR CONSPIRACY AND TRIAL AT NUREMBERG. London, Bodley Head, 1953. 373 p.

4474 Falkenhorst, Nikolaus von, defendant.
TRAIL OF NIKOLAUS VON FALKENHORST, FORMERLY GENERALOBERST IN THE GERMAN ARMY. Edited by E. H. Stevens; foreword by Sir Norman Birkett. London, Hodge, 1949. 278 p. (War Crimes Trials)

4475 Fishman, Jack.
THE SEVEN MEN OF SPANDAU. London, Allen, 1954. 224 p.

Other edition:
New York, Rinehart, 1954. 276 p.

4476 Fritzsche, Hans.
THE SWORD IN THE SCALES. As told to Hildegard Springer; translated by Diana Pyke and Heinrich Fraenkel; foreword by Frank Owen. London, Wingate, 1953. 335 p.

4477 Gallagher, Richard.
NUREMBERG: THE THIRD REICH ON TRIAL. New York, Avon Book Division, Hearst Corp., 1961. 255 p.

4478 Germany. Heer.
THE CASE AGAINST GENERAL HEUSINGER: DOCUMENTS ILLUSTRATING THE CHARGES OF THE USSR AGAINST FORMER LIEUTENANT-GENERAL ADOLF HEUSINGER, FORMER OPERATIONS CHIEF OF THE WEHRMACHT HIGH COMMAND. Chicago, Translation World Publishers, 1961. 175 p.

4479 Germany (Territory under Allied Occupation, 1945- U.S. Zone). Military Tribunals.
TRIALS OF WAR CRIMINALS BEFORE THE NUERNBERG MILITARY TRIBUNALS UNDER CONTROL COUNCIL LAW NO. 10, NUERNBERG, OCTOBER 1946-APRIL 1949. Washington, U.S. Government Printing Office, 1949-53. 15 v.

4480 Gibb, Andrew D.
PERJURY UNLIMITED: A MONOGRAPH ON NUREMBERG. Edinburgh, Green, 1954. 62 p.

4481 Gilbert, Gustav M.
NUREMBERG DIARY. New York, Farrar, Straus, 1947. 471 p.

Other edition:
London, Eyre and Spottiswoode, 1948.

4482 Glueck, Sheldon.
THE NUREMBERG TRIAL AND AGGRESSIVE WAR. New York, Knopf, 1946. 121 p.

4483 Harris, Whitney R.
TYRANNY ON TRIAL: THE EVIDENCE AT NUREMBERG. Introduced by Robert H. Jackson; foreword by Robert G. Storey. Dallas, Southern Methodist University Press, 1954. 608 p.

4484 Heydecker, Joe J., and Johannes Leeb.
THE NUREMBERG TRIAL: A HISTORY OF NAZI GERMANY AS REVEALED THROUGH THE TESTIMONY AT NUREMBERG. Translated and edited by R. A. Downie. London, Heinemann; Cleveland, World Publishing Co., 1962. 398 p.

4485 International Military Tribunal.
TRIAL OF THE MAJOR WAR CRIMINALS BEFORE THE INTERNATIONAL MILITARY TRIBUNAL, NUREMBERG, 14 NOVEMBER 1945 - 10 OCTOBER 1946. Nuremberg, 1947. 42 v.

4486 Jackson, Robert H.
THE CASE AGAINST THE NAZI WAR CRIMINALS: OPENING STATEMENT FOR THE UNITED STATES OF AMERICA BY ROBERT H. JACKSON, AND OTHER DOCUMENTS. New York, Knopf, 1946. 216 p.

4487 Jackson, Robert H.
THE NÜRNBERG CASE, AS PRESENTED BY ROBERT H. JACKSON, CHIEF COUNSEL FOR THE UNITED STATES, TOGETHER WITH OTHER DOCUMENTS. New York, Knopf, 1947. 268 p.

4488 Janeczek, E.
NUREMBERG JUDGEMENT IN THE LIGHT OF INTERNATIONAL LAW. Geneva, Imp. Populaires, 1949. 142 p.

4489 Kelley, Douglas McG.
22 CELLS IN NUREMBERG: A PSYCHIATRIST EXAMINES THE NAZI CRIMINALS. London, Allen; New York, Greenberg, 1947. 245 p.

4490 Kenny, John P.
MORAL ASPECTS OF NUREMBERG. Washington, D.C., Pontifical Faculty of Theology, Dominican House of Studies, 1949. 168 p. (Thomistic Studies)

4491 Kinter, Earl W. (ed.).
THE HADAMAR TRIAL: TRIAL OF ALFONS KLEIN AND SIX OTHERS. London, Hodge, 1949. 250 p. (War Crimes Trials)

4492 Knieriem, August von.
THE NUREMBERG TRIALS. Translated from German by Elizabeth D. Schmitt; special preface by Max Rheinstein. Chicago, Regnery, 1959. 561 p.

4493 Kramer, Josef, defendant.
TRIAL OF JOSEF KRAMER AND FORTY-FOUR OTHERS: THE BELSEN TRIAL. Edited by Raymond Phillips. London, Hodge, 1949. 749 p. (War Crimes Trials)

4494 Lunau, Heinz.
THE GERMANS ON TRIAL. New York, Storm, 1948. 180 p.

4495 Macdonald, Bruce J. S.
THE TRIAL OF KURT MEYER. Toronto, Clarke, Irwin, 1954. 216 p.

4496 Trainin, Aron Naremovich.
HITLERITE RESPONSIBILITY UNDER CRIMINAL LAW. Edited by A. Y. Vishinski; translated by Andrew Rothstein. London and New York, Hutchinson, 1945. 108 p.

4497 Translation World Publishers, Chicago.
THE CASE AGAINST GENERAL HEUSINGER: DOCUMENTS ILLUSTRATING THE CHARGES OF THE USSR AGAINST FORMER LIEUTENANT-GENERAL ADOLF HEUSINGER, FORMER OPERATIONS CHIEF OF THE WEHRMACHT HIGH COMMAND. Chicago, 1961. 175 p.

4498 U.S. Chief of Counsel for the Prosecution of Axis Criminality.
NAZI CONSPIRACY AND AGGRESSION. Washington, U.S. Government Printing Office, 1946. 8 v.

Supplement A-B:
Washington, U.S. Government Printing Office, 1947-48. 2 v.

4499 West, Rebecca (pseud.).
A TRAIN OF POWDER. New York, Viking Press, 1955. 310 p.

Other edition:
London, Macmillan, 1955. 331 p.

4500 Woetzel, Robert K.
THE NUREMBERG TRIALS IN INTERNATIONAL LAW. London, Stevens; New York, Praeger, 1960. 287 p.

Other edition:
2d ed. (with a postscript on the Eichmann case). 1962.

4501 Zeuss, Wolfgang, defendant.
TRIAL OF WOLFGANG ZEUSS AND OTHERS: THE NATZWEILER TRIAL. Edited by Anthony M. Webb. London, Hodge, 1949. 233 p. (War Crimes Trials)

C. JAPAN

4502 Fixel, Rowland W.
TRIAL OF JAPAN'S WAR LORDS. n.p., 1959. 249 l.

4503 Hanayama, Shinsho.
THE WAY OF DELIVERANCE: THREE YEARS WITH THE CONDEMNED JAPANESE WAR CRIMINALS. Translated by Hideo Suzuki, Eiichi Noda, and James K. Sasaki; translation revised by Harrison Collins, New York, Scribner, 1950. 297 p.

Other edition:
London, Gollancz, 1955. 297 p.

4504 Kenworthy, Aubrey S.
THE TIGER OF MALAYA: THE STORY OF GENERAL TOMOYUKI YAMASHITA AND "DEATH MARCH" GENERAL MASAHARU HOMMA. New York, Exposition Press, 1953. 112 p.

4505 Kodama, Yoshio.
SUGAMO DIARY. Translated from the Japanese by Taro Fukuda. Tokyo, 1960. 275 p.

4506 Mallal, Bashir A. (ed.).
THE DOUBLE TENTH TRIAL: WAR CRIMES COURT. Singapore, Malayan Law Journal Office, 1947. 652 p.

4507 Reel, Adolf F.
THE CASE OF GENERAL YAMASHITA. Chicago, University of Chicago Press; Cambridge, Eng., Cambridge University Press, 1949. 323 p.

4508 Sleeman, Colin (ed.).
TRIAL OF CAPTAIN GOZAWA SADAICHI AND NINE OTHERS. London, Hodge, 1948. 245 p. (War Crimes Trials)

4509 Sumida, Haruzo, defendant.
TRIAL OF SUMIDO HARUZO AND TWENTY OTHERS: THE "DOUBLE TENTH" TRIAL. Edited by Colin Sleeman and S. C. Silkin. London, Hodge, 1951. 324 p. (War Crimes Trials Series)

4510 Supreme Commander for the Allied Powers. Government Section.
THE CASE OF GENERAL YAMASHITA: A MEMORANDUM. Written by Courtney Whitney, Chief, Government Section. Tokyo, 1950. 82 p.

4511 Yamada, Otozo, defendant.
MATERIALS ON THE TRIAL OF FORMER SERVICEMEN OF THE JAPANESE ARMY, CHARGED WITH MANUFACTURING AND EMPLOYING BACTERIOLOGICAL WEAPONS. Moscow, Foreign Languages Publishing House, 1950. 534 p.

D. EICHMANN TRIAL

4512 Arendt, Hannah.
EICHMANN IN JERUSALEM. New York, Viking Press, 1963. 275 p.

4513 Gollancz, Victor.
THE CASE OF ADOLF EICHMANN. London, 1961. 61 p.

4514 Hull, William L.
THE STRUGGLE FOR A SOUL. Garden City, N.Y., Doubleday, 1963. 175 p.

4515 Linze, Dervey A.
THE TRIAL OF ADOLF EICHMANN. Los Angeles, Holloway House, 1961. 224 p.

4516 Pearlman, Maurice.
CAPTURE AND TRIAL OF ADOLF EICHMANN. New York, Simon and Schuster, 1963. 666 p.

4517 Robinson, Jacob.
AND THE CROOKED SHALL BE MADE STRAIGHT: THE EICHMANN TRIAL, THE JEWISH CATASTROPHE, AND HANNAH ARENDT'S NARRATIVE. New York, Macmillan, 1965. 406 p.

4518 Russell, Edward F. L. Russell, baron.
THE TRIAL OF ADOLF EICHMANN. London, Heinemann, 1962. 324 p.

Other edition:
THE RECORD: THE TRIAL OF ADOLF EICHMANN FOR HIS CRIMES AGAINST THE JEWISH PEOPLE AND AGAINST HUMANITY. New York, Knopf, 1963. 351 p.

4519 Zeiger, Henry A. (ed.).
THE CASE AGAINST ADOLF EICHMANN. Foreword by Harry Golden. New York, New American Library, 1960. 192 p. (Signet Books)

INDEX

AUTHORS AND MAJOR SERIES

Abbott, Delmas W., 1430
Abbott, Harry P., 1106
Abend, Hallett E., 3323
Aberdeen. City Council. 3343
Abshagen, Karl H., 400
Adamic, Louis, 2935
Adams, Leonard P., 3675
Adamson, Hans C., 1481, 2626, 2628, 2629
Adamson, Iain, 1876
Addis, C. T.
Adler, Marta, 3781
Agar-Hamilton, John A. I., 1540, 1541, 1602
Agrafiotis, Cris J., 1616
Agriculture monograph, 3704, 3735, 3742
Ahluwalia, Gian C., 3402
Ahnfeldt, Arnold L., 706
Ahrenfeldt, Robert H., 611
Aikawa, Taksaki, 3078
Air Force and Space Digest, 1986
Aitken, Edward F., 877
Albemarle County Historical Society. War History Committee, 3520
Alcorn, Robert H., 724
Aldouby, Zwy, 3827
Aldridge, Joanna M., 2932
Alessandro, Guilietta d', 3064
Alethea (pseud.), 3256
Alexander, Charles W., 4460
Alexander, Harold R. L. G., 338
Alexander, Michael, 3967
Alexander, Peter, 878
Alfieri, Dino, 2989
Allan, James, 3853
Allan, Sherman, 557
Allbury, Alfred G., 4086
Allchin, Frank, 879
Allen, Ethan P., 3676, 3677
Allen, George E., 3466
Allen, Gwenfread E., 3521
Allen, Hugh, 3678
Allen, Maury, 4146
Allen, Max S., 695
Allen, Robert S., 1108
Allen, Ted, 612
Allen, William E. D., 1634
Allied Commission, 4239
Allied Forces, 1690, 1926, 4375
Allied Forces. Mediterranean Theatre, 1691, 1692
Allied Forces. Southeast Asia Command, 1927
Allied Forces. Southeast Asia Command. Women's Auxiliary Service (Burma), 1928
Allied Forces. Southwest Pacific Area, 2877
Allied Forces. Supreme Headquarters, 284, 1693, 4397
Allied Forces. Supreme Headquarters. Air Defense Division, 2996
Allied Forces. Supreme Headquarters. Mission to Norway, 1694
Allied Forces. Supreme Headquarters. Psychological Warfare Division, 468
Allied Forces. 15th Army Group, 1109
Allied Forces. 21st Army Group, 469, 3782
Allied Forces. 21st Army Group. Medical Services, 613
Allison, Errol S., 339
Allward, Maurice F., 2198
Almond, Gabriel A., 2799
Alsop, Stewart J. O., 725
Altieri, James, 1110

Ambrière, Francis, 3854, 3855
American Academy of Political and Social Science, Philadelphia, 3149, 4240
American Book Center for War Devastated Libraries, 4411
American Council of Voluntary Agencies for Foreign Service. Survey Committee on Displaced Persons, 4194
American Forces in Action, 1609, 1854, 1855, 1864, 1983, 2732
American Historical Association. Committee for the Study of War Documents, 59
American Jewish Conference, 3783
American University, Washington, D.C. Special Warfare Research Division, 2822
Amery, Julian, 2761
Amory, Robert, 1111
Amoury, Daisy, 4307
Amrine, Michael, 470
Anders, Leslie, 1929
Anders, Wladyslaw, 1462, 1635
Andersen, Hartvig, 726
Anderson, Margaret K., 3679
Anderson, Oscar E., 524
Anderson, Robert C. B., 923
Anderson, Trazzvant W., 1112
Anderson, Verily (Bruce), 3344
Anderson, William, 2082
Andreas-Friedrich, Ruth, 2800
Andrieu d'Albas, Emmanuel M.A., 2547
Angell, Joseph W., 2071
Angier, John C., 1695
Anscomb, Charles, 2389
Ansel, Walter, 423
Anshen, Melvin, 3731
Anson, Thomas V., 614
Appel, John W., 618
Appleman, John A., 4454
Appleman, Roy E., 2548
Arbib, Robert S., 3345
Arbing, Børge W., 1636
Archard, Theresa, 615
Arendt, Hannah, 4512
Argent, Jack N. L., 880
Arkwright, Albert S. B., 4024
Armed Forces Chemical Association, 471
Armenian General Benevolent Union of America, 3467
Armstrong, Anne, 3324
Armstrong, Anthony (pseud.). See Willis, Anthony A.
Armstrong, Colin N., 3856
Armstrong, Hamilton F., 3205
Armstrong, John A., 2841, 2842
Armstrong, Warren (pseud.). See Bennett, William E.
Army Air Forces Aid Society, 1113
Army Times, 1114
Arndt, Karl, 4461
Arne, Sigrid, 3325
Arnold, Elliott, 2226
Arnold, Henry H., 451, 1987
Arnold, Ralph C. M., 424
Arnold, Richard, 727
Arnothy, Christine, 3095
Aron, Robert, 1696, 3177
Arrington, Grady P., 285
Arrol, Anthony M. (pseud.). See Pont-Alain, C. M.
Arthos, John, 1333
Ash, Bernard, 1482, 2549

·195·

Ashburner, D., 1469
Ashton, Dean H., 3522
Ashworth, William, 3619
Aslanis, Anastasios, 3857
Associated Press, 103
Association of Jewish Refugees in Great Britain, 4195
Astier De La Vigerie, Emmanuel D', 728
Aston, Walter H., 4025
Astrup, Helen, 2851, 2852
Attiwill, Kenneth, 1904, 4087
Attlee, Clement R., 2936
Atwell, Lester, 1697
Auerbach, Frank L., 4196
Augé, J. N., 226
Augspurger, Owen B., 1115
Auphan, G. A. J. Paul, 2272
Aurén, Sven A.G., 1698
Aurthur, Robert A., 1116
Austin, Alexander B., 1699
Australia. Army. 2/13th Infantry Battalion, 881
Australia. Royal Australian Air Force, 1988, 2083
Australia in the War of 1939-1945. Series 1 (Army), 281, 1578, 1626, 2569, 2634
Australia in the War of 1939-1945. Series 2 (Navy), 2588
Australia in the War of 1939-1945. Series 3 (Air), 2010, 2144, 2240
Australia in the War of 1939-1945. Series 4 (Civil), 3418, 3627, 3656
Australia in the War of 1939-1945. Series 5 (Medical), 714-717
Australian War Memorial, 227, 228
Ausubel, Nathan, 3293
Automobile Manufacturers Association, 3680
Aviation History Unit, 1989
Aye, Lillian, 4241
Aylin, Robert N., 2273

Babcock, Myles S., 2550
Babington-Smith, Constance, 729
Baclagon, Uldarico S., 1894
Badoglio, Pietro, 3065
Baer, Alfred E., 1117
Baggaley, James, 1930
Bagnall, Stephen, 1700
Bahnemann, Gunther, 401
Bailey, Charles W., 535
Bailey, James, 2084
Bailey, James R. A., 2212
Baillie-Grohman, H. T., 1624
Baker, Benjamin, 3620
Baker, Blanche E., 4242
Baker, E. R., 586
Baker, Edgar C. R., 1900, 2085
Baker, Gilbert, 3250
Baker, Gladys L., 3751
Baker, John V. T., 3621
Baker, Peter, 730, 1701
Baker, Richard B., 1702
Baker, Botts, Andrews and Walne, Houston, Texas, 3681
Baldwin, Hanson W., 2893
Balison, Howard J., 2274
Ball, Adrian, 198
Ball, Edmund F., 1703
Ball, Lamar Q., 3527
Ballantine, Duncan S., 472
Ballantine, W. M., 3346
Ballou, Robert O., 4419
Bamm, Peter (pseud.). See Emmrich, Kurt
Band, Claire, 1877
Band, William, 1877
Bank, Bertram, 4088
Bankson, Budd, 4378
Bannister, Sybil, 2997
Bar-Adon, Dorothy R., 3784
Baratinsky, Viacheslav, 4197
Barber, Donald H., 1542
Barclay, Cyril N., 425, 924-929, 1543
Barclays Bank (Dominion, Colonial and Overseas), 3622
Baring, Norah, 4243

Barkas, Geoffrey, 473
Barker, A. J., 1931
Barker, Frank R. P., 930
Barker, John S., 1118
Barker, Ralph, 2086-2089
Barlow, Randle, 4026
Barnard, Jack, 1932
Barnes, Gladeon M., 474
Barnett, Correlli D., 1544, 1545
Barnett House, Oxford, 4244
Barnhart, Edward N., 4
Barns-Graham, John W., 2551
Barrett, Neil H., 1933
Bartimeus (pseud.). See Ritchie, Lewis A. da Costa
Bartlett, Dorothy A., 616
Bartlett, N., 159
Bartley, Whitman S., 2718
Bartz, Karl, 731, 2090
Bassett, George, 3096
Bates, F. E., 99
Bates, Joan, 2275
Bates, Leonard, 2275
Bates, P. W., 475
Battaglia, Roberto, 2828
Baudouin, Paul, 2937
Bauer, Josef M., 4027
Baumbach, Werner, 2091
Baurdzhan, Momysh-Uly, 1638
Bawden, William T., 4412
Bayles, William D., 2801
Bayliss, W. C., 906
Bazna, Elyesa, 732
Beach, Edward L., 2552
Beal, Edwin, 9
Beamish, John, 1934
Beard, Charles A., 180
Beardwell, M. F., 4245
Beaton, Cecil W. H., 2938, 2939
Beattie, Edward W., 3858
Beck, Henry C., 1109
Beck, Levitt C., 2092
Becker, George H., 3312
Becker, Hans (pseud.), 3859
Beddie, James S., 2900
Beddington, William R., 931
Beebe, Gilbert W., 617, 618
Beecher, Henry K., 619
Beecher, John, 2390
Befeler, Murray, 154
Begin, Menahem, 3860
Behan, John M., 476
Behrens, Catherine B. A., 2277
Beidler, Francis, 4430
Beith, John H., 229, 3623, 4198
Bekker, Cajus D. (pseud.). See Berenbrok, Hans D.
Belfield, Eversley M. G., 1704, 1743, 2174
Belgion, Montgomery, 4462, 4463
Bell, Archibald C., 932
Bell, Frank F., 1120
Bell, George K. A., 4308
Bell, H. E., 4386
Bell, Leslie, 733, 4090
Bell, Richard, 2940
Bell, Robert, 3624
Bellamy, Francis R., 3682
Belleau Wood (Aircraft Carrier), 2553
Bellegarde, Carlo de, 4028
Bellett, Aubrey C., 882
Bellini delle Stelle, Pier L., 1705
Belot, Raymond de, 2391
Benda, Harry J., 3251, 3252
Benedek, Therese, 620
Beneš, Eduard, 2941
Bengtson, John R., 3111
Benham, Hervey, 3366
Ben Line Steamers, Ltd., 2278

Bennett, Donald C. T., 2093
Bennett, Edwin G., 1121
Bennett, John M., 2094
Bennett, Lowell, 3861
Bennett, William E., 2279
Benoist-Méchin, Jacques G. P. M., 1483
Benson, James, 2380, 2539, 2540, 4091
Benson, S. E., 883
Bent, Rowland A. R., 1463
Benton, Brantford B., 2675
Benton, Wilbourn E., 4464
Bentwich, Norman de M., 2942, 3326, 4199, 4200
Benuzzi, Felice, 3862
Benyon-Tinker, W. E., 2392
Berenbrok, Hans D., 2393, 2394
Berenstein, Taliana, 4246
Berg, Mary, 1474
Bergier, Jacques, 734
Bergman, Paul, 1269
Berkowitz, Sarah B., 3785
Berlin, Sven, 1706
Bernadotte of Wisborg, Folke, greve, 2998, 4247
Bernard, Jean-Jacques, 4002
Bernard, John T., 4089
Berneri, Marie L., 2894
Bernstein, Victor H., 4465
Bernstein, Walter S., 1707
Bertelsen, Aage, 3168
Berthold, Will, 2395
Bertram, James M., 4092
Best, Sigismund P., 735, 3863
Bestic, Alan, 3993
Bethel, Elizabeth, 66
Bettelheim, Bruno, 4309
Betzler, J. E., 2369
Bewley, Charles H., 2999
Bharucha, P. C., 1546
Bickers, Emma P., 3403
Bickers, Richard T., 2095
Bickersteth, Anthony C., 1935
Biddle, Francis B., 4466
Bilainkin, George, 2943
Bill, Alan, 3332
Billany, Dan, 4029
Billingsley, Chris, 4201
Bīlmanis, Alfreds, 3233, 3234
Binder, Jenane (Patterson), 2096
Binkoski, Joseph, 1122
Bird, Michael J., 2772
Bird, William R., 2773
Birdwood, Christopher B. B., 933
Birdzell, Bill C., 1398
Birkenhead, Frederick W. F. Smith, 477
Bishop, Edward, 1508, 2097
Bisson, Thomas A., 3591, 3592
Blackater, C. F., 4093
Blackeley, Al Ethelred (pseud.). See Blake, Alfred E.
Blackman, Michael J. D'Arcy, 3864
Blake, Alfred E., 3404
Blake, George, 934
Blake, John W., 3347
Blamey, Arthur E., 1547
Blau, George E., 1639
Bledsoe, Marvin V., 2098
Bleicher, Hugo E., 736
Blight, Gordon, 935
Bliven, Bruce, 2554
Block, Geoffrey L. B., 1484, 2099
Bloemertz, Gunther, 2100
Blond, Georges, 1991, 2396, 3000
Bloom, Ursula H., 3348
Blore, Trevor, 478, 2397
Blum, John M., 2944
Blumenson, Martin, 1708-1710
Blumentritt, Guenther, 402
Board of Deputies of British Jews, 3786

Boardman, Thayer M., 76, 576
Boas, J. H., 2762
Boder, David P., 4202
Boehm, Eric H., 2802
Boesch, Paul, 1711
Boggs, Charles W., 2255
Bohmler, Rudolf, 1712
Boice, William S., 1123
Bolce, William J., 519
Boldizsár, Ivan, 2827, 3313
Boldt, Gerhard, 3001
Boles, Antonette, 479
Bolitho, Hector, 2101-2103
Bonaparte, Marie, 621
Bond, Geoffrey, 2398
Bond, Harold L., 1713
Bone, Sir David W., 2280
Bongartz, Heinz, 1640
Boom, Corrie ten, 3865
Boorman, Henry R. P., 1509, 3349
Borden, Mary, 622
Borghese, Junio V., 2399
Borman, Clifford A., 1078
Bormann, Martin, 2945
Borodin, George (pseud.). See Milkomane, George A. M.
Borsody, Stephen, 2895
Borth, Christy, 3683
Borthwick, James, 936
Bosanquet, Mary, 4248
Boscolo, Armando, 4180
Bose, Subhas C., 3405
Boss-Walker, Geoffrey, 884
Bossing, Nelson L., 4413
Boston, Bernard, 1124
Boswell, Rolfe, 480
Bourne, Dorothea St. H., 481
Bouskell-Wade, George E., 937
Boussel, Patrice, 1714
Bove, Arthur P., 1125
Bowden, Jean, 623
Bowen, Frank C., 2281
Bowler, Douglas, 1909
Bowman, Benjamin L., 4312
Bowman, Gerald, 1992
Bowman, Waldo G., 482
Boyce, Joseph C., 483
Boyd, William B., 590
Boyington, Gregory, 2213
Boyle, Martin, 4094
Boyle, Patrick R., 1936
Braddock, David W., 1548
Braddon, Russell, 737, 2104, 2774, 4095, 4096, 4310
Braden, Thomas, 725
Bradford, Ernie, 2400
Bradford, J. S., 1486
Bradley, Omar N., 286
Bragadin, Marc' A., 2282
Braham, John R. D., 2105, 2106
Braham, Randolph L., 5, 3787
Braibanti, Ralph J. D., 40
Braly, William C., 4097
Braman, Oscar, 1126
Bramsted, Ernest K., 3115
Bramwell, James G., 340
Brand, George, 4467
Brand, Joel, 3788
Brandon, Lewis, 2107
Brandt, Karl, 3593
Brashear, Alton D., 624
Braziller, George, 1347
Bregstein, Herbert L., 1739
Brelis, Dean, 1971
Brelsford, William V., 1464
Brennand, Frank, 2401
Brennecke, Hans J., 2402, 2403, 2404, 2468
Brent, Rafer, 230

Brereton, Lewis H., 1993
Brett-James, Anthony, 1070, 1071, 1946
Brewer, Philip P., 69
Brewster, Ralph H., 3097
Briant, Keith, 938
Brickhill, Paul, 2108, 2109, 4030-4032
Bridges, Antony, 2405
Bridgland, R. J., 898
Briggs, David G., 4249
Briggs, G.G.B., 4303
Briggs, Margaret Y., 3253
Briggs, Richard A., 1127, 1715
Bright, Joan, 939, 940
Bright, Pamela, 625
Brilhac, Jean, 4033
Britain at War Series, 268, 2292
British Battle S Series, 1552, 1553, 1762, 2495
British Iron & Steel Federation, 3625
Britnell, George E., 3626
Brittain, Vera, 4314
Broad, John E., 4034
Broad, Lewis, 104
Brodd, Lawrence J., 1431
Brodrick, Alan H., 231
Bromme, Vincent, 2775
Brookes, Ewart, 2283, 2284, 2406
Brookhouser, Frank, 105
Brookings Institution, Washington, D.C. International Studies Group, 3327
Broom, Leonard, 4181, 4182
Brophy, Leo P., 484, 485
Brosse, Thérèse, 4414
Brou, Willy C., 2285
Broughton, Douglas G., 4098
Brower, David R., 1128
Brown, Brendan F., 4455
Brown, David T., 287
Brown, Ernest F., 169
Brown, Robert M. V., 4099
Brown, Winifred, 2407
Bruckberger, Raymond L., 4311
Brueckner, Leo J., 4413
Brundage, Helen, 288
Brunn, Geoffrey, 3575
Brusselmans, Anne, 2763
Bruvold, H. P., 2633
Bryan, J., 298
Bryan, John N. L., 4100
Bryan, Joseph, 2214, 2555
Bryan, Julien H., 1475
Bryans, John Lonsdale. See Lonsdale Bryans, John.
Bryant, Sir Arthur, 341, 1716
Bryant, Benjamin, 342
Buber, Margarete, 4003
Buchanan, Albert R., 2077, 3468
Buchheim, Hans, 3002
Buckeridge, Justin P., 1129
Buckley, Christopher, 1485, 1549, 1617, 1717
Buckmaster, Maurice J., 738, 2776
Budish, Jacob M., 3121
Buenafe, Manuel E., 1895
Buggy, Hugh, 2556
Bulcock, Roy, 4101
Bulkley, Robert J., 2286
Bull, Peter, 2408
Bullard, Oral, 1130
Bullen, Roy E., 941
Bullmore, Francis T. K., 2110
Bullock, Alan L. C., 2918, 3003
Bunnell, Sterling, 626
Burchard, John E., 486, 581, 4415, 4439
Burchett, Wilfred G., 1937, 2878
Burdon, Randal M., 1079
Burford & Fullbrook Women's Institute, 3350
Burgers, Nelly M., 3150
Burgess, Alan, 3789

Burhans, Robert D., 1131
Burke, Edmund, 2111
Burman, Ben L., 1550
Burmetz, Paul, 3098
Burne, Alfred H., 426
Burney, Christopher, 3776, 3866
Burns, John, 885
Burr, Samuel E., 1878
Burt, Kendal, 4035
Burtness, Paul S., 211
Burton, Eli F., 487
Burton, Reginald G., 4102
Burwell, Lewis C., 1132
Busch, Fritz O., 2409, 2410
Busch, Harald, 2411
Busch, Tristan (pseud.). See Schuetz, Arthur
Bush, Byron O., 1311
Bush, Lewis W., 4103, 4104
Bushell, Thomas A., 2287
Bustos, Felixberti G., 3254
Butcher, Harry C., 289
Butler, Ewan, 739, 1486
Butler, James R. M., 427
Butler, Pierce, 4416
Butlin, Sydney J., 3627
Butow, Robert J. C., 212, 3079
Buttinger, Joseph, 2803
Byford-Jones, W., 2823, 3004
Bykofsky, Joseph, 488
Byrnes, James F., 2946
Byrnes, Laurence G., 1338
Byrom, James (pseud.). See Bramwell, James G.
Bytniewska, Irena, 3122

Caffin, James, 2866
Caidin, Martin, 2112, 2113, 2152, 2215, 2241, 2244
Caillou, Alan (pseud.). See Lyle-Smythe, Alan
Cain, T. J., 2412
Calder-Marshall, Arthur, 3206
Caldwell, Daniel T., 4312
Caldwell, John C., 3255
Calkin, Homer L., 80
Callinan, Bernard J., 886
Callison, Talmadge P., 1718
Calmel, Jean, 1994
Calvert, Michael, 343, 1938
Calvocoressi, Peter, 4468
Cameron, Ian C. (pseud.). See Payne, Donald G., 942, 2114, 2413
Cameron, John, 4469
Caminada, Jerome, 3867
Campbell, Alfred S., 4250
Campbell, Archibald B., 2288
Campbell, Arthur F., 1939
Campbell, Sir Ian, 2414
Campbell, Levin H., Jr., 3684
Campbell, Robert F., 3685
Canada. Army. Governor General's Horse Guards, 914
Canada. Army. 5th Canadian Light Anti-Aircraft Regiment, 913
Canada. Department of National Defence. General Staff, 232, 233
Canada. Department of Reconstruction, 3628
Canada. Royal Canadian Air Force, 1995, 1996
Canadian Bank of Commerce, 3629
Canadian Institute of International Affairs, 3406
Canadian Jewish Congress, 3407
Cannon, M. Hamlin, 1896
Cant, Gilbert, 234, 2289, 2557
Capa, Robert, 1719
Capka, Joseph, 2115
Caplan, Jack, 4105
Capleton, Eric W., 943
Cardif, Maurice, 740
Cardigan, Chandos S. C. Brudenell-Bruce, earl of, 4036
Cardwell, Ann Su (pseud.). See Super, Margaret L.
Carell, Paul, 1551, 1641, 1720
Carew, John M., 344, 1879
Carew, Tim (pseud.). See Carew, John M.

Carlisle, John M., 1721
Carlson, Alvin O., 4313
Carman, Ernest D., 3441
Carmer, Carl L., 2558
Carnahan, Floyd L., 4417
Carne, Daphne, 2116
Carpenter, Iris, 1722
Carpenter, Newt, 1175
Carre, Mathilde (Belard), 741
Carrigg, John J., 4398
Carroll, Gordon, 235
Carroll, Wallace, 3569
Carroll-Abbing, John P., 4203
Carter, B. Noland, 697
Carter, Barbara B., 3066
Carter, Joseph, 1133
Carter, Percy V., 2216
Carter, Ross S., 1134
Carter, Worrall R., 489, 490
Carver, Michael, 1552, 1553
Carver, Richard M. P., 944
Casey, Richard G., 2947
Casey, Robert J., 290, 2290
Caskie, Donald C., 3868
Casper, Bernard M., 945
Casper, Jack A., 1135
Cass, Bevan G., 1136
Cassidy, George L., 915
Castagna, Edwin, 1137
Castens, Edward H., 1409
Castillo, Edmund L., 491
Castle, John (pseud.), 3869
Cate, James L., 2069
Cates, Tressa R., 4106
Catholic Church, 4251
Catlin, George E. G., 4314
Catton, Bruce, 3469
Caulfield, John, 1339
Caulfield, Malachy F., 2415
Cave, Floyd A., 181
Cave, Hugh B., 1997
Caverhill, William M., 1723
Cavert, Inez M., 11
Celt, Marek, 1724
Central Commission for Investigation of German Crimes in Poland, 3790
Ceylon. Ministry of Agriculture and Lands, 3630
Chalmers, William S., 345, 346
Chamberlain, John, 2745
Chamberlain, Thomas H., 428
Chamberlin, William C., 3769
Chamberlin, William H., 3470
Chambers, George W., 3870
Chambliss, William C., 2559
Chance, John N., 2117
Chandler, Lester V., 3686
Chaphekar, Shankarrao G., 236, 1905, 1940
Chapin, John C., 1138
Chaplin, Howard D., 946
Chapman, Edward A., 742
Chapman, Frederick S., 1906
Chapman, Ivan, 3871
Chapman, Robert B., 4315
Charles, Roland W., 2291
Charlott, Rupert, 887
Charlton, Lionel E. O., 1998
Charlwood, Donald E., 2118
Charteris, John, 3351
Chatterton, Edward K., 2292
Chatterton, George J. S., 2119
Chaya, Prem, 3256
Cheesman, E. C., 2120
Chell, Randolph A., 2416
Chenango (U.S. Aircraft Carrier), 2560
Cheng, H. M., 1913
Chennault, Claire L., 291
Chernoff, Howard L., 3523
Cherry, Alex H., 2417
Chester, Daniel N., 3631
Chiang Kai-shek, 3257
Chiesl, Oliver M., 3872
Chin Kee Onn, 1907
Chisholm, Roderick, 2120
Chrisp, John, 4037
Christian, John L., 1941
Christian Science Publishing Society, 4316
Chu Tê, 1880
Chuikov, Vasilii I., 1642
Churchill, Peter, 743, 744, 4038
Churchill, Sir Winston L. S., 2948-2950, 3352-3357
Chutter, James B., 3873
Ciano, Galeazzo, conte, 2951, 2952, 2990
Ciechanowski, Jan, 3123
Clabby, J., 947
Clare, Thomas H., 3408
Clark, Alan, 1529, 1643
Clark, Mark W., 292
Clark, Ronald W., 492, 493, 494, 1510
Clark, Russell S., 4107
Clark, Thomas B., 2889, 3256
Clarke, Comer, 429, 1487, 3791
Clarke, D. H., 1999
Clarke, Dudley, 745, 948
Clarke, Edward B. S., 949
Clay, Ewart W., 950
Cleveland, Reginald M., 2000
Clifford, L. E., 2561
Clifton, George, 3874
Cline, Ray S., 430
Clissold, Stephen, 3207
Clostermann, Pierre, 2122, 2123
Clough, Wilson O., 4418
Coakley, Robert W., 539
Coast, John, 1921, 4108
Coates, John B., 627, 628, 697, 698, 699, 701, 702, 703, 705, 707, 709
Cobb, Ivo G., 3358
Cocchia, Aldo, 2418, 2419
Cochrane, Rexmond C., 484
Cocks, Edith M. S., 629
Codman, Charles R., 1725
Cody, Joseph F., 1080, 1081, 1554
Cohen, Bernard C., 3328, 3772
Cohen, Elie A., 3773
Cohen, Jerome B., 3594
Cohlmia, Kenneth, 1116
Cohn, David L., 237
Colaković, Rodoljub, 2867
Cole, Howard N., 495, 630
Cole, Hugh M., 1726, 1727
Cole, John A., 3116
Cole, Wayne S., 3471
Coleman, Herbert A., 657
Coleman, John M., 496
Coll, Blanche D., 497
Colledge, J. J., 2334
Collier, Basil, 1511, 1728, 3359
Collier, Richard, 1488, 1512, 2777
Collins, Charles, 3235
Collins, Larry, 1729
Collis, Maurice, 1942
Collis, William R. F., 4004, 4204, 4205
Colonna, Jerry, 4377
Columbia Broadcasting System, 1730, 2562
Columbia University. Bureau of Applied Social Research. War Documentation Project Study, 85
Colvin, Ian G., 199, 746, 747, 748
Combined Production and Resources Board (United States, Great Britain, and Canada), 3610
Combray, P. G., 4303
Comeau, Marcel G., 1530
Commager, Henry S., 106

Committee on Public Administration Cases, Washington, D.C., 3687, 3688
Compton's Pictured Encyclopedia, 107
Condit, D. M., 2822
Condit, Kenneth W., 498
Congdon, Don, 238, 239
Conn, Stetson, 240, 3472
Connell, Brian, 2563
Connell, Charles, 499, 1731
Connell, John (pseud.). See Robertson, John H.
Connelly, Kenneth A., 4317
Conner, Howard M., 1140
Connery, Robert H., 3689
Connor, R., 549
Connor, William H., 3524
Conover, Helen F., 49, 52, 54
Considine, Robert, 332
Contractors Pacific Naval Air Bases, 4252
Control Commission for Germany (British Element), 4379
Cook, Gene, 2657
Cooke, Elliot D., 631
Cooke, Kenneth, 2420
Cookridge, E. H. (pseud.). See Spiro, Edward
Coombes, J.H.H., 1908
Cooper, B. W., 4470
Cooper, Diana M., Viscountess Norwich, 2953
Cooper, Dick, 749
Cooper, George T., 4109
Cooper, Herston, 241
Cooper, John P., 1141
Cooper, John St. J., 1732
Cooper, Maurice Z., 3772
Cooper, Page, 632
Coox, A. D., 2600
Cope, Harley F., 2293
Cope, Sir Zachary, 633, 634
Corbett, Edmund V., 2294
Corbo, Dominick R., 1142
Cornelius, Mary D., 4110
Cornell University. State School of Industrial and Labor Relations. Bulletin, 9
Corpe, Hilda R., 4111
Cortvriend, V. V., 3241
Cosgrove, Edmund, 2001
Coulter, Jack L., 635
Council of King George's Jubilee Trust, 3360
Council of Polish Political Parties, 3792
Council on Books in Wartime, 4419
Court, William H. B., 3632
Covell, Sir Gordon, 647
Covington, Henry L., 1143
Cowburn, Benjamin, 750
Cowie, J. S., 500
Cowin, John N., 1465
Cowles, LeRoy E., 4420
Cowles, Virginia S., 1555
Cox, Geoffrey, 1733
Craf, John R., 3690
Crankshaw, Edward, 3005
Cranz, F. Edward, 1161
Cras, Hervé, 1734, 2272, 2538
Craven, Wesley F., 2069
Crawford, John G., 3633
Crawley, Aidan, 4039
Creedy, Brooks S., 4253
Creighton, Sir Kenelm, 2295
Cremor, W. E., 889
Creswell, John, 431, 2296
Cretzianu, Alexandre, 3099
Crew, Francis A. E., 636, 637
Crichton-Stuart, Michael, 1556
Crisp, Dorothy, 3361
Crisp, Robert, 1557, 1618
Crispin, K. E., 906
Croce, Benedetto, 2954
Crocker, George N., 3473
Croft-Cooke, Rupert, 1558
Cronin, Francis D., 1144

Cross, John, 2879
Cross, Robert, 1919
Cross, Wilbur, 2297
Crowl, Philip A., 2564, 2565, 2615
Crown, John A., 2712, 2721
Crowther, James G., 4421
Croydon Times, 3362
Crozier, Stephen F., 951
Cuddon, Eric, 4471
Cumming, Michael, 2124
Cunkle, Arthur L., 3691
Cunliffe, Marcus F., 952, 1736
Cunningham, Andrew B., 347
Cunningham, Winfield S., 2566
Current, Richard N., 3474
Curtis, Alberta, 3573
Cushing, Emory C., 4422
Cyprian, Tadeusz, 3124
Czapski, Józef, 3875
Czebe, Jenö, 3100
Czechoslovak Republic. Ministerstvo Zahranicnich Veci, 3794

Dabrowski, Roman, 3067
Dahlerus, Johan B. E., 2896
The Daily Mail, London, 3777
Daily Telegraph, London, 86
Dalderup, Leo, 3876
Dalgleish, John, 1735
Dallin, Alexander, 6, 2844, 3442, 3443
Dallin, David J., 751, 3282
Daly, Hugh C., 1318
Dangerfield, Elma, 3795
Dangerfield, Royden, 3576
Danishevsky, I., 1675
Darby, Hugh, 1736
D'Arcy-Dawson, John, 1737
Darwin, Bernard R. M., 501
Dasch, George J., 752
Daugherty, William E., 502
David, Claude, 3006
David, Lily M., 3755
Davidson, Basil, 2868
Davidson-Houston, James V., 753
Davies, Arfor T., 638
Davies, Edmund F., 1619
Davies, John, 2421, 2422
Davies, Raymond A., 3444, 3796
Davies, "Trotsky," (pseud.). See Davies, Edmund F.
Davin, Daniel M., 1531
Davis, Albert H., 1145
Davis, Franklin M., 1738
Davis, Kenneth S., 3475
Davis, Mac, 3476
Davis, Russell G., 2567
Davy, George M. O., 953
Dawie, David, 4029
Dawson, Raymond H., 3477
Dawson, Robert M., 2409
Dawson, W. Forrest, 1146
Dawson, William D., 1082
Day, D., 554
Deakin, Frederick W., 2991
Dealey, Ted, 3080
Dean, Basil, 4380
Dean, Charles G. T., 954
Deane, John R., 3478
Deane-Drummond, Anthony, 4040
Deb, J. N., 3410
De Bakey, Michael E., 617, 641, 720
Deborin, Grigorii A., 108
De Chant, John A., 2002
De Courcy, John, 955
Dedijer, Vladimir, 2869
Deedes, W. F., 1059
Deere, Alan C., 2125
De Gruchy, Francis A. L., 109

De Guingand, Sir Francis W., 348, 432
Delaney, John P., 1147
Delarue, Jacques, 3007
Delaware. Public Archives Commission, 3524

Delmayne, Anthony, 4041
Delmer, Sefton, 3570, 3571
Delzell, Charles F., 2829
Dembitzer, Salamon, 4206
DeMendelssohn, Peter, 3008, 3112
Demetriades, Phokion, 1620
Dempster, Derek, 2209
Denham, Elizabeth, 754
Dennett, Raymond, 3283, 3333
Dennis, Clyde H., 4318
Dennis, Geoffrey P., 110
Denny, John H., 1943
De Polnay, Peter, 3178
De Polo, Taber, 1148
DeRoussy de Sales, Raoul J.J.F., 3284
Derry, Kingston, 1489
Derry, Sam, 4042
De Schweinitz, Dorothea, 3692
Detmers, Theodor, 2423
Detroit News, 87
Detzer, Karl W., 146
De Valera, Eamonn, 4446
Devanny, Jean, 3411
Deveikis, Casey, 1149
Devereux, James P.S., 2568
Devigny, André, 4043
Devilliers, Catherine, 1644
DeWeerd, Harvey A., 135, 312
De Wet, Hugh W.A.O., 3877
Dewey, Albert P., 1490
Dexter, David, 2569
Diamond, Gerald, 498
Dibold, Hans, 1645
Dickey, Charles W., 293
Dickson, Robert K., 2298
Dietrich, Otto, 3009
Dimbleby, Richard, 3364
Dinerstein, Herbert S., 1651
Di Phillip, John, 2424
Dirksen, Herbert von, 3010
Disabled American Veterans, 147
Divine, Arthur D., 1491
Divine, David, 1492
Divine, Robert A., 182
Dixon, C. Aubrey, 2845
Dobran, Edward A., 3878
Dollmann, Eugen, 349
Domke, Martin, 3693
Donald, William, 2425
Donat, Alexander, 3879
Doneaux, Jacques, 2764
Dönitz, Karl, 403
Donker, P. A., 3151
Donnison, Frank S. V., 4255
Donohoe, James, 2804
Donovan, John, 3797
Donovan, Robert John, 2570, 2571
Doody, John, 1559
Dorling, Henry T., 2426
Dornberger, Walter, 2127
Dornbusch, Charles E., 7, 8
Doromal, Jose D., 2880
Dos Passos, John, 2572
Douie, Vera, 4256
Doulton, Alfred J. F., 1072
Dourlein, Pieter, 755
Dove, Patrick G. G., 2427
Doward, Jan S., 4319
Downes, Donald C., 756
Downey, Fairfax D., 503
Downing, Rupert, 1493
Doyle, Howard J., 1171
Draper, Theodore, 1150, 1494

Drawbell, James W., 3634
Droste, Chris B., 1922
Drum, Karl, 2128
Drummond, Donald F., 183
Drummond, John D., 956, 2299, 2428, 2853
Drury, Allen, 3480
Drury, Betty, 4423
Dryden, Clarence A., 3525-3526
DuBois, Josiah E., 4472, 4473
Duffus, Louis, 3412
Dugan, James, 2129
Duggan, Stephen, 4423
Duggan, Thomas V., 1151
Duke, Madelaine (pseud.), 757
Duke, Neville, 2003
Dull, Paul S., 60
Dulles, Allen W., 2805
Dunbar, John, 4044
Duncan, Michael, 4045
Duncan, Peter, 758
Duncan, Sylvia, 758
Duncan, William E., 957
Dunlop, Daphne, 2768
Dunlop, John T., 3694
Dunn, Cuthbert L., 639
Dunn, Frederick S., 3329
Dunning, George, 3880
Dupuy, Richard E., 1152, 1739
Dupuy, Trevor N., 242, 1944, 2130, 2429, 2573
Durand, Algernon T. M., 958
Durand, Ralph A., 3242
Duren, Theo van, 2765
Durnford, John, 4046
Durnford-Slater, John, 759
Durrani, Mahmood K., 760
Dutourd, Jean, 3179
Duvall, Elmer E., 490
Dwyer, John P., 1400
Dye, John T., 294
Dyer, George, 1306
Dyer, H. G., 350
Dynowska, Wanda, 1476
Dziuban, Stanley W., 243, 244

Eade, Charles, 3352, 3354-3357
Eades, Prince Alvah, 4320
East, William, 1153
Easton, Alan, 2430
Ebenstein, William, 3011
Eckberg, J. M., 2584
Eden, Sir Anthony, 2955, 2956
Edgar, Louise E., 2574
Edge, Geraldine, 640
Edinger, Lewis J., 3012
Edlmann, Edmund G., 761
Edmonds, Walter D., 2217
Edwards, Kenneth, 433, 1740, 2292
Edwards, L. R., 1154
Edwards, W. Earle, 4071
Eeles, Henry J., 959
Egan, Eileen M., 4257
Eggers, Reinhold, 4005
Eggleston, Wilfrid, 4424
Egoroff, Pavel P., 3770
Ehrenburg, Il'ia G., 1647, 3798
Ehrlich, Blake, 2778
Ehrlich, Hans J., 2542
Eichelberger, Robert L., 2575
Eide, Richard B., 4399
Einsiedel, Heinrich, Graf von, 3881
Eisenhower, Dwight D., 295
Ekart, Antoni, 3882
Eldridge, Fred, 1945
Elgey, Georgette, 3177
Eliot, Thomas S., 3125
Eliscu, William, 762

Elkin, Daniel C., 641
Ellenberger, G. F., 960
Ellis, Albert F., 2576
Ellis, Jean M., 4258
Ellis, Lionel F., 961, 1495, 1741
Ellsberg, Edward, 1560, 1561, 1742
Ellsworth, Lyman R., 2577
Eloy, Victor, 2766
Elsbree, Willard H., 3081
Elvin, Harold, 3445
Embry, Sir Basil E., 351, 2004, 4047
Emmens, Robert G., 3883
Emmrich, Kurt, 642
Encyclopedia Americana, 111
Engelman, Rose C., 3472
Ensor, Robert C. K., 112
Epstein, Melvin L., 1258, 1351
Eremenko, Andrei I., 173
Erskine, David H., 962
Esposito, Vincent J., 276
Essame, Hubert, 963, 1704, 1743
Essex (Aircraft Carrier), 2578
Essex County Standard, Colchester, England, 3366
Eton, Peter, 3208
Eubank, Keith, 200
Evans, Alfred John, 4048
Evans, Sir Geoffrey C., 964, 1562, 1946
Evans, Jack, 763
Evatt, Herbert V., 3413
The Evening Bulletin, Philadelphia, 148
Evening News, London, 149
Evstigneev, Georgii Vasil'evich, 3884
Ewing, Joseph H., 1155
Eyre, Donald C., 1909
Eyre, James K., 434

Fadeev, Aleksandr A., 1648
Fahey, James J., 2579
Fainsod, Merle, 3446
Fairchild, Byron, 240, 3472, 3695
Fairclough, H., 890
Fairfax, Ernest, 3635
Fairfax, John, 352
Fakui, Shizuo, 2618
Falk, Stanley L., 4112
Falkenhorst, Nikolaus von, defendant, 4474
Falls, Cyril, 113
Fancy, John, 4049
Fane, Francis D., 2300
Fantin, Renée, 3739
Farago, Ladislas, 296, 764, 765, 2301
Faramus, Anthony C., 3885
Farley, Edward I., 2580
Farmer, Paul, 3180
Farnum, Sayward H., 1156
Farran, Roy A., 353, 1744
Farrell, Harry G., 1157
Fasola, Cesare, 4381
Fauteux, Claire, 3886
Faviell, Frances, 3367
Feakes, Henry J., 2581
Fearnside, Geoffrey H., 881, 891
Feasby, W. R., 643
Fedorov, Aleksei F., 2846
Fehler, Hein, 2431
Fehling, Helmut M., 3887
Fehrenbach, T. R., 1745
Feis, Herbert, 213, 2582, 3259, 3285, 3296, 4447
Feld, Mischa Jac (pseud.), 3236
Feldt, Eric A., 766
Fellowes-Gordon, Ian, 1947
Fenno, Richard F., 3297
Fenston, Joseph, 114
Ferguson, Ion, 3888
Ferguson, Sheila, 4259
Fergusson, Bernard E., 965, 1948-1950, 2302

Fernau, Joachim, 1649
Ffrench Blake, R.L.V., 966
Fiedler, Arkady, 2432
Field, Ellen, 4113
Field, James A., 2583
Fielding, W. L., 1466
Fielding, Xan, 2824
Fighting forces series, 312
Finch, Percy, 2684
Finch, Peter, 967
Finkelstein, Samuel M., 1158
Finnie, Richard, 3696
Firbank, Thomas, 354
Firkins, Peter C., 892
Firmin, Stanley, 767
First, Edythe W., 3697
Fischer, George, 3447
Fischer, Louis, 2897
Fishbein, Morris, 644
Fisher, Anne M. R., 4183
Fisher, Douglas A., 3698
Fisher, Richard, 2433
Fishman, Jack, 4475
Fiske, Marjorie, 3573
Fittkau, Gerhard, 3889
Fitzgerald, Desmond J. L., 969
Fitzgerald, Earl A., 4114
Fitzgerald, Hilde, 4259
FitzGibbon, Constantine, 1513, 2806
Fitzroy, Olivia, 970
Fixel, Rowland W., 4502
Fjellbu, Arne, 3173
Flackes, William D., 371
Flanagan, Edward M., 1159
Fleming, Peter, 435, 436
Fleming, Raymond H., 3719
Flender, Harold, 2854
Fletcher, Harry R., 2175
Fletcher, Leonard, 4400
Flight Lieutenant Herbert (pseud.). See Meissner, Janusz
Florentine, Eddy, 1746
Flower, Desmond, 115, 971
Flowers, Wilfred S., 645
Flynn, Thomas F., 3542
Foley, Cedric J., 1747
Foley, Charles, 768
Food, Agriculture and World War II. See Studies on Food, Agriculture and World War II
Food Research Institute, Stanford University, War-Peace Pamphlets. See War-Peace Pamphlets
Food Research Institute, Stanford University. Studies on Food, Agriculture and World War II. See Studies on Food, Agriculture, and World War II
Foote, Alexander, 769
Forbes, Alexander, 2005
Forbes, Donald, 2434
Forbes, George K., 4115
Forbes, Patrick, 972
Ford, Corey, 770, 2006
Forester, Cecil S., 2435-2437
Formidable (Aircraft carrier), 2303
Forrest, Alec J., 4207
Fortescue, Winifred B., 4261
Fortune, Charles H., 88
Foster, John M., 2218
Fotitch, Constantin, 3209
Fowke, Vernon C., 3626
Fowler, Elizabeth, 4050
Fox, Annette B., 2898
Fox, Sir Frank, 973
Fox, John, 771
Fraenkel, Heinrich, 2812, 3035, 3036
Francis, Charles E., 2007
Francis, Devon E., 2131
Frank, Anne, 3152
Frank, Gerold, 2584

Frank, Wolfgang, 2304, 2438, 2514
Frankel, Stanley A., 1160
Frankland, Noble, 2132, 2206
Franks, Ivan B., 2996
Fraser, Ian E., 2439
Freeman, Kathleen, 184
Freidin, Seymour, 447
French, Herbert E., 3182
Fried, John H. E., 3595
Friedberg, G., 1242
Friedheim, Eric, 2133
Friedman, Filip, 4006
Friedman, Philip, 30, 1477, 3800, 4208
Friedmann, Tuvyah, 3801
Friedrich, Carl J., 4262
Friend, John F., 1951
Friends, Society of. American Friends Service Committee, 4321
Frischauer, Willi, 2440, 3013, 3014
Fritzsche, Hans, 4476
Frumkin, Grzegorz, 4209
Fuchida, Mitsuo, 2585
Fuchs, James R., 75
Fučik, Julius, 3900
Fuel Research Station, 504
Fuermann, George M., 1161
Fuller, Grace H., 51, 53
Fuller, Jean O., 772, 2779-2781
Fuller, John F. C., 245
Funk, Arthur L., 3183
Furer, Julius A., 505
Furman, John, 4051
Furmanski, H.R.R., 3901
Furnia, Arthur H., 201
Furr, Arthur, 3481

Gafencu, Grigory, 202, 2992
Galang, Ricardo C., 3260
Galantai, Maria, 1748
Gallagher, Matthew P., 174
Gallagher, O'Dowd, 246
Gallagher, Richard, 1749, 4477
Galland, Adolf, 2134
Gallant, Thomas G., 2586
Gallegos, Adrian, 3902
Gallery, Daniel V., 2305, 2306, 2441
Gallico, Paul, 2135
Gallin, Mary A., 2807
Gandar Dower, Kenneth C., 1563
Gander, Leonard M., 355
Gant, Roland, 3903
Gantenbein, James W., 185
Garby-Czerniawski, Roman, 773
Gardner, Brian, 247, 2899
Garrad-Cole, E., 4052
Garrenton, John S., 4322
Gates, Lionel C., 974
Gaulle, A. J. Noel de (pseud.). See Graff, Klaas de
Gaulle, Charles de, 2957
Gaunt, Howard C. A., 4425
Gavin, James M., 2136
Gayn, Mark, 3255
Gayre, George R., 4263
Gazel, Stefan, 2833
Gebler, Robert T., 506
Genovese, Joseph G., 2008
Gensuibaku Kinshi Nihon Nyōgikai, 2261
Genung, Albert B., 3699
George, Alexander L., 3117
George, John B., 2587
Georgetown University, Washington, D.C. School of Foreign Service. Institute of World Policy, 3774
Georgia. World War Historian, 3527
Gerahty, Leslie M., 2137
Gerken, Mable R., 4264
German Report Series, 1478, 1621, 1622, 1646, 1650, 1667, 1669, 1676, 1680, 1682

Germany. Auswärtiges Amt, 186, 2900, 3015, 3016
Germany. Heer, 4478
Germany. Kriegsmarine. Oberkommando, 437
Germany. Wehrmacht. Oberkommando, 438, 439
Germany (Territory under Allied Occupation, 1945- U. S. Zone). Military Tribunals, 4479
Gerstein, Irving, 1366
Gerstel, Jan, 3904
Geve, Thomas, 4007
Ghent, Donald, 9
Gibb, Andrew D., 4480
Gibbs, Sir Gerald, 2009
Gibbs, Patrick, 4053
Gibson, Charles E., 2442
Gibson, Guy P., 2138
Gibson, Hugh, 2951
Gibson, John F., 2443
Gibson, Ronald, 1750
Gibson, Walter, 4116
Gideon, C. Edward, 1432
Gigon, Fernand, 2262
Gilbert, Felix, 438
Gilbert, Gustav M., 4481
Gilbert, Price, 2729
Gilchrist, R. T., 975
Giles, Dorothy, 2859
Giles, Henry E., 1751
Giles, Janice Holt, 1751
Gill, George H., 2588
Gillespie, Oliver A., 2589
Gillies, Frederick W., 1162
Gillison, Douglas, 2010
Gilmour, Oswald W., 3261
Gilroy, Maxwell L., 2590
Gilson, D. C., 1031
Gimenez, Pedro M., 3262
Gimpel, Erich, 774
Gingerich, William F., 3118
Ginter, Maria, 3126
Gise, Benjamin, 1382
Gisevius, Hans B., 2808
Giskes, H. J., 775
Giusti, Ernest H., 3068
Glasfurd, Alexander L., 2444
Glasser, Arthur F., 4323
Gleason, S. Everett, 2908, 2910
Gleason, William F., 1153
Gleeson, James J., 248, 2379
Glenn, John G., 893
Glines, Carroll V., 2011, 2219
Glover, Charles C., 89
Glover, Edwin M., 1910
Gluck, Gemma La Guardia, 3905
Glue, W. A., 1102
Glueck, Sheldon, 4482
Godfrey, John T., 2139
Godwin, George S., 507
Goebbels, Joseph, 2958
Gold, Bela, 3700
Goldman, Jack B., 38
Goldmann, Gereon K., 4324
Goldsmith, Myron B., 1901
Goldstein, Bernard, 3802
Gollancz, Victor, 4513
Gollwitzer, Helmut, 2809, 3906
Golovko, Arsenii G., 2445
Good, Mabel T., 3414
Goodbody, Ernest, 356
Goodhart, David, 894
Goodhart, David W., 1564
Goodhart, Philip, 3286
Goodman, Cecily, 4008
Goodman, Wilfred H., 3648
Goodrich, Leland M., 3330
Goodwin, Ralph B., 4117, 4118
Gordon, David L., 3576

Gordon, Ernest, 4119, 4120
Gordon, Gary, 3082
Gordon, Oliver L., 2591
Gordon-Cumming, H. R., 2369
Gorecki, J. (pseud.). See Kaminski, Aleksander
Goris, Jan A., 3153-3155
Görlitz, Walter, 404
Gosset, Renée P., 1565, 1566
Goudsmit, Samuel, 508
Gouré, Leon, 1651, 1652, 1653
Goutard, Adolphe, 1496
Gowing, M. M., 3641, 3642
Goyal, S. N., 2012
Graaf, Klaas de, 2767
Grabowski, Zbigniew, 2959
Graebner, Walter, 1502
Graham, Andrew, 976
Graham, Burton, 2220
Graham, Cosmo M., 357
Graham, Cuthbert A. L., 1074
Graham, Frank D., 3597
Graham, Frederick C. C., 977
Graham-Murray, James, 2901
Granovsky, Anatoli M., 776
Grant, Douglas, 3368
Granville, Wilfred, 2446
Graves, Charles, 509, 1753, 3636
Graves, John, 1000
Graves, Philip, 139
Gray, Brian, 1467
Gray, Jesse G., 297
Great Battles of History Series, 1581, 1708, 1777
Great Britain. Admiralty, 2307
Great Britain. Air Ministry, 510, 511, 978, 2221
Great Britain. Army. Anti-Aircraft Command
Great Britain. Army. Corps of Royal Engineers, 512
Great Britain. Army. East Lancashire Regiment, 979
Great Britain. Army. Grenadier Guards, 980
Great Britain. Army. Princess Louise's Kensington Regiment. Regimental Old Comrades' Association, 981
Great Britain. Army. Royal Army Service Corps, 982
Great Britain. Army. Royal Artillery. 7th Medium Regiment. Historical Committee, 983
Great Britain. Army. 79th Armoured Division, 984
Great Britain. British Information Services, 151, 2308
Great Britain. Cabinet Office. Historical Section, 513
Great Britain. Central Office of Information, 1567, 2447, 4265
Great Britain. Central Statistical Office, 3637
Great Britain. Colonial Office, 2592
Great Britain. Committee on the Preservation and Restitution of Works of Art, Archives and Other Material in Enemy Hands, 4382, 4383
Great Britain. Ministry of Food, 3638
Great Britain. Ministry of Information, 2593
Great Britain. Ministry of War Transport, 2309
Great Britain. War Office, 514, 646
Greatorex, Wilfred, 1865
Green, Alex, 2222
Green, Constance McLaughlin, 515
Green, Francis H. K., 647
Green, William, 2013, 2014
Greenberg, Eugene M., 1393
Greenfield, Kent R., 175, 440, 463, 516
Greenwall, Harry J., 1497
Gregory, Andrew G., 1163
Grenfell, Russell, 2448, 2594, 3369
Gretton, Sir Peter W., 2449
Gribble, Leonard R., 2015
Grider, George, 2310
Griffin, Alexander R., 648
Griffin, Clarence W., 3528
Griffith, Samuel B., 2595
Griffiths, Bernard, 2450
Griffiths, Owen E., 3415
Grimm, Georg, 4464
Grinnell-Milne, Duncan W., 441, 3184

Grodzins, Morton, 4184
Gross, Feliks, 3604
Grossman, Jonathan, 3695
Grossman, Moishe, 3907
Grossman, Vasilii S., 1654, 3448
Grosvenor, Joan (pseud.). See Bates, Joan
Groth, John, 152
Groult, Benoîte, 3185
Groult, Flora, 3185
Grove, Lee, 2343
Groves, Leslie R., 517
Grygier, Tadeusz, 649
Guareschi, Giovanni, 3908
Guderian, Heinz, 405
Guest, Francis H., 3909
Guest, Freddie, 4121
Guild, Frank H., 1164
Guillain de Bénouville, Pierre, 2782
Guillaume, Augustin L., 1655
Guirey, E. L., 4122
Gulick, Luther H., 3482
Gunning, Hugh, 985
Gupta, S. C., 2016
Gurley, Frank, 1165
Gurney, Gene, 2017-2019
Guttery, David R., 986
Guyol, Philip N., 3529
Gwiazdowski, Alexander P., 3910
Gyalistras, Sergios A., 3222

Haape, Heinrich, 1656
Haarer, Alec E., 518
Hachiya, Michihiko, 2263
Hadar, Alizia R., 3127
Hadow, Maria, 3911
Hafer, Harold F., 4325
Hagen, Renate, 3058
Hager, Alice, 2223
Haggerty, James E., 4326
Haines, C. Grove, 187
Haire, T. B., 1405
Hajsman, Jan, 3778
Halder, Franz, 406, 442
Halifax, Edward F. L. Wood, 3370
Hall, George L., 3530
Hall, Grover C., 1166
Hall, H. Duncan, 3611, 3612
Hall, Roger, 777
Hall, Walter P., 116
Halley, David, 1952, 3912
Halsey, William F., 298
Halton, Matthew H., 3416
Hambre, Edward, 3330
Hamilton, James W., 519
Hamilton, Thomas, 650
Hammer, David H., 2596
Hammond, Ralph C., 1754
Hammond, Richard J., 3639, 3640
Hampshire, Arthur C., 1808, 2311, 2451
Hampton, Oscar P., 651
Hamson, Denys, 1623
Hamzavi, Abdol H., 3287
Hanayama, Shinsho, 4503
Hancock, Kenneth R., 3417
Hancock, William K., 3641
Hankey, Maurice P. A., baron, 2902
Hanley, Gerald, 1953
Hansen, Harold A., 117
Hanser, Richard, 3017
Hanson, Alice C., 3701
Hara, Tameichi, 2597
Harbinson, Robert, 4210
Hardison, Irene, 652
Hardman, Leslie H., 4008
Hardy, Alfred C., 2312
Hardy, William, 1339

Hare, Judith, Countess Listowel, 802, 3128
Hare-Scott, Kenneth, 520
Hargest, James, 4054
Hargreaves, Eric L., 3642
Haring, Clarence H., 4448
Harkins, Philip, 2881
Harkness, Sir Douglas, 3643
Harling, Robert, 2452, 2453
Harr, Bill, 1755
Harrington, Joseph D., 2748
Harris, Arthur T., 2140
Harris, Charles R. S., 4266
Harris, George H., 4055
Harris, Jack W., 4402
Harris, Lionel H., 521
Harris, Seymour E., 3702
Harris, Whitney R., 4483
Harrison, Derrick I., 2141
Harrison, Ernest J., 3237
Harrison, Gordon A., 1756
Harrison, Michael, 1757
Harrisson, Thomas H., 1923
Harrity, Richard, 157
Harrod, Roy F., 522
Hart, Kitty, 3913
Hart, Sydney, 2313, 2454
Hartendorp, A.V.H., 4123
Hartley, Arthur B., 523
Hartley, Francis J., 895
Hartley, Peter G., 4124
Hartmann, Frederick H., 4449
Hartmann, Vera, 2455
Hartt, Frederick, 4384
Hartzell, Karl D., 3531
Harvard University. Porcellian Club, 4426
Harvell, Ursel P., 1396
Hashimoto, Mochitsura, 2598
Hasler, H. G., 1813
Hasluck, Eugene L., 118
Hasluck, Paul, 3418
Hassel, Sven (pseud.). See Arbing, Børge W.
Hassell, Ulrick von, 2960
Hassett, Edward C., 1377
Hassett, William D., 3483
Hasson, Joseph S., 1344
Hastain, Ronald, 4125
Hastings, Robert P., 2224
Hastings, Robin H.W.S., 958, 987
Hatch, Alden, 299
Hatchette, Antonio A., 1514
Hathaway, Dame Sibyl M.C.B., 3243
Hatlem, John C., 153
Hauge, Eiliv O., 778, 2455
Haugland, Vern, 2225
Haukelid, Knut, 1498
Haverhill, Massachusetts. War Records Committee, 3532
Havighurst, Robert J., 3703
Hawaiian Sugar Planters' Association, 3533
Hawkins, Desmond, 1758
Hawkins, Jack, 4126
Hawkins, John, 1167
Hawkins, Maxwell, 2599
Hawkins, Ward, 1167
Hay, Ian (pseud.). See Beith, John Hay
Hayashi, S., 2600
Hayes, Carlton J. H., 4450
Hayes, Denis, 4327
Haynes, George L., 1298
Haywood, E. V., 896
Healiss, Ronald, 2456
Heaps, Leo, 1759
Hearn, Cyril V., 779, 780
Heavey, William F., 1168
Hechler, Kenneth W., 1760
Hecimovic, Joseph, 3914
Heckstall-Smith, Anthony, 1568, 1624, 2314

Heidenheimer, Arnold J., 1169
Heilbrunn, Otto, 781, 2845
Heilmann, Will, 2142
Heimler, Eugene, 3915
Heinl, Robert D., 2713, 2720
Heinz, Grete, 61
Heisler, J. B., 1657, 4056
Heller, Bernard, 188
Heller, Francis H., 3534
Helm, Thomas, 2601
Helton, H. Stephen, 71, 74
Hemphill, William E., 2649
Henderson, Harry B., 160
Henderson, James H., 1083, 1084, 3916
Henderson, Sir Neville, 2961
Henn, Peter, 1761
Henrey, Mrs. Robert, 1515, 3186, 3187
Henrey, Robert (pseud.). See Henrey, Mrs. Robert
Henri, Raymond, 2602, 2603
Henriques, L. Q., 358
Henry, Frank M., 2143
Henry, Mike (pseud.). See Henry, Frank M.
Henry, R. L., 897
Henslow, Miles, 4401
Herbert, Flight Lieutenant (pseud.). See Meissner, Janusz
Herge, Henry C., 4427
Herington, John, 2144
Hernandez, Al, 782
Herndon, John G., 117
Herring, Robert R., 1402
Hersey, John R., 2264
Hershberger, Guy F., 4328
Hess, Rudolf, 3917
Hesse, Fritz, 3018
Hetherington, John A., 359
Hewitt, Robert L., 1170
Hewlett, Richard G., 524
Heydecker, Joe J., 4484
Heydte, Friedrich A., Baron von der, 1532
Heyst, Axel (pseud.). See Grabowski, Zbigniew
Hibbert, Christopher, 1762, 3069
Hichens, Robert P., 2145
Hickcox, Percy M., 4329
Hickey, Raymond M., 4330
Higgins, Benjamin H., 3644
Higgins, Edward T., 2604
Higgins, John F., 1354
Higgins, Trumbull, 3371
Higgs, Dorothy P., 3244
Hilberg, Raul, 3803
Hill, Anthony, 1911
Hill, Arthur D., 3694
Hillary, Richard, 2146
Hills, Reginald J. T., 988
Hillson, Norman, 360
Hind, Robert R., 4127
Hine, Al, 1763
Hines, Eugene G., 2605, 2606
Hingston, Walter G., 989
Hinshaw, David, 4267
Hinsley, Francis H., 443, 2315
Hiroshima Gembaku Shōgai Kenkyūkai, 2265
Hiroshima Research Group of Atomic Bomb Casualties. See Hiroshima Gembaku Shōgai Kenkyūkai
Hirsch, Phil, 119, 300, 2020
Hirschmann, Ira A., 4211
Hislop, John, 3372
Historical Reports on War Administration, 536, 3509, 3517, 3739, 3756, 3760
Historical Reports on War Administration: War Production Board. Special Study, 3676, 3677, 3697, 3710, 3711, 3721-3724, 3736, 3741, 3766
History of the King's Own Yorkshire Light Infantry, 960, 989
History of the Second World War. United Kingdom Civil Series, 554, 564, 2277, 3583, 3632, 3637, 3639, 3641, 3642, 3650, 3658-3660, 3666, 4282

History of the Second World War: United Kingdom Civil Series; War Production Series, 3611, 3612, 3619, 3645-3647, 3667
History of the Second World War: United Kingdom Medical Series, 633, 634, 635, 636, 637, 639, 647, 660, 675
History of the Second World War: United Kingdom Military Series, 427, 1489, 1495, 1537, 1741, 2206, 2359, 3359
History of the Second World War: United Kingdom Military Series; Civil Affairs and Military Government Series, 4266
Hitler, Adolf, 444, 3019
Ho Yung-chi, 1954
Hoare, Robert J., 4057
Hobbs, Leslie, 1764
Hodge, Clarence L., 154
Hodges, Sheila, 4314
Hodson, James L., 2309, 2962, 3484
Hoegh, Leo A., 1171
Hoehling, Adolph A., 214
Hoemberg, Elisabeth S., 3020
Hoess, Rudolf, 4009
Hoettl, Wilhelm, 783, 784
Hofer, Walther, 189
Hoffman, Carl W., 2724, 2725
Hoffman, Ross J. S., 187
Hoffmann, Heinrich, 3021
Hogan, Edward L., 3753
Hogan, John J., 301
Hogan, Thomas L., 1427
Hoge, Peyton, 1172
Hogerzeil, Han, 4004
Holborn, Hajo, 4268
Holborn, Louise W., 3331
Holles, Everett, 249
Hollis, Sir Leslie, 445
Holmaas, Arthur J., 3704
Holman, Dennis, 361, 1912, 2882, 4109
Holman, Gordon, 2316, 2317
Holt, Edgar, 120
Hood, Stuart, 2830
Hoover, Herbert C., 3705
Hoover Institution on War, Revolution and Peace. See Stanford University. Hoover Institution on War, Revolution and Peace
Hoover Institution Studies. See Stanford University. Hoover Institution on War, Revolution and Peace
Hopkins, Harold, 2607
Hopkins, John A. H., 90
Horan, James D., 2584, 2608
Horikoshi, Jiro, 2241
Hornby, William, 3645
Hornsby, Henry H., 1173
Horrabin, James F., 170
Horrocks, Sir Brian, 362
Horsley, Terence, 2021
Horst, Kate A., 1765
Horstmann, Lali von S., 3022, 3023
Hosford, Bowen I., 3365
Hosoda, Mosaburo, 3598
Houart, Victor, 1569
Hougen, John H., 1174
Hough, Donald, 2226, 4331
Hough, Frank O., 2609, 2610, 2709, 2712
Hough, Richard Alexander, 2318
Houston, Karl H., 1175
Hovelsen, Leif, 2855
Hovsepian, Aramais A., 302
Howard, Clive, 2227
Howard, Michael E., 992
Howard, Richard A., 2611
Howard-Williams, Ernest L., 1516
Howarth, David A., 785, 1766, 2457-2459
Howarth, Patrick, 786
Howe, Ellic, 3024
Howe, George F., 1176, 1570
Howe, Thomas C., 4385
Howell, Edgar M., 2847
Howell, Edward, 1625
Howell, Nathaniel R., 3535

Howgrave-Graham, Hamilton M., 3373
Howlett, R. A., 2612
Howseman, Robert S., 1373
Hsueh Chun-tu, 10
Huddleston, Sisley, 3188, 3189
Hugessen, Sir Hughe M. K., 2963
Hughes, Pennethorne, 1571
Hughes, Richard, 3667
Hughes, Robert, 2460
Hughes, William R., 4332
Hugill, J. A. C., 1767
Huie, William B., 2266, 2613
Hull, Cordell, 2964
Hull, William L., 4514
The Humanist Library Series
Hungary. Külügyminiszterium, 4212
Hunt, George P., 2614
Hunt, Gordon, 1955
Hunt, Leslie, 1085
Hunter, Anthony, 2526
Hunter, Charles N., 1956
Hunter, Kenneth E., 153, 250, 1768
Hunter, Kenneth H., 3753
Huot, Louis, 3210
Hurkala, John, 1177
Hurstfield, J., 3646
Husted, H. H., 91
Huston, James A., 1178, 1769
Hutak, Jakub B., 3804
Hutchings, B. L. B., 1010
Hutchinson, Walter, 155
Hutnik, Joseph J., 1327
Hutton, Clayton, 4058, 4059
Huxley-Blythe, Peter J., 4213
Huzar, Elias, 3485
Huzel, Dieter, 525
Hyde, Harford M., 787, 788
Hytier, Adrienne D., 3190

Icardi, Aldo, 789
Icenhower, Joseph B., 2319
Ickes, Harold L., 2965
Idriess, Ion L., 526
Ignatov, Petr K., 2848
Iklé, Frank W., 2993
Ileana, Princess of Rumania, 653
Illustrated History of World War II, 242, 1944, 2130, 2429, 2573
Ind, Allison, 790
India. War Department. Director of Public Relations, 1957
Indiana. War History Commission, 3536
Ingersoll, Ralph McA., 1770
Ingham, Travis, 2883
Inks, James M., 3211
Inman, Peggy, 3647
Inoguchi, Rikihei, 2228
Insh, George P., 4269
Instone, Gordon, 2783
Inter-Allied Conferences on War Medicine, London, 654
International Commission for the Teaching of History, 1
International Conference on the History of the Resistance Movements, 1st, Liège, (1958), 2749
International Conference on the History of the Resistance Movements, 2d, Milan, (1961), 2750
International Council for Philosophy and Humanistic Studies, 3025
International Military Tribunal, 4485
International Social Service, 4215
International Tracing Service, 3779, 4216
Inter-University Case Program, 3707, 3708
Iran. Ministry of Foreign Affairs, 3298
Irgang, Frank J., 1771
Irikura, James K., 3252
Ironside, William E., 2966
Irvin, Anthony S., 1958
Irvin, John G., 1179
Irving, David J. C., 2147, 2148
Irwin, Dudley M., 3537

Isakov, Ivan S., 2320
Isely, Jeter A., 2615
Isenberg, Carl, 1383
Ismay, Hastings Lionel, baron, 363
Isserman, Ferdinand M., 4270
Ito, Masanori, 2616
Iványi-Grünwold, Béla, 3332
Izbicki, John, 2810

Jablon, Seymour, 658
Jablonski, Edward, 2022
Jackson, C. O. Badham, 3419, 4271
Jackson, Henry C., 1572
Jackson, Robert, 2440, 2861, 4060
Jackson, Robert H., 4486, 4487
Jackson, Seymour, 718
Jacob, Alaric, 3449
Jacob, Naomi E., 3374
Jacob, Philip E., 4356
Jacobs, James W., 898
Jacobsen, Hans A., 251, 2816
Jacot, B. L., 2851, 2852
Jakobson, Max, 1525
Jamar, K., 1468
James, David, 2465, 3918
James, David H., 3083
James, Leonard F., 4428
James, Meyrich E. C., 791
James, Robert W., 3613
James, Stefan (pseud.), 2229
James, Walter D., 3375
James, Sir William M., 2321, 2322
Jameson, K., 1649
Jameson, William, 2461
Jameson, Sir William S., 2323
Jamieson, John A., 4429
Janeczek, E., 4488
Janeway, Eliot, 3709
Janis, Charles G., 3919
Janowitz, Morris, 502
Janta, Alexander, 3920
Japan. Hikiage Engochō. Fukuinkyoku, 527
Japan. Hikiage Engochō. Fukuinkyoku. Dai 2 Fukuinkyoku Zammu Shoribu, 2617
Japan. Second Demobilization Bureau, 2618
Japan Council against Atomic and Hydrogen Bombs. See Gensuibaku Kinshi Nihon Kyogiki
Japanese American Citizen's League, 4185
Japanese monograph, 1891, 1893, 1925, 2253
Japanese Studies on Manchuria, 1890, 1892
Jarman, Thomas L., 3026
Jaworski, Leon, 3805
Jeanty, Ninette H., 3921
Jecchinis, Chris, 2825
Jedrzejewicz, Waclaw, 3376
Jeffcott, George F., 655
Jeffrey, Betty, 4128
Jeffrey, William F., 1959
Jenkins, Ford, 3377
Jenkinson, Hilary, 4386
Jennings, Cyril O., 4129
Jensen, Oliver O., 2619
Jerusalem. Yad va-shem, 3806
Jervois, Wilfrid J., 993
Jewell, Norman L. A., 2462
Jewish Black Book Committee, 3807
John, Evan (pseud.). See Simpson, Evan J.
Johnen, Wilhelm, 2149
Johns, Glover S., 1772
Johnson, Amanda, 1499
Johnson, Chalmers A., 792
Johnson, Charles M., 917
Johnson, Edward, 4472, 4473
Johnson, Frank, 2150
Johnson, Franklyn A., 303
Johnson, Gerden F., 1180

Johnson, James E., 2023, 2151
Johnson, Joseph E., 3283
Johnson, Robert S., 2152
Johnson, Roy F., 994
Johnston, Bruce F., 3598
Johnston, Denis, 1573
Johnston, Doris R., 4130
Johnston, Frank, 2083
Johnston, Mary E., 640
Johnston, Richard W., 1181
Johnston, Stanley F., 2230
Jolly, Alan, 995
Jolly, Cyril, 4061
Jones, Arthur J., 996
Jones, Drummond, 3710
Jones, Ewart C., 3922
Jones, Francis C., 3084
Jones, Francis S., 4062
Jones, Ira, 997
Jones, Ken, 1182
Jones, Major W., 2871
Jones, W. A., 3923
Jones, William E., 1183
Jong, Louis de, 793
Jordan, George R., 3614
Jordan, Z., 3314
Joslen, H. F., 528
Josowitz, Edward L., 1275
Joswick, Jerry J., 304
Joubert de la Ferté, Philip B., 529, 2024, 2463
Jovichić, Lenka A., 3212
Józef Pilsudski Institute of America for Research in the Modern History of Poland, New York. Documents series, 3376
Jubelin, André, 2153
Jucker, Ninetta, 3191
Jullian, Marcel, 2464
Junod, Marcel, 4272

Kadar, Alfred F., 1184, 1356
Kahn, Ely J., 305, 1185, 2620
Kalijarvi, Thorsten V., 3518
Kalinin, Mikhaid I., 3450
Kállay, Miklós, 3103
Kalyanasundaram, V., 2903
Kamenetsky, Ihor, 3113, 3451
Kaminski, Aleksander, 2834
Kammen, Michael G., 2074
Kammerer, Gladys M., 3486
Kapetanović, Nikola, 2872
Kaplan, Chaim A., 2025
Kaps, Johannes, 3027, 3028
Karabatsos, Dick G., 3538
Karaka, Dosoo F., 998, 3420
Kardorff, Ursula von, 3029
Karig, Walter, 2293, 2324
Karolevitz, Robert F., 1310
Karski, Jan (pseud.), 3129
Kase, Toshikazu, 2904, 3085
Kathigasu, Sybil D., 2884
Kato, Masuo, 3086
Katz, Ephraim, 3827
Katz, Samuel I., 588
Kauffman, Russell W., 2325
Kaufman, Aubrey, 3127
Kaufman, Isidor, 3487
Kawai, Michi, 3087
Kay, Robin L., 1086
Keast, William R., 551
Keating, Bern, 2326
Keating, Lawrence A., 304
Keats, John, 2885
Kecskemeti, Paul, 2905
Keeble, L. A. J., 2327
Keenan, Joseph B., 4455
Keitel, Wilhelm, B.J.G., 407
Keith, Agnes N., 4131

Keith, Jean E., 497
Kellett, Wanda L., 4132
Kelley, Douglas McG., 4489
Kelly, Frank, 3924
Kelly, Robin A., 2446
Kemp, James C., 999
Kemp, Norman, 530
Kemp, Peter K., 794, 795, 1000, 1001, 2328
Kempe, A.B.C., 3378
Kemsley, Walter, 1002
Kendrick, Douglas B., 698
Kennard, Coleridge, 3925
Kennedy, Sir John, 306
Kennedy, John de N., 531
Kennedy, Joseph P., 3156
Kennedy, Robert M., 1478
Kenney, George C., 307, 2231
Kenney, William, 3488
Kenny, John P., 4490
Kent, George D., 64
Kent, William, 4387
Kent Hughes, Wilfrid S., 4133
Kenworthy, Aubrey S., 4504
Keogh, E. G., 1574
Kephart, Rodney, 4134
Keplicz, Klemens, 3299
Ker, Frederick I., 3648
Kerilles, Henri de, 3192
Kern, Erich (pseud.). See Kernmayr, Erich
Kernmayr, Erich, 1658
Kerr, Colin G., 899
Kerr, George F., 532
Kerr, James L., 2329, 2465
Kershner, Howard E., 4273
Kersten, Felix, 2967
Kertész, István, 3104
Kertzer, Morris N., 4333
Kerwin, Paschal E., 2466
Kessel, Alexander W. L., 668
Kessel, Joseph E., 3030
Kesselring, Albert, 408
Keyes, Elizabeth, 364
Khan, Shah N., 3421, 3422
Kidson, Arthur L., 1087
Kimche, David, 4217
Kimche, Jon, 796, 4217
Kimmel, Husband E., 215
Kimmins, Anthony M., 365
King, Alison, 2154
King, Ernest J., 366, 451
King, Spencer B., 3539
King, William, 2467
Kingston-McCloughry, Edgar J., 446
Kinnaird, Clark, 92, 3808
Kinsella, Patrick, 367
Kintner, Earl W., 4491
Kinzie, George R., 3711
Kippenberger, Sir Howard, 368
Kirby, Edward M., 4402
Kirby, Stanley W., 252
Kirk, John, 533
Kishi, Kōichi, 3252
Kitsuse, John I., 4181
Klee, E., 534
Klefos, Brede, 2856
Klein, Alexander, 797
Klein, Burton H., 3599
Klein, Gerda W., 3926
Kleist, Peter, 2906
Klem, Per, 1481
Klemme, Marvin, 4274
Klemow, Sid, 1353
Klestadt, Algert, 1897
Klinger, Fred, 1325
Klose, Kevin, 3952
Knapp, Stefan, 3927

Knebel, Fletcher, 535
Knieriem, August von, 4492
Knight, Sir Henry, 3649
Knight, Peter, 1003
Knoke, Heinz, 2155
Knoll, H. B., 4432, 4433
Knox, Robert S., 3489
Kobrick, Leonard, 1327
Kodama, Yoshio, 416, 4505
Koehl, Robert L., 3031
Koestler, Arthur, 3928
Kogan, Norman, 2907
Kogon, Eugen, 3780
Kohan, C. M., 3650
Kohrs, Walter E., 4335
Komorowski, Tadeusz, 2836
Konijnenburg, Emile van, 3157
Konoye, Fumimaro, Prince, 2968
Koop, Theodore F., 4403
Kopp, Hans, 4135
Koppel, Helga, 3042
Korbel, Josef, 3105
Korbonski, Stefan, 2836
Koriakov, Mikhail M., 3929
Korson, George G., 4275
Korwin-Rhodes, Marta, 1479
Kospoth, B. J., 3930
Kournakoff, Sergei N., 1659
Kousoulas, Dimitrios G., 3223
Kovpak, Sydir A., 1660
Koyen, Kenneth A., 1186
Krabbe, Henning, 3379, 4404
Král, Václav, 3809
Kramer, Josef, defendant, 4493
Krancke, Theodor, 2468
Krasnov, Nikolai N., 3931
Krauskopf, Robert W., 81
Krausnick, Helmut, 3037
Krebs, Richard J. H., 1187
Kreipe, Werner, 447
Kress, Andrew J., 3712
Kriege, Uys, 4063
Kriger, Evgenii G., 1661
Kroese, A., 2330
Krueger, Walter, 1188
Krylov, Ivan N. (pseud.), 1662
Krzesinski, Andrew J., 3130
Kučan, Viktor, 3217
Küchler-Silberman, Lena, 4218
Kuhlmann, Albert W., 694
Kuhn, Kathe, 2809
Kulkielko, Renya, 3810
Kurcz, F. S., 1470
Kusumi, Yoshio, 3598
Kuter, Laurence S., 3300
Kuznets, Simon S., 3713

Lachs, Manfred, 4456
La Farge, Oliver, 2026
Laffin, John, 1575
Lake Forest University, Lake Forest College, 4430
Lallemant, Raymond, 2156
Lambermont, Paul Marcel, 2157
Lambert, D., 4219
Lambert, Eric, 4136
Lamensdorf, Rolland G., 1189
Lamer, Mirko, 3577
Lampe, David, 2857
Lanchbery, Edward, 2158
Lancum, Frank H., 3651
Land, Emory, 2331
Landau, Rom, 2159
Landis, Benson Y., 11
Landis, James M., 3156
Landsborough, Gordon, 1576, 2469
Lane, Frederic C., 536

Langelaan, George, 798
Langer, William L., 2908-2910
Langmaid, Kenneth J. R., 2332
Langmaid, Rowland, 2470
Langsam, Walter C., 121
Lanux, Pierre Combret de, 3540
Lapierre, Dominique, 1729
Larsen, Colin R., 2621
Larsen, Otto M., 3932
Larson, Harold, 488
Larson, Taft A., 3541
Larteguy, Jean, 2232
Lasker, Bruno, 4220
Lassen, Suzanne, 2471
Lattre de Tassigny, Jean de, 1471
Latviešu Tautas Palidziba, 3811
Lauer, Walter E., 1190
Laughlin, Austin, 799
Launay, Jacques de, 2911
Lauterbach, Richard E., 3452
Lavagnino, Emilio, 4388
Lavender, Don E., 1191
La Violette, Forrest E., 4186
Lawrence, Christie N., 2873
Lawrence, W. J., 1004
Lawrence, William L., 537
Lawson, Don, 3490
Lawson, J.H.W., 2233
Lawson Ted W., 2234
Lazar, Albert O. (pseud.), 3933
Lazzaro, Urbano, 1705
Leach, Charles R., 1192
League of Nations, 2912, 3578, 3579
League of Nations. Secretariat. Economic, Financial and Transit Department, 3580
Leahy, William D., 2970
Leasor, James, 2913, 3208, 4035
Leasor, Thomas J., 3032
Leber, Annedore, 2811
LeBlanc, A. O., 1154
Leblanc, Cyrille, 3542
Leckie, Robert, 2622-2624
Lee, Alvin T. M., 3714
Lee, Arthur S. G., 2027
Lee, Asher, 1517, 2028, 2160
Lee, Dwight E., 3575
Lee, James, 2029
Lee Kung-sam, 1881
Lee, Norman, 2333
Leeb, Johannes, 4484
Leeming, John F., 3934, 3935
Leffelaar, Hendrik L., 4137
Legendre, Gertrude S., 3936
Legg, Frank, 369, 4405
Lehmann, John, 3380
Lehmann, Leo H., 4334
Lehmkuhl, Dik, 3174
Leigh, Randolph, 538
Leighton, Alexander H., 4187
Leighton, Barbara E., 3293
Leighton, Richard M., 539
Leiss, Amelia C., 3333
Leitgeber, Witold, 253
Leive, Max, 1269
Lemon, Adele M., 3543
Lengyel, Olga, 4010
Lenton, H. T., 2334
Lepotier, Adolphe, 800
Lerner, Adolf R., 3812
Lerner, Daniel, 540, 3033, 3572
Lerner, Max, 3491
Leslie, Anita, 656
Leslie, Donald, 1061
Lestchinsky, Jacob, 3813, 3814
Lett, Gordon, 2831
Leuschner, Martin L., 4335

Lévai, Jeno, 3815
Lever, Harry, 3715
Levering, Robert W., 4138
Leverkuehn, Paul, 801
Levi, Maxine, 2751
Levi, Primo, 3937, 4011
Le Vien, Jack, 122
Levin, Max, 704
Levitt, Theodore, 3716
Levy, Alan, 1887, 3816
Levy, Arnold, 3381
Lewis, David D., 2472
Lewis, Peter J., 1005
L'Herminier, Jean, 2473
Liang Yen (pseud.). See Briggs, Margaret Y.
Lias, Godfrey, 3938
Lichauco, Marcial P., 3263
Liddell Hart, Basil H., 413, 448, 449
Liebling, Abbott J., 1773, 2784
Life (Chicago), 156
Lim, Janet, 4139
Lin Yutang, 3264, 3265
Lincoln, Fredman A., 2335
Lincoln, John (pseud.). See Cardif, Maurice
Lind, Andrew W., 3544
Lind, Ragnar G., 1399
Lindsay, Martin, 1006
Lindsay, Thomas M., 1007
Linebarger, Paul M. A., 541
Link, Mae M., 657
Linklater, Eric R. R., 1744
Linze, Dervey A., 4515
Lipschutz, Norman, 3131
Lipscombe, Frank W., 2474
Liquor Store & Dispenser, 3717
Lisiewicz, M., 2126
Listowel, Judith Hare, countess of. See Hare, Judith, Countess Listowel
Little, Eric H., 2625
Liveroidge, Douglas, 2475
Livry-Level, Philippe, 2161
Ljubljana. Znanstveni Institut, 4064
Llewellyn, Bernard, 3266
Lloyd, Edward M. H., 3581
Lloyd, Sir Hugh P., 1533
Lloyd Owen, David, 1577
Lochner, Louis P., 2958
Lockhart, Sir Robert H. B., 803, 1008
Lockridge, Richard, 310
Lockwood, Charles A., 2626-2629
Lockwood, Theodore, 1193
Lodge, O. R., 2723
Lodwick, John, 370, 2476
Loewenheim, Francis L., 203
Loh, W. G., 912
Lomax, C. E. N., 955
Lomax, Sir John G., 2971
Lombard, Helen C. C., 3492
Lombroso, Silvia, 3070
Londerville, J. D., 3652
London. Imperial War Museum. Library, 12, 13, 14, 15, 16, 17, 18, 19, 20, 21, 22, 23, 24, 25, 26
London. Instytut Historyczny imienia Generala Sikorskiego, 2914
Long, Basil K., 3423
Long, Clarence D., 3582
Long, Esmond R., 658
Long, Gavin M., 1578, 1626
Lonsdale Bryans, James, 804
Loo Pin-Fei, 2886
Look, 3718, 4389
Loomis, Robert D., 2030
Loomis, William, 254
Lord, John, 122
Lord, Walter, 216
Lord, William G., 1194
Lorraine, Jacques, 3193

Lott, Arnold S., 2336, 2630
Louisiana. Department of Military Affairs, 3719
Louisville. (U.S. Heavy Cruiser), 2631
Love, Edmund G., 1195, 1196, 2565, 2632
Lovell, Stanley P., 805
Low, N. I., 1913
Lowery, Tom, 1379
Lowrie, Donald A., 4221
Lowry, M. A., 1009
Ludden, Robert W., 4012
Luey, Allen T., 2633
Lugol, Jean, 1579
Lumer, Hyman, 3720
Lunau, Heinz, 4494
Lundin, Charles L., 3106
Lusar, Rudolf, 542
Lusseyran, Jacques, 3939
Lutz, Alma, 4276
Lutz, Francis E., 3545
Luukkanen, Eino A., 1526
Luzzatto, Riccardo, 2832
Lyle-Smythe, Alan, 3940
Lynip, G. Louise, 4336
Lynn, Rita Le B., 4337
Lyon, Allan, 1775
Lytton, Victor A.G.R. Bulwer-Lytton, 2d earl of, 3334

Maahs, Arnold M., 4338
Maas, Henry S., 659
Macardle, Dorothy, 4222
McAleer, James A., 3721, 3722
MacArthur, Douglas, 308, 309
Macartney, Carlile A., 3107
McAvity, J. M., 918
MacBain, Alastair, 770, 2006
McCabe, Graeme, 4140
McCallum, Neil, 1776
McCarthy, Dudley, 2634
McCauley, Maryclaire, 3723
McClendon, Dennis E., 2162
McCloskey, Mark A., 4277
McClymont, W. G., 1627
McCormac, Charles, 4141
McCorquodale, D., 1010
McDermott, R. B., 3546
Macdonald, Bruce J. S., 4495
MacDonald, Charles Brown, 1777-1780
MacDonald, Elizabeth P., 806
MacDonald, Florence, 4278
MacDonald, John F., 1580, 3424
Macdonnell, James E., 2337, 2635
McDougall, Murdoch C., 807
McDougall, William H., 4142, 4143
McElwee, William L., 1011, 1781
Mcfarlan, Graeme, 904
McFetridge, Elizabeth M., 697, 698
McGee, John H., 1898
McGeoch, W. Percy, 1012
McGill, Michael C., 371
McGovern, James, 1782
McGrane, Reginald C., 3724
McGrann, Roy T., 1198
MacGregor, Harold, 1197
Machlejd, Wanda, 723
MacHorton, Ian, 1960, 1961
Macinnes, Charles M., 3382
MacInnes, Colin, 372
McInnes, Edgar, 123
Macintyre, Donald G.F.W., 1500, 2031, 2338, 2339, 2351, 2414, 2477-2479
McIntyre, Stuart H., 3493
McIvor, Russel C., 3653
Mackaye, Milton, 2575
McKee, Alexander, 1518, 1783, 2480, 2481
McKee, Ilse, 3034
McKee, Philip, 2032

McKelvie, Roy, 1962
Mackenzie, Compton, 3425
MacKenzie, Kenneth P., 4144
McKeogh, Michael J., 310
McKerracher, Mac, 1444
McKie, Ronald, 2636, 2637
Mackiewicz, Joseph, 3817
McKinsey, William L., 1260, 1355
McLane, Charles B., 3453
Maclean, Fitzroy, 373, 2972
McLemore, Henry, 1185
Macleod, Colonel Roderick, 2966
McLintock, James D., 1963
McLuskey, James F., 2163
McMath, J. S., 1013
McMillan, Archibald M., 4339
McMillan, George, 1199, 2638
Macmillan, Norman, 2033
McMillan, Richard, 1784
McMinn, John H., 704
McNair, Sir Arnold D., 3654
MacNalty, Arthur S., 660, 4279
Macneil, Calum, 2482
McNeill, William H., 3224
McWane, Frederick W., 311
Madan, N. N., 1964
Madden, B.J.G., 1014
Magener, Rolf, 4145
Maguire, Eric, 1785
Magyar Harcosok Bajtársi Közössége. Hadifogolyszolgálat, 3941
Maiskii, Ivan Mikhailovich, 2915
Majdalany, Fred, 1581, 1786, 1787
Maks, Leon, 2837
Malaparte, Curzio (pseud.), 1665
Malcolm, Alec D., 1015
Mallal, Bashir A., 4506
Malone, Richard S., 3426
Malthe-Bruun, Kim, 2858
Mann, Edna, 1501
Mannerheim, Carl G. E., 409
Mansfield, Alan, 543
Manstein, Erich von, 450
Mant, Gilbert, 1914
Manus, Max, 2859, 2860
Manvell, Roger, 2812, 3035, 3036
Mao Tse-tung, 1882
Maratoff, Paul, 1634
Marek, Stephen, 4122
Margolin, Leo J., 544
Maritain, Jacques, 3194
Maritsky, Victor (pseud.). See Baratinsky, Viacheslav
Markey, Morris, 2639
Markham, Reuben H., 3214
Marquez, Adalia, 1899
Mars, Alastair, 2483, 2484
Marsh, Charles F., 3563
Marsh, Garry (pseud.). See Gerahty, Leslie M.
Marshall, Alan J., 901
Marshall, Bruce, 2785
Marshall, George C., 312, 451
Marshall, Samuel L. A., 1788, 1789
Martel, Giffard Le Q., 545
Martelli, George, 808
Martens, Allard, 2768
Martienssen, Anthony K., 452
Martin, David, 3215
Martin, Edward F., 77
Martin, Hugh Gray, 1016
Martin, James J., 3494
Martin, Pete, 685
Martin, Ralph G., 157, 158, 2640
Martin, Thomas A., 1017
Martovych, Oleh (pseud.), 2849
Maruyama, Michirō, 2641
Maryland Historical Society. War Records Division, 3547
Masel, Philip, 902

Maskelyne, Jasper, 546
Mason, Francis K., 2034
Mason, Henry L., 3159
Mason, Walter W., 3775
Masters, David, 1018, 2164, 2340, 2341
Masters, John, 3427
Mathews, Sidney T., 1780
Matloff, Maurice, 453
Matson, Clifford H., 1200
Matsumoto, Toru, 4340
Matthews, Allen R., 2642
Matthews, Geoffrey F., 1965
Matthews, Russell, 903
Matthews, Walter R., 4341
Mau, Hermann, 3037
Maugeri, Franco, 419, 3071
Maugham, Frederic H. M., 4457
Maugham, Robin, 1582, 2973
Mauldin, William H., 313
Maule, Henry, 374, 1960, 1961
Maund, Loben E. H., 2342
Maupin, Jere W., 3605
Maurel, Micheline, 3942
Maxon, Yale C., 3088
Mayer, Milton S., 3038
Mayo, Andrew R., 1790
Mazur, Tadeusz, 3148
Meadows, Maureen C., 3428
Medd, Peter N., 4065
Medical Department, U.S. Army: Surgery in World War II.
   See U.S. Army Medical Service, The Medical Department of the
   U.S. Army, in World War II: Surgery in World War II
Medical Research Council (Great Britain), Special Report Series, 682
Medlicott, William N., 3583
Medvedev, Dmitrii N., 2850
Meeking, Charles, 159
Meerloo, Joost A. M., 3160
Meier, Maurice, 3818
Meiggs, Russell, 3655
Meinecke, Friedrich, 3039
Meissner, Janusz, 2165
Mejak, J., 3318
Mellenthin, Friedrich W. von, 454
Melling, Leonard, 1019
Mellor, David P., 3656
Mellor, W. Franklin, 4279
Melville, Alan (pseud.). See Caverhill, William M.
Mendès-France, Pierre, 3943
Menon, Vapal P., 3429
Mentze, Ernst, 3169
Mepham, Clement R., 1020
Mercer, Asja, 2861
Mercey, Arch A., 2343
Merke, O., 534
Merley, David, 86
Merriam, Robert E., 1791
Merrill, James M., 2235
Mersey Docks and Harbour Board, Liverpool, 3384
Merton, Robert K., 3573
Merton, Thomas, 2267
Metcalf, George R., 4342
Methodist Church (U.S.). Commission on Chaplains, 4343
Methuen, Paul A., 4390
Metzler, Jost, 2485
Meyer, Hershel D., 2916
Meynell, Laurence W., 4066
Michelsen, Kaj C. B., 3170
Michie, Allan A., 1502, 1792, 1793
Mick, Allan H., 1342
Middleton, Drew, 314, 1519
Midlam, Don S., 2236
Mielke, Fred, 665
Mihovilović, Ive, 3314
Mikes, George, 3216
Mikhailov, Nikolai N., 3454
Mikolajczyk, Stanislaw, 3132

Miksche, F. O., 2752
Milbourne, Andrew R., 664
Miles, Wyndham D., 484
Milford, N. H. War Memorial Book Committee, 3548
Military History of World War II, 2573
Milkomane, George A. M., 809
Millar, George R., 2786
Miller, Ernest B., 2643
Miller, Everett B., 708
Miller, Francis T., 124, 315
Miller, John, 2644, 2645
Miller, Jordan Y., 588
Miller, Lee G., 4406
Miller, Max, 2486, 2487, 2646
Miller, Merle, 2268
Miller, Norman M., 2237
Millett, John D., 1201
Millin, Sarah G., 1794-1798
Millington, Geoffrey, 2166
Millington-Drake, Sir Eugen J.H.V., 2488
Millis, Walter, 217, 1799
Mills-Roberts, Derek, 810
Milner, Samuel, 2647
Milward, Alan S., 3600
Minco, Marga, 3161
Minney, Rubeigh J., 811
Minott, Rodney G., 1800
Misselwitz, Henry F., 3089, 3495
Mitchell, Alan W., 2003, 2167
Mitchell, Sir Harold P., 2974
Mitscherlich, Alexander, 665
Mittelman, Joseph B., 1202
Moellering, Ralph L., 4344
Moen, Petter, 3945
Mohr, Ulrich, 2489
Mollet, Ralph, 3245
Momeyer, William E., 3549
Monaghan, Forbes J., 3267
Monks, John, Jr., 2648
Monks, Noel, 2490, 4407
Monsarrat, Nicholas, 2491
Monsey, Derek, 4067
Montagu, Ewen E. S., 812
Montgomery, Bernard L., 375, 1583, 1801
Moody, Dallas D., 2649
Moody, Samuel B., 4146
Moore, Don, 2300
Moore, Edith, 4345
Moore, Harriet L., 3455
Moorehead, Alan McC., 1584, 1802
Morača, Pero, 3217
Mordal, Jacques (pseud.). See Cras, Hervé
Morgan, Sir Frederick E., 1803
Morgan, Guy, 3946
Morgan, H. Gerthon, 3703
Morgan, Henry G., 455
Morgan, John D., 3725
Morgan, Murray C., 2650
Morgan, William J., 813, 814
Morgenstern, George E., 218
Morin, Raul, 3496
Morison, Samuel E., 456, 457, 2344, 2345
Morris, Arthur H. M., 1021
Morris, David E., 1883
Morris, Herman C., 160
Morris, Richard B., 3497
Morrison, Ian, 1966
Morrison, Jack K., 1203
Morrison, Wilbur H., 1204, 2238
Morrow, James E., 1397
Morton, Gertrude B., 4280
Morton, Louis, 2, 458, 1900
Morzik, Fritz, 2168
Moseley, Wendell F., 2011
Mosenson, Moshe, 1585
Moskop, Roy L., 1205

Mosley, Leonard O., 815
Moss, William S., 816, 1534, 3601
Mote, Frederick W., 27
Motter, Thomas H. V., 1586
Mottram, E., 1022
Mouchotte, René, 2169
Moule, William R., 4147
Moulton, James L., 1804
Mowat, Farley, 919
Moxon, Oliver, 376, 2239
Moyzisch, L. C., 817
Mueller, Chester, 547
Mueller, Ralph, 1206
Muggeridge, Malcolm, 2990
Muir, Augustus, 1023
Mukerji, Girija, 3430
Mulgan, John, 377
Munro, Ross, 1805
Munsell, Warren P., 1207
Munson, Kenneth G., 2035, 2036, 2170
Munthe, Malcolm, 2862
Muranjan, Sumant K., 3657
Murphy, Audie, 1806
Murphy, Henry B. M., 4223
Murphy, Henry C., 3726
Murphy, Thomas D., 1208
Murphy, W. E., 1587
Murray, Keith A. H., 3658
Murray, Mary, 4148
Museum of Modern Art, New York, 161
Musmano, Michael A., 3040, 3819
Musser, W. Daniel, 3727
Mussolini, Benito, 3072
Muus, Fleming B., 2863
Myers, Debs, 282
Myers, Edmund C. W., 3225
Myers, Hugh H., 4149

Nabarro, Derrick, 3947
Nadich, Judah, 4224
Nagai, Takashi, 2269
Nakajima, Commander Tadashi, 2228
Nalder, Reginald F. H., 1024
Namier, Lewis B., 204, 205
Nance, Curtis H., 1303
Nansen, Odd, 3948
Napa (Attack Transport), 2651
Napp, Ralph R., 412
Narracott, Arthur H., 1520, 2037
Nash, George C., 548
National Broadcasting Company, 1807
National Bureau for Industrial Protection, 3728
National Lutheran Council, 4346
National Nuclear Energy Series. Manhattan Project Technical Section, 666
Neave, Airey, 2769, 4068
Neil, Roy S., 2874
Neilson, Francis, 93, 198
Nelson, Donald M., 3729
Nelson, Ralph W., 4347
Neprud, Robert E., 2038
Netherlands. Department van Financiön, 3606
Neumann, Inge S., 28
Neumann, Peter, 1668, 3041
Neumann, Robert, 3042
Neumann, William L., 3301
Neville, James E. H., 1025
Neville, Ralph, 818
New Canaan, Connecticut. War Records Committee, 3550
Newcomb, Alan H., 3949
Newcomb, Richard F., 2652, 2653
Newman, Bernard, 1521, 2917
Newman, Judith S., 4013
Newnes, George, Ltd., 162
Newport News, Virginia. History Commission, World War II, 3551
Newsome, Noël F., 2918

Newsweek, 2919
Newton, Don, 1808
New York City Committee for Service Men, 4281
New York Herald Tribune, 94
New York City Museum of Modern Art. See Museum of Modern Art, New York
The New Yorker, 125
New Zealand. Army. 3d Division. Histories Committee, 1088-1100
New Zealand. Department of Internal Affairs. War History Branch, 3431, 3432
New Zealand. Prime Minister's Department. Information Section, 255
Nicholas, Elizabeth, 819
Nicholas, M., 2171
Nicholas, N., 2171
Nichols, Charles S., 2722
Nichols, Lester M., 1209
Nicholson, Walter N., 1026
Nickerson, Hoffman, 459
Nicoll, Peter H., 126
Nielander, William A., 3730
Niescior, Leon, 4014
Nikitin, M. N., 3820
Nilsson, John R., 1210
Nimitz, Chester W., 2349, 2662
Nirenstein, Albert, 2838
Noel-Baker, Francis E., 3228
Noel de Gaulle (pseud.). See Graff, Klaas de
Noguères, Henri, 206
Noia, Joseph, 4225
Noonan, William, 1884
Nork, Karl, 3950
Norman, Albert, 1809
Norman, Kathleen, 1535
North, John, 1810
Norton, Conrad, 4031
Norton, Frazer D., 1101
Norton-Taylor, Duncan, 2654
Norway. Norske Regjerings Informasjonskontor, 2492
Norwood, Arthur, 1223
Nova Scotia, 3433
Novick, David, 3731
Novitch, Marian, 2753
Noyes, John H., 2655
Noyes, William A., 549, 4431
Nu, U, 3268
Nyberg, Clifford W., 692
Nyiszli, Miklos, 4015

Oatts, Lewis B., 1967
Ober, Warren U., 211
O'Brien, John W., 905
O'Brien, Terence H., 4282
O'Callaghan, Sean, 820
O'Callahan, Joseph T., 2656
Ochsner, Charly R., 4451
Odgers, George, 2240
Odic, Charles J., 3195
Offenberg, Jean, 2172
Official History of the Indian Armed Forces in the Second World War, 1939-45. Campaigns in the Eastern Theatre, 1964, 1972, 1973
Official History of the Indian Armed Forces in the Second World War, 1939-45. Campaigns in the Western Theatre, 1546, 1589
Official History of the Indian Armed Forces in the Second World War, 1939-45. General war administration and organisation, 555, 2016
Official History of the Indian Armed Forces in the Second World War, 1939-45. Medical services, 671, 672
Official History of New Zealand in the Second World War, 1939-45, 475, 614, 686, 687, 688, 1078-1084, 1087, 1101-1105, 1531, 1554, 1587, 1598, 1604, 1627, 1815, 2382, 3432, 3440, 3621, 3775
Ogburn, Charlton, 1212
Ogden, Graeme, 2493
Ogden, Michael, 2494
Ogle, Mary S., 4150
Oglivy-Dalgleish, James W., 1027
Okubo, Miné, 4188
Okumiya, Masatake, 2241, 2585

Oldfield, Barney, 4408
O'Leary, Cedric P., 4151
Oleck, Howard L., 256
Oliphant, Sir Lancelot, 3951
Oliver, Philip G., 1213
Olsen, Oluf R., 2864
Olsson, Carl, 257
Ommanney, Francis D., 2346
O'Neill, Herbert C., 127, 128, 259, 1811, 2920
O'Neill, Hester, 4226
Onslow, William A. B. Onslow, 6th earl of, 1588
Oras, Arts, 3238
Orbaan, Albert, 2754
Orde, Roden, 1028
Order of battle series, 1414
Organ, F. P., 1446
Origo, Iris M., 3073
Orme, Alexandra, 3133
Orska, Irena (pseud.). See Bytniewska, Irena
Osada, Arata, 2270
O'Sheel, Patrick, 2657
Osman, W. H., 550
Oughterson, Ashley W., 666
Outze, Børge, 3171
Owen, Frank, 1915, 1968
Owen, Roderic, 2173
Owens, Walter E., 1215
Oxford University. Institute of Statistics, 3615

Pabel, Reinhold, 4189
Pabst, Helmut, 1670
Pack, Stanley W. C., 2495
Packe, Michael St. J., 1029
Paddock, Robert H., 1216
Padmanabhan, C. E., 129
Padover, Saul K., 3574
Padre (pseud.). See Wuest, Karl A.
Page, Robert C., 1969
Paget, Mrs. K. M., 4152
Paget, Reginald T., 410, 4152
Pakštas, Kazys, 3239
Pal, Dharm, 1589
Palmer, Robert R., 516, 551
Palta, Krishan R., 3434
P'an Chao-Ying, 3269
Paneth, Philip, 3108, 3227, 3821
Pankhurst, E. Sylvia, 3316
Pankhurst, Richard K. P., 3316
Panlilio, Yay, 2887
Panther Veterans Organization, 1217
Papagos, Alexandros, 1628
Pape, Richard, 4069, 4070
Papen, Franz von, 2975
Paquin, Grete, 3058
Parham, Hetman J., 2174
Paris, Edmond, 3822
Parker, Henry M. D., 3659
Parkin, Ray, 2658, 4153
Parkinson, Cyril N., 1030
Parnes, Herbert S., 3732
Parrish, Thomas D., 2347
Parsons, Anthony D., 1031
Parsons, Laurence M. H. (pseud.). See Rosse, Lawrence M. H. Parsons, 6th earl of
Parsons, Robert P., 667
Partridge, Eric, 177
Paterson, Thomas T., 3584
Patton, George S., 316
Patton, William, 552
Paul, Daniel (pseud.). See Kessel, Alexander W. L.
Paul, William P., 1033
Paull, Raymond, 2659
Pavey, Walter G., 920
Pavillard, Stanley S., 4154
Pavlov, Dimitrii V., 1661
Pawle, Gerald, 553, 3385

Pawlowicz, Sala K., 3952
Pay, Don R., 1218
Payne, Donald G., 2039, 2496
Payne, Pierre S. R., 3270
Peacock, Geraldine, 1970
Pearl, Jack, 317, 2040
Pearlman, Maurice, 4516
Pearson, Michael, 860
Pearson, Ralph E., 1219
Peaslee, Budd J., 1220
Peck, Graham, 3271
Peers, William R., 1971
Peillard, Léonce, 2497
Peis, Gunter, 872, 1480
Pelékis, K. (pseud.), 3240
Pendar, Kenneth W., 3498
Penfold, A. W., 906
Peniakoff, Vladimir, 1536
Pennsylvania. Historical and Museum Commission, 3552, 3553
Pensacola. (Cruiser), 2660
Percival, Arthur E., 1916
Percival, Winifred D., 3953
Pereira, Jocelyn, 378
Perl, Gisella, 4016
Permenter, Donald, 4099
Perrault, Gilles, 1812
Perrin, Henri, 3954
Perusse, Roland I., 29
Peter II, King of Yugoslavia, 2976
Peterman, Ivan H., 3236
Peters, Clarence A., 4227
Peterson, Agnes F., 61
Pethö, Tibor, 3100
Peto, Marjorie, 669
Petrov, Vladimir, 3456
Peyton, Green (pseud.). See Wertenbaker, Green P.
Pezas, Mikia, 3228
Phillips, Cecil E. L., 1590, 1813, 1814
Phillips, Claire, 1901
Phillips, Dean, 2604
Phillips, Neville C., 1815
Phillips, Norman C., 821
Phillips, Raymond, 4493
Philpot, Oliver L. S., 3955
Pick, Frederick W., 3302
Pickersgill, J. W., 2977
Pickles, Dorothy M., 3196
Pile, Sir Frederick A., 1522
Piliar, Iurii E., 3956
Pineau, Roger, 2228, 2597, 2616
Pinkett, Harold T., 72
Pinkus, Oscar, 3134
Pinto, Oreste, 822-826
Piquet-Wicks, Eric, 827
Pirie, Anthony, 828
Pirinsky, George, 3499
Pitkin, Thomas M., 597
Pitman, Stuart, 1034
Pitt, P. W., 1035
Pitt, Roxane, 829
Pitt-Rivers, Julian A. L., 1036
Plant, Arthur, 1122
Playfair, Ian S. O., 1537
Pleasants, Eric, 380
Plocher, Hermann, 2175
Pocock, Arthur, 2498
Pogue, Forrest C., 460
Pokryshkin, Aleksandr I., 2176
Poland. Biuro Odszkodowań Wojennych, 3135
Poland. Committee of Enquiry into the Question of the Polish Prisoners of War from the 1939 Campaign, Missing in the U.S.S.R., 3823
Poland. Ministerstwo Informacji, 3136
Poland. Polskie Siły Zbrojne Armia Krajowa, 2839
Pole, Aline, 3137
Polevoi, Boris N., 1662, 1663
Poliakov, Léon, 3824, 3825

Polish American Congress, 3500
Pollock, George, 2499
Pollock, P. Hamilton, 4348
Pompe, Cornelia A., 4458
Pondera (transport), 2661
Pondera (Transport), 2661
Pont-Alain, C. M., 3246
Pool, Ithiel de Sola, 3033
Poolman, Kenneth, 2041, 2177, 2348, 2500-2502
Pope, Dudley, 2503-2505
Popham, Hugh, 2178
Poppe, Janus, 3272
Popple, Charles S., 3733
Portway, Christopher, 3957
Postan, Michael M., 554, 3660
Potiphar (pseud.), 3585
Potter, Elmer B., 2349, 2662
Potter, John D., 417, 418
Potts, Charles, 1591
Powell, Lyle S., 670
Powell, Michael, 2506
Prasad, Bisheshwar, 1972, 1973
Prasad, Sri N., 555
Pratt, Fletcher, 260, 2663-2665
Presseisen, Ernst L., 2994
Prest, Alan R., 3586
Preuss, Ernst G., 207
Price, Harvey L., 3734
Price, John, 3661
Priest, Barbara, 830
Prince, Morris, 1221
Pringle, Dave J. C., 1102
Pringle, Patrick, 261, 2042
Pritt, Denis N., 2921
Prittie, Terence C. F., 2813, 4071
Prosser, David G., 2787
Proudfoot, Malcolm J., 4228
Prüller, Wilhelm, 411
Pryce, J. E., 3958
Psimeno, H., 3232
Psychoundakis, George, 1629
Pubols, Ben H., 3735
Pudney, John, 2179
Pugh, Marshall, 2350
Pugsley, A. F., 2351
Puleston, William D., 2352
Pumphrey, Bevan, 3662
Purcell, Richard J., 3736
Purdue University, 4432, 4433
Pury, Roland de, 3959
Pyle, Ernest T., 1818, 2666

QMC Historical Studies, 576
Qualter, Terence H., 556
Quant, Willis C., 3755
Queen-Hughes, R. W., 921
Quigley, Martin, 3074
Quilter, D. C., 1037
Quinterley, Esmond, 2043

R. A. F. Flying Review, 2044, 2045, 4072
Rabin, Gilbert, 4392
Rabinowitz, Louis I., 1592
Rachlis, Eugene, 831
Rademaker, John A., 3554
Radlovic, I. Monte, 3218
Raeder, Eric, 2507
Raina, Bishen L., 671, 672
Rainier, Peter W., 1593
Ramsey, Guy H. W., 262
Ramsey, Pauline C., 3376
Randall, Howard M., 1819
Randolph, John H., 1222
Rangsdove, William B., 117
Rankin, Howard, 3388
Ranz, Jochanan, 3138

Rao, Raghunath, 3663
Rapport, Leonard, 1223
Rasmussen, Albert H., 2353
Rasmussen, Wayne D., 3751
Ratchford, Benjamin U., 3335
Rauch, Basil, 3501
Raven, Hélène J., 3960
Rawicz, Slavomir, 3961
Rawnsley, Cecil F., 2180
Ray, Cyril, 1038
Ray, Jefferson F., 4283
Ray, Samuel H., 4349
Raymond, Ernest, 3336
Raymond, Patrick, 3336
Rayner, Denys A., 2508
Rayner, Louisa, 3219
Read, Frances W., 4350
Reader's Digest, 130, 832
Reading, Geoffrey, 2667
Rebec, Estelle, 78
Robert, Richard R., 1224
Recto, Claro M., 3273
Red Cross. Finland. Finlands Röda Kors, 4284
Red Cross. International Committee, Geneva, 4285, 4286
Red Cross. U.S. American National Red Cross, 4287-4289
Red Cross. U.S. American National Red Cross. Hawaii Chapter, 4290
Reed, Douglas, 2922
Reed, Philip, 2214
Reel, Adolf F., 4507
Rees, John R., 673, 674
Reeves, James, 115
Rei, August, 2923
Reichers, Louis, 2181
Reid, Francis, 1630
Reid, Ian D., 4073
Reid, John P. M., 2046
Reid, Patrick R., 4074-4077
Reiner, Ella L., 3962
Reiners, Wilfred O., 3963
Reinhold, William J., 2668
Reiss, Mary C., 4258
Reitlinger, Gerald R., 3043, 3457, 3826
Rémy (pseud.). See Renault-Roulier, Gilbert
Renaud, Alexandre, 1820
Renault-Roulier, Gilbert, 833, 834, 2161, 2788, 3964
Rendel, Alexander M., 835
Renne, Louis O., 4155
Rennel, Francis J. Rennel Rodd, baron, 4291
Rentz, John N., 2711, 2719
Reoch, Ernest, 1503
Rexford-Welch, Samuel C., 675
Reyburn, Wallace, 1821
Reyes, José G., 4156
Reynaud, Paul, 3197
Reynolds, Bart, 318
Reynolds, Leonard C., 2509
Reynolds, Quentin J., 1523, 2669, 3827, 4078
Rhode, Gotthold, 3317
Rhodes-Wood, Edward H., 1039
Rhys, Lloyd, 2670, 3274
Ribbentrop, Joachim von, 2978
Richard, Dorothy E., 95
Richards, Benjamin J., 2671
Richards, Denis, 2047
Richards, James M., 4391
Richards, Van Ness, 1382
Richardson, Anthony, 420, 4047
Richardson, Eudora R., 557
Richardson, Hal, 836
Richardson, William, 447
Rickman, Thomas H., 4277
Riddell, James, 558
Rieber, Alfred, 3198
Riegelman, Carol, 3737
Riegelman, Harold, 2672
Riemer, Ruth, 4182

Riesco, M. R., 1002
Riesenberg, Felix, 2354
Riess, Curt, 3044, 3045, 3838
Rigby, Francoise L., 2770
Rigoni Stern, Mario, 1664
Ringelblum, Emanuel, 3828
Rissik, David, 1040
Ristig, James F., 1257, 1348
Ritchie, Lewis A. da Costa, 1594
Rittenhouse, William H., 3965
Ritter, Gerhard, 2814
Rivas, Richard C., 2182
Rivett, Rohan D., 4157
Robbins, D.I.M., 1031
Robbins, Robert A., 1226
Roberts, Eric S., 3664
Roberts, Michael R., 1075
Robertson, Bruce, 2048, 2049
Robertson, Esmonde M., 3046
Robertson, John H., 381, 3435
Robertson, Terence, 1822, 2510-2513
Robinett, Paul M., 1127
Robinson, A.S.L., 1874
Robinson, Clinton F., 559
Robinson, Georgette, 837
Robinson, Jacob, 30, 4517
Robson, Walter, 382
Rodenhauser, Reiner, 412
Rofe, Cyril, 3966
Rogers, Edward K., 4351
Rogers, Hugh C. B., 560
Rogers, Lindsay, 676
Rogge, Bernhard, 2514
Rogin, Martin, 78
Rohatyn Association of Israel, 3829
Rohwer, Jürgen, 251
Roll, Erich, 3616
Rolo, Charles J., 1974
Romanus, Charles F., 461, 1885, 1975
Romilly, Giles, 3967
Rommel, Erwin, 413
Rontch, Isaac E., 319
Rooney, Andrew A., 263
Roosenburg, Henriette, 3968
Roosevelt, Elliott, 3303
Roosevelt, Franklin D., 3502, 3503
Root, Waverly L., 2924
Rootham, Jasper, 2875
Rorimer, James J., 4392
Roscoe, Theodore, 2355, 2356
Rose, Joseph R., 561
Rosen, Josef, 3771
Rosen, S. McKee, 3617
Rosen, Victor, 419
Rosenfeld, Else R. B., 3969
Rosenman, Samuel I., 4292
Rosenthal, Herbert H., 497
Rosinger, Lawrence K., 3275, 3276
Roskill, Stephen W., 2357-2359, 2515
Ross, Allen M., 79
Ross, Angus, 1103
Ross, John M. S., 2050, 2063
Ross, William D., 3335
Rosse, Laurence M. H. Parsons, 6th earl of, 1041
Rossi, Angelo (pseud.). See Tasca, Angelo
Rothberg, Abraham, 131
Rothfeder, Herbert P., 31
Rothfels, Hans, 2815
Rothstein, Andrew, 208, 3458
Rousset, David, 3970, 3971
Rowan, Richard W., 838
Rowan-Robinson, Henry, 264, 1823
Rowdon, Maurice, 383
Rowe, Albert Percival, 562
Rowe, Vivian, 1504

Rowland, Buford, 590
Rowse, Alfred Leslie, 191
Roxan, David, 4393
Roy, Claude, 1824
Roy, Jules, 2183
Royal Air Force Journal, 2051
Royal Institute of International Affairs, 96, 3337
Royce, Hans, 2816
Rozek, Edward J., 3288
Rubel, George K., 1128
Rudel, Hans U., 2184
Rudnicki, Adolf, 3830
Ruge, Friedrich, 2360
Rumpf, Hans, 2185
Rundell, Walter, 3738
Ruppenthal, Roland G., 563
Rusk, Howard L., 1509
Russell, Edward F. L. Russell, 2d baron, 3831, 4158, 4581
Russell, Judith, 3739
Russell, Ruth B., 3338
Russell, Wilfrid W., 2243
Russell, William B., 907
Russell-Roberts, Denis, 1917
Russia. Komissiia po Izdaniiu Diplomaticheskikh Dokumentov, 3289
Russia. Sovetskoe Informatsionnoe Biuro, 176
Rutkowski, Adam, 4246
Ryan, Allen L., 1229
Ryan, Cornelius, 1825
Ryan, Peter, 1924
Ryder, Robert E. D., 1826
Rygg, Andrew N., 4293

Saber, Clifford, 1595
Sabey, Ian, 3972
Sabrillo, Jacques, 3825
Saelen, Frithjof, 839
Saint Exupéry, Consuelo de, 3199
Saint John, John, 668
Saint John, Joseph F., 2674
Saint John, Robert, 1631, 4409
Saint Joseph News-Press, 97
Saito, Fred, 2244, 2597
Sakai, Saburo, 2244
Sakamaki, Kazuo, 219
Salerno, Attilio M., 3075
Saliège, Jules Géraud, Cardinal, 3200
Salisbury-Jones, Sir Guy, 320
Salmond, James B., 1042
Salomon, Henry, 2361
Salvemini, Gaetano, 192
Salvesen, Sylvia, 3973
Salwey, Ruth, 3974
Samain, Bryan, 1827
Samarin, Vladimir D. (pseud.), 3459
Sampson, Francis L., 2186, 2187
Samson, Gerald, 1886
Samwell, H. P., 384
Sanborn, Frederic R., 193
Sanders, Jacquin, 2516
Sanderson, James D., 2755
Sandes, Edward W. C., 1043, 1076
Sandford, Kenneth, 385
San Francisco Examiner, 98
Sano, Bunichiro, 2261
Sansom, William, 3386
Saporiti, Piero, 3076
Saraphēs, Stephanos, 2826
Sargent, Frederic O., 1230
Satō, Tasuku, 4353
Saturday Evening Post, 265
Saundby, Sir Robert H.M.S., 2052
Saunders, Hilary A. St. G., 840, 1044, 2047, 2188, 3665, 4294, 4295
Savage, Christopher I., 564
Savage, Katharine, 132, 133
Savary, Gladys S., 3277
Savin, William A., 1231

Savo Island (aircraft carrier), 2675
Saward, Dudley, 2189
Sawicki, James A., 565
Sawicki, Jerzy, 3124
Sawyer, John, 1828
Sayers, Michael A. K., 3047
Sayers, Richard S., 3666
Sayers, William C. B., 3387
Sayre, Joel, 1596
Scaevola (pseud.), 3139
Scanlon, Helen L., 32
Scanlon, J. J., 3597
Schaeffer, Heinz, 2517
Schechtman, Joseph B., 4229
Scheer, Charles H. E., 587
Schellenberg, Walter, 841
Schertl, Alfons, 2190
Scheufler, Karl W., 1362
Schimanski, Stefan, 386
Schlabrendorff, Fabian von, 2817, 2818
Schlegel, Marvin W., 3555
Schlotterbeck, Friedrich, 2819
Schmidt, Heinz W., 1597
Schmidt, Paul, 3048
Schnabel, Ernst, 3162
Schneider, Norris F., 3556
Schneider, Reinhold, 2809
Schoenberner, Franz, 4230
Schoenholtz, E. R., 2080
Schofield, Brian B., 2518
Schofield, Stephen, 842
Schofield, William G., 2519
Schramm, Wilhelm, 2820
Schreiber, Thomas, 33
Schreurs, Johannes J.M.H., 3163
Schrire, I., 3975
Schroeder, Paul W., 194
Schröter, Heinz, 1677
Schubart, William H., 2676
Schueller, George K., 3033
Schuetz, Arthur, 843
Schull, Joseph, 2362, 2363
Schultz, Paul L., 1232
Schulze-Holthus, Bernhard, 844
Schütz, William W., 4394
Schwabedissen, Walter, 2191
Schwartz, Andrew J., 3290
Schwarz, Leo W., 3832
Schwarzwalder, John, 845
Science in World War II: Office of Scientific Research and Development, 483, 486, 549, 581, 596, 4431, 4439
Scifres, Charles, 1435
Sclater, William, 2520
Scotland, A. P., 846
Scott, Douglas, 4079
Scott, J. D., 554
Scott, Jay (pseud.), 266
Scott, John D., 3667
Scott, Lionel, 2789
Scott, Peter T., 1352, 2521
Scott, Robert L., 2245
Scoullar, J. L., 1598
Scrivener, Jane (pseud.), 1829
Seabrook, William C., 2364
Seabury, Paul, 3049
Seagrave, Gordon S., 677, 678
Seasholes, Henry C., 2677
The Second World War, 1939-1945: A Popular Military History Series, 229, 1485, 1549, 1617, 1810
Second World War, 1939-1945, Series, 1774
Seddon, Richard, 4395
Sedmak, V., 3318
Seger, Gerhart, 3050
Selby, David, 2678
Seldman, Joel I., 3740
Seligman, Adrian C. C., 2522

Sellar, Robert J. B., 1045
Sellman, Roger R., 134
Sellwood, Arthur V., 2365, 2523
Semmes, Harry H., 321
Semmler, Rudolf, 3051
Senger und Etterlin, Fridolin von, 414
Seramgard, Arthur K., 322
Serle, R. P., 908
Seth, Ronald S., 209, 847, 848, 1046, 1678, 1679, 2524, 2525, 2756, 2757
Sevareid, A. Eric, 323
Sewell, William G., 4159
Sexton, Winton K., 4080
Seydewitz, Max, 3052
Seymour, Harold J., 4296
Shankland, Peter, 2526
Shapiro, Lionel S. B., 1830
Sharon, Henrietta B., 679
Sharp, John C., 35
Shaw, Carroll K., 3741
Shaw, Frank H., 2366, 2367
Shaw, Henry I., 2722
Shaw, James, 1976
Shaw, William B. K., 1599
Shears, Philip J., 1047
Sheean, Vincent, 324
Sheehan, Fred, 1831
Shelton, John B., 2926
Shennan, Alexander F., 1832
Sheppard, Eric William, 268
Sherbrooke-Walker, Ronald, 2192
Sheridan, Jack W., 1234
Sheridan, Martin, 2679
Sherman, Frederick C., 2680
Sherrod, Robert L., 2053, 2681, 2682
Sherwood, Robert E., 3504
Shiomi, Saburo, 3602
Shipley, S. Paul, 3388
Shirer, William L., 2527, 3053
Shirey, Orville C., 1235
Sholty, Alva H., 4354
Shomon, Joseph J., 566
Shores, Louis, 2054
Short, Stanley W., 1977
Shrimpton, John A., 3976
Shropshire (Cruiser), 2528
Shugg, Roger W., 135
Shulman, Milton, 1833
Sibley, Mulford Q., 4355, 4356
Silkin, S. C., 4509
Sill, Van R., 567
Silvera, John D., 269
Silverstone, Paul H., 2368
Sim, Katharine, 1918
Simmons, Kenneth W., 3977
Simms, Frank, 4065
Simon, Leslie E., 4434
Simonds, Peter, 1834
Simons, Jessie E., 4160
Simons, Thurlow B., 1250
Simpson, Evan J., 568, 1600
Simpson, William, 680
Sims, Edward H., 2055, 2056
Sims, Grover J., 3742
Sims, Lydel, 2566
Sinclair, Donald W., 1104
Sinclair, William B., 2246
Sinel, Leslie P., 3247
Sinevirskii, Nikolai, 849
Singer, Kurt D., 850, 851
Singh, Bishan, 1978
Singh, Gurchan, 2888
Sington, Derrick, 4017
Sinton, Russell L., 1236
Sired, Ronald, 2529
Sisters of Our Lady of the Sacred Heart, 4357

Skimming, Sylvia, 4297
Skorzeny, Otto, 852, 853
Skrine, Clarmont P., 1601
Sledziński, Waclaw, 3140
Sleeman, Colin, 4508, 4509
Slim, William Slim, 1st viscount, 1979
Small, Robert O., 3743
Smaller War Plants Corporation, 3744
Smeeton, Miles, 387
Smirnov, Sergei S., 1681
Smith, Bruce L., 36
Smith, Chester L., 2683
Smith, Clarence McK., 681
Smith, Dean A., 682
Smith, Donald, 4161
Smith, Dudley G., 4298
Smith, Edwin S., 1394
Smith, Frank E., 1237
Smith, Gaddis, 3505
Smith, Herbert A., 3587
Smith, Holland M., 2684
Smith, Nicol, 2889
Smith, Norman D., 1524
Smith, Ralph E., 3745
Smith, Robert R., 1902, 2685
Smith, Stanley E., 2686-2688
Smith, Waldo E. L., 4358
Smith, Walter B., 462
Smyth, Frank, 2220
Smyth, Henry DeW., 569
Smyth, Sir John George, 270
Sneed, Bessie, 4162
Snell, Edwin M., 453
Snell, John L., 195, 2927, 3291, 3304
Snow, Sir Charles P., 4436, 4437
Snow, Edgar, 2928
Snow, John H., 854
Snyder, Earl A., 1238
Snyder, Louis L., 136, 137, 3054
Snyder, Robert S., 4359
Sobel, Robert, 3506
Social Science Research Council. Committee on Civil-Military Relations Research, 37, 684
Society for the Propagation of the Faith, 4360
Soltikow, Michael, 855
Somerhausen, Anne S., 3164
Somers, Herman M., 3746
Sonnabend, H., 3978
Sontag, Raymond J., 2900
Sosabowski, Stanislaw, 421
Sosnowski, Kiryl, 4231
Soupault, Philippe, 3979
South, Oron P., 683
South Africa. Director-General of Supplies, 570
South Africa. Prime Minister's Department. Union War Histories Section, 1602, 2369
South Africa. Railways and Harbours Board, 571
South African Jewish Board of Deputies, 3436
South Dakota. World War II History Commission, 3557
Southall, Ivan, 572, 2057, 2193, 2247
Southard, Frank A., 3588
Southon, Alfred, 3980
Spaight, James M., 2058
Sparrow, John C., 573
Sparrow, John H. A., 992
Spears, Sir Edward L., baronet, 2979
Special Libraries Association. Military Libraries Division, 38
Speidel, Hans, 1835, 1836
Spellman, Francis J., 4361
Spencer, Floyd A., 50
Spencer, John H., 1538
Spencer, Louis R., 2890
Spencer, Robert A., 922
Spender, Stephen, 4299
Spenser, James (pseud.). See Guest, Francis H.
Spier, Eugen, 3981

Spier, Henry O., 3
Spiro, Edward, 856, 857
Spitzer, Abe, 2268
Spooner, Anthony, 2194
Spurling, R. Glen, 700
Stacey, Charles P., 1837
Stafford, Edward P., 2689
Stahl, Alfred J., 4163
Stainforth, Peter, 2195
Stalin, Iosif, 3460
Stamps, T. Dodson, 276
Standard Oil Company, 2370
Stanford, Alfred B., 1838
Stanford Research Institute; Stanford University, 2059
Stanford University. Hoover Institution on War, Revolution, and Peace, 39
Stanford University. Hoover Institution on War, Revolution, and Peace. Bibliographical Series, 10, 27, 61
Stanford University. Hoover Institution on War, Revolution, and Peace. Documentary Series, 3181
Stanford University. Hoover Institution on War, Revolution, and Peace. Hoover Institution Studies. Series B; Elite Studies, 3033
Stanford University. Hoover Institution on War, Revolution, and Peace. Publications, 64, 3079
Stanley Clarke, Edward B., 1048
Stark, Flora, 3982
Stark, Freya, 1603, 2980
Starr, Chester G., 1239
The Stars and Stripes, 138
Startup, Robin McG., 574
Stauffer, Alvin P., 575
Stead, Philip J., 858
Stědry, Vladimír, 3388
Steele, Theodore M., 1240
Steere, Edward, 576
Steichen, Edward, 2690, 2727, 2728
Stein, Elliot K., 1200
Steinbeck, John, 271
Stembridge, Jasper H., 171
Stephan, Enno, 859
Stephanides, Theodore, 1539
Stericker, John, 4164
Sterling, Dorothy, 272
Sterling, Forest J., 2691
Stern, James, 3055
Stetson, Arthur W., 1371
Stettinius, Edward R., 3305
Steven, Walter T., 4362
Stevens, E. H., 4474
Stevens, Edmund, 3461
Stevens, Frederic H., 4165
Stevens, William G., 388, 1105, 1604
Stevenson, Eleanor, 685
Stewart, Carroll, 2129
Stewart, George, 273
Stewart, Ian M., 1049
Stewart, Irvin, 4438
Stewart, Sidney, 4166
Stibbe, Philip, 4167
Stiles, Bert, 2196
Stilwell, Joseph W., 325
Stipp, John L., 3114
Stockman, James R., 2710
Stokes, Richard L., 3614
Stone, Isidor F., 4232
Storrs, Ronald, 139
Stoughton, Bradley, 3747
Stout, Thomas D. M., 686, 687, 688
Stout, Wesley W., 577, 578
Strahl, Fred M., 1241
Strategicus (pseud.). See O'Neill, Herbert C.
Strathern, Robert F., 1605
Stratton, Roy O., 2693
Straubel, James H., 1986
Straus, Jack M., 1242
Strauss, Cyril A., 389

Strauss, Harold, 3306
Street, Arthur G., 3390
Stroop, Jürgen, 3834
Strootman, Ralph E., 1243
Strutton, Bill, 860, 2876
Stuart, Gilbert, 1887
Studies on Food, Agriculture, and World War II, 3577, 3581, 3590, 3598, 3616, 3633, 3640, 3649, 3669
Studnitz, Hans-Georg von, 1839
Stussman, Morton J., 1244
Stypułkowski, Zbigniew, 3983
Suchenwirth, Richard, 2197
Sumida, Haruzo, defendant, 4509
Summersby, Kathleen, 326
Sunderland, Riley, 461, 1885, 1975
Sunderman, James F., 2060
Super, Margaret L., 3141, 3142
Supreme Commander for the Allied Powers. Government Section, 4510
Survey of International Affairs, 2930
Sutton, Barry, 2248
Sutton, Harry T., 1050
Svābe, Arveds, 3835
Svaz Protifašistických Bojovníků, 3836
Swanwick, Francis W., 3391
Sweet-Escott, Bickham A. C., 861, 3229
Swiecicki, Marek, 1840, 1841
Sykes, Christopher, 327
Synge, William A. T., 1051
Syrkin, Marie, 2758
Szalet, Leon, 4018
Szaz, Zoltan M., 3319
Szende, Stefan, 3837
Szmaglewska, Seweryna, 4019
Szner, Zui, 3799
Szoskiis, Henryk J., 3838
Szymczyk, Norbert J., 3143

Tabori, Paul, 2981, 3392
Tackley, Margaret E., 250
Tailliez, Philippe, 3984
Tainsh, Alsadair R., 1980
Tanner, Väinö A., 1527
Tantri, K'tut, 4168
Tartière, Dorothy, 2790
Tasca, Angelo, 2925
Tashjian, James H., 3507
Tauras, K. V. (pseud.), 2865
Taylor, Alan J. P., 196
Taylor, Anna M., 178
Taylor, Frank J., 3748
Taylor, Geoff, 3985
Taylor, Henry Jr., 328
Taylor, Jeremy L., 1053, 1054
Taylor, Joe G., 1981
Taylor, John E.S.R., 2530, 2531
Taylor, John W. R., 2198
Taylor, Philip H., 40
Taylor, Samuel W., 2133
Taylor, Telford, 1505, 3056
Taylor, Theodore, 329, 2371
Tchok, Ivan M., 2791
Teare, T.D.G., 862
Tedder, Arthur W., 2061
Teissier du Cros, Janet, 3201
Tempest, Victor (pseud.), 2062
Temple Historical Society, Temple, N. H., 3558
Templeton, Kenneth S., 1245
Templewood, Samuel J. G. Hoare, 4452
Tenenbaum, Joseph L., 2840, 3839
Tenenbaum, Sheila, 3839
Tennien, Mark A., 1888, 4353
Terasaki, Gwen H., 3090
Ter Braak, Harry F., 1246
Terrell, Edgar A., 1247
Terrell, Edward, 579

Terrett, Dulany, 580
Texas (Battleship), 2532
Thatcher, Dorothy, 1919
Thayer, Charles W., 2982
Theobald, Robert A., 220
Thiesmeyer, Lincoln R., 581, 4439
Think, 3508
Thomas, Charles W., 2533
Thomas, David A., 2372, 2373
Thomas, Dorothy S., 4190
Thomas, John, 2792
Thomas, Lowell J., 2249
Thomas, Robert C. W., 1606
Thomas, Walter B., 1632
Thompson, Clary, 582
Thompson, Douglas W., 3986
Thompson, George R., 583
Thompson, Henry L., 2063
Thompson, James A., 2694
Thompson, Kenneth, 2534
Thompson, Reginald W., 390, 1842-1846
Thompson, Walter H., 3393
Thomson, David, 3202
Thomson, George P., 4410
Thomson, R. H., 3987
Thorburn, Don, 2250
Thorburn, Lois, 2250
Thorne, Bliss K., 2251
Thorne, Charles B., 2759
Thorne, Leon, 3988
Thornton, Willis, 1847
Thorwald, Jürgen, 1683
Tickell, Jerrard, 863, 864, 2199
Tillott, A. T., 1048
Tilman, Harold W., 2760
The Times, London, 3668
Timothy, Patrick H., 1848
Tinley, James M., 3669
Tipton, Laurance, 1889
Tischer, Werner, 2200
Titmuss, Richard M., 4300
Tōgō, Shigenori, 3091
Toland, John, 1849, 2252
Tolischus, Otto D., 3092
Tomlinson, Henry M., 2696, 3394
Tompkins, Dorothy L.C.C., 41
Tompkins, Peter, 865, 3204
Tong, Hollington K., 3278
Topolski, Feliks, 166
Toschi, Elios, 4169
Toulmin, Harry A., 3749
Toynbee, A. J., 2930
Toyne, John, 866
Traffrail (pseud.). See Dorling, Henry T.
Trahan, E. A., 1248
Trainin, Aron Naremovich, 4496
Transill, Charles C., 221
Translation World Publishers, Chicago, 4497
Travers, Pamela L., 4233
Treadwell, Mattie E., 1249
Treece, Henry, 386
Trefousse, Hans L., 197, 222
Tregaskis, Richard W., 2697
Trevelyan, Mary, 4301
Trevelyan, Raleigh, 1850
Trevor-Roper, Hugh R., 439, 2945, 3057
Trew, Cecil G., 689
Trice, Frasia D., 1250
Trinka, Z'dena, 3840
True, 274
Truman, Harry S., 2983
Trumbull, Robert, 2271, 2698
Truppner, W. C., 3731
Truscott, Lucian K., 330
Tsuchida, William S., 690
Tsuji, Masanobu, 1920, 3093

Tuker, Sir Francis I. S., 1055
Tuleja, Thaddeus V., 2535, 2699
Tully, Andrew, 1851
Tumey, Ben, 331
Tungay, Ronald W., 1472
Tunnell, James M., 1607
Tun Pe, U, 3279
Turk, Jerry, 1206
Turnbladh, Edwin T., 498
Turner, Ernest S., 3395
Turner, John F., 584, 585, 1852, 2064, 2065, 2374-2376, 2536, 2537, 3989
Turner, Leonard C. F., 1540, 1541, 1602, 2369
Turville, William H. H., 713
Tushnet, Leonard, 3144
Tweed, George R., 2700
Tyson, Geoffrey W., 1982

Ulanoff, Stanley M., 2066
Ulasek, Henry T., 73
Umadevi (pseud.). See Wanda Dynowska
Umemura, Michael Takaaki, 60
Umiastowski, Roman, 2932
Underhill, M. L., 4364
Underhill, William E., 1056
Union Club of the City of New York, 3559
United Committee of South-Slavs in London, 3220
United Nations, 3339
United Nations. Communications and Records Division. Archives Section, 62
United Nations. Dag Hammerskjöld Library. Bibliographical Series, 42
United Nations. Department of Conference and General Services, 63
United Nations Archives Reference Guides, 62, 63
United Nations Information Office, New York, 43
United Nations Monetary and Financial Conference, Bretton Woods, New Hampshire, 1944, 3618
United Nations Relief and Rehabilitation Administration. Central Tracing Bureau. Documents Intelligence, 3841
United Nations Relief and Rehabilitation Administration. Chief Historian, 4302
United Nations War Crimes Commission, 4459
United Party, South Africa, 3437
University of Michigan. Center for Japanese Studies. Occasional Papers, 60
Unsdorfer, S. B., 3990
Upton, Anthony F., 1528
Uren Malcolm, John L., 909
Urquhart, Fred, 278
Urquhart, Robert E., 1865
U.S. Adjutant-General's Office. Administrative Services Division, 44
U.S. Aerospace Studies Institute. Concepts Division, 2067
U.S.A.F. Historical Studies, 1981, 2128, 2168, 2191, 2197, 2203, 2204
U.S. Air Force. School of Aviation Medicine, 691
U.S. Air Force. USAF Historical Division, 2069, 2070, 2071
U.S. Air Force. 20th Fighter Bomber Wing, 1251
U.S. Air University, 99
U.S. Air University. Documentary Research Study, 683
U.S. Armed Forces Information School, Carlisle Barracks, Pennsylvania, 3340
U.S. Army. Chaplain Corps, 4365
U.S. Army. Chemical Corps, 586
U.S. Army. Corps of Engineers. Great Lakes Division, 1252
U.S. Army. Corps of Engineers. 2d Combat Battalion, 1253
U.S. Army. Corps of Engineers. 2d Special Brigade, 1254
U.S. Army. Corps of Engineers. 9th Command, 1255
U.S. Army. Corps of Engineers. 48th Combat Battalion, 1256
U.S. Army. Corps of Engineers. 155th Combat Battalion, 1257
U.S. Army. Corps of Engineers. 187th Combat Battalion, 1258
U.S. Army. Corps of Engineers. 256th Combat Battalion, 1259
U.S. Army. Corps of Engineers. 291st Combat Battalion, 1260
U.S. Army. Corps of Engineers. 320th Battalion, 1261
U.S. Army. Corps of Engineers. 373d Regiment, 1262
U.S. Army. Corps of Engineers. 654th Topographic Battalion, 1263

U.S. Army. Corps of Engineers. 816th Aviation Battalion, 1264
U.S. Army. Corps of Engineers. 1374th Petroleum Distribution Company, 1265
U.S. Army. Corps of Engineers. 1629th Construction Battalion, 1266
U.S. Army. Corps of Engineers. 1880th Aviation Battalion, 1267
U.S. Army. European Command. Historical Division, 45
U.S. Army. Evacuation Hospital No. 12, 693
U.S. Army. Evacuation Hospital No. 41, 694
U.S. Army. Evacuation Hospital No. 77, 695
U.S. Army. Far East Command, 2706
U.S. Army. Forces in the European Theater, 1268
U.S. Army. Forces in the Far East, 1890-1893, 2253
U.S. Army. Forces in the Pacific, 867, 2707, 4366
U.S. Army. Japan. Headquarters, 1925
U.S. Army. Mediterranean Theater of Operations, 696
U.S. Army. Military Government Detachment F-13, 1269
U.S. Army. Signal Corps. 43d Battalion, 1270
U.S. Army. Signal Corps. 116th Signal Radio Intelligence Company, 1271
U.S. Army. Signal Corps. 439th Battalion, 1272
U.S. Army. Signal Corps. 803d Training Regiment, 1273
U.S. Army. Tank Corps. 81st Battalion, 1274
U.S. Army. Tank Corps. 601st Destroyer Battalion, 1275
U.S. Army. Tank Corps. 628th Destroyer Battalion, 1276
U.S. Army. Tank Corps. 644th Destroyer Battalion, 1277
U.S. Army. Tank Corps. 701st Battalion, 1278
U.S. Army. Tank Corps. 717th Battalion, 1279
U.S. Army. Transportation Corps. 13th Port, 1280
U.S. Army. II Corps, 1301
U.S. Army. 2d Chemical Mortar Battalion, 1281
U.S. Army. 2d Military Government Regiment, 1282
U.S. Army. 2d Mobile Radio Broadcasting Company, 1283
U.S. Army. III Corps, 1302
U.S. Army. 3d Armored Division, 1284
U.S. Army. Third Army, 1285-1287
U.S. Army. 3d Division, 1288
U.S. Army. IV Corps, 1303
U.S. Army. Fifth Army, 1289
U.S. Army. 5th Division, 1290
U.S. Army. Sixth Army, 1291, 1903
U.S. Army. 6th Division, 1292
U.S. Army. Eighth Army, 1293, 2701-2705
U.S. Army. Ninth Army, 1294
U.S. Army. 9th Division, 1295
U.S. Army. 9th Engineer Command, 1296
U.S. Army. 10th Infantry, 1297
U.S. Army. XI Corps, 1304
U.S. Army. 11th Cavalry, 1298
U.S. Army. 11th Field Hospital, 692
U.S. Army. XII Corps, 1305, 1306
U.S. Army. Twelfth Army, 1299
U.S. Army. Fifteenth Army, 1300
U.S. Army. XVI Corps, 1307
U.S. Army. XX Corps, 1308, 1309
U.S. Army. 25th Division, 1310
U.S. Army. 29th Infantry, 1311
U.S. Army. 30th Division, 1312
U.S. Army. 31st Division, 1313
U.S. Army. 33d Division, 1314
U.S. Army. 34th Division, 1315
U.S. Army. 35th Division, 1316
U.S. Army. 40th Division, 1317
U.S. Army. 42d Division, 1318
U.S. Army. 43d Signal Battalion, 1319
U.S. Army. 45th Division, 1320
U.S. Army. 47th Infantry Regiment, 1321
U.S. Army. 56th Antiaircraft Artillery Brigade, 1322
U.S. Army. 65th Armored Field Artillery Battalion, 1323
U.S. Army. 67th Armored Regiment, 1324
U.S. Army. 71st Division, 1325
U.S. Army. 75th Division, 1326
U.S. Army. 76th Division, 1327
U.S. Army. 78th Division, 1328
U.S. Army. 81st Chemical Mortar Battalion, 1329
U.S. Army. 81st Division, 1330
U.S. Army. 81st Tank Battalion, 1331
U.S. Army. 83d Division, 1332
U.S. Army. 85th Division, 1333

U.S. Army. 88th Division, 1334
U.S. Army. 89th Division, 1335
U.S. Army. 90th Division, 1336
U.S. Army. 92d Division, 1337
U.S. Army. 94th Division, 1338
U.S. Army. 95th Armored Field Artillery Battalion, 1339
U.S. Army. 100th Division, 1340
U.S. Army. 101st Cavalry Group, 1341
U.S. Army. 102d Division, 1342
U.S. Army. 106th Cavalry Group, 1343
U.S. Army. 114th Infantry, 1344
U.S. Army. 119th Field Artillery Group, 1345
U.S. Army. 129th Infantry, 1346
U.S. Army. 133d Antiaircraft Artillery Battalion, 1347
U.S. Army. 155th Engineer Combat Battalion, 1348
U.S. Army. 174th Field Artillery Group, 1349
U.S. Army. 184th Antiaircraft Artillery Battalion, 1350
U.S. Army. 187th Engineer Combat Battalion, 1351
U.S. Army. 194th Field Artillery Battalion, 1352
U.S. Army. 195th Antiaircraft Artillery Battalion, 1353
U.S. Army. 271st Infantry, 1354
U.S. Army. 291st Engineer Combat Battalion, 1355
U.S. Army. 305th Field Artillery Battalion, 1356
U.S. Army. 305th Infantry, 1357
U.S. Army. 320th Engineer Battalion, 1358
U.S. Army. 324th Infantry, 1359
U.S. Army. 345th Field Artillery Battalion, 1360
U.S. Army. 350th Infantry, 1361
U.S. Army. 355th Antiaircraft Searchlight Battalion, 1362
U.S. Army. 358th Infantry, 1363
U.S. Army. 375th Field Artillery Battalion, 1364
U.S. Army. 376th Infantry, 1365
U.S. Army. 387th Antiaircraft Artillery Battalion, 1366
U.S. Army. 413th Infantry, 1367
U.S. Army. 457th Antiaircraft Artillery Battalion, 1368
U.S. Army. 506th Infantry, 1369
U.S. Army. 536th Antiaircraft Artillery Battalion, 1370
U.S. Army. 573d Antiaircraft Battalion, 1371
U.S. Army. 611th Ordnance Base Armament Maintenance Battalion, 1372
U.S. Army. 612th Ordnance Base Armament Maintenance Battalion, 1373
U.S. Army. 628th Tank Destroyer Battalion, 1374
U.S. Army. 644th Tank Destroyer Battalion, 1375
U.S. Army. 693d Field Artillery Battalion, 1376
U.S. Army. 701st Tank Battalion, 1377
U.S. Army. 716th Railway Operation Battalion, 1378
U.S. Army. 778th Antiaircraft Artillery Battalion, 1379
U.S. Army. 790th Field Artillery Battalion, 1380
U.S. Army. 834th Engineer Aviation Battalion, 1381
U.S. Army. 863d Antiaircraft Artillery Battalion, 1382
U.S. Army. 951st Field Artillery Battalion, 1383
U.S. Army. 1629th Engineer Construction Battalion, 1384
U.S. Army Air Forces, 3094
U.S. Army Air Forces. Historical Office, 2254
U.S. Army Air Forces. Matériel Command, 3750
U.S. Army Air Forces. Mediterranean Theater of Operations, 2201
U.S. Army Air Forces. Office of Statistical Control, 2072
U.S. Army Air Forces. Personnel Narratives Division, 2073
U.S. Army Air Forces. 8th Photo Squadron, 1385
U.S. Army Air Forces. IX Air Defense Command, 1386
U.S. Army Air Forces. 9th Air Force, 1387-1389
U.S. Army Air Forces. 13th Air Force, 1390
U.S. Army Air Forces. 14th Air Force, 1391
U.S. Army Air Forces. 15th Air Force, 1392
U.S. Army Air Forces. XIX Tactical Air Command, 1393
U.S. Army Air Forces. 34th Bombardment Group, 1394
U.S. Army Air Forces. 42d Bombardment Group, 1395
U.S. Army Air Forces. 44th Bombardment Group, 1396
U.S. Army Air Forces. 61st Service Squadron, 1397
U.S. Army Air Forces. 67th Troop Carrier Squadron, 1398
U.S. Army Air Forces. 79th Fighter Group, 1399
U.S. Army Air Forces. 95th Bombardment Group, 1400
U.S. Army Air Forces. 100th Bombardment Group, 1401
U.S. Army Air Forces. 308th Bombardment Wing Heavy, 1402
U.S. Army Air Forces. 326th Service Group, 1403

U.S. Army Air Forces. 345th Bombardment Group, 1404
U.S. Army Air Forces. 386th Bombardment Group, 1405
U.S. Army Air Forces. 435th Troop Carrier Group, 1406
U.S. Army Air Forces. 440th Troop Carrier Group, 1407
U.S. Army Air Forces. 444th Bombardment Group, 1408
U.S. Army Air Forces. 446th Bombardment Group, 1409
U.S. Army Air Forces. 487th Bombardment Group, 1410
U.S. Army Air Forces. 493d Bombardment Group, 1411
U.S. Army Air Forces. 497th Bombardment Group, 1412
U.S. Army in World War II: The Army Ground Forces, 516, 551
U.S. Army in World War II: The Army Service Forces, 1201
U.S. Army in World War II: China-Burma-India Theater, 461, 1885, 1975
U.S. Army in World War II: The European Theater of Operations, 460, 563, 587, 588, 1709, 1726, 1727, 1756, 1779
U.S. Army in World War II, Medical Department. See U.S. Army Medical Service
U.S. Army in World War II: The Mediterranean Theater of Operations, 1570
U.S. Army in World War II: The Middle East Theater, 1586
U.S. Army in World War II: Pictorial Record, 153, 250, 1768
U.S. Army in World War II: Special Studies, 102, 243, 1249, 1780
U.S. Army in World War II: Technical Services, 484, 485, 488, 497, 515, 575, 580, 583, 597, 605, 681, 1453
U.S. Army in World War II: The War Department, 430, 453, 539, 3695, 3745
U.S. Army in World War II: The War in the Pacific, 458, 1896, 1900, 1902, 2564, 2565, 2644, 2645, 2647, 2685
U.S. Army in World War II: The Western Hemisphere, 240, 3472
U.S. Army Medical Service, 697-709
U.S. Army Medical Service. Medical Department of the U.S. Army in World War II, 655, 698, 702, 704, 705, 706, 708, 709, 720
U.S. Army Medical Service. The Medical Department of the U.S. Army in World War II: Surgery in World War II, 626, 628, 641, 651, 696, 697, 700, 701, 703, 707
U.S. Army Medical Service. Preventive Medicine in World War II, 627
U.S. Army Service Force. Information and Education Division, 589
U.S. Bureau of Aeronautics. Navy Department, 2074
U.S. Bureau of Agricultural Economics, 3751
U.S. Bureau of Community Facilities, 3752
U.S. Bureau of Foreign and Domestic Commerce. Office of Industry and Commerce, 3753
U.S. Bureau of Indian Affairs, 3510
U.S. Bureau of Labor Statistics, 3754, 3755
U.S. Bureau of Labor Statistics Bulletin, 3701, 3754
U.S. Bureau of Medicine and Surgery, 710, 711
U.S. Bureau of Ordnance. Navy Department, 590
U.S. Bureau of Ships, 591
U.S. Bureau of the Budget, 3509
U.S. Bureau of the Budget. Library, 46
U.S. Bureau of Yards and Docks, 592
U.S. Chief of Counsel for the Prosecution of Axis Criminality, 4498
U.S. Civilian Production Administration, 3756
U.S. Coast Guard Reserve, 1413
U.S. Congress. House. Committee on Veterans' Affairs, 1853
U.S. Congress. Joint Committee on the Investigation of the Pearl Harbor Attack, 223
U.S. Congress. Senate. Committee on Foreign Relations, 3511
U.S. Counter Intelligence Corps School, Baltimore, 868
U.S. Department of Agriculture. Agriculture Monograph. See Agriculture Monograph
U.S. Department of Agriculture. Graduate School, 3512
U.S. Department of Agriculture. War Records Monograph, 3714
U.S. Department of Commerce, 3757
U.S. Department of Defense, 464
U.S. Department of State, 3307-3309, 3341, 3513-3515
U.S. Department of State. Foreign Relations of the U.S.: Diplomatic Papers, 3307-3309
U.S. Department of State. Historical Office, 64
U.S. Department of State. Interim Research and Intelligence Service. Research and Analysis Branch, 3603, 3607
U.S. Department of State. Office of Public Affairs. Division of Historical Policy Research, 3310

U.S. Department of State. Publication: European Series, 3341, 3515
U.S. Department of the Army. Office of Military History, 47, 48, 65, 463, 593, 1414, 1854, 1855
U.S. Department of the Army. Pamphlet, 1639, 2847
U.S. Displaced Persons Commission, 4234
U.S. Joint Army-Navy Assessment Committee, 2708
U.S. Library of Congress. European Affairs Division, 49, 50
U.S. Library of Congress. General Reference and Bibliography Division, 51, 52, 53, 54
U.S. Marine Corps, 2255, 2709-2725
U.S. Marine Corps. 9th Regiment, 1415
U.S. Marine Corps Institute, Washington, D.C., 2726
U.S. Military Academy, West Point. Department of Military Art and Engineering, 275, 276, 277, 1506, 1608, 1685, 1856-1858
U.S. National Archives, 66, 67, 68, 69, 70, 71, 72, 73, 74, 75, 76, 77, 78, 79, 80, 81
U.S. National Archives. Inventories of World War II Records, 69
U.S. National Archives. Preliminary Inventories, 71, 72, 73, 74, 75, 76, 77, 78, 79, 80, 81
U.S. National Archives. Reference Information Papers, 70
U.S. National Historical Publications Commission, 55
U.S. National Security Resources Board, 82
U.S. Naval Air Station, Lakehurst, N. J., 2075
U.S. Naval Air Transport Service, 594
U.S. Naval History Division, 100
U.S. Naval Special Hospital, Yosemite National Park, California, 712
U.S. Navy, 2727, 2728
U.S. Navy. Air Group 86, 1416
U.S. Navy. Construction Battalion Detachment No. 1050, 1450
U.S. Navy. Construction Battalion Maintenance Unit 635, 1449
U.S. Navy. Escort Carrier Force, 2729
U.S. Navy. Fleet Hospital No. 108, 713
U.S. Navy. Pacific Fleet and Pacific Ocean Areas, 2730
U.S. Navy. 4th Construction Battalion, 1417
U.S. Navy. 6th Construction Battalion, 1418
U.S. Navy. 7th Amphibious Force, 1419
U.S. Navy. 8th Construction Battalion, 1420
U.S. Navy. 18th Construction Battalion, 1421
U.S. Navy. 21st Construction Battalion, 1422
U.S. Navy. 24th Construction Battalion, 1423
U.S. Navy. 25th Construction Battalion, 1424
U.S. Navy. 30th Construction Battalion. Special, 1425
U.S. Navy. 34th Construction Battalion. Special, 1426
U.S. Navy. 42d Construction Battalion, 1427
U.S. Navy. 43d Construction Battalion, 1428
U.S. Navy. 50th Construction Battalion, 1429
U.S. Navy. 55th Construction Battalion, 1430
U.S. Navy. 57th Construction Battalion, 1431
U.S. Navy. 58th Construction Battalion, 1432
U.S. Navy. 62d Construction Battalion, 1433
U.S. Navy. 82d Construction Battalion, 1434
U.S. Navy. 85th Construction Battalion, 1435
U.S. Navy. 90th Construction Battalion, 1436
U.S. Navy. 91st Construction Battalion, 1437
U.S. Navy. 94th Construction Battalion, 1438
U.S. Navy. 96th Construction Battalion, 1439
U.S. Navy. 102d Construction Battalion, 1440
U.S. Navy. 105th Construction Battalion, 1441
U.S. Navy. 107th Construction Battalion, 1442
U.S. Navy. 116th Construction Battalion, 1443
U.S. Navy. 121st Construction Battalion, 1444
U.S. Navy. 130th Construction Battalion, 1445
U.S. Navy. 135th Construction Battalion, 1446
U.S. Navy. 136th Construction Battalion, 1447
U.S. Navy. 143d Construction Battalion, 1448
U.S. Office of Air Force History, 2076, 2077
U.S. Office of Community War Services, 3516
U.S. Office of Contract Settlement, 3758
U.S. Office of Defense Transportation, 595
U.S. Office of Education, 4440
U.S. Office of Foreign Agricultural Relations, 3759
U.S. Office of Inter-American Affairs, 3517
U.S. Office of Naval History, 101
U.S. Office of Naval Intelligence, 2731
U.S. Office of Naval Operations. Naval History Division, 2077, 2256, 2377
U.S. Office of Scientific Research and Development. Science in World War II. See Science in World War II
U.S. Office of Strategic Services. Research and Analysis Branch, 3280
U.S. Office of Temporary Controls, 3760
U.S. Office of War Information, 1859
U.S. Provost Marshal General's School, Camp Gordon, Georgia, 4235
U.S. Quartermaster Corps, 597
U.S. Quartermaster School, Fort Lee, Virginia, 598
U.S. Strategic Bombing Survey, 83, 84
U.S. War Department. General Staff, 172, 599, 600, 1609, 1860-1864, 1983, 2732, 2733
U.S. War Department. General Staff. Military Intelligence Division, 140, 601
U.S. War Manpower Commission, 3761
U.S. War Production Board, 56, 3560
U.S. War Relocation Authority, 4191-4193
U.S. 62d Quartermaster Base Depot, 1451

VA Medical Monograph, 658, 718, 3772
Vaculik, Serge, 422
Vagin, P. I., 3820
Vaidya, Suresh, 3438, 3991
Valinger, Leon de, 3524
Vallance, Ute, 3059
Valtin, Jan (pseud.). See Krebs, Richard J. H.
Vance, Robert T., 1116
Van der Post, Laurens, 4170
Van Dusen, Henry P., 4367
Van Paassen, Pierre, 3165
Vanport City, Oregon. Schools, 4236
Van Sinderen, Adrian, 141
Vansittart, Robert G., 4368
Van Woerdan, Peter, 2771
Varney, Joyce J., 3396
Vatican. Biblioteca Vaticana, 4441
Vaughan, Elizabeth H., 4171
Vaughan-Thomas, L. J. Wynford, 1866
Veale, Frederick J. P., 3842
Verney, Gerald L., 1057, 1058
Verney, John, 391
Verni, Vicente, 142
Vian, Sir Philip, 2378
Victoria, Australia. Forests Commission, 3670
Vietor, John Adolf, 4020
Vigneras, Marcel, 602
Villari, Luigi, 1867
Vincent, Adrian, 3992
Viorst, Milton, 3292
Virski, Fred, 1686
Volckmann, Russell W., 2891
Vomécourt, Philippe de, 2793
Von Roeder, George, 1452
Voss, Vivian, 910
Voznesenskii, Nikolai A., 3674
Vrba, Rudolf, 3993
Vulliez, Albert, 2538

Waage, Johan, 1507
Wade, Harry F., 3439
Wadge, D. Collett, 603
Wagner, Wolfgang, 3317, 3320
Wainwright, Jonathan M., 332
Wake, Sir Hereward, 1059
Waldheim-Emmerick, Ragnhild Schurer von, 2794
Waldron, Thomas J., 248
Waldron, Thomas J., 2379
Walker, Alden D., Major, 1252
Walker, Allan S., 714-717
Walker, Arthur E., 718
Walker, David E., 870
Walker, Edward R., 3671
Walker, K. A., 1610
Walker, Reginald F., 4369

Walker, Roy, 3175
Wallace, Brenton G., 1868
Wallace, Graham, 2202
Wallace, Robert N. A., 4370
Wallace, Walter, 4172
Waller, George M., 224
Walt, Harry P. van, 3166
Waltcher, Gladys, 9
Walter, Gérard, 3204
Walters, Anne M., 2795
Walton, Francis, 3762
Walton, Frank L., 3763
Wandrey, Ralph H., 2257
Wandycz, Piotr S., 2933
Wanless, Alexander, 3397
Wanstall, Ken, 4393
War Crimes Trials Series, 4467, 4469, 4471, 4474, 4501, 4508, 4509
Warbey, William, 3176
Warburg, James P., 604
Ward, Edward, 3994
Ward, Irene, 1060
Ward, Robert S., 3281
Wardlaw, Ada, 4355
Wardlow, Chester, 605, 1453
Waren, Helen, 3843
Warfield, Gaither, 3145
Warfield, Hania, 3145
Warhaftig, Zorach, 4237
Warlimont, Walter, 3060
Warmbrunn, Werner, 3167
Warmington, Eric H., 4442
Warner, Harold P., 279
War-Peace Pamphlets, 3770, 3771
Warrack, Graeme, 4081
Warren, Charles E. T., 2380, 2539, 2540
Warren, John C., 2203, 2204
Warren, Shields, 666
Washington (Battleship), 2734
Wasp (aircraft carrier, 2d of the name), 2735, 2736
Waters, John C. A., 2078
Waters, Sydney D., 2381, 2382
Watkins, J. Harold, 1061
Watson, Mark S., 465
Watsonian Club, Edinburgh, 4443
Watson-Watt, Sir Robert A., 606, 607
Watt, Sholto, 2205
Watters, Mary, 3561
Watts, Franklin, 3293
Watts, John C., 719
Watts, Stephen, 3398
Wavell, Archibald P., 392
Wdowinski, David, 3844
Weaver, William G., 608
Webb, Anthony M., 4501
Webber, A. J., 1788
Weber, Wayne M., 3399
Webster, Sir Charles K., 2206
Wechsberg, Joseph, 3110
Wedemeyer, Albert C., 333
Weedon, Martin, 4173
Weeks, Sir Ronald M., 609
Weinberg, Gerhard L., 85, 2934
Weinstock, Eugene, 4021
Weir, Sir Cecil McA., 3672
Weiss, Reska, 3995
Weissberg, Alex, 3788
Weizäcker, Ernst H., 2984
Welch, Robert H. W., 334
Welker, Robert H., 335
Welles, Sumner, 3294
Wells, Leon W., 3845
Wemyss, David E. G., 2541
Wendel, Else, 3061
Wentzel, Fritz, 4082
Werner, Morris R., 2790
Werstein, Irving, 1870, 1871, 2737-2740

Wertenbaker, Green P., 2258
Werth, Alexander, 1687, 3462
West, Adam, 393
West, Charles O., 1357
West, Rebecca, 3119, 4499
Westover, J. G., 1788
Westphal, Siegfried, 280
Wettern, Desmond, 4174
Wettlin, Margaret, 3463
Wetzel, Friedrich, 2821
Weygand, Maxime, 394, 395
Weyher, Kurt, 2542
Whayne, Tom F., 720
Wheatley, Dennis, 466
Wheatley, Ronald, 167
Wheeler, Charles M., 1633
Wheeler, Keith, 721, 2741
Wheeler, Richard, 2742
Wheeler, William R., 3562
Wheeler-Bennett, Sir John W., 210, 3063
Whimpey, Albert, 75
Whipple, Chandler, 2743
Whitcomb, Edgar D., 4175
Whitcombe, Fred, 167
White, Dorothy S., 3295
White, John B., 871
White, Nathan W., 1454
White, Oliver G. W., 1062
White, Osmar E. D., 2744
White, Theodore H., 325
White, Walter F., 1872
White, William L., 3464
Whitecross, Roy H., 4176
Whitehall, Walter M., 366
Whitehouse, Arthur G. J., 2079, 2383, 2384
Whiting, George F., 4177
Whitley, Joe, 2227
Whitnell, Lewis, 2207
Whitney, Cornelius V., 336
Whitney, Courtney, 337, 4510
Whitney, Hans, 4178
Whitty, H. Ramsden, 1063
Wicklow, W.C.J.P.J.P.H., 396
Widdington, Richard, 4421
Wieck, Fred, 1683
Wieneke, James, 911
Wiener Library, 57, 58, 143, 3589
Wiener Library, London. Catalogue Series, 57
Wiesel, Eliezer, 3846
Wighton, Charles, 872, 873, 3847
Wigmans, Johan H., 3996
Wigmore, Lionel, 281
Wilber, Edwin L., 2080
Wilcox, Francis O., 3518
Wilcox, W. A., 1984
Wilcox, Walter W., 3764
Wiley, Bill I., 516, 551
Wilkinson, Burke, 2385
William and Mary College, Williamsburg, Virginia. Hampton Reads-Peninsula War Studies Committee, 3563
Williams, Annabelle R., 4304
Williams, Eric E., 4083-4085
Williams, Francis, 2985
Williams, Jack J., 1455
Williams, Mary H., 102
Williamson, Catherine E., 3400
Williamson, Hugh A. F., 1064
Willis, Anthony A., 1065
Willison, Arthur C., 1611
Willoughby, Charles A., 2745
Willoughby, Malcolm F., 3564
Wilmot, Chester, 144
Wilson, Earl B., 3765
Wilson, Earl J., 2746
Wilson, Henry M. Wilson, baron, 397
Wilson, Hugh R., 2986

INDEX

AUTHORS AND MAJOR SERIES

Abbott, Delmas W., 1430
Abbott, Harry P., 1106
Abend, Hallett E., 3323
Aberdeen. City Council. 3343
Abshagen, Karl H., 400
Adamic, Louis, 2935
Adams, Leonard P., 3675
Adamson, Hans C., 1481, 2626, 2628, 2629
Adamson, Iain, 1876
Addis, C. T.
Adler, Marta, 3781
Agar-Hamilton, John A. I., 1540, 1541, 1602
Agrafiotis, Cris J., 1616
Agriculture monograph, 3704, 3735, 3742
Ahluwalia, Gian C., 3402
Ahnfeldt, Arnold L., 706
Ahrenfeldt, Robert H., 611
Aikawa, Taksaki, 3078
Air Force and Space Digest, 1986
Aitken, Edward F., 877
Albemarle County Historical Society. War History Committee, 3520
Alcorn, Robert H., 724
Aldouby, Zwy, 3827
Aldridge, Joanna M., 2932
Alessandro, Guilietta d', 3064
Alethea (pseud.), 3256
Alexander, Charles W., 4460
Alexander, Harold R. L. G., 338
Alexander, Michael, 3967
Alexander, Peter, 878
Alfieri, Dino, 2989
Allan, James, 3853
Allan, Sherman, 557
Allbury, Alfred G., 4086
Allchin, Frank, 879
Allen, Ethan P., 3676, 3677
Allen, George E., 3466
Allen, Gwenfread E., 3521
Allen, Hugh, 3678
Allen, Maury, 4146
Allen, Max S., 695
Allen, Robert S., 1108
Allen, Ted, 612
Allen, William E. D., 1634
Allied Commission, 4239
Allied Forces, 1690, 1926, 4375
Allied Forces. Mediterranean Theatre, 1691, 1692
Allied Forces. Southeast Asia Command, 1927
Allied Forces. Southeast Asia Command. Women's Auxiliary Service (Burma), 1928
Allied Forces. Southwest Pacific Area, 2877
Allied Forces. Supreme Headquarters, 284, 1693, 4397
Allied Forces. Supreme Headquarters. Air Defense Division, 2996
Allied Forces. Supreme Headquarters. Mission to Norway, 1694
Allied Forces. Supreme Headquarters. Psychological Warfare Division, 468
Allied Forces. 15th Army Group, 1109
Allied Forces. 21st Army Group, 469, 3782
Allied Forces. 21st Army Group. Medical Services, 613
Allison, Errol S., 339
Allward, Maurice F., 2198
Almond, Gabriel A., 2799
Alsop, Stewart J. O., 725
Altieri, James, 1110

Ambrière, Francis, 3854, 3855
American Academy of Political and Social Science, Philadelphia, 3149, 4240
American Book Center for War Devastated Libraries, 4411
American Council of Voluntary Agencies for Foreign Service. Survey Committee on Displaced Persons, 4194
American Forces in Action, 1609, 1854, 1855, 1864, 1983, 2732
American Historical Association. Committee for the Study of War Documents, 59
American Jewish Conference, 3783
American University, Washington, D.C. Special Warfare Research Division, 2822
Amery, Julian, 2761
Amory, Robert, 1111
Amoury, Daisy, 4307
Amrine, Michael, 470
Anders, Leslie, 1929
Anders, Wladyslaw, 1462, 1635
Andersen, Hartvig, 726
Anderson, Margaret K., 3679
Anderson, Oscar E., 524
Anderson, Robert C. B., 923
Anderson, Trazzvant W., 1112
Anderson, Verily (Bruce), 3344
Anderson, William, 2082
Andreas-Friedrich, Ruth, 2800
Andrieu d'Albas, Emmanuel M.A., 2547
Angell, Joseph W., 2071
Angier, John C., 1695
Anscomb, Charles, 2389
Ansel, Walter, 423
Anshen, Melvin, 3731
Anson, Thomas V., 614
Appel, John W., 618
Appleman, John A., 4454
Appleman, Roy E., 2548
Arbib, Robert S., 3345
Arbing, Børge W., 1636
Archard, Theresa, 615
Arendt, Hannah, 4512
Argent, Jack N. L., 880
Arkwright, Albert S. B., 4024
Armed Forces Chemical Association, 471
Armenian General Benevolent Union of America, 3467
Armstrong, Anne, 3324
Armstrong, Anthony (pseud.). See Willis, Anthony A.
Armstrong, Colin N., 3856
Armstrong, Hamilton F., 3205
Armstrong, John A., 2841, 2842
Armstrong, Warren (pseud.). See Bennett, William E.
Army Air Forces Aid Society, 1113
Army Times, 1114
Arndt, Karl, 4461
Arne, Sigrid, 3325
Arnold, Elliott, 2226
Arnold, Henry H., 451, 1987
Arnold, Ralph C. M., 424
Arnold, Richard, 727
Arnothy, Christine, 3095
Aron, Robert, 1696, 3177
Arrington, Grady P., 285
Arrol, Anthony M. (pseud.). See Pont-Alain, C. M.
Arthos, John, 1333
Ash, Bernard, 1482, 2549

Ashburner, D., 1469
Ashton, Dean H., 3522
Ashworth, William, 3619
Aslanis, Anastasios, 3857
Associated Press, 103
Association of Jewish Refugees in Great Britain, 4195
Astier De La Vigerie, Emmanuel D', 728
Aston, Walter H., 4025
Astrup, Helen, 2851, 2852
Attiwill, Kenneth, 1904, 4087
Attlee, Clement R., 2936
Atwell, Lester, 1697
Auerbach, Frank L., 4196
Augé, J. N., 226
Augspurger, Owen B., 1115
Auphan, G.A.J. Paul, 2272
Aurén, Sven A.G., 1698
Aurthur, Robert A., 1116
Austin, Alexander B., 1699
Australia. Army. 2/13th Infantry Battalion, 881
Australia. Royal Australian Air Force, 1988, 2083
Australia in the War of 1939-1945. Series 1 (Army), 281, 1578, 1626, 2569, 2634
Australia in the War of 1939-1945. Series 2 (Navy), 2588
Australia in the War of 1939-1945. Series 3 (Air), 2010, 2144, 2240
Australia in the War of 1939-1945. Series 4 (Civil), 3418, 3627, 3656
Australia in the War of 1939-1945. Series 5 (Medical), 714-717
Australian War Memorial, 227, 228
Ausubel, Nathan, 3293
Automobile Manufacturers Association, 3680
Aviation History Unit, 1989
Aye, Lillian, 4241
Aylin, Robert N., 2273

Babcock, Myles S., 2550
Babington-Smith, Constance, 729
Baclagon, Uldarico S., 1894
Badoglio, Pietro, 3065
Baer, Alfred E., 1117
Baggaley, James, 1930
Bagnall, Stephen, 1700
Bahnemann, Gunther, 401
Bailey, Charles W., 535
Bailey, James, 2084
Bailey, James R. A., 2212
Baillie-Grohman, H. T., 1624
Baker, Benjamin, 3620
Baker, Blanche E., 4242
Baker, E. R., 586
Baker, Edgar C. R., 1900, 2085
Baker, Gilbert, 3250
Baker, Gladys L., 3751
Baker, John V. T., 3621
Baker, Peter, 730, 1701
Baker, Richard B., 1702
Baker, Botts, Andrews and Walne, Houston, Texas, 3681
Baldwin, Hanson W., 2893
Balison, Howard J., 2274
Ball, Adrian, 198
Ball, Edmund F., 1703
Ball, Lamar Q., 3527
Ballantine, Duncan S., 472
Ballantine, W. M., 3346
Ballou, Robert O., 4419
Bamm, Peter (pseud.). See Emmrich, Kurt
Band, Claire, 1877
Band, William, 1877
Bank, Bertram, 4088
Bankson, Budd, 4378
Bannister, Sybil, 2997
Bar-Adon, Dorothy R., 3784
Baratinsky, Viacheslav, 4197
Barber, Donald H., 1542
Barclay, Cyril N., 425, 924-929, 1543
Barclays Bank (Dominion, Colonial and Overseas), 3622
Baring, Norah, 4243

Barkas, Geoffrey, 473
Barker, A. J., 1931
Barker, Frank R. P., 930
Barker, John S., 1118
Barker, Ralph, 2086-2089
Barlow, Randle, 4026
Barnard, Jack, 1932
Barnes, Gladeon M., 474
Barnett, Correlli D., 1544, 1545
Barnett House, Oxford, 4244
Barnhart, Edward N., 4
Barns-Graham, John W., 2551
Barrett, Neil H., 1933
Bartimeus (pseud.). See Ritchie, Lewis A. da Costa
Bartlett, Dorothy A., 616
Bartlett, N., 159
Bartley, Whitman S., 2718
Bartz, Karl, 731, 2090
Bassett, George, 3096
Bates, F. E., 99
Bates, Joan, 2275
Bates, Leonard, 2275
Bates, P. W., 475
Battaglia, Roberto, 2828
Baudouin, Paul, 2937
Bauer, Josef M., 4027
Baumbach, Werner, 2091
Baurdzhan, Momysh-Uly, 1638
Bawden, William T., 4412
Bayles, William D., 2801
Bayliss, W. C., 906
Bazna, Elyesa, 732
Beach, Edward L., 2552
Beal, Edwin, 9
Beamish, John, 1934
Beard, Charles A., 180
Beardwell, M. F., 4245
Beaton, Cecil W. H., 2938, 2939
Beattie, Edward W., 3858
Beck, Henry C., 1109
Beck, Levitt C., 2092
Becker, George H., 3312
Becker, Hans (pseud.), 3859
Beddie, James S., 2900
Beddington, William R., 931
Beebe, Gilbert W., 617, 618
Beecher, Henry K., 619
Beecher, John, 2390
Befeler, Murray, 154
Begin, Menahem, 3860
Behan, John M., 476
Behrens, Catherine B. A., 2277
Beidler, Francis, 4430
Beith, John H., 229, 3623, 4198
Bekker, Cajus D. (pseud.). See Berenbrok, Hans D.
Belfield, Eversley M. G., 1704, 1743, 2174
Belgion, Montgomery, 4462, 4463
Bell, Archibald C., 932
Bell, Frank F., 1120
Bell, George K. A., 4308
Bell, H. E., 4386
Bell, Leslie, 733, 4090
Bell, Richard, 2940
Bell, Robert, 3624
Bellamy, Francis R., 3682
Belleau Wood (Aircraft Carrier), 2553
Bellegarde, Carlo de, 4028
Bellett, Aubrey C., 882
Bellini delle Stelle, Pier L., 1705
Belot, Raymond de, 2391
Benda, Harry J., 3251, 3252
Benedek, Therese, 620
Beneš, Eduard, 2941
Bengtson, John R., 3111
Benham, Hervey, 3366
Ben Line Steamers, Ltd., 2278

U.S. Department of State. Publication: European Series, 3341, 3515
U.S. Department of the Army. Office of Military History, 47, 48, 65, 463, 593, 1414, 1854, 1855
U.S. Department of the Army. Pamphlet, 1639, 2847
U.S. Displaced Persons Commission, 4234
U.S. Joint Army-Navy Assessment Committee, 2708
U.S. Library of Congress. European Affairs Division, 49, 50
U.S. Library of Congress. General Reference and Bibliography Division, 51, 52, 53, 54
U.S. Marine Corps, 2255, 2709-2725
U.S. Marine Corps. 9th Regiment, 1415
U.S. Marine Corps Institute, Washington, D.C., 2726
U.S. Military Academy, West Point. Department of Military Art and Engineering, 275, 276, 277, 1506, 1608, 1685, 1856-1858
U.S. National Archives, 66, 67, 68, 69, 70, 71, 72, 73, 74, 75, 76, 77, 78, 79, 80, 81
U.S. National Archives. Inventories of World War II Records, 69
U.S. National Archives. Preliminary Inventories, 71, 72, 73, 74, 75, 76, 77, 78, 79, 80, 81
U.S. National Archives. Reference Information Papers, 70
U.S. National Historical Publications Commission, 55
U.S. National Security Resources Board, 82
U.S. Naval Air Station, Lakehurst, N.J., 2075
U.S. Naval Air Transport Service, 594
U.S. Naval History Division, 100
U.S. Naval Special Hospital, Yosemite National Park, California, 712
U.S. Navy, 2727, 2728
U.S. Navy. Air Group 86, 1416
U.S. Navy. Construction Battalion Detachment No. 1050, 1450
U.S. Navy. Construction Battalion Maintenance Unit 635, 1449
U.S. Navy. Escort Carrier Force, 2729
U.S. Navy. Fleet Hospital No. 108, 713
U.S. Navy. Pacific Fleet and Pacific Ocean Areas, 2730
U.S. Navy. 4th Construction Battalion, 1417
U.S. Navy. 6th Construction Battalion, 1418
U.S. Navy. 7th Amphibious Force, 1419
U.S. Navy. 8th Construction Battalion, 1420
U.S. Navy. 18th Construction Battalion, 1421
U.S. Navy. 21st Construction Battalion, 1422
U.S. Navy. 24th Construction Battalion, 1423
U.S. Navy. 25th Construction Battalion, 1424
U.S. Navy. 30th Construction Battalion. Special, 1425
U.S. Navy. 34th Construction Battalion. Special, 1426
U.S. Navy. 42d Construction Battalion, 1427
U.S. Navy. 43d Construction Battalion, 1428
U.S. Navy. 50th Construction Battalion, 1429
U.S. Navy. 55th Construction Battalion, 1430
U.S. Navy. 57th Construction Battalion, 1431
U.S. Navy. 58th Construction Battalion, 1432
U.S. Navy. 62d Construction Battalion, 1433
U.S. Navy. 82d Construction Battalion, 1434
U.S. Navy. 85th Construction Battalion, 1435
U.S. Navy. 90th Construction Battalion, 1436
U.S. Navy. 91st Construction Battalion, 1437
U.S. Navy. 94th Construction Battalion, 1438
U.S. Navy. 96th Construction Battalion, 1439
U.S. Navy. 102d Construction Battalion, 1440
U.S. Navy. 105th Construction Battalion, 1441
U.S. Navy. 107th Construction Battalion, 1442
U.S. Navy. 116th Construction Battalion, 1443
U.S. Navy. 121st Construction Battalion, 1444
U.S. Navy. 130th Construction Battalion, 1445
U.S. Navy. 135th Construction Battalion, 1446
U.S. Navy. 136th Construction Battalion, 1447
U.S. Navy. 143d Construction Battalion, 1448
U.S. Office of Air Force History, 2076, 2077
U.S. Office of Community War Services, 3516
U.S. Office of Contract Settlement, 3758
U.S. Office of Defense Transportation, 595
U.S. Office of Education, 4440
U.S. Office of Foreign Agricultural Relations, 3759
U.S. Office of Inter-American Affairs, 3517
U.S. Office of Naval History, 101
U.S. Office of Naval Intelligence, 2731
U.S. Office of Naval Operations. Naval History Division, 2077, 2256, 2377
U.S. Office of Scientific Research and Development. Science in World War II. See Science in World War II
U.S. Office of Strategic Services. Research and Analysis Branch, 3280
U.S. Office of Temporary Controls, 3760
U.S. Office of War Information, 1859
U.S. Provost Marshal General's School, Camp Gordon, Georgia, 4235
U.S. Quartermaster Corps, 597
U.S. Quartermaster School, Fort Lee, Virginia, 598
U.S. Strategic Bombing Survey, 83, 84
U.S. War Department. General Staff, 172, 599, 600, 1609, 1860-1864, 1983, 2732, 2733
U.S. War Department. General Staff. Military Intelligence Division, 140, 601
U.S. War Manpower Commission, 3761
U.S. War Production Board, 56, 3560
U.S. War Relocation Authority, 4191-4193
U.S. 62d Quartermaster Base Depot, 1451

VA Medical Monograph, 658, 718, 3772
Vaculik, Serge, 422
Vagin, P. I., 3820
Vaidya, Suresh, 3438, 3991
Valinger, Leon de, 3524
Vallance, Ute, 3059
Valtin, Jan (pseud.). See Krebs, Richard J. H.
Vance, Robert T., 1116
Van der Post, Laurens, 4170
Van Dusen, Henry P., 4367
Van Paassen, Pierre, 3165
Vanport City, Oregon. Schools, 4236
Van Sinderen, Adrian, 141
Vansittart, Robert G., 4368
Van Woerdan, Peter, 2771
Varney, Joyce J., 3396
Vatican. Biblioteca Vaticana, 4441
Vaughan, Elizabeth H., 4171
Vaughan-Thomas, L. J. Wynford, 1866
Veale, Frederick J. P., 3842
Verney, Gerald L., 1057, 1058
Verney, John, 391
Verni, Vicente, 142
Vian, Sir Philip, 2378
Victoria, Australia. Forests Commission, 3670
Vietor, John Adolf, 4020
Vigneras, Marcel, 602
Villari, Luigi, 1867
Vincent, Adrian, 3992
Viorst, Milton, 3292
Virski, Fred, 1686
Volckmann, Russell W., 2891
Vomécourt, Philippe de, 2793
Von Roeder, George, 1452
Voss, Vivian, 910
Voznesenskii, Nikolai A., 3674
Vrba, Rudolf, 3993
Vulliez, Albert, 2538

Waage, Johan, 1507
Wade, Harry F., 3439
Wadge, D. Collett, 603
Wagner, Wolfgang, 3317, 3320
Wainwright, Jonathan M., 332
Wake, Sir Hereward, 1059
Waldheim-Emmerick, Ragnhild Schurer von, 2794
Waldron, Thomas J., 248
Waldron, Thomas J., 2379
Walker, Alden D., Major, 1252
Walker, Allan S., 714-717
Walker, Arthur E., 718
Walker, David E., 870
Walker, Edward R., 3671
Walker, K. A., 1610
Walker, Reginald F., 4369

Walker, Roy, 3175
Wallace, Brenton G., 1868
Wallace, Graham, 2202
Wallace, Robert N. A., 4370
Wallace, Walter, 4172
Waller, George M., 224
Walt, Harry P. van, 3166
Waltcher, Gladys, 9
Walter, Gérard, 3204
Walters, Anne M., 2795
Walton, Francis, 3762
Walton, Frank L., 3763
Wandrey, Ralph H., 2257
Wandycz, Piotr S., 2933
Wanless, Alexander, 3397
Wanstall, Ken, 4393
War Crimes Trials Series, 4467, 4469, 4471, 4474, 4501, 4508, 4509
Warbey, William, 3176
Warburg, James P., 604
Ward, Edward, 3994
Ward, Irene, 1060
Ward, Robert S., 3281
Wardlaw, Ada, 4355
Wardlow, Chester, 605, 1453
Waren, Helen, 3843
Warfield, Gaither, 3145
Warfield, Hania, 3145
Warhaftig, Zorach, 4237
Warlimont, Walter, 3060
Warmbrunn, Werner, 3167
Warmington, Eric H., 4442
Warner, Harold P., 279
War-Peace Pamphlets, 3770, 3771
Warrack, Graeme, 4081
Warren, Charles E. T., 2380, 2539, 2540
Warren, John C., 2203, 2204
Warren, Shields, 666
Washington (Battleship), 2734
Wasp (aircraft carrier, 2d of the name), 2735, 2736
Waters, John C. A., 2078
Waters, Sydney D., 2381, 2382
Watkins, J. Harold, 1061
Watson, Mark S., 465
Watsonian Club, Edinburgh, 4443
Watson-Watt, Sir Robert A., 606, 607
Watt, Sholto, 2205
Watters, Mary, 3561
Watts, Franklin, 3293
Watts, John C., 719
Watts, Stephen, 3398
Wavell, Archibald P., 392
Wdowinski, David, 3844
Weaver, William G., 608
Webb, Anthony M., 4501
Webber, A. J., 1788
Weber, Wayne M., 3399
Webster, Sir Charles K., 2206
Wechsberg, Joseph, 3110
Wedemeyer, Albert C., 333
Weedon, Martin, 4173
Weeks, Sir Ronald M., 609
Weinberg, Gerhard L., 85, 2934
Weinstock, Eugene, 4021
Weir, Sir Cecil McA., 3672
Weiss, Reska, 3995
Weissberg, Alex, 3788
Weizäcker, Ernst H., 2984
Welch, Robert H. W., 334
Welker, Robert H., 335
Welles, Sumner, 3294
Wells, Leon W., 3845
Wemyss, David E. G., 2541
Wendel, Else, 3061
Wentzel, Fritz, 4082
Werner, Morris R., 2790
Werstein, Irving, 1870, 1871, 2737-2740

Wertenbaker, Green P., 2258
Werth, Alexander, 1687, 3462
West, Adam, 393
West, Charles O., 1357
West, Rebecca, 3119, 4499
Westover, J. G., 1788
Westphal, Siegfried, 280
Wettern, Desmond, 4174
Wettlin, Margaret, 3463
Wetzel, Friedrich, 2821
Weygand, Maxime, 394, 395
Weyher, Kurt, 2542
Whayne, Tom F., 720
Wheatley, Dennis, 466
Wheatley, Ronald, 167
Wheeler, Charles M., 1633
Wheeler, Keith, 721, 2741
Wheeler, Richard, 2742
Wheeler, William R., 3562
Wheeler-Bennett, Sir John W., 210, 3063
Whimpey, Albert, 75
Whipple, Chandler, 2743
Whitcomb, Edgar D., 4175
Whitcombe, Fred, 167
White, Dorothy S., 3295
White, John B., 871
White, Nathan W., 1454
White, Oliver G. W., 1062
White, Osmar E. D., 2744
White, Theodore H., 325
White, Walter F., 1872
White, William L., 3464
Whitecross, Roy H., 4176
Whitehall, Walter M., 366
Whitehouse, Arthur G. J., 2079, 2383, 2384
Whiting, George F., 4177
Whitley, Joe, 2227
Whitnell, Lewis, 2207
Whitney, Cornelius V., 336
Whitney, Courtney, 337, 4510
Whitney, Hans, 4178
Whitty, H. Ramsden, 1063
Wicklow, W.C.J.P.J.P.H., 396
Widdington, Richard, 4421
Wieck, Fred, 1683
Wieneke, James, 911
Wiener Library, 57, 58, 143, 3589
Wiener Library, London. Catalogue Series, 57
Wiesel, Eliezer, 3846
Wighton, Charles, 872, 873, 3847
Wigmans, Johan H., 3996
Wigmore, Lionel, 281
Wilber, Edwin L., 2080
Wilcox, Francis O., 3518
Wilcox, W. A., 1984
Wilcox, Walter W., 3764
Wiley, Bill I., 516, 551
Wilkinson, Burke, 2385
William and Mary College, Williamsburg, Virginia. Hampton Reads-Peninsula War Studies Committee, 3563
Williams, Annabelle R., 4304
Williams, Eric E., 4083-4085
Williams, Francis, 2985
Williams, Jack J., 1455
Williams, Mary H., 102
Williamson, Catherine E., 3400
Williamson, Hugh A. F., 1064
Willis, Anthony A., 1065
Willison, Arthur C., 1611
Willoughby, Charles A., 2745
Willoughby, Malcolm F., 3564
Wilmot, Chester, 144
Wilson, Earl B., 3765
Wilson, Earl J., 2746
Wilson, Henry M. Wilson, baron, 397
Wilson, Hugh R., 2986

Wilson, Michael C. D., 1874
Wilson, R. D., 1066
Wilson, Richard C., 1985
Wilson, Robert E., 1456
Wilson, Roger C., 4305
Wilton, Eric, 1067
Wiltse, Charles M., 702, 3766
Winant, John G., 398, 2987
Wingerfield, Rex M., 1875
Winncroft, Eileen, 3061
Winston, Robert A., 2259
Winterton, Paul, 3465
Wiskemann, Elizabeth, 2995, 3321
Wistrand, R. B., 2260
Wittlin, Tadeusz, 3848, 3997
Wittmer, Felix, 3311
Woetzel, Robert K., 4500
Wohlstetter, Roberta, 225
Wojcik, Andrzej J., 3322
Wolf, Abraham, 4444
Wolfe, Don M., 722
Wolfert, Ira, 2892
Wolff, Leon, 2208
Wolff, Perry S., 1457
Wood, A. Mervyn, 1473
Wood, Alan, 3248
Wood, Derek, 2209
Wood, Frederick L. W. 3440
Wood, Jerry E. R., 4022
Wood, Mary, 3248
Wood, Sterling A., 1458
Wood, Winifred, 2081
Woodbury, David O., 610, 3767
Woodhall, Barnes, 700
Woodhouse, Christopher M., 3230
Woodress, James, 3497
Woodrooffe, Thomas, 2543, 2544
Woodruff, Michael F. A., 682
Woodward, Comer Vann, 2747
Woodward, David, 399, 2545, 2546
Woodward, Sir Ernest L., 3401
Woodward, Paul B., 3568
Wooldridge, John de L., 2210
Woollcombe, Robert, 1068, 1612
Woolley, Sir Charles L., 4396
Woolton, Frederick J. Marquis, 1st earl of, 3673
Woozley, A. D., 1010
World Peace Foundation, Boston, 3342
World University Service, 4445
Worsley, Thomas B., 3768
Wrench, Sir Evelyn, 2988
Wright, Bertram C., 1459
Wright, Lawton, 3748
Wright, Robert, 2180
Wright, Robert J., 4179
Wrigley, C. C., 3612
Wuest, Karl A., 4371
Wuorinen, John H., 3101
Wyatt, Horace M., 3249
Wykeham, Peter, 2211
Wyndham, Hon. Humphrey, 1069
Wynne, Barry, 2796, 2797
Wyss, M. de, 3077

Xydis, Stephen G., 3231

Yad Washem Martyrs' and Heroes' Memorial Authority, Jerusalem.
  Yivo Instituto for Jewish Research, New York. Joint documentary
  projects. Bibliographical series, 5, 30
Yamada, Otozo, defendant, 4511
Yamamoto, Tomomi, 3998
Yank, The Army Weekly, 282
Yeates, James D., 912
Yeats-Brown, Francis C. C., 268, 1613
Yen, Liang (pseud.). See Briggs, Margaret Yang
Yindrich, Jan H., 1614
Yoder, Samuel A., 4306
Yokota, Yutaka, 2748
Youell, George, 4372
Young, Arthur N., 3608
Young, Desmond, 415
Young, Edward P., 2387, 2388
Young, George G., 874, 2798, 4453
Young, Joseph, 3715
Young, Peter, 875
Young, Ramsay F., 3999
Young, Robert, 533
Young, Roland A., 3519
Young, Scotty (pseud.). See Young, Ramsey F.
Younger, Calton, 4000
Yovitchitch, Lena A., 3221
Yugoslavia. Jugoslavenski Informacione Kiro u Londonu, 3850
Yugoslavia. Poslanstvo, U.S., 4373
Yugoslavia. War Reparations Commission, 3609
Yunnie, Park, 1515
Yust, Walter, 145

Zacharias, Ellis M., 876
Zachodnia Agencja Prasowa, 723
Zagorov, Slavcho D., 3590
Zagórski, Waclaw, 3146
Zahn, Gordon C., 4374
Zajaczkowska, Anna, 3147
Zammit, Romeo M., 4001
Zandvoort, Reinard W., 179
Zawodny, Janusz K., 3851
Zeiger, Henry A., 4519
Zeman, Z.A.B., 3120
Zeuss, Wolfgang, defendant, 4501
Ziegler, Junior G., 1460
Ziegler, Richard, 168
Zielinski, Henry K., 4238
Ziemke, Earl F., 283
Zieser, Benno, 1688, 1689
Zimmerman, John L., 2715
Zimmermann, Erich, 2816
Zitridou, Pipitsa C., 3232
Zuckerman, Isaac, 3852
Zufelt, Edwin J. H., 1461
Zummach, Charles F., 4335
Zwiazek Bojowników o Wolność i Demokracje, 3148
Zywulska, Krystyna, 4023

Ref
Z
6207
W8
Z5

SEP 24 1971